Sociocultural Anthropology

A PROBLEM-BASED APPROACH

FOURTH CANADIAN EDITION

Richard H. Robbins
State University of New York at Plattsburgh

Rachel Dowty
New Haven University

Maggie Cummings
University of Toronto

Karen McGarry
McMaster University

Australia • Brazil • Canada • Mexico • Singapore • United Kingdom • United States

***Sociocultural Anthropology: A Problem-Based Approach,* Fourth Canadian Edition**
Richard H. Robbins, Rachel Dowty, Maggie Cummings, Karen McGarry

Sr. Director, Product: Jackie Wood

Sr. Portfolio Manager: Leanna Maclean

Product Marketing Manager: Sydney Pope

Director, Content and Production: Toula DiLeo

Content Development Manager: Gail Brown

Sr. Content Production Manager: Imoinda Romain

Sr. IP Analyst: Christine Myaskovsky

Production Service: SPi Global

Copy Editor: Matthew Kudelka

Compositor: SPi Global

Text Designer: Liz Harasymczuk

Cover Designer: Diane Robertson

Cover Image: "The Grand Entrance" by Daphne Odjig (2010, art card). Used with permission.

Library and Archives Canada Cataloguing in Publication:

Title: Sociocultural anthropology : a problem-based approach / Richard H. Robbins, State University of New York at Plattsburgh, Rachel Dowty, New Haven University, Maggie Cummings, University of Toronto, Karen McGarry, McMaster University.
Other titles: Cultural anthropology
Names: Robbins, Richard H. (Richard Howard), author. | Dowty, Rachel, author. | Cummings, Maggie, author. | McGarry, Karen, author.
Description: Fourth Canadian edition. | Previous editions published under title: Cultural anthropology. | Includes bibliographical references and index.
Identifiers: Canadiana (print) 20200311115 | Canadiana (ebook) 20200311131 | ISBN 9780176870997 (softcover) | ISBN 9780176875343 (PDF)
Subjects: LCSH: Ethnology—Textbooks. | LCGFT: Textbooks.
Classification: LCC GN316 .R63 2020 | DDC 306—dc23

ISBN-13: 987-0-17-687099-7
ISBN-10: 0-17-687099-7
Ebook ISBN-13: 978-0-17-687534-3
Ebook ISBN-10: 0-1-7687534-4

Cengage Canada
1120 Birchmount Road
Toronto, ON M1K 5G4
Canada

Cengage is a leading provider of customized learning solutions with employees residing in nearly 40 different countries and sales in more than 125 countries around the world. Find your local representative at **www.cengage.com.**

To learn more about Cengage platforms and services, register or access your online learning solution, or purchase materials for your course, visit **www.cengage.ca.**

A Note about the Book's Cover

The publisher of *Sociocultural Anthropology: A Problem-Based Approach*, Fourth Canadian Edition, hopes that the inquiry-based approach of this book will guide students as they develop an inquisitiveness and openness to cultural diversity. The cover features "The Grand Entrance" (1989) by Daphne Odjig, a Canadian artist of Indigenous ancestry.

Printed in Canada
Print Number: 01 Print Year: 2020

Brief Contents

Contents

Preface

A Note to Students: How to Read This Textbook

"How can you begin to think like an anthropologist?" Each of the chapters in this book addresses a series of questions and problems that are of concern to contemporary anthropologists. This text provides you with the necessary anthropological concepts and tools to begin to think "anthropologically" about these problems. For most of you, thinking anthropologically will involve re-evaluating and critiquing many core ideas and values you have probably been taught are "true," "right," or "natural." Through cross-cultural examples and case studies, you will learn to appreciate the diversity of beliefs, traditions, and experiences of different cultures. This appreciation, in turn, will challenge you to think differently about aspects of your own culture, upbringing, and beliefs.

Each of the nine chapters in this text includes a problem, chapter questions, "Beyond the Book" exercises, a new "Applying Anthropology" feature, chapter questions, summary and review questions, critical thinking questions, and key terms definitions with a glossary of terms listed with page numbers. Think of these as a "toolkit" to guide you through the text.

Each chapter opens with a brief epigraph (a short quotation) and an opening image related to the problem the chapter addresses. Together, they are meant to evoke, visually and in literary terms, the issue at hand. Keep them in mind as you read through the chapter. The chapter then begins with a specific "problem." While reading a chapter, you should keep the relevant problem in mind so that, once you are finished reading, you will understand how the various cultural examples in the text can help you critically address the central problem or issue of the chapter. To make the broad issues in the chapter manageable, we break down the problem into a series of related questions. These chapter questions will help you think anthropologically and more specifically about the problem.

The Beyond the Book exercises interspersed throughout each chapter are derived from the chapter content. These exercises are intended to help you focus your attention on a meaningful critique of contemporary social practices and to allow you to apply the new knowledge and skills you are learning to particular social concerns. You should therefore do the exercises after you have read the chapter's corresponding section. The new feature, Applying Anthropology, further illustrates the practical aspect of anthropology by presenting real-world examples of how anthropology is applied in today's world.

In the end-of-chapter material you will find a summary and review questions for each chapter question to help you check your understanding of the material. In addition, critical thinking questions are provided to help you reflect on the broad issues discussed in the chapter. These questions should be considered only after you have read the entire chapter thoroughly. They also make excellent study questions. The end-of-chapter section ends with a list of key terms, with page numbers for quick and easy reference. You will find key terms in bold font with definitions throughout this text. These are foundational concepts and ideas in anthropology, and it is important to understand how these key ideas are defined within the discipline. (For instance, most people use the term "gender" in everyday language. However, "gender" has a unique meaning in anthropology.) A full glossary of key terms with definitions is provided at the end of the book.

For Instructors

This text introduces students to the key concepts and methods utilized by sociocultural anthropology. Although the first and second Canadian editions were titled *Cultural Anthropology: A Problem-Based Approach*, we have replaced the term "cultural anthropology" in the third and fourth editions with "sociocultural anthropology." We feel that this change better reflects the combined influences of British and American anthropology on Canadian anthropological traditions. One of our goals in writing this text is to encourage students to read, think, and write critically. Indeed, we believe that one of the main objectives of first-year sociocultural anthropology courses is to teach students to think differently about the world around them. The text facilitates this by encouraging students to analyze and critique many basic assumptions they have brought with them to the course. For example, many of us are taught to think about our sense of identity, which encompasses gender, class, race, ethnicity, nationality, and family, as natural, biological, or fixed—as something we are born with. In this text, however, we place particular emphasis on the culturally constructed nature of our world: on the idea that many identities, as well as beliefs and practices, that we view as natural are both learned and the consequences of cultural differences.

We thus adopt a "problem-based approach" to the study of anthropology. Richard Robbins wrote the original edition of *Cultural Anthropology: A Problem-Based Approach* in the hope that such an approach would foster a classroom culture that, regardless of class size and instructional technique, would actively involve students in the learning process, promote critical thinking, and impress on students that they, along with the other people and cultures of the world, are cultural animals worthy of study.

Each chapter is organized around an intellectual "problem" and then subdivided into a series of questions that address the problem from an anthropological perspective. We hope that after reading this text, students will appreciate that culture, as the way that human beings make their lives meaningful, is fluid, dynamic, contradictory, and subject to critique. Moreover, we hope that students who read this book will understand why and how anthropology *matters* for anyone who wants to understand, and perhaps make a difference in, the contemporary world.

As mentioned, the material in this text is organized by problems and questions rather than by topics. Each chapter focuses on a specific problem of anthropological as well as general concern:

- How can people begin to understand beliefs and behaviours that are different from their own?
- How do sociocultural anthropologists learn about culture?
- How do we explain the transformation of human societies over the past 10,000 years from small-scale, nomadic bands of hunters and gatherers to large-scale, urban-industrial states?
- Why do people believe different things, and why are they so certain that their view of the world is correct and that others are wrong?
- What do we need to know before we can understand the dynamics of family life in other societies?
- How do people determine who they are, and how do they communicate who they think they are to others?
- Why are modern societies characterized by social, political, and economic inequalities? How are certain gender, class, racial, and other identities privileged or marginalized in various social contexts?
- What is the relationship between globalization, the nation-state, and national identity? What are the economic and cultural effects of globalization?
- How do societies give meaning to and justify various forms of conflict resolution, both peaceful and violent?

These problems have no definitive solutions, yet they drive much intellectual inquiry. Each problem/

chapter is broken down into a series of specific questions, each of which can be "answered" by focusing on the ethnographic and theoretical contributions of anthropologists. Such questions include the following:

- Is it possible to see the world through the eyes of others?
- How do people come to accept social hierarchies as natural?
- What are the characteristics of peaceful societies?

Although the problems and questions included in the text are not exhaustive, those that we have selected are central to the concerns of the discipline and include the topics and issues typically covered in an introductory sociocultural anthropology class. We have chosen problems and questions that we hope will capture students' imaginations and whet their appetite for further study in the discipline. The Topic and Question Correspondence chart, which links topics to questions considered in the text, can be used in guiding discussion and in course planning.

TOPIC AND QUESTION CORRESPONDENCE

Topic	Corresponding Chapter or Question
Applied Anthropology	Question 1.5
Caste	Question 7.1
Colonialism	Question 2.1; Question 2.2; Question 3.2; Question 3.3; Question 4.4; Question 4.5; Question 6.2; Question 6.6; Question 8.2; Question 8.3; Question 8.4; Question 9.3; Question 9.4
Conflict	Chapter 9
Corporations	Question 8.1; Question 8.2
Cultural Relativism	Question 1.2
Culture Change	Chapter 3
Culture Concept	Chapter 1
Ecology	Question 1.5; Question 3.3; Question 8.1; Question 8.3
Economic Anthropology	Chapter 3; Chapter 7; Chapter 8
Education	Question 6.1; Question 8.3
Ethnocentrism	Question 1.2
Family Organization	Chapter 5
Feminist Anthropology	Question 5.5; Question 6.5; Question 7.3; Question 9.3
Fieldwork	Chapter 2
Food Production	Question 2.3; Question 3.1; Question 8.2
Foragers	Question 3.1; Question 9.2
Gender	Question 2.2; Chapter 7; Question 6.1; Question 7.3; Question 9.3
Gift Giving	Question 5.3; Question 6.5
Globalization	Chapter 8; Question 3.2; Question 3.3
Human Rights	Question 1.2; Question 7.5
Identity	Chapter 6
Indigenous Peoples	Question 1.5; Question 3.2; Question 3.3; Question 3.4; Question 4.1; Question 4.2; Question 4.3; Question 4.4; Question 4.5; Question 5.5; Question 6.1; Question 6.5; Question 6.6; Question 8.3; Question 8.4; Question 9.1; Question 9.2; Question 9.3
Industrialization	Question 3.2; Question 3.3
Inequality	Chapter 7
International Development	Question 2.5; Question 3.3; Question 6.6

(Continued)

TOPIC AND QUESTION CORRESPONDENCE *(Continued)*

Topic	Corresponding Chapter or Question
Kinship	Chapter 5
Language and Culture	Question 1.3; Question 4.1; Question 6.3; Question 7.3; Question 9.5
Law and Anthropology	Question 1.5
Marriage	Chapter 5
Medical Anthropology	Question 1.5; Question 3.4
Nation-State	Chapter 8; Question 9.4
Neoliberalism	Chapter 8
Peasants	Question 3.1; Question 3.3; Chapter 5
Political Ecology	Question 1.5
Political Organization and Control	Chapter 7; Question 7.5; Question 9.2; Question 9.3; Question 9.4
Race and Racism	Question 7.2; Question 7.4
Religion/World View	Chapter 4; Question 1.1; Question 1.2; Question 9.1
Ritual	Question 1.3; Question 1.4; Question 4.2; Question 4.3; Question 6.4; Question 6.5
Sexuality	Question 5.3; Question 5.5; Question 6.1; Question 7.3
Social Stratification	Chapter 7
Status and Rank	Chapter 7; Question 3.1; Question 3.2; Question 3.4; Question 9.1
Subsistence Techniques	Question 3.1; Question 3.2
Symbolism	Question 1.1; Question 1.3; Question 1.4; Question 4.1; Question 4.2; Question 4.3; Question 6.4; Question 6.5
Systems of Exchange	Question 6.5
Tourism	Question 2.5; Question 8.4

A key pedagogical feature of this text is the inclusion of Beyond the Book exercises that give students the opportunity to go beyond the textbook and apply what they have read, to think about the implications of the material for their own lives, and to think about various problems "like an anthropologist." These exercises are interspersed throughout the text and can be used in various ways by students and instructors. They might serve as discussion questions in lectures, tutorials, or online discussion posts, or they could be used as the basis for group work. They could also be treated as informal writing assignments, with students preparing brief reading responses based on the exercises, which would then be used as a starting point for classroom discussion. However they are used, the exercises are designed to give students a chance to engage in intellectual debate and to highlight the real-world implications of what they have learned. Each chapter ends with a new Applying Anthropology section, which uses real-world examples to illustrate the ways in which a problem-based approach and anthropological perspective can be used outside academia.

In addition to the pedagogical features discussed, each chapter concludes with an end-of-chapter section that includes a review of the chapter questions, several critical thinking questions, and a list of key terms from the chapter. The chapter questions review includes a brief summary of the key points relating to that question, along with a few review questions. The critical thinking questions provide students with the opportunity to rethink the material in a way that underscores what they have learned through the problem-based approach. The key terms (which appear in bold throughout the chapter) are listed with page numbers for quick reference and to allow students to review each chapter's key material—names, terms, and theories—quickly.

Sociocultural Anthropology: A Problem-Based Approach begins with a discussion of the development of cartography and the different map projections throughout the world. This exemplifies one of the key pedagogical goals of an introductory anthropology class: to show how one's entire world is shaped by one's cultural perspective. In addition to these maps, each of the chapters includes two or three smaller maps, each of which corresponds with one of the ethnographic examples in the text. These are intended to help orient students toward the material, especially for places that, in our teaching experience, students tend to be less familiar with (the Trobriand Islands, for example).

Another key feature that contributes to learning stems from Richard Robbins's conviction—evident in the earlier editions and maintained here, and which we share—that students learning about the cultures of others cannot fully appreciate them without first understanding something of their own cultural perspective. In order to appreciate that other people construct their worlds, they must appreciate that they themselves do so as well. Accordingly, we have included numerous comparisons of world cultures with North American cultures, both in the text and through the exercises.

New in This Edition

One of the goals of this Fourth Canadian Edition of *Sociocultural Anthropology: A Problem-Based Approach* is to highlight the ways in which the research that anthropologists do can be applied to help understand and enrich people's lives. In the new Applying Anthropology features, for instance, we showcase the work of a number of anthropologists, such as Paul Farmer's work in Haiti and Daniel Miller's multisited and collaborative project on the use of smartphones among the elderly. In keeping with this goal, we have also updated and added new Beyond the Book exercises that encourage students to reflect upon and actively experiment with the practical application of anthropological techniques and principles on their own terms. We continue to retain the spirit of Richard Robbins's account of what anthropology is all about. We further build on Sherrie Larkin's efforts in the first Canadian edition to provide interesting and important examples of the research that Canadian anthropologists are doing, both in Canada and beyond. Larkin's strong focus on Canadian anthropological work with First Nations, Inuit, and Métis peoples remains important and has been further strengthened with more relevant and timely examples.

In addition, we have made the following chapter-specific changes.

Chapter 1

- The discussion of the concept of "culture" has been expanded.
- New and updated Beyond the Book exercises encourage students to think about their own lives in terms of culture and to apply what they are reading to examples from their everyday lives.
- The new Applying Anthropology feature discusses career possibilities in the growing field of user experience (UX) design.

Chapter 2

- The significance of gender in fieldwork is now discussed in greater depth, with particular reference to the idea that there can be more than one "native's point of view."
- The discussion of issues of representation and essentialism has been expanded and enhanced.
- A new Beyond the Book exercise on social media ethnography has been added.
- The new Applying Anthropology feature discusses representation and indigeneity.

Chapter 3

- There is greater emphasis throughout the chapter on the relationship of progress and development to contemporary environmental

- issues and the climate crisis, including an updated and expanded discussion of economic development and environmental and cultural devastation in Brazil and Paraguay.
- The section on illness/health anthropology has been updated to include a discussion on vaccines and how the COVID-19 pandemic highlighted how increased global inequality has led to increased global health disparities.
- The new Applying Anthropology section discusses Fort McMurray Métis and the reclaiming and restoring of oil sands.

Chapter 4

- The chapter includes an expanded discussion of the coexistence of secular and religious worldviews, with a new Beyond the Book exercise on Quebec's Bill 21.
- New material on nonreligious rituals has been added, including a discussion of the symbolic aspects of face masks during the COVID-19 pandemic and a Beyond the Book exercise that asks students to think about wedding symbols and rituals from an anthropological perspective.
- The new Applying Anthropology feature explores the conflict between Native Hawaiian activists and proponents of the Thirty Meter Telescope on Mauna Kea, and also serves as a case study of potential conflicts between religious and secular worldviews.

Chapter 5

- New material on polygyny and polyamory has been added, including a discussion of the case in Bountiful, British Columbia.
- The concepts of "kin term" and "kin type" are discussed and differentiated.
- The lengthy section in the previous edition on HIV and medical anthropology has been reduced and incorporated into the new Applying Anthropology feature.

Chapter 6

- This chapter provides a new discussion of the concept of ethnicity in relation to the Québécois in Canada.
- There is a new section on social media and identity in relation to Indigenous protests.
- The new Applying Anthropology feature explores the role of smartphones and social media in constructing identities among the elderly in relation to health.

Chapter 7

- The section on race and intelligence has been revised and pared down.
- Statistics on poverty in Canada are updated.
- New expanded discussions on the #MeToo movement and on transgender and third gender have been added.

Chapter 8

- A new discussion on nationalism, populism, and Brexit has been added.
- A new discussion on the effects of globalization and the COVID-19 pandemic is included.
- Statistics have been updated throughout.
- The section on the nation-state (formerly Section 8.3) has been moved to the beginning of the chapter, so that the nation-state is discussed prior to neoliberalism and globalization.
- The new Applying Anthropology feature discusses Indigenous resistance to globalization.

Chapter 9

- The section on the relationship between horses, warfare, and rank among the Kiowa has been updated.
- A new section on the rise of alt-right movements has been added.
- The new Beyond the Book exercises highlight real-world cases such as the Mi'kmaq Warrior Society shale gas protests in

New Brunswick and feature the research of anthropologist Lawrence Ralph, who studied violent conflict among gangs and its effect on communities.

- The new Applying Anthropology feature examines gender-based violence in Belize.

Finally, in addition to the new pedagogical features and the new material discussed above, many of the photographs and chapter openers have been changed. They have, however, been added in such a way that they complement a key strength of the book—the inclusion of many in-depth case studies and examples that engage readers and bring anthropology to life. This text should appeal to visual learners, active learners, and those who learn through reading. These learning styles come together in the opening pages for each chapter, each of which includes a visual element (such as a photo) that is explicitly connected, in its caption, to a text element (the epigraph), which, in turn, exemplifies the issues for active learning articulated in the chapter problem.

Acknowledgments

We remain indebted to Richard Robbins, Rachel Dowty, and Sherrie Larkin for their work on earlier editions of this text. In the first Canadian edition, published in 2007, Sherrie Larkin did an excellent job of adapting Robbins's text for a Canadian readership. Much of this fourth edition is an extension and elaboration of their earlier efforts.

We also thank Leanna Maclean, Senior Portfolio Manager; Sydney Pope, Product Marketing Manager; Gail Brown, Content Development Manager; Imoinda Romain, Senior Content Production Manager; and Aurelio Zappia, Digital Project Manager at Cengage Canada for their encouragement, patience, and support throughout the development and production of this fourth edition. Thanks also go to the copy editor, Matthew Kudelka.

Maggie would like to thank Karen, as always, for being an imaginative, inspiring, and patient co-editor and a wonderful colleague. And Karen thanks Maggie for her patience, organization, and creativity during the planning, writing, and editing of this text.

We would also like to thank the reviewers, past and present, for their valuable feedback:

Anna K. Boshnakova, Sheridan College
Sean Connaughton, Kwantlen Polytechnic University
Marley Duckett, University of Saskatchewan
Ellen Facey, University of Northern British Columbia
Edward J. Hedican, University of Guelph
Chris Holdsworth, University of Calgary
Teresa Holmes, York University
Karen Hutton, UNB Fredericton & St. Thomas University
Branka Maleševi, University of Windsor
Sam Migliore, Kwantlen Polytechnic University
Bruce Miller, University of British Columbia
Brian Pegg, Kwantlen Polytechnic University
Amali Philips, Wilfrid Laurier University
Blair Rutherford, Carleton University
Patricia Kelly Spurles, Mount Allison University
James Stinson, Trent University
Mark Tate, Memorial University
Charisma A. Thomson, University of Regina
Marilyn Walker, Mount Allison University
Sandra Widmer, York University
Barbara Wilkes, University of Calgary
Saulesh Yessenova, University of Calgary
Kaitlin Young, University of Alberta

We would be very grateful to receive questions, comments, and suggestions for improvement from instructors and students. Our e-mail addresses are maggie.cummings@utoronto.ca and mcgarry@mcmcaster.ca.

Maggie Cummings and Karen McGarry

Ancillaries

Instructor Resources

The following instructor resources have been created for *Sociocultural Anthropology*, Fourth Canadian Edition. Access these ultimate tools for customizing lectures and presentations at http://login.cengage.com.

Test Bank

This resource was updated and revised by Darlene Balandin, Western University. It includes over 280 multiple-choice questions. Included, as well, are more than 135 true/false, 140 short answer, and 65 essay-type questions.

The test bank is available in a cloud-based platform. **Testing Powered by Cognero®** is a secure online testing system that allows instructors to author, edit, and manage test-bank content from anywhere Internet access is available. No special installations or downloads are needed, and the desktop-inspired interface, with its drop-down menus and familiar, intuitive tools, allows instructors to create and manage tests with ease. Multiple test versions can be created in an instant, and content can be imported or exported into other systems. Tests can be delivered from a learning management system, the classroom, or wherever an instructor chooses. Testing Powered by Cognero for *Sociocultural Anthropology*, Fourth Canadian Edition, can also be accessed through http://login.cengage.com.

PowerPoint

Microsoft® PowerPoint® lecture slides were revised and updated by Amali Philips, Wilfrid Laurier University. There is an average of 25 to 30 slides per chapter, many featuring key figures, tables, and photographs from *Sociocultural Anthropology*, Fourth Canadian Edition. Instructor notes have been incorporated throughout, making it simple for instructors to customize the deck for their courses.

Image Library

This resource consists of digital copies of figures, short tables, and photographs used in the book. Instructors may use these jpegs to customize the PowerPoint slides or create their own PowerPoint presentations.

Instructor Guide

This resource was updated and revised by Charisma A. Thomson, University of Regina. It is organized according to the textbook chapters and addresses key educational concerns, such as typical stumbling blocks student face and how to address them. Other features include responses to the text's Critical Thinking Questions.

About the Authors

RICHARD H. ROBBINS is a Distinguished Teaching Professor of Anthropology at the State University of New York College at Plattsburgh. His research interests include the anthropological study of religion and belief, the social and cultural consequences of globalization, the anthropology of economic growth, technology and culture, and the culture of the classroom. He has conducted research among Indigenous peoples of Canada and fishing communities in northeastern New Brunswick. His books include *Debt as Power* (with Tim DiMuzio); *Global Problems and the Culture of Capitalism* (6e); *Talking Points on Global Issues: A Reader*; *Darwin and the Bible: The Cultural Confrontation* (with Mark Nathan Cohen); and *Globalization and the Environment* (with Gary Kroll). He is the co-editor with Luis Vivanco of the series Creative Teaching and Learning in Anthropology and the Anthropology of Stuff, published by Routledge Press. Professor Robbins is the recipient of the 2005 American Anthropological Association Award for Excellence in Undergraduate Teaching.

RACHEL DOWTY is Visiting Assistant Professor in Emergency Management at the University of New Haven, Connecticut. Her research interests revolve around the social and anthropological study of crises and disasters, organizations, and science and technology. She co-authored *Cultural Anthro* (2nd edition, with Richard H. Robbins). She co-edited a volume titled *Dynamics of Disaster: Lessons on Risk, Response, and Recovery* (2011, with Barbara Allen) and has authored numerous book chapters and articles. She has taught a variety of university courses for the past 17 years, focusing on understanding culture through hands-on civic engagement and reflection. In her spare time, she enjoys hiking, landscaping, and spending time with her family.

MAGGIE CUMMINGS is an assistant professor, teaching stream, in the Department of Anthropology at the University of Toronto, Scarborough (UTSC). For more than a decade, she has done fieldwork on gender, modernity, and social change in Vanuatu. More recently, her research interests have expanded to include the ethnography of social media and the institutional ethnography of the contemporary university. Since beginning her teaching career in 2006, she has designed and taught more than a dozen undergraduate anthropology courses, including "Introduction to Anthropology," "Fieldwork in Sociocultural Anthropology," "Race and Racism," and "Culture through Film and Media." She has also been involved in several fieldwork-based student learning initiatives at UTSC, including an interdisciplinary project on citizenship, belonging, and urban life in East Scarborough. In 2019, she won a UTSC Teaching Award.

KAREN McGARRY is an Associate Professor of Anthropology at McMaster University in Hamilton, Ontario. Her research focuses on two areas: the anthropology of sport, and educational anthropology. Her fieldwork on sport involves ethnographic studies of elite, high-performance sports like figure skating, with an emphasis on the production, distribution, and reception of particular representations of athletes' bodies in the mass media. Broadly speaking, she is interested in the intersections among gender, race, class, ethnicity, and Canadian nationalism. In the field of educational anthropology, her interests lie within the realm of multicultural education and educulturalism. At McMaster, she teaches introductory anthropology courses ("Sex, Food, and Death" and "Race, Religion, and Conflict"), as well as anthropological theory, and a fourth-year undergraduate course, "The Anthropology of Zombies and the Undead."

Problem-Based Pedagogical Framework

One doesn't need to change one's instructional approach to adopt a problem-based book. If you'd like your students to question, inquire, think critically, and analyze material, the problem-based pedagogical framework of this text can support that intention.

A Thorough, Robust Map Program

Expanding students' geographical awareness can be achieved through a comprehensive map program. Global ethnographic examples within the chapters are grounded by maps. The maps give students a visual sense of both the global diversity of human culture and the geographical breadth of anthropology as a discipline. These maps also help to orient students toward the material, especially for places with which, in the authors' teaching experiences, students tend to be less familiar.

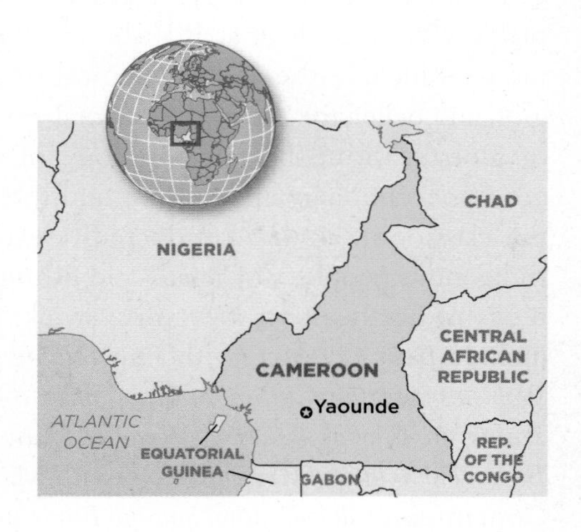

PROBLEM 2

How do sociocultural anthropologists learn about culture?

Problems

At the centre of the problem-based approach is the problem that frames each chapter. The material in this text is organized by problems rather than by topics to encourage students to make connections between pressing issues, anthropological lenses, and anthropologists' work. Each of the nine chapters of the book focuses on a specific problem of anthropological, as well as general, concern. Although these problems may have no definitive solutions, they drive much intellectual inquiry.

Questions

Each problem/chapter is broken down into a series of specific questions, each of which can be "answered" by focusing on the ethnographic and theoretical contributions of anthropologists. These questions are revisited at the end of the chapter with a brief summary and review questions to provide key takeaways and help students check their understanding.

QUESTIONS

3.1 How and why did foraging societies switch to sedentary agriculture?

3.2 How can we explain the vast inequality between the rich and the poor?

3.3 How does economic development affect inequality and cultural diversity?

3.4 Have progress and development improved human health?

Beyond the Book

A key pedagogical feature of this text is the inclusion of exercises that give students the opportunity to apply what they have read, to think about the implications of the material for their own lives, and to try to think about various problems "like an anthropologist." These can be assigned for homework, worked through in class, or posted to your learning management system. Students can complete them in groups or individually.

BEYOND THE BOOK 4.3

1. What skills are most valuable in the wake of an imagined zombie apocalypse? In zombie myths, who becomes the hero, and who is zombie fodder? What does this suggest about our anxieties related to our contemporary ways of making a living in North America?
2. The vampire genre is as popular, if not more so, than myths and stories about zombies. Why do you think this is the case? What do contemporary vampires tell us about ourselves?

Critical Thinking Questions

To extend the inquiry-based philosophy of the text, the authors have provided critical thinking questions at the end of each chapter. The questions encourage students to review what they have learned by giving students the opportunity to rethink the material in a way that underscores what they have learned through the problem-based approach. These questions can be assigned for homework or used for in-class discussion.

CRITICAL THINKING QUESTIONS

1. If worldview is culturally and socially constructed, can there be such a thing as objective truth? What are the implications of taking a social constructionist approach to reality for the pursuit of knowledge? Is objectivity possible? What obstacles might

Applying Anthropology

This new feature illustrates how anthropological knowledge and ethnographic expertise matter in the real world and how they are put into practice. As well, this feature is intended to encourage students to consider how anthropology can be applied to solve social, economic, and political problems throughout the world.

APPLYING ANTHROPOLOGY

Mediating Worldviews on Mauna Kea

When anthropologists learn to interpret, understand, and take seriously different worldviews, and to communicate such worldviews to those who are unfamiliar with them, they are practising a valuable skill that has innumerable applications in a world in which peoples with varying worldviews frequently share territory and resources. Anthropologists can act as cultural mediators when conflicts arise and often as advocates for or collaborators with those whose ways of knowing are marginalized, misunderstood, or disparaged. Many anthropologists apply their knowledge and skills on behalf of Indigenous peoples whose ways of knowing the world around them (as discussed in Section 4.3) are at odds with dominant understandings of the relationship between humans and nature. The applied and public anthropology of Ty Tengan, an anthropologist and *Kanaka Maoli* (Native Hawaiian) who teaches at the University of Hawaii at Manoa, provides one example of the significance of this kind of work.

The opening image of this chapter captures the beauty and wonder of the Milky Way as viewed from the top of Mauna Kea, the tallest peak in Hawaii at 4302 metres above sea level (indeed, if measured from the sea floor, Mauna Kea is the tallest mountain in the world). Also pictured is the Gemini Northern Telescope, one of thirteen large telescopes atop the mountain, which is a coveted location for astronomical observation due (TMT), part of a new class of extremely large telescopes (EMTs) that will allow astronomers to observe faint light in distant galaxies for the first time, opening up the possibility of answering new and even unanticipated questions about the origins of the universe, black holes, exoplanets, and dark matter.

For many Native Hawaiians, however, the peak of Mauna Kea is a sacred place, home to several deities and birthplace to *Wakea*, an ancestor whose domain is the sky (Case 2019, 168). It is also revered for its role in "collecting the waters that sustain life" (Goodyear-Ka'ōpua 2017, 189), as it sits atop the island's principle aquifer. Since the TMT was proposed, therefore, opponents have fought to prevent its construction on the grounds that it is a desecration of sacred space, environmentally unsound, and the most recent example of a long history of threats to Native Hawaiian sovereignty. Since 2009, these opponents have made a case against the telescope in the media and in the courts. In 2019 the conflict came to a head when final approval was given for the construction of the telescope. A group of protesters, or protectors, established a road block at the sole access point to the peak, effectively halting construction of the TMT. In the media coverage of the blockade and the preceding years of protest, one common narrative often prevailed, one that pitted specifically Hawaiian cultural interests against the "universally applicable" lessons

Running Glossary

This edition continues to have a running glossary in which key terms are highlighted and defined on the page where they first appear. The glossary (whose terms appear in bold throughout the chapter) allows students to review quickly the chapter's material: names, terms, and theories.

worldview
An encompassing picture of reality based on shared cultural assumptions about how the world works.

Indigenism
Refers to an international, collaborative movement that aims to protect the rights and livelihoods of Indigenous peoples.

Putting the World in Perspective

Although all humans that we know about are capable of producing accurate sketches of localities and regions with which they are familiar, ***cartography*** (the craft of mapmaking as we know it today) had its beginnings in sixteenth-century Europe, and its subsequent development is related to the expansion of Europeans to all parts of the globe. From the beginning, there have been two problems with maps: the technical one of how to depict on a two-dimensional, flat surface a three-dimensional spherical object, and the cultural one of whose worldview maps reflect. In fact, the two issues are inseparable, for the particular projection one uses inevitably makes a statement about how one views one's own people and their place in the world. Indeed, maps often shape our perceptions of reality as much as they reflect them.

In cartography, a ***projection*** refers to the system of intersecting lines (of longitude and latitude) by which part or all of the globe is represented on a flat surface. There are more than a hundred different projections in use today, ranging from polar perspectives to interrupted "butterflies" to rectangles to heart shapes. Each projection causes distortion in size, shape, or distance in some way or another. A map that correctly shows the shape of a landmass will of necessity misrepresent the size. A map that is accurate along the equator will be deceptive at the poles.

Perhaps no projection has had more influence on the way we see the world than that of Gerhardus Mercator, who devised his map in 1569 as a navigational aid for mariners. So well suited was Mercator's map for this purpose that it continues to be used for navigational charts today. At the same time, the Mercator projection became a standard for depicting landmasses, something for which it was

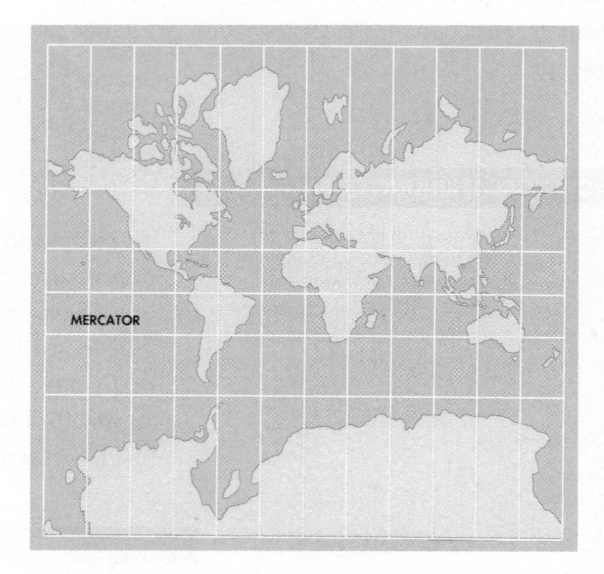

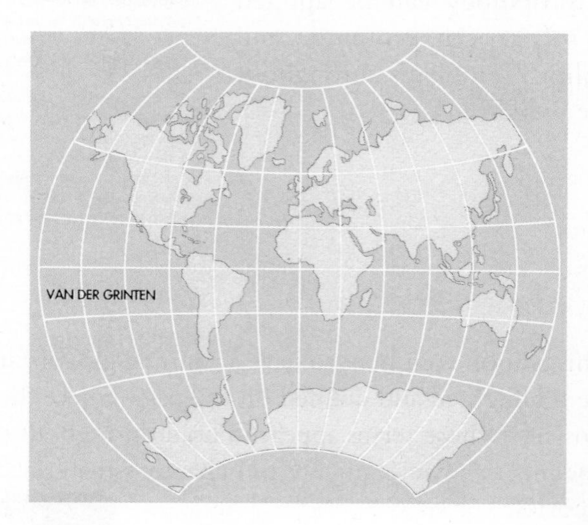

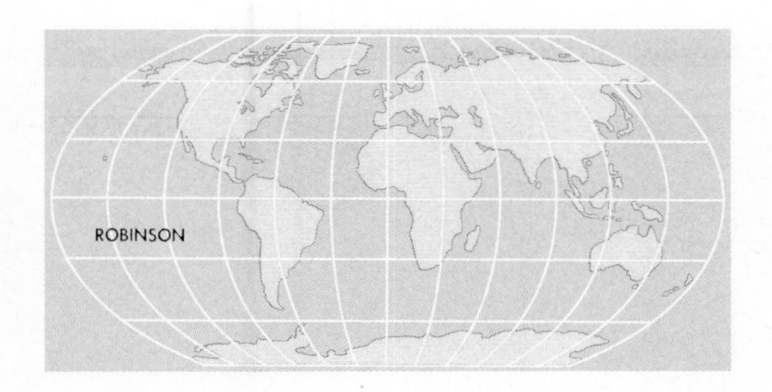

never intended. Although an accurate navigational tool, the Mercator projection greatly exaggerates the size of landmasses in higher latitudes, giving about two-thirds of the map's surface to the northern hemisphere. Thus, the lands occupied by Europeans and European descendants appear far larger than those of other people. For example, North America (19 million square kilometres) appears almost twice the size of Africa (30 million square kilometres), while Europe is shown as equal in size to South America, which actually has nearly twice the landmass of Europe.

A map developed in 1805 by Karl B. Mollweide was one of the earlier ***equal-area projections*** of the world. Equal-area projections portray landmasses in correct relative size, but as a result, they distort the shapes of continents more than other projections. They most often compress and warp lands in the higher latitudes and vertically stretch landmasses close to the equator. Other equal-area projections include the Lambert Cylindrical Equal-Area Projection (1772), the Hammer Equal-Area Projection (1892), and the Eckert Equal-Area Projection (1906).

The Van der Grinten Projection (1904) was a compromise aimed at minimizing both the distortions of size in the Mercator and the distortions of shape in equal-area maps such as the Mollweide. Although an improvement, the Van der Grinten still emphasizes the lands of the northern hemisphere at the expense of the southern. For example, it shows Canada and the former Soviet Union at more than twice their actual size.

The Robinson Projection, which was adopted by the National Geographic Society in 1988 to replace the Van der Grinten, is one of the best compromises to date between the distortions of size and those of shape. Although an improvement over the Van der Grinten, the Robinson Projection still depicts lands in the northern latitudes as proportionally larger than those of the southern, that is, the developing world. And like European maps before it, the Robinson Projection places Europe at the centre with the Atlantic Ocean and the Americas to the left, thus emphasizing the cultural connection between Europe and North America, while neglecting the geographic closeness of northwestern North America to northeastern Asia.

Each of the maps on the following pages conveys quite a different cultural message. In addition to the Robinson Projection there is the Peters Projection, an equal-area map that has been adopted as the official map of UNESCO (the United Nations Educational, Scientific, and Cultural Organization) and a Japanese map that shows us how the world looks from the other side.*

*From Haviland/Prins/McBride/Walrath, *Cultural Anthropology, 13e*. Cengage Learning Inc. Reproduced by permission. www.cengage.com/permissions

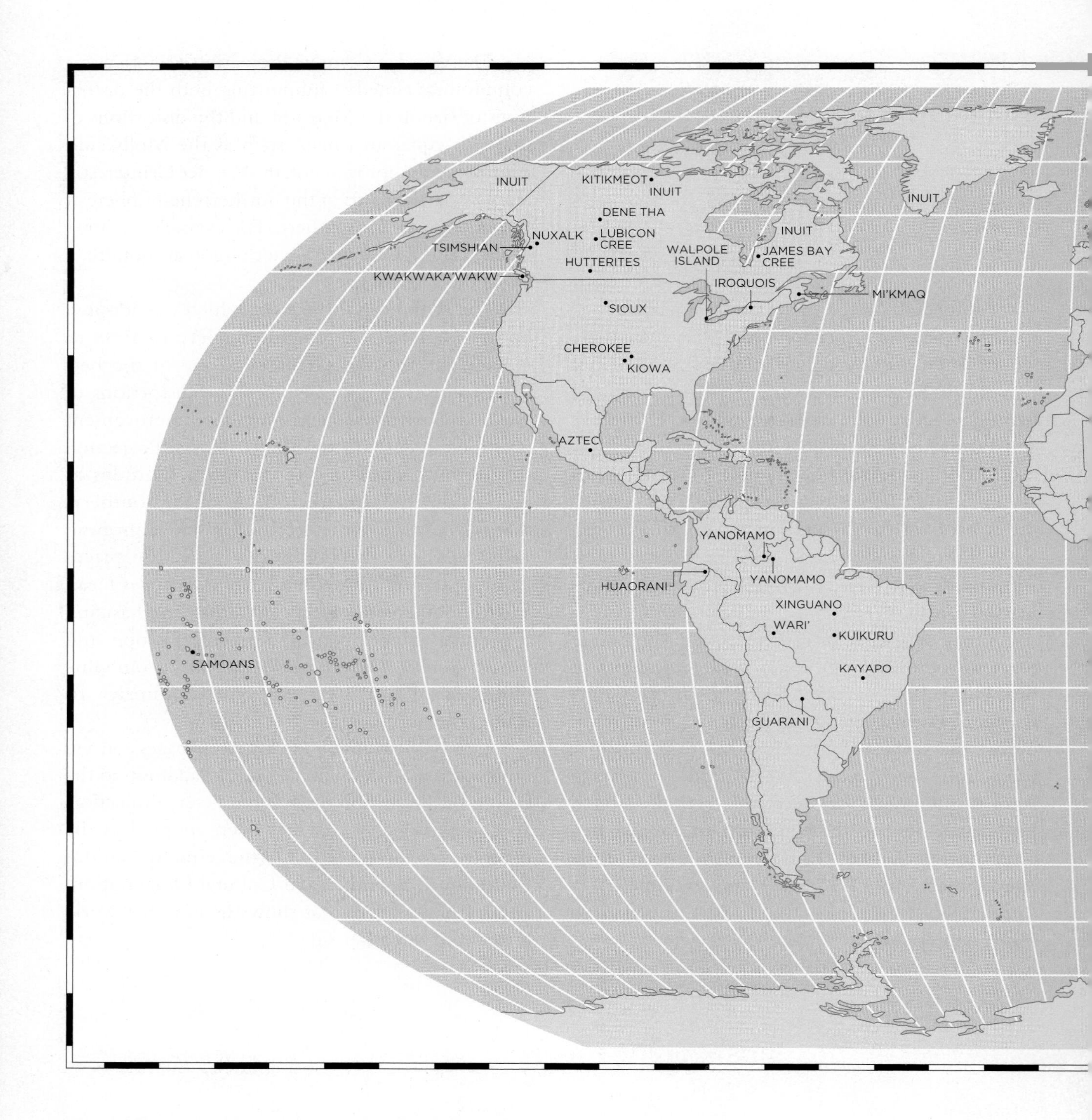

The Robinson Projection

This projection is used today by the National Geographic Society and Rand McNally. Although it distorts the relative size of landmasses, it does so much less than most other projections. Still, it places Europe at the centre of the map. This textbook uses the Robinson.

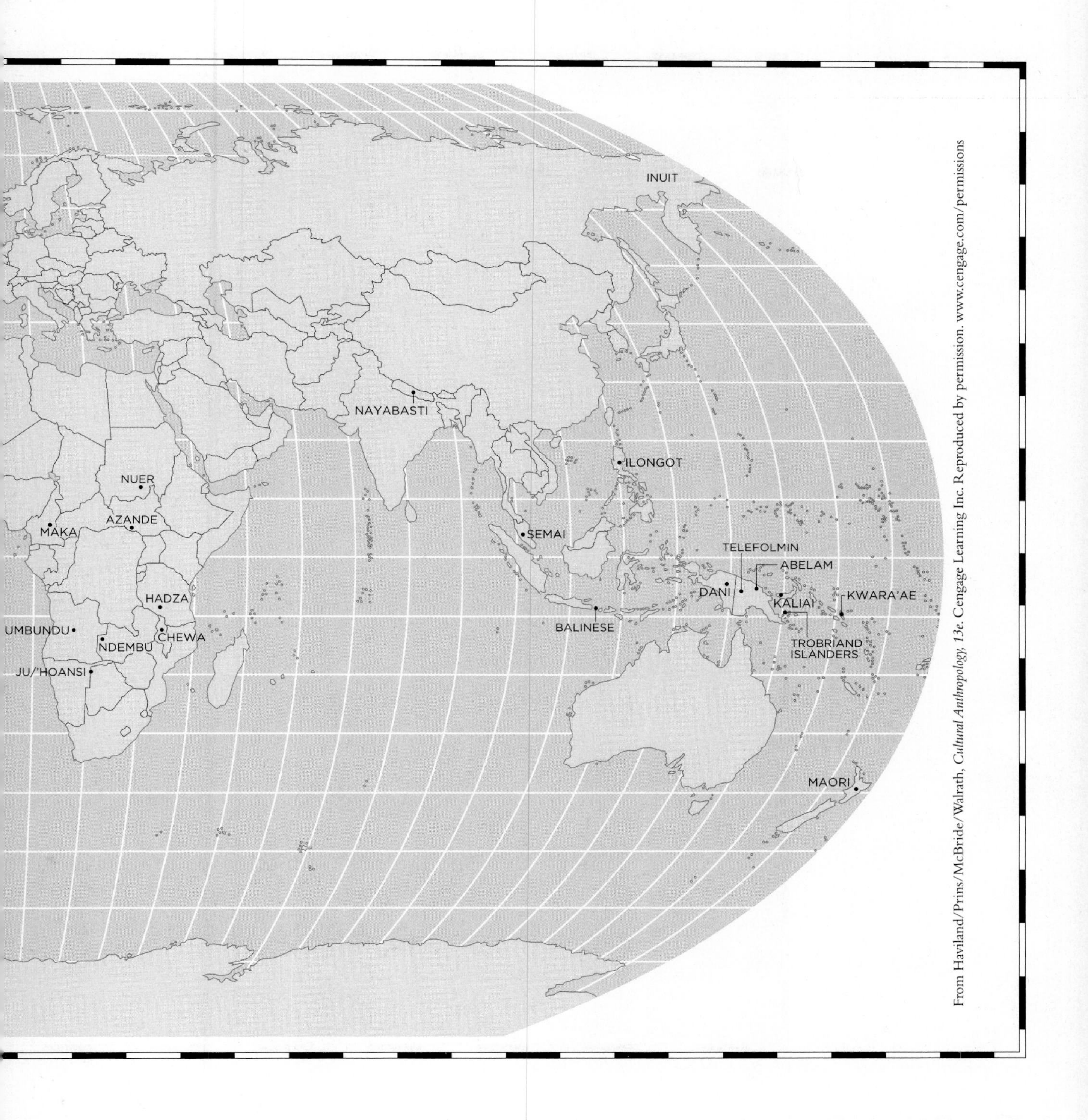

From Haviland/Prins/McBride/Walrath, *Cultural Anthropology, 13e.* Cengage Learning Inc. Reproduced by permission. www.cengage.com/permissions

The Peters Projection

This projection is based on the Peters. It distorts the continents (countries near the equator are vertically elongated by a ratio of 2 to 1), but it does show all the continents according to their correct relative sizes. Europe is still at the centre but is not shown as larger than the rest of the world.

RUSSIA
ESTONIA
LATVIA
LITHUANIA
AZERBAIJAN
ARMENIA
GEORGIA
UKRAINE
MOLDOVA
BULGARIA
MONTENEGRO
MACEDONIA
ALBANIA
TURKEY
KAZAKHSTAN
KIRGHIZSTAN
TAJIKISTAN
UZBEKISTAN
TURKMENISTAN
MONGOLIA
NORTH KOREA
SOUTH KOREA
JAPAN
PEOPLE'S REPUBLIC OF CHINA
SYRIA
IRAQ
IRAN
AFGHAN-ISTAN
JORDAN
KUWAIT
BAHRAIN
PAKISTAN
NEPAL
BHUTAN
INDIA
MYANMAR
TAIWAN
QATAR
SAUDI ARABIA
OMAN
UNITED ARAB EMIRATES
LAOS
BANGLA-DESH
THAILAND
YEMEN
VIETNAM
PHILIPPINES
CAMBODIA
DJIBOUTI
ETHIOPIA
BRUNEI
MALAYSIA
SRI LANKA
SOMALIA
UGANDA
SINGAPORE
PAPUA NEW GUINEA
INDONESIA
KENYA
TANZANIA
MALAWI
MADAGASCAR
ZIMBABWE
MOZAMBIQUE
AUSTRALIA
NEW ZEALAND
ANTARCTICA

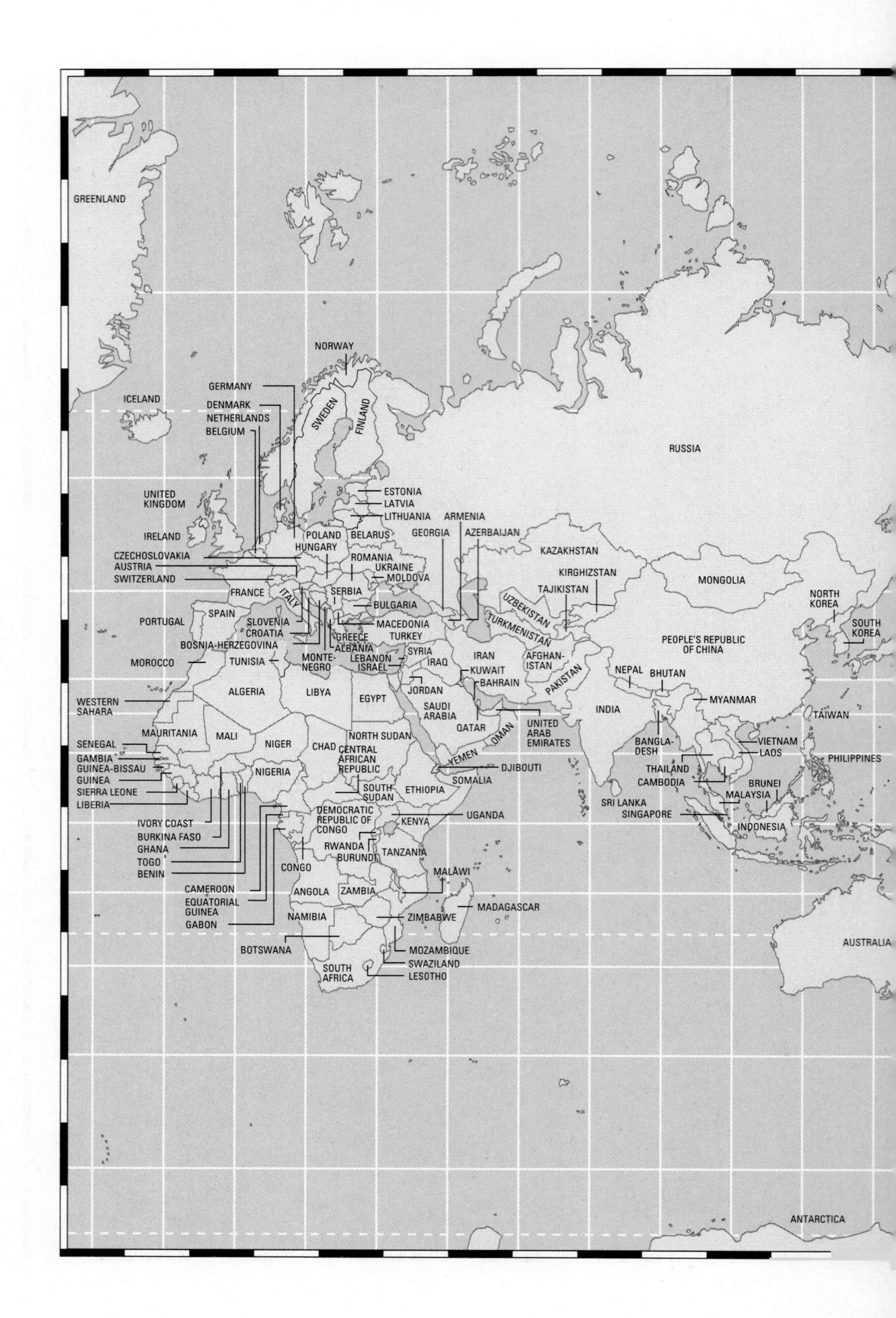

Japanese Map

Not all maps place Europe at the centre of the world. This map, besides reflecting the importance the Japanese attach to themselves in the world, has the virtue of showing the geographic proximity of North America to Asia—a fact easily overlooked when maps place Europe at their centre.

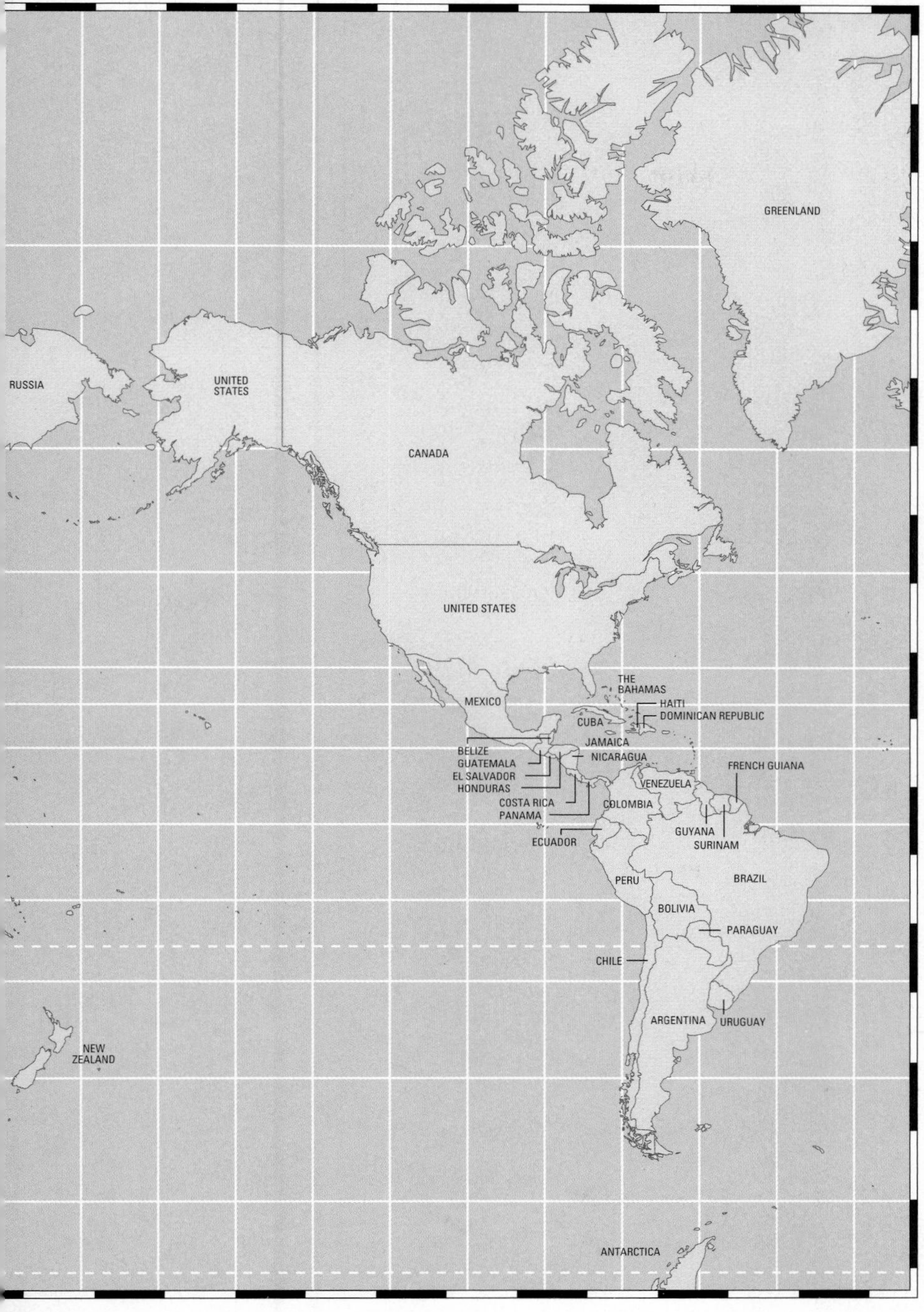
GREENLAND
RUSSIA
UNITED STATES
CANADA
UNITED STATES
THE BAHAMAS
HAITI
DOMINICAN REPUBLIC
MEXICO
CUBA
JAMAICA
BELIZE
GUATEMALA
EL SALVADOR
HONDURAS
NICARAGUA
COSTA RICA
PANAMA
FRENCH GUIANA
VENEZUELA
COLOMBIA
GUYANA
SURINAM
ECUADOR
BRAZIL
PERU
BOLIVIA
PARAGUAY
CHILE
ARGENTINA
URUGUAY
NEW ZEALAND
ANTARCTICA

CHAPTER 1

Culture and Meaning

KIKE CALVO/Alamy Stock Photo

As noted in the epigraph by Rupert Ross, it is nearly impossible to accurately interpret people's acts when we do not understand the meanings they attribute to those acts. This photo of two Inuit teens, dressed in traditional clothing, demonstrates the potential pitfalls of misinterpretation. What do you see when you look at the photo? Is this everyday dress, or is this for a special occasion? What is the significance of their clothing? Unless you are well versed in Inuit culture and history, it is likely that your interpretation says more about your own cultural context than that of the Inuit. Understanding human beliefs and behaviours requires a similar attention to meaning in context.

Acts are never merely acts. They are also signals of attitude. Those signals, however, are often culture specific. When acts are seen, but their signal-content misinterpreted, it is impossible to avoid forming inaccurate interpretations of others. Until we understand what particular acts mean to the other, we will continually ascribe motivations and states of mind that are well off the mark.

—Rupert Ross, *Dancing with a Ghost*

PROBLEM 1

How can people begin to understand beliefs and behaviours that are different from their own?

Introduction

The World Behind Everyday Appearances

In **sociocultural anthropology** we strive to look beyond the world of everyday experiences to discover the patterns and meanings that lie behind that world. Take, for example, the typical classroom chair with attached desk.

In our taken-for-granted, everyday world, this piece of furniture is a utilitarian object: something to sit on, or to write on, or even to put our feet on. But for the sociocultural anthropologist, as the epigraph to this chapter suggests, acts are never merely acts, nor are objects, even classroom chairs, merely objects; both are signals whose meaning is culturally specific. The classroom chair tells some interesting tales and poses some interesting questions. For example, why do we have chairs at all? Many societies don't; instead, people sit or squat on the ground or the floor or sit on stools or benches. Historically, the chair likely first appeared in Europe or the Near East, but it wasn't common even in Europe until the eighteenth century. Another question: Why does the classroom chair take the form it does? One feature of the chair that anthropologists might explore as they try to decipher the meaning of the classroom chair with writing surface is the erect position into which it forces the body, compelling it, in effect, to "pay attention." We might take a clue from the French philosopher Michel Foucault, who refers to the shaping of the human body as a "political anatomy." By this, he means that people's bodies are controlled by others to operate with the necessary speed and efficiency. Political anatomy produces, he says, "docile bodies."

An anthropologist might suggest that the classroom chair with desk is part of the political anatomy of educational settings—part of the system of relations that gives meaning to the classroom. In other words, this piece of furniture forms the body into a shape that prepares it (or forces it) to attend to a teacher and not to others in the same room. Moreover, it is appropriate to its unique setting in the classroom, as are other objects of furniture. Imagine, for example, replacing classroom chairs with bar stools, whose main purpose is to promote bodily mobility and conversation with others.

Once alert to the idea that the classroom chair might serve as an instrument of control, we might notice other ways in which classroom design serves as a mode of discipline. The distribution of people in space, with each person in a particular

sociocultural anthropology
A comparative approach to the study of societies and cultures that focuses on differences and similarities in the ways that societies are structured and cultural meanings are created.

"spot" in neat, ordered rows, serves to discipline people to "pay attention" to the classroom centre and not to others around them. We might also notice the distinctive ordering of time and the use of clocks, bells, and whistles to control the movement and activities of people in school settings. We can even take our analysis a step further and examine the discipline of the school setting sequentially, from kindergarten through high school. Contrast, for example, the wide-open space of the kindergarten classroom, with its open, movable chairs and tables and teacher's desk set off to the side, with the enclosed, partitioned space of a second- or third-grade classroom, with its neatly arranged desks facing the centred desk of the teacher. This is the evolution of classroom discipline.

Students, of course, do not always obey the subtle commands that direct their bodies to do certain things at certain times. One only has to examine the strange bodily contortions of students as they resist the form into which the classroom chair tries to force them. We also try, occasionally, to resist the isolation imposed by the arrangement of classroom furniture or the timetables set by clocks, bells, and whistles.

The ways in which specific societies order behaviour through the arrangement of space and time is but one small area examined by sociocultural anthropology, but it serves as an example of how, from an anthropological perspective, we cannot take anything about even our own beliefs and behaviour for granted, let alone the behaviour and beliefs of those whose backgrounds and histories differ from our own.

Sociocultural anthropologists find patterns of meaning even in objects as simple as a classroom chair.

This book is about how sociocultural anthropology can help us see beyond our taken-for-granted world. We will be examining how sociocultural anthropology helps us understand others and, in the process, better understand ourselves. We will also be examining how knowledge of others and ourselves is relevant to careers in social and economic development, public policy and planning, education, medicine, and conflict resolution.

BEYOND THE BOOK 1.1

On your own, or with a group of classmates, take a close look around the room where you have your lecture and/or tutorial. Take note of as many details about design or setup of the classroom as possible. For instance, consider the following questions:

- What direction do chairs face? Are they fixed, or can they be moved? What kinds of behaviours and interactions does the setup encourage or discourage?
- What kinds of technologies does the space use or encourage? Where are there outlets, lights, screens, blackboards, whiteboards? Who uses these, and when?
- Is there a lectern? A podium? A microphone? Who gets to use them, and how do you know?

Discuss your answers with your classmates. What might an anthropologist learn about how we value and share knowledge based on the design of the classroom? If possible, spend some time moving around the classroom, using space in ways that you normally would not during class time. How does it feel to do this? Does it change your perception of the space?

A Multifaceted Discipline

The term "anthropology" comes from two Greek words: *anthropos*, meaning "human beings," and *logia*, meaning "the study of" or "the knowledge of." This study of, or knowledge of, human beings includes everything that humans do currently or have done in the past. It also includes collecting evidence of how and when we became human and comparing humans to other organisms in the world. If asked to describe a typical anthropologist, you might envision an intrepid explorer, like Indiana Jones, searching for priceless artifacts or painstakingly excavating ancient fossils. But it would be more realistic to imagine a sociocultural anthropologist equipped with a notebook and a voice recorder rather than a shovel or a trowel. The kind of knowledge about human beings that interests sociocultural anthropologists is acquired by spending time with people, talking to them, observing what they do, and trying to understand their lives—as anthropologist Bronislaw Malinowski aptly put it—"from the native's point of view" (see Section 1.2).

In North America, anthropology is divided into four different approaches to the study of humans. Although these four subdisciplines address some of the same questions about what it means to be human, they focus on different aspects of the anthropological question (hence, the differences among the tools—notebooks versus shovels—used by different kinds of anthropologists). The subdisciplines are biological anthropology, archaeology, linguistic anthropology, and sociocultural anthropology (known as "cultural anthropology" in the

© Don Smith/Alamy Stock Photo

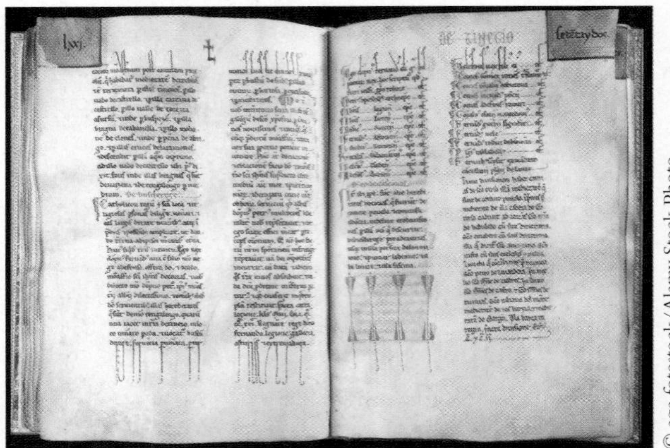

© age fotostock/Alamy Stock Photo

© Private Collection/Leemage/Bridgeman Images

© Richard Lord/The Image Works

Most anthropologists specialize in one or more of anthropology's four subfields. Clockwise from the top left, these are biological anthropology, linguistic anthropology, sociocultural anthropology, and archeology.

United States and "social anthropology" in Britain; in Canada the discipline is influenced by both these traditions). To understand what makes sociocultural anthropology unique among the subdisciplines (and among the social sciences in general), it is important first to understand the points of convergence and divergence among these subdisciplines.

Biological anthropology, the oldest of the four subdisciplines, focuses on the study of the evolution, function, and health of the human body and our closest primate ancestors across time and space. There are many areas of specialization within the field of biological anthropology, three of which are discussed here. Some biological anthropologists, for instance, specialize in *paleoanthropology*, which is the study of the fossilized remains of the earliest humans, and endeavour to understand the history of human biological evolution. Paleoanthropologists excavate ancient sites of early human activity or habitation, and they study fossil remains in laboratories.

Through close examinations of fossil records in Africa, Europe, and parts of Asia, paleoanthropologists study mostly extinct, transitional species between apes and humans called "hominids." Hominids are bipedal primates that first evolved in Africa ("bipedal" refers to the ability to walk on two feet for extended periods). They subsequently spread throughout the rest of the world. Although the history of hominid evolution is changing rapidly as new fossils are discovered, it is currently believed that hominids evolved more than 4 million years ago.

By studying and comparing the anatomy of hominid feet and leg joints, as well as preserved footprints, paleoanthropologists can reconstruct such things as the height, gait, and locomotion patterns of ancient hominids. At the site of Laetoli in Tanzania, for instance, famed paleoanthropologist Mary Leakey discovered evidence of bipedalism from hominid footprints preserved in volcanic ash that date to approximately 3.7 million years ago. Other paleoanthropologists study the cranial anatomy of hominids. Tooth structure and tooth wear can help us reconstruct hominid diets. Reconstructions of the physical structure of hominids can also provide evidence for their migrations and ancient interactions. Based upon his excavation and study of Neanderthal sites, Canadian anthropologist Eugene Morin argues that Neanderthals and humans interacted with each other between 30,000 and 40,000 years ago. This interaction may have included interbreeding.

Other biological anthropologists specialize in primatology, or the study of our closest nonhuman relatives. One of the most famous primatologists is Jane Goodall. In 1960, she went to Gombe Stream National Park in Tanzania, where she began a lifetime study of the behavioural patterns of wild chimpanzees. Given that humans and chimpanzees are closely related genetically, many primatologists believe that the study of apes can help glean information about the behaviour of early hominids that lived between 4 and 5 million years ago. Today, Goodall continues her research. She has worked tirelessly to help establish safe chimpanzee sanctuaries, and she speaks out against the destruction of their ecosystems.

The newest branch of biological anthropology is forensic anthropology, which is the study of human remains for identification and cause of death. Forensic anthropologists can often determine the age, sex, health status, height, and cause of death by examining human skeletal material and its surrounding context. Many forensic anthropologists assist with human rights cases, excavating human bones found buried in mass graves. By excavating remains found in war-torn areas of the world, such as the former Yugoslavia, Rwanda, and Darfur, forensic experts can document cases of genocide. This information, in turn, can be used in international human rights tribunals to establish the guilt or innocence of various parties. In addition, by identifying missing individuals, forensic anthropologists are able

biological anthropology
A subdiscipline of anthropology that focuses on the evolution, function, and health of the human body and those of our closest primate ancestors.

to provide many families with a sense of closure through confirmation of the death of a loved one. Other forensic experts work on active criminal investigations in tandem with the police in an effort to identify human remains that may be associated with a criminal case.

Archaeology is the branch of anthropology that studies human history and its artifacts. Archaeologists typically look at the material remains of human groups in order to learn how people lived. Tools, pottery shards, and other artifacts offer clues about the social and cultural lives of societies that existed thousands of years ago. Archaeologists excavate archaeological sites (areas that display evidence of past human activity).

Although archaeologists are often romanticized as treasure hunters within our pop culture, they do not keep any artifacts they find. All artifacts discovered are carefully mapped and recorded at a site to preserve their provenience, or specific location in space. For example, it is important to note where an artifact is found inside a house. Is it in the kitchen, a storage room, a bathroom, or a midden (refuse area)? By mapping out the horizontal locations of artifacts, archaeologists can make inferences about the functions of different spaces on a site. Some areas, for instance, might be used for cooking, others for making weapons, and still others for weaving or producing textiles. When recording provenience, archaeologists also record vertical provenience, or how far below the surface an artifact is discovered. Often, different layers of soil (called "strata") are connected to different dates of occupation. So it is important to map both vertical and horizontal provenience to understand spatial functions as well as time periods.

Once an archaeological site is excavated, the artifacts discovered are taken to labs, where they are washed and further analyzed. Decorations on pottery, for instance, can help date the pot (and, by extension, the site) and may also reveal other information about past lifestyles. Occasionally, residue may even be discovered inside an artifact such as a pot. Archaeologist Pat McGovern, for instance, conducts chemical analyses on the residue of ceramic pots. In the process, he has discovered (and re-created) some of the world's oldest alcoholic beverages. In Iran, he found the world's oldest barley beer, dating to approximately 3400 BCE, as well as the oldest wine made from grapes, from 5400 BCE. Brewing ancient beverages for modern consumers may sound exciting, but more than that, the ingredients in such beverages can tell us a lot about ancient life. For instance, we can learn about trade routes and migrations of people by examining the ingredients in beer. If a particular ingredient is not locally available, archaeologists can trace its source to other cultural areas and try to understand past human interactions, such as trade, on a wider scale.

Linguistic anthropology involves examining the relationship between language and culture. Linguistic anthropologists explore how people use language, both in a physical sense with regard to how communication is structured, and in a historical sense with regard to how different languages have developed and spread throughout history. Linguistic anthropologists are interested in studying all languages across time and space, although most focus on language use within a particular cultural framework. Sociolinguists, for instance, are interested in how various aspects of culture shape how we use language. They may analyze the structure and vocabulary used within speech, the study of accents, and even the study of topics of conversation. Language is informed by a society's views on gender, class, race, and other factors such as the context of

archaeology
The branch of anthropology that studies human history and its artifacts. Archaeologists typically look at the material remains of human groups in order to learn how people lived.

linguistic anthropology
A study of the relationship between language and culture. Linguistic anthropologists explore how people use language, both in a physical sense with regard to how communication is structured, and in a historical sense with regard to how different languages have developed and spread throughout history.

speaking. Think, for example, about how you may speak differently (in terms of vocabulary choice, intonation, and conversation topics) when you have a conversation with your grandmother versus your best friend.

An early and famous sociolinguistic study was conducted by American linguist William Labov, who studied the speech of sales associates working in department stores in Manhattan. Interested in the connection between social class and speech, Labov (1966) studied speech differences among sales associates at three department stores: *S. Klein*, which offered low-priced merchandise; *Macy's*, which appeals typically to middle-class consumers; and *Saks*, a high-end, expensive retailer. Labov noted that sales associates in each store talked differently, with associates from Saks putting greater emphasis on preconsonantal r's, found in such words as "beer" or "floor." A strong emphasis on the pronunciation of "r" is considered to be a subtle and unconscious form of prestige, and it is an emphasis mainly used in upper-class speech in Manhattan.

Historical linguists study the origins of languages and changes in language over time. For example, Canadian anthropologist John Colarusso received international media attention in 2014 when he deciphered writings on an ancient Greek vase referred to as the "New York Goose Play Vase" in New York's Metropolitan Museum of Art. An expert on the ancient Circassian language, Colarusso translated the meanings of ancient scribbles and graffiti on pottery that dates to more than 3000 years ago.

The above examples from the fields of biological anthropology, archaeology, and linguistic anthropology highlight the diversity of interests within anthropology. Given that anthropologists study all aspects of humanity across time and space, it is not uncommon to find an anthropologist studying ancient Egyptian hieroglyphics, observing homeless people in Toronto, or excavating archaeological sites in Peru.

Although all anthropologists specialize in the study of particular peoples, places, and issues, they also tend to work collaboratively, when necessary, to understand various societies. An archaeologist excavating an ancient site in Turkey, for instance, will most certainly call in biological, or physical, anthropologists when and if skeletal material is uncovered. Similarly, a historical linguist, like John Colarusso, will work with archaeologists or art historians to help decipher writings on ancient pottery. But what, then, is sociocultural anthropology, the primary focus of this text? How do the research interests and methods of sociocultural anthropologists differ from those of other anthropologists?

What Makes Sociocultural Anthropology Unique?

Sociocultural anthropologists look at how societies are structured and how cultural meanings are created. Although these anthropologists are interested in differences among peoples throughout the world, they also look for similarities in how people construct their own versions of what it means to be human. Sociocultural anthropologists, then, explore both the universal and the particular, moving back and forth between these two levels of inquiry and analysis in their work. They do fieldwork and ethnography among the societies and cultures they study (see Chapter 2), gathering data by talking to people and by participating in and observing their day-to-day lives.

This focus on social structures and cultural meanings, in all their forms, is what makes sociocultural anthropology unique among the subdisciplines. Many people, including some anthropologists, wonder whether sociocultural anthropology should be characterized as a science or as one of the humanities. At its best, sociocultural anthropology incorporates aspects of both: the methodological and analytical rigour of the sciences, and the interpretive insights and nuances of the humanities. Eminent anthropologist Eric Wolf (1964, 88) perhaps put it best when he described anthropology as "the most scientific of the humanities, [and] the most humanistic of the sciences." This combination of versatility and breadth is precisely what makes anthropology such an interesting and dynamic discipline.

Moreover, the unique perspective on humanity provided by sociocultural anthropology is well suited to thinking about the complexity of the contemporary world and the human condition. This book is organized around nine general problems that arise from the human condition—problems such as how to understand people with different beliefs and behaviours; why ways of life change; how people justify violence; and whether solving problems of social inequality is possible. These problems concern everyone, not just sociocultural anthropologists, but definitive solutions are not possible. So the goal, instead, is to achieve a greater understanding of why those problems exist and what might be done to address them. Sociocultural anthropologists can ask specific questions about them, applying their unique disciplinary perspective and methodologies. We will be focusing on these nine general problems in this text. At various points you will be asked to supply your own answers to questions and, perhaps, to discuss your answers with others.

Understanding others requires you to recognize that your behaviours and beliefs, as well as those of people in other societies, are socially patterned and constructed. For that reason, you will find in this text many comparisons between North American life and life in other societies. Whether or not you pursue a career in anthropology or a career that explicitly requires anthropological expertise, learning to approach and understand human beliefs and behaviour from an anthropological perspective is a valuable skill in the contemporary world.

QUESTIONS

1.1 Why do human beings differ in their beliefs and behaviours?
1.2 Is it possible to see the world through the eyes of others?
1.3 How can the meanings that others find in experience be interpreted and described?
1.4 What can learning about other peoples tell anthropologists about their own societies?
1.5 How can an anthropological perspective be used outside academia?

Question 1.1: Why Do Human Beings Differ in Their Beliefs and Behaviours?

From an anthropological perspective, members of a **society** view the world in a similar way because they share the same **culture**; people differ in how they view the world because their cultures differ. What do anthropologists mean by "culture"? A good place to start to understand the concept is with the fact that members of all human societies experience specific life events such as birth, death, and the quest for food, water, and shelter. All societies have what are for them appropriate rules for courtship, ideas about childrearing, procedures for exchanging goods, methods of food production, techniques for building shelters, and so on. But from one society to the next, the meanings people assign these events differ. We learn these meanings from, and teach these meanings to, other members of our culture.

Our working definition of culture, therefore, is as follows: "culture is the system of meanings about the nature of experience that is shared by a people and passed from one generation to another." This definition encompasses the meanings people give to things, events, activities, and people. Anthropologists have debated—and often disagreed about—the substance of culture and the best ways to study it (as we discuss in further detail in Chapter 2). Our working definition of culture highlights those aspects of this complicated and contentious term upon which most anthropologists can agree: culture is about meaning; cultural meanings must be

society
The social structures and organization of a group comprised of people who share a territory and culture.

culture
The system of meanings about the nature of experience that are shared by a people and passed on from one generation to another, including the meanings that people give to things, events, activities, and people.

learned; and, once learned, meanings are shared by members of a particular culture. It is also worth noting that most anthropologists today also agree on what culture is not. First, and foremost, culture is not a singular, quantifiable entity; it is not something that exists to a greater or lesser degree in certain groups. From the perspective of contemporary anthropology, no one people can be "more cultured" than another. From this follows a key second point: although anthropologists today tend to think in terms of "cultures," plural, rather than "Culture," singular, this does not mean that different cultures are separate, bounded entities, impervious to change or mutual influence. And finally, anthropologists are wary of discussions of culture that make it sound like a thing, or a possession ("the people of X do ritual Y because it is part of their culture"). Rather, it is important to remember that culture is a concept, or a tool, for understanding shared perceptions of experience ("by looking at ritual Y, performed by people X, we can see shared cultural understandings of Z"). Anthropologist Michel-Rolph Trouillot reminds us that, as a noun, often "the word culture blurs more than it elucidates the facts to be explained" (Trouillot 2003, 115). Methodologically speaking, the use of the word culture might suggest that that we are looking for one specific thing. Much better, Trouillot suggests that we rethink our focus to include

> *style, taste, cosmology, ethos, sensibility, desire, ideology, aspirations, or predispositions [, which] often better describe the facts that need to be studied because they tend to better limit the range of traits and patterns covered and are ... more grounded in the details that describe living, historically situated, localized people. (Trouillot 2003, 115)*

Culture, and the desires, ethos, and sensibilities it entails, enables human beings to make sense of their life experiences and to understand those experiences as meaningful in particular ways. Human beings share certain basic experiences: hunger and death, for example. Why, though, do people from different backgrounds understand these experiences in different ways? Thinking about culture begins to suggest an answer to this question.

Attitudes toward death provide one example. For some people, death marks the passage of a person from one world to another. For others, death is an ending, the final event in a life span. Still others view death as part of a never-ending cycle of birth, death, and rebirth. The Kwakwaka'wakw of British Columbia, for example, believe that when a person dies, the soul leaves the body and enters the body of a salmon. When a salmon is caught and eaten, a soul is released and is free to enter the body of another person.

Some societies fear the dead; others revere them. In rural China until recently, each household contained a shrine to the family ancestors. Before any major family decision, the head of the household addressed the shrine to ask the ancestors' advice, thus making the dead part of the world of the living. In southern Italy, by contrast, funeral customs were designed to discourage the dead from returning. Relatives placed useful objects such as matches and small change near the body to placate the soul of the deceased and to ensure that it did not return to disturb the living.

In some societies, death is accepted as natural and inevitable; in others, death is always attributed to the malevolent act of some person, often involving sorcery. In these societies, every death elicits suspicion and a demand for vengeance. Still other societies require great demonstrations of grief and mourning for the deceased. Thus, the Dani of New Guinea require a close female relative of a recently deceased person to sacrifice part of a finger. In most North American societies, survivors of the deceased are expected to restrain their grief almost as if it were a contagious disease. For many North Americans, the sight of southern Italian women pulling their hair and being restrained from flinging themselves into an open grave is as bewildering as their own restraint of grief would be to southern Italians.

Food provides another telling example of how a culture takes the "raw materials" of human life and makes them meaningful. All humans need to eat; however, no society accepts all items in their edible universe as "good to eat." Only a relatively few items are so designated. Insects such as grubs, beetles, and ants are acceptable fare in some societies, while people in others are horrified by the thought of eating insects. Most North Americans like and are encouraged to drink milk, yet some people in China consider milk undrinkable. Conversely, the Chinese raise dogs for meat—something that would horrify most North Americans. North American children who have raised pet guinea pigs would have a hard time accepting the Peruvian practice of raising guinea pigs for food.

Of all the 2 million or so species of living organisms that inhabit Earth, only humans dwell largely in worlds that they themselves have created by giving meanings to things. This creation is what anthropologists mean by the term "culture." Human beings are cultural animals; they ascribe meanings of their own creation to objects, persons, behaviours, emotions, and events and then proceed to act as if those meanings are real. All facets of their lives—death, birth, courtship, mating, food acquisition and consumption—are suffused with meaning.

FABRICE COFFRINI/AFP via Getty Images

Packs of precooked insect burgers based on protein-rich mealworm are seen on a supermarket shelf on 21 August 2017 in Geneva, Switzerland. Swiss food safety laws were changed in 2017 to allow for the sale of food items containing three types of insects: crickets, grasshoppers, and mealworms.

Clifford Geertz suggests that human beings are compelled to impose meaning on their experiences because without those meanings to help them comprehend experience and impose an order on the universe, the world would seem a jumble, "a chaos of pointless acts and exploding emotions" (1973, 46). When people share the meanings they give to experiences, they share and participate in the same culture.

Differences in culture arise, in part, from the fact that different groups of human beings, for various reasons, create, share, and participate in different realities; as a consequence, they assign different meanings to death, birth, marriage, and food. Objects, persons, behaviours, emotions, and events in a human world have meanings ascribed to them by those who share, use, or experience them. The clothes people wear, the foods they eat (or refuse to eat), even their gender, are defined through the meanings that people give them. Understanding culture, and the culturally situated meanings that flourish in various cultural contexts, is therefore the main object of anthropological study. In the next section, we will explore how anthropologists have approached the study of culture.

BEYOND THE BOOK 1.1

Mere edibility is not enough to determine what counts as food. Food is a cultural creation; that is, human beings define what is and is not food. Consider, for example, the items listed below, all of which serve as food among one group of people or another. Which of these would you eat, and which would you not eat? If there are any you would not eat, explain why.

	Yes	No
eel		
kangaroo tail		
dog		

	Yes	No
guinea pig		
raw squid		
sea urchin (sea slugs)		
ants		
monkey brains		
grubs		
opossum		
rattlesnake		
iguana		
horse		
dolphin		
pickled pig's feet		
haggis (stuffed intestines)		
cow brains		
blood sausage		
raw steak		
armadillo		

Question 1.2: Is It Possible to See the World through the Eyes of Others?

This question lies at the heart of the anthropological enterprise. The anthropologist must be able to look beyond everyday appearances to decipher the often hidden meanings of beliefs, objects, and behaviours, while setting aside her or his preconceptions about what is normal or proper. In addition to that, the anthropologist must also learn one culture and then relate what he or she has learned to members of another culture in order to translate the meanings of one world into the meanings of another. In the process, many anthropologists experience cultural traditions and values vastly different from their own. In this section, we explore the intricacies of two key concepts in anthropology: ethnocentrism and cultural relativism.

How Do People Explain the Beliefs and Behaviours of Others?

Richard Scaglion (1990) is fond of telling the story of his friend, a member of the Abelam tribe of Papua New Guinea, who was looking through an issue of *Sports Illustrated*. The friend, dressed in full ceremonial regalia with a feather through his nose, was laughing uncontrollably at a woman shown in a liquor advertisement. When he managed to stop laughing long enough to explain what he thought was so funny, he said, "This white woman has made holes in her ears and stuck things in them." When Scaglion pointed out that his friend had an ornament in his nose, the reply was "That's different. That's for beauty and has ceremonial significance. But I didn't know that white people mutilated themselves."

Scaglion's friend was confronting a problem that many do when the behaviour or beliefs of others seem to differ from their own, and his response was not unusual. He was both shocked and mystified at the strange behaviour. And this suggests a dilemma: Since there are so many versions of what the world is like, how do we go about trying to understand each of them without making positive or negative judgments? Which version of the world is correct? Are there any such versions we *can* reject or condemn? Can we say, as so many have, that one culture is superior to another?

In the catalogue of human behaviours and beliefs, it is not difficult to find practices or ideas that may seem bizarre or shocking even to trained anthropologists. Sociocultural anthropologists have described the beliefs of the Ilongots of the Philippines, who must kill an enemy to obtain a head that they can throw away in order to diminish the grief and rage they feel at the death of a kinsman or kinswoman. They have studied the historical records of the Aztecs in Mexico, who believed that the universe underwent periodic destruction and that the only way to ward off disaster was to pluck the hearts from live sacrificial victims to offer to the gods. They have also studied modern states that

© Rita Willaert/http://www.flickr.com/photos/rietje

Abelam villager in ceremonial costume.

routinely engage in or sanction torture, terror, and genocide. How, then, should we react to practices and beliefs such as these?

The Ethnocentric Fallacy and the Relativist Fallacy

If we do condemn or reject the beliefs or behaviours of others, we may be embracing the **ethnocentric fallacy**, or the idea that our beliefs and behaviours are right and true, while those of other peoples are wrong or misguided. Sociocultural anthropologists have long fought against **ethnocentrism**, that is, the tendency to judge the beliefs and behaviours of other cultures from the perspective of one's own. They try to show that what often appears on the surface to be an odd belief or a bizarre behaviour is functional and logical in the context of a particular culture. They find the ethnocentric fallacy *intellectually* and *methodologically* intolerable; if everyone everywhere thinks that they are right and that others must be wrong, an intellectual and social dead end is inevitable. Furthermore, if we, as anthropologists, assume that we have all the right answers, our study of other cultures becomes simply the study of other people's mistakes.

Because of the intellectual and methodological implications of ethnocentrism, sociocultural anthropologists emphatically reject this position. But the opposite pole to ethnocentrism, **cultural relativism**, raises issues of its own. Cultural relativism, simply stated, holds that no behaviour or belief can be judged to be odd or wrong simply because it is different from our own; instead, we must try to understand a culture on its own terms and to understand behaviours or beliefs for the purpose, function, or meaning they have to people in the societies in which we find them. In other words, cultural relativism holds that a specific belief or behaviour can be understood only in relation to the culture—the system of meanings—in which it is embedded.

However, relativism poses a *moral* predicament. Once we concede, say, that it is permissible to rip out the hearts of living human beings, provided that you believe it necessary to save the world, or that it is permissible to subject young girls to genital

ethnocentric fallacy
The mistaken notion that the beliefs and behaviours of other cultures can be judged from the perspective of one's own culture.

ethnocentrism
The tendency to judge the beliefs and behaviours of other cultures from the perspective of one's own culture.

cultural relativism
The effort to understand the beliefs and behaviours of other cultures in terms of the culture in which they are found.

modification to protect family reputations, we find ourselves falling quickly into the **relativistic fallacy**, or the idea that it is impossible to make moral judgments about the beliefs and behaviours of others. This standpoint, of course, seems morally intolerable because it implies that no beliefs or behaviours can be condemned. So we are left with two untenable positions: the ethnocentric alternative, which is intellectually and methodologically unsatisfactory, and the relativistic alternative, which is morally unsatisfactory. How do we solve this problem?

Putting Cultural Relativism into Practice

Virginity Testing in Turkey and Beliefs about Reproduction

To illustrate further the dilemma of relativism and the difficulty of appreciating the cultures of others without making moral judgments, consider this incident. Some time ago a human rights group based in the United States issued a report condemning the practice of virginity testing in Turkey. Traditionally, young women in Turkey, as in some other cultures, are expected to avoid sexual relations prior to marriage, although the same rule does not apply to men. In this tradition, the bride's virginity is revealed by displaying, the morning after the wedding, the sheet that was spread on the couple's wedding bed with the telltale hymeneal blood stain. The human rights report condemns the traditional testing as well as the reported practice of forcing tests on hospital patients, students, and applicants for government jobs. As anthropologists, we must ask: Is the human rights group being ethnocentric in judging Turkish customs by North American cultural norms, or is it correctly identifying abuses of women that must be corrected? Might it help if we better understood the logic behind the belief?

In her book on Turkish village society, *The Seed and the Soil*, anthropologist Carol Delaney (1991) describes how virginity testing relates to the way in which Turkish villagers conceptualize and explain the reproductive process. They see producing children as analogous to the planting and growing of crops; the man provides the "seed" with his semen, and the woman serves as the "soil" in which the seed germinates and grows. As a metaphor for reproduction, the idea of the seed and the soil provides villagers with a way of thinking about and understanding reproduction. However, the metaphor of seed and soil has at least one important implication; since seeds do not have a limited life span, as we know semen to have, villagers believe that once planted, the seed (semen) may grow at any time. Consequently, if a woman has had sexual relations with a man other than her husband at any time prior to her marriage, the paternity of the child will be in doubt. Since descent in traditional Turkish villages is closely tied to many things, including property rights, uncertainty about the identity of the true father can have major implications. Thus, in the context of Turkish beliefs about procreation, virginity testing may be said to make sense.

Furthermore, Turkish beliefs about conception are not that far removed from our own, since our language draws from the same agricultural metaphors as those of Turkish villagers to explain reproduction. We talk about women being "fertile" or "barren" and semen "fertilizing" "eggs." "Sowing one's oats," as an expression of sexual activity, is still heard in parts of the United States and Canada. Furthermore, these views are reinforced by religious proscription, legitimized in the Koran and the Hebrew Scriptures. Thus, before we either condemn or accept the Turkish villagers for their treatment of women, we need to examine what their beliefs tell us about our own. Our own may be equally problematic.

relativistic fallacy
The idea that it is impossible to make moral judgments about the beliefs and behaviours of members of other cultures.

Cannibalism among the Wari' and Beliefs about Death

But what of cannibalism, such as the Wari' practice of roasting and eating the dead? Surely, there is no way to justify that! Cannibalism, as Beth Conklin (2001) points out in her study of Wari' cannibalism, *Consuming Grief*, pushes the limits of cultural relativism, guaranteeing reactions of revulsion and fascination. But in addition to that, it has political implications: for centuries, cannibalism was the ultimate smear tactic. To accuse one's enemies or people one wanted to degrade or dominate of cannibalism was the ultimate justification for conquest, domination, and exploitation. In 1503, Queen Isabella of Spain decreed that Spaniards could legally enslave specifically those American Indians who were cannibals. Pope Innocent IV, in 1510, ruled that Christians could punish, by force of arms, the sin of cannibalism. By claiming moral superiority in this way, Christians were claiming the right to decide ultimately what is right and what is wrong. Armed with that power, they felt justified in imposing their own views and way of life.

What Queen Isabella and Pope Innocent IV conveniently overlooked, however, was that Europeans at the time practised cannibalism. As Conklin notes, medicinal cannibalism—the consumption of human body parts for curative purposes—had a long tradition in Europe. Up until two centuries ago, European physicians prescribed the consumption of human flesh, heart, bones, and other body parts as cures for such afflictions as arthritis, reproductive disorders, sciatica, warts, and skin blemishes. Human blood was thought to be a cure for epilepsy, and physicians recommended that it be drunk immediately after the supplier died. Physicians also thought that the blood of someone who died violently was particularly effective.

The people of medieval Europe accepted in their own lives the same types of practices they condemned in others; furthermore, they failed to understand the practices from the point of view of the others. The Wari' ate their dead, for example, because they believed it was the compassionate thing to do. As Conklin puts it, "[m]ore painful than having the corpse eaten would have been to have it not eaten" (2001, 81). For the Wari', a corpse left intact was a painful reminder of the deceased. People unrelated to the deceased ate the corpse, even when the smell or taste repulsed them, in the belief that it would help family members come to terms with their loss.

The Western practice of burying the dead (which missionaries and government officials forced the Wari' to do after contact) was almost as horrific to the Wari' as their cannibalism might have been for non-Wari'. "It's cold in the earth," a father who had recently lost a two-year-old son explained to Beth Conklin. "We keep remembering our child, lying there, cold. We remember and we are sad. It was better in the old days, when the others ate the body. Then we did not think about our child's body much. We did not remember our child as much, and we were not so sad" (xv). Burying the body also violated many fundamental Wari' values. For them, the ground was "dirty" and "polluting." They never sat directly on the dirt, and discarding things on the ground was considered disrespectful. Special ritual objects were never supposed to touch the ground.

Without a deeper understanding of Wari' culture, we cannot know how consuming the dead aligns with the meaning they impose on their world, including how they deal with their emotions. By consuming the dead, Wari' are trying to obliterate the painful memories of their loss. The memory of the body is painful, but equally painful are the material objects associated with the deceased and the very mention of the deceased's name. Thus, the Wari' not only consume the body but also burn the house and personal possessions of the deceased. For most North Americans, a dead body is only a shell, its soul or spiritual essence gone. However, the dead are nonetheless memorialized in a variety of ways that are meaningfully linked to both the lives of the dead and to those still alive, as the roadside memorial depicted in the photo demonstrates. The Wari', by contrast, want to separate the dead from the living,

Jeffrey Isaac Greenberg 4/Alamy Stock Photo

Roadside memorials in North America are a poignant way to remember the dead and send a message to the living: in this case, to "drive safely." Specifically, white-painted "ghost bikes" mark locations where cyclists died in collisions with motor vehicles.

so obliterating their memories is perfectly logical. The point, then, is that when we impose our own meanings on practices such as cannibalism and fail to see those practices the way others do, we miss a great deal.

BEYOND THE BOOK 1.2

In their funeral practices, Wari' attempt to obliterate the memory of the dead, as do many other societies. Other societies, however, memorialize the dead; forgetting them would be an act of disrespect. Think about your own cultural background and whether or not you are encouraged to preserve the memory of the dead. List the ways you try to keep the memory of deceased persons alive, and speculate as to why you do that instead of trying to forget them. If you are encouraged to forget the dead, how is that accomplished? Why? Compare your beliefs and practices with those of your classmates.

But does this mean that *any* practice or belief, once we understand it from "the native's point of view," is acceptable? Does understanding the cultures of others require that we accept and justify all beliefs and practices?

Objectivity and Morality

For anthropologists, the conflict between ethnocentrism and relativism is not just theoretical. When choosing their research subjects, anthropologists may face this dilemma: Should they maintain a "moral distance" from those they are studying and remain "objective," or should they engage in criticizing behaviour or beliefs they encounter (e.g., virginity testing)?

The contradiction between "objective" anthropology and a politically committed anthropology became apparent to Nancy Scheper-Hughes when she returned as an anthropologist to a shantytown in Brazil where, previously, she had worked as a community organizer. The women with whom she had worked in the past became angry. Why, they asked, was she now, as an anthropologist, so passive, so indifferent to the destruction around her when as a community organizer, she had helped them fight for clean water, decent wages, and protection from police brutality? She tried to explain that as an anthropologist, she was there now to observe, document, and write about their lives as truthfully as she could. The women refused to accept this view of her work and insisted that, if they were to work with her, she would have to work with them to fight for better lives. "What," they said, "is anthropology to us?"

On the basis of that experience, Scheper-Hughes (1995, 416) now argues for a politically committed, morally engaged, and ethically grounded anthropology. "Those of us who make our living observing and recording the misery of the world," she writes, "have a particular obligation to reflect critically on the impact of the harsh images of human suffering that we foist upon the public."

Scheper-Hughes proposes what she calls a more "womanly-hearted" anthropology, one that is concerned with how people treat one another. Cultural relativism, she says, is no longer appropriate to the world in which we live, and anthropology, if it is to be worth anything, must be "critically grounded." Anthropologists cannot ignore the massacres and disappearances of vulnerable people that often occur in the communities in which anthropologists work. They must, she insists, serve as witnesses and reporters of human rights abuses and of the suffering of the poor and the oppressed. Witnessing, rather than just observing, therefore, requires not simply that we approach our subjects from a relativist perspective, but that we employ **critical cultural relativism**, through which anthropologists engage directly with questions of inequality, ethics, and power.

But serving as a witness for the poor and oppressed can itself lead to moral dilemmas for the anthropologist when the people with whom the anthropologist works engage in behaviour that may appear morally questionable. Scheper-Hughes confronted this question when she discovered and reported that impoverished women in the Brazilian shantytowns sometimes allowed their starving infants to die in the belief that they were doomed anyway. When Philippe Bourgois (2003) studied the world of crack dealers on the Upper East Side of New York City, he worried about the negative images he would be conveying if he reported the personal violence, sexual abuse, addiction, and alienation he witnessed. He recalled the advice of anthropologist Laura Nader, who advised others not to study the poor and powerless because whatever you say will be used against them.

Human rights activists, in particular, are skeptical about cultural relativism. If, they say, we must tolerate the beliefs and practices of other cultures because to do otherwise would be ethnocentric, how can we ever criticize what seem to be violations of basic human rights, such the right to bodily integrity, or the right to be free from torture, arbitrary imprisonment, slavery, and genocide? Cultural relativism, they say, makes arguments about human rights meaningless by legitimizing almost any behaviour. Critical cultural relativism, on the other hand, might allow us to understand cultural beliefs and practices on their own terms without ignoring the cultural power dynamics that allow them to "make sense" within a given culture.

Elizabeth Zechenter, who makes the argument for universal principles of human rights, says that cultural relativists are right to contend that endorsing or rejecting some foreign customs risks imposing one's cultural prejudices on others. She adds, however, that the idea we can make no judgments without being ethnocentric is illusory: "One simply cannot avoid making judgments when faced with oppression and brutality masquerading under the guise of cultural tradition. Such a non-judgmental tolerance of brutality is actually an ultimate form of ethnocentrism, if not an outright ethical surrender" (1997, 336).

There is obviously no easy answer to the question of when, if ever, it is proper to judge the beliefs and practices of others to be right or wrong, or when, if ever, it is proper to work to change behaviours or beliefs judged to be wrong. Ideally, our attempts to understand what, at first, seemed puzzling in some cultures, and our arrival at some solution to that puzzle, should lead us to ask ourselves what made the behaviour or belief puzzling in the first place. We also need to bear in mind that when cultures order the world in certain ways for their members, they are, in effect, masking other ways of viewing things. We need to appreciate that there are perspectives different from our own and that our ethnocentric biases may blind us to those alternatives. In other words, while culture provides us with certain meanings to give to objects, persons, behaviours, emotions, and events, it also shields us from alternative meanings. What our culture hides from us may be more important than what it reveals.

critical cultural relativism
An alternative perspective on cultural relativism that poses questions about cultural beliefs and practices in terms of who accepts them and why, who they might be disproportionately harming and benefiting, and the cultural power dynamics that enable them.

BEYOND THE BOOK 1.3

Think of a cultural practice or belief that you have heard about (from the media, from acquaintances, from places you have travelled) that challenges your sense of cultural relativism. What aspects of this practice or belief are problematic for you, and why? What aspects of your cultural background (e.g., religion, class, gender) inform the judgments you are inclined to make in this case? What information do you need in order to better understand your example within its own cultural context? Do you think it is possible for us (as anthropologists and anthropology students) to overcome our ethnocentric biases? Support your opinion and compare your answers with those of your classmates.

Question 1.3: How Can the Meanings That Others Find in Experience Be Interpreted and Described?

In one Sherlock Holmes detective story, Dr. Watson, Holmes's assistant, decides to teach the great detective a lesson in humility. He hands Holmes a pocket watch owned by Watson's late brother and challenges Holmes to infer from the watch the character of its owner. Holmes's interpretation: "[Your brother] was a man of untidy habits—very untidy and careless. He was left with good prospects, but he threw away his chances and finally, taking to drink, he died."

Watson, astounded at the accuracy of Holmes's description of his late brother, asks if it was guesswork. "I never guess," replies Holmes.

"I began by stating that your brother was careless. When you observe the lower part of the watch case, you notice that it is not only dented in two places, but it is cut and marked all over from the habit of keeping other hard objects, such as coins or keys, in the same pocket. Surely it is no great feat to assume that a man who treats [an expensive] watch so cavalierly must be a careless man. Neither is it a very far-fetched inference that a man who inherits one article of such value is pretty well provided for in other respects."

"But what about his drinking habits?" asks Watson.

Holmes responds: "Look at the innerplate which contains the keyhole [where the watch is wound]. Look at the thousands of scratches all around the hole-marks where the key has slipped. What sober man's key could have scored those grooves? But you will never see a drunkard's watch without them. He winds it at night, and he leaves these traces of his unsteady hand. Where is the mystery in all this?"

Had Holmes been an anthropologist, he might have been tempted also to draw some inferences about the society in which the watch was manufactured, particularly about its conceptions of time. For example, in some societies, time is task oriented, not clock oriented; time might be measured by how long it takes to cook rice, as in Madagascar. In other societies, time patterns depend on natural events such as the rising of the sun or the ebb and flow of tides. British anthropologist E.E. Evans-Pritchard, in his classic account of the Nuer of the Sudan, noted,

> *the Nuer have no expression equivalent to "time" in our language, and they cannot, therefore, as we can, speak of time as though it were something actual, which passes, can be wasted, can be saved, and so forth. I don't think they ever experience the same feeling of fighting against time because their points of reference are mainly the activities themselves, which are generally of a leisurely character. Events follow a logical order, but they are not controlled by an abstract system, there being no autonomous points of reference to which activities have to conform with precision. Nuer are fortunate. (Evans-Pritchard 1940, 103)*

An anthropologist might also infer that clocks are instruments of discipline; they tell us when to get up, when to go to bed, when to eat, when to start work, and when to stop work. Our work patterns are defined by clocks, and our wages may depend on the constant repetition over time of a particular task. Historian E.P. Thompson (1967) notes that until the

Modern notions of clock-based time tell us a great deal about the culture we live in. Workers like these were required to punch a timecard at the start and end of their shifts, for their wages may have depended on a particular task or tasks being completed over a particular time. What measures of time are most important in your life as a student?

institution of modern notions of time and the need to measure it with clocks, work patterns were characterized by alternating bouts of intense labour and idleness, at least whenever people were in control of their own working lives. He even suggests that this pattern persists today, but only among a few self-employed professionals such as artists, writers, small farmers, and, he suggests, university students.

Watson's brother's watch was a product of Western society, part of its culture. Holmes "read" the watch as if it were a collection of symbols or words, a **cultural text** that revealed the character of its owner. He could just as easily have viewed it as a text inscribed with the symbols that revealed the ideas about time and work that characterized the civilization that produced it.

One way to think about culture is as a text of significant symbols: words, gestures, drawings, natural objects—anything, in fact, that carries meaning. To understand another culture we must be able, as Holmes was with a pocket watch, to decipher the meanings of the symbols that comprise a cultural text. We must be able to interpret the meanings embedded in the language, objects, gestures, and activities that are shared by members of a society. Fortunately, the ability to decipher a cultural text is part of being human; in our everyday lives we both read and maintain the text that makes up our own culture. We have learned the meanings behind the symbols that frame our lives, and we share those meanings with others. Our task in understanding another culture is to take the abilities that have enabled us to dwell in our own culture and use them to understand the cultures of others.

Deciphering the Balinese Cockfight

To illustrate how an anthropologist might decipher a cultural text, imagine yourself coming upon a cockfight on the island of Bali. You see a ring in which two roosters with sharpened metal spurs attached to their legs are set at each other until one kills the other. Surrounding the fighting cocks are men shouting encouragement to their favourites, each having placed a wager that his favourite will kill its opponent.

FIGURE 1.1 Bali

cultural text
A way of thinking about culture as a text of significant symbols, such as words, gestures, drawings, and natural objects, all of which carry meaning.

In Balinese society, cockfighting is a major sporting event that is closely tied to cultural interpretations of manhood, competition, and status.

What do you make of this? Your first reaction might be shock or disgust at the spectacle of the crowd urging the cocks to bloody combat. After a while you might begin to find similarities to events that are meaningful to you, such as some North American sports. But what if, like Sherlock Holmes—or like Clifford Geertz (1972), from whom this example is taken—you want to understand the meaning of what is happening and what that meaning tells you about how Balinese view their world? If you assume that the cockfight is a feature of Balinese culture, a Balinese text filled with symbols that carry meaning about what it is to be Balinese, how might you proceed to read this text?

You might begin by finding out the language the Balinese use to talk about the cockfight. You would no doubt discover that the double-entendre of cock both as a synonym for rooster and as a euphemism for penis is the same for the Balinese as it is for North Americans. The double-entendre even produces, says Geertz, the same jokes, puns, and obscenities in Bali as it does in North America. You would discover that *sabung*, the Balinese word for cock, has numerous other meanings and is used metaphorically to mean hero, warrior, champion, political candidate, bachelor, dandy, lady-killer, or tough guy. Court trials, wars, political contests, inheritance disputes, and street arguments are compared with cockfights. Even the island of Bali is thought of as being cock-shaped (in this case, meaning the fowl). You would also find that men give their fowls inordinate attention, spending most of their time grooming them and even feeding them a special diet. As one of Geertz's Balinese informants put it, "We're all cock crazy."

Having discovered the importance of cockfights to the Balinese and the connections they make between cocks and men, you next examine the cockfight itself. You learn that cockfights are public events held in arenas of about 4.7 square metres from late afternoon until after sundown. Handlers, expert in the task, attach sharp spurs to the cocks' legs; for a cock thought to be superior to an opponent, the spurs are adjusted in a slightly disadvantageous position. The cocks are released in the centre of the ring and fly at each other, fighting until one kills the other. The owner of the winning cock takes the carcass of the loser home to eat; the losing owner is sometimes driven in despair to wreck family shrines. You discover that the Balinese contrast heaven and hell by comparing them to the mood of a man whose cock has just won and the mood of a man whose cock has just lost.

You find out that while the Balinese place odds on cockfights, there are strict social conventions that dictate the wagering. For example, a man will never bet against a cock that is owned by someone of his family group or village or a friend's family group or village, but he will place large bets against a cock owned by an enemy or the friend of an enemy. Rarely is a cockfight without social significance (e.g., between two outsiders), and rarely do cocks owned by members of the same family or village fight each other. Moreover, the owners of the cocks, especially in important matches, are usually among the leaders of their communities. You might learn that cockfights come close to encouraging open expressions of aggression between village and kin-group rivals, but not quite, because the cockfight is, as the Balinese put it, "only a cockfight."

Given the social rules for betting and the ways in which odds are set, you might reason, as Geertz did, that the Balinese rarely make a profit betting on cockfights. Geertz says, in fact, that most bettors just want to break even. Consequently, the meaning of the cockfight for a Balinese has little to do with economics. The question is what meaning the cockfight *does* have for the Balinese. What is the cockfight really about, if it is not about money?

Geertz concludes that the Balinese cockfight is, above all, about status, about the ranking of people vis-à-vis one another. The Balinese cockfight is a text filled with meaning about status as the Balinese see it. Cocks represent men—more specifically, their owners; the fate of the cock in the ring is linked, if only temporarily, to the social fate of its owner. Each cock has a following consisting of the owner, the owner's family, and members of the owner's village, and these followers "risk" their status by betting on the cockfight. Furthermore, Geertz maintains that the more a match is between near equals, personal enemies, or high-status individuals, the more the match is about status. And the more the match is about status, the closer the identification of cock and man, the finer the cocks, and the more exactly they will be matched. The match will inspire greater emotion and absorption, and the gambling will be more about status and less about economic gain.

For Geertz, the cockfight is like any art form; it takes a highly abstract and difficult concept—status—and depicts it in a way that makes it comprehensible to the participants. The cockfight is meaningful to the Balinese because it tells them something real about their own lives, but in a way that does not directly affect their lives. They see the struggle for status that is part of everyday life vividly portrayed, even though, in the cockfight itself, no one really gains or loses status in any permanent sense.

A few words of caution are necessary concerning what we might learn about the Balinese from this particular cultural text. First, it would probably be a mistake to assume that the people gain status by being on the winning side or lose it by being on the losing side. The status outcomes of the cockfight do not translate into real life any more than the victory of your favourite sports team increases your status. Instead, says Geertz, the cockfight illustrates what status is about for the Balinese. The cockfight is a story the Balinese tell themselves about themselves. It would also be a mistake to assume that the character of the Balinese can be read directly from the cockfight; any conclusion that the cockfight is indicative of an aggressive, competitive, violent national character would quickly be dispelled. The Balinese are shy about competition and avoid open conflict. The slaughter in the cockfight is not how things are literally, but about how they could be. Finally, the cockfight reveals only a segment of the Balinese character, just as Watson's brother's watch revealed only a segment of its owner's character. The culture of a people, like the possessions of a person, is an ensemble of texts—collections of symbols and meanings—that must be viewed together to achieve a full understanding.

Question 1.4: What Can Learning about Other Peoples Tell Anthropologists about Their Own Societies?

Anthropologists do not limit themselves to the study of cultures that are different from their own. They often apply concepts and techniques that are useful in understanding and interpreting other cultures as a means to understand and interpret their own. One objective of studying other cultures is to help us recognize the meanings we impose on our own experiences.

BEYOND THE BOOK 1.4

Anthropologists often learn about culture through cross-cultural comparisons, but an important "side effect" of taking an anthropological perspective on the world is that it encourages us to see our own society and culture in a new light. The questions below, which you can answer alone, with a partner/small group, or as a class discussion, encourage this kind of thinking about the often elusive concept of "Canadian culture":

1. What are some uniquely Canadian practices, beliefs, or values? Are these widely agreed upon, or up for debate?
2. What are some of the key symbols or texts of Canadian culture? How might you interpret the meanings behind them?
3. Can you think of cases where the "Canadianness" of certain beliefs, values, symbols, or practices has become a matter of debate or disagreement? What can we infer about Canadian culture from such debates?
4. What Canadian practices or beliefs might be most shocking or difficult to understand to someone who was not familiar with them? Why?

A Balinese Anthropologist Studies Canadian Hockey

Whether we approach other cultures as anthropologists, as travellers, or as professionals who need to communicate with people of other cultures, the confrontation with other ways of believing and behaving should cause us to reflect on our way of viewing the world. To illustrate, try to step outside yourself and objectify an experience whose meaning you take for granted. Pretend you are a Balinese anthropologist who suddenly comes upon a spectacle as important in its way to Canadians as the cockfight is to Balinese: a hockey game.

As a Balinese, you might first react to this Canadian text with horror and revulsion at seeing men and women speeding from one end of an ice sheet to the other with long wooden sticks in their hands, rudely pushing one another out of the way while thousands cheer them on. As you settled in, however, you would soon find some obvious similarities between the hockey game and the cockfight you are familiar with at home. Both are spectator sports in which the spectators sort themselves into supporters of one side or the other. In fact, in hockey, the sorting is even more carefully arranged, since fans of one team are often seated on one side of the arena and fans of the other on the opposite side.

Your next step (as in interpreting the cockfight) would be to examine the language Canadians use to refer to the hockey game. You discover that they use similar expressions in talking about hockey and fighting, for example, roughing and slashing. Coaches talk about getting "revenge" for defeats, as generals might talk about getting revenge on battlefields. You conclude that Canadians seem to feel the same way about hockey as they do about fighting. If you attend several hockey games, you will most likely witness players of opposing teams taking off their protective gloves and beginning to punch each other.

You soon discover that winning and losing hockey games is as important to Canadians as winning and losing cockfights is to Balinese. Winners engage in frenzied celebrations called "victory parties," and losers are often despondent in defeat. As anthropologists know, this behaviour is not always the case in other societies. For example, when the Gahuku-Gama of the Highlands of New Guinea started playing soccer, they always played until a committee of elders decided that the score was tied; the match was then considered completed. So you speculate that hockey is also about the meanings that Canadians give to the idea of success. You learn that success in Canada (like status in Bali) is a highly abstract idea; because it is abstract, its meaning is embedded in activities understood by members of the society. You need to find answers to certain questions about the meaning of success in Canadian society: How is success defined? How is it obtained? Why doesn't everyone who follows all the rules for gaining success attain it?

Through your fieldwork, you find that most North Americans believe that "all men are created equal" and that every person has (or at least should have) an equal opportunity to succeed. People compete for success, and they ought to compete on an equal footing, on a "level playing field," as some put it. Success, North Americans believe, comes from hard work, sacrifice, and self-denial. But you wonder why North Americans believe that hard work, sacrifice, and self-denial bring success. Aren't there instances where they do not? How do North Americans explain why women and minorities succeed less often than white males do? Why do some people achieve more success than others? You conclude that it is impossible to prove directly in real life the correctness of this North American success model. Faith in the value of work and self-denial must be generated in other ways. As a Balinese anthropologist studying the Canadian custom of hockey, you conclude, then, that the meaning of Canadian hockey lies in its demonstration of the North American success model as it is supposed to work. But the Canadian game of hockey is more than simply a mirror of society: Canadian hockey is also a ritual that creates meaning.

© AP Photo/Julio Cortez

An anthropologist might suggest that the meaning of hockey, for North Americans, is tied to our cultural understandings of success.

Rituals do not just reflect society. As Yngve Lithman (2004) suggests, they also draw attention to something and provide an explanation for something. Anthropologist Noel Dyck points out that Canadian hockey "is not only one of Canada's proudest contributions to the world of sport but also a national passion" (2000, 10). Hockey becomes important to children very early in life, and it involves the whole family. Tiny players, called "Tim Bits," sponsored by the Tim Hortons coffee shops throughout Canada, begin their training so young that their mothers or fathers, or even their grandfathers or grandmothers, help them put on their protective clothing in the dressing rooms. Young teams of children are grouped according to age into categories such as novice, atom, peewee, bantam, and midget, all progressing to secondary school and university teams. Those working toward professional play are called "Junior" and progress from Junior D to Junior A. At the other end of the life cycle, older players play on teams for "old timers," which are also grouped according to age.

Canadian hockey is also a ritual that, anthropologists Peter Collings and Richard Condon suggest, helps people adjust to sudden change by providing a way for players to gain status, achievement, and self-esteem. In the Kitikmeot region of the Northwest Territories, society is no longer based on hunting as a way of life, but communities are not yet fully integrated into the North American capitalist economy. In the Canadian Arctic, hockey has become a recreational activity that helps bridge this gap, and for most communities, it is a passion.

At first, when radio and television were introduced to the Arctic, and to the community of Holman, where Collings and Condon did their fieldwork in the 1980s, children played hockey on the snow-covered streets. Later, when a sporting organization in Yellowknife sent skates to Inuit communities, children began playing hockey on ice ponds. The initial hockey games were played Inuit style, with little emphasis on winning or losing, and were governed by flexible rules. Eventually, however, a league was established, and teams from different communities began to compete with one another.

With the formalization of hockey as a competition, violence became a standard feature of the game. Collings and Condon found that significantly more injuries were sustained playing hockey than during any other activity, including hunting, trapping, or fishing. Furthermore, being injured during a hockey game was a sure way to gain prestige, especially if an injured player returned to the ice before his injury was healed. Collings and Condon argue that the game of hockey, as it is played in Holman, models the values of achievement and self-reliance: "If achievement and self-reliance cannot be expressed in the conduct of everyday life, then it can be expressed on the ice while competing with one's peers. Status and control, so elusive to these young people in real life, become attainable goals when modeled in the context of play" (1996, 258).

Collings and Condon acknowledge the positive aspects of sports. Games like hockey affirm the value of success, besides providing a dramatic set of instructions on how to attain it. The games help build character and teach young people about cooperation. But Collings and Condon (1996) also suggest that there is a "darker side" to hockey. For some people, "games can teach violence, verbal aggression, subterfuge, cheating, poor sportsmanship, and other undesirable traits" (261). At the same time, hockey demonstrates the limits of acceptable violence. When players break the rules of the game, they incur penalties, just as citizens are penalized for breaking the laws in Canada. When players score a high number of points, they are rewarded with both prestige and, in the case of professional hockey, wealth. Violence and competition are part of Canadian life, and the game of hockey shows how both are important to Canadians, as well as that both must be controlled.

Anthropologists, therefore, can conclude (as did Collings and Condon) that hockey provides for Canadians, as the cockfight does for the Balinese, a small-scale rendering of concepts too complex to be directly comprehended (status and success for Canadians, status only in the case of the Balinese). The audience for a hockey game is led to believe that if the rules that govern the world of hockey are equated with the rules that govern success outside the rink, then the principles that govern success on the hockey rink must also apply in the outside world. If hard work, dedication, submission to authority, and teamwork lead to success in a game, then surely they will lead to success in real life. The rules by which success is achieved in hockey can also be applied to life to succeed in the real world.

Of course, hockey is also a game people enjoy. Analyzing it should not reduce our enjoyment of it but rather should heighten our fascination with it. By looking at hockey from the same perspective that Geertz viewed the cockfight, we should gain an understanding of why the meaning carried by the game is important. Understanding the cockfight heightens our appreciation of the hockey game, but it also helps us see similarities between Canadians and Balinese. If you were shocked by the cockfight, seeing the similarities to hockey should lessen that shock, at the same time making hockey seem just a bit more exotic.

BEYOND THE BOOK 1.4

In 2019, the Toronto Raptors basketball team won the National Basketball Association (NBA) championship, prompting many sports and cultural commentators to ask, "Could basketball overtake hockey as Canada's national sport?" (Bogart 2019). Basketball, some suggest, is more accessible and appeals to a broader segment of Canada's increasingly multicultural population than hockey. Do an Internet search for some of these kinds of commentaries. Based on what you find, and your own opinions and experience, how would you answer the following questions:

1. How does basketball differ from hockey as a "cultural text" in Canada? In what ways are they similar?
2. What does the potential shift from one national sport to another reflect about Canadian culture?

An Anthropologist Looks at a "Happy Meal"

Nothing is too mundane to provide some insights into the culture of which it is a part. Take the "Happy Meal" advertised by one of the many fast food establishments in North America. It consists of a hamburger, French fries, a cola drink, and a plastic toy, which is often gendered—one chooses a "girl" toy or a "boy" toy. What can we learn about the culture of North America by looking beyond the taken-for-granted quality of this meal? Among other things, we can gain some idea of North American demographic and ecological patterns, agricultural and industrial history, and gender roles.

Why, for example, is meat the centre of the meal? Most cultures have diets centred on some complex carbohydrate—rice, wheat, manioc, yams, taro—or something made from these—bread, pasta, tortillas, and so on. It is the spices, vegetables, meat, or fish that when added to these foods gives cuisine its distinctive taste. Meat and fish are, however, generally at the edge, not the centre, of the meal. And why is beef the main ingredient in the Happy Meal rather than, say, pork?

Anthropologists Marvin Harris and Eric Ross note that one advantage of beef is its suitability for the outdoor grill, which became more popular as people moved from cities into suburbs. Suburban cooks soon discovered that pork patties crumbled and fell through the grill, whereas beef patties held together better. In addition, to reduce the risk of trichinosis, pork had to be cooked until it was grey, which makes it tough.

In the United States, beef farmers, as well as the farmers who grew the corn that was fed to cattle to achieve a desirable fat content, benefited from the definition of a hamburger set by the US Department of Agriculture: "'Hamburger' shall consist of chopped fresh and/or frozen beef with or without the addition of beef fat as such and/or seasonings, shall not contain more than 30 percent fat, and shall not contain added water, phosphates, binders, or extenders. Beef cheek (trimmed Beef cheeks) may be used in the preparation of hamburgers only in accordance with the conditions prescribed in paragraph (a) of this section" (Harris 1998, 124).

As Marvin Harris noted, we can eat ground pork and ground beef, but we can't combine them into a patty and call it a hamburger. Hamburgers also cannot be made exclusively of lean beef, for if they were, they would fall apart during cooking. Fat must be added as a binder, and the fat must come from beef scraps, not from vegetables or a different animal. This definition of the hamburger protects both the beef industry and the corn farmer, whose income is linked to cattle production. Moreover, it helps the fast food industry by allowing inexpensive scraps of fat from slaughtered beef to make up to 30 percent of a hamburger. In this way, an international beef patty that has overcome the "pig's natural superiority as a converter of grain to flesh," as Harris (1998, 126) puts it, has been created.

The cola drink that accompanies the hamburger is the second part of the fat- and sugar-centred diet that has come to characterize our culture. People in Canada consume, on average, about 38.6 kilograms of sugar a year. Why so much? Sugar, as anthropologist Sidney Mintz (1985) suggests, has no nutritional properties, but it provides a quick and inexpensive energy boost for hard-working labourers with little time for a more nutritious meal. Sugar also serves as an excellent complement to the fat in hamburgers: it has what nutritionists call "go-away" qualities that remove the fat coating and the beef aftertaste from the mouth.

From the Happy Meal, we also learn that a fat-and-sugar diet is highly environmentally destructive. Beef raising is among the most environmentally inefficient and destructive forms of food raising. For example, the amount of water used to produce 4.5 kilograms (10 pounds) of steak equals the household consumption of a family for an entire year. Thirty-three times more water is needed to produce a kilogram of beef protein than an equivalent amount of plant protein.

Cattle raising is playing a major role in the destruction of tropical forests in Brazil, Guatemala, Costa Rica, and Honduras, where forests have been levelled to create pasture for cattle. Since most of the forest is cleared by burning, the creation of cattle pasture also generates carbon dioxide, which is contributing significantly to global warming.

Sugar is no less destructive a crop. Sugar production alters the environment in a number of ways. Forests must be cleared to plant sugar, wood or fossil fuel must be burned during the evaporation process, waste water is produced when sucrose is extracted from the sugar cane, and more fuel is burned in the refining process. Contemporary sugar production in Hawai'i has destroyed forests, and waste products from processing have severely damaged marine environments. "Big Sugar," as the sugar industry is called in Florida, is largely responsible for the pollution, degradation, and almost total destruction of the Everglades.

Thus, one of the "texts" that anthropologists can read from a Happy Meal relates to the extent to which consumption patterns associated with our culture create waste and environmental damage. Because of these consumption patterns, the average child born in Canada or the United States will, over the course of his or her lifetime, do twice the environmental damage of a Swedish child, 3 times that of an Italian child, 13 times that of a Brazilian child, 35 times that of an Indian child, and 280 times that of a Chadian or Haitian child.

And what of gendered toys—dolls for girls and toy cars for boys? Clearly, there is a message here about gender roles, given that dolls are expected to be chosen by girls and cars by boys. But if you look closely enough, you can deduce even more about our culture from this meal.

Question 1.5: How Can an Anthropological Perspective Be Used Outside Academia?

What Can You Do with a B.A. in Anthropology?

Students taking anthropology classes often say, "I like anthropology, but what can I do with it?" A more or less typical response is "Anything that you can do with any liberal arts major." That doesn't get us very far, though. Being a professional anthropologist—teacher, researcher, consultant—generally requires an advanced degree. However, an anthropological perspective and methodology can be invaluable in all sorts of career areas. For instance, "Why the World Needs Anthropologists" is a yearly conference for practising and applied anthropologists whose members work in diverse fields, including user design, architecture, sustainable community-building, information and communication technology, and urban planning. The demand for candidates with ethnographic skills is on the rise. In 2020, a LinkedIn search using "ethnography" as a keyword yielded many hits that included jobs at *Netflix, Canada Post, Microsoft, Royal Bank of Canada, Canadian Tire,* and *Google.* These examples are all from the corporate world; many anthropologists are employed in the public sector or by nongovernmental organizations (NGOs), as well. Why are these companies looking for ethnographers? Anthropology, like any discipline, deals with problems and questions. In the contemporary lingo of human resources departments, ethnographers "add value" to the companies they work for by bringing a unique perspective to bear on the problems and questions they address. They often have distinctive insights and are able to suggest innovative solutions that accountants, marketers, doctors, or lawyers cannot. In particular, students of anthropology should graduate equipped with at least three problem-solving "tools" unique to the discipline:

- anthropological methods, especially close observation and detailed description and documentation of behaviour, as discussed in Chapter 2;
- anthropological concepts, which are useful for understanding what observed behaviours, such as rites of passage (Chapter 6), kinship (Chapter 5), and reciprocity (Chapter 7), mean to the people studied; and
- anthropological theories, which aim to explain why human beings organize their experiences into meaningful categories in the ways that we do.

Culture, our core disciplinary concept, is a tool that enables anthropologists to go beyond describing what people do and what it means to them to explain the deeper significance of *why* people do what they do. What kinds of problems can anthropologists help solve with their anthropological "toolkit"? People in management must address the problem of how to structure relationships among staff; people in government must address problems involved in designing public policy initiatives, such as reducing juvenile crime. Someone in a medical field may face the problem of how to educate the young regarding sexually transmitted disease, while someone employed in the tourist industry must address the problem of how to minimize the negative consequences of tourism for local populations. The solutions to all of these and other problems can benefit from an anthropological perspective because all involve the ways that people give meaning to their experiences. Throughout the rest of this book, we will be examining various examples of how anthropological perspectives are applied to real-world problems by anthropologists working both within and outside academia.

Applied Anthropology

The best way to understand what anthropology is and how ethnographic insights have problem-solving potential is to look at what anthropologists and ethnographers do and at how they approach various kinds of social problems. *Applied anthropology* is the subdiscipline of anthropology that specializes in putting anthropological knowledge into practice outside academia. Sociocultural anthropology is, in part, about social and cultural differences, whether between countries or within a single classroom. The fact that different peoples assign different meanings to events, objects, individuals, and emotions is a source of considerable conflict, miscommunication, and misunderstanding. Anthropologists seek to explain this diversity, to help people understand one another better, and, in the process, to apply their experience and knowledge to solving social, economic, educational, business, and political problems encountered in our diverse and increasingly interconnected world.

Applied anthropologists therefore work in a variety of areas and settings. Almost anything of interest to academic anthropologists may also be the focus of applied anthropologists. In practice, some branches of anthropology or areas of study lend themselves particularly well to applied anthropology: these include Indigenous issues, political anthropology, environmental anthropology, medical anthropology, and corporate ethnography. The examples of applied anthropology discussed below demonstrate the important ways in which anthropological knowledge and ethnographic expertise matter in the real world. They also begin to suggest some (but certainly not all) of the ways that anthropology can be put to use outside academia.

Indigenous Issues

Regna Darnell and Julia Harrison (2006), scholars of the history of Canadian anthropology, have argued that, although the growth of anthropology in Canada has been influenced by the French, British, and American scholarly traditions, one thing that marks the Canadian disciplinary tradition as distinct is the strong focus on Indigenous peoples. They also suggest that an emphasis on applying research findings in order to serve the needs of the Indigenous communities that have been studied—that is, applied anthropology—has been a defining feature of the discipline in Canada.

Edward Hedican writes that more and more First Nations band administrations are employing anthropologists to conduct research in areas that the bands themselves find useful, such as research that helps document the validity of First Nations land claims. Such collaborations makes anthropological research easier because, as Hedican suggests, "people will certainly be more willing to cooperate with researchers if they are able to see that the work has some direct relevance to their lives" ([1995]2008, 253).

Dawn Martin-Hill is a Canadian anthropologist and filmmaker of Mohawk ancestry whose work with the Lubicon Cree is discussed in detail in Chapter 3. Much of her research has focused on exploring the lingering effects of colonialism on First Nations groups. She also has a particular interest in understanding the historical and cultural basis of First Nations' land claims. In her 2008 film *Sewatokwa'tshera't: The Dish with One Spoon*, she documents and lends her support to the Haudenosaunee, who are involved in disputes with the federal and Ontario governments over land claims.

In February 2006, in what would come to be known as the Grand River Land Dispute, Haudenosaunee from the Six Nations of Grand River began public protests and road blockades. Their goal was to bring greater public awareness to a 40 hectare plot of land near Caledonia that had been granted to them in 1754. The protests were sparked by the impending threat that the land was about to be developed into a residential suburb by Henco Industries Ltd., which claimed to have purchased it in 1841 from what was then called "Canada West." The dispute is ongoing, and it is relevant to note that throughout the ordeal, the Haudenosaunee have been portrayed in the mainstream media as violent, irrational, aggressive, and potentially dangerous. Such depictions function to garner public support and sympathy for the developers and to delegitimize the validity of Haudenosaunee land claims.

In response to overwhelmingly negative representations in the mainstream media, Martin-Hill has organized numerous peaceful protests. Many of these have included not only Haudenosaunee protesters but also supportive members of the academic community. Such initiatives draw attention to the ways in which the agency and legal rights of Haudenosaunee community members have been threatened and at times delegitimized by both government and corporate interests.

Another way that anthropologists working with Indigenous peoples often apply their knowledge and insights is through efforts to influence and improve relevant public policy. One prominent example is the government-commissioned Hawthorne–Tremblay Report, published in two volumes in 1966 and 1967. This was the largest applied research project in Canadian anthropology. Titled A Survey of the Contemporary Indians of Canada: Economic, Political, and Educational Needs and Policies, the report was the result of a collaborative project that involved 35 researchers, both faculty and graduate students, who conducted interviews and surveys in Indigenous communities. The study differed from more traditional scholarly projects in several ways: it was written in readable language rather than academic jargon; it was expressly intended to address the concerns of bureaucrats and government officials rather than scholars; and it provided 151 recommendations with the potential to be implemented by the federal government (Dyck 2006, 82–83). As Dyck states: "Although the discussion of the report was pre-empted by the abortive White Paper proposals of 1969, it did popularize the concept of 'citizen plus,' a formulation firmly endorsed by provincial and territorial Indian organizations in their opposition to the Trudeau government's new Indian policy" (83).

Today, making contributions to land claims and to public policy pertaining to Indigenous peoples is a high-demand field for applied anthropologists. The Firelight Group, based in British Columbia, is a research cooperative that provides community-based research and technical support, most often to First Nations clients, on projects that are designed to support reconciliation between Indigenous and non-Indigenous interests, or to facilitate the inclusion of Indigenous perspectives on decision making and public policy. The anthropologists employed by the Firelight Group work on a range of projects that include social, economic, and cultural impact assessments and traditional knowledge and land use studies.

Legal Anthropology

Another important branch of sociocultural anthropology involves the area of law and society and is sometimes called "legal anthropology." Sally Falk Moore describes this approach as one that

> *inquires into the context of enforceable norms: social, political, economic, and intellectual. This includes, but goes farther than, what Western governments and courts define as law. In anthropology, while the 'socio-legal' includes formal juridical institutions and their social surroundings, it also encompasses law-like activities and processes of establishing order in many other social domains, formal and informal, official and unofficial, in our own society and in others. (2005, 1)*

Anthropologists who study legal issues in a particular place ask questions about power, such as "who makes the rules, who can undo them, how are they normalized and enforced, and how are they morally justified" (Moore 2005, 2). These questions were first asked in egalitarian societies where legal institutions, such as courts and police, were absent; anthropologists tried to understand what prevented total chaos. Other questions are now being asked in relation to the possible lasting effects of colonialism on "native laws," as the colonial powers enforced their own sense of what was right and just.

In his book *Culture Meets Power*, Stanley Barrett argues that globalization has increased conflict throughout the world and that anthropology's interest in the political is likely to grow. He suggests that "power, authority, influence, manipulation, and coercion (or force) constitute the basic terms in this field of inquiry" (2002, 19). With these concepts in mind, anthropologists have extended their interest in legal issues to include, for example, intellectual property issues and global human rights. They also look at global issues that involve international labour, immigration patterns and obstacles, and development schemes, continually asking: "Who is in control? Whose interests are being served?" We will touch on many of these issues in the chapters that follow.

Rosemary Coombe possesses both anthropology and law degrees, and much of her career has focused on questions pertaining to how law, ethics, and culture relate to one another. How do we come to believe that our systems of rules, regulations, and laws are "right," or natural? Moreover, how is our legal system changing in response to globalization and other phenomena?

Anthropologists like Coombe are beginning to explore the volatile world of intellectual property law. In an increasingly globalized, digitized, and mediated world in which the flow of images of celebrities and commodities is unimpeded by geographical borders, Coombe's work (see Coombe 2013) asks how changing notions of ownership and authorship are understood in different societies. How, for instance, are representations of athletes or movie stars appropriated for different political causes or by advertisers? In the process, how do the meanings of their bodies change, and who owns the appropriated images? In these contexts, differing cultural understandings of "ownership" have legal implications. To affect change and to educate current policy makers about the cultural implications of changing notions of intellectual property rights, Coombe conducts workshops with lawyers, law societies, government officials, and law schools. Through these efforts, she seeks to bridge the gap between theory and practice. For instance, if practising lawyers do not possess an understanding of the theoretical underpinnings of cultural notions of appropriation and ownership, then it becomes difficult if not impossible to represent the diverse needs of clients or to create culturally sensitive and appropriate legislation.

Political Ecology

A relatively new branch of sociocultural anthropology that is gaining popularity is *political ecology*, defined by Blaikie and Brookfield (1987, 17) as a field of study that "combines the concerns of ecology and a broadly defined political economy." One direction this approach has taken has involved challenging dominant explanations for environmental degradation and contesting some of the popular solutions to environmental problems (Paulson, Gezon, and Watts 2003, 205). Analyzing the politics of environment may uncover the interests of powerful elites that profit from directing public inquiry away from their activities and toward those of less powerful peoples, such as Indigenous groups, who are forced into the rainforest, where they clear plots of land to grow subsistence products.

Although political ecology usually focuses on land scarcity and access to material resources, two anthropologists at McMaster University have included community identity in their study of peri-urban political ecology. Tina Moffat and Beth Finnis combine a focus on access to land with access to education in a "squatter" community of 300 people called Nayabasti, in Kathmandu, Nepal. As in many such communities, most of Nayabasti's people lack both sewers and indoor plumbing and build houses out of rudimentary materials. The people of Nayabasti were given the land informally by the municipal government more than 30 years ago, but they have no legal documentation, and the only improvement that has been made is the partial installation of indoor toilets (unconnected to sewers) by a Danish nongovernmental organization (NGO). When the community was first formed, there were few others close by. However, the area now includes monasteries built by Tibetan refugees, as well as the homes of wealthy urbanites who have moved from the core of Kathmandu to the outskirts because the land is cheaper and the air is cleaner. The arrival of these newcomers, who have clear title to their land, has placed the community of Nayabasti at even more risk.

Moffat and Finnis discuss the difficulties the community has faced in its efforts to provide education for local children. In 1998, the residents pooled their resources and set about searching for a place to build their own school. After a period of negotiation with the municipal government, a plot of land was found. The community provided almost all the labour to build the school, with Lumanti, a local NGO, providing financial support. Moffat and Finnis caution that it is still uncertain whether the school will be sustainable, but the project has reinforced community identity, and the community's "ability to get this far is evidence of the incredible capacity of slum and squatter dwellers" (2005, 465).

Medical Anthropology

Medical anthropology is another branch of anthropology in which anthropologists are able to put their ethnographic skills and perspectives to good use. According to the Society for Medical Anthropology, it is

> *a subfield of anthropology that draws upon social, cultural, biological, and linguistic anthropology to better understand those factors which influence health and well being (broadly defined), the experience and distribution of illness, the prevention and treatment of sickness, healing processes, the social relations of therapy management, and the cultural importance and utilization of pluralistic medical systems. (http://www.medanthro.net/blog/about-the-blog)*

This area of anthropology has moved in many directions. Medical anthropologists may analyze the politics of health care access, local interpretations and experiences of health and illness, the cultural and historical context of contemporary medical practice and policies, or perceptions and experiences of risk and stigma related to various illnesses.

Naomi Adelson is a medical anthropologist who has done fieldwork with the James Bay Cree of northern Quebec. In her ethnography, Being Alive Well, she notes that the Cree do not have a word that readily translates into what we call "health" in English. Rather, they talk about miyupimaatisiiun, or "being alive well." For the Cree, being alive well has less to do with individuals and physiology than with social and political relations. Adelson's informants asked, rhetorically, "If the land is not healthy, then how can we be?" (2000, 1). The Cree understanding and experience of health is grounded in what it means to "be Cree," which is itself grounded in connections to the land and to the past (25). The James Bay Cree once travelled and hunted across a vast swath of land in northwestern Quebec, but today many live in the village of Whapmagoostui at the mouth of the Great Whale River, hunting in the bush only on weekends. Since the 1970s, the Cree have been fighting with the provincial government of Quebec over the appropriate uses of the land and its resources, most famously in the building of the James Bay I hydroelectric dam and the failed James Bay II project. While the Quebec government saw the land as underused and underpopulated and as an untapped source of wealth and power, the Cree knew that the projects would drastically alter the ecosystem surrounding Whapmagoostui, changing the migration and survival patterns of land and sea mammals, fish, and birds. What would it mean to be Cree in the face of such changes? How could they manage to "be alive well"? Adelson (2000, 1) argues that "all definitions of health . . . are laden with ideological nuances and can never be separated from cultural norms and values."

Since Adelson conducted her initial fieldwork, there has been a fusing, at the local level, of health and politics. Adelson distributed copies of her research to local political and health authorities, and her use of "being alive well" to explain Cree understandings of health has been incorporated, via *The James Bay Experience: A Guide for Health Professionals Working among the Cree in Northern Quebec*, into the vocabulary of doctors, dentists, and other health care workers in the area (115).

In her work on the social determinants of health among migrant farm workers in Ontario who come to Canada under the Seasonal Agricultural Workers Program (SAWP), anthropologist Janet McLaughlin (2009) bridges the gap between scholarly and applied anthropology. Her work exemplifies the potential overlap between several of the branches of anthropology we have described here, addressing concerns of medical anthropology, political ecology, and legal anthropology. McLaughlin notes that although health, or at least access to the highest attainable standard of health, is a human right, transnational migrant workers are in a paradoxical position when it comes to exercising this right. Although human rights are meant to be universally applicable, "they are also primarily premised on the relationship between individuals and the obligations of the state to respect, protect and fulfill the rights of citizens. What then are the implications for people who live and work in nations in which they are not citizens?" (McLaughlin 2009, 1). The health of migrant workers is shaped by a number of factors related to the nature of their employment, including the work they do, their working conditions, their access to health care, language barriers, and the type of housing in which they stay while in Canada. Yet they are also more vulnerable and neglected in terms of their health care needs because of the temporary nature and precarity of their employment, their transnational mobility, and their status as noncitizens. In addition to writing about these migrant workers for audiences that include other anthropologists and scholars of development, McLaughlin applies and disseminates her knowledge and findings beyond academia by writing policy papers and newspaper articles and working with several community groups that address the needs of migrant workers. Beyond that, she is the co-founder of the Migrant Worker Health Project (www.migrantworkerhealth.ca), a website that provides a collection of resources and information for health care workers to assist them in providing care to migrant workers.

Corporate Ethnography

Increasingly, corporations recognize that anthropologists possess many unique and beneficial skills that can assist with the marketing and advertising of products. Specifically, anthropologists possess excellent qualitative research skills (discussed in Chapter 2), a commitment to cultural relativism, problem-solving skills and approaches unique to the discipline, and a focus on cross-cultural and multicultural understandings of the world. As such, corporations realize that anthropologists can often assist them in marketing particular products to people of specific demographics. If *McDonald's*, for example, is experiencing low revenue on the sale of a particular product in Norway, they may hire an anthropologist to go to Norway and interview potential consumers to understand why the product is not meeting target sales goals. The anthropologist may learn that the product does not appeal to Norwegian food preferences, that the product is perceived as too expensive, or that the advertising campaign is, perhaps for cultural reasons, failing to appeal to its target demographic.

The relationship between consumerism, culture, and "taste" (in terms of cultural preferences for certain foods, clothing styles, or particular aesthetic trends) is explored by Canadian anthropologist, corporate ethnographer, and blogger Grant McCracken (see McCracken 2005). McCracken has conducted fieldwork for a wide variety of corporations, including Nike, Ikea, and the Ford Foundation. His goal is to harness the unique perspectives and fieldwork methods of sociocultural anthropology for analyses of consumer trends. He is hired by large corporations to ask and answer questions such as these: How and why do consumers make the purchases that they do? Why is a particular product not meeting sales expectations? How can a product be redesigned to make it more appealing to the consumer? Large companies hire McCracken to increase their net sales and revenues; his approach involves interviewing consumers about their shopping and consumption habits, then synthesizing this information with analyses of broader cultural trends with respect to consumption.

The alignment of anthropology with corporate interests, however, raises a number of ethical problems. As we will learn in Chapter 2, anthropologists have a primary ethical responsibility to ensure that their work does not harm their informants. Many people, including many anthropologists, would argue that the ultimate purpose of marketing and advertising is to manipulate people into mindless consumerism. From this perspective, the use of ethnography to increase corporate profits is harmful to those consumers who are being studied. Moreover, as we will discuss in Chapter 8, the rampant consumption that characterizes contemporary capitalism has global consequences that consumers often do not see, or at least do not consider—for example, environmental degradation, increased global inequality, and poor working conditions for the people who produce the goods we are encouraged to consume. Is it ethical to use our ethnographic problem-solving skills for corporate ethnography, when consumer culture might itself be considered a problem? On the other hand, as we discuss in the Applied Box below, it is worth considering that not all anthropologists who work as corporate ethnographers try to increase sales of soft drinks or cars or sneakers. Some corporate ethnographers work in fields such as design, user experience, urban development, education, and health care.

APPLYING ANTHROPOLOGY

Keeping the Human Experience Front and Centre

One example that confounds easy adjudication of the ethics of corporate ethnography is the work conducted by Lisa Reichenbach and Amy Maish (2006) on how pharmaceutical companies might best meet the needs of Type 2 diabetics while simultaneously maximizing their profits. They argue that ethnography, with its focus on lived experience, is the best way to improve and encourage patient-focused health care and pharmaceutical interventions. In their ethnographic work on Type 2 diabetes patients as health care clients, they discovered that the key to understanding the illness experience was to realize that coping with diabetes entails a series of life transitions—from healthy to ill, and from dependent patient

(Continued)

to self-care practitioner (through the self-administration of insulin).

The theorization of life transitions, as they are facilitated by what anthropologists call "rites of passage" (see Chapter 6), is an example of how these corporate ethnographers are able to bring the unique tools of anthropology to bear on a problem that is of interest to both patients and health care practitioners: how to improve the experience of taking insulin and thereby increase patient compliance. Of course, this work also addresses a challenge for pharmaceutical companies: to sell more insulin. Reichenbach and Maish suggest that the insights gleaned during their research may ultimately benefit both patients and pharmaceutical companies, though not necessarily to the same degree. The key question, they say, when addressing the issue of business opportunities, is not just "What is your overall opportunity as a brand?"; it is also "How do I realize that opportunity in the real and often painful world of the diabetic?"

User experience (UX) design is another field in which corporations have much to gain, and to learn, from anthropologists. Of course, because of the very nature of UX design, which aims to create better experiences for "regular" people as they interact with corporations online, the insights of anthropologists have the potential to have impacts beyond the corporate bottom line. Fatimah Richmond is a design anthropologist who has worked for *LinkedIn*, *Microsoft*, and *Google*. According to Richmond, the power of design anthropology is that it "provides an ever-evolving tool set for generating insights that ensure the human remains central in the quest to solve the right complex business problems" (Reyero 2018). At *Google*, these "complex business problems" included improving the usability of its Google Currents software (for internal enterprise communication). She has also applied her anthropological toolkit to more ethically

huePhotography/E+/Getty Images

Anthropologists who use their ethnographic skills in the field of user experience (UX) work with designers and potential end users to ensure that online interactions maintain a "human" element that makes them both functional and enjoyable.

pressing questions about designing user experiences with an eye for equity and diversity, such as: "Can we build products and services for people of all races? Can we sound the alarm before racism becomes codified in those products and services?" (Richmond and Ladner 2017). When asked about the future direction of user experience research, Richmond points out that as artificial intelligence (AI) becomes a more common part of our everyday lives, design anthropologists will be at the forefront of bridging complex human thought with complex AI algorithms and solving problems, in part by paying heed to how uniquely human norms, rituals, and customs play out in "trans-human" contexts and encounters (Reyero 2018).

Conclusions

This chapter has considered five questions. Some have had to do with the problem of how to understand ways of life that are different from our own, others with the problem of how to better understand our own lives. Why do human beings differ in what they believe and how they behave? One answer is that human beings, unlike other animals (or, at least, to a greater extent than other animals), create their own worlds and ascribe meanings to objects, persons, behaviours, emotions, and events: meanings that together constitute a culture. As Geertz (1973) suggests, human beings are compelled to create meanings if only to instill some sense of order in their lives.

The judgments we make about the beliefs and behaviours of other people create a dilemma. If, on the one hand, we assume that the meanings that others give to their experiences are wrong, silly, or absurd simply because they are different from ours, we are committing the ethnocentric fallacy. Ethnocentrism is intellectually awkward because it allows everyone to believe that their views are correct and that the views of others are wrong. This mindset would make any kind of intercultural understanding virtually impossible. If, on the other hand, we conclude that the beliefs and behaviours of others can be judged only in the context of their cultures, we are confronted with the relativistic fallacy, which implies that any belief or behaviour is acceptable, provided it makes sense to the people of the society in which it occurs. This viewpoint places us in a moral dilemma because we must then accept virtually any belief or behaviour.

One way we describe and interpret the meanings other people find in their experiences is to consider a culture as a text inscribed with symbols whose meanings can be deciphered. We can examine virtually any cultural activity in this way and find in it a portion of the overall view of the world of a people. If we approach our own culture in the same way we approach other cultures, we should gain a better understanding of the meanings we give objects, persons, and events. If we objectify our own beliefs and behaviour in the same way that we objectify the beliefs and behaviours of others, our own culture should become more exotic, while the cultures of others become less strange, shocking, or bizarre. It is this ability to make the familiar exotic and the exotic familiar that makes the anthropological perspective so interesting and able to serve you well whether you go into a career as a professional anthropologist or simply apply your new-found insights to the world around you.

Regardless of your career path, the anthropological approach developed in this text should provide you with critical thinking skills. You will perhaps question your own beliefs and understandings of the world as you study, and recognize that much of what we are taught to accept as "natural" is really the by-product of enculturation. In other words, our identities and world views are culturally constructed. This understanding encourages us to recognize the dangers of thinking about our beliefs as "natural' or "biological." Ultimately, by recognizing how culture shapes our experiences, we are in a better position to understand both ourselves and others around us.

QUESTIONS: REVIEW

Introduction

In this introduction to the chapter, and to the text as a whole, we introduce the idea of anthropology as discipline that looks beyond everyday appearances to discover the underlying meanings of commonsense beliefs and practices. In this section we also briefly discuss the broader context of four-field anthropology as a discipline that holistically studies what makes us human.

Review Questions

1. What are the four subdisciplines of anthropology?
2. What are the unique features of sociocultural anthropology as a subdiscipline?

1.1 Why do human beings differ in their beliefs and behaviours?

In this section we discuss the significance of the term culture to the anthropological endeavour. All human beings have to deal with many of the same basic experiences and needs: birth, death, companionship, and hunger, for example. The culture concept helps us to understand why people from different backgrounds make these experiences meaningful in such different ways. According to Clifford Geertz, without our ability to use culture to impose meaning on our experiences, we humans would perceive the world as chaotic and pointless.

Review Questions

1. What is culture?
2. How do anthropologists use the concept of culture to explain why human beings differ in their beliefs and values? What are some examples of these differences discussed in the text?

1.2 Is it possible to see the world through the eyes of others?

The discipline of anthropology is premised on the belief that it is possible and worthwhile (though often challenging) to see the world through the eyes of others. Doing so means avoiding ethnocentrism and practising cultural relativism. The examples in this section about virginity testing in rural Turkey and ritual funerary cannibalism among the Wari' of Bolivia demonstrate the importance of contextualizing unfamiliar or unsettling beliefs and practices within the system of cultural meanings from which they emerge. However, it would be a fallacy to believe we must therefore accept and justify all beliefs and practices. Critical cultural relativism is one way to situate and critique dangerous or oppressive practices while still remaining attuned to the cultural context from which they emerge.

Review Questions

1. What is the difference between ethnocentrism and cultural relativism?
2. What is critical cultural relativism, and how might it help us avoid the relativistic fallacy? Use examples from this section to explain your answer.

1.3 How can the meanings that others find in experience be interpreted and described?

Many anthropologists find it productive to approach culture as a text whose underlying or unifying meanings can be interpreted by the anthropologist and shared with others. The key example in this section is of Clifford Geertz's work on the Balinese cockfight, which he interprets as a cultural text, or "a story the Balinese tell themselves about themselves," whose key underlying meaning pertains to the significance of status to Balinese society.

Review Questions

1. What does it mean to think of culture as a text? How does this approach shape how an anthropologist tries to understand and describe a culture?
2. Describe in detail the circumstances surrounding a typical Balinese cockfight. How does the cockfight help the Balinese comprehend the significance of status for their daily lives?

1.4 What can learning about other peoples tell anthropologists about their own societies?

Anthropology is not only about understanding cultures that are unfamiliar to us; an anthropological approach can also be used to better understand and interpret one's own culture. In this section, we use an anthropological approach to unpack two everyday or commonsense aspects of Canadian culture: hockey as national sport, and the Happy Meal, both of which are laden with meanings that often go unspoken.

Review Questions

1. If an anthropologist were to interpret hockey in Canada as a text, what meanings would emerge as most significant, and why?
2. What does the popularity of the Happy Meal suggest to anthropologists about gender roles, consumption patterns, and environmental practices?

1.5 How can an anthropological perspective be used outside academia?

Most the anthropologists you meet as an undergraduate will be professors, but there are many other fields in which anthropological expertise and skills might be applied. In this section, we discuss the transferable, and valuable, problem-solving skills acquired through anthropological training, and give example of various fields in which these have been successfully applied.

Review Questions

1. What are the three problem-solving skills unique to the discipline of anthropology?
2. Describe the way that anthropological problem-solving skills have been applied to at least two different issues or settings outside of academia.

CRITICAL THINKING QUESTIONS

1. In the introduction, we discussed the way that an anthropologist might find cultural meaning in a classroom chair. Think about the kinds of classroom spaces you are taking classes in—lecture halls, labs, seminar rooms. What other aspects of the classroom setup can you rethink from an anthropological perspective? How might an anthropologist explain your findings?
2. Anthropologists explore the ways in which human beings make their experiences meaningful through culture. Is it possible to imagine life without systems of meaning to help us make sense of it? What would a life without culture be like?
3. Which of the subfields of applied anthropology do you think has the most potential applications in today's globalized world, and why? If you could choose a contemporary social problem to address from the perspective of one of these subfields, what would it be and why?

KEY TERMS

archaeology (p. 6)
biological anthropology (p. 5)
critical cultural relativism (p. 16)
cultural relativism (p. 12)
cultural text (p. 18)
culture (p. 8)
ethnocentric fallacy (p. 12)
ethnocentrism (p. 12)
linguistic anthropology (p. 6)
relativistic fallacy (p. 13)
society (p. 8)
sociocultural anthropology (p. 2)

CHAPTER 2

Doing Fieldwork in Sociocultural Anthropology

REUTERS/Mark Blinch

As noted below in the quotation from the famous American anthropologist Margaret Mead, the process of doing sociocultural anthropology, called "ethnographic fieldwork," requires both open-mindedness and a capacity for astonishment. The work of Jeremy Dutcher (pictured above at the piano) embodies these qualities. Dutcher (whose work we discuss at the end of this chapter) was astonished to discover an archive of long-forgotten recordings of Maliseet traditional songs (themselves recorded by an anthropologist 100 years earlier). He reworked the songs with contemporary arrangements and his own operatic singing; the resulting music demands an open mind about musical genres and about Indigenous culture. Dutcher's music evokes Mead's description of anthropology as a discipline that demands that we "look, listen, and record."

Anthropology demands the open-mindedness with which one must look and listen, record in astonishment and wonder that which one would not have been able to guess.★

—Margaret Mead

★Cited in Boellstorff (2010, 71)

PROBLEM 2

How do sociocultural anthropologists learn about culture?

Introduction

One of the best ways to understand what anthropology *is*, as a discipline, is to begin by thinking about what anthropologists *do*. What makes sociocultural anthropology unique among the social sciences, and what determines the kinds of knowledge anthropologists produce, is our unique methodological approach. **Ethnographic fieldwork** (often referred to simply as "fieldwork") is one of the defining features of sociocultural anthropology and something that has historically distinguished it as a unique field of inquiry, for although anthropologists do make careful use of other anthropological tools, such as surveys and census data, these tools are usually a supplement to fieldwork. Ethnographic fieldwork typically involves various forms of long-term engagements (often a year or more) and interactions with a particular cultural group or community. This work many include participating in daily activities such as gardening and household tasks, attending religious ceremonies, or conducting interviews with community members. It also involves learning the local language in order to be able to communicate directly and effectively with people without the use of translators. As we will discuss in Chapter 3, understanding the local language also provides unique insights into the cultural transmission of beliefs and values.

Ethnographic fieldwork is a form of **qualitative research**, which makes it different in its aims and scope from methods of **quantitative research** such as surveys, experiments, or closed-ended questionnaires, which are analyzed through statistical analysis. The qualitative nature of ethnographic research and analysis make it particularly suitable for the kinds of questions that anthropologists explore. By way of comparison of these two kinds of research and their uses, think about what sometimes happens when your cellphone rings and you forget to check call display. It's a telemarketer, and you're faced with a request to complete a survey. While the immediate reaction for many people is to hang up the phone, sometimes you may "give in" and answer the telemarketer's questions. If you are busy or indifferent to the topic being discussed, you will probably not give much thought to your

ethnographic fieldwork
A research method in which sociocultural anthropologists have intensive, long-term engagements with a group of people. It may involve the use of both qualitative and quantitative methods, including interviews, participant observation, and survey-based research.

qualitative research
Research methods that aim to explore, rather than measure, various phenomena, often through forms of observation such as interviews, focus groups, and direct participant observation.

quantitative research
Research methods that involve the generation of statistical data. Examples include surveys and censuses.

responses. Perhaps you are trying to relax, doing schoolwork, making dinner, or otherwise occupied. Because you do not know the individual who is asking you questions, you may have no feeling of interest or responsibility to engage with that person, or to be involved in the study.

This lack of connection with the surveyor is one of the potential methodological shortcomings of quantitative research in terms of getting an in-depth, nuanced picture of human beliefs, attitudes, and motivations. Moreover, because the telemarketer knows little or nothing about you, and cannot see you and judge your body language as you respond to the survey questions, it is entirely possible that you might simply lie, that your responses will be taken out of context, or that there might be contradictions between what you say and do that the telemarketer is unaware of. When a telemarketer asks you, for instance, to rank your responses to questions on a scale from 1 to 5, there is seldom any room to elaborate upon why you feel the way you do about a particular issue. Oftentimes, our answers to surveys are brief and given under time pressure. Telemarketing surveys may work well for answering questions about the *what* of certain behaviours and preferences; however, on their own, they are a much less appropriate tool for answering the kinds of how and why questions that anthropologists ask about cultural meanings, values, and beliefs.

Over time, anthropologists conducting fieldwork often develop a sense of **rapport** with the groups they work with. In other words, they feel a sense of affinity with them and have a general concern for their well-being; friendships often develop. It is precisely this sense of rapport that allows anthropologists to obtain an in-depth understanding of various facets of culture. For example, while many people may feel uncomfortable or indifferent about responding to questions provided by an anonymous telemarketer, they are more likely to engage in open debates or frank discussion over coffee with someone who, they feel, cares about them, and vice versa. For this reason, most anthropological research necessitates the use of long-term fieldwork. Long-term engagements with people allow anthropologists to understand aspects of culture from an insider's perspective, or what is termed an **emic perspective**. Coming to understand a culture from an emic perspective requires that an anthropologist make use of the principle of cultural relativism. Once the anthropologist has conducted fieldwork and grasped the insider's understanding of a culture, the task is then to situate this understanding within an **etic perspective**, that is, from the perspective of an outside observer. Ideally, anthropologists shift back and forth between these two perspectives when they write, analyze, and present their findings.

In the past, one feature that distinguished anthropology from other disciplines in the social sciences was its focus upon non-Western peoples and places. Closely affiliated with and enabled by European colonialism (discussed in Chapter 3), European and North American anthropologists often went to live, as guests of colonial administrators, among Indigenous peoples in the South Pacific, Africa, or the Americas. At the turn of the twentieth century, anthropology was thus defined as the study of non-Western peoples and places. This focus would gradually shift throughout the twentieth century, and today you are just as likely to see

rapport
A feeling of affinity, friendship, and responsibility between an anthropologist and an informant. It is often developed through the use of long-term ethnographic fieldwork.

emic perspective
Traditionally refers to an "insider's perspective." The goal of most fieldwork is to employ cultural relativism to understand an issue or perspective from the point of view of one's informants.

etic perspective
Refers to the analysis of an aspect of culture using comparative categories, explanations, and interpretation from the perspective of an outside observer.

anthropologists studying their own cultures as the cultures of others. Some North American anthropologists, for instance, use ethnographic fieldwork to tackle important social issues or problems at home, such as racism, homelessness, poverty, and the gentrification of cities. Others study aspects of pop culture, such as the globalization of music industries, dance, or fashion.

Once an anthropologist has spent a sufficient time in the field and has generated enough data, in the form of field notes, photographs, and video recordings, or a combination thereof, the next step is to disseminate an analysis of the fieldwork experiences for the benefit of a broader audience. Dissemination often takes written forms—for example, journal articles, books, or popular culture forms of writing such as magazine or newspaper articles. Some anthropologists also produce films about their fieldwork experiences, or they publish photographs, or other forms of visual media.

The production of anthropological knowledge based on ethnographic fieldwork is not without its potential pitfalls. What, for instance, are the ethical implications and responsibilities that arise from the unique situation of ethnographic fieldwork? Another issue in the production of anthropological knowledge is that of **representation**, which refers to the ways in which anthropologists depict a particular group of people. Whenever we write about a cultural group, we are crafting particular representations for public consumption, and it is important to recognize that this privilege is connected to power. In other words, our representations will have an impact on how people perceive others, and negative representations may have long-term, deleterious consequences for various peoples. In this chapter, we explore the history of anthropological fieldwork and the way it has changed over the last century. We also discuss the various practical, ethical, intellectual, and representational challenges that arise during the process of doing and writing about ethnographic fieldwork.

QUESTIONS

- **2.1** How did ethnographic fieldwork develop during the formative years of anthropology?
- **2.2** How has fieldwork changed over the past century?
- **2.3** What are some of the challenges of conducting fieldwork?
- **2.4** What are the responsibilities of anthropologists toward the people they work with? What does it mean to "act ethically" as an anthropologist?
- **2.5** How do anthropologists represent the people they study and work with? Why is representation an important issue within anthropology?

Question 2.1: How Did Ethnographic Fieldwork Develop during the Formative Years of Anthropology?

Anthropology from an Armchair

Anthropology began at a particular time in history: "the Age of Exploration," which was launched by Christopher Columbus when he arrived in the Americas in 1492 and which lasted until the early seventeenth century. It was during these centuries that Europeans first encountered people who looked and behaved very differently than themselves (Barrett 1996, 3). Travellers and explorers returned home with stories about the seemingly "strange" people they had met in faraway places, sometimes bringing back live native "specimens" as well. Those at home debated at length whether these beings were fully human.

European countries established colonies throughout the world, often sending missionaries along to "civilize" the strange people; those

representation
The way in which a group of people is depicted in writing or through images. Anthropologists are increasingly conscious of the fact that when they write about a group of people, they are constructing particular representations that may have positive or negative long-term effects for a group of people.

missionaries then documented their encounters. One of the most famous of these accounts is the *Jesuit Relations*, first published in 1632, which describes the interactions between the Jesuit missionaries and the Indigenous peoples in what is now southern Ontario. These missionaries' writings were a type of proto-anthropology, though it must be added that missionaries and anthropologists today have very different motivations for the work they do. For most missionaries, cultural understanding is a necessary means toward an end goal of changing or even eradicating certain beliefs; for most anthropologists, such understanding is an end in and of itself.

Notwithstanding these early cross-cultural interactions, anthropology did not emerge as a formal discipline until 1883, when Edward Tylor was appointed to the first academic position of anthropology in Britain, at Oxford. Decades later, in 1925, Thomas F. McIlwraith became the first anthropology appointment at the University of Toronto. Canada's first Department of Anthropology was founded at the same university in 1936.

In the late 1800s, as anthropology grew in popularity throughout Europe and North America, many early anthropologists, such as Tylor, engaged in what contemporary anthropologists like to call **armchair anthropology**. That is, instead of visiting various peoples and conducting their own first-hand research, they stayed at home and amassed diaries, reports, and various documents written by Europeans or Euro-Americans who had come in contact with non-Western peoples. Sitting in their "armchairs," or perhaps at their university office desks, these anthropologists applied a comparative method to explore differences and similarities in social institutions and belief systems among a variety of societies. This approach often included a comparison of family structures, political and economic organizations, and religious or spiritual beliefs, among other things. Based on their comparisons, armchair anthropologists would try to make cross-cultural generalizations about such things as warfare, marriage patterns, religion, and other phenomena. These comparisons and generalizations were based entirely on etic interpretations and analysis.

Tylor relied on the travellers' and missionaries' accounts as sources of information for *Primitive Culture* (1871). But he did so uncritically—that is, he did not acknowledge the inherent biases in their writings—taking their work at face value (as did many other armchair anthropologists of his day). Indeed, without any first-hand experience or emic understanding of the cultures he was reading about, it would have been difficult for him to detect or refute these biases.

It is worth noting the ways in which Tylor's own definition of culture reflected the methodological approach that he shared with his fellow armchair anthropologists. According to Tylor, "culture or civilization, taken in its wide [comparative] ethnographic sense, is that complex whole which includes knowledge, belief, art, morals, law, custom, and any other capabilities and habits acquired by man as a member of his society" (1871, 1). As in our working definition of culture outlined in Chapter 1, Tylor's definition emphasized the shared and learned aspects of culture; however, he and other Victorian anthropologists wrote about culture in the singular, believing that some peoples or cultural groups might have more or less culture or civilization than others. In this sense, both their methodology and their understanding of culture were not merely comparative, but hierarchical as well. At the time, ranking and ordering different cultural groups, many of whom were the subjects of colonialism, was an integral part of the logic of and intellectual justification for colonial endeavours. (These links between colonialism, ethnocentrism, and early anthropology are discussed more fully in Chapter 3.) Of relevance here is that contemporary anthropologists remain interested in the differences and similarities between cultures but no longer employ hierarchies when comparing human beliefs and behaviours.

armchair anthropology
Refers to an approach to the study of various societies that dominated anthropology in the late 1800s. It involved the collection, study, and analysis of the writings of missionaries, explorers, and colonists who had sustained contact with non-Western peoples. Armchair anthropologists used these documents to make comparisons and generalizations about the ways of life of various groups.

Ethnographic Fieldwork

Anthropologists like Bronislaw Malinowski and Franz Boas (often regarded as the "fathers" of social and cultural anthropology, respectively) would soon move beyond the armchair anthropology of Tylor and his contemporaries. Boas sought first-hand knowledge among the Inuit and the Kwakwaka'wakw of Canada, while Malinowski conducted much of his early fieldwork in the South Pacific. After Malinowski went to live in the Trobriand Islands during the First World War, extended periods of fieldwork became the required methodology of sociocultural anthropology.

Anthropologists, like other social scientists, use surveys, written documents, historical accounts, and questionnaires as part of their research toolkit. But the unique feature of sociocultural anthropology is the ethnographic method: investigators immerse themselves in the lives of the people they are trying to understand, systematically observe their day-to-day lives, and thereby attain some level of understanding of the meanings those people ascribe to their existence. This immersion process entails **participant observation**, defined as the active participation of observers in the lives of their subjects.

The ethnographic method is only the beginning of the anthropological enterprise. The anthropologist also seeks to explain why people view the world the way they do and to contribute to the understanding of human behaviour in general by sharing findings with other anthropologists and the broader public. But this enterprise begins with fieldwork, which involves the meeting of at least two cultures: that of the researcher, and that of the people the researcher is trying to understand. Anthropological researchers must set aside their own views of things and endeavour to see the world in a new way. In many respects, they must assume the demeanour and status of children, students, or novices, who must be taught by their elders the proper view of the world.

Bronislaw Malinowski (1884–1942), born in Poland and trained in Britain, was one of the first anthropologists to abandon the armchair approach.

Bronislaw Malinowski in the midst of Trobriand Islanders. Malinowski was one of the first anthropologists to conduct long-term fieldwork.

He revolutionized anthropology by stressing the primacy of fieldwork. Malinowski's discovery of the efficacy of fieldwork for understanding culture could be described as something of an accident. In 1914, he travelled to New Guinea as part of a team of researchers; then the First World War broke out and he found himself unable to travel back to Britain, for he was a citizen of the Austro-Hungarian empire and, therefore, an enemy of the state. He decided to stay and conduct long-term research, alone, in the Trobriand Islands as the guest of British colonial officials.

Soon after his arrival, Malinowski concluded that it would be necessary to spend each day with the Trobrianders if he hoped to obtain a comprehensive understanding of their daily lives. So he left the comfort of his colonial household, acquired a tent, and set up camp in a nearby Trobriand village. By living with Trobrianders, learning their language, and observing and participating in their daily tasks, he established the importance of participant observation as a fieldwork strategy.

Participant observation requires long-term engagement with a group of people and their daily lives. It may involve living with group members as

participant observation
An element of fieldwork that can involve participating in daily tasks and observing daily interactions among a particular group.

well as observing and participating in daily tasks, no matter how mundane. This fieldwork technique has become a defining feature of contemporary anthropological fieldwork. Even today, anthropologists regularly observe and participate in such things as gardening, harvesting, cooking, recreation, and various rituals and ceremonies.

Conducting participant observation is a balancing act that requires the anthropologist to shift back and forth between, or even attempt to simultaneously inhabit, two different roles: that of the participant, and that of the observer. Becoming too closely involved in participation may mean losing one's ability to see things from an etic, or outsider's, perspective; focusing too much energy on observation and note-taking may mean missing out on the details and nuances that are such an important part of gaining first-hand experience of the emic point of view.

As one of the first people to conduct this kind of fieldwork, Malinowski established the template for managing this balancing act, one that most anthropologists continue to follow today. He took detailed field notes by hand during his participatory interactions with Trobriand Islanders. In the evenings, he typed up his notes and spent more time thinking about his observations. Later, he would transform these into an **ethnography**, defined as a written description and analysis of an anthropologist's experiences and interactions with a group of people. In essence, the ethnography is the end product of a fieldwork experience. For Malinowski (1961, 3), the measure of a good ethnography was the extent to which the reader was able to follow the anthropologist's analytic shifts between the emic and etic perspectives:

> *I consider that only such ethnographic sources are of unquestionable scientific value, in which we can clearly draw a line between, on the one hand, the results of direct observation and of native statements and interpretations, and on the other, the inferences of the author, based on his common sense and psychological insight.* ([1992]1961)

Malinowski felt that by carefully documenting their experiences and observations with field notes, and combining this with participant observation and other qualitative fieldwork techniques, anthropologists would be able to obtain "the native's point of view" (Malinowski 1961, 25), his evocative term for the emic perspective. The differences between Edward Tylor's definition of *culture* and Malinowski's reflect the differences between armchair anthropology and ethnographic fieldwork. Malinowski was less interested in hierarchical comparisons than in understanding each culture on its own terms. His view was that cultures arise in order to meet the particular needs of specific peoples. Culture, in this sense, can be understood as plural. For Malinowski (1944, 36), culture was

> *the integral whole consisting of implements and consumers' goods, of constitutional charters for the various social groupings, of human ideas and crafts, beliefs, and customs. Whether we consider a very simple or primitive culture or an extremely complex and developed one, we are confronted by a vast apparatus, partly material, partly human, and partly spiritual, by which man is able to cope with the concrete, specific problems that face him.*

When Malinowski returned to Britain, he took up a position teaching anthropology at the London School of Economics. The ethnography he wrote based on his Trobriand Islands fieldwork, *Argonauts of the Western Pacific* ([1922]1961), was considered groundbreaking at the time and remains a classic today. Malinowski is credited with being one of the first anthropologists to both utilize and formalize participant observation and long-term fieldwork, and he went on to train a wide range of influential anthropologists in these methods in the first half of the twentieth century.

ethnography
A written description and analysis of a particular group of people, usually based upon anthropological fieldwork.

> **BEYOND THE BOOK 2.1**
>
> Fieldwork involves a great deal of preparation and study before arriving in "the field." If you were asked to travel to the Trobriand Islands to study family relationships in a small village for a year, what steps would you take to prepare yourself for your fieldwork?

Question 2.2: How Has Fieldwork Changed over the Past Century?

Changing Notions of Fieldwork

Malinowski's insistence on long-term fieldwork and participant observation would have lasting effects on the discipline. These days, PhD students in anthropology are still required to spend at least a year in the field, and they often incorporate participant observation as a fieldwork technique. However, fieldwork has also changed over the last century, and many of Malinowski's original ideas about fieldwork have been challenged. Nonetheless, his systematic approach to the collection and analysis of data, which resulted in an evocative and eloquent presentation of Trobriand Islands culture, remains key to the ethnographic endeavour today.

In the late nineteenth century, anthropology was about the study of non-Western peoples and places. Most anthropologists were upper-class, well-educated, white men from Europe, Australia, Canada, and the United States. From their perspective, Indigenous peoples were the most appropriate subjects of study. In a somewhat paternalistic way, these early anthropologists viewed Indigenous peoples as groups in need of "rescue." Thus, a great deal of early-twentieth-century anthropology in North America was an outgrowth of **salvage anthropology**, an idea espoused by Franz Boas, among others, who felt that Indigenous peoples throughout the world were undergoing rapid assimilation and would eventually disappear (Darnell 1998a, 23). He felt that anthropologists had an obligation to document and collect

Diamond Jenness (1886–1969) is recognized as an early pioneer of Canadian anthropology. Chief of Anthropology at the National Museum of Canada between 1926 and 1948, he sought to expand the museum's collections and its international reputation. He also lobbied the federal government to fight against racism toward Indigenous peoples and to advocate for better living conditions for people living on reserves.

the various traditions and cultures of these groups. Boas and his students began documenting Inuit and Northwest Coast Indigenous cultures so to "preserve" them before they disappeared (which they never did).

Museums at the time took on the same task. Indeed, museums became integral to this culture of collecting and would play a prominent role in the development of Canadian anthropology. In 1911, the Anthropology Division of the Geological Survey of Canada was established, with Edward Sapir, Marius Barbeau, and Diamond Jenness on its staff. In the 1920s, this unit became part of the

> **salvage anthropology**
> An approach to anthropology that arose in the late 1800s when anthropologists witnessed the extinction or assimilation of Indigenous peoples throughout the world. In response, some anthropologists, such as Franz Boas, suggested that anthropologists rapidly document the oral stories, songs, histories, and other traditions of Indigenous peoples before they disappeared.

National Museum of Canada, since renamed the Museum of Civilization (Ervin 2001, 15).

Regna Darnell, an anthropologist at the University of Western Ontario who has conducted extensive research on the history of Canadian anthropology, contends that, although there are no features of Canadian anthropology that set it apart as utterly unique, "the national discipline combines features of disciplinary organization and historical context in patterns that *are* unique" (1998b, 155). It is difficult to define exactly what is "Canadian" about Canadian anthropology, but Darnell has an interesting suggestion: "In Canada, a critical mass of First Nations languages and cultures maintains them [traditional cultures] with a saliency in the national forum unparalleled in the United States" (2000, 170). Many Canadian anthropologists continue to focus on Indigenous peoples, but they also conduct research in Latin America, the Caribbean, Asia, Africa, Europe (Eastern and Western), New Zealand, Australia, Melanesia, Polynesia, and the Middle East. Throughout this book, we will be looking at the work of many Canadian anthropologists as well as that of anthropologists in other parts of the world.

The flow of anthropologists is still predominantly *from* former colonial powers *to* former colonies, despite the fact that most of the world's former colonies have achieved independence over the last century. However, ideas about appropriate "field sites" and subjects of study have changed since the days of Malinowski and Boas. Anthropologists no longer restrict themselves to the study of non-Western peoples and places; more anthropologists today are studying "up" rather than "down" in terms of power relationships. Today, Canadian anthropologists are just as likely to study aspects of their own communities.

This shift in thinking has had consequences for how anthropologists conduct their fieldwork. The field "site" is no longer necessarily a faraway place. Anthropologists might study office culture in Vancouver, homelessness in Toronto, or separatist ideologies in Quebec. As such, they do not necessarily travel long distances for fieldwork, and many no longer live among their informants for extended periods of time. Furthermore, studying up, or at least "sideways," often leads anthropologists to research sites that are the locus from which to study uneven global connections and intersecting flows of people, things, or ideas. Thus, a field site might be chosen in order to study ecotourism in Costa Rica, the migration of refugees and asylum seekers across the Mediterranean Sea, factories that produce goods destined for global markets, or the flow of music genres and styles around the world. New topics, sites, and power relationships mean that it is often less accurate to talk about research "informants"; people studied may well be "participants," "collaborators," or "key cultural consultants."

Perhaps the greatest transformations in the kinds of research anthropologists do, the research sites we choose, and the questions we ask have been made to address concurrent transformations in social and cultural life as a result of processes of globalization (discussed in further depth in Chapter 8). For instance, a key difference between the anthropology of today and that of Malinowski's time has had to do with how we think of the "native" in the "native's point of view." Anthropologists today are more likely to interrogate the difference between an insider's point of view and an outsider's, not least because the people we study may negotiate more than one cultural point of view in their daily lives. Kirin Narayan (1993), for example, famously asked, "How native is a 'native' anthropologist?" She was inspired to ask the question by her own position, as the daughter of a German-American mother and an Indian father. When she conducted fieldwork in India, she was considered a "native" anthropologist, even though she did not necessarily see herself as native. So she questioned the oversimplified dichotomy between native and non-native; she also argued that, due to globalization and the interpenetrating communities and power relations that flow from it, identities might better be thought of, studied, and written about as hybrid and in flux. Furthermore, regardless of the extent to which either an anthropologist or a "native" identifies as an insider or outsider, there are many other factors, such as gender, sexuality, education, race, and class, that mean that the category of "native" may be better thought of as plural rather than singular (671–72).

A striking example of the significance of gender, for example, for understanding the "native's point of view" comes from Annette Weiner's work in the Trobriand Islands. Conducted nearly 60 years after Malinowski's famous fieldwork, Weiner's research set out to revisit what has become a "sacred place" in anthropology. In addition to conducting pioneering fieldwork and participant observation, Malinowski famously wrote about Trobriand Islanders' kula exchange (which involves the circulation of shell necklaces and bracelets among trading partners in a ring of islands off the coast of Papua New Guinea). *Argonauts of the Western Pacific* remains a classic text in economic anthropology; in Chapter 6 we discuss the kula ring as an example of the relationship between reciprocity and identity. Malinowski's analysis of Trobriand economics focused on men's exchanges of wealth, and he saw wealth exchange as exclusively the domain of men. Yet according to Weiner, "he never considered that this significance was underwritten by women's own wealth because he did not systematically investigate women's productive activities" (Weiner 1988, 5). When she turned her ethnographic focus to women, women's lives, and particularly women's exchanges, Weiner realized that women too conduct elaborate exchanges (for instance, of banana leaf skirts and bundles of banana leaves during funerary rituals). In doing so, they both produce and circulate their own form of wealth, with all the attending political and economic ramifications. Wealth, status, and identity have the potential to look very different in the Trobriand Islands, depending on which "native's point of view" we take.

Another key shift in the discipline and its methodologies over the past century has to do with the focus on a single research site. Malinowski advocated in-depth research in one specific location, but anthropologists today often conduct multi-locale fieldwork, or fieldwork in multiple locations. Other anthropologists advocate the use of multi-sited fieldwork, a term coined by George Marcus in 1995. **Multi-sited fieldwork** involves connecting the localized events and experiences of a community with broader regional, national, or global processes. This approach often goes hand in hand with multi-locale approaches. For instance, Canadian anthropologist Andrew Walsh (2010) has studied the commodification of sapphires and the growing preference for "natural" gems (sapphires that have not been subject to heat treatment to enhance their colour) from multiple perspectives. He has interviewed Malagasy miners and local sapphire traders in Madagascar as well as gemologists and jewellers in North America. His work has taken him not only to Madagascar but also to international gemological trade shows. In essence, Walsh is endeavouring to track the multiple meanings and relationships that form around the international sapphire trade, and to that end, he has explored how international demand for "natural" sapphires is affecting the lives of miners in local communities in Madagascar. Sapphires "mean" different things to different groups of people, and the mining industries have different economic, political, social, and health consequences for different groups depending on one's position within this complex international web of sapphire procurement, distribution, and consumption.

BEYOND THE BOOK 2.2

As an anthropologist, you have been employed by a non-governmental organization to study issues of homelessness in a mid-sized Canadian city. Your fieldwork will last one year, and you must try to incorporate the perspectives of homeless people, municipal politicians, homeless shelter workers, social workers who work with homeless people, and others. Outline how you would conduct fieldwork in this situation.

multi-sited fieldwork
This term, coined by George Marcus in 1995, refers to the process of connecting localized experiences of fieldwork with broader, global processes. It necessitates understanding various issues from multiple "sites," or perspectives.

Finally, the internet, online gaming, and social media have changed the ways we form and maintain social relationships, and some anthropologists have adjusted their methods accordingly. Today we are creating a sense of community not only through face-to-face interactions but also through internet sites, Reddit forums, online games, Skype, and Instagram, among others. Given that our contemporary interactions are mediated by technology, we increasingly see anthropologists conducting fieldwork online as well as face to face.

Tom Boellstorff's ethnography *Coming of Age in Second Life* (2008), for example, documents his research on, and in, the three-dimensional, online gaming world of "Second Life." Boellstorff conducted all of his fieldwork online. He justified this by stating that this virtual space is a productive one for studying the unique "cultural logic" of gaming and gamers. In other words, the online communities created by gamers are just as valid an object of study as traditional face-to-face communities have been. Interestingly, Boellstorff cites Tylor's understanding of culture as a "complex whole," asking, "What is a virtual world if not a complex whole, however networked?" (2008, 66). He goes on to explain that he is not studying "virtual culture," but rather "culture in virtual worlds" (66). He also emphasizes the similarity between his research "site" and more traditional field sites by paying homage to Malinowski's famous "arrival" scene in his book about the Trobrianders. In his own ethnography, Boellstorff asks the reader to

> *imagine yourself suddenly set down surrounded by all your gear, alone on a tropical beach close to a native village while the launch or dinghy which has brought you sails away out of sight . . . You have nothing to do, but to start at once your ethnographic work. Imagine further that you are a beginner, without previous experience, with nothing to guide you and no one to help you.*

Thus far, his arrival is a verbatim transcript of Malinowski's, which, Boellstorff says, "exactly describes my first initiation into field work in Second Life" (2008, 3).

Clearly, fieldwork has undergone changes since Malinowski's time. However, the *content* of fieldwork, or data collection, has barely changed. What counts as a site, or what counts as the emic or insider's point of view, may have changed, but as Raymond Madden (2010, 32) has aptly put it, "being ethnographic" remains in many ways the same: "Being with people . . . in their time and space, in all their strangeness and in their mundane and quotidian flow, is still one of most valued ways to build a qualitative understanding of the particulars and generalities of the human condition."

Another key aspect of doing anthropology that remains relatively unchanged is that, as anthropologists, through our ethnographies we create bodies of knowledge about the people we are studying. Issues of how to accurately and ethically represent human beliefs and behaviours therefore remain central to the discipline.

Tom Boellstorff conducted his fieldwork for *Coming of Age in Second Life* entirely online.

BEYOND THE BOOK 2.3

With social media being such a ubiquitous part of our daily lives, anthropologists are exploring ways to approach social media as a field "site." One way has been through tracking the social life of hashtags. How do people choose and use hashtags? Why? How do they circulate? What is the relationship between the cultural "work" that hashtags do online and their possible effects in the "real" world? Yaramir Bonilla and Jonathan Rosa (2015) conducted fieldwork on hashtag activism, including #Ferguson and #IfTheyGunnedMeDown. They demonstrated that hashtag activism has the power to create a shared political time and space among users and to draw attention to the real-world consequences of police brutality.

By yourself, or with a partner in class, choose a popular hashtag that you have used or are familiar with. Go online and "follow" the life of the hashtag through time and across users and platforms. What do you notice about the way the hashtag circulates? What kinds of connections does it make or suggest? Does the hashtag's meaning shift from user to user or platform to platform? How does it draw on, and affect, life in the offline world? Compare your results with those of the rest of the class.

Question 2.3: What Are Some of the Challenges of Conducting Fieldwork?

Ethnographic fieldwork is often frustrating and lonely. It can also involve elements of **culture shock** and miscommunication. *Culture shock* refers to a feeling of disorientation in the initial stages of fieldwork as the anthropologist adjusts to a new language, beliefs, foods, and even climate. In the early stages of fieldwork, an anthropologist may also misinterpret the intent of his or her informants, which can lead to awkward or embarrassing situations. In Jean Briggs's ethnography of her years of fieldwork with the Inuit of Canada's Arctic, titled *Never in Anger* (1970), she recounts some of her most crucial mistakes. Her research documented the importance, for the Inuit, of controlling one's emotions, and especially one's anger. She recounts her adoptive father's disappointment with her when she was unable to prevent herself from visibly demonstrating her anger. However, as Briggs has noted in retrospect: "Everything that happens is data. Mistakes are a good thing. You can learn more from making mistakes than from getting it right" (Sullivan 2016).

The following ethnographic vignettes from Richard Scaglion (1990) and Michael Kearney (1991) highlight the importance of long-term ethnography when it comes to interpreting the belief systems of other cultures. In many ways, the anthropologist becomes a student during fieldwork. It is through our mistakes and breaches of etiquette that we learn socially appropriate behaviours and ways of being and acting within a cultural group. Fieldwork is also a time when we can begin to challenge our own taken-for-granted assumptions about the world.

The Embarrassed Anthropologist

Awkwardness and embarrassment are a part of fieldwork as well as a part of the process through which the fieldworker learns about another culture. Richard Scaglion (1990) spent more than a year with the Abelam of Papua New Guinea. Shortly after he arrived in the field, he observed and photographed an Abelam pig hunt in which the men set out nets and waited while the women and children made lots of noise to drive the pigs into the nets. Soon after, he was invited by the Abelam to participate in a pig hunt, and he took this as a sign of acceptance, that the people "liked him." He started to go with the men, but they told him they wanted him to go with the women and children to beat the bush, explaining, "We've never seen anyone who makes as much noise in the jungle as you." Later, wanting to redeem himself, Scaglion offered to help an Abelam who was planting crops

culture shock
Refers to a feeling of disorientation in the initial stages of fieldwork when an anthropologist is adjusting to a new language, beliefs, food, or even climate.

with a digging stick. A crowd gathered to watch as he used a shovel to try to dig a demonstration hole. After he had struggled for several minutes to get the shovel into the hard-packed soil, someone handed him a digging stick, and he was amazed at how easy it was to use. Later, he found out that several Abelam had shovels but rarely used them because they didn't work.

After months of answering Scaglion's questions about their view of the natural world, such as the moon, sun, and stars, some Abelam asked him about *his* views of the universe. Feeling on safe ground, he gave the usual grade-school lecture about the shape of Earth, its daily rotation, and its travels around the sun. Using a coconut, he showed them the relative positions on Earth of New Guinea, Australia, Europe, and the United States. Everyone listened intently, and Scaglion thought it had gone well—until a week later, when he overheard some elders wondering how it was that North Americans walked upside down!

Beginning again, Scaglion used the coconut to explain how, as Earth rotates, sometimes the United States is upright and New Guinea is on the bottom. The Abelam rejected this because they could see that they were not upside down, and no one, not even some of the old people in the community, remembered ever having walked upside down. Scaglion began to draw on the physics he had learned at university. As he tried to explain Newton's law of gravity (or "grabity," as his friends pronounced it), he suddenly realized that he didn't understand "grabity" either. The concept, something he had accepted since grade 3, was one that even physicists take for granted.

Confronting Witchcraft in Mexico

Awkward or embarrassing moments in the field may help anthropologists understand a culture and even question their own view of the world. But the question of whether one can ever see the world through others' eyes remains contentious among anthropologists. Obviously, to communicate with anyone—even members of their own society—people must share some of the meanings they ascribe to objects, persons, behaviours, emotions, and events. What happens, then, when views of the world are completely different?

Michael Kearney (1991) travelled to the town of Santa Catarina Ixtepeji in the valley of Oaxaca, Mexico (Figure 2.1), with the intention of studying the relationship between the people's view of the world and their social arrangements and environment. He began his work secure in his knowledge of the scientific and materialist view of the world—a view he had been raised to accept—but he was often fascinated by the differences between his view and that of the people of Santa Catarina Ixtepeji. Their world was controlled by mystic notions of "fate" and the will of God, and by malevolent witches and other harmful and sometimes lethal spiritual forces. He became familiar with the Ixtepejanos' world view, never doubting that it was "unscientific"—albeit justified, perhaps, by a life in which suffering, disease, and death were common.

FIGURE 2.1 Mexico

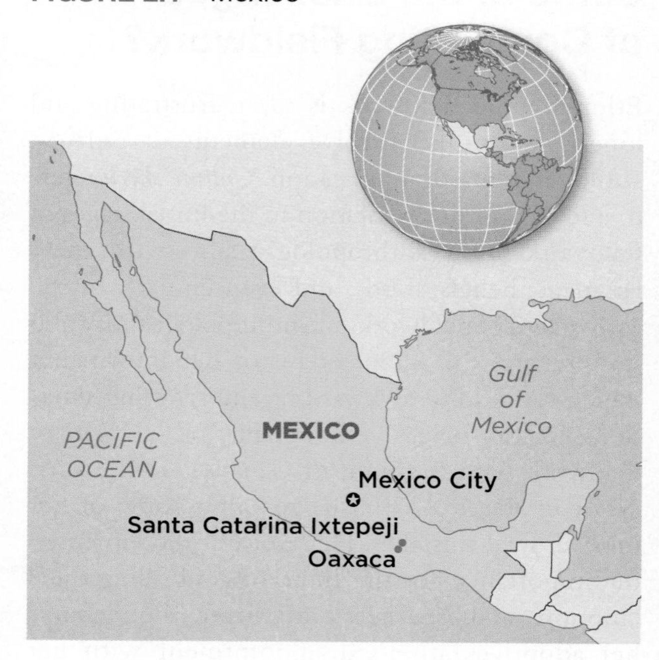

Kearney's faith in his own worldview was momentarily shattered by an incident that began innocently enough. While walking to an appointment, he came upon an obviously distressed woman, Doña Delfina. She was known as a witch, and Kearney had been trying unsuccessfully to interview her. When they met she explained that her sister-in-law had a "very bad disease in her arms" and that she wanted him to help. Kearney accompanied Doña Delfina to her house, where he found that the sister-in-law's arms were ulcerated with deep, oozing lesions that looked to him like infected burns. They rejected his offer to take the sick woman to a doctor for medical treatment, so Kearney said he had some ointment that might help, and they eagerly agreed that he should use it. He got the ointment, which contained an anaesthetic, and daubed it on the woman's sores. Much to the amazement of Doña Delfina, her sister-in-law immediately felt better. By the afternoon, her arms had greatly improved; by the following morning, scabs had formed; the day after, she had completely recovered.

Kearney was credited with a "miraculous cure" but encountered an unexpected reaction. The same day, an Ixtepejano friend asked Kearney what he had done, and the anthropologist proudly explained. The friend replied: "Why did you do that? It was not a good thing to do." The sick woman, he said, had been the victim of black magic; another woman, Gregoria, was trying to take Delfina's brother away from his wife and was using black magic to make Delfina's sister-in-law sick. Delfina was using *her* magic to keep her brother in the household, but Gregoria was winning. Now, the friend explained to Kearney, he had intervened, tipping the balance of power back to Delfina but creating a powerful enemy in Gregoria. "Maybe you should leave town for a while until Gregoria calms down," Kearney's friend suggested.

Kearney did not take the danger seriously, and he might never have done so were it not for two incidents that occurred soon afterward. A young doctor in town asked Kearney, who had medical training, to assist in an autopsy of a man who had died in a fall off a truck. It was a particularly long and gory autopsy, conducted with rusty carpenter's tools in a dimly lit room. Images of the scene and the cadaver disturbed Kearney's sleep over the next few days. One night, about a week later, as the wind beat cornstalks against his house, Kearney felt an itching on his arm. Rolling up his sleeve, he discovered several angry welts that seemed to be growing as he watched. Immediately, he thought of the chancrous arms of Delfina's sister-in-law, and remembered at the same time that Gregoria's house was only 50 metres from his. Could she be trying to kill him? "She got me!," he thought. The image of the cadaver on the table jumped into his mind, followed by a wish that he had got out of town while there was still time. As Kearney put it, he was witnessing the disintegration of his scientific, materialist view of the world and grappling with forces with which he was unprepared to deal.

Kearney is not sure how long his initial terror lasted—seconds, perhaps minutes. As he struggled against it, he realized that he was suspended between two worlds: his own and that of the Ixtepejanos. He was questioning a world of meanings that he had until then taken for granted. Kearney is not sure how long he was able to truly believe that the world was as the Ixtepejanos saw it, but as he retrieved his own view of the world, the Ixtepejanos' world view, filled with witchcraft and magic, ceased to be only intellectually interesting. It had acquired a reality and a sense of legitimacy for him that it had not had before he experienced the real fear that he had been bewitched. He came to realize through his experience that any system of belief is eminently reasonable when viewed from within that system.

The experiences of these anthropologists, Kearney and Scaglion, highlight certain features of the ethnographic method. They especially illustrate anthropologists' efforts to appreciate the views of others while at the same time questioning their own views of the world. They also illustrate what makes the ethnographic method unique: by participating in the lives of others and in their cultural practices, anthropologists can take themselves as subjects of investigation. Those who succeed in seeing the world as others do, if only for a brief moment, find it far easier to understand and describe that world. It also helps the anthropologist understand how others can believe what they do. Claude Lévi-Strauss, one of the greatest anthropologists of the twentieth century, once said that anthropologists' efforts to immerse themselves in the worlds of others turn them into "marginal" men or women. They are never completely native because they cannot totally shed their own cultural perceptions, but they are never the same again after having glimpsed alternative visions of the world. Anthropologists are, as Roger Keesing put it, outsiders who know something of what it is to be insiders.

Scaglion and Kearney both succeeded because they were able to see things, at least temporarily, from the native's point of view or an insider's perspective. Doing this is by no means easy, especially when we are faced with practices and beliefs that we find incredible or troublesome. We may be able to overcome our initial shock or bewilderment on confronting different cultures if we understand something about why cultural differences exist. But how should we react if the meanings that others ascribe to experiences differ from our own? It is difficult enough to look beyond everyday appearances at our own beliefs and behaviours; it is far more difficult when we confront beliefs and behaviours of others that we initially consider wrong, horrible, or bizarre.

BEYOND THE BOOK 2.4

Thinking back to the discussion on *The Embarrassed Anthropologist*, consider some awkward or embarrassing situation created by something you did or didn't do, said or didn't say. What was inappropriate about your behaviour, and why did it lead to misunderstanding or embarrassment? What did you learn from the experience about the meaning of your behaviour or that of others?

Question 2.4: What Are the Responsibilities of Anthropologists toward the People They Work With? What Does It Mean to "Act Ethically" as an Anthropologist?

As the previous sections have demonstrated, fieldwork is challenging—to an anthropologist's worldview, sense of well-being, and even ego. In this section, we discuss another set of challenges: the ethical challenges of living with others and gathering data during fieldwork, and the related challenges of accurately and fairly representing informants in one's written (or visual) ethnography.

The ethical challenges posed by fieldwork, and especially by participant observation, arise from the fact that, rather than simply conducting naturalistic observations of behaviour, fieldwork is inherently interventionist. This characteristic is especially evident in applied anthropology, where anthropologists conduct their research with the goal of solving a particular problem. But it is just as true of "regular" anthropology: our presence in the field will inevitably have an effect on those we study. We get involved in the day-to-day lives of our research subjects, we develop a rapport, and we negotiate relationships with our informants. Even at the best of times, human relationships are complicated and unpredictable (besides being rewarding and fulfilling). Relationships during ethnographic fieldwork are unique because ethnography, by definition, gives the ethnographer the power to create knowledge about the people he or she is studying. The power dynamic involved in ethnographic fieldwork, therefore, adds an additional layer of responsibility to relationships in the field.

One way that anthropologists working in various institutions (e.g., universities, hospitals, and community groups) address the potential ethical dilemmas of fieldwork is by participating in an institutional ethics review process, which involves writing a proposal, reviewed by one's peers, that explains how the ethnographer will ensure that the ethical standards of the discipline (and the institution) are maintained.[1] Although these proposals consist of a series of elements that must be addressed, it might be better to think of fieldwork not as having an ethical element that must be present, but rather as including "an ethical commitment from the very outset, and through all phases of ethnographic research and writing" (Madden 2010, 34). Here, we discuss not so much the various ethical elements that might appear in one's ethics review at a particular institution, but rather, the various ethical considerations that must be taken into account in fieldwork.

First and foremost, anthropologists are expected to "do no harm" to their informants. In other words, anthropological fieldwork must not result in any physical, psychological, or emotional harm to those who participate in our studies. To protect the rights of informants, anthropologists are required to obtain **informed consent** before conducting research. This requires them to disclose their identity, the goals of the project, and any potential risks involved. This requirement is a large part of what differentiates anthropologists from spies or investigative journalists: our informants must always know about and understand our presence in the field; with rare exceptions, we need to make certain of this even when it means that knowledge of our presence and our goals may change how people interact with us.

Ahead of our own goals and even ahead of our disciplinary pursuit of knowledge is our responsibility to our informants. This emphasis on ensuring the well-being of one's informants is why building rapport is so important to fieldwork. Anthropologists must also obtain permission to conduct any form of fieldwork, and while the use of written permission forms or letters is common, that permission can occasionally take the form of verbal consent. Individuals must also be told that they may withdraw from the project at any time, and to protect informants' confidentiality, people (and often places) are usually given pseudonyms. Furthermore, research participants have a right to know how an anthropologist will store and protect their data.

Our ethical commitments to our participants can lead to difficult situations and hard choices. For example, Philippe Bourgois (2003) has conducted fieldwork in El Barrio, New York, among gangs of Puerto Rican crack dealers and their families and communities. It took Bourgois more than two years to obtain the trust and loyalty of various crack dealers, and the goal of his project was to examine how poverty and urban economic restructuring (among other things) contributed to their choice to become crack dealers. Given the sensitive nature of his project, and the fact that the information he collected during his fieldwork (which details the names and addresses of dealers as well as the locations of crack houses) would be an invaluable resource to police, he found it necessary to change the names of informants and the specific locations where he conducted fieldwork. Indeed, because anthropologists, unlike journalists, do not have the legal right to protect their "confidential sources" in court, many anthropologists who find themselves in situations where they may witness illegal behaviour choose to remove themselves from the situation altogether. This decision may result in a "loss" of potentially rich data, but it may also be the only way to protect the rights of their participants and live up to their ethical responsibilities to those people with whom they have long-term relationships and commitments.

informed consent
The ongoing process of ensuring that research participants understand the goals, methods, and potential outcomes of the research process and give permission for the researcher to conduct said research.

[1] For instance, all Canadian researchers who conduct research with human subjects, regardless of the discipline, must act in accordance with the Tri-Council Policy Statement: Ethical Conduct for Research Involving Humans. Interested readers can access the statement here: http://www.pre.ethics.gc.ca/pdf/eng/tcps2/TCPS_2_FINAL_Web.pdf

Question 2.5: How Do Anthropologists Represent the People They Study and Work With? Why Is Representation an Important Issue within Anthropology?

Representation and Culture

Because they create knowledge about culture and relay other people's stories about themselves to a wider audience, anthropologists are concerned about issues of *representation*. All ethnographic depictions are based on interpretation rather than the mere presentation of raw data, and as such those depictions are shaped to varying degrees by the perspectives and assumptions of the author. That is why anthropologists try to think critically about how they depict the people they are studying, be it in writing, photographs, art, films, and other media, or on the internet. Representations can be created by anthropologists, by the media, or by the informants themselves. Increasingly, anthropologists are speaking out against racist, sexist, and homophobic representations produced by the mass media and even by other anthropologists. In the wake of 9/11 and the 2014–15 armed conflicts/air strikes against ISIS, for example, many mainstream American media outlets depicted Islamic people (especially men) as violent terrorists or as "uncivilized," "backward," and "primitive." The mass media have tended to resort to **essentialism** when representing particular groups. In essentialist representations, groups of people are depicted in ways that tend to homogenize and stereotype them (Mattingly, Lawlor, and Jacobs-Huey 2002). When essentialist representations are consumed by a public that is too often uncritical, racism is perpetuated and domestic and foreign policy are often affected for the worse. Because of their expertise and first-hand experience, anthropologists are well positioned to challenge the accuracy of such representations and analyze their repercussions.

Mass tourism is one social realm that tends to rely heavily on essentialist images and depictions of non-Western peoples. Such images are frequently circulated in brochures, on websites, and in other forms of advertising by airlines, hotels, and tour operators. Tourist brochures and websites often lure middle-class Canadians to tropical islands by representing the island and its people as "primitive," "timeless," and "exotic." In fact, the tourist industry is built around producing marketable images or representations of particular peoples and places to attract foreign tourists (and their dollars). In many developing nations, non-white peoples (especially Indigenous peoples) are frequently depicted as "primitive." We are often so accustomed to hearing this term used in uncritical ways and in association with Indigenous peoples, for instance, that we fail to understand how representations of particular groups as exotic or primitive are ethnocentric.

Let's analyze what the term "primitive" means. The term hearkens back to the colonial era, when non-Western peoples were erroneously positioned as "backward" and as inferior to white Westerners in a biological, technological, and social sense. It is thus used to denote a group of people who are considered inferior, stuck in "another time," "uncivilized." The problem, of course, is that there are no primitive peoples, because the concept itself is simply a representation or a depiction of another group of people based on a subjective and often biased comparison with one's own society. Moreover, as we discuss in Chapter 3, markers of what is viewed as progress in our society (e.g., access to technology) are not necessarily viewed as desirable or necessary in other types of societies. So, the very criteria that are often used to label a group as "primitive" are themselves problematic.

Nevertheless, we still see the term "primitive" employed frequently in travel brochures. Since Western tourists tend to view themselves as civilized,

essentialism
The act of creating generalizations or stereotypes about the behaviour or culture of a group of people.

they may feel it is exciting and adventurous, not to mention a break from the stresses of modern life, to travel the world viewing seemingly simple, "primitive" peoples. If, however, you perceive another group of people as primitive, then mistreating and exploiting them becomes justified. Throughout her fieldwork in Sosua in the Dominican Republic, Denise Brennan (2004) explored the relationships that developed among heterosexual Afro-Dominican and Latina women and white, foreign male sex tourists. Sosua has become a magnet for sex tourism. Heterosexual men, in particular, travel to Sosua to engage in sexual relations with local women, who often come from marginalized backgrounds and rely on sex tourism for a stable income. When the men are asked why they come so far to engage in sex, they argue that the Dominican women are highly sexualized and are "exotic," "hot," and "primitive" (Brennan 2004, 45) compared to white women back home. The bodies of Dominican women thus become objectified, and their supposedly "exotic" and "primitive" nature is highlighted as a central component of their being. Representations of sex workers as "primitive" have led to their sexual exploitation and mistreatment, ranging from physical abuse at the hands of male sex tourists, to the pervasive view among Westerners that the lives of such women are somehow expendable, given their seemingly inferior, socially marginalized status.

With respect to representation, anthropologists also turn a critical lens upon themselves. An anthropologist who takes a photograph or writes an ethnographic account is crafting a particular representation of a group of people. Anthropologists must therefore ask themselves: Who has the right to produce representations of another group of people, and is there such a thing as a misrepresentation?

The people whom anthropologists study are becoming increasingly vocal in their concerns about how they are depicted. American anthropologist Margaret Mead travelled to American Samoa in 1925 to study adolescent girls' sexual habits; this research led to the publication of her now famous ethnography, *Coming of Age in Samoa* (1928). Throughout her book, Mead painted a picture of Samoan society as peaceful; she also noted that the girls were free to experiment with premarital sex. This acceptance contrasted sharply with American attitudes at the time regarding sexuality, which viewed premarital sex as taboo. Her ethnography, which was widely read by anthropologists, students, and the mainstream public, cultivated (perhaps unintentionally) a romanticized and "exotic" representation of Samoans for a largely Western audience. Later generations of Samoans critiqued her work, often denying that teenagers engaged in gratuitous sex (Marshall 1993). Some anthropologists are quick to point out that the "missionization" of Samoans has contributed to the development of moral strictures on sexuality–structures that in turn have affected their perceptions of Mead's text. Even so, their objections raise some interesting questions for anthropology students. What if the anthropologist's interpretations of culture differ from those of his or her informants? And what are the consequences of the representations cultivated by anthropologists?

There are no clear-cut answers for those questions, but it is worth noting that the representations crafted by anthropologists can have long-term ill consequences for the groups being depicted. For example, Napoleon Chagnon studied the Yanomamö, an Amazonian Indigenous group in Brazil and Venezuela. He often labelled them as "fierce" and warlike. In fact, the title of his ethnography about them is *Yanomamo: The Fierce People* (1968). Other anthropologists who have studied the Yanomamö (e.g., Ferguson 1995; Turner 2005) have challenged his interpretation of the Yanomamö as fierce. Terence Turner (2005) has argued that representations of the Yanomamö as "fierce" have done them harm. For instance, in the early 1990s, the British government wanted to provide financial assistance to various Amazonian groups for education and medical clinics. But after reading Chagnon's work, they decided that the money would be better spent on reducing levels of "violence" in the community.

© Gerard Sioen/Anzenberger/Redux

Sue Cunningham Photographic/Alamy Stock Photo

Images like the one on the left depict the Yanomamö as fierce and warlike and have resulted in essentialist representations of the tribe. Compare with the photo on the right. If more depictions of the Yanomamö looked like this one, how might our impressions of them have been different?

In addition to taking issues of essentialism and representation very seriously in their own work, many anthropologists strive to identify, analyze, and offer ethnographically informed alternatives to essentialist representations that circulate in "the real world." As we have seen, such representations can have significant negative effects on those represented, and during their fieldwork, anthropologists often witness those effects first-hand. For instance, many anthropologists have written about the essentialist figure of the "starving African child." You may have come across such depictions in the imagery for fundraising campaigns for various NGOs, charities, and religious missions. Anthropologist Bianca Dahl has written about the influence and unexpected consequences of the use of the image of the "starving orphan" by the Bathusi Orphan Day Care Centre in Lentswê, Botswana, which began as a modest feeding program for children orphaned by HIV/AIDS:

> *The iconography of the African AIDS orphan, captured in National Geographic–style images of what Catherine Lutz and Jane Collins (1993, 181) call "starving ungendered children"—that is, wide-eyed toddlers with distended bellies and flies buzzing around their orifices—constitutes the motivating stereotype behind much of the well-intentioned flow of money from the West toward organizations*

like Bathusi. Such institutions operate on the presumption of poverty, neglect, and/or abandonment of orphans by their relatives. As James Ferguson (1990, xiii) has suggested, in Western perceptions "the bloated bellies of African children are the signs of social as well as nutritional deficiency." Despite partial convergence between donors and locals about the needs of orphans, discontent began to arise in Botswana when NGOs started to provide a quantity of these material services that far exceeded the mere avoidance of starvation. Their mandate extended to empowering children through educational support and self-esteem-building activities, and increasingly gifting orphans not just food but also fashionable clothes, toys, and even cell phones. (Dahl 2014, 635–36)*

The use of essentialist representations of "starving orphans" was strategically useful for the NGO's fundraising, so much so that it was able to offer greater aid and programming. Ironically, villagers anxious about this influx of relative wealth and opportunity critiqued the program (and the children themselves) in the same essentialist terms that had made the NGO so successful, claiming that the children in question were "too fat to be orphans" (Dahl 2014).

In Canada, and in North America more broadly, another common essentialist representation that you have probably encountered is that of the veiled Muslim woman as the subject of religious oppression. Such representations and the discourses that accompany them tend to equate veiling, and Islam, with oppression; they are also essentialist in that they suggest that all Muslim women wear the veil all the time; that only Muslim women cover their heads; that veiling is always forced and always oppressive; and that, in short, Muslim women need to be "saved" by secularists, by feminists, or by non-Muslim men.

Regarding these essentialist representations, and especially regarding how they have increased in North America since 9/11, anthropologist Lila Abu-Lughod has asked: "Do Muslim women really need saving?" (Abu-Lughod 2002). The anthropological response to essentialist representations is generally to counter them with more complicated depictions based on ethnographic evidence. Like Abu-Lughod, Canadian anthropologist Homa Hoodfar addressed the kinds of assumptions that many Canadians often make about women who veil, arguing that "the veil in their minds" and the veil "on our heads" were two very different things (Hoodfar 2001). In her fieldwork with young Muslim women living in Canada (from a wide variety of backgrounds and with a wide range of religious beliefs and practices), Hoodfar found that women chose to veil (or not) for a variety of reasons, including for modesty's sake, as a means to assert their cultural and religious identity (see Chapter 6), or to avoid non-Muslim suitors. None of her informants reported being forced by their father or other relatives to wear the veil. Perhaps most importantly, many women claimed that part of the reason that they chose to veil (even when they came from families where no one else did so) had to do with "talking back" to essentialist representations of Muslim women. Hoodfar writes,

As the data indicates, the continued negative portrayal of Islam and Muslims in the West has, in fact, motivated some women to take up the veil. They do so, not only because of their personal religious beliefs, but also out of a wish to assert openly the presence of the Muslim community. (Hoodfar 2003, 39)

Clearly, representations put forward by anthropologists, the mass media, and others have social, economic, and political consequences for various groups. So it is important for anthropologists to consider the long-term impact of their work in various communities. Increasingly, the writings, films, and other visual and print media produced by anthropologists are read or viewed not only by academics but also by their informants and their communities,

---

APPLYING ANTHROPOLOGY

Challenging Essentialist Representations through Music

In 2018, Jeremy Dutcher won Canada's prestigious Polaris Music Prize for his first album, *Wolastoqiyik Lintuwakonawa* (Our Maliseet Songs). Dutcher is a classically trained operatic tenor and a member of the Tobique First Nation, one of six Wolastoqiyik (pronounced "Wuh-last-o-key-yik") or Maliseet Nation reserves in New Brunswick. He also has a dual BA in Social Anthropology and Music from Dalhousie University.

The songs on the album combine traditional Wolastoqivik melodies with Dutcher's operatic singing and contemporary orchestration from a wide range of genres. The result defies easy categorization into one musical genre or tradition. Dutcher may not be a professional anthropologist, but his work is informed, in part, by an anthropological sensibility and challenges essentialist representations of Indigenous peoples and what "Indigenous" music might sound like.

As an undergraduate, Dutcher was a relative latecomer to anthropology. In his music degree program, he had been frustrated by the relative absence of any discussion or inclusion of Indigenous music. In his fourth year, he took an Introductory Anthropology class. According to Liesl Gambold, the professor, he came to her and said, "I have a problem. I am two semesters way from graduating with a degree in Music, but I realize after a few days in class that I need to study anthropology" (Radice, Noble, and Gambold 2018). Inspired by this realization, he took an extra year to finish a B.A. in Anthropology, writing an honours thesis titled "Traditional Music in a Contemporary Moment: Musical Pan-Indigeneity as Revitalization in the Wabanaki Region" (2012). It was during research for this thesis that Maliseet elder Maggie Paul made him aware of a collection of wax cylinder recordings, made by anthropologist William Mechling in 1900. These are the recordings that Dutcher sampled and re-envisioned on his award-winning album. Mechling's collection could be considered a work of salvage anthropology (see Section 2.2), and perhaps a prescient one: the 1876 Indian Act had limited the public expression of Indigenous art and music, and many of these songs had all but disappeared from living memory (the recordings were forgotten in an archive). Dutcher breathed new life into these traditional songs and introduced them to a new generation of Wolastiquyik speakers (and as the album's popularity demonstrates, to many others as well). By combining genres and voices in novel ways, and by breaking down barriers between traditional/contemporary music and indigenous/settler/classical music, Dutcher's work challenges essentialist representations of Indigenous peoples, their cultures, and their art. An article about Dutcher and *Wolastoqiyik Lintuwakonawa* in the Guardian's "Opera" column noted

> *Dutcher says part of his role is to "break down people's misunderstandings." He wants to show everyone—from the reservation to the opera house, and even the white hobbyists who dress up as "Indians" in historical re-enactments—that the only things gone from this world forever are the old limitations placed on Indigenous peoples. As he concludes: "I'm not the Indian you wanted, but I am the Indian you need." (Darville 2019)*

Dutcher's work may not be a typical example of applied anthropology, but therein lies its significance: an anthropological sensibility (not to mention collaborative and Indigenous methodologies) might successfully be applied in myriad settings and workplaces, to a wide variety of issues or problems.

by journalists, by government and nongovernmental organizations, and by others. As such, anthropologists have a responsibility to the people they work with to ensure that the work they produce does not cause them any harm.

BEYOND THE BOOK 2.5

Find a Canadian news article that discusses a particular event involving a "minority" group. Outline how the author of the article represents this group. What words does the author use? What sorts of pictures (if any) are displayed? What is the tone of the article? Who was it written by, and for what audience?

Conclusions

Over the past century, ethnographic fieldwork has emerged as a defining feature of sociocultural anthropology. To understand cultural phenomena from the perspectives of those whom we work with and study, we must go into the field (whether or not this is a singular, physical locale or site) to learn about them first-hand. Through long-term fieldwork and the use of various qualitative methods such as interviews and participant observation, anthropologists develop a nuanced understanding of the different beliefs and cultural practices they encounter in various societies. In addition, fieldwork helps us comprehend how various societies are influenced by broader social processes, such as globalization and colonialism.

As discussed throughout this chapter, Bronislaw Malinowski is often credited as one of the first anthropologists to break away from the "armchair" anthropology that dominated the discipline in the late nineteenth century. He immersed himself in Trobriand communities, living with his informants, learning the local language, participating in various cultural traditions, and observing aspects of daily life. Malinowski's emphasis on participant observation stressed the importance of obtaining first-hand knowledge of and developing a sense of rapport with people. Under Malinowski, anthropology developed as a discipline that emphasized qualitative research methods such as participant observation, and the importance of long-term fieldwork in a single locale, and that focused largely on the study of Indigenous and non-Western peoples.

Given that anthropology at the turn of the twentieth century was heavily influenced by colonialism and that Malinowski himself went to the Trobriand Islands as a guest of colonial administrators, it is not surprising that most early anthropologists "studied down." By this, we mean that there was a tendency to conduct fieldwork among peoples who were less powerful economically, socially, and politically than the anthropologist. Over the last century, however, we have seen gradual changes in anthropological methods and goals.

Anthropology has indeed grown and changed over the past century. Although there still exists a tendency for anthropologists from First World or developed nations to study those in developing nations, anthropologists are certainly no longer restricted to the study of "non-Western" peoples and places. Anthropologists are also increasingly cognizant of relationships of power, and more anthropologists "study up," which includes studying corporate elites, celebrities, politicians, and others in positions of power and authority. Increasingly, anthropologists conduct fieldwork that is multi-locale and/or multi-sited, which allows them to better address questions about globalization and its implications for cultural beliefs, values, and practices. Despite these changes, the central tenets of ethnography remain the same: anthropologists still strive to systematically collect data that reflect and illuminate an emic point of view, while presenting and analyzing these data from an etic point of view for an audience of (mostly) outsiders. Ethnographic fieldwork, and especially participant observation, involves negotiating complex relationships and requires an ethical commitment on the part of the anthropologist to fairly and accurately treat and depict research subjects at all stages of the research process.

QUESTIONS: REVIEW

Introduction

Here we introduce the significance of ethnographic fieldwork to the discipline of anthropology. It is our key methodology, one that sets us apart from other social sciences.

Review Questions

1. Compare and contrast quantitative and qualitative methodologies. What kinds of questions or topics are best explored with each?
2. What is the difference between the *emic* and *etic* perspectives?

2.1 How did ethnographic fieldwork develop during the formative years of anthropology?

In this section, we discuss the history of anthropological methods, beginning with "proto-anthropologists," such as culturally minded explorers, travellers, and missionaries, who observed and wrote about the beliefs and practices of people they encountered who were unfamiliar to them. Many of the first professional anthropologists read and compared these kinds of second-hand accounts in order to compare different cultures, often with the goal of ranking them in a hierarchy of civilizations. We then discussed the enduring significance of Bronislaw Malinowski's work in the Trobriand Islands. After conducting long-term fieldwork and participant observation, Malinowski determined that this kind of first-hand experience was critical for understanding "the native's point of view." He trained a generation of students to do the same, and today, ethnographic fieldwork remains the methodological underpinning of sociocultural anthropology.

Review Questions

1. What are some of the differences between armchair anthropology and participant observation?
2. What was E.B. Tylor's definition of culture, and how did it reflect the kinds of research methods he used?
3. Name at least three characteristics of ethnographic fieldwork.

2.2 How has fieldwork changed over the past century?

The world has changed a great deal since Malinowski first conducted his fieldwork, and although many aspects of fieldwork still draw on Malinowski's example, much about this method has changed, as well. Today, anthropologists are just as likely to study "at home" as they are to study in an unfamiliar place; and many anthropologists study "up" rather than "down"; we often study global cultural flows rather than particular cultural "sites." Increasingly, anthropologists are doing fieldwork online, as well.

Review Questions

1. Discuss some of the changes to fieldwork that have taken place over the past century. What factors do you think are responsible for some of these changes?
2. What are some of the shortcomings of thinking of the "native's point of view" as singular rather than plural?
3. What is multi-sited fieldwork, and why might an anthropologist choose to do it?

2.3 What are some of the challenges of conducting fieldwork?

In this section, we discuss some of the difficulties anthropologists face when they first enter the field and while they are conducting their fieldwork. Adjusting to the field means overcoming culture shock, possibly learning a new language, establishing rapport and gaining trust, and learning from one's mistakes. The examples in this section demonstrate that as they try to figure out an unfamiliar cultural context, anthropologists may end up feeling embarrassed, at best, or being endangered, at worst.

Review Questions

1. What is culture shock?
2. Using examples from this section, discuss the ways in which making mistakes can help an anthropologist to better understand "the native's point of view."

2.4 What are the responsibilities of anthropologists toward the people they work with? What does it mean to "act ethically" as an anthropologist?

In this section of the chapter, we explored the ethical obligations faced by anthropologists in the field, in their writings, and beyond. Fieldwork is unique because it requires sustained and often very close contact between the researcher and the researched. Anthropologists must be certain that they "do no harm" and obtain informed consent. There is great power (and power imbalance) in writing about people's lives and creating authoritative knowledge about "cultures." Anthropologists therefore strive to avoid essentialist or primitivist representations of the people they study, and often strive to counter such representations outside the discipline, as well.

Review Questions

1. What is informed consent in the context of conducting research, and why is it important?
2. Define *essentialism* and give examples of essentialist cultural representations.

2.5 How do anthropologists represent the people they study and work with? Why is representation an important issue within anthropology?

Anthropologists base their depictions on interpretations of the data they collect during fieldwork; in doing so, they effectively create knowledge about those they study, and this knowledge is taken seriously because of the anthropologists' expertise. Anthropologists therefore have a great responsibility to take the issues of representation seriously, and especially to avoid essentialisms in their representations of those they study. In this final section of the chapter, we discussed examples of the repercussions that inaccurate or essentialist representations by anthropologists and others have had on Samoans, the Yanomamö, orphans in Botswana, and Muslim women in Canada.

Review Questions

1. Why are some Samoans and contemporary anthropologists critical of Margaret Mead's depictions of Samoan culture in Coming of Age in Samoa?
2. What are some of the negative repercussions of Napolean Chagnon's depictions of the Yanomamö as fierce and warlike?
3. How do the ethnographic research findings of Bianca Dahl and Homa Hoodfar challenge popular media representations of orphans in Botswana and veiled Muslim women in Canada, respectively?

CRITICAL THINKING QUESTIONS

1. In section 2.1, we discuss participant observation, in which the anthropologist both observes and takes part in daily life in order to understand an emic, or "native's," point of view. Is this objective knowledge or subjective knowledge or something in between? List the reasons for your answer.
2. Discuss some of the changes to fieldwork that have taken place over the past century. What factors do you think are responsible for some of these changes?

KEY TERMS

armchair anthropology (p. 40)
culture shock (p. 47)
emic perspective (p. 38)
essentialism (p. 52)
ethnographic fieldwork (p. 37)
ethnography (p. 42)
etic perspective (p. 38)
informed consent (p. 51)
multi-sited fieldwork (p. 45)
participant observation (p. 41)
qualitative research (p. 37)
quantitative research (p. 37)
rapport (p. 38)
representation (p. 39)
salvage anthropology (p. 43)

CHAPTER 3

The Meaning of Progress and Development

REUTERS/Arko Datta

As economic inequality within and between the world's nations becomes more and more pronounced, scenes such as this one from India (where 1 percent of the population holds 73 percent of the wealth) are becoming more and more common. How, in an age of unprecedented progress and development, have so many people been left on the outside looking in? Below, in the epigraph to this chapter, John Isbister points out that modern technology has penetrated the developing world, but the results have not always been positive or evenly distributed.

One of the myths prevalent about third-world people is that they are unchanging, that their societies are static. One often hears the word traditional used to describe the network of relationships in which they seem trapped. The opposite is true, however. The third world is undergoing rapid and sometimes chaotic social change: populations are growing and becoming more urbanized. Public health measures are lowering death rates . . . Modern technology has penetrated the third world and transformed production. Education at all levels is spreading.

The lives of people in the third world are changing. They are not improving, however, at least for the majority. One can find privileged groups, or even entire countries and regions, in which economic conditions have progressed and human and political rights are respected . . . These are exceptions, though; most people in the third world are desperately poor.

—John Isbister, *Promises Not Kept* (2003)

PROBLEM 3

How do we explain the transformation of human societies over the past 10,000 years from small-scale, nomadic bands of foragers to large-scale, urban-industrial states?

Introduction

What Do We Mean When We Talk about Progress?

For thousands of years, all human beings lived as bands in small, nomadic groups of 30 to 100 people, gathering wild vegetable foods and hunting large and small game. Ten thousand years ago, however, most human societies began to move away from this mode of livelihood and form of social organization. Today, no human beings anywhere in the world live exclusively by hunting and gathering, although every society in existence is descended from such people.

Today's world is radically divided into wealthy nations and poor nations. Some enjoy a standard of living that gives them abundant food, comfortable shelter, and a plethora of consumer goods, but more than a billion people worldwide suffer from hunger and poverty, live in urban and rural slums, and lack even the basics of health care.

The gradual shift from a type of society that flourished for thousands of years, and the accompanying creation of a world divided into the wealthy and the poor, poses both a riddle and a moral predicament. The riddle is this: Why, after thousands of years of living as foragers, did some societies begin to change their way of life? Why did they begin to domesticate plants and animals and exchange their nomadic existence for a sedentary life in villages and towns? And how, over the next 10,000 years, did these villages and towns come to be divided into rich and poor states? The moral predicament involves our perceptions of the few remaining small-scale societies that exist today and of the millions of people who go hungry each day. Should we assume—as many have and still do—that human beings chose to abandon a nomadic, foraging life because they discovered better ways of living? Should we assume that the few remaining small-scale tribal societies are remnants of an inferior way of life and that, given the opportunity, their members would adopt modern farming, wage labour, or urban life? Should we assume that we can explain the world's division of wealth by saying that some nations have progressed while others have not? Or is the concept of **progress**—namely, that human history has been a steady advance from a life dependent on nature's whims to a life of control and domination

progress
The idea that human history is the story of a steady advance from a life dependent on the whims of nature to a life of control and domination over natural forces.

over natural forces—a fabrication of contemporary societies based on ethnocentric notions of technological superiority?

Throughout this chapter, we will seek to understand the monumental shift that has occurred in modes of livelihood and social organization over the past 10,000 years without relying on an uncritical use of the concept of progress. Many anthropological ideas about modes of livelihood can be put to good use outside the academy in the area of development; however, we will also see that "development" only works when we question the assumptions often inherent in the idea of progress. What, exactly, does progress mean, and for whom? And who determines what counts as progress and what does not?

QUESTIONS

3.1 How and why did foraging societies switch to sedentary agriculture?
3.2 How can we explain the vast inequality between the rich and the poor?
3.3 How does economic development affect inequality and cultural diversity?
3.4 Have progress and development improved human health?

Question 3.1: How and Why Did Foraging Societies Switch to Sedentary Agriculture?

A thumbnail sketch of what we know about the course of cultural history, modes of livelihood, and social organization will provide a useful starting point for understanding the meaning of progress and development. We will combine what we have learned about human history from the work of archaeologists and historians with information provided by cultural anthropologists who have worked among contemporary foraging and tribal societies to create a relatively clear picture of **culture change**. Until around 10,000 years ago, humans were scattered in nomadic **bands** of 30 to 100 people, who made their livelihood as **foragers**, gathering wild plants and hunting small and large game. Because the search for food required mobility, it was probably not unusual for them to move every few days. Generally, people had few personal possessions or other forms of material culture. Such items would have been liabilities, hindering the ability to travel. With groups that were small and mobile, simple economic, social, and political arrangements sufficed: formal leaders were not needed, and there was little occupational specialization. If there was a specialist, it was likely to be a person who was believed to have special spiritual powers that could be used to cure illness or (if used malevolently) to cause illness or death. Kinship served as the main organizing principle of these societies, and social differences among people were based largely on age and gender. Because there was little occupational specialization and little difference in individual wealth or possessions, relations among people likely were egalitarian.

At some point in history, some foragers began to plant crops and domesticate wild animals. These groups became **sedentary**, living in permanent or

culture change
The changes in meanings that a people ascribe to experience and changes in their way of life

bands
A term used by anthropologists to refer to egalitarian units of social organization, found mostly among foragers; these units usually consist of fewer than 100 people.

foragers
A term used by anthropologists to refer to societies that make their livelihood through gathering plants, hunting, or fishing.

sedentary
Refers to the practice of living in permanent or semi-permanent settlements.

semi-permanent settlements of 200 to 2,000 people. They practised **slash-and-burn, or swidden, agriculture**; they cleared forests by burning the trees and brush and then planted crops among the ashes. This land would be cultivated for one to three years; after that, another plot of land would be burned and planted.

Larger, more sedentary groups required more formal leadership. One member would assume the role of chief or elder, with the authority to make decisions and resolve disputes. Simple occupational roles developed. Villages consisted of extended family groups, and people organized themselves into **clans**, or groups of 200 to 500 people who claimed descent from a common ancestor. Now that leadership roles had developed, members of some groups were ranked in importance.

Later in history, perhaps because of a need to defend themselves against other groups, settlements combined themselves under common leaders to form **states** consisting of many thousands of persons. The development of agriculture intensified, and slash-and-burn techniques were replaced by plough or **irrigation agriculture**. Leaders organized labour for the purpose of constructing public works such as roads (the Inca Highway), fortifications (the Great Wall of China), and religious structures (pyramids in Mexico, cathedrals in medieval Europe). Hereditary leaders emerged, settlements grew into cities, and competition between groups over available resources spurred the development of standing armies.

As technological complexity increased, people began to develop specific skills and to specialize in occupational tasks (e.g., herder, baker, butcher, warrior, potter); that occupational specialization led to increased trade and to the evolution of a merchant class. Some 300 years ago, some of these hierarchical societies began to develop into large-scale, industrialized states, which are now found all over the world. Table 3.1 summarizes this sketch of human social and cultural history.

Does the Idea of Progress Help Us Understand the Shift from Foraging to Sedentary Agriculture?

As we have seen, the shifts in modes of livelihood from foraging to horticulture to agriculture were accompanied by major social and cultural shifts. From the earliest days of their discipline, anthropologists have sought to explain these shifts. One possible explanation for why societies transformed themselves in this way is that human inventions resulted in better ways of doing things; in other words, human culture progressed. However, more recently, anthropologists have begun to question the idea that the foraging life was harsh and difficult. In this section, we discuss the work of two early and influential anthropologists, Lewis Henry Morgan and Leslie White, who developed explanations of culture change based on the idea of progress. We then explore case studies of foraging, slash-and-burn, and industrial agriculture; finally, we discuss the work of anthropologists who argue that agriculture is *not* the easiest mode of livelihood, nor is it the most efficient. If the notion of the steady march of progress through time does not adequately explain the shift in modes of livelihood, what does?

slash-and-burn, or swidden, agriculture
A mode of livelihood in which forests are cleared by burning trees and brush, and crops are planted among the ashes of the cleared ground.

clans
Unilineal descent groups whose members claim descent from a common ancestor.

states
Forms of society characterized by a hierarchical ranking of people and centralized political control.

irrigation agriculture
A form of cultivation in which water is used to deliver nutrients to growing plants.

TABLE 3.1 Summary of the Development of Societies from Foragers to Agricultural States

	FORAGERS	HORTICULTURALISTS	STATE SOCIETIES
Population density	Approximately 1 person per 2.6 square kilometres.	Approximately 10 to 15 people per 2.6 square kilometres.	Approximately 300 people per 2.6 square kilometres.
Subsistence	Hunting, gathering, and fishing.	Slash-and-burn agriculture with mixed livestock herding.	Plough or irrigation agriculture.
Work, labour, and production	Very high yield relative to labour expended.	High yield relative to labour expended.	High labour needs relative to yield. High degree of occupational specialization.
Political organization	Informal political organization. Few, if any, formal leaders. Conflict controlled by limiting group size, mobility, and flexibility of group membership. Little intergroup conflict.	More formalized political organization, often with well-established leaders or chiefs. Increased population density and wealth result in increased potential for conflict. Intergroup warfare, motivated by desire for wealth, prestige, or women, is common.	Highly developed state organization with a clear hierarchy of authority. Often a two-class society with rulers (landowners) and peasants. Authority of the elite backed by organized use of force (police or army). Warfare for purpose of conquest is common. Well-established mechanisms for resolving conflict (e.g., courts) exist side by side with informal mechanisms.
Social organization	Small family groups, whose major purpose is economic cooperation. Few status distinctions other than those of sex and age. Marriage for economic partnership and interfamily alliance.	Emphasis on extended family groups. Descent important for the distribution of wealth and property. Status distinctions based on wealth are common, but status mobility is usually possible.	Emphasis on nuclear family. Family is strongly patriarchal, with women holding low status. Strong bonds of intergenerational dependence are built on inheritance needs. Social distinctions between people are emphasized, sometimes based on occupations. Little or no status mobility.

Evolutionary Explanations for Culture Change: Lewis Henry Morgan and Leslie White

One possible reason why foragers chose at some point to settle down and domesticate plants and animals is that sedentary agriculture was an easier, less dangerous, and more productive way to get food. People who discovered that they could plant and harvest crops and domesticate animals instead of searching for their food began to do so. According to this explanation, they had *progressed*.

The idea that change occurs because of a desire to progress is entrenched in Western societies, and beginning in the nineteenth century, anthropologists contributed significantly to this view. Many early anthropologists in the mid- to late- nineteenth century were inspired by the work of British naturalists Charles Darwin and Herbert Spencer and their ideas of evolution.

In the 1830s, Darwin embarked on a scientific voyage around the world on the HMS *Beagle*. Among other things, he documented physical variations in different species of nonhuman animals and plants, arguing that such processes as **natural selection** contributed to the formation of new

natural selection
Refers to Darwin's idea that the survival of different species of organisms is partly contingent upon how well adapted they are to their physical environments. Those with favourable physical traits are more likely to survive to reproduce.

species. Darwin published his theory of evolution in 1859 in *On the Origin of Species*. Within the developing academic discipline of anthropology, many scholars misappropriated many of Darwin's ideas and applied them to the study of human societies. While Darwin's original publication dealt with notions of *biological* evolution—that is, physical, bodily changes over time—some scholars felt that his ideas could be applied to the study of social change, or how *societies* changed over time.

Meanwhile, the British philosopher and naturalist Herbert Spencer was working on his own theories of evolution; he suggested that change can be understood as progress over time and, moreover, that an end point, or final goal, exists for human societies. Spencer felt that, like biological organisms, societies grow, expand, and increase in complexity over time, and that the more complex and "advanced" a society was, the more "evolved" it was. While this link between social change and progress is considered ethnocentric by today's anthropological standards, notions of social progress would influence many early anthropologists via the theory of **unilineal evolution**.

Lewis Henry Morgan, for instance, was influenced by, and became a proponent of, unilineal evolutionary ideas, which posit that all societies go through a series of uniform, standardized stages of social evolution. Such theories typically (and ethnocentrically) positioned Western societies at the apex of a "ladder of civilization" and were informed by Morgan's own culturally informed notions of progress. Morgan, a lawyer in Rochester, New York, took a great interest in the historical evolution of culture, and he offered his own variant of unilineal evolution to explain how humankind had progressed. Morgan sent out questionnaires to travellers and missionaries all over the world asking them about the family organization and kinship terminology of the cultures they visited.

In *Ancient Society* (1877), Morgan postulated a unilineal theory of human development in which human societies evolved through three stages that he labelled savagery, barbarism, and civilization. He further divided savagery and barbarism into early, middle, and late stages. Some societies—notably the settler populations of the United States, according to Morgan's theory—had evolved completely to civilization; others had yet to complete their transformation and remained in the stage of savagery or barbarism. The passage of societies from one stage to the next, Morgan reasoned, required some major technological invention. Thus, the advance from early to middle savagery was marked by the control of fire; from middle to late savagery, by the invention of the bow and arrow; from late savagery through late barbarism, by the invention of pottery, agriculture, and animal domestication; and so on. Eventually, some societies had progressed to civilization.

Particularly problematic with this model is the erroneous notion that "progress" can be universally defined by, and reduced to, technology. We must remember that Morgan, like all anthropologists, was a product of his times; he was influenced by developments that were occurring in Western nations like his own at the time of his writing. For example, the **Industrial Revolution** and the growth and dissemination of capitalism as the world's dominant economic model would undoubtedly have had an impact upon how he interpreted various societies. One consequence of the Industrial Revolution was the proliferation and dissemination of cheap, mass-produced goods—the result of standardization and mechanization in the context of factory labour—and the development of a middle class of mass consumers. In this context, the accumulation

unilineal evolution
A late-nineteenth-century theory of social evolution which posited that all societies go through a series of standardized stages of change. It ethnocentrically positioned Western societies at the apex of a "ladder of civilization."

Industrial Revolution
A period of European history, generally identified as occurring in the late eighteenth century, marked by a shift in production from agriculture to industrial goods, urbanization, and the factory system.

of material things would become a measure and marker of one's "success" or social progress.

Think about how many people in our society today, for instance, measure their success through the purchase and/or consumption of material culture: obtaining the "right" car or house, or having a particular brand of clothing or mobile phone. Although technology and material culture (for better or worse) are distinctive markers of success and progress within Western nations such as Canada, can we apply such notions of progress universally? What about nomadic foraging societies, for whom material culture and the accumulation of possessions may be a liability? The use of technology as a defining feature and marker of progress may be ethnocentric; even so, ideas about unilineal evolution have had a lasting impact on how we think about different societies and culture change. Indeed, other writers—including many anthropologists—elaborated on Morgan's scheme, assuming, as he did, that humankind was progressing and would continue to do so.

For example, in the mid-twentieth century, Leslie White formulated what would become one of the more influential evolutionary schemes to explain the historical development of culture. Like Morgan, White saw technology as the driving force of cultural evolution, Specifically, he focused on the human capacity to harness energy through technology and to transform that energy into things required for survival, such as food, clothing, and shelter. By means of technology, energy was put to work, and the amount of food, clothing, or other goods produced by the expenditure of energy was proportional to the efficiency of the technology available. Because foragers had only their own muscle power to work with, the amount of energy produced by their work was limited. Once technological advances, such as the plough, the water wheel, and the windmill, enabled people to grow more crops and to domesticate animals, they were able to harness more and more energy for their own use. Still later, new forms of energy as in coal, oil, and gas were harnessed by means of steam engines and internal combustion engines, and the amount of energy human beings could control again leaped forward.

From White's perspective, cultural development varied directly with the efficiency of the tools employed. Technology that was more efficient allowed human societies to transform more energy to fulfill their needs; these societies could then produce more food and support larger populations. At some point, increased efficiency in food production allowed a few people to produce enough food for everyone, freeing others to develop different skills and thereby promoting occupational specialization. Specialization led to widespread trade and the development of commerce. Population growth and increased contacts among groups led to the development of states capable of coordinating group activities and organizing armies to defend group wealth.

What Are the Shortcomings of These Theories of Progress?

As with Morgan, White's theories encapsulated a point of view that many people hold to this day: that technology is the true measure of progress, and that the more energy human societies can harness through the development of new power sources, the more social, economic, and political problems they will solve. Of course, this view is not universal. In the early twenty-first century, in the face of global warming and the climate crisis caused by humanity's overdependence on the energy produced by burning fossil fuels, more and more non-anthropologists have begun to question the wisdom and sustainability of equating energy consumption with progress. Nonetheless, technological progress remains a popular explanation for why societies transformed themselves, and many people continue to view technology as the solution to ongoing world problems.

Even during the twentieth century, some anthropologists were questioning the progress theory. Spurring these doubts were studies of foraging societies that suggested the life of a nomadic

BEYOND THE BOOK 3.1

Take 10 to 15 minutes (in class, in tutorial, or at home) to do an Internet search to see how ideas of "progress" with respect to energy use are invoked and circulated by one (or more) of the following: (a) climate activists; (b) climate change deniers; (c) advocates for renewal energy sources; (d) advocates for the fossil fuel industry. Compare and contrast your results with those of your classmates. What are some of the key differences in what "progress" means to each group? Are there any similarities? How do your findings challenge or reinforce Leslie White's theories about the relationship between energy use and human progress?

forager was not nearly as harsh and dangerous as had been supposed. The supposition that foragers often went hungry proved to be unfounded. Apparently, they had plenty of food. Moreover, contrary to popular opinion, they did not have to work very hard to get it. In fact, some anthropologists, such as Marshall Sahlins (1968), suggested that foraging represented "the original affluent society," with minimal work and plenty of leisure time. These findings raise two questions: Why *did* most foragers shift away from their mode of livelihood? And why do we often continue to explain this shift in terms of progress?

Life among Foragers: The Ju/'hoansi

The Ju/'hoansi[1] peoples of Namibia's Kalahari Desert are a foraging society that has contributed extensively to what anthropologists have learned about small-scale societies. Lorna Marshall, assisted by her children Elizabeth and John, began research among the Ju/'hoansi in the 1950s. Their work, along with intensive studies by Richard Lee and others, has provided us with a good description of Ju/'hoansi foraging activities. There is some controversy in anthropology over whether the Ju/'hoansi have always been foragers, but that was the way they lived when they were visited by the Marshalls and Lee during the 1960s.

Ju/'hoansi groups lived around water holes, from which they would wander as far as 10 kilometres in search of plant and animal foods. Their groups numbered from 30 to 40 people during the rainy season, when water holes were full and plentiful, but increased to 100 to 200 during the dry season, when only the larger holes retained water. Lee (1969) found that the food quest was constant among the Ju/'hoansi. They did little food processing, so they had to get food supplies every third or fourth day. Vegetable foods constituted 60 to 80 percent of the diet, and women gathered most of it, producing two to three times as much food as men.

Lee reports that the Ju/'hoansi never exhausted their food supplies. The major food source was the mongongo nut, which is far more nourishing than our own breakfast cereals and contains five times the calories and ten times the protein of cooked cereals. Mongongo nuts provided more than 50 percent of the Ju/'hoansi caloric intake; there are 1,260 calories and 56 grams of protein in 300 nuts. Ju/'hoansi territory contained more than 80 other species of edible plants, most of which they did not even use; they did, however, eat about 20 species of roots, melons, gums, bulbs, and dried fruits. In addition, meat was provided by an occasional giraffe, antelope, or other large game animal, as well as by the more usual porcupine, hare, or other small animal. Their meat intake was between 80 and 90 kilograms per person per year—an amount comparable to the meat consumption in wealthy state societies.

In other words, Lee (1969) found that the environment of the Ju/'hoansi provided ample readily accessible food. Their diet consisted of some 2,300 calories a day, with a proper balance of protein, vitamins, and minerals. If the Ju/'hoansi diet was deficient, it was in carbohydrates, since there was no equivalent to our white bread, pasta, rice, or sugar.

The Ju/'hoansi did not spend much time getting food. Lee conducted a careful study of Ju/'hoansi work habits. During the first week in which he recorded the time spent getting food, he found

[1] The terms that societies use to refer to themselves are often different from those assigned by others. Unfortunately, the latter sometimes become more widely accepted than the former. The Ju/'hoansi, for example, were referred to as "Bushmen" by Europeans and later as "!Kung" by anthropologists.

© David Cayless/Getty Images

Readily available plant foods were the mainstay of the Ju/'hoansi diet. Here, Ju/'hoansi women gather plant resources.

that individuals averaged 2.3 days at this work, with a typical working day of six hours. Overall, the average time spent getting food was 2.4 days, or less than 20 hours of work per week. The most active person Lee observed worked at obtaining food an average of 32 hours a week. Other time was spent doing housework or mending tools.

Lee concluded that, contrary to the stereotype that foragers struggle with limited technology to obtain the food they need for survival, they do not have to work hard to make a living. He added that the idea that foraging societies struggle for existence is an ethnocentric notion that assumes that our own technologically oriented society represents the pinnacle of development. If Lee, and others, are correct about foragers' ease of survival, and if their life is not harsh and dangerous, why did those foragers of 10,000 years ago abandon their old practices, begin to domesticate crops and animals, and settle in permanent villages and towns?

BEYOND THE BOOK 3.2

Make a list of what you think are the advantages and disadvantages of life 10,000 years ago. Compare it to a list of what you think are the advantages and disadvantages of contemporary life in an industrialized society. Which way of life do you consider more affluent, and why? Partner up with a classmate and compare your lists and your explanations.

The Transition to Agriculture

There is a perspective on cultural change that views the gradual shift from foraging to modern, industrial society less as development or progress and more as a necessary evil. This perspective emphasizes the influences of population growth and **population density**—defined here as the number of people living in a given area. To understand this point of view, we need to examine the transition from foraging to agriculture while also exploring the reasons for the eventual change from relatively simple slash-and-burn agriculture to more complex, labour-intensive irrigation agriculture. Comparing modern agricultural techniques with less complex methods used in the production of potatoes will also illustrate the point.

Anthropologist Mark Cohen set out to explain why individuals or groups abandoned foraging for agriculture and why so many did so in a relatively short time. First, he examined the reported food-gathering strategies of foraging societies. Foragers settle in a given area to collect food; then, as food resources decline in one spot, they enlarge the area within which they travel in search of them. Imagine this area as a series of concentric circles; as the outer circles are approached from the centre, the group may decide to move to another area where food is more plentiful in order to reduce the distance that members must travel. Cohen suggests that when population density in a given geographical area reached a point where different groups began to bump into one another, or found they had to travel farther and farther to get enough food to feed a growing population, they began to cultivate their own crops. He notes that anthropological and archaeological evidence suggests that they knew how to do this all along, but chose instead to gather crops until the labour involved in travelling to new food sources surpassed the labour involved

population density
The number of people in a given geographic area.

in growing crops. In other words, the historical transition from foraging to simple agriculture was a necessary consequence of population growth rather than a consequence of a discovery or invention that was adopted because it made life better. In a limited way, of course, this transition from gathering to cultivating did make life easier; when people began to harvest crops in a limited area and remained in villages, groups no longer needed to travel as much. However, Cohen and others argue that agriculture did not improve life at all; in fact, it made life worse (a claim we explore later in this chapter).

In most parts of the world, when societies abandoned foraging, they likely began to adopt slash-and-burn agricultural techniques. Slash-and-burn, or swidden, agriculture can be practised by relatively small, kinship-based groups. As a way to grow crops, it is highly efficient and productive. The Kuikuru, who inhabit the central Brazilian rainforest, annually produce about 5 million calories per hectare of land farmed—enough to feed five people more than 2,700 calories per day for a year. Moreover, the Kuikuru work only about two hours a day.

Swidden agriculture, by contrast, requires large tracts of available land because after a plot is farmed for a couple of years, it must lie fallow for 20 to 30 years to allow the brush and trees to grow back so that it can be used again. If the population and thus the amount of land needed to feed it both increase, plots must be used more frequently, perhaps every five or ten years. When land is cultivated more frequently, though, the yield per acre declines. Thus, swidden agriculture is efficient only as long as the population and the amount of land available remain constant.

Farmland may become scarce not only because of increasing population but also because of environmental changes or the encroachment of other groups. Then new agricultural techniques must be developed to increase the yield on the available land. The digging stick may be replaced with the plough, or irrigation systems may be devised, and developments like these require a great deal of labour. In other words, the more food the group has to produce, the more complex the technology needed to produce it; the more complex the technology, the greater the amount of work involved. Note that this contradicts the idea that the shift from simple to complex technologies always makes life easier.

Tables 3.2 and 3.3 demonstrate the relationships among land, labour, population, and methods of agriculture. Table 3.2 indicates that the amount of labour required to produce a harvest increases with the complexity of agricultural techniques. For example, it requires up to ten times more labour to produce a harvest with irrigation agriculture than it does to produce one with swidden agriculture.

Why, then, abandon swidden agriculture? The answer: There is not enough land to support the population. Table 3.3 lists the amount of land needed to feed 100 families using various agricultural methods. For example, as little as 36.5 hectares of land are required to feed 100 families if irrigation agriculture is used, while around 1,200 hectares are needed if swidden agriculture is used. If a group has enough land, it might as well keep its farming

TABLE 3.2 Days of Labour per Acre per Harvest by Type of Agriculture

TYPE OF AGRICULTURE	DAYS OF LABOUR PER ACRE
Advanced swidden	18–25
Plough cultivation	20
Hoe cultivation	58
Irrigation agriculture	90–178

Source: Data from Wolf (1966).

TABLE 3.3 Land Needed to Feed 100 Families Using Different Agricultural Methods

AGRICULTURAL METHOD	NUMBER OF HECTARES NEEDED TO FEED 100 FAMILIES
Swidden agriculture	1,200*
Swidden with garden plots	650*

*Includes unworked land that must be allowed to lie fallow to regain fertility.

Source: Data from Wolf (1966).

methods simple, changing them only if population increases or the supply of land decreases.

But the history of humankind has been marked by an increase in population and an increase in the ratio of people to land. Robert L. Carneiro (1978) outlines the consequences of population density for cultural change.

The increase in the number of people relative to the available land creates two problems. First, if there are more people than there is available land to feed them, conflict may arise between people vying for the available resources. Second, if a growing population decides to intensify methods of growing crops, there is a need for greater societal organization. Irrigation agriculture, for example, requires the digging of ditches, the building of pumps to bring water to the fields and to drain water from them, and the coordination of one, sometimes two harvests a year. Thus, whether a society deals with an increasing ratio between land and people by intensifying efforts to produce more food, or addresses the problem by denying some people access to the necessary resources, the groundwork is laid for a stratified society to emerge, with the concomitant need for a state organization.

Anthropologists such as Cohen and Carneiro are suggesting, then, that the change from foraging to gradually more labour-intensive methods of agriculture was not a matter of choice. Slash-and-burn agriculture wasn't easier than foraging, and plough and irrigation agriculture was not more efficient than slash-and-burn agriculture. Rather, changes in food production techniques were necessary responses to increases in population or population density, and these, in turn, created the need for more formal, more elaborate political and social institutions, both to organize labour and to maintain order among more and more people.

We might conclude from this—which not all anthropologists do—that the transition from foraging to complex agriculture, and the associated social, political, and economic transformations, do not represent progress. But is it not safe to say that at the very least, Western societies, particularly in North America, use agricultural techniques that are vastly superior to those of small, tribal societies? Those who claim that modern food production techniques are far more efficient than any others point out that in Canada and the United States, only 1 calorie of human energy is needed to produce 210 calories for human consumption; by contrast, foragers produce fewer than 10 calories of food for every calorie they use collecting the food. Others, however, argue that these figures are deceptive. At the same time that we have vastly decreased the amount of human labour required to produce food, they say, we have vastly increased the amount of nonhuman energy required. From that perspective, we expend 1 calorie of nonhuman energy in the form of non-renewable fossil fuels (e.g., oil and coal) for every 8 calories we produce.

Industrial Agriculture: Producing Potato Calories

To make this point about energy, John H. Bodley (1985) compared the production of sweet potatoes in New Guinea with potato production in the United States.

In New Guinea, people cultivate sweet potatoes by slash-and-burn agriculture; plots of land are burned, cleared, and planted using digging sticks. When the crops are ready, sweet potatoes are cooked in pits and eaten. In one New Guinea community, sweet potatoes accounted for 21 percent of the diet of 204 people. Some of the sweet potatoes were fed to pigs, thus producing protein and accounting for an even larger proportion of the diet. The people used only 10 percent of the arable land, and there was no danger of resource depletion. With their agricultural techniques, the New Guinea farmers could produce about 12.4 million calories per hectare.

Potato farms in Canada and the United States produce more than twice as many calories per acre as New Guinea farmers—about 29.6 million calories per hectare. However, as Bodley points out, in addition to the human energy that goes into

North American farming, vast amounts of non-human energy are expended. Chemicals must be applied to maintain soil conditions and to control insects and fungus. For example, in the Washington State in the 1960s, 60 percent of the potato acreage was airplane-sprayed five to nine times per season to control insects; another 40 percent was treated for weeds. American potato farmers need specialized machines to cut, seed, harvest, dig, and plant. In 1969, 36,000 tons of fertilizer were applied to 25,300 hectares—more than 1120 kilograms per hectare. Thus, while the American system produced more potatoes, the actual energy costs per calorie were lower in New Guinea. Moreover, all kinds of hidden costs from consequences such as soil erosion and pollution were incurred in the United States.

North Americans must also deal with distribution costs, which are minimal in traditional cultures, where most households consume what they themselves produce. In modern industrial societies, where 95 percent of the population is urban, the energy expended in distributing the food now exceeds the energy expended in producing it. If we take the food-producing process as a whole—the manufacture and distribution of farm machinery, trucks, and fertilizer; irrigation projects; food processing; packaging; transportation; truck manufacturing; industrial and domestic food preparation; and refrigeration—we'd discover that the American food industry expends 8 to 12 calories of energy to produce a single calorie of food!

Question 3.2: How Can We Explain the Vast Inequality between the Rich and the Poor?

Even if we agree that foragers don't struggle for food and that simpler forms of agriculture are more efficient than modern techniques, we still have not explained the vast divisions in the modern world between the rich and the poor. The bar graphs in Figure 3.1 illustrate the economic disparities in the world economy. The bottom tier of the first bar consists of the roughly 70 percent of the world's people (most of them in developing nations) who make less than $10,000 per year. As the second bar shows, that 70 percent of the population controls only 2.7 percent of the world's wealth.

If progress is not the reason for this unequal distribution, why do most people in the industrial world enjoy a higher standard of living than people in developing countries? That question requires a complex discussion of 300 years of world history, with a specific focus on the links between capitalism, industrialism, and colonialism and the rise of all three. Rather than try to pack three centuries into the next few pages, let's see what we can learn from the story of the expansion of one industry, in one country, during one phase of its development: the textile industry in England in the last half of the eighteenth century and the first half of the nineteenth. This period coincides with the advent of colonialism and the Industrial Revolution, which was marked by urbanization, by the factory system, and by a shift in production away from agriculture toward industrial goods.

The arrival of Christopher Columbus in the Americas and the subsequent "Age of Discovery" marked the beginning of a period of European colonialism that has had a lasting impact on world economics, politics, and ideologies. When Europeans encountered various Indigenous cultures, they often did not know how to interpret the vast differences in customs, religion, kinship, and political organization (among other things) that they experienced. Many even questioned whether Indigenous groups were fully human.

Such attitudes, which are clearly ethnocentric by today's standards, are what fuelled the implementation and dissemination of colonial rule. If you position yourself as morally superior to or even as more "human" than other peoples, then it becomes easy to justify colonial atrocities such as slavery. As we

FIGURE 3.1 World Economic Disparities

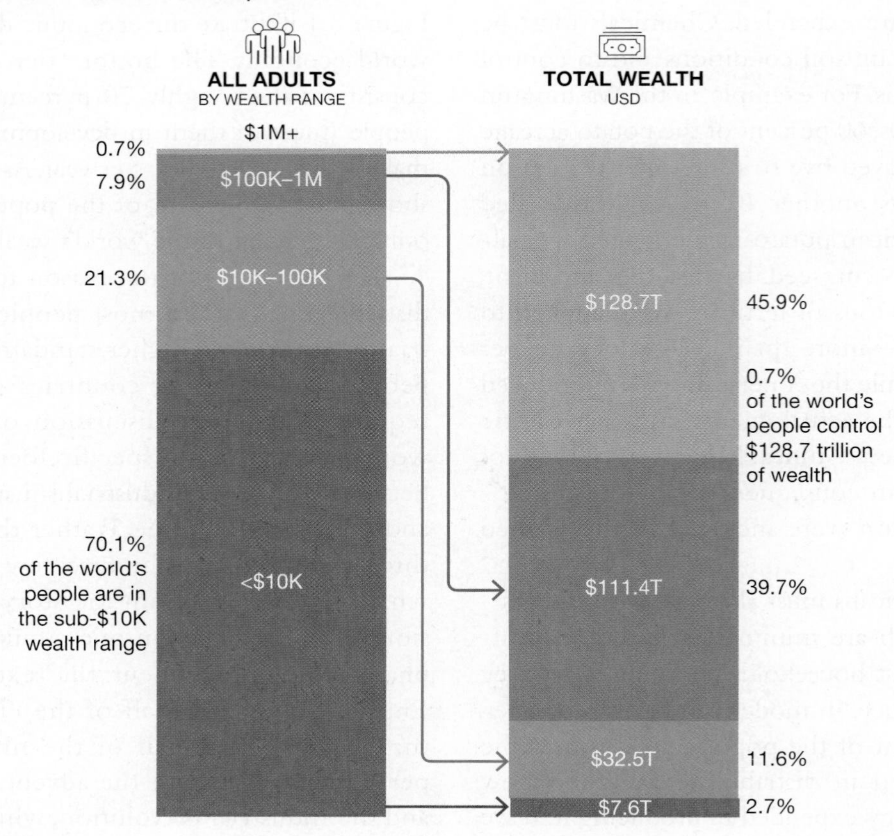

Source: Nick Routley, "Top-Heavy Wealth Spectrum," World Economic Forum, 7 January 2019, https://www.weforum.org/agenda/2019/01/visualizing-the-extreme-concentration-of-global-wealth. Originally published in "Visualizing the Extreme Concentration of Global Wealth," *Visual Capitalist*, 26 December 2018, https://www.visualcapitalist.com/global-wealth-concentration.

will see below, European **colonialism** was a system predicated on exploitative relationships between colonizer and colonized. Without the natural resources and raw materials supplied through slavery or the imposition of exploitative forms of labour on local populations, European colonies would not have been able to expand their wealth. Indeed, the root of many contemporary global inequalities can be attributed to European colonialism and the advent of the Industrial Revolution.

Before the Industrial Revolution in Europe, the world was significantly different in its distribution of wealth. China was arguably the richest country in the world during the sixteenth and seventeenth centuries as gold and silver taken from the mines of South America by the Spanish and Portuguese were funnelled to China to pay for Chinese silks, spices, teas, and luxury goods; India was developing a thriving cotton textile industry as Indian calicoes flooded into Europe. Wealthy states developed in western Africa, and Islamic traders thrived from Africa to Southeast Asia. Seventeenth-century England was a largely rural and agricultural country; even by 1700, only 13 percent of the population

colonialism
Refers to the acquisition of new territories throughout the world by European powers from 1492 until approximately 1945. Colonizers often imposed new forms of politics, economics, and religion upon colonized Indigenous or other cultures, and frequently exploited local populations for their labour.

lived in towns of 5,000 or more. England, however, had long enjoyed a thriving trade in raw wool and inexpensive wool textiles.

In its early days, textile production was largely a handicraft industry, and most steps in the production of wool cloth, from cutting and degreasing the wool, to dying and spinning the thread, to weaving the cloth, were in the hands of rural families or small cooperatives. The finished cloth or wool product might be sold at a local market or fair; more often, though, it was sold to urban-based merchants or traders for resale at fairs or for shipment overseas.

The trade in home-produced textiles was profitable for all; however, traders and merchants discovered that they needed to better control the type, quantity, and quality of cloth produced by spinners and weavers. The merchants' first solution to this problem was the **"putting out" system**, whereby merchants supplied weavers with materials and required them to produce cloth of the desired type. Some merchants supplied only the wool, cotton, or linen, while others supplied everything, including the looms. The merchants delivered the supplies and tools and picked up the finished products, generally paying the producers for each piece produced. Putting out had many advantages for textile merchants: it gave them more control over production; it ensured cheap labour, for it brought women and children into the production process; and if demand for textiles slackened, the merchants could easily control how much was produced by limiting the materials they put out.

Increasingly, however, beginning in the eighteenth century, English merchants found it expedient to transform the "putting out" system into a **factory system** by bringing the spinners, weavers, and others together in one location to produce the cloth. Factories were neither new nor unique to England—factories employing more than 15,000 workers existed in France as early as 1685. Furthermore, merchants were not particularly anxious to invest in factories. Profits from manufacture were not nearly as great as profits from trade, especially long-distance exchange. Moreover, removing people from home-based families to urban-based factories required new mechanisms of discipline and control—a fact that explains why early factories were modelled on penal workhouses and prisons. Finally, the entrepreneur, who in the past could have halted putting out when demand slackened, now had to keep his factories busy to pay for his investment in buildings and technology. Consequently, he had to create demand for his products.

The only things that made a manufacturing investment attractive were various government subsidies, or laws (e.g., vagrancy laws requiring people to have jobs) that ensured a flow of cheap labour. Textile manufacturers were able to draw on workers who had been forced from their land by the enclosure laws, which were pushing peasant farmers off their common lands at the behest of landowners, who wished to grow crops to sell to England's growing population. Since there were no minimum wage laws or laws restricting child labour, factory owners could exploit the cheap labour of women and children; thus, by 1834, children under 13 represented 13 percent of the British cotton industry, and by 1838, only 23 percent of textile factory workers in England were adult men. In addition, government played a major role in creating and defending overseas markets as well as sources of raw materials such as cotton.

The expansion of the textile industry had multiple effects. For one thing, it fuelled the growth of cities: by 1800, one-quarter of the English population lived in towns of 5,000 or more; and Manchester, a textile-manufacturing centre, grew from 24,000 inhabitants in 1773 to more than 250,000 by 1851.

"putting out" system
A means of production, common in the sixteenth and seventeenth centuries and surviving today, in which a manufacturer or merchant supplies the materials and sometimes the tools to workers, who produce the goods in their own homes.

factory system
A system of production characterized by the concentration of labour and machines in specific places. It is associated with the Industrial Revolution.

Moreover, factories spurred technological development. Mechanization of the textile industry began in earnest with Kay's flying shuttle in 1733, which doubled the weavers' output.

Spinners could not keep up with the need for thread for the new looms, however, so bottlenecks developed. To meet this need, James Hargreaves introduced, in 1765, the spinning jenny. In 1769, Richard Arkwright invented the water frame; then, in 1779, Samuel Crompton developed a spinning mule that combined features of the water frame and the jenny. Finally, in 1790, steam power was added to the production process. These inventions generated a staggering increase in textile production. A hand spinner in eighteenth-century India took more than 50,000 hours to process 100 pounds of cotton into thread; in England, Crompton's mule reduced that to 2,000 hours; the power-assisted mules of around 1795 reduced this time still further, to 300 hours. By 1825, it was taking only 135 hours to process 100 pounds of cotton.

The growth of the textile industry produced great wealth and employed millions of workers but led to two problems. In economic terms, the growth transformed England into the wealthiest country in the world. And textiles were not, of course, the only industry that expanded—trade, the manufacture of iron, and food production further increased the wealth of the growing British Empire. But where was the market for all these textile products to be

© Hine, Lewis Wickes (1874-1940)/Private Collection/Bridgeman Images

© Universal History Archive/UIG/Bridgeman Images

© Look and Learn/Bridgeman Images

Three inventions that revolutionized the textile industry (clockwise from top left): the flying shuttle, the water frame, and the spinning mule. These inventions were intended to increase product output and human efficiency. Both adults and children served as labourers in the textile industry.

found? And where were the raw materials—notably the cotton—to come from?

Some historians point to the large domestic market available to English textile producers in the wake of the growth of the English population from 6 million in 1700 to 9 million in 1800. Moreover, English textile manufacturers were able to sell much of their product to markets in Europe as well as to the growing markets of the Americas. But there was still competition for these markets. England was not the only textile producer; Holland, France, and Spain were busy competing (and often fighting among one another) for overseas markets as well as for sources of raw materials. This competition, and the growing military superiority of Western Europe, often had dire consequences for once-prosperous industries in other parts of the world. The story of textiles in India is instructive.

The British in India

Mughal India of the seventeenth century was founded by Turks from Turkestan, who made their chief, Babur, the first Mughal emperor in 1527. India was a major trading country, and centuries-old trade networks linked India to Europe, the Islamic world, and China. In 1690 the British East India Company was granted a monopoly in East Asian trade by the British government. A relative latecomer to the Indian trade, it established a trading centre in Bengal, in the city of Calcutta (now Kolkata). "John Company," as it came to be known, soon had some 150 posts in India, which traded for fine silks, cotton, sugar, rice, saltpetre, indigo, and opium.

In the 1750s the British provoked the rulers of Bengal into war, and defeated them conclusively in 1757. In the aftermath of their victory in Bengal, they plundered the state treasury of some £5 million and gained control of 10,000 Bengali weavers. By 1765, John Company was the civil administration of Bengal. It promptly increased the tax burden on peasants and artisans, which led to serious famines in 1770 and 1783. Meanwhile, from its base in Bengal, the company began to extend its control over much of the Indian subcontinent.

Before the British military takeover, India had been producing cloth that was cheaper and better than English textiles; in fact, Indian cottons and calicoes—named after the city of Calicut—were the craze of Europe. To meet this challenge, the British government prohibited the British East India Company from importing calicoes into England. To take advantage of the import restriction, English factories began producing copies of popular Indian textiles for sale both in England and abroad. In addition, India was required to admit English manufacturers free of tariffs. These actions effectively destroyed what had been a thriving Indian textile industry. Although India was still a major producer of raw cotton, Indian cotton was not preferred or favoured by English or American manufacturers; however, China was willing to import plenty of it.

The British, and Western European nations in general, had a problem with trade into China. Chinese products, notably tea, were in high demand, but the Europeans were producing little that the Chinese wanted or needed. There was a market in China for opium, however, and by 1773, the British East India Company had a monopoly over opium sales. Opium was illegal in China, but the Chinese state seemed incapable of cutting off supplies. Smuggling opium into China was hugely profitable for British merchants, as well as for the Americans and the French. When the Chinese government tried to halt the trade in 1839 by seizing opium held by British merchants in warehouses in Canton, the British government intervened militarily and forced the Chinese government to stop enforcing its own opium laws. An analogy today might be the government of Colombia sending troops to the United States or Canada to force acceptance of Colombian cocaine shipments. Moreover, the British demanded and received additional trading rights into China, further opening a market, not only for opium but for textiles as well.

The British-led opium trade from India to China had three results. First, it reversed the flow of money between China and the rest of the world: during the first decade of the nineteenth century, China was still enjoying a yearly trade surplus of 26 million silver dollars; by the third decade, 34 million dollars per year were leaving China to pay for opium. Second, estimates are that by the end of the nineteenth century, one out of every ten Chinese was addicted to opium. Finally, textile exports from England to India and China increased from 6 percent of total British exports in 1815, to 22 percent in 1840, 31 percent in 1850, and more than 50 percent after 1873.

Cotton, Slavery, and the Trail of Tears

Cotton and the British textile industry also figure into the story of slavery and the removal of thousands of Native Americans from their homeland in the United States. The British were able to sell raw Indian cotton to China, but Indian cotton was not acceptable to European and North American markets. Indian cotton produced a shorter fibre, whereas cotton produced elsewhere, notably in Egypt and the southern United States, produced a longer, more desirable fibre. Cotton production in the Americas was labour intensive, however, and to be profitable, it required slave labour.

Slavery was not created by the need for cotton—as an institution, it was far more ancient than that. It was never uncommon for groups at war to turn captured enemies into slaves. However, the slave trade grew rapidly between the fifteenth and nineteenth centuries in response to Europe's economic expansion and the demands of trade. The Spanish required workers for their silver mines; the Spanish, Portuguese, British, and French required cane cutters and millers for their sugar plantations in Brazil and the Caribbean; and Georgia, Alabama, Louisiana, Texas, and Mississippi required labourers for their cotton plantations. Between 1451 and 1600, some 275,000 slaves were taken from Africa to what is now the United States and to Europe and its colonies. During the seventeenth century, 1.3 million slaves were forcibly exported from Africa; between 1701 and 1810, the figure was around 6 million. Another 2 million were taken from Africa between 1810 and 1870, many destined for Cuba.

Reliance on slave labour in the United States was closely tied to the rise of the British textile industry. Here, a slave family picks cotton on a plantation near Savannah, Georgia, during the early 1860s.

The production of cotton using slave labour fuelled the Industrial Revolution in the United States. England had long imported raw cotton from its possessions in the West Indies and from Turkey; by 1807, however, half its supply was from the United States. In fact, between 1815 and 1860, raw cotton constituted half the value of domestic exports from the United States.

The American cotton industry grew so rapidly, in part, because of Eli Whitney's cotton gin, an invention that efficiently separated the seeds from the raw cotton fibre. The gin allowed a person to clean cotton 50 times more quickly than in the past. American cotton production increased enormously as a result: from 3,000 bales in 1790 to 178,000 in

1810, 732,000 in 1830, and 4.5 million in 1860. But to be competitive, cotton production required cheap labour, and slave labour was half the price of wage labour. Each plantation required between 50 and 200 slaves, depending on the quality of the soil.

The British demand for American cotton was obviously not the cause of slavery, but it ensured its continuance in the United States into the second half of the nineteenth century. Between 1790 and 1860, 835,000 slaves were moved from Maryland, Virginia, and the Carolinas to Alabama, Louisiana, Mississippi, and Texas in one of the greatest forced migrations of all time. But this migration was not the only forced one spurred by the world demand for cotton. Another was the forced removal in the 1830s of 125,000 Native Americans from their homes in Georgia, Alabama, and Mississippi to the Oklahoma Territory, along the route known as the "Trail of Tears" (see Figure 3.2).

The story of the forced removal of the Cherokee (and other Native American nations) in the United States does much to explain why some of the world's people enjoy greater wealth than others. The Cherokee had always been viewed as among the more "advanced" Native American groups—the early European settlers had counted them as one of the "civilized tribes" of North America. They were horticulturists, living in large, autonomous villages and, after the American Revolution, occupying large tracts of fertile land from North Carolina into Georgia. In 1802, to persuade the southeastern states to give up claims to territory in the west, President Thomas Jefferson instituted what became known as the "Georgia Compact of 1802." The Compact called for Georgia and the Carolinas to give up claims to western territories in exchange for land held by southeastern Indigenous groups, including the Cherokee. The Indigenous people fought the

FIGURE 3.2 Map of the Trail of Tears, Showing the Cherokee Removal

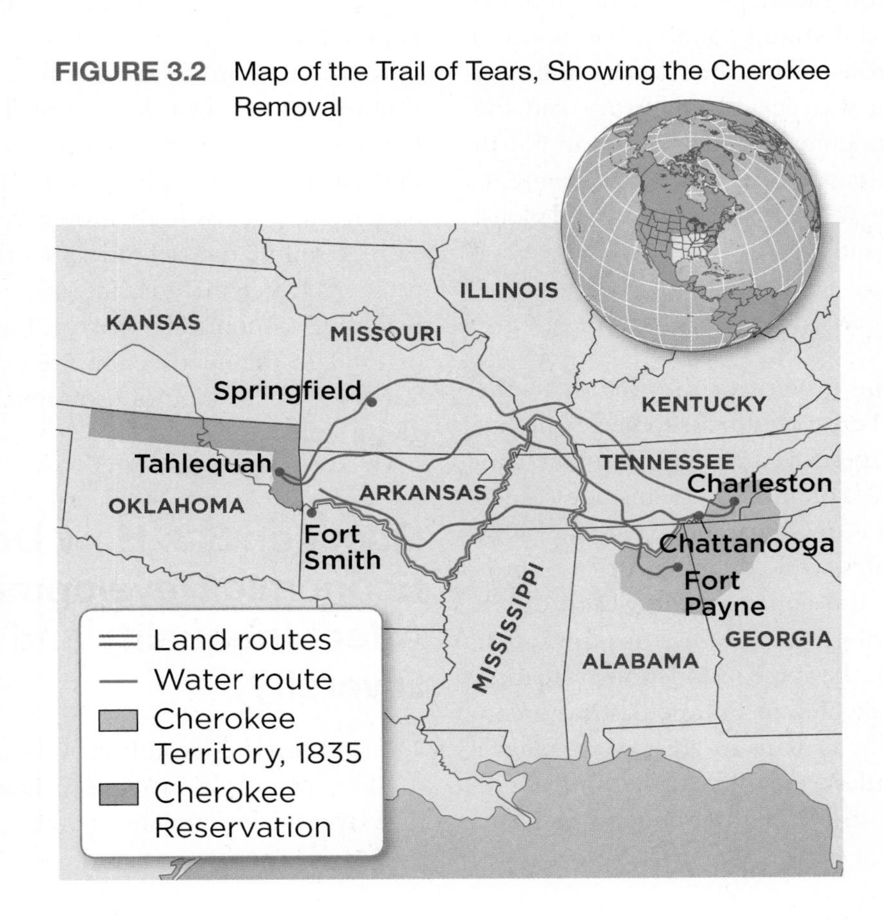

removal, embarking on a modernization plan; within a decade the Cherokee had built plantations, were holding slaves, and had their own newspaper, schools, and alphabet. They were also among the soldiers who served under Andrew Jackson in the War of 1812.

The Cherokee lobbied the US Congress extensively to repeal the Georgia Compact, but to no avail. Andrew Jackson, who had made the removal of Native Americans a cornerstone of his presidential campaign in 1828, signed the final order. The army was sent in to forcibly move the population as land speculators flooded onto what had been prosperous Cherokee farms and plantations. Thousands of additional acres of what had been Cherokee land were taken over or converted to cotton production by white farmers using black slaves. In this way, white farmers using Native American land and African labour to produce cotton for the British and American textile industries created much of the future wealth of the young country. The political economy of cotton production, slavery, and land alienation during this period of history laid the groundwork for ongoing systemic racism in North America, as we discuss in Chapter 7. For a contemporary perspective on the textile industry and global inequality, see Chapter 8.

Progress for Whom?

To summarize, the growth of the British textile industry produced great wealth for some people, but in the process, it destroyed textile manufacturing in India, led to the colonization of India, escalated imports of opium into China, and extended slavery in the United States while draining Africa of productive labour; it also enhanced the wealth of US settlers while driving Native Americans from their lands. In addition, the mass production of textiles in Britain and elsewhere in Europe destroyed textile manufacture by artisans in areas of the world where British textiles were sold. Furthermore, since women were the main textile producers in many societies, we might also speculate that the textile trade led to a decline in the status of women in these societies.

In assessing progress, we must also broaden our scope beyond a single industry. Britain was not the only producer of textiles, nor was it the only country seeking to open and control overseas markets. France, Germany, the Netherlands, and (later) the United States also had thriving textile industries. It is important to remember, too, that the textile industry was only one industry among many in Western Europe that required raw materials and new markets. As a result of the growing European demand for sugar, cocoa, palm oil, tobacco, and coffee, millions of hectares around the world were converted from subsistence farming to cash crop farming; in turn, self-sufficient peasant farmers became dependent wage labourers or unemployed poor. Finally, remember that we have examined only a brief period of time. The high point of European colonial expansion came later than the events described here, in the last quarter of the nineteenth century and the first decades of the twentieth. By looking at the bigger picture, we can begin to understand why the problems of the nonindustrial nations are due less to their own shortcomings than to the exploitative activities of others, and why a peasant farmer in India in 1400 was significantly better off economically than his Indian counterpart of 1960. In the next section, we explore the manifestations of this kind of economic "progress" on a global scale.

Question 3.3: How Does Economic Development Affect Inequality and Cultural Diversity?

The Industrial Revolution radically transformed the lives of people in Western Europe and North America as the vast majority of the population went from being farmers to labourers. Usually, the change of job was not a matter of choice: people began selling their labour not because wage labour offered a better life, but because they no longer possessed land on which to secure a livelihood. Moreover, the availability of jobs was subject to the whims of the market and the rise and fall in the demand for products. As long as there was a demand for products, jobs were secure; when demand slackened, people were thrown out of work.

Overall, however, the rate of economic growth and technological advancement was astonishing and resulted in a dramatic improvement in the standard of living of most people in Western countries. Nevertheless, many in the industrialized world did not enjoy increased wealth, and people in the low-income countries often saw their living standards decline further as their countries fell under the influence of European powers.

As countries began to achieve independence from their former colonial rulers, new national leaders promised to improve the lives of their people, and the leaders in the rich countries promised to help; hence, the push for what became known as "**economic development**" ensued. Yet as John Isbister, whom we cite in this chapter's epigraph, argues in *Promises Not Kept: Poverty and the Betrayal of Third World Development*, these promises were empty.

The ideology of economic development included the assumption that the world's nonindustrial countries were backward and needed to progress or develop—*develop* being largely a code word for "Westernize." Tania Li, an anthropologist at the University of Toronto, documented how a development project in Indonesia typically began: "First, it is necessary to identify a target group with a deficiency to be rectified . . . Second, there needs to be an agency tasked with planning and executing the appropriate development fix" (1999b, 298).

There flourished in the West an unprecedented resolve to know everything about the developing world, which experienced a massive invasion of experts, all of whom were tasked with investigating, measuring, and theorizing about every aspect of these societies. In *Encountering Development: The Making and Unmaking of the Third World*, Arturo Escobar suggests that

> *development fostered a way of conceiving of social life as a technical problem, as a matter of rational decision and management to be entrusted to that group of people—the development professionals—whose specialized knowledge allegedly qualified them for the task. Instead of seeing change as a process rooted in the interpretation of each society's history and cultural tradition . . . these professionals sought to devise mechanisms and procedures to make societies fit a preexisting model that embodied the structures and functions of modernity. (1995, 52)*

Three key assumptions shaped the idea of economic development that emerged: (1) economic growth and development is the solution to national as well as global problems; (2) global economic integration will contribute to solving global ecological and social problems; and (3) foreign assistance to undeveloped countries will make things better. Thus, countries that wished to develop sought foreign loans and investments to create an industrial infrastructure—dams, power stations, ports, roads, and railways, and so on—as well as schools for training local people to operate these. The loans, then, would allow undeveloped

economic development
The term used to identify an increase in level of technology, and by some, standard of living of a population. Others view it as an ideology based on three key assumptions: (1) that economic growth and development is the solution to national as well as global problems; (2) that global economic integration will contribute to solving global ecological and social problems; and (3) that foreign assistance to undeveloped countries will make things better.

countries to produce export goods such as cotton, sugar, palm oil, tobacco, coffee, and cocoa (as well as other cash crops) as well as oil, metal ores, lumber (and other natural resources). This theory of economic development was nothing new; what *was* different was the degree of apparent support that the wealthier nations were offering the poorer. One major Western institution that promoted economic development was the **World Bank**.

The World Bank was founded in 1944 in Bretton Woods, New Hampshire, at a meeting of the representatives of major industrial nations. At the time of this conference, the Allied powers were still at war with Germany and Japan (which, of course, were not invited). The task of those attending was to develop plans for the economic reconstruction of those countries that were being devastated by the war and to develop a postwar plan for worldwide economic and monetary stability. It was decided at Bretton Woods to establish the **International Monetary Fund (IMF)** and the International Bank for Reconstruction and Development (the World Bank). Funds for the bank were to be provided by member nations, largely in the form of loan guarantees. The bank would lend money to governments for specific projects: highways, dams, power plants, factories, and the like; those governments would agree to pay back the loans over a set time. The charter also specified that the loans must be made without regard for political or noneconomic factors and that the bank must not interfere in the political affairs of any member or debtor nation.

The World Bank began operating in 1946, with the initial loans going to European countries. But soon the World Bank was making huge loans to countries such as Brazil, India, and Indonesia—loans that were supposed to transform their economies, generate wealth, and alleviate poverty. Many people have argued since that however benign their intentions, these loans only *increased* poverty and led to environmental and cultural devastation. How could this have happened?

Economic Development, Environmental Devastation, and Cultural Devastation in Brazil and Paraguay

Brazil has been a major recipient of World Bank loans. In the 1960s the Brazilian government made a conscious decision to industrialize. Using loans from the World Bank and other Western lenders, along with money from private investors, Brazil built dams, roads, factories, and industries. It also modernized its agriculture, becoming a world leader in the export of crops such as soybeans. The economy surged, and Brazil became a model of modern industrialization: factories created jobs, and people flocked to the cities for employment as Brazil's cities began to rival any in the West.

But there was a downside: to repay its debts, Brazil needed to earn foreign income. Consequently, landowners were encouraged to expand their production of cash crops, especially those that could be sold in North America and Europe. Since the West already produced more than enough food (American farmers were being paid by the government not to grow food crops), Brazilian farmers turned to crops with other uses, such as soybeans, sisal, sugar, cocoa, and coffee. To grow more of these products required modern farming techniques and lots of land. Small farmers, forced off their land, had to find farm employment growing cash crops or migrate to the cities in search of jobs that, for the most part, did not exist. Moreover, those who found

World Bank
One of the institutions created at the 1944 Bretton Woods, New Hampshire, meeting of Allied nations. The World Bank (or the Bank for Reconstruction and Development) functions as a lending institution to nations largely for projects related to economic development.

International Monetary Fund (IMF)
Created as an outcome of the 1944 Bretton Woods Conference to regulate currency transactions among countries. The IMF now makes loans and regulates the economies of lending countries.

jobs on the large farms were not paid enough to purchase the food they had once grown themselves on their small plots. Brazil did increase production of some food crops, notably beef, but because poor Brazilians could not pay as much for beef as relatively wealthy North Americans and Europeans could, most Brazilian beef was exported. In 2018, Brazil was the world's top exporter of beef, providing close to 20 percent of the world's beef exports.

To make matters worse, in the mid-1980s, Brazil and other debtor countries discovered that they could not keep up their payments to the World Bank and other Western financial institutions. To help these countries avoid default, the World Bank allowed them to renegotiate their loans. First, though, they had to agree to reduce their government spending—and typically, the targets for spending cuts were public education, welfare, housing, and health. These cutbacks resulted in still greater hardships for the poorest citizens.

In the wake of its program for economic development, Brazil has increased its total wealth. Some people have become very rich, but it is estimated that more than 26 percent of Brazilians are still living in poverty. And Brazil is not unique; most of Central and South America, Africa, and Southeast Asia followed the same formula for development, and most of these countries also experienced increased poverty and hunger for the majority of their people.

Economic development has brought environmental destruction as well. Between 1981 and 1983, the World Bank began delivering payments on a loan for Brazil to construct a road through the Amazon rainforest and to build new settlements. The economic goal of this project was to open vast tracts of Amazon rainforest for settlement by displaced peasants, thereby transforming the forest into a cash producer. Nearly half a million settlers flooded into the area between 1981 and 1986. The government, however, was not prepared for that level of migration, and the new migrants were forced to burn forests to grow food to survive. The poor soil of the rainforests would not support agriculture for more than a couple of years, however, and people ultimately were left with worthless land. The only activity that proved worthwhile was cattle ranching, and that required the burning of still more rainforest. The area went from 1.7 percent deforestation in 1978 to 16.1 percent in 1991. Although rates of deforestation slowed in the 1990s and early 2000s, they have since re-escalated; the current rate of deforestation is close to 20 percent, and the Climate Observatory (Observatório do Clima)—a not-for-profit climate change network—calculated that in 2017, 46 percent of Brazil's greenhouse gas emissions were the result of deforestation.

Often, the same economic forces (and discourses of progress and development) that are promoting environmental destruction are also undermining traditional cultures. A case in point is that of the Guaraní, most of whom live in Paraguay, but also in Brazil, Argentina, and Bolivia. There are about 15,000 Guaraní. For centuries, their lives centred

Victor Moriyama/Getty Images

In this aerial image, a fire burns in a section of the Amazon rainforest in August 2019, in the region near Porto Velho, Brazil.

on the rainforest, where they gathered tree crops, grew food crops, raised animals, and hunted and fished. The first European governor of the area described them, in 1541, as "the richest people of all the land and province both for agriculture and stock raising." They quickly entered into trade with Europeans, mostly by gathering and selling a caffeine-bearing plant called *yerba mate*. These trade arrangements did not greatly affect Guaraní life, since they would gather and sell yerba mate only when they needed some Western trade item, such as a metal pot. Consequently, Guaraní culture was able to sustain itself and thrive. Just as important, the Guaraní exploited the rainforest in sustainable ways by adapting to it rather than trying to change it. Then in the 1970s, due largely to international trade arrangements, both the Guaraní and the rainforest began to decline.

In the 1970s, Paraguay, like most developing countries, enjoyed an economic boom fuelled largely by loans from the World Bank and other international lenders. Increasing production of crops such as soy, wheat, and cotton also fuelled the boom. The "economic miracle" was accomplished by bringing more land under cultivation; this, however, involved cutting down forests, selling the timber, and converting the cleared land into farmland or pasture. The rate of rainforest destruction accelerated rapidly. Between 1970 and 1976, Paraguayan rainforests were reduced from 6.8 to 4.2 million hectares. Since then, Paraguay has continued to have one of the highest rates of deforestation in the world; the Guaraní have disproportionately suffered the negative effects of this deforestation.

Guaraní culture has been one more casualty of global capitalism and "economic development." This group's livelihood has been destroyed, and new roads through the rainforest have brought with them thousands of new settlers eager to stake claims to some portion of the forest, clear it of trees, and grow cash crops. Unfortunately, rainforest soil quickly loses its nutrients once the forest canopy that protects it is destroyed. Furthermore, all the animals and plants that the Guaraní once depended on have been decimated. As a result, the Guaraní have been displaced to squatter settlements in towns and cities or along the roads that have been built through the rainforests. The wages they can make working for farmers or in other odd jobs are inadequate to support families; illness and disease have increased; and suicide rates between 2000 and 2013 have more than tripled over the previous ten years (Lyons 2015).

Finding Hope in the Face of Cultural Devastation

The experiences of peoples such as the Guaraní raise an important question: What does it mean to experience cultural devastation? This question is important, not only for what it tells us about the experiences of other people, but also for how we understand what culture is and what culture change can mean. Clearly, all cultures are vulnerable. People's views of the world, what they count as important, what they value, and what the good life means to them, are all subject to sudden upheaval.

Popular discourses of progress and economic development suggest that for Indigenous peoples, adaptation to new modes of livelihood and ways of being is the solution. However, what counts as "adaptation" is not particularly straightforward, especially once we recognize that, for many Indigenous peoples, it has generally been the colonizers who have defined the terms of engagement. Dawn Martin-Hill's work with the Lubicon Cree of Alberta (Figure 3.3) provides an instructive example of what it means to go from being an independent hunting society to one struggling for recognition, self-determination, and cultural survival within the Canadian nation-state.

For centuries, the Lubicon Cree have lived, hunted, and trapped within a 110-kilometre radius of Lubicon Lake in northern Alberta. Because of their relative isolation, the Lubicon avoided much contact with white settlers until the end of the nineteenth century. Then, in 1899, Lubicon elders, wanting to

FIGURE 3.3 Map of Proposed Lubicon Reserve and Unceded Lubicon Territory in Alberta

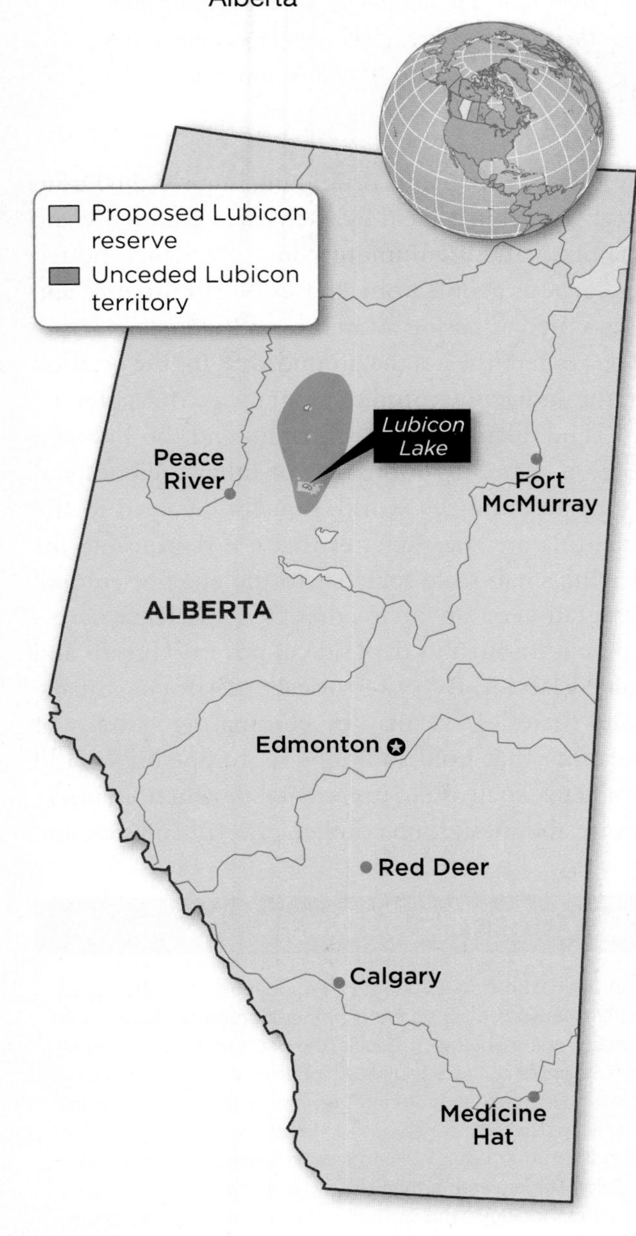

secure their territory against the encroachment they saw happening elsewhere, approached the Canadian government about signing a treaty. The treaty, however, failed to materialize over the following years. In 1939, the Lubicon were finally recognized as a band under federal law, and the groundwork was laid for establishing a reserve of 65 square kilometres. But World War II created a shortage of surveyors, and the required survey never happened. The Lubicon population was decimated by illness in the first half of the twentieth century, and in 1942, many remaining Lubicon were removed from the band registry by the Department of Indian Affairs. As a result of that, they were deemed too small a population to warrant a treaty or a reserve (Martin-Hill 2004, 315–16).

The Lubicon elders decided that their young people should learn English in order to pursue their land claims. One of these youth, Walter Whitehead, was elected chief in the early 1970s and began to lay the legal groundwork for the land claim. Unfortunately, he was doing so at the same time that oil exploration was beginning in northern Alberta. Since then, the Lubicon Cree have been embroiled in an unsettled land claim. Meanwhile, oil and gas corporations have been extracting resources from land that the Lubicon have never legally relinquished, all the while contaminating it. In their struggle for recognition, the Lubicon had to walk a fine line between trying to work within the Canadian legal system on the one hand and maintaining their own Indigenous knowledge on the other. In 2018, the Lubicon Lake band finally reached a settlement with the governments of Alberta and Canada. The settlement awards the Lubicon 246 square kilometres of land, plus more than $100 million in compensation.

As Martin-Hill points out, "from the West's perspective, Indigenous peoples [like the Lubicon] are always standing in the way of progress, development, and civilization" (2008b, 153). She also points to the Lubicon's determination to reach a fair deal with the Canadian government; their resolve was "rooted in their firm belief that good always overcomes bad" (158). They use their own Indigenous knowledge to their advantage (as best they can under the circumstances), "restructuring their damaged traditional system by recreating a modern anti-colonial community" (159). Martin-Hill recounts a conversation, excerpted here, with Albert Laboucon, a Lubicon elder, who explained the transformative possibilities of such a community:

> *I met Albert Laboucon [a Cree-speaker in his seventies] during my second trip to Little Buffalo in December 1989 . . . I asked Albert to tell me about himself, and for his thoughts on the land claim. His answers were short and often direct.*
>
> *"I was raised in the bush, trapping, hunting, a hard life but a good one. There has been much change. No more animals, no wildlife, everything is disappearing, our ways are. They came . . . in the road and destroyed everything in their path. They cut right through trap lines, right through everything. Everything is dirty, water and animals are not so clean. I want the children, [the] grandchildren, to have something, that's why I stay with it. I think they are trying to wipe us out . . . I never thought that really before—to wipe us out . . . just [to] get us out of the way. They are greedy, greed like we don't know. There is nothing for me, just doing this for my grandchildren now . . . This has been going on a long time, since I was young. I thought it would all be okay; we would get our reserve, no big deal. They seem to want to wipe us out instead, don't know why. I think they have money, no word for the money they have. We don't want much . . . A lot they do doesn't make sense, destroying the land, water, air. No matter, they think they're above all this—they're not. They're needing air, water, food, and they can't see what will happen to us will happen to them too. They don't think about their children either. What will these young ones have to drink if all the water no good? Maybe if we keep hollering they will hear us . . . if we keep making enough noise. It's good that other Indians like you [Martin-Hill is Mohawk] come here and help. We need to help one another the way the Creator intended. I feel better when there are other Indians helping."*
>
> *I asked Albert to tell me what he wanted me to take back to my people, what to tell them from him. He sat quietly for a long time and then said in Cree, "We should put our voices together, our drum, it will be heard across the country." (117–18)**

Albert Laboucon's drumming inspired the Drum Beat Conference, held by McMaster University and the Six Nations community in 1989, which hosted Indigenous people from all over North America and was aimed at raising awareness of Indigenous issues. The conference laid the groundwork for the creation of the Indigenous Studies program at McMaster.

The dilemma of the Guaraní and the Lubicon Cree is shared by thousands of other societies and groups around the world. Equally involved in the dilemma are the societies that are responsible for driving small-scale societies to the edge of cultural devastation or are forcing them to experience development through its dark side of poverty, disease, and forced labour. By systematically destroying small-scale societies, we may be eliminating systems of meaning that hold solutions to compelling world problems, such as environmental destruction, intergroup and intragroup conflict, poverty, and sickness.

BEYOND THE BOOK 3.3

In 2006, the New Economics Foundation, and UK-based think tank, named Vanuatu (a low-income or developing nation in the Southwest Pacific) the Happiest Place on Earth, as its citizens had a relatively high level of well-being but a low environmental footprint. Inspired by this top happiness ranking, Vanuatu began its own study: a pilot test to come up with "Alternative Indicators of Well-Being for Melanesia." Ralph Regenvanu, a member of parliament (with a degree in anthropology) who worked on developing the indicators, describes the project in the video "Vanuatu: Another Kind of Wealth" (https://www.youtube.com/watch?v=sXhftm_tifQ). Search for the video online, and after watching it, answer (and/or discuss) these questions:

---

*From *The Lubicon Lake Nation: Indigenous Knowledge and Power*, by Dawn Martin-Hill, © University of Toronto Press, 2008. pp. 117-118. Reprinted with permission of the publisher.

1. Based on what you have read in this chapter, make a list of the reasons why one of the world's "least developed countries" might have ranked at the top of this index.
2. How do these indicators challenge the ideas of progress and economic development critiqued throughout this chapter?
3. If you could choose your own comparable indicators of well-being, what would they be?

Question 3.4: Have Progress and Development Improved Human Health?

Illness and Inequality

Are the world's people better off now than they were before the Industrial Revolution? Obviously, the answer depends on who you are. If you are fortunate enough to be a labourer, business person, or professional in a wealthy country, you are likely to be materially better off than your counterpart of five centuries ago, provided that the price you pay in health risks because of a damaged environment does not offset your material gains. If you are a labourer or small farmer in one of the world's poor countries, it is hard to see how you could be better off than your peasant counterpart of centuries past. If you are among the world's landless, unemployed, or underemployed, or one of the billion without enough food, it is difficult to see how your life could be an improvement over that of your counterpart two centuries before.

Even if the *economic* changes of the past two centuries have not improved many people's lives, can't we at least assume that *some* technologies—notably medical technologies—have done so? To answer this question, we need to consider two things: first, whether we have progressed in our ability to treat disease (using the **biomedical model**); and second, whether we fully understand the traditional medical techniques that modern medicine has sought to replace.

An apparent triumphs of modern society has been the treatment and cure of disease. Life expectancy more than doubled in the twentieth century. In 1900, world life expectancy was around 30 years; by 2016, it was 72 years. Antibiotics and vaccines save millions of people from death each year, and modern diagnostic methods and equipment allow medical practitioners to identify the onset of disease more easily. Yet the progress we often take for granted is not available to all. For instance, children from the poorest 20 percent of the world's households are twice as likely to die before their fifth birthday as children from the richest 20 percent of households; in addition, 99 percent of annual maternal deaths, and 95 percent of annual deaths from tuberculosis, occur in developing countries (WHO 2017). In fact, the single most important determinant of a country's ability to protect its citizens from disease is the degree of economic equality.

We can, perhaps, better judge the extent to which we have "progressed" by examining what it takes for us to die of an infectious disease. At least four things have to happen. First, we have to come into contact with some **pathogen** or **vector** that carries a disease. Second, the pathogen must be virulent—that is, it must be able to kill us. Third, if we come into contact with a deadly pathogen, it must evade our body's immune system. Finally, the pathogen must be able to circumvent whatever measures our society has developed to prevent it from doing harm. As we will see, our chances of dying are affected at every step by social and cultural patterns, particularly by the degree of economic and social inequality.

biomedical model
Also known as *Western medicine*, *scientific medicine*, or *modern medicine*, the model combines biology with the diagnosis and treatment of illness and views the body as a machine, independent of social context, that must be repaired periodically.

pathogen
An infectious agent such as a bacteria or a virus that can cause disease.

vector
An organism, such as a mosquito, tick, flea, or snail, that can transmit disease to another animal.

Cultural complexity has increased our exposure to infectious agents. Large, permanent settlements attract and sustain vermin such as rats and fleas, which serve as hosts for microorganisms and ensure their survival and spread. Permanent settlements also result in the buildup of human waste and refuse. Sedentary agriculture requires altering the landscape in ways that can increase the incidence of disease. Schistosomiasis, for example, is a disease caused by worms and snails, which thrive in irrigation ditches. The domestication of animals such as dogs, cats, cattle, and pigs increases contact between people and disease-causing microorganisms. Large populations must store and process their food, which also increases the likelihood that disease-causing agents will survive and spread.

Coming into contact with an infectious pathogen is not in itself enough for death to ensue: the pathogen must be deadly. But this, too, depends on your social and cultural situation, including your income. Generally, it is not to the advantage of pathogens—viruses, bacteria, parasites—to kill their hosts; pathogens find it advantageous to allow their hosts to live and supply nutrients. However, if the pathogen does not need its host in order to survive, it can evolve into a more deadly form. Such is the case with waterborne infections. Pathogens that spread by contaminated water can survive regardless of how sick their host becomes, and by reproducing extensively in their host, they make it more likely that they can contaminate water supplies—for example, through bodily wastes. All of this means that you are far more likely to contract a deadly disease if you lack access to clean and treated water.

Even if you come into contact with a deadly pathogen, your immune system is designed to prevent it from killing you. The strength of your immune system, however, is clearly a function of diet, and diet is determined largely by income level. In this respect, we have not progressed. In 1950, 20 percent of the world's people (500 million) were malnourished. Today some 50 percent (3.5 billion) are malnourished. Insufficient food is one of the principal causes of immune system failure. Fortunately for many, in the twentieth century vaccines, which work to strengthen one's immune system against future infections by particular diseases, were developed for a wide array of deadly pathogens. The effect on infectious disease transmission has been tremendous. For instance, the reported incidence, globally, of measles has been reduced by 83 percent since 2000, preventing 21.1 million deaths. (Strategic Advisory Group of Experts on Immunization 2019, 5). However, the benefits of vaccination are unequally shared, and key factors that determine low vaccine coverage are economic inequalities and social marginalization (11). In 2020, more vaccines are more widely available than ever before, but over the past decade, an increase in extreme poverty and a rapid increase in the number of people displaced by the effects of conflict and climate change have led to a plateau with regard to access to vaccines and their health benefits.

Finally, societies have developed methods to cure illnesses that our immune systems have failed to ward off. There is little doubt that the discovery of cures for infectious diseases is one of the great success stories of modern culture. Unfortunately, access to these cures is determined largely by individual wealth. This reality suggests why the United States, the wealthiest country in the world overall, ranks 38th in the world in life expectancy (UNDP 2019). It is no coincidence that the United States has the largest income gap between the rich and the poor of any industrialized country. Japan, which has the lowest gap between the rich and the poor, also has the highest life expectancy, even though Japanese are three times heavier smokers than Americans.

In sum, although we have indeed made dramatic progress in understanding, preventing, and curing infectious disease, we have made no progress—and, indeed, have gone backward—in terms of our ability to provide equitable access to these cures. At the same time, we have increased global exposure to infectious pathogens. As we write this edition of the textbook in spring 2020, the world is in the throes of the COVID-19 pandemic. The reach of this virus is truly global, and no places or peoples are immune; however, that does not mean that COVID-19 is a great equalizer. Even from the vantage point of the "middle" of the pandemic, at least two things about the virus seem clear—it is a disease that can be "spread" by inequality, and it is likely that its effects and aftermath will exacerbate existing inequalities. Take, for instance, the Pacific island nation of Vanuatu. Vanuatu (1,750 kilometres northeast of Australia), is a small, developing nation whose economy relies heavily on tourism, remittances from temporary foreign workers, and foreign aid. As of April 2020, it had no cases of COVID-19; it took early preventative measures such as closing its borders and implementing physical distancing. However, doing so has effectively closed down its tourism industry, and those working temporarily overseas have been put out of work. Together, these two things could well cripple its economy, yet they have been deemed necessary, for the nation has little capacity to deal with an outbreak (its hospital does not have any ventilators, for example).

In early April 2020, Vanuatu was hit by a Category 5 hurricane, "super" Cyclone Harold. Many residents of Vanuatu were left without access to shelter and potable water, and the effects of the cyclone on local agriculture meant that many people faced food shortages as well. So Vanuatu faced a Catch-22 after the cyclone: open the border to allow foreign aid to enter (especially in the form of aid workers and volunteers) and risk the possibility of being overwhelmed by COVID-19; or turn away foreign workers and volunteers and their much-needed assistance, and hope that residents could get back on their feet before food and water ran out (or another cyclone struck). The situation in Vanuatu is just one example of the myriad ways that increased global inequality has led to increased global health disparities.

Interpersonal Theories of Health and Illness

Even if we conclude that modern societies are more susceptible to contagious diseases, have they not at least improved their technologies for preventing and curing illness? In answering this question, it is important to grasp that the meanings members of different societies give to illness vary as much as the meanings they give to other aspects of their lives. In mainstream North American society, illness is viewed as an intrusion by bacteria or viruses. Our curing techniques emphasize eliminating those agents. Death can occur, we believe, when we have failed to do so.

In many other societies, interpretations of illness are completely different. Illness may be attributed to witchcraft—that is, a witch or sorcerer has used magic to inflict illness on another person. Or it may be attributed to soul loss, or the soul having left the body. Or it may be attributed to spirit possession, the idea that a foreign spirit has entered the patient. These explanations are not mutually exclusive; for example, the soul may flee the body as the result of witchcraft or sorcery.

These theories of illness—soul loss, spirit possession, sorcery, and witchcraft—have one thing in common: all are expressions of the **interpersonal theory of disease**. Simply stated, in the

In a healing ceremony designed to restore the patient to his proper place in the world, a traditional Navajo doctor paints an image of the universe with coloured sand on an earthen floor.

interpersonal theory of disease
A view of disease in which it is assumed that illness is caused by tensions or conflicts in social relations.

interpersonal theory of disease it is assumed that illness is caused not by microorganisms but rather by tensions or conflicts in social relations. In this view, witches, spirits, and souls are mediating agents that link a social cause—tension and conflict—to a physical result—illness or death.

Those who believe that illness has spiritual or magical causes do not believe that a witch or sorcerer strikes at random, that the soul leaves the body without cause, or that a spirit will possess just anyone. Rather, they believe there must be a social reason for these things to occur.

For instance, witchcraft involves relationships between people: the witch voluntarily or involuntarily afflicts someone who has caused offence or who has breached a rule of conduct. The Chewa of Malawi in southeastern Africa contend that illness and death are induced by witchcraft when someone fails to observe some social norm. Whereas Canadians react to illness or death by seeking the disease or accident responsible, the Chewa ask what wrong the victim has committed, with whom the victim has quarrelled, or who is jealous of the victim. The Chewa explicitly recognize the connection between sorcery and social tension.

If an illness has social causes, then the cure, too, must be at least partly social. A Chewa who becomes ill consults a diviner to discover the cause of the illness. During the consultation, the patient and the diviner discuss the social roots of the illness. The diviner needs to know about the patient's relationships with kin and, if ancestral spirits may be responsible, the genealogy of the patient. Thus, Chewa medical theory, although couched in the idiom of sorcery, is a social theory of illness, not simply a supernatural one.

The example of the Ndembu, an agricultural society in northwestern Zambia studied by Victor Turner (1967), also illustrates the significance of repairing social problems to cure illnesses that reflect social tensions or conflicts. The Ndembu believe that a persistent or severe illness is caused either by the punitive action of some ancestral ghost or by the secret malevolence of a sorcerer or witch. The ghosts punish people when they forget to make a ritual offering to their ancestors or when, as the Ndembu put it, "kin are not living well together."

To effect a cure, the Ndembu patient consults a native doctor. The doctor first inquires about the patient's social relations: Has he or she quarrelled with anyone? What is the state of the patient's marital relations? Is anyone jealous of the patient? The doctor asks those with whom the patient has quarrelled to participate in the ceremony, which is a dramatic affair with chanting and drumming, sometimes lasting for hours. People who have complaints about the patient's social behaviour may come forward, and the patient may report grudges against neighbours. At the climax, the doctor may dramatically extract from the patient's body some object that could have been causing the illness.

The Ndembu recognize, at least implicitly, that social strain and stress may produce physical illness and that one way to treat illness is to treat the sources of social strain. Western medicine also recognizes the negative health effects that stress can have. Events such as the death of a spouse, the loss of a job, relocation to a new home, or even holidays such as Christmas can increase the chances of illness. These are the same kinds of events that can trigger the need for ceremonial cures in some societies. Thus, rather than viewing the healing practices of traditional societies as inferior, it makes far more sense to recognize that they focus on social stress as a cause of illness.

Cost is another consideration. Ethnomedical cures not only can be beneficial but also are affordable. One consequence of biomedical advances is increasing dependence on expensive technology. Consequently, while significant advances have been made in medicine, the cost to patients of many such advances has made them unavailable to all but a small percentage of the world's population. In societies where healing is everyone's responsibility instead of a commodity to be purchased, it follows the moral values of a social obligation rather than those of business.

APPLYING ANTHROPOLOGY

Oil Sands Reclamation in Northern Alberta

As we have seen, efforts by countries to "progress" and modernize have often undermined the lives of Indigenous peoples (as well as the lives of craftspeople and small farmers). The idea of progress clearly contains some ethnocentric assumptions about what constitutes the "good life." Clearly, there is much for anthropologists to contribute to the field of development to mitigate these types of assumptions. Many anthropologists make a living by lending their expertise to development organizations, governments, and policy-makers, often with the specific goal of addressing the negative, unwanted, or culturally inappropriate effects of "economic development."

Anthropologist Tara L. Joly's work on oil sands reclamation in northern Alberta provides one important example of the significance of this kind of work, as well as possible career trajectories for those interested in applying anthropological knowledge to address the often detrimental environmental and cultural impacts of economic progress and development. Much of Joly's research (2017a, b) focuses on the "aftermath" of extractive resource development: Who decides what counts as reclamation or restoration of the post-extractive Athabasca oil sands landscape, and why?

The Government of Alberta requires that when extractive projects such as mining or oil sand extraction are finished, the companies that ran them must "reclaim" the land for other uses such as agriculture, forestry, recreation, and Indigenous land use (Alberta 2000, cited in Joly 2017b). As we have seen in the case of the Lubicon Cree, many areas with a heavy presence of extractive industries nonetheless remain Indigenous homelands. Frequently, environmental impact assessments justify extraction by suggesting that although it will negatively affect Indigenous land uses such as hunting and fishing, the promised reclamation will fully restore the land for these uses. However, Joly found that competing discourses of "productivity" recirculate in reclamation practices. What counts as "making land productive" post-extraction? Joly found that more often than not, settler-colonial views of productivity are privileged over those of the McMurray Métis, who have their own perspectives on the best "use" and value of their homeland. Joly's work suggests that neither reclamation nor, more broadly, reconciliation can truly happen if the perspectives of Indigenous peoples are not taken seriously and given weight in policy-making and reclamation practices.

MARK RALSTON/AFP via Getty Images

Monitoring equipment in a reclaimed forest on the site of a former Syncrude oil sands mine near Fort McMurray, Alberta.

Joly's findings demonstrate the relevance and practical significance of anthropological expertise for a wide range of audiences. Based on her fieldwork, she has written ethnography for scholarly audiences, but she has also written policy recommendations for governments and lawmakers, as well as cultural and environmental impact assessments aimed at amplifying the voices and protecting the rights of her Métis interlocutors. She has been employed as a researcher in a university setting, but she has also worked for Willow Springs Strategic Solutions, Inc., which provides community-based research and services to clients with a stake in the social, economic, and cultural impacts of resource development. A key finding of her ethnographic research is that the McMurray Métis see the post-extraction landscape as part of a relationship that needs healing rather than reclamation. Part of Joly's job as a consultant is to translate this ethnographic finding, and others like it, into "real life" policy change and action. For instance, in a report about the diminished stock of freshwater clams in the lower Athabasca region, commissioned by the Fort McMurray Métis, Joly sets out a framework for stakeholders (the Métis, but also government scientists and representatives of other agencies) to "learn together" about this problem. "Learning together" has meant creating a "Clam Team" comprising not just scientists, but also Métis with traditional knowledge of the social significance of clams in local life (Hopkins et al. 2019). The team conducted community-based participatory research to figure out "where the clams have gone"; the voices of Indigenous knowledge were on equal footing with those of the non-Indigenous experts; all parties shared ownership of the research process, outcomes, and decision-making. The report Joly wrote on this commissioned project (one of several such advisory reports she has written based on research in the Athabasca region) provides a toolkit for healing the lower Athabasca region by finding and supporting the clam stocks, but also for conducting research in which reconciliation is front and centre throughout the life of the project. This is a prime example of the applicability of anthropological insights, methodologies, and expertise to environmental development, reclamation, and healing, and especially of the possibilities for collaborative fieldwork.

Conclusions

We began this chapter by noting that over the past 10,000 years, human societies have shifted away from a way of life that had survived for some 100,000 years. Why did so many societies begin to change from nomadic foraging to sedentary agriculture? Some anthropologists, such as Lewis Henry Morgan and Leslie White, have suggested that the need to progress and develop better ways of living may explain the change. Studies of forager societies, however, reveal that they live quite comfortably and with minimum effort. Indeed, Marshall Sahlins referred to the foraging way of life as "the original affluent society," characterized by minimal work coupled with ample leisure time.

If we reject the straightforward narrative of progress, how are we to explain the transformation of human societies over the past 10,000 years? It is possible that an increase in population or population density fuelled the transition of societies from foraging to swidden agriculture and then to plough or irrigation agriculture. But although the transition to more labour-intensive forms of agriculture may have been the result of population pressure, other anthropologists have argued that newer forms of agricultural technology may be simply better or more efficient. John Bodley's analysis of the energy expenditures of modern agriculture suggests, however, that it is difficult to conclude that it is, in fact, simply better.

Explanations that equate culture change with progress have heavily influenced the trajectory of global economic development. These explanations, though, fall short when we try to understand the gap between the wealthy and poor nations of the world. We find that we must consider the history of the economic expansion of Europe, as well as the military, political, and social exploitation of the countries of Asia, Africa, and the Americas. We find that hunger is not so much due to a lack of modern agriculture; rather, it is a consequence of poverty and attempts to industrialize. The need to repay bank loans secured for industrialization has led countries such as Brazil to encourage the development of large farms that grow mainly cash crops for export. As a result, people are dispossessed of their land and left without enough money to buy food.

For many small-scale societies, global economic development has led to cultural devastation at the hands of "civilized" countries. Unfortunately, notions of progress may simply be a convenient rationale for one society to impose its economic and political will on others. Perhaps when we talk about culture change in terms of progress, we should remember to ask: Progress for whom? In the last section of the chapter, we explored the implications of an anthropological understanding of progress for thinking critically and cross-culturally about health and illness. It may seem self-evident that Western standards of health care are higher than those of less developed societies. Researchers have concluded, however, that infectious diseases are more common in industrialized societies and that human behaviours associated with industrialization, modernization, and the unequal distribution of wealth often promote the incidence and spread of contagious disease. Moreover, traditional theories of illness and curing ceremonies can be effective in the diagnosis and treatment of illness or disease, and these approaches are often more cost-effective and accessible than Western medical expertise and technologies.

QUESTIONS: REVIEW

3.1 How and why did foraging societies switch to sedentary agriculture?

In this section, we provided an overview of the major shift, 10,000 years ago, that most human societies made from foraging and nomadism to agriculture and sedentary life. We traced the changes to social organization that happened when people gave up foraging. In this section, we also consider various anthropological perspectives on why this shift happened, and whether or not it can be adequately described as "progress."

Review Questions

1. Compare foraging, slash-and-burn (swidden) agriculture, and state societies in terms of their modes of livelihood, population size, amount of labour relative to yield, and types of social and political organization.
2. According to Cohen and Carniero, what is the relationship between population density, modes of livelihood, and social organization?
3. How did Henry Lewis Morgan and Leslie White apply Darwin's theories of natural selection and evolution to culture?
4. What did Marshall Sahlins mean when he suggested that foragers were "the original affluent society," and why did he make this argument?

3.2 How can we explain the vast inequality between the rich and the poor?

In this section, we discuss the vast and growing inequality between the rich and the poor that has occurred despite high levels of "progress." Using the case study of the textile industry in Britain, and by closely tracing the links between this industry and the textile industry in India, the opium trade in China, and slavery and land alienation in the United States, we suggest some of the reasons why the shift away from agriculture toward industrial production over the last 300 years has increased global wealth disparities.

Review Questions

1. What is the difference between the putting-out system and the factory system of textile production? How did the shift from the former to the latter increase inequality in Britain and beyond? Give examples.
2. What was the Trail of Tears (Cherokee Removal)? How was it related to slavery and cotton production in the United States in the eighteenth century?
3. What is colonialism? What role has it played in the rise of global wealth inequality? Give examples.

3.3 How does economic development affect inequality and cultural diversity?

In this section, we demonstrate how economic development, particularly as practised by the World Bank and the International Monetary Fund, has had devastating environmental, economic, and cultural repercussions for small-scale and Indigenous societies. The examples in this section focus on Brazil, the Guarani of Paraguay, and the Lubicon Cree of Alberta.

Review Questions

1. What is economic development? What roles have the World Bank and the IMF played in economic development?
2. How might economic development lead to economic and/or cultural devastation? Give at least two detailed examples.
3. Why, and by whom, have the Lubicon Cree been considered "in the way of progress"? How have they restructured their community and beliefs in the face of such considerations?

3.4 Have Progress and Development Improved Human Health?

Have forms of progress and development in the realm of health and illness, most notably medical technologies such as vaccines and antibiotics, improved human health? In this section, we demonstrate that, again, it depends who you are, where you live, and under what circumstances. Access to the benefits of modern medicine is not equally distributed, and poor, marginalized, and vulnerable populations are less able to access this form of "progress." Moreover, as we discuss in the second half of this section, many cultures have their own ways of making sense of, and treating, illness that do not necessarily fit with the Western medical model. This section focuses on illness and healing among the Chewa of Malawi and the Ndembu of Zambia, for whom many illnesses have social causes that require social treatments that also serve as social interventions.

Review Questions

1. What is the biomedical model of health and illness? List and discuss at least three reasons why access to biomedicine has not necessarily increased health for everyone in the world.
2. What is the interpersonal theory of disease? Explain how the perceptions and treatments of illness and healing among the Chewa and the Ndembu exemplify this theory.

CRITICAL THINKING QUESTIONS

1. In Chapter 1, we discussed the concept of cultural relativism. How might you apply the idea of cultural relativism to the twin concepts of progress and development?
2. Western environmental activists often point to Indigenous cultures and modes of livelihood as examples of a more environmentally friendly way to live. What are the possible advantages and disadvantages of this approach, both from the perspective of the environmentalists and from that of the Indigenous groups to whom they refer?
3. Given what you have learned about how population, urbanization, agriculture, and technology relate to one another, what predictions might you make about future modes of livelihood and food production?
4. Canadians are starting to take the idea that "mental health is health" more seriously. What might we learn about the causes and treatments of poor mental health if we applied the interpersonal theory of disease instead of, or in addition to, a Western medical perspective?

KEY TERMS

bands (p. 62)
biomedical model (p. 85)
clans (p. 63)
colonialism (p. 72)
culture change (p. 62)
economic development (p. 79)
factory system (p. 73)
foragers (p. 62)
Industrial Revolution (p. 65)
International Monetary Fund (IMF) (p. 80)
interpersonal theory of disease (p. 87)
irrigation agriculture (p. 63)
natural selection (p. 64)
pathogen (p. 85)
population density (p. 68)
progress (p. 61)
"putting out" system (p. 73)
sedentary (p. 62)
slash-and-burn, or swidden, agriculture (p. 63)
states (p. 63)
unilineal evolution (p. 65)
vector (p. 85)
World Bank (p. 80)

CHAPTER 4

Constructing Realities

Michele Falzone/Stockbyte/Getty Images

For Native Hawaiians, the peak of Mauna Kea is sacred. It is also considered special by astronomers, for its height and lack of light pollution make it one of the best sites in the world for astronomical observation. Astronomers believe that the research done in the peak's observatories will provide invaluable information about the origins of the universe. For Native Hawaiians, however, the ongoing construction of observatories is an affront to the gods and ancestors (and to Hawaiian sovereignty). How do people come to have such different beliefs about the same place? What happens when these beliefs appear to be at odds with each other? Rather than regarding unfamiliar beliefs with amusement or incredulity, as the Jesuit missionary cited in the epigraph did with Amerindians, an anthropologist would approach these beliefs with intellectual curiosity and an open mind.

> *It is amusing to hear them speak of their souls ... They think of the soul as divisible, and you would have all the difficulty in the world to make them believe that our soul is entire in all parts of the body ... God of truth, what ignorance and stupidity!*
>
> —Jesuit reaction to Amerindian beliefs about life after death

PROBLEM 4

Why do people believe different things, and why are they so certain that their view of the world is correct and that other views are wrong?

Introduction

The Central Question

How is it that people can believe in a God whose existence cannot be proven? How can they believe in the existence of ancestor spirits, or witches, or devils, or believe in the power of magic to call forth spirits of the dead? Although there is no material proof, people do believe these things, and even take these beliefs for granted. Many North Americans, for example, believe in the existence of God, and some firmly believe in the existence of Satan and the possibility of demonic possession. Such beliefs need not be tied to religion. For example, many North Americans daily consult their horoscope, believing that the position of the stars at their birth somehow affects their destiny.

When people try to make sense of their experiences, they do so by drawing from shared cultural assumptions about how the world works. These shared, learned cultural assumptions create an encompassing picture of reality (which can be religious or secular). This picture is called a **worldview**.

Worldviews differ significantly between cultures. For example, E. E. Evans-Pritchard, a famous British anthropologist, is famous to this day for his 1920s fieldwork among the Azande of southern Sudan. Evans-Pritchard (1937) found that witchcraft was "ubiquitous" among the Azande and that they tended to explain many acts of misfortune, such as death, illness, or even a bad hunt, as due to witchcraft. In other words, they claimed that someone was bewitching them, causing them misfortune. In contrast, in our society, many people may also experience misfortune, perhaps falling down and getting a bad cut that causes infection. The Azande might use witchcraft to explain the infection, whereas we might argue that the individual was clumsy for falling or that he or she had the "bad luck" to fall and get hurt. So, while many experiences are universal—sickness, death, the birth of an infant, a host of other life events—we all interpret those experiences based on our worldview. Unfortunately, many people tend to think that their worldview is the only correct one for interpreting their reality, and this often leads to ethnocentric assumptions about other cultures and their beliefs. These assumptions can range from believing that your religion is correct and that the spiritual beliefs of others are irrational

worldview
An encompassing picture of reality based on shared cultural assumptions about how the world works.

or incorrect, to accepting that your model of politics or economics is "right" or better than that of others.

Anthropologists have long had to consider how to deal with differing worldviews and beliefs. For example, early anthropological studies of religion sought to explain how people could believe in things that seemed illogical, such as witchcraft. Edward Tylor, considered by some to be the founder of modern anthropology, wrote in *Primitive Culture* (1870) that religion and a belief in the supernatural developed through people's efforts to explain basic phenomena, such as death and dreaming. Tylor imagined early human beings thinking, "What is the difference between a live person and a dead one, between a sleeping person and someone who is awake?" They must have reasoned that there was something, some kind of essence, that left the body at the moment of death or that travelled to distant places in the dreams of sleep. According to Tylor, from this reasoning came a belief in the idea of a soul that animated the body but that fled the body in death and in sleep. In his view, this understanding was why the word for breath and the word for soul are the same or similar in so many languages. And it was not unreasonable, said Tylor, for these early philosophers to imagine that other animals and things were animated by souls as well.

Once people arrived at a belief in souls, it was a small step to reason that there were places where departed souls resided and an even smaller step to believe that souls became gods. It was logical, then, for human beings to appeal to these departed spirits for help in controlling life's uncertainties. For Tylor, then, beliefs in gods and spirits developed through the efforts of human beings to explain certain events, to understand why things happened as they did.

In his classic work *The Elementary Forms of Religious Life* ([1912]1961), French sociologist Emile Durkheim asked what led to the concept of God. Durkheim, like Tylor, speculated that the secret must lie in the beliefs of early human beings. Durkheim thought that the lives of these people could best be studied by looking at contemporary small-scale societies whose social organization was considered "simple." He decided to read about the religious beliefs of the Indigenous peoples of Australia, particularly their beliefs about **totemism**. The totem, said Durkheim, was some element of nature—an animal, an insect, a plant, or some celestial phenomenon—that served as a symbol for a group or clan. The totem was worshipped and was considered sacred and holy by the members of the group. It also served as a concrete representation of the group. If members of the group worshipped the totem and if the totem was a symbol of the group, was it unreasonable to suppose, asked Durkheim, that the group—the clan itself—was the object of worship?

What, however, would suggest to people that the totem had sacred power? The answer, said Durkheim, lay in the constraints that people feel are imposed on them by the group and by society and in the special power that people feel when groups come together in celebration and **ritual**. And if in small-scale societies people worship the group through their symbolic representations, as clans worship themselves through their totems, is it not reasonable to suppose that in large-scale societies people worship society through their god or gods? That God is society?

Early anthropologists approached the questions of God, in particular, and religion, in general, with the assumption that such beliefs were mistaken or irrational. Nevertheless, they believed that religious beliefs served some purpose: the beliefs and rituals may have increased group cohesion or provided supernatural sanctions for the violation of group norms.

totemism
The use of a symbol, generally an animal or a plant, as a physical representation for a group, generally a clan.

ritual
A dramatic rendering or social portrayal of meanings shared by a specific body of people in a way that makes them seem correct and proper. (See also symbolic actions.)

Recent anthropological efforts to understand differing beliefs and worldviews have built on these early efforts, but as Michael Lambek (2002, 5) argues:

> *If many of the nineteenth-century thinkers saw members of smaller-scale societies mired in superstition, ignorance, bliss, or folly, the personal connections forged in decent ethnographic fieldwork immediately deprived westerners of any illusions of intellectual or moral superiority ... Theorists began to realize that rather than compare nonwestern systems of thought directly to western science, it was much more sensible to compare religion, common sense, and specialized knowledge about the world within any given society ... and to compare western religious practices with nonwestern ones.*

Today, anthropologists' efforts to understand belief rarely start from the premise that other peoples' beliefs are irrational or incorrect. Rather, anthropologists try to understand the nature of belief or religious practice and how it is that people come to believe that their view of the world is correct.

In order to explain and contextualize people's beliefs in any cultural context, and regardless of how strange or familiar such beliefs seem, we need to examine a number of concepts. **Metaphor** is one of the tools we apply to make our knowledge meaningful to ourselves and to others; in that regard, it plays a major role in giving us a sense of the universe and ourselves. As we will see, **symbolic actions**—all the rituals, myths, arts, stories, and music that we enjoy or participate in—play a role in organizing and making concrete a particular worldview. We also need to explore how people learn to view the world as they do and how they defend their beliefs against skeptics who challenge a particular view of the world. What we believe must also be, in some way, a product of our social, economic, and political lives. In addition, we need to ask and explain why people sometimes radically change what they believe. Finally, it is also worth thinking about how secular and religious belief systems can coexist within the same society, what challenges this might pose, and how anthropologists view these challenges.

QUESTIONS

4.1 How does the use of metaphor affect the meanings people assign to experience?
4.2 How does symbolic action reinforce a particular view of the world?
4.3 How does the way we live affect our beliefs and rituals?
4.4 What happened to local worldviews when they were confronted by the religions of the European colonizers?
4.5 How can people reorder their view of the world if it becomes unsatisfactory?
4.6 How can secular and religious worldviews coexist?

Question 4.1: How Does the Use of Metaphor Affect the Meanings People Assign to Experience?

Borrowing Meaning with Metaphors

One major characteristic of language is its economy; the same words we use to describe one area of experience can also be used to describe another. This capability is exercised primarily through metaphor. Metaphors take language from one **domain of experience**, such as the domain of the body or the domain of animals, and apply it to another domain,

metaphors
Figures of speech in which linguistic expressions are taken from one area of experience and applied to another.

symbolic actions
The activities—including ritual, myth, art, dance, and music—that dramatically depict the meanings shared by a specific body of people.

domain of experience
An area of human experience (e.g., business, war, science, family life) from which people borrow meaning to apply to other areas.

such as landscape features or persons. For example, "the shoulder of the road" is a metaphoric extension of a body part used to refer to landscape, while "Jeff is a dog" represents an extension from the animal world to the human world.

Metaphors are valuable tools for constructing worldviews. By directing attention to certain aspects of experience, while downplaying or ignoring others, metaphors can reinforce people's beliefs, as well as their understandings of reality, which ultimately come to be taken for granted as correct and true. To put it another way: "Through metaphors we understand the abstract in terms of the concrete" (Lakoff and Johnson 1980, 112).

When language is extended from one domain to another, meaning is also extended. In other words, metaphor involves not only speaking of one experience in terms of another but also understanding one experience in terms of another. For example, when those of us who speak English in North America describe an argument, we might say, "His point was right on target," or "Your claims are indefensible," or "She attacked my argument, and I had to defend my position." We might say, "She shot down my argument," or "I think I won the argument." We speak of argument in terms of conflict, taking the language from the domain of war and applying it to the domain of conversation. But we have not only transferred words; we have also transferred meaning. We don't simply talk about arguments in terms of war: we win and lose arguments.

Alternatively, think about the way the conception of illness is embedded in the language used to describe it. North Americans who speak English take language from the domain of war and use it to talk about health. We build our defences against illness; we get ill because our resistance was low. We fight a cold, destroy germs, wage war on cancer, and have heart attacks. The language that AIDS researchers use is full of metaphors drawn from war. Recent research reports that the AIDS virus weakens the "immune system attack force," and that "killer cells" are meant to "destroy virus-stricken cells." As one HIV researcher put it: "If you want to think of it with a war analogy, it's as though the soldiers are still on maneuvers, but they no longer have their weapons: When they encounter the enemy, they lose their weapons" (cited in Kolata 1995). It is worth thinking about the implications of the metaphors we use to discuss disease: How does our North American anglophone way of speaking of illness in terms of war and battle affect the kinds of treatment for illness that we devise and seek? Does this metaphor imply the need for cures that destroy the agent of disease rather than restore the patient to health?

The human body and war, of course, are not the only domains from which North American anglophones borrow to assign meaning to other areas of experience. North Americans who speak English borrow also from the domain of economic exchange. In English, time is spoken of not only as if it were a distinct thing, but also as if it were a specific type of thing: "Time is money," "You're wasting my time," "This gadget will save you hours," "I don't have the time to give you," "That flat tire cost me an hour," "You need to budget your time," "He's living on

Rick Madonik/Toronto Star via Getty Images

When North Americans use the term "slam dunk" to refer to ensured success, they are borrowing meaning from the domain of sports to make sense of another domain of experience.

borrowed time," "Is that worth your while?" Time in North American cultures is a valuable commodity, a scarce resource that is quantified, invested, and spent.

BEYOND THE BOOK 4.1

North American anglophones often borrow heavily from the domain of sports in their use of metaphor. Create a list of the sports-related metaphors with which you are familiar. How do such metaphors shape your understanding of experiences of romance, success, and failure? Can you think of alternative metaphors that might also describe those experiences? How might a shift in metaphor change your understanding of those experiences?

The fact that English speakers in North America borrow so heavily from the domains of war and economic exchange for metaphors suggests another way to understand how language operates to influence people's views of the world. Most societies seem to have one or more domains from which they borrow extensively for metaphor. These domains become **key metaphors** that give to each culture a style or cast that makes the culture distinctive. When a culture's members think and speak of many domains of experience in terms of a particular domain, that culture's meanings achieve a certain coherence, and a coherence of belief is thereby achieved as well.

Kwakwaka'wakw Metaphors of Hunger

Perhaps one of the most spectacular expressions of the elaboration of both a key metaphor and the human imagination is found among the Kwakwaka'wakw (once called the "Kwakiutl") of British Columbia (Figure 4.1).

Stanley Walens (1981) suggests that the act of eating is a key metaphor for the Kwakwaka'wakw. A fundamental meaning the Kwakwaka'wakw find in their experience is that the universe is a place in which some beings must die so that other beings may eat them and live. Eating gives life in at least two ways: it provides nutrition, and it frees souls. The Kwakwaka'wakw believe that when a person dies, the soul leaves the body and enters the body of a salmon. But the soul cannot be freed until the physical body is destroyed. For this reason the Kwakwaka'wakw place their dead on scaffolds where the body can be devoured by ravens and other birds. Once the soul enters the body of a salmon, it remains there, living in a salmon world that socially resembles the human world. When the salmon is caught and eaten by human beings, however, the soul is once again freed and enters the body of a newborn child. Thus, for the Kwakwaka'wakw, the act of eating serves as a metaphor through which much of their life is understood and described.

The importance of eating as a metaphor that orders experience is evident in the dominance

FIGURE 4.1 Kwakwaka'wakw Territory in British Columbia

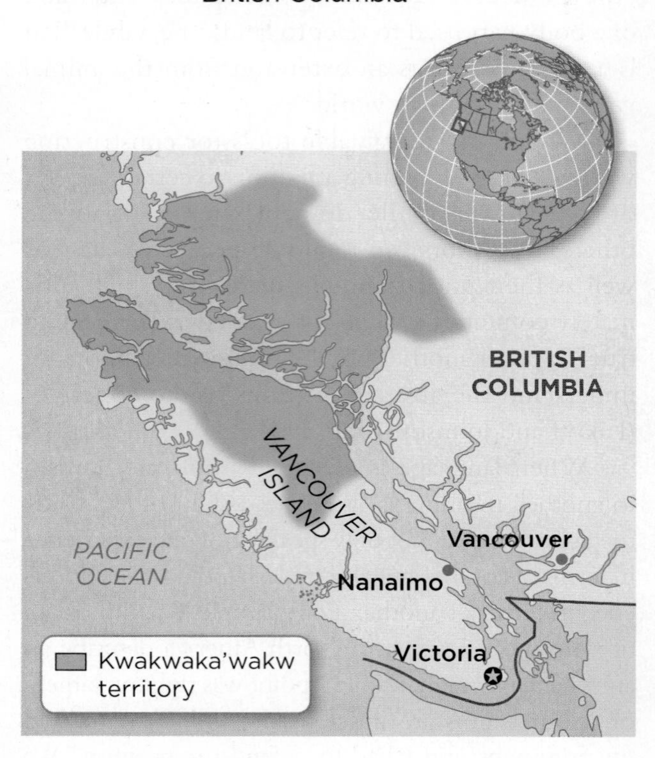

key metaphors
A term to identify metaphors that dominate the meanings that people in a specific culture attribute to their experience.

of mouths in Kwakwaka'wakw art, ritual, and **myth**. Their art is filled with the gaping jaws of killer whales, the fangs of wolves and bears, and the tearing beaks of hawks, eagles, and ravens. Dancers wear masks of cannibal birds with three-metre-long beaks that shatter human skulls to suck out the brains. In their myths, wild women with protruding lips inhabit the woods, waiting to rip apart travellers and misbehaving children. It is a world where suckling infants turn into monsters and devour their mothers.

The Kwakwaka'wakw use the eating metaphor to give meaning to a wide range of their experiences. Hunger is associated with greed, which, like unrestrained hunger, causes people to accumulate wealth far beyond what they need. Hunger is also associated with immorality, in that the Kwakwaka'wakw believe that human desires create conflict and destruction that can quickly get out of hand—people must work together to prevent and control conflict before it threatens to destroy the group. People who hoard food are, in effect, hoarding souls, preventing the return of a soul from the spirit world. Consequently, the Kwakwaka'wakw place great emphasis on gift giving and generosity. Hunger is also associated with children, who constantly demand to be fed and who will, if allowed, devour all the family's food.

The full impact of a metaphor lies in the fact that people are trying to impose order on their lives by describing the world according to a particular domain of experience. The Kwakwaka'wakw believe that greed, conflict, and childrearing can be solved by controlling hunger. Eating is thus highly ritualized and controlled. Food must be carefully handled and generously given to others to avoid accusations of greed. In fact, wealthy persons are said to vomit forth goods, vomit being for the Kwakwaka'wakw a life-giving substance. Animals that regurgitate their food, such as wolves and owls, occupy a special place in the Kwakwaka'wakw world. The socialization techniques of the Kwakwaka'wakw are geared toward teaching children to control their hunger. In sum, a single domain of experience—eating—has been elaborated by the Kwakwaka'wakw to give to their world meaning.

The Metaphors of Contemporary Witchcraft and Magic

A metaphor is a theory, a system of interpretation that, once understood in the context of one domain of experience, can then be transferred to others. The metaphors may also be embedded in myth and history as well as everyday experience. Mutually sustaining metaphors work to reinforce belief systems and worldviews. A good example of that is witchcraft and magic.

Witchcraft refers to the belief that an individual (the witch) has the ability to help or harm others through the manipulation of powerful substances or words—in other words, through **magic**. In North American society, most people have come to associate the term "witch" with particular stereotypes: the witch is assumed to be elderly, female, dressed in black, riding on a broomstick, and able to cast nefarious spells on seemingly innocent people. Such stereotypes are rooted in the witch hunts that were carried out in Europe during the Inquisition and the Reformation, a time when many women accused of witchcraft were tortured or killed. It is important to note, however, that witches can also be healers, revered for their wisdom. Furthermore, witchcraft beliefs are widespread and found on all

myth
A story or narrative that portrays the meanings people give to their experience.

witchcraft
Refers to the belief that an individual (the witch) has the ability to help or to cause harm to others through the manipulation of powerful substances.

magic
Refers to the manipulation of words or substances to influence spiritual beings for good or evil purposes.

continents and in a variety of types of societies. When anthropologists compare witchcraft beliefs cross-culturally, they find that people of all ages and genders can be labelled witches. In almost all societies, however, witchcraft beliefs function as metaphors that reinforce people's understandings of their world.

Ritual Magic in Twentieth-Century England

Modern Western forms of witchcraft persist in many parts of Europe and North America. Although in most contexts, witches are perceived as inherently evil, modern European forms of witchcraft draw upon aspects of New Age spirituality, and practitioners use witchcraft as a form of personal healing and as a means to achieve a sense of well-being. Anthropologist Tanya M. Luhrmann details the link between modern, urban witchcraft and worldview in *Persuasions of the Witch's Craft: Ritual Magic in Contemporary England* (1989). Luhrmann joined various covens and groups in England whose members are middle-class urbanites who situate their magic in "New Age" ideology, the "Age of Aquarius." They are people who place an emphasis on natural foods, good health, and personal stability and whose magical practices consist largely of conjuring spirits, reading the tarot, and magical healing.

A key metaphor embedded in modern witchcraft and magic is that of stratification, of "planes" and "levels." For the follower of good witchcraft, or magic, or the tarot, the universe is a complex system of entities and beings, each of which exists on a different "plane," "astral plane," or "level," of which the everyday plane of material life is but the lowest. After death, for example, the soul does not die, but goes to exist on another plane, with some souls remaining in contact with the material world. Other magical forces exist on other levels, and they, too, can be harnessed by human beings to influence events on the everyday plane of existence. Moreover, the properly trained human mind can, simply by imagining it, create forms on the "astral plane" that may, in turn, affect things in the material world.

Becoming a magician, Luhrmann says, requires the acquisition of specialized and esoteric knowledge; consequently, magicians read books, arrange and attend rituals, go to meetings, and learn astrology, mythology, and seventeenth-century Gaelic cures, as well as how to read tarot cards.

The tarot deck consists of 78 cards that comprise an elaborate and complex system of metaphoric associations that together link various domains of experience. These domains range from the planets and other celestial objects (e.g., sun, moon), to colours, material elements (e.g., mercury, iron, gold), emotions, personal qualities, and mythological beings. Each tarot card is said to have some meaning that is determined by its association with a specific planet, an element, an emotion or human quality, and so forth. The magician uses the tarot cards to divine the future, but the cards also provide ways for people to interpret their own lives. The cards, says Luhrmann, provide people with a symbolic map with which to interpret and understand themselves as they transfer the meanings of the cards to their own lives and experiences. Thus, some may associate themselves with the Empress, calm and fecund, or they may say that someone has the temperament of the Magician, mercurial and unpredictable. In associating themselves with a particular card, people also associate themselves with a specific planet (e.g., Mars—dominant and aggressive) or colour (e.g., red—emotional and passionate). In a sense, one may begin to define oneself in terms of the tarot and become the person whom the cards delineate. The transfer of meaning also creates meaning.

In examining the power of metaphor to define our realities and reinforce our beliefs, we must remember that there is no necessary connection between the domains from which people draw metaphors and the domains to which they apply them. There is no natural connection between commodities and time, war and health, eating and immortality, the tarot's Empress and someone's personality. These borrowings are the products of the human imagination. Many different metaphors can be applied to a specific experience, and one domain can never be the exact replica of the other. No man is really a tiger, no woman really a fox. On some level, then, metaphoric borrowings are intrinsically absurd. Yet we constantly seem to confuse one domain with another: we really do fight disease; we really win arguments. And so, as anthropologists, we need to explore by what cultural means people are convinced that by controlling one domain of experience (e.g., eating), they can really control another (e.g., greed). In the next section, we explore how symbolic actions reinforce worldviews.

Question 4.2: How Does Symbolic Action Reinforce a Particular View of the World?

Metaphors are not the only way that we mediate between our senses and the meanings we assign to experience. We also participate in activities that express a particular view of the world and that reinforce particular beliefs about the way the world works. Especially important are symbolic actions such as ritual, myth, literature, art, games, and music. Symbolic actions carry bundles of meanings that represent public displays of a culture. They are dramatic renderings and social portrayals of the meanings shared by a specific body of people. More important, symbolic actions render particular beliefs and views of the world in a way that makes them seem correct and proper. A closer look at the Kwakwaka'wakw Hamatsa dance provides a good example of how ritual portrays, reinforces, and provides evidence for a particular view of the world. In addition to rituals, popular stories and myths—such as those about zombies and vampires in contemporary North America—are embedded with meanings that are closely intertwined with a particular worldview. Stories about zombies alone are not likely to convince anyone that the world works in the way it is portrayed in the stories. Instead, the meanings that characterize a culture are repeated again and again in other symbolic actions. Objects of material culture can also take on symbolic meanings, and their use and circulation may become a form of symbolic action, as we see at the end of this section with the example of personal protective face masks.

The Kwakwaka'wakw Hamatsa Dance

The Kwakwaka'wakw view of the world, as we noted previously, rests on the metaphor of hunger and is graphically displayed in their language, myth, art, and ritual. One of the most important Kwakwaka'wakw rituals is the Cannibal Dance.

The Cannibal Dance is a four-day spectacle that serves as the highlight of the Kwakwaka'wakw Winter Ceremonial, a period of celebration and ritual observance in which all worldly activities cease. It is a time when the spiritual world of the Kwakwaka'wakw, filled with powerful beings and animal spirits, intersects with the real world. The dance varies in some detail from group to group, but in all, it is the focal point of a youth's initiation into the Cannibal Society, a group responsible for performing certain rituals. In the ceremony, the initiate plays the role of the cannibal dancer, or *hamatsa*. Members of the Cannibal Society and others gather in a ceremonial house to call back the cannibal to the human world from his sojourn in the realm of Man Eater, one of the most important of the supernatural beings in the Kwakwaka'wakw pantheon of spirits.

At the beginning of the ceremony, the *hamatsa* is believed to be in the woods frantically searching for human flesh to devour. Some early ethnographic accounts of the dance report that he would actually eat human mummified remains.

Meanwhile, members of the Cannibal Society gather around a fire in the ceremonial house to sing and recite prayers to entice the *hamatsa* into the house, periodically sending out men to see if he is approaching the village. Finally, the prayers and calls of the Cannibal Society attract the *hamatsa*, who arrives, dressed in branches of the hemlock tree, pushing aside roof boards and jumping down among the celebrants. Jumping through the roof is supposed to symbolize descent from the spirit world above to the world of the living below. In a seeming frenzy, the *hamatsa* runs around the fire and then into an adjacent room, leaving behind only the sacred hemlock branches he had worn. During the four days of the ceremony, the celebrants try by various means to entice him back into the house and, in effect, tame and socialize him, convincing him to forsake his craving for human flesh and accept normal food. In one part of the ceremony, the *hamatsa* flees the house and a member of the Cannibal Society is sent as the bait to attract him. The *hamatsa* rushes upon him, seizes his arm, and bites it. Each time he bites someone, he dashes into a secret room and vomits, an act that is repeated various times during the ceremony.

During pauses, members of the audience exchange gifts. Later, the *hamatsa* appears naked and is given clothes, but he flees again. At another point a woman who serves as a co-initiate appears naked, carrying mummified remains. She dances backward, trying to entice the *hamatsa* to enter the house, but she fails. Finally, the group succeeds in subduing the *hamatsa* by bathing him in the smoke of cedar bark that has been soaked in menstrual blood. After the conclusion of the public part of the Cannibal Dance, the initiate and a few members of the Cannibal Society go to another house and eat a normal meal, the final symbol that the *hamatsa* has been tamed.

Ritual can be viewed as a symbolic representation of reality. In another sense, ritual presents participants with solutions to real problems, in the same way that symbolic representations suggest real solutions. For the Kwakwaka'wakw, the *hamatsa* is the ultimate projection of the power of hunger, and his desire for human flesh is a manifestation of the forces that can destroy society. The participants in the ritual, by symbolically taming the hunger of the *hamatsa*, are asserting their moral responsibility to control greed and conflict. The ritual is the acting out of the group's successful efforts to overcome forces that threaten their society. Here is how Walens (1981, 162) puts it:

> *The hamatsa's hunger is fearsome; but it is the same hunger felt by every human, and thus every human has the power to control it. Ultimately the hamatsa and the bestial ferocity he embodies can be conquered ... The winter ceremonials prove that no matter how terrible the power of hunger, no matter how many fearsome guises it assumes, no matter how many masks it wears, and no matter how many voices it speaks with, morality will be the ultimate victor. So long as humans have the knowledge to use food correctly, they need never fear hunger nor its awful accompaniment, death.*

The Cannibal Dance also contains a powerful message about socialization. Children, like the *hamatsa*, come from the spirit world and enter the physical world naked. Like the *hamatsa*, children have a female assistant, their mother, who must feed and socialize them. Children come into the world hungry, threatening to devour their parents' wealth. Thus, in the Kwakwaka'wakw view of things, all humans are cannibals who must be socialized and tamed. Through swaddling, ritual fasting, denial of food, and other actions, parents transform their children from cannibals into moral human beings. Through ritual enactment, the Kwakwaka'wakw have made their symbols real.

Rituals, like this one, or like those enacted in thousands of mosques, churches, temples, and synagogues across North America, are special occasions that not only involve the enactment of key metaphors but also serve as special events set aside from everyday existence. Such events draw participants into an emotional involvement with the metaphors. Rituals really do produce special feelings; people are carried away with the symbolism, the music, and the social communion with others, and it is easy in this situation to come to believe that it is not the ritual that produces these feelings, but the forces or powers that the ritual is believed to summon or embrace.

BEYOND THE BOOK 4.2

Think/Pair/Share: The Hamatsa Dance may seem "exotic," but rituals are a key part of more familiar world religions as well (prayer is one example). Rituals can also be secular (graduation ceremonies, for instance). Some rituals can be both or either (weddings).

1. **Think** of a ritual that you have participated in and that was meaningful to you. Take a few minutes to write down a description of the ritual. What are some of the symbolic aspects of the ritual? What meanings are produced through the use of symbolism, and how? How do you feel when you practise it? What is its significance to your belief system?
2. **Pair** with a partner. Compare what you've written about. If there are aspects of your partner's ritual that you do not understand, or symbolic meanings that are not obvious to you, ask them to try to explain further.
3. **Share** your findings with the class. What were some of the challenges you faced in trying to unpack the unspoken symbolic aspects of your ritual, and to explain them to someone less familiar with them?

Zombies Are "Good to Think With"

Contemporary witchcraft and magic draw heavily from myth and literature for their language, symbols, and metaphors. When anthropologists speak of myth, they are not referring to stories that are untrue. Myths, like histories, are accounts that explain the past from a particular point of view. Luhrmann reports that many of the magicians she came to know were first attracted to their beliefs when they read J.R.R. Tolkien's *Lord of the Rings*, or Ursula LeGuin's Earthsea Trilogy, or Marion Zimmer Bradley's *Mists of Avalon*. The themes of many of these books, and of contemporary witchcraft and magic in general, are contained in North American popular culture. These books and movies contain **key scenarios**, stories, or myths that, like ritual, portray certain values and beliefs. In the same sense that people act out and communicate their view of the world through ritual and come to learn how to feel in that world, they can be said to act out the scenarios contained in their myths and histories.

Claude Lévi-Strauss (1964), a key scholar of myth and meaning, coined the phrase "good to think with" to refer to the way that humans use aspects of the material world as a reservoir of metaphorical and symbolic meanings. Zombies may not be part of the material world as we know it, but zombie stories and myths are certainly good to think with. The proliferation of zombie movies, books, television shows, and video games in the 2010s in North America suggests that the "zombie apocalypse" genre contains key scenarios that embody how we think about our world today.

What is it about zombies that we find so compelling, and why now? Zombies, unlike their popular undead cousins, vampires, are barely recognizably human. Zombies are mindless wanderers; zombies are tireless; and zombies are almost uncontrollably contagious—turning loved ones against one another in an instant, creating a pandemic, producing hordes of relentless consumers with insatiable, never-ending appetites.

Anthropologists Jean and John Comaroff suggest that contemporary zombie stories have much to do with "the implosion of neoliberal capitalism at the end of the twentieth century" (2009, 451).

key scenarios
Dominant stories or myths that portray the values and beliefs of a specific society.

The Comaroffs were interested in the proliferation of zombie stories in late twentieth-century South Africa, but their insights are applicable to the North American case as well. Stories of a zombie apocalypse tap into our fears of what they call "millennial capitalism": zombies, like North Americans, consume relentlessly (think of shopping malls during the holidays), and zombies "work" without ceasing and for little reward (like "ideal" offshore workers under global capitalism). Furthermore, with rare exceptions, zombies do not possess a sense of consciousness and thus lack critical thinking abilities. This characteristic mirrors the oftentimes voracious and uncontrolled consumption habits of contemporary shoppers, with their seemingly "senseless" desire to possess particular brands of clothing or other commodities.

There is a rising pop-culture interest in zombie pandemics, which are modelled after diseases such as the avian flu, Ebola, and more recently COVID-19. These diseases make intimate contact with and global flows of people and goods dangerous, even deadly. Zombie stories are thus linked with contemporary fears of the mobile "other" and function as a commentary on phenomena such as immigration, which is frequently blamed for the spread of disease and other social ills. Zombie stories are a metaphorical exploration of our fears and desires in today's global, capitalist economy.

Pictorial Press Ltd/ Alamy Stock Photo

How might we explain the contemporary popularity of zombie and vampire myths and stories?

BEYOND THE BOOK 4.3

1. What skills are most valuable in the wake of an imagined zombie apocalypse? In zombie myths, who becomes the hero, and who is zombie fodder? What does this suggest about our anxieties related to our contemporary ways of making a living in North America?
2. The vampire genre is as popular, if not more so, than myths and stories about zombies. Why do you think this is the case? What do contemporary vampires tell us about ourselves?

The Meaning of Face Masks during a Global Health Pandemic

Human cultures also imbue objects with symbolic meaning, and objects often play a key role in our rituals and stories. Understanding the ways that objects can take on symbolic meanings regardless of their material characteristics can help us make sense of behaviours and practices that might otherwise seem nonsensical, even irrational. Take, for instance, the personal protective face mask. According to medical anthropologist Gideon Lasco (2020), this mundane object took on myriad new meanings in the early days of the 2020 COVID-19 pandemic. In early 2020, the overwhelming majority of COVID-19 cases were in China, and the spread of the virus was considered a "global health emergency," but not yet a pandemic, by the World Health Organization. Nonetheless, writing from the perspective of the Philippines, Lasco asked, "Why are face masks going viral"? On the day that the first case of COVID-19 was diagnosed in the Philippines, he noticed that more than half the people he saw in public were wearing personal protective masks, ranging from lightweight disposable surgical masks to N95 respirators. The latter are effective for preventing the spread of the disease by health care professionals and patients, but at the time there was little evidence that surgical masks, which, in the Philippines are an unregulated commodity, provide more than minimal protection against viruses. Although health agencies were advising against wearing face masks, people in the Philippines (and soon, throughout the world) were hoarding them. Why? According to Lasco, "people's motivation for wearing these masks goes far beyond simple considerations of medical efficacy. Cultural values, perceptions of control, social pressure, civic duty, family concerns, self-expression, beliefs about public institutions, and even politics are all wrapped up in the 'symbolic efficacy' of face masks" (Lasco 2020).

In the Philippines, the symbolic efficacy of face masks takes many forms. Many of the Filipinos Lasco asked suggested that wearing the mask gave them a sense of control, besides serving as a physical reminder of their values: "Even if doctors say it's not necessary, I will wear it anyway because my family is at stake." On a darker note, Lasco also notes that face masks are also often linked to various forms of othering: a Filipino-Chinese colleague recounted to him that when he went to a restaurant, other patrons began to discreetly put their masks on. "They think all Chinese are contagious." Wearing a face mask becomes, in such situations, and regardless of their efficacy, a "risk ritual," one that provides comfort, quells anxiety, and symbolizes solidarity in both positive and negative forms.

Photo by Ezra Acayan/Getty Images

Filipino Catholics wearing protective masks attend services at a church in February 2020 in Paranaque city.

BEYOND THE BOOK 4.4

Weddings offer a great example of the significance of symbolic objects. Most weddings, whether they are religious or secular, formal or informal, large-scale celebrations or intimate events, will have, at the very least, special clothes, special jewellery, and special certificates. The Canadian Museum of History has a vast collection of wedding-related objects that represent a wide variety of cultural backgrounds and practices. The collection can be viewed online at https://www.historymuseum.ca/cmc/exhibitions/tresors/immigration/imf0500e.html, or search online for the Canadian Museum of History and "Wedding Rituals."

Take some time to browse the collection. Which items are familiar to you? Which are not? Are these objects practical, symbolic, or some combination of both? Think about the wedding rituals you are familiar with: What types of objects are involved? What symbolic meanings are attached to them? Can you imagine a wedding in which there are no ritual objects? Why, or why not?

Question 4.3: How Does the Way We Live Affect Our Beliefs and Rituals?

In answering this question, anthropologist Marshall Sahlins wrote:

> *When we were pastoral nomads, the Lord was our Shepherd. We were his flock, and he made us lie down in green pastures ... When we were serfs and nobles, the Lord was our king. Sat regnant on the throne of heaven, His shepherd's crook now a jeweled sceptre ... Finally we are businessmen—and the Lord is our accountant. He keeps a ledger on us all, enters our good deeds in black and debits our sins in red. (1968, 96)*

Perhaps it is too easy to say, as Sahlins goes on to point out, that people create gods in their own image or, as Emile Durkheim suggested, that "God is another name for society." Nevertheless, clearly the way we live, the organization of our social, economic, and political lives, must influence what we believe, how we represent those beliefs, and how we act them out. We need to understand, also, how our beliefs and the manner in which we act them out serve to maintain and reproduce certain patterns of social, political, and economic relations.

We tend to think that our own worldviews and ways of living are "natural" and, by extension, normal. In North American society, for instance, we have been enculturated to see capitalism and its attending effects as normal. Think, for instance, about how the notion of time is affected by capitalism. As we discussed in Chapter 3, ever since the Industrial Revolution, capitalism has stressed effective time management—a productive worker is a timely and efficient worker. Time has thus come to be commodified, and to maximize productivity and profit, workers in office jobs or factories are encouraged to manage their time effectively. We value disciplined workers, and we use phrases such as "time is money." Time is also something that can be "wasted" or "saved." This commodification and valuation of time affects all areas of our lives. Think, for instance of how most of us set our daily tasks to calendrical and clock-based time, and how, with the advent of smartphones and calendar apps, we increasingly micromanage our time to achieve greater productivity.

This commodification of time affects worldviews surrounding such seemingly "natural" processes as labour and birth, and is reflected in and reinforced by contemporary birthing rituals. Robbie Davis-Floyd (2004), for instance, has explored how Western, capitalist notions of time inform American hospital births. Davis-Floyd argues that most American women's experiences of birth are informed by a "technocratic" model that stresses the need for biomedical interventions such as ultrasound, Cesarean sections, epidurals, and intravenous infusions of pitocin (a synthetic form of oxytocin used to induce or speed up the labour process). Davis-Floyd suggests that while many of these procedures are often medically necessary, such as the use of Cesarean sections in emergency situations, most are not. Pitocin, for instance, is given to the vast majority of women who experience hospital births, and its purpose is to speed up the labour process and to allow for an "efficient" and timely labour that fits neatly within the obstetricians' schedules. In addition, when women labour for long periods of time, they become tired and are more prone to be "difficult" or demanding patients. According to Davis-Floyd, these procedures, through their predictability and repetition, turn hospital birth into a ritual, one that serves to reinforce fundamental beliefs about the superiority of technology over nature. Birth as a ritual is particularly effective because it is one of a category of rituals called **rites of passage**, special kinds of rituals (discussed in further detail in Chapter 6) that marks one's transition from one social state or status to another. In this case, birth as a rite of passage marks a woman's transition to motherhood. Ultimately, such interventions are naturalized and perceived as necessary for mother and baby, but in fact, they reflect dominant Western capitalist worldviews about time and efficiency. So how we live (in this case, in a capitalist economic system where efficiency is highly valued) affects our beliefs about how we manage our bodies. To try to understand how what we believe is related to how we live, let's examine some other ways of knowing that challenge Euro-Canadians' beliefs about the world and their place in it.

Ways of Living and Ways of Knowing among the Dene Tha

In *Ways of Knowing: Experience, Knowledge, and Power among the Dene Tha* (1998), Jean-Guy Goulet writes of his own experience learning about a worldview very different from the one he acquired as a child. For the Dene Tha living in three communities in northwestern Alberta—Bushe River, Meander River, and Chateh (Figure 4.2)—learning comes

rites of passage
The term coined in 1908 by Arnold van Gennep to refer to the category of rituals that accompany changes in status, such as the transition from boyhood to manhood, living to dead, or student to graduate.

FIGURE 4.2 Dene Tha Territory

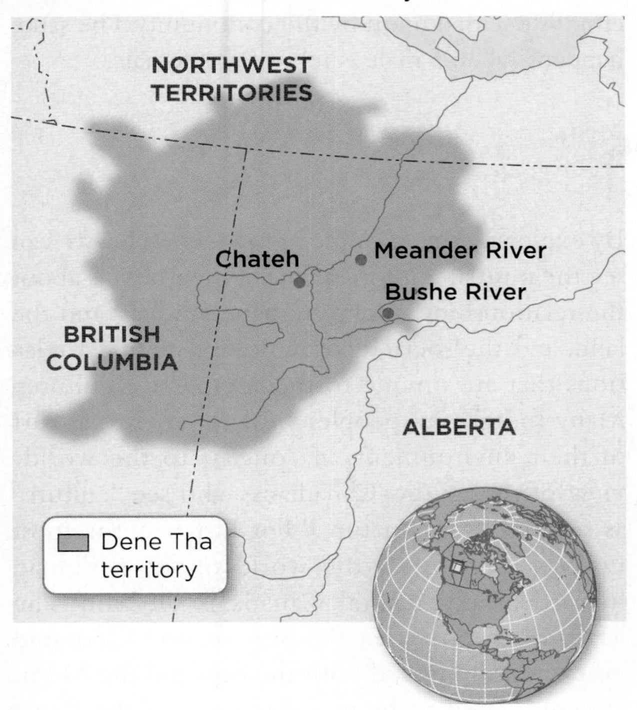

only through direct experience. In Chateh, the community where Goulet lived while he was a student of the Dene Tha, an adult cannot teach a child how to hunt or cook or perform a ritual by simply giving verbal instructions: to replace personal experience with objectified instruction is to turn knowledge into a commodity. All Dene Tha must learn by observing and by doing or imitating what they see when watching others. In the Dene Tha view, the only true knowledge is personal knowledge. While Dene Tha stories can also contain knowledge, the narrator is careful to avoid making claims about the truthfulness of the story if it is not part of his or her own personal experience.

Along with the importance of personal knowledge comes the right of every Dene Tha to personal autonomy and the responsibility to respect the autonomy of others, including non–Dene Tha. Someone who interferes with another's direct experience is viewed as infringing on the other's right to gain knowledge properly. This understanding extends to small children as well as adults. Dene Tha children are allowed to explore their world in ways that Euro-Canadian children are not. For instance, setting and enforcing a particular bedtime for a child is considered by Euro-Canadians to be a sign of good parenting, but for a Dene Tha parent, this practice is a sign of an irresponsible parent who is blocking the child's access to knowledge and personal autonomy.

Dene Tha notions of power also differ from those of Euro-Canadians. In the Dene Tha worldview, "when Dene speak of a power, they think of a powerfulness inherent in plants, animals, or other substances, which can affect human beings knowingly or unknowingly" (Goulet 1998, 60). Dene Tha distinguish between two different "lands": ndahdigeh, "our land," and echuhdigeh, "the other land." Plants and animals in the bush are manifestations of the other land in our land; therefore, Dene Tha must be very respectful of all forms of life, human and nonhuman.

Sometimes "our land" interacts directly with "the other land." An example given by Goulet is that of a young man's violent death, which produced an angry storm, which was said to be the result of the man's feelings. In another example, when the animal helpers of a Dene Tha healer felt let down because a patient did not bring proper gifts, the village was covered with low clouds and drizzle for three days.

Dene Tha communicate with the other world through dreams and gain important knowledge about healing using plants and animal parts. If a piece of bark is taken from a tree or a plant is taken from the ground for its roots, a small portion of tobacco is placed at the bottom of the tree or in the ground at the spot the plant once grew.

In addition to providing meat for humans, animals are important because of their ability to share power with humans. This relationship of sharing goes back to a time when animals and humans were not as separated as they are now and when they married, spoke the same language, and lived together. Although this is no longer the case, the Dene Tha still view animals as superior to humans and believe that animals give to humans only the powers they no longer need.

© Arctic Photo/All Canada Photos

A Dene hunter goes out to check his traplines.

Dreaming is the way that the Dene Tha gain powerful knowledge. When elders travel to the other land, they sometimes return with songs, which are then used in healing ceremonies. Dreams are also the process by which one can see the future and even take steps to avoid misfortune. Dreams may have a very pragmatic use, as when a Dene Tha hunter learns where to find animals that are willing to give themselves to humans. For the Dene Tha, the mind, or soul, is where one's will, memory, and intellect reside. One's mind receives a power to heal or to cause harm from an animal helper. Although one's body may die, one's mind can choose to return to "this land" and become born again in a new body. In other words, human bodies are only temporary, but human minds are permanent.

Dreaming is understood by the Dene Tha as a journey in which the soul leaves the body and travels to other places in this land or spends time with relatives in the other land. If, however, the soul stays away too long, the body may become ill and a healer may be required to bring the soul back. If the soul doesn't return, the body will eventually die. For the Dene Tha in Chateh, some people (but not all) choose to come back to Earth once they die. Reincarnation in Chateh is a process whereby the spirit of a relative enters a woman's body to be born again. If the spirit was a female in her previous life and is born again as a male, family members may call the boy by female kinship terms such as "my sister" or "my daughter," once the former identity of the child is decided upon by the community. The same happens when a male is reborn as a female.

Nature, "Ways of Knowing," and Indigeneity

By exploring the example of the Dene Tha, we can see the mutual reinforcement of their beliefs about the relationships among humans, animals, and the land, and the social, economic, and political relations that are unique to their respective cultures. Many Indigenous peoples view themselves as part of their environment, in contrast to the worldview of most Euro-Canadians, who see "culture" as separate from "nature." For instance, the most important being in the world of the Mi'kmaq in eastern and coastal Canada is the Sun. The Mi'kmaq believe that the Sun created Earth and everything on it, and both the Sun and the Moon are considered to be manifestations of the Great Spirit. When a person dies, that person's soul climbs the Milky Way to the land of the dead. Another prominent being of the Mi'kmaq spirit world is Glooscap, who was once on Earth and who created the natural features of the Mi'kmaq land. Glooscap also taught the Mi'kmaq how to make tools and weapons, and before he left Earth to become the assistant of the Great Spirit, he predicted the arrival of the Europeans.

In *Do Glaciers Listen?* (2005), Julie Cruikshank explains how Indigenous women who lived inland from the Saint Elias Mountains of Yukon told her stories in which glaciers had human-like qualities and interacted with humans: "The women I know portrayed glaciers as conscious and responsive to humans. Glaciers, they insisted, are wilful, sometimes capricious, easily excited by human intemperance but equally placated by quick-witted human responses" (2005, 8). In this worldview, the behaviour of humans could have grave consequences for the behaviour of the "natural" world. Cruikshank was told by local women that glaciers had a keen sense of smell and disliked the odour of cooking fat. These women warned against cooking bacon for breakfast when near a glacier because the glacier might react by causing a surge that produced ear-splitting sounds.

Indigenous peoples in other parts of the world have strikingly similar beliefs about their physical environments. For instance, the worldview of the Maori of New Zealand contains an origin story in which Sky Father and Mother Earth were joined together and produced many children. These children became the spirit beings of the sea, the winds, forests, plants, animals, and humans. Thus, Maori do not see themselves as separate from the physical world. As Manuka Henare (2001, 202) explains: "the resources of the earth do not belong to humankind; rather humans belong to the earth. While humans as well as animals, birds, fish, and trees can harvest the bounty of Mother Earth's resources, they do not own them."

These "ways of knowing" about the world and one's place in it differ greatly from the worldviews of Euro-North Americans, who believe that humans are superior to all other entities in the world and that everything in the world belongs to humans. The Euro-North American notion of human ownership of Earth's resources creates a very different way of interacting with the physical environment and justifies the ways of those who take resources from Earth—minerals, trees, animals, plants—without acknowledging any reciprocal responsibility.

BEYOND THE BOOK 4.5

1. Take a few minutes to think about your own beliefs about the relationship between the cultural life of humans and the natural world. Are they connected to a particular religious or secular worldview (or both)? How do these beliefs reinforce the life you live (and vice versa)?
2. If you believed that all the entities of the world are somehow connected and have the same rights as humans, how would this belief change the way you think about resources, such as the foods you eat, the gas you put in your car, and the electricity and water you use in your house, as well as the disposal of your garbage?

Coping with the Unknown: Modernity and Witchcraft in Cameroon

The examples in the previous section show the significance, for many Indigenous peoples, of knowing the world through first-hand knowledge and experience. However, not all humans in the world are able at all times to "know," through direct observation, what is happening around them. For instance, the major and unprecedented political, economic, and social transformations wrought by colonialism and postcolonialism have often happened rapidly and at the behest of a relatively small but powerful elite. Local people may not be able to investigate directly because they lack access to the information they would need to do that. Here, we look at an example from Cameroon, where one way that people cope with not knowing is by using witchcraft to explain the conflicts wrought by modernity and state formation.

Peter Geschiere, who has been doing fieldwork among the Maka people in southeastern Cameroon (Figure 4.3) since 1971, found that witchcraft had not decreased with modernization, as had been forecast by development experts. Quite

FIGURE 4.3 Cameroon

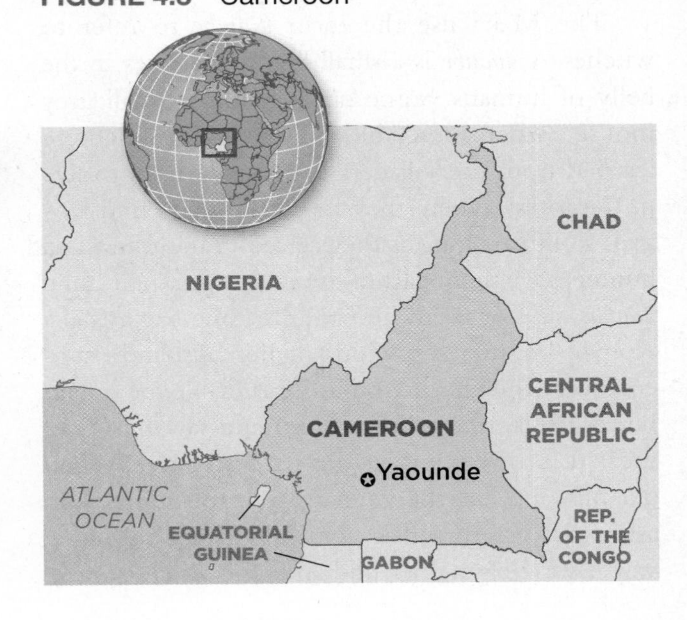

the opposite: Cameroon newspaper reports about the "nightly escapades" of witches had multiplied since Cameroon became an independent state in 1960. In *The Modernity of Witchcraft: Politics and the Occult in Postcolonial Africa* (1997), Geschiere asked himself why. One of his Maka companions repeated a saying he had heard from a Dutch missionary: "Where there is electric light, witchcraft will disappear" (1997, 2). Yet this man had been threatened by the occult in towns that were well lit by electricity.

It is perhaps the ambiguity of witchcraft in Cameroon that enhances its connection to politics. In the Maka worldview, all events are the result of human action. Nothing happens simply by chance. If someone becomes ill, meets with misfortune, becomes wealthy, or gains a prominent position in politics, the cause is witchcraft. Witchcraft is the process whereby inequalities are both created and overcome; indeed, the new elites are believed to have gained their wealth through witchcraft. To gain access to wealth and power, a politician must have connections to the occult.

This ambiguity extends into the realm of kinship. Witchcraft is said to be "the dark side of kinship." The Maka believe that one's kin are the only people one can really trust, yet it is kin who trade the hearts of their kin for the favours of witches.

The Maka use the term *djambe* to refer to witches. A *djambe* is a small being that lives in the belly of humans. Some say it is like a small grey mouse; others describe it as a crab. Geschiere learned from the villagers that *djambe* used to live in the forest, where they helped hunters find animals to kill. As long as they stayed in the forest and hunters gave them part of the meat from their hunt, *djambe* did not harm humans. But one day a Maka woman became suspicious of her husband's success every time he went hunting. Unable to contain her curiosity, she followed him and saw him feed meat to a tiny being at the base of a tree. When her husband left, the woman went to the tree and asked the creature if it would help her the same way it was helping her husband. The *djambe* agreed, and the woman took it home. Once in the village, the *djambe* demanded that the woman feed it meat; when no more animal meat was to be found, it demanded that she feed it her children. Now that the *djambe* was in the village, it became the source of both fortune and misfortune.

In principle, all humans have a *djambe* in their belly, and as long as it is not activated, it does neither good nor harm. But the Maka say that no one can function without some connection with the occult. The way to activate one's *djambe* is to make it "go out" of one's body so that its flies around and meets other *djambe*. To become a witch and be part of the nocturnal feasts held in the forest, one must sacrifice the hearts of one's parents, because witches have an insatiable appetite for human flesh. Also, a highly developed *djambe* has a second pair of eyes and can see things not visible to those who are not witches.

In an effort to control witchcraft, the state justice system now involves itself in accusations of witchcraft. Unlike during colonial times, the state is anxious to prosecute witches to show its citizens that it is legitimate. However, because many of those who are employed by the state owe their good fortune to witchcraft, such prosecutions are paradoxical. As an example of how deep beliefs in witchcraft run in Cameroon, Geschiere tells of a civil servant, himself suspected of having connections to the occult because of his position, who accused villagers of using witchcraft to sabotage government projects.

Witchcraft in Cameroon exemplifies some of the tensions that have accompanied the end of colonialism and the incorporation of newly independent countries into the global capitalist market as individual entities. Beliefs about witchcraft help the Maka explain, in terms they understand, the changes that have taken place now that their own people are filling state positions and capitalism is creating previously inconceivable wealth. The existing worldview explains the sudden affluence of the elite that coexists with the poverty of the majority. This process of evaluating the unknowable by using what is knowable (witchcraft, in this case) produces explanations that make sense in local terms, those they may seem totally illogical to outsiders who do not share their beliefs. The power of an anthropological perspective is that it provides us with methodological and theoretical tools with which to contextualize and understand worldviews other than our own.

Question 4.4: What Happened to Local Worldviews When They Were Confronted by the Religions of the European Colonizers?

As we saw above in the example of witchcraft in postcolonial Cameroon, the new political, social, and economic conditions that accompanied the introduction of new forms of inequality implicitly challenged or unsettled local ways of knowing the world. It is also the case that, in most colonial encounters, some form of Christianity challenged the local worldviews of the colonized or Indigenous peoples with regard to their spiritual beliefs. Christianity, with its close links to capitalism, was part of the bedrock of colonial rule. Many early anthropologists assumed that Christianity was such a powerful force that it destroyed all forms of indigenous worldviews. Recent research has shown that this is not always the outcome, which in turn raises a question: How do Indigenous or colonized peoples fit religions such as Christianity into their existing worldviews?

The Dene Tha and Christianity

Jean-Guy Goulet tells us that the Dene Tha inhabit a social context that presents many challenges to their worldview. Western institutions, such as "the school, the police station, the nursing station, and the church" (1998, 193), expect the Dene Tha to absorb the worldview of Euro-Canadians. The Dene Tha do accept some Euro-Canadian ways and incorporate them in a complementary fashion into Dene Tha ways of knowing.

Before the arrival of Europeans, many indigenous cultures of the Americas practised variants of **shamanism**, and shamanism continues to be an important aspect of traditional spirituality. Shamanism is the oldest spiritual belief system in the world. It has many variants, but in general terms, it is a belief system in which spiritual practitioners, or "shamans," enter into an altered state of consciousness to seek guidance from spiritual beings. They work on behalf of an individual or on behalf of an entire community. In shamanic societies, spirituality and healing are closely intertwined, and the shaman is seen as having specialized knowledge of medicine, health, and healing. He or she can thus diagnose illness and help cure a patient.

With the advent of European colonialism in Canada, however, many Indigenous peoples were converted to Christianity. But they did not completely abandon their traditional shamanic beliefs. Indeed, many contemporary Indigenous societies are a syncretism, or blend, of shamanic and Christian elements.

For instance, most Dene Tha say they are Christians, usually Roman Catholic or Anglican, but they still abide by their original worldview as well. It is not so much that missionaries and priests convinced them to reject their own view of the world; rather, the Dene Tha determined that some aspects of Christianity made sense when evaluated by a Dene Tha worldview. For instance, the Christian figure of Jesus Christ is often incorporated into the category of those who now live in *echuhdigeh*, or "the other land," and who communicate with the living through dreams. The crucifix (or cross) has been accepted, and some shamans use it as a personal symbol, in conjunction with the drum.

The Dene Tha assign an especially powerful role to the Roman Catholic rosary. A young Dene Tha told Goulet that "they were encouraged by

shamanism
Refers to a spiritual belief system whereby spiritual practitioners called "shamans" enter into an altered state of consciousness to seek guidance from spiritual forces.

the Elders to carry a rosary on their person as a protection against other Dene who might attack them with their power" (1998, 204). The rosary has a different meaning when used by the Dene Tha, who interpret it according to their own worldview, as a prophet explained to Patrick Moore and Angela Wheelock (1990, 62): "Each large bead represents a place where the Son of God came to earth. He walked along the earth and then went back to heaven. He did this many times, and each of the small beads represents his tracks on earth."

When the rosary is used in the Prophet Dance in conjunction with the dominant symbols of the circle and the path, it takes on the meaning of that ritual. In the Prophet Dance the circle represents social and cosmic order; it takes its shape from important concepts and objects in Dene Tha life: the Sun, Earth, and the drum. Participants dance together in a circle around a fire in three or four rows. The path represents the journey between "our land" and "the other land," and the dancing performed during the Prophet Dance is believed to influence the quality of the journey the dancers will take when they die. The Dene Tha believe that when they dance, *Ndawota* (God) watches their feet and measures their steps; the more steps a dancer takes during the Prophet Dance, the fewer he or she will have to take on the journey to heaven. The same belief applies to the rosary: each bead of the rosary represents one prayer and one step on the way to heaven.

At the same time, the Dene Tha reject some of the most fundamental Christian beliefs. One of the most foreign to the Dene Tha is the belief in original sin and in the Christian "hell," with its implication that one is never forgiven for some sins and that punishment continues into eternity. The introduction of Christianity into the cultural world of the Dene Tha did not result in the wholesale abandonment of their existing beliefs and worldview; rather, they successfully incorporated certain aspects (but not others) of a Christian worldview into their own belief system.

All reinterpretations of Christianity depend on local histories and local experiences. As discussed in the next example, Jamaicans living in poverty saw the European version of Christianity as intimately linked to colonialism and to the oppressiveness of the capitalist world system. This perspective was then reflected in the reinterpretation of the Christian Messiah in a new religion, Rastafarianism.

Rastafari in Jamaica

In 1834, slavery officially ended in the British West Indies, although there would be four more years of a bondage system known as *apprenticeship* before ex-slaves were able to leave the plantations. In places such as Jamaica, many of the newly freed people moved away from the sugar estates and began new lives on small plots of land where they could grow their own food and sell the surplus at community markets. In the early 1900s, however, the United Fruit Company moved into Jamaica to start new plantations, employing the small-scale farmers as wage labourers. Within a few years, United Fruit was undercutting the prices of the surplus foods the small-scale farmers had been selling. By the mid-1930s, so many of the rural farmers had lost their lands that a vast pool of landless, unemployed people, numbering in the hundreds of thousands, had left the countryside and moved to the city of Kingston in search of jobs. When they arrived and found that the jobs were not there, they settled on the fringes of the city and tried to survive.

In 1930, Ras Tafari was crowned emperor Haile Selassie I of Ethiopia. The Jamaicans living in extreme poverty on the fringes of Kingston followed the crowning of a black king with great enthusiasm, for this event provided a clear sign that black men were not always destined to be at the bottom of society. During the coronation ceremonies, Ras Tafari was proclaimed King of Kings and Lion of Judah. For the poor living in Kingston, Haile Selassie was either the Messiah or the living God and a symbol of hope and salvation for all black people. His coronation fulfilled the biblical prophecy that a saviour would come for them and lead them back to Africa.

As Rastafari became organized, Rasta leaders founded communities in and around Kingston that emphasized what they understood to be traditional African values: cooperative work efforts, respect for life, and the unity of all peoples of African descent. Through their belief in their messiah, Rasta returned to what they saw as their African beliefs and rejected the values of capitalist society and the capitalist market. By the time Selassie was overthrown in 1974, the Rasta belief system was so widespread that the loss of the messiah had little effect. Rasta continued to reject the capitalist world, which they called Babylon, and to create their own understanding of the Christian Bible, in which they were heroes. Their present oppression (downpression in Rasta terms) comes from the United States, which has taken over the role as the centre of Babylon from Britain. The Rasta believe that eventually Jah (God) will truly set them free (Henry 1997).

The Rastafari response to colonial and postcolonial forms of domination resonated with oppressed peoples around the globe. The continued global popularity of the reggae music of Bob Marley is evidence of this resonance. As discussed in Section 4.2, key scenarios, such as rituals, share and perpetuate values and beliefs; popular music often embodies these key scenarios. Bob Marley's extensive discography has been aptly named "Songs of Freedom," and his music remains both relevant and incredibly popular four decades after his death (in 1981). According to Jason Toynbee (2007), Marley can be considered the "herald of a post-colonial world." Toynbee points out that Marley is #12 on Forbes magazine's "Top-Earning Dead Celebrities List" (Kafka 2005), with tens of millions worth of albums sold, and that his music is most popular in the global South, where "most people listen to him on cassettes, generally copied and distributed outside of official music industry channels. No statistics are available for this activity. Nor is there any way to quantify the circulation of images of Marley in the form of posters and drawings, or the spread of stories about him" (2007, 8).

Bob Marley.

How can we explain Marley's ongoing global superstar status? Toynbee (2007, 27–28) elaborates:

> *Marley was among a handful of musicians who challenged the unwritten rules (the "mental slavery") that kept the great masses of the world in bondage to the rich and powerful. As he sang it:*
>
> *Today they say that we are free*
> *Only to be chained in poverty*
> *Good god, I think it's all illiteracy*
> *It's only a machine that makes money*
> *—Bob Marley, "Slave Driver"**
>
> *That these lines sound compelling and poignant is a testament to Marley's extraordinary creative powers ... Marley combined an appreciation of the embeddedness of oppressive social relations with affirmation of the autonomy of human beings, and of their facility to "act back" upon the world in order to change it.*

The case of Bob Marley's reggae, and of Rastafari more generally, provides a powerful example of the often unexpected ways in which people incorporate introduced beliefs into existing belief systems, and of the ways in which one's living conditions shape and are shaped by one's worldview. Rather than ask, as some early anthropologists did, how European religions have destroyed the cultures of local people who have lived through colonization, anthropologists are now asking how colonized peoples have interpreted the colonial religion in the context of their own worldviews. Although the arrival of colonial religions may change local people's worldviews, it is rarely the case that the beliefs and values that have worked to explain the ways of the world for a long time are readily or completely discarded.

Question 4.5: How Can People Reorder Their View of the World If It Becomes Unsatisfactory?

The meanings that people assign to their experiences do not change easily. We very much take for granted that the view of the world created by the interaction of our own experiences of the world with the mediums of language, symbolic actions, humour, and collective judgments is the right view. But beliefs do change. Changes in the meanings that people assign to their experiences are often triggered by social upheavals, during which old ways of looking at the world, for whatever reason, are no longer satisfactory. Such social upheavals, and the resulting unease, are often the direct result of colonial encounters and subsequent inequalities. If sufficient numbers of people share this unease, they may together try to change both their view of the world and the organization of society. This may lead to a new or revised belief system that promises to return the society to a real or mythical previous state, or that offers a new vision of the world that promises to relieve oppression or frustration. During such social upheavals, the usual explanations for events are unsatisfactory, traditional solutions to problems no longer work, and rituals may be abandoned. Doubts generated by social upheaval are replaced with new certainties born of religious fervour or conversion. Here are two key ways in which this happens: through revitalization movements, or through syncretism. We discuss each of these below by exploring the ethnographic examples of the Ghost Dance and Haitian Vodou, respectively.

Revitalization Movements: Wovoka and the Ghost Dance

Anthropologist Anthony F.C. Wallace (1966) suggests the term "**revitalization movements**" for efforts by people to construct a more satisfying culture. The escalating political, economic, and cultural colonization of Indigenous peoples over the past few centuries has inspired a multitude of revitalization movements. These movements promise liberation from oppression by foreign powers and tend to incorporate and rework elements of precolonial culture. Wallace developed his theory in the context of North American Indigenous peoples, but his framework has since been applied to colonial contexts around the world. It enriches our understanding of the effects of colonial contact on existing belief systems.

As settlers moved west in the nineteenth century, they came into contact with hundreds of Native American groups. As more and more people migrated west, conflicts over land triggered wars between these groups and US military forces. The Indian Wars lasted from about 1850 to 1880. During those decades, the US government negotiated and signed treaties with Native American groups, promising financial compensation as well as food and other provisions and guaranteeing their rights over areas of land.

However, as more white settlers moved onto Native American territories, the US government insisted on renegotiating treaties when land that had been given to Native American groups was desired by settlers. For example, the Sioux were given rights to the Black Hills of South Dakota, but after gold

revitalization movements
The term suggested by Anthony F.C. Wallace for attempts by a people to construct a more satisfying culture.

was discovered there, the government unilaterally renegotiated the treaties, reducing the land of the Sioux by more than half in 1889. (In this case, however, the courts later ruled that the government's act was illegal and that the Sioux never ceded their rights.) In addition, the buffalo were virtually exterminated, sometimes in a conscious effort by the US military to destroy the economic basis of Native American society.

As a result of the Indian Wars, treaty negotiations, government deceit, and the influx of new settlers, Native American groups were restricted to reservations, made dependent on government rations, and denied traditional pursuits such as hunting and horse raiding. Government deliveries of food and provisions were often late or did not arrive at all, and diseases brought to the New World by European settlers, to which the Indigenous population had little resistance, decimated the population. Children were taken to boarding schools away from the reservations and prohibited from speaking their first languages. Government agents, often at the insistence of Christian missionaries, banned traditional ceremonies and rituals. In brief, the social fabric of Indigenous society was virtually destroyed. Those traditional things that help filter experience—language, ritual, and the ability of groups to collectively sustain particular views of the world—virtually vanished.

Revitalization movements usually receive their impetus from a prophet who claims to have received a vision or dream about a new way of viewing the world or a set of moral injunctions governing people's lives. The major prophet for the Ghost Dance was a Paiute named Wovoka. In 1889, Wovoka had a vision in which he was taken up to heaven, where he saw God and all the people who had died performing their traditional games and activities. God told him he must go back and tell people to live in peace with whites and with one another. Wovoka was also given instructions for a ritual dance. He was told that if this dance were performed for five days and nights, people would be reunited with their friends and relatives in the other world.

Nevada Historical Society

Wovoka (Jack Wilson), Northern Paiute prophet of the Ghost Dance, Yerington, Nevada, ca. 1915.

Converts to Wovoka's message spread the word from Nevada to Native American groups throughout the United States and Canada. Wovoka's message was sometimes reinterpreted as it spread from one Indigenous group to another. In some versions, the world would be destroyed and only the Native Americans brought back to life; in others, Euro-Americans and Native Americans would live together in harmony. In some versions, the buffalo would return. In some cases, a specific date was set for the millennium (4 July was one date; another was the time of a major traditional ceremony). In some versions, Wovoka was even said to be the son of God. Whatever the interpretation, the Ghost Dance, as it came to be called, was adopted by many groups that were seeking a revival of a way of life disrupted by Euro-American expansion.

Among the groups that enthusiastically adopted the Ghost Dance were the Sioux. They had sent emissaries in 1889 to visit Wovoka; those emissaries had returned with descriptions of his vision and power. One account of the delegate's report is contained in James Mooney's *The Ghost Dance Religion and the Sioux Outbreak of 1890* (1897). An anthropologist working for the Bureau of American Ethnology, Mooney travelled around the country interviewing key figures, including Wovoka, and collecting first-hand accounts of the dance from Euro-Americans and Native Americans. Here is his description of the report of the Sioux delegates:

> *They were gone all winter, and their return in the spring of 1890 aroused an intense excitement among the Sioux, who had been anxiously awaiting their report. All the delegates agreed that there was a man near the base of the Sierras who said that he was the son of God, who had once been killed by the whites, and who bore on his body the scars of the crucifixion. He had now returned to punish the whites for their wickedness, especially for their injustice toward the Indians. With the coming of the next spring (1891) he would wipe the whites from the face of the earth, and would then resurrect all the dead Indians, bring back the buffalo and other game, and restore the supremacy of the aboriginal race. (Mooney [1897]2011, 64)*

Based on these messages, the Sioux began to dance in October 1890, but for them, the Ghost Dance turned into a tragic reminder of Euro-American oppression. Frightened that the dance might turn into open rebellion, the Indian agent on one of the Sioux reservations called in the military. Some of the Sioux fled the reservation, chased by the Seventh Cavalry, General George Custer's group, which had been decimated by a combined Native American army at Little Bighorn in 1876. After being promised a safe return to their reservation, the fleeing Sioux surrendered their arms at a place called Wounded Knee, where they were surrounded by the Seventh Cavalry equipped with Gatling guns. As soldiers rummaged through the Sioux shelters searching for guns, someone fired a shot and the army opened fire, killing hundreds of men, women, and children.

The Ghost Dance virtually ceased among the Sioux after the massacre at Wounded Knee, but it continued among other groups, each of which hoped for the return of their traditional culture. Today it represents one attempt of a people to build a new culture, a new system of meaning after the destruction of an earlier one.

Syncretism and Haitian Vodou

Another way people cope with drastic changes in their lives is by developing a different worldview. Doing so entails combining elements of a new view with those of an older one. Anthropologists use the term **syncretism** for the process by which elements of two or more worldviews are combined to produce a new way of understanding lived experience. In Haiti, Africans from many different parts of the continent were forcibly brought together by the slave trade. Having been captured inland, the Africans were taken to the coast, where they were sold to slave traders, loaded onto ships, and taken across the "Middle Passage" to a foreign land, where they were sold on to plantation owners. These Africans could not bring any of their belongings with them across the Middle Passage, but they could bring their beliefs and worldviews, stored in their memories. After they reached Haiti and were divided among individual plantations, they were unlikely to meet anyone from their own community; as a consequence, much of the initial adjustment they had to make involved learning to communicate with other slaves from other parts in Africa. Once new systems of communication had been established, Africans

syncretism
The term given to the combination of old beliefs or religions and new ones (often introduced during colonization) to create a new worldview.

could create a distinctive Caribbean culture based on their former beliefs and those of the French planters. In this totally new world it must have been immediately obvious to all African slaves that their old worldviews would not work to explain their new experiences in Haiti.

The new worldview that Africans created in Haiti, then, was a **creole** view based on their lived experiences in their new world. That world was filled with work and suffering, first as slaves and then later as peasants living in a country that today is still the poorest in the Western Hemisphere. Karen McCarthy Brown explains that Haitians created Vodou to find a way to live in conditions that to this day are among the worst in the world: "Vodou is the system they have devised to deal with the suffering that is life, a system whose purpose is to minimize pain, avoid disaster, cushion loss, and strengthen survivors and survival instincts" (1991, 10).

Although the French introduced Roman Catholicism during the colonial period, the slaves they owned worshipped their Vodou deities in secret. After the Haitian Revolution ended in 1804, free Haitians combined the two religions to produce a third that looks like Catholicism on the outside but is something quite different. Haitians believe in the Christian God, whom they call "Bondye." They believe that this god created all things and that he is supreme. But they also believe that he is a European god who has many Europeans to attend to and is therefore much too busy to bother with poor Haitians. So, instead of trying to interact with Bondye directly, Haitians use African spirits, or *lwa*, to intercede for them. These *lwa* have names that connect them to Catholic saints: the Virgin Mary is Ezili, Saint Patrick is Danbala, Saint James is Ogou, Saint Gerard is Gede, and Isidore is Azaka. But this is where the similarities end, for Haitian *lwa* are anything but saintly.

Vodou *lwa* present models for Haitian life and address issues that real Haitians face. For example, Azaka, the poor peasant farmer, teaches Haitians to remember their roots: their land and their ancestors. In the worldview of rural Haitians, land, ancestors, and spirits are all the same thing. Azake also reminds people of the importance of family, and part of what urban Vodou congregations do is provide families for those who have migrated to the cities.

As another model, Ezili represents women, and because women play various roles in Haiti, she has various manifestations. Three important Ezili manifestations are Ezili Danto, Ezili Freda, and Lasyrenn. Ezili Danto is the hard-working black single mother. She presents and works through the problems that single Haitian mothers face. Ezili Freda is the rich white woman who represents white privilege in Haiti. Freda is usually posed reclining on a sofa, dressed in beautiful clothes, covered with jewellery, and eating chocolates. This image reaffirms for Haitians the uselessness of white sensuality, because Freda does nothing except pose. Lasyrenn, often associated with the African "mammy water," is both black and white and lives just below the surface of the water, which Haitians say is "the back of the mirror." If one were to lean over a calm pool, one might catch a glimpse of Lasyrenn, but doing this is dangerous because sometimes she pulls people into the water and they disappear; some say she takes them back to Ginen (Africa). Sometimes, Lasyrenn will pull women under the water and keep them for several days, or as long as one year. When the women return, they are changed by the sacred knowledge they have learned and may become priestesses. Lasyrenn resembles the carved figureheads that slave trading ships had on their bows. This image may mean that she reminds Haitians of the traumatic Middle Passage and slavery.

Danbala, Ogue, and Gede are male *lwa* who represent oppositions in Haitian life.

Danbala is the oldest and most respected of the *lwa* and, like Saint Patrick, is associated with snakes. The difference between Saint Patrick and Danbala is that snakes are creatures that have important survival

creole
A term used commonly to refer to the formation of slave societies in the Caribbean in which elements of African and European cultures were merged, blended, or combined into something uniquely Caribbean.

skills. Snakes can curve their bodies to go over obstacles, and if a snake puts its tail in its mouth it becomes a circle with no beginning and no end. Thus, Danbala represents life, death, and rebirth in a continuous cycle. He also mediates opposites: as the symbol of the rainbow, Danbala is said to have one foot in the ocean and one in the Haitian mountains. Haitians say that Danbala is becoming angry with politics in Haiti and that he has taken his foot out of the water. People say that Haiti will now wither and die.

Ogue is a warrior who has subdivided into at least seven figures. In one of his manifestations, he is the handsome soldier riding a beautiful white horse who faces battle fearlessly. In another he is a liar and a beggar. In others he is a drunk or a coward. Ogue presents the lesson that while power may liberate, it also corrupts, as has happened to many of Haiti's leaders.

Gede is the master of the cemetery and is said to have one foot in life and one foot in death. Gede is a trickster, always making jokes, and he teaches that one way to overcome misfortune is to make fun of it. It should come as no surprise, then, that Gede is an important healer.

Haitian Vodou, then, is not just a set of exotic rituals, as it is often portrayed in the media. It is a worldview that helps Haitians cope with a life of poverty and hardship. Furthermore, as Brown argues, Haitian Vodou is a system of healing that applies to a variety of areas in the lives of its followers, including troubled social relationships, physical illness, and the pain of the past in which families were torn apart by slavery.

Question 4.6: How Can Secular and Religious Worldviews Coexist?

The Rise of Western Secularism

Increasingly, many Western industrialized nations, including Canada, are reporting higher rates of **atheism** and a preference for **secularism**, or the

atheism
Refers to a lack of belief in supernatural forces or beings.

secularism
Refers to the separation of political and economic realms of society from religion or spirituality.

Mama Lola, the subject of Karen McCarthy Brown's (2001) ethnography, *Mama Lola: A Vodou Priestess in Brooklyn.*

separation of spirituality/religion from government, economics, and politics. Atheists do not identify as "religious," and most do not believe in the existence of deities or spiritual forces. In 2011, the Canadian census reported that 23.9 percent of Canadians declared that they did not have any religious affiliation. This statistic raises interesting questions about the future of religion in a multicultural society like Canada. Increasingly, many influential scientists and thinkers, like best-selling author and evolutionary biologist Richard Dawkins (2006), are labelling religion a "delusion" and a source of unnecessary violence and cultural conflict.

Atheism and secularism, like religious beliefs, constitute worldviews. Moreover, like the other worldviews we have discussed throughout this chapter, Western secularism developed in a particular political, economic, and indeed religious context. According to Talal Asad (2003), secularism as is understood in the West is informed by European history *and* religion, as it grew out the Enlightenment, the French Revolution, and Protestant theology. Secularism is not the absence of religion, but takes its meaning from its comparative relationship to religion in a particular context, with some religious worldviews better able to coexist with secularism than others.

What will be the future of religion in an increasingly globalized, multicultural, and secular world? It may be that the rise of atheism and the trend toward the abandonment or dismissal of organized forms of religion as "irrational" or "primitive" beliefs in favour of strictly scientific understandings of the world will lead to increasing intolerance of and ethnocentrism toward adherents of religion.

Such attitudes were apparent in responses to the 2015 *Charlie Hebdo* shootings in Paris. On 7 January 2015, two gunmen (later identified as adherents of Al-Qaeda in Yemen) entered the headquarters of the satirical newsmagazine with the goal of assassinating cartoonists, artists, and key production team members. Eleven people were killed and 11 more were injured. Five more people were killed and 11 wounded in additional attacks in other areas of Paris. *Charlie Hebdo*, renowned for its secular, irreligious, and irreverent political stance, had published satirical caricatures that mocked the Islamic prophet Muhammad. In the aftermath of this tragedy, interpretation and response became divided along religious/secular lines. The secular mainstream French and Western public honoured and commemorated the deceased *Charlie Hebdo* employees for their secularism, bravery, and defence of freedom of speech. Many adherents of Islam, however, felt that the organization, through its publications, had committed hate crimes, as it is considered sacrilegious to depict Muhammad in pictorial representations; in addition, the paper depicted Islam and its adherents as primitive, backward, and uncivilized. (Note that *Charlie Hebdo*'s religious satire is not limited to Islam; Catholicism, for example, has also been a target.)

This example draws our attention to the contested role of religion (or irreligion) in an increasingly globalized world. In the West, atheist worldviews are on the rise and religiosity is increasingly being undermined by the rise and proliferation of scientific narratives. How can anthropological principles of cultural relativism be applied to mitigate the proliferation of ethnocentric assumptions about different religions and worldviews? And how can such anthropological principles be used to combat, or at least understand and address, secular/religious violence and conflict?

The work of anthropologist Mayanthi Fernando (2014) exemplifies one possibility. Fernando's ethnography of the paradoxes of being a Muslim French citizen in contemporary secular France reminds us that there is no single way of practising either Islam or secularity, and that seemingly universal ideas about freedom of speech are differently inflected in different cultural, social, and historical contexts. In a blogpost written as an anthropologically informed response to the *Charlie Hebdo* incident, Fernando (2015) suggests:

> *We should not deny the horror of January 6. But, in its aftermath, rather than uncritically reaffirm French national identity and wring our*

hands about Muslims' refusal to integrate, we should use this moment of reflection to understand the various ways in which Muslims are consistently excluded from the [French] nation.

Clearly, anthropologists and anthropology students have much to offer with respect to debates about the rise and proliferation of secularism in the coming years.

BEYOND THE BOOK 4.6

In 2019, Quebec passed Bill 21, "An Act respecting the laicity [secularism] of the State." Laicity (the English translation of *laicité*, a term rooted in the French Revolution), as defined in the bill, is based on four principles: the separation of state and religions, the religious neutrality of the state, the equality of all citizens, and freedom of conscience and freedom of religion. The most contentious part of the bill has to do with the proposed ban on religious symbols in the public sector.

1. Do some research on Bill C-21, and reactions to it from the perspective of different Canadians. Share your findings with a partner or group members.
2. What kinds of assumptions about secularism and religious belief systems underpin this bill?
3. Who might be disproportionately affected (negatively or positively) by Bill 21?
4. What do Bill 21, and public discourse about it, suggest about the challenges of separating state and religion in a multicultural society?

APPLYING ANTHROPOLOGY

Mediating Worldviews on Mauna Kea

When anthropologists learn to interpret, understand, and take seriously different worldviews, and to communicate such worldviews to those who are unfamiliar with them, they are practising a valuable skill that has innumerable applications in a world in which peoples with varying worldviews frequently share territory and resources. Anthropologists can act as cultural mediators when conflicts arise and often as advocates for or collaborators with those whose ways of knowing are marginalized, misunderstood, or disparaged. Many anthropologists apply their knowledge and skills on behalf of Indigenous peoples whose ways of knowing the world around them (as discussed in Section 4.3) are at odds with dominant understandings of the relationship between humans and nature. The applied and public anthropology of Ty Tengan, an anthropologist and *Kanaka Maoli* (Native Hawaiian) who teaches at the University of Hawaii at Manoa, provides one example of the significance of this kind of work.

The opening image of this chapter captures the beauty and wonder of the Milky Way as viewed from the top of Mauna Kea, the tallest peak in Hawaii at 4302 metres above sea level (indeed, if measured from the sea floor, Mauna Kea is the tallest mountain in the world). Also pictured is the Gemini Northern Telescope, one of thirteen large telescopes atop the mountain, which is a coveted location for astronomical observation due to its height, lack of light pollution, good weather, and latitude. In 2009, an international consortium of stakeholders in the field of astronomy chose Mauna Kea as the location for its proposed new observatory, which will be eighteen stories tall and take up five acres on the peak. It will house the Thirty-Meter Telescope (TMT), part of a new class of extremely large telescopes (EMTs) that will allow astronomers to observe faint light in distant galaxies for the first time, opening up the possibility of answering new and even unanticipated questions about the origins of the universe, black holes, exoplanets, and dark matter.

For many Native Hawaiians, however, the peak of Mauna Kea is a sacred place, home to several deities and birthplace to *Wakea*, an ancestor whose domain is the sky (Case 2019, 168). It is also revered for its role in "collecting the waters that sustain life" (Goodyear-Ka'ōpua 2017, 189), as it sits atop the island's principle aquifer. Since the TMT was proposed, therefore, opponents have fought to prevent its construction on the grounds that it is a desecration of sacred space, environmentally unsound, and the most recent example of a long history of threats to Native Hawaiian sovereignty. Since 2009, these opponents have made a case against the telescope in the media and in the courts. In 2019 the conflict came to a head when final approval was given for the construction of the telescope. A group of protesters, or protectors, established a road block at the sole access point to the peak, effectively halting construction of the TMT. In the media coverage of the blockade and the preceding years of protest, one common narrative often prevailed, one that pitted specifically Hawaiian cultural interests against the "universally applicable" lessons of astronomy; sacred knowledge against scientific knowledge. These two worldviews are depicted not just as incompatible but as having unequal truth value: the sacred is seen as specific to Hawaiians, while science is seen as secular therefore and more widely applicable.

Ty Tengan is an anthropologist who specializes in the Native Hawaiian cultural renaissance and a respected university professor whose expertise is widely acknowledged across many audiences. He is also a Native Hawaiian "who for numerous cultural, political, and ethical reasons opposes the construction of the Thirty-Meter Telescope"; nonetheless, he "strives to bring out both sides of these debates" in his teaching and media appearances (Tengan 2018, 135). He has become an important and influential educator and cultural mediator in debates about the TMT. Tengan's interventions in debates about the conflict are numerous and diverse: he has long been active on Twitter and gives interviews for podcasts, television, newspapers, YouTube programs, and radio. More recently, the camp of protectors blocking the access road to the TMT construction site has grown into a semi-permanent and self-sustaining community. Tengan acts as the spokesperson for the Mauna Kea protectors at the University of Hawaii (whose community is deeply divided on the matter of the TMT). The protectors have established the *Pu'uhonua o Pu'uhuluhulu* or Pu'uhuluhulu University, which offers classes in Hawaiian language and culture classes to members of the camp community, and Tengan has joined Hawaiian educators, elders, and scholars to run classes there as well.

Tengan's interventions and mediations tend to focus on two particular themes: explaining why Mauna Kea is a special place for Native Hawaiians, and dispelling the idea that the conflict is about sacred culture beliefs versus secular scientific knowledge. As Tengan told *Manoa Now*:

> *To say that Hawaiians are anti-scientific is really to have a poor understanding of what Hawaiian religious and spiritual practices are based upon ... In actuality, much of indigenous thought and belief is very scientific in the sense that it's based on observations that are testable. Hypotheses are drawn up about how certain phenomenon in the environment work ... that is at the core of indigenous beliefs ... Hawaiians — the protectors — are not against science. They're against bad science that's being done in a harmful way. (Ladao 2017)*

Tengan points out that TMT supporters and protesters both have a tendency to lean on the science-versus-religion binary when it suits their purposes. When viewed through the anthropological perspective in terms of worldview, however, this binary dissolves: astronomers practise science informed by their worldview(s), and Native Hawaiians have long practised their own science (including astronomy) informed by theirs. And both sides view Mauna Kea as a place that is special because it potentially holds answers to the questions that all humans try to answer through culturally informed worldviews, whether they are religious or secular: Who are we? Why are we here? What is the origin and meaning of the life and the universe?

Thus far, the efforts of Tengan (and countless others) have succeeded in terms of raising awareness and beginning to change the narrative about Mauna Kea to one that is more nuanced and takes the Native Hawaiian worldview seriously. Although the TMT project has not yet been cancelled, it has also not proceeded, and the protectors continue to provide education at Pu'uhululu University (both in person and online at https://www.puuhuluhulu.com/learn and on the Pu'uhonua o Pu'uhuluhulu Maunakea Facebook page).

Conclusions

We began the chapter by asking how it is that people can believe in things that cannot be proven—why, for example, people are convinced of the presence of God, the existence of unseen spirits, or the powers of witchcraft. As we have seen, to answer this question requires us to examine aspects of social life such as metaphor, ritual, and myth, along with other features of social life that persuade people of the correctness of their beliefs or that convince them to change what they believe.

How does metaphor affect the meanings we assign to our experience? The selection of metaphors has an impact on the meanings we assign to experience. By taking the language from one domain of experience and applying it to another, we carry the meaning of one domain to another domain. Any effort to understand another culture (or to turn our anthropological analysis on our own culture) requires that we pay close attention to key metaphors.

The social and cultural construction of reality does not happen through metaphor alone. Symbolic actions also reinforce a particular view of the world. Ritual, for example, symbolically depicts a certain view of reality in such a way that it convinces us of the truth of that reality. Recall, for example, the Hamatsa Dance of the Kwakwaka'wakw, which portrays the values of Kwakwaka'wakw society and provides members with a way to control their lives. Recall, as well, the rituals of contemporary English magic and witchcraft, which convince participants that mental forces can influence the material world.

The culturally informed stories we tell ourselves, about zombies, vampires, or the power of face masks, are also forms of symbolic action that reinforce what we understand about our reality.

Relevant metaphors and rituals do not come out of nowhere, and not just any metaphor or ritual will be meaningful or effective in a particular cultural context. The way we live (including social, political, and economic forces) influences what we believe and how we act out those beliefs. "Ways of knowing" among Indigenous peoples differ from the kinds of knowledge that Euro-North Americans take for granted as correct because of the different ways these groups make their livelihood. People tend to act based on what they know about the world around them, which is shaped by their worldview. Sometimes, as we have seen in from the case of the Maka of Cameroon, people are forced to speculate about what they cannot know—for example, why some people are rich while others remain poor. The Maka speculate using the tools provided to them by their existing worldview, such as witchcraft. These explanations may not make sense to an outsider, but knowing what we as anthropologists know about how belief systems work helps us begin to take such explanations seriously instead of dismissing them out of hand.

We also looked at two examples (Dene Tha Christianity and Rastafari in Jamaica and beyond) of how people reinterpret new European religions using the worldviews that helped them explain their experiences before colonization or slavery. In most cases, people actively select parts of the new religion to incorporate into their own worldview. The global popularity of Bob Marley illustrates that as a result of forces of globalization (see Chapter 8), and local responses to those forces, many people around the world have had to reorient their belief systems in similar ways, despite differences in local histories and local experiences.

Under certain conditions, people may be led to radically change what they believe. The experience of social upheaval may lead, as it did among the Plains Indians, to a new belief system that promises to reorder society—and, in the case of the Ghost Dance, to resurrect the past. In the case of Haitian Vodou, a new worldview has been constructed to help people cope with the new conditions of a life they don't believe they can change.

Finally, we explored the effects of the rise of Western secularism and atheism. We saw how secularism often contributes to the development of new struggles over competing worldviews (occasionally in the form of violence, as in the *Charlie Hebdo* case), as well as the development of problematic binaries between notions of a spiritual and a secular world. Overall, the key significance of understanding how and why people come to believe what they do is that doing so gives us insight into one of the things that makes us human: our desire—and, indeed, our need—to make our lives meaningful.

QUESTIONS: REVIEW

Introduction

We began the chapter by asking the main question that anthropologists have always asked when it comes to belief systems: Why do people hold steadfastly to beliefs that cannot be proven? The answer is: worldview. Those who share this encompassing picture of reality share beliefs about how the world works and why. But why do different cultures have different worldviews? Here we introduced various theories about religion and belief systems proposed by early anthropologists, including Evans-Pritchard, Tylor, and Durkheim. Today, rather than trying to figure out why some belief systems are more evolved or rational than others, anthropologists try to contextualize how worldviews come into existence in particular cultural settings. Focusing on symbolic action is one of the key ways in which to do so.

Review Questions

1. Define and discuss the significance of the following terms: *worldview, ritual, totemism, animism,* and *symbolic action.*

4.1 How does the use of metaphor affect the meanings people assign to experience?

Metaphors use language from one domain of experience to describe another domain of experience; for instance, if we say, "I shot down his argument", we are using a metaphor from the domain of warfare to describe the domain of disagreement. In this way, metaphors are valuable tools for constructing worldviews. By emphasizing the significance of some domains of experience over others, we reinforce our beliefs and come to see them as natural or commonsense. In this section, we explore the centrality of the metaphor of hunger among the Kwakwaka'wakw, as well as the way that witches in contemporary England come to share a worldview based on the metaphor of "planes" of existence and interpreting life through the metaphorical meanings of the tarot deck.

Review Questions

1. How do the metaphors of eating and hunger effect the ways the Kwakwaka'wakw (a) socialize their children; (b) think about death and dying; c) understand greed?
2. What is witchcraft? What is magic?
3. How and why do witches in England use tarot cards to interpret their daily lives and those of others?

4.2 How does symbolic action reinforce a particular view of the world?

In addition to metaphor, symbolic actions such as rituals and storytelling are important ways by which we express and reinforce what we believe to be true about the world we live in. Taken literally, such symbolic actions may make little sense, especially to outsiders, but closer interpretation can yield insights into how they convey meaning. In this section, we discussed several examples of symbolic action in action, including the Kwakwaka'wakw Hamatsa Dance, zombie and vampire stories in contemporary North America, and the ritual meaning and significance of wearing facemasks, regardless of the "real" risk of infection, during a pandemic.

Review Questions

1. Describe the various "steps" in the four-day ritual of the Kwakwaka'wakw Hamatsa/Cannibal Dance. What does each step symbolize, and how? What lessons does this ritual teach the Hamatsa about the socialization of children?
2. Why are zombies and vampires "good to think with"? What issues are being thought about in each case?
3. Describe the "symbolic efficacy" of face masks in the Philippines. Why might some people take comfort in the ritual of wearing a face mask during a health crisis?

4.3 How does the way we live affect our beliefs and rituals?

In this section, we looked at the relationships between ways of life and ways of knowing. Cultural rituals and beliefs emerge in the context of particular ways of making a living and in particular political, economic, and social systems.

Review Questions

1. What is a rite of passage? How does medicalized childbirth in North America, as a rite of passage, reflect North American ways of living?
2. What is knowledge according to the Dene Tha, and how does one obtain it?
3. How do Dene Tha view the power dynamics between humans and animals, and humans and the environment in which they live?
4. What is the significance of dreaming for the Dene Tha?
5. A Dutch missionary once said to the Maka of Cameroon, "Where there is electric light, witchcraft will disappear." Why has this proven not to be the case, and what does it have to do with inequality?

4.4 What happened to local worldviews when they were confronted by the religions of the European colonizers?

In this section, we explored what happens when Christianity, through colonial encounters the world over, came into contact with and challenged various local worldviews. Many early anthropologists assumed that Christianity would inevitably destroy local worldviews. However, the examples in this section, of Christianity among the Dene, and of Rastafari, especially in Jamaica, demonstrate that this is not always the case, and that Indigenous and colonized peoples often fit religions such as Christianity into their existing worldviews in culturally creative ways.

Review Questions

1. What is shamanism? How did the Dene Tha meld their shamanistic practices and beliefs with those of Catholicism and Anglicanism? Give examples.
2. Who was Ras Tafari? How did his coronation lead to a new belief system among the poor descendants of slaves in Kingston, Jamaica?
3. Why does Bob Marley, through his music, continue to resonate with oppressed peoples around the globe?

4.5 How can people reorder their view of the world if it becomes unsatisfactory?

Although worldviews are resilient, and not easy to change, it is nonetheless the case that changing a worldview is possible, especially it no longer provides satisfactory explanations of reality for the people who share it. Two key ways in which worldviews can change are through revitalization movements, such as the Ghost Dance, and through syncretism, such as Haitian Vodou. In both cases, new worldviews arose that provided better, more effective explanations and practices for dealing with new realities.

Review Questions

1. What is a revitalization movement? Who was Wokova, and how does the Ghost Dance exemplify the way that a revitalization movement deals with cultural dissatisfaction?
2. What is syncretism? How does Haitian Vodou, as a syncretic belief system, help Haitians cope with and make sense of poverty and hardship?

4.6 How can secular and religious worldviews coexist?

In the final section of this chapter, we draw attention to the fact that secularism, which is on the rise in Canada, is a worldview with its own unique history and accompanying beliefs about the links between religion, the state, and citizenship. Using the example of the *Charlie Hebdo* shootings in France in 2015, we demonstrate both the challenges faced by the concurrent rise of secularism, globalization, and multiculturalism, and how anthropologists might address such challenges.

Review Questions

1. Is secularism the absence of belief, or is it a worldview itself?
2. How were explanations for the 2015 *Charlie Hebdo* shootings in France explained in different ways by the religious and secular perspectives?
3. How might an anthropological perspective change how we look at the *Charlie Hebdo* incident, according to Mayanthi Fernando?

CRITICAL THINKING QUESTIONS

1. If worldview is culturally and socially constructed, can there be such a thing as objective truth? What are the implications of taking a social constructionist approach to reality for the pursuit of knowledge? Is objectivity possible? What obstacles might this present for the anthropological study of culture?
2. Do we need to believe in rituals in order for them to be effective? Explain why or why not.
3. How have the forces and circumstances of globalization shaped belief systems around the world?

KEY TERMS

atheism (p. 118)
creole (p. 117)
domain of experience (p. 96)
key metaphors (p. 98)
key scenarios (p. 103)
magic (p. 99)
metaphors (p. 96)
myth (p. 99)
revitalization movements (p. 114)
rites of passage (p. 106)
ritual (p. 95)
secularism (p. 118)
shamanism (p. 111)
symbolic actions (p. 96)
syncretism (p. 116)
totemism (p. 95)
witchcraft (p. 99)
worldview (p. 94)

Constructing Families and Social Relationships

©Danita Delimont/Alamy Stock Photo

This soapstone sculpture by Inuit artist Jonasie Quarqortoq Faber, simply titled "Family," depicts a family unit–mother, father, and child–that many North Americans would identify as the "typical" nuclear family. However, the dynamics of the Inuit nuclear family are not necessarily the same as the nuclear family dynamics described in the epigraph below by Whately. Indeed, as we will see throughout this chapter, family dynamics and configurations vary widely from culture to culture.

If ever thou purpose to be a good wife, and to live comfortably, set down this with thyself: mine husband is my superior, my better, he hath authority and rule over me; nature hath given it to him ... God hath given it to him.

—W. Whately, A Bride-Bush, or, A Wedding Sermon: London, 1617

PROBLEM 5

What do we need to know before we can understand the dynamics of family life in other societies?

Introduction

Family Relations in North American Popular Culture

Anthropologists can learn a great deal about changing North American family relations by watching popular TV shows from different eras. For instance, by comparing contemporary shows like *Modern Family* with sitcoms from the 1970s like *All in the Family*, and paying attention to the reasons for domestic strife, the choices characters make, and the impact those choices have on family members, we can better understand the changing composition of families and the challenges they face. Furthermore, an anthropologist would learn much by paying close attention to viewers' reactions to the show: What did they find plausible, scandalous, or relatable? What exactly was it about this family that made its members both typical and compelling?

We can also look to events in mainstream digital media to help us understand changing cultural conceptions of families. These days, for instance, many would be unfazed by the inclusion of divorced or gay characters in social media, or in the daily news, and the discussions they evoke. For instance, in May 2012, US President Barack Obama publicly declared his support for same-sex marriage (which has been legal in Canada since 2005). In an interview with ABC News, he explained that he had taken his cue from his two young daughters, who had schoolmates whose parents were gay and who could not imagine why they would be denied the right to marry. President Obama's statement echoed the growing public support for same-sex marriage; nonetheless, it generated much controversy. For instance, Bristol Palin, daughter of 2008 Republican vice-presidential candidate Sarah Palin, criticized the president in her blogpost titled "Hail to the Chiefs: Malia and Sasha Obama." She suggested that Obama's daughters had watched too many episodes of *Glee*—a popular television show with several prominent gay characters—and that President Obama should be a "proper" father and leader, teaching his daughters what to do and think rather than allowing them to teach him. In 2015, same-sex unions acquired increasing support and legitimacy when the US Supreme Court's *Obergefell vs. Hodges* case ruled that same-sex individuals have a legal right to marry, thereby making same-sex marriage available in every American state. In 2017, however, with the election of Donald Trump as president, we witnessed a resurgence of Palin's conservative perspective on family. During his tenure as president, Trump has been criticized for deliberately nominating Supreme Court justices who are unsupportive of LGBTQ rights, including same-sex marriage, and he has publicly stated that he would like to see *Obergefell v. Hodges* overturned. The multitude of conflicting opinions surrounding cases like same-sex marriage over time and across space gives us pause to consider questions such as these: Whose version of the North American family is the "correct" one? How are contemporary politics intertwined with mainstream notions of family structure? How do changing notions of gender and/or sexuality impact how notions of family are perceived and constructed?

The study of **kinship**, including family composition, descent, and marriage, has long been central to sociocultural anthropology. Franklin and McKinnon (2001, 1) argue that, in fact, "the study of kinship is itself symbolic of the anthropological tradition." Kinship has long intrigued anthropologists because it relates so closely to social organization. Many early anthropologists assumed that kinship was more important in small-scale societies, where it provided the entire basis of social organization, than in large-scale societies. But as we will find later in this chapter, contemporary kinship studies have demonstrated that kinship remains a meaningful element of social life in large-scale societies as well. When we study kinship, we are interested both in classifications—who is considered a relative and who is not—and in the ways people make particular relationships meaningful. Anthropologists who study family relations often begin by exploring the composition of a typical family and how it is formed and maintained. They examine how the themes of sexuality, love, and wealth are dealt with and what kinds of situations or conflicts can disrupt family life. However, as we can see from the example above, the typical family is just that: an ideal type that may or may not closely align with people's everyday experiences. Questions about what does or does not count as a family, what kinds of rights various members should have, and who should be the head of the household can be contentious. By exploring both the typical family *and* the debates about its composition, however, we can learn much about a given society.

When exploring kinship, anthropologists stress the importance of cultural relativism. For example, practices such as polygyny (a form of plural (or polygamous) marriage where a man has multiple wives, discussed further below), which is illegal in Canada, have received abundant media coverage in North American contexts in recent years due to the linkages of some high-profile cases with misogynist behaviours and the abuse of women and children. In 2011, for instance, Winston Blackmore and James Oler, two male leaders of a fundamentalist Mormon polygamous sect in Bountiful, BC, were charged with polygamy; six years later, in 2017, they were convicted. Collectively, they had 27 wives and 145 children. The nuclear, heterosexual monogamist Canadian family is increasingly coming under challenge; but at the same time, cases of polygamy are often sensationalized and labelled as deviant in North American contexts. Ultimately, however, anthropologists recognize that it is important to avoid assuming that polygyny is always equated with the mistreatment of women. It is only through ethnographic fieldwork that anthropologists can understand the unique perspectives of different interest groups in various cultures.

To manage the task of understanding patterns of family relations cross-culturally, we will focus first on family life in three societies: the Ju/'hoansi of Namibia and Botswana, the Trobriand Islanders of the South Pacific, and a rural Chinese farm family in Taiwan. These have been selected for three reasons. First, they represent very different levels of social, cultural, and technological complexity. The Ju/'hoansi are gatherers and hunters living in small, mobile groups; the Trobriand Islanders are horticulturists living in villages of up to 400 people; and the rural Chinese in Taiwan represent a large agricultural society. Second, family structure and roles vary significantly among the three, as do notions

kinship
Refers to the anthropological, cross-cultural study of family composition, marriage, and descent patterns.

about the bases of kinship relations and how kinship terms, such as mother, father, sister, and brother, are used. Finally, the three societies have been well studied in the anthropological literature. We will discuss these societies in what anthropologists refer to as the **ethnographic present**; that is, although the actual descriptions may refer to situations that existed in the past, they will be described as if they still exist. In reality, the Ju/'hoansi, the Trobriand Islanders, and the rural Chinese are, to varying degrees, very different today than they were when they were studied by the anthropologists whose work we will mention. After this review, we will look at more recent kinship studies by anthropologists to show some of the problems they have encountered and the new directions they have taken.

QUESTIONS

5.1 What is the composition of the typical family group?
5.2 How are families formed, and how is the ideal family type maintained?
5.3 What are the roles of sexuality, love, and wealth?
5.4 What threatens to disrupt the family unit?
5.5 How has the anthropological study of families changed?

Question 5.1: What Is the Composition of the Typical Family Group?

To understand family composition in different societies, we need certain concepts and tools. One place to begin is by examining how unmarried North Americans would typically respond if asked about the composition of their families. They would likely list their mother, father, brothers, and sisters. If asked, "Who else?" they would likely add grandparents, aunts, uncles, and cousins. If married, they would add their spouse and children. Figure 5.1 shows how this family structure would be diagrammed using genealogical notations.

David Schneider was one of the first anthropologists to study American kinship systematically, and his 1968 study led him to conclude that kinship, in North America and elsewhere, is a cultural system, not a set of biological facts. For instance, although Americans talk about kinship in terms of biological relatedness (often using the metaphor of shared blood), in practice, kinship is not dictated by any biogenetic reality. Often, we call people kin who are not related to us biogenetically. Many of us, for instance, grow up referring to close friends of our parents as "aunt" or "uncle" despite the fact that we are not biologically related to them. Such relationships can even extend to companion animals. Many people think about their dogs or cats in terms of kinship. Dogs, for instance, are often perceived as family members, with owners taking on the role of "parents" and with dogs as their "kids." Conversely, we often deny kinship status to biogenetic relatives (Feinberg 2001, 8). Family members can become "estranged" as a result of familial disagreements or a family member's participation in illegal or seemingly unethical activities. Ultimately, we employ the language of blood, of love, and of solidarity strategically to determine whom we consider kin and whom we do not.

Certain features of some North American families stand out for the anthropological observer. Many North Americans consider themselves equally

BEYOND THE BOOK 5.1

Using the genealogical notations introduced in Figure 5.1, draw a kinship diagram of your own family. Include as many generations and as many kin as are relevant to your own family life. When you are done, answer these questions:

1. Would you include anyone who is not biologically related to you?
2. Have you left out someone who is a "blood" relative but whom you do not consider kin?
3. How do you explain these inclusions and exclusions in your family?

ethnographic present
Use of the present tense to describe a culture, although the description may refer to situations that existed in the past.

FIGURE 5.1 Composition and Development of the Canadian Nuclear Family

1. The traditional Canadian household generally begins with a husband and wife pair moving from the households of their parents.

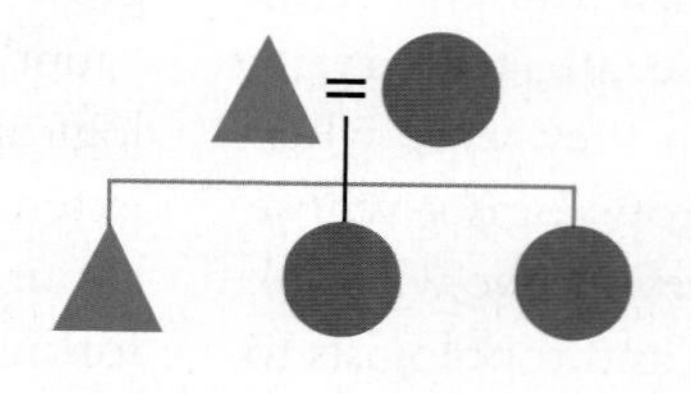

2. The arrangement is formalized with the birth of children, which produces a new nuclear family.

3. At some point the household might be composed of three generations, as married children join the household with their children.

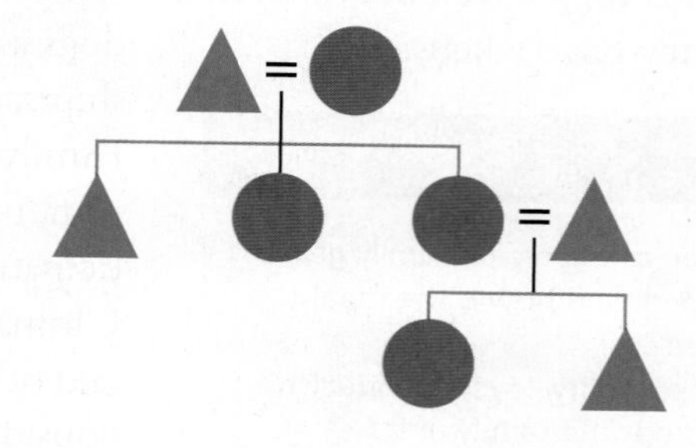

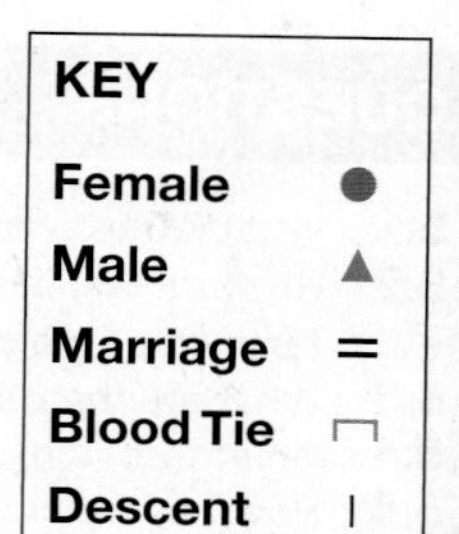

4. At a later stage, the household might consist of the original couple or a single person.

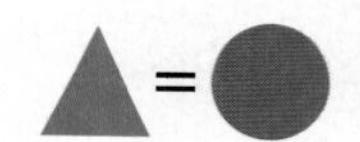

tied by kinship to both their mother and their father, and to both their maternal and their paternal kin. In other words, North Americans generally recognize **bilateral kinship**, or kinship through both parents. As we will see, however, not all societies do. Second, many North Americans make no linguistic distinction between the mother's siblings and the father's siblings; both are referred to as *aunt* or *uncle*, as are the spouses of their parents' siblings. Nor do they distinguish linguistically the children of aunts and uncles; all are referred to as *cousins*. For many North Americans, the most important family grouping is the **nuclear family**—the group that traditionally consists of father and mother and their biological or adopted children.

Notions of what constitutes a nuclear family, however, change over time. Increasingly in Canadian society, for instance, the concept of the nuclear family has shifted to also encompass same-sex partners who live with their biological or adopted children. Now that same-sex partnerships are becoming more and more accepted, and that they have become legal under the *Civil Marriage Act* of 2005, the nuclear family does not necessarily imply the existence of heterosexual unions.

bilateral kinship
A system in which individuals trace their descent through both parents.

nuclear family
The family group consisting of father, mother, and their biological or adopted children.

Families in other societies may be composed very differently. For example, other societies may place greater emphasis on ties to one parent or the other. In some cases, only people related through *either* the mother *or* the father are considered family. Societies that emphasize persons' ties to their mother are said to have **matrilineal kinship** systems; those that emphasize persons' ties to their father are said to have **patrilineal kinship** systems. Few societies ignore an individual's relationship to one side of the family or the other; rather, in most societies, relationships with mothers' families and fathers' families are viewed differently. For example, North Americans traditionally inherit their surnames from their fathers, which reflects the patrilineal principle; in cases of divorce, however, North American legal systems usually give priority to the matrilineal principle by awarding custody of the child to the mother.

When studying how different groups classify how their members are related to one another, anthropologists make a distinction between **kin types** and **kin terms**. Kin types are etic terms that are used by anthropologists (and not necessarily the people they study) to make sense of family relationships. Kin types usually imply a biological relationship between people and include terms like *mother, father, brother, sister, son, husband*, and so on. In contrast, a kin term is an emic category, which means it is a term used by one's interlocutors to refer to an individual they consider to be a member of their family. By exploring when, how, and in what contexts people employ various kin terms, anthropologists can better understand how those we study and engage with perceive and categorize family members. Kin terms are thus specific to each culture. Kin terms may include kin types like *brother* or *father*, but they may also include concepts and vocabulary that are culture specific. The term *cousin*, for instance, does not correspond to one stable kin type or biological relationship. In North America, for example, cousin can refer to one's mother's sister's daughter, or one's father's brother's son, and so on. The kin terms we might use in North America, then, are not universally applicable; indeed, they vary significantly from culture to culture.

FIGURE 5.2 Ju/'Hoansi Territory in Botswana and Namibia

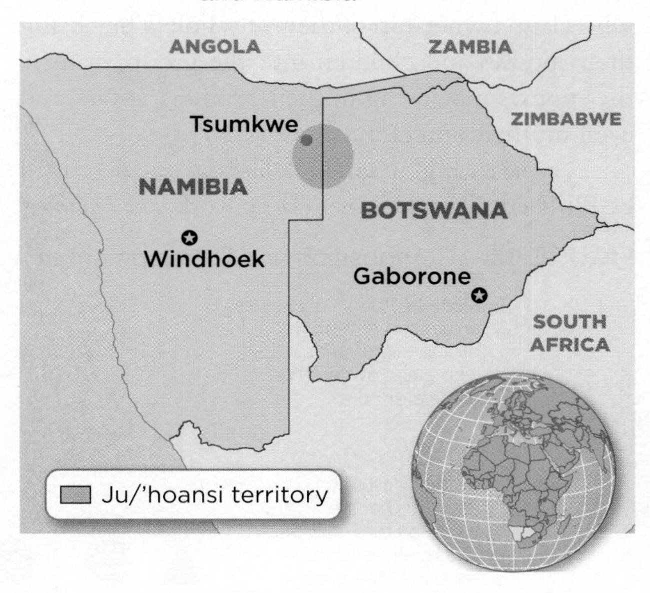

Each of the three societies discussed in this chapter—the Ju/'hoansi, the Trobrianders, and the rural Chinese—has its own way of defining what a family is and how its members relate to one another.

The Family Composition of Ju/'hoansi

For most of the year, the Ju/'hoansi (Figure 5.2) live in groups numbering from 10 to as many as 40 people, who are bilaterally related (through both parents), and who hunt and gather in a territory

matrilineal kinship
A system of descent in which persons are related to their kin through the mother only.

patrilineal kinship
A system of descent in which persons are related to their kin through the father only.

kin type
Terms used by anthropologists to denote biological relationships among family members.

kin term
Culture-specific vocabulary to denote family relationships. These terms may or may not correspond to an anthropologist's kin type.

associated with a particular water hole. Camp groups are often organized around a brother-and-sister pair, who claim ownership of the water hole. They bring their spouses and children into the group; in turn, the spouses may bring in their brothers, sisters, and even mothers and fathers.

A typical camp might look like the one described by Elizabeth Thomas in her classic work *The Harmless People* (see Figure 5.3). Membership in a camp is fluid. People move freely from camp to camp based on hunting alliances or because conflict develops in the group. Within the camp, however, the basic family group is the nuclear family of husband, wife, and children. Children spend most of their time with their mothers. The Ju/'hoansi acknowledge that pregnancy results from sexual intercourse (not

FIGURE 5.3 Composition and Development of a Ju/'Hoansi Camp

1. Most Ju/'hoansi camps are organized around brother/sister pairs who claim ownership of a water hole.

2. Brother and sister are joined at the camp by their spouses and relatives of their spouses. The nuclear family is the main economic unit.

3. Bridegrooms join the camp of brides' parents for brideservice.

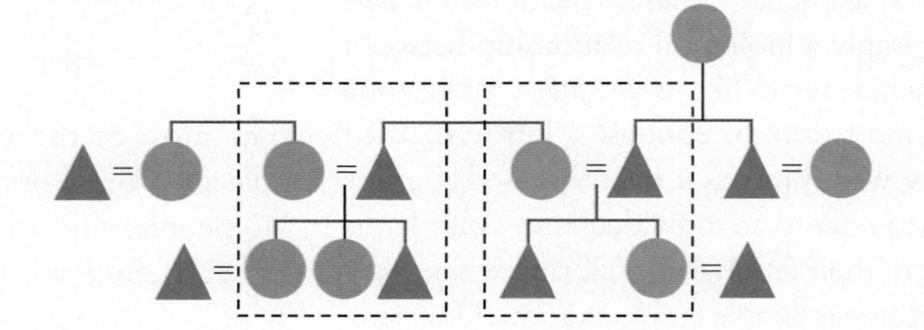

4. Camp composition changes as a result of changing social relations.

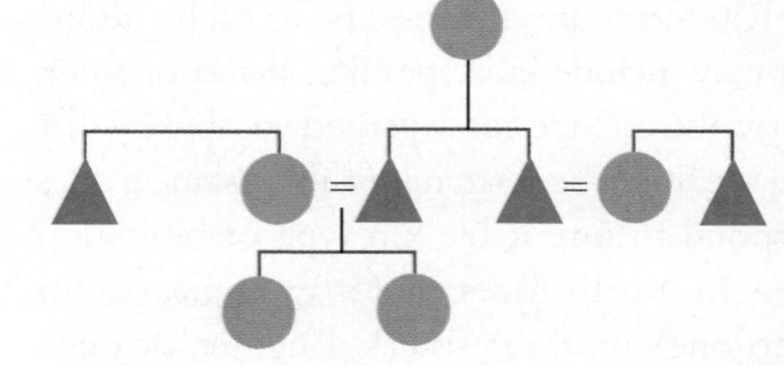

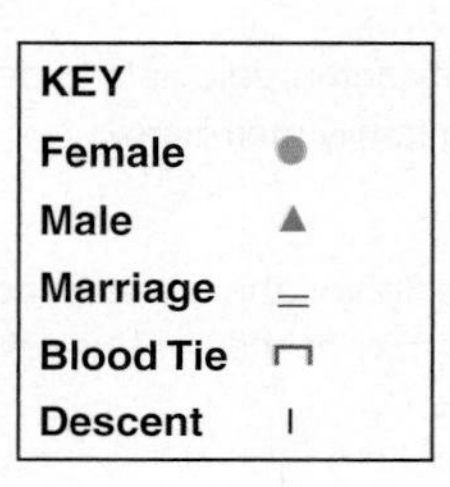

the case in all societies). They also believe that conception takes place at the end of the woman's menses, when the man's semen joins with the last of the menstrual blood.

A feature of Ju/'hoansi society that figures prominently in the dynamics of family life is the custom of **brideservice** at marriage, which requires that a groom work for the bride's parents for a specified time. Among the Ju/'hoansi, when a couple marries, the groom is expected to come and live in the bride's parents' camp and work for her parents for as long as ten years. Tales of Ju/'hoansi family life are often built around the effects of this arrangement on family dynamics.

The Family Composition of Trobriand Islanders

The people of the Trobriand Islands (Figure 5.4) live in some 80 villages, whose populations range from 40 to 400. Each village is surrounded by water holes, fruit trees, palm groves, and cultivated fields of yams, taro, and other crops. Each is further divided into hamlets, and each hamlet ideally consists of a **matrilineage**, or *dala*, as Trobrianders call it—that is, a group of men related to one another through the female line, along with their wives and unmarried children.

FIGURE 5.4 Papua New Guinea

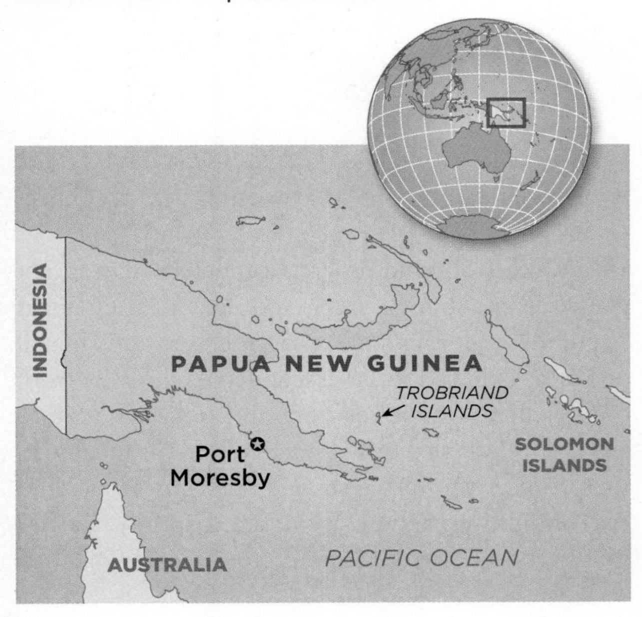

The matrilineages are ranked relative to one another, and each village has a chief who is the eldest male of the highest-ranking matrilineage. Since each person is a member of the lineage of his or her mother, neither a man's wife nor his children can be members of his own *dala* (see Figure 5.5).

Trobrianders' mythology and beliefs about procreation dramatically depict the matrilineal element in their lives. Their mythology contains stories of how, a long time ago, pairs of brothers and sisters emerged from the ground to begin each *dala*. *Dala* members trace their descent back to their mythological ancestors, and they base their claims to specific plots of land on the fact that it was from there that their ancestors emerged. There is obviously an element of incest in Trobriand myth, since the originators of each lineage were brothers and sisters; however, Trobriand theories of procreation ostensibly deny a role to men in conception. They reinforce the matrilineal principle as well as the tie between brothers and sisters.

Trobrianders say that when a person dies, the soul or spirit becomes young and goes to live on an island called Tuma. There the soul ages, but it regenerates itself by bathing in the sea. As the skin is sloughed off, a spirit child, or baloma, is created, which returns to the world of the living and enters the womb of a woman of the same matrilineage as itself. In effect, a Trobriand matrilineage exists in perpetuity, as souls and spirits travel back and forth between the land of the living and the island of the dead.

The baloma may enter the woman through her head, or it may be carried by water into her womb. In some areas of the Trobriand Islands, if a woman wishes to become pregnant, a pail of water is brought

brideservice
The requirement that when a couple marries, the groom must work for the bride's parents for some specified time.

matrilineage
A lineage that is formed by tracing descent in the female line.

FIGURE 5.5 Composition of a Trobriand Island Dala and Household

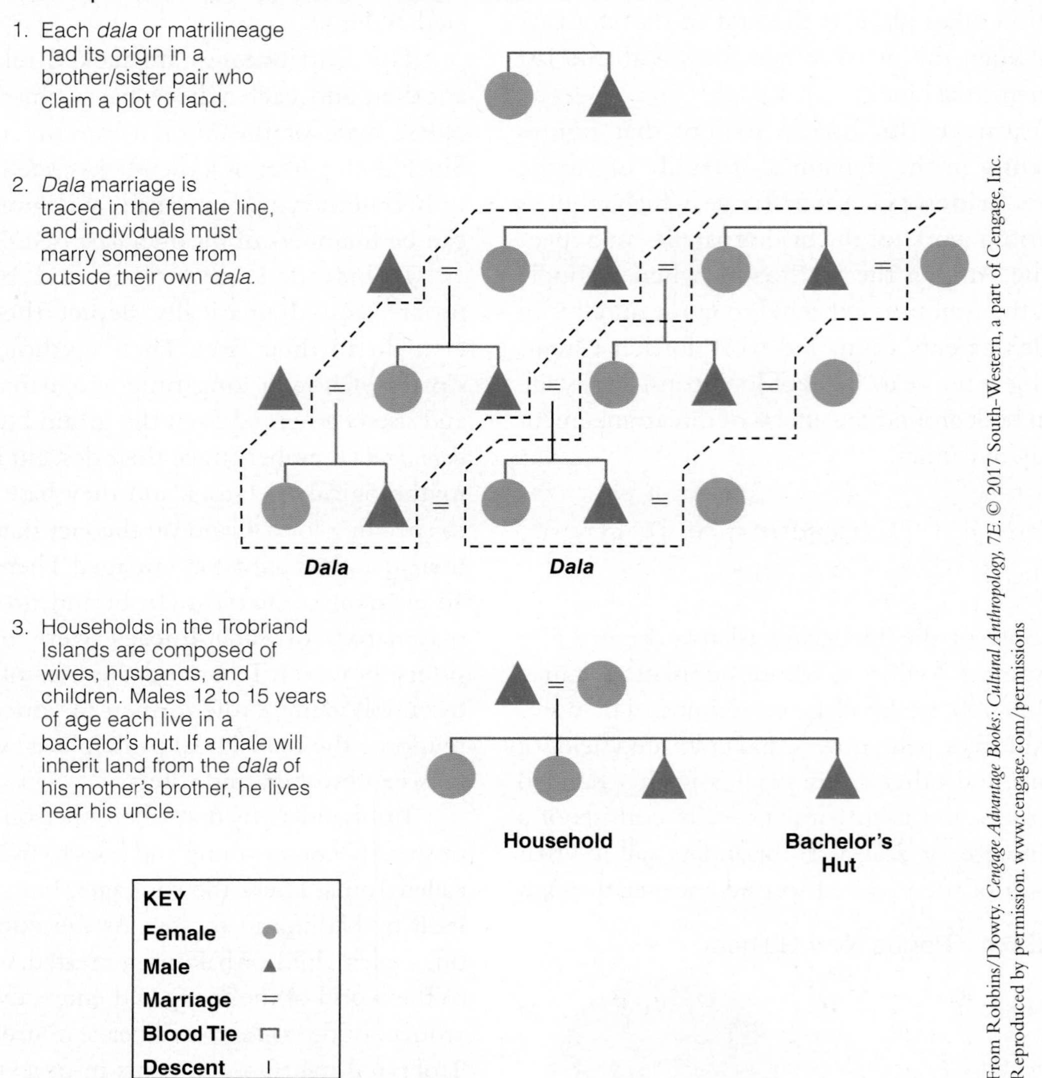

to her dwelling by her brother. In fact, a woman cannot conceive without the "permission" of her brother. Consequently, the act of conception among Trobrianders is a matter of three agencies: a woman, the spirit or baloma of a deceased ancestor, and the woman's brother. Sexual intercourse is said to play no role in conception, but it does play a role in the development and growth of the fetus. Trobrianders believe that the man's semen provides food and nourishment for the fetus, and that is why children physically resemble their fathers. Sexual intercourse is also said to open the womb for the child to emerge.

While Trobriand procreation beliefs may, at first glance, seem strange, in the context of their ideas about descent they make perfect sense. When a person is believed to be descended exclusively from the mother, possible relations and ties to the father are excluded not only socially but physically as well. In fact, we find in strongly patrilineal societies corresponding beliefs about conception. Earlier in this book, we examined how Carol Delaney

(1991, 26) explained how Turkish villagers had a "monogenetic" theory of procreation. "It is the males," she wrote, "who give life; women merely give birth." Turkish villagers use an agricultural metaphor to describe procreation: men provide the seed, and women are the soil. It is the seed that contains life; the soil simply nurtures it. The man is believed to plant the seed, and the woman is said to be the field in which the seed is planted. In this way, the male role in the patrilineal family system of the Turkish village is emphasized and the female role is diminished.

Trobrianders find it easy to rationalize and "prove" their beliefs about procreation. Bronislaw Malinowski, who spent four years studying the Trobrianders, tells of their response when he suggested to them that sexual intercourse plays a role in procreation:

> *I sometimes made myself definitely and aggressively an advocate of the truer physiological doctrine of procreation. In such arguments the natives would quote, not only positive instances of women who have children without having intercourse; but would also refer to the many cases in which an unmarried woman has plenty of intercourse and no children. This argument would be repeated over and over again, with specially telling concrete examples of childless persons renowned for profligacy, or of women who lived with one white trader after another without having any baby. (Malinowski 1929, 185–86)*

To what extent Trobrianders really deny a role to men in procreation is a matter of some debate. Annette Weiner, who worked with them in the early 1970s, some 50 years after Malinowski's pioneering work, reported that they no longer denied that men played a direct role in conception. However, she also reported a case where a grandmother claimed she had used magic to make her granddaughter pregnant when the woman conceived during her husband's absence.

Regardless of the extent to which Trobrianders recognize the role of coitus, their ideas about descent and procreation reflect important features of the composition of their families. First, the key family relationship for them is not, as it is among the Ju/'hoansi, between husband and wife; it is between brother and sister. Second, the father of the family is an outsider to his children, a member of another family group. His interest, ideally, is in his sister's children, since it is they who are members of his matrilineage. Third, since the matrilineal **extended family** group, the *dala*, is more important than the nuclear family, Trobrianders merge certain people under the same kin term the same way many North Americans refer to different kinds of kin as aunt, uncle, or cousin. In the Trobrianders' case, a person refers to all women of his or her matrilineage of the same generation by the same term; for example, a man refers to his mother, as well as his mother's sisters, by the term *ina*. A woman refers to her brother and to all other men of her matrilineage and generation as *luta*. Thus, a man has many "sisters," and a woman has many "brothers."

BEYOND THE BOOK 5.2

The procreation beliefs of the Trobriand Islanders prompted debate among anthropologists about whether the Trobrianders really did believe that men played little or no role in reproduction or whether, to emphasize the matrilineal principle, they pretended not to acknowledge the male role. In either case, we would expect to find in societies that emphasize the patrilineal principle that a woman's role in reproduction is de-emphasized. What kind of belief about reproduction might deny the importance of the female? How does this compare with the biological roles of men and women in North American societies?

extended family
A family group based on blood relations of three or more generations.

The Family Composition of Rural Chinese

Family life in rural China revolves around the patrilineal extended family household of a married couple, their married sons and daughters-in-law, and their grandchildren and unmarried daughters (see Figure 5.6). To understand a rural Chinese family, you have to understand the idea of *temporal depth*, for in China, the **patrilineage** exists

FIGURE 5.6 Composition and Development of a Rural Chinese Family

1. The traditional Chinese family exists in time as well as in space. Descent is traced patrilineally for generations.

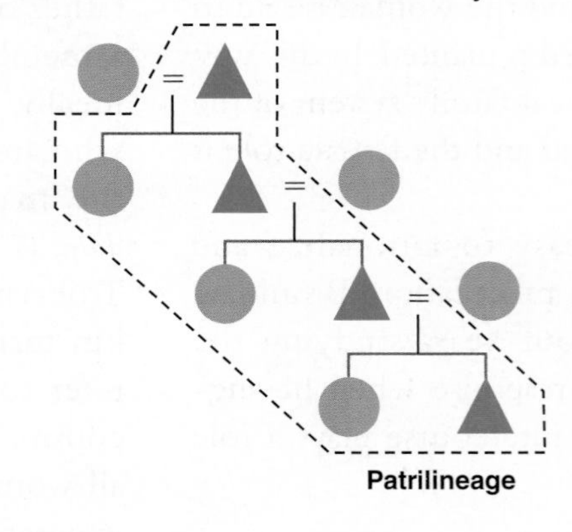

2. An ideal family would be similar to that of the Lim household in Taiwan.

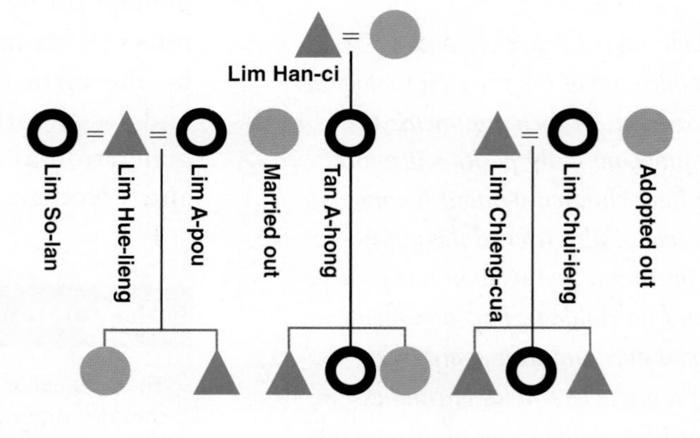

3. Most Chinese extended households eventually break up into separate nuclear family units, with wives of sons joining their husbands' households.

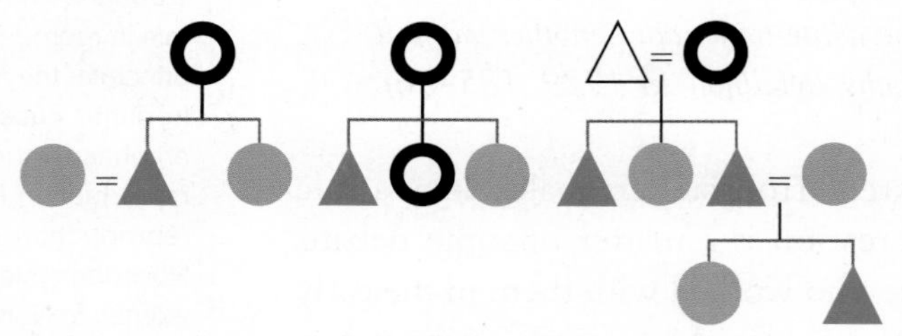

KEY
- **Female** ●
- **Male** ▲
- **Marriage** =
- **Blood Tie** ⊓
- **Descent** |
- **Adopted Daughter** O

as much in time as it does in space, and the family includes a long line of patrilineal ancestors. A patrilineage is a lineage that is formed by tracing descent in the male line. Anthropologist Francis L.K. Hsu notes that the identity of each male is defined by his relations to the dead as much as it is by his relations to the living. His social worth and destiny are but reflections of the actions of his ancestors. He thus exists, as Hsu (1967) says, "under the shadow of his ancestors." Likewise, the spirits of the dead are dependent on the contributions of the living. These contributions are ceremonially made at altars, prominently positioned in each home, from which people send gifts to their ancestors by burning paper money, paper clothes, or other paper articles.

Given the interdependence between the living and the dead men of the patrilineage, it is apparent why Chinese males deem it essential to have male descendants to look after their well-being and to provide for them in the afterworld. Male children and grandchildren are living proof to a man that his line will continue. For this reason, unlike the Ju/'hoansi or the Trobrianders, the Chinese express a marked preference for male children. Males are needed to maintain the patrilineal descent group, for if the only children born are daughters whose children will, in turn, belong to the patrilineage of their husbands, a family line will die out. A son, as some Chinese put it, is a major happiness; a daughter is but a small happiness.

In addition to a long line of male ancestors, an ideal rural Chinese household should include several generations of fathers and sons sharing a common hearth or cooking stove and an ancestral altar: the symbols of the household. In the architecture of Peihotien (Figure 5.7), the village where Margery Wolf (1968) did her fieldwork, houses are constructed in such a way that they can easily be extended to accommodate additional sons and grandsons, who bring their wives to live in the family home. In reality it is very difficult to maintain this ideal; most households in villages such as Peihotien are small, consisting of a married couple and several dependent patrilineal relatives.

FIGURE 5.7 Peihotien

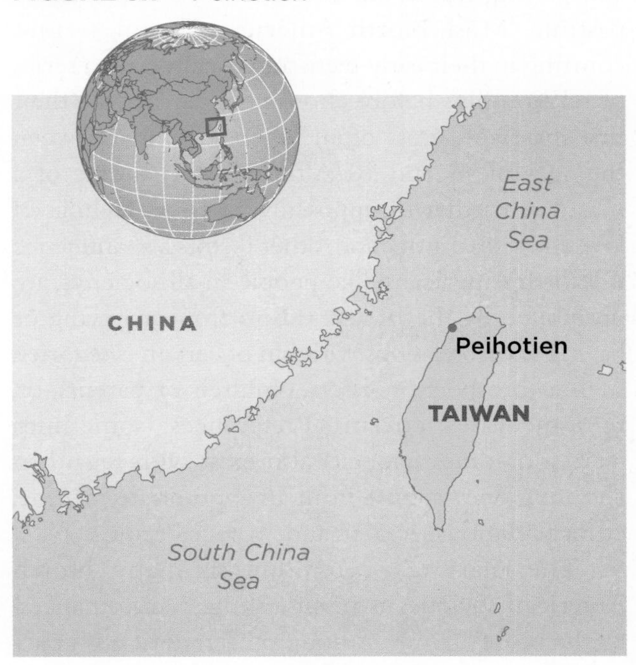

Question 5.2: How Are Families Formed, and How Is the Ideal Family Type Maintained?

Regardless of the size of family units or descent systems, most societies require the socially recognized union of a male and a female (we will discuss the exceptions later in this chapter). Generally, this union takes the form of marriage, a publicly recognized joining of two people or two families. However, while marriage makes or sustains families, the manner in which such an arrangement comes about varies significantly between societies. In North American societies, for example, many children begin learning about courtship and marriage at an early age: five- and six-year-olds are teased about their "boyfriends" or "girlfriends,"

patrilineage
A lineage that is formed by tracing descent in the male line.

and playing house together is a popular preschool pastime. Most North Americans begin serious courting in their early teens and usually have a series of relationships before choosing a partner for their first marriage, most often when they are between the ages of 18 and 30. Although the choice of a marriage partner is supposedly based on feelings of love and sexual attraction, other factors also influence it. North Americans, like people in all societies, are prohibited by the **incest taboo** from marrying or having sexual relations with kin of certain categories, such as brothers or sisters, children or parents, or, in some cases, cousins. Preferences (sometimes tacit, sometimes explicit) also exist with regard to choosing one's spouse from an appropriate income, ethnic, religious, gender, and/or racial group.

The marriage ceremony in many North American societies is often arranged and financed by the bride's family, although this tradition is gradually changing. After the honeymoon, the couple ideally establishes an independent residence. Their relationship based on love expressed through regular sexual intercourse is later transformed by the arrival of one or more children, when a wife becomes a mother and a husband, a father. However, the cycles of events that create or sustain the family among the Ju/'hoansi, the Trobrianders, and the rural Chinese illustrate the diversity of such arrangements.

The Family Cycle of Ju/'hoansi

Ju/'hoansi men and women, like most North Americans, begin to learn about courtship, sex, and marriage early in life. Because there is little privacy in a Ju/'hoansi camp and children sleep with their parents, they soon are playing at marriage and imitating the bodily movements of parents making love. Most young men and women have had sexual experiences by the time they are 15.

Ju/'hoansi men usually marry for the first time between the ages of 18 and 25, when they are able to hunt and work for their wives' parents. Marriage is important for a man for a number of reasons. It marks him as an adult worthy of taking part in

Roger De La Harpe/Gallo Images/Corbis

In Ju/'hoansi culture, most marriages are arranged by the couple's parents, and the bride-to-be frequently objects to the chosen spouse or to the prospect of marriage itself.

Ju/'hoansi public life, he gains a sex partner, and he gains a mate to provide his food. While men are obligated to share and formally distribute the meat they obtain in the hunt with everyone in the camp, women are not obligated to share what they gather outside their nuclear family group, and women gather from 60 to 80 percent of the food in a camp.

Women often marry as early as 12 to 14 years of age, generally before their first menstruation, which occurs at about 17. Girls have fewer reasons to marry than men. Single or married men are always available as sex partners, and since the product of male labour, meat, is widely shared, a woman need not have a husband to ensure her share of the hunt. A girl's parents, however, have good reasons for getting her married as soon as possible. The earlier she is married, the longer she and her husband will remain with her parents until she is of age, and the longer her husband will work for her parents. Moreover, the bride's family gains an alliance with another family and is less likely to get involved in open conflict between men over their daughter.

incest taboo
A rule that prohibits sexual relations among kin of certain categories, such as brothers or sisters, parents and children, or, in some cases, cousins.

Marriages are almost always arranged by the couple's parents. Typically, the mother or father of the male approaches the family of the girl with a proposal for marriage. If the girl's parents approve of the match, the families exchange gifts to indicate their agreement. An appropriate husband for a daughter is a man who is not too much older, is not yet married, is a good hunter, and is willing to accept responsibility. The prospective groom should also be cooperative, generous, and unaggressive.

The Ju/'hoansi avoid choosing a spouse who is a close kinsperson; they are also are restricted in the choice of a marriage partner by their naming system. There are only about 30 to 40 names that can be chosen for newborns, and people with the same first name consider themselves connected, regardless of their actual kinship relation to one another. For example, if two people are named Toma, then everyone related by kinship to one Toma will be considered related in the same way to the other Toma. Consequently, if a man's name is Toma, all the brothers and sisters of everyone else named Toma are considered his brothers and sisters, all the sons and daughters of any other Toma are considered his sons and daughters, and so on. Therefore, a marriage partner should occupy neither an actual prohibited kinship category nor one created by the naming system. A woman, for example, could not marry a man with the same name as her father or a man whose father had the same name as her father, since she and the man would refer to themselves as brother and sister. When Richard Lee (1984) was working with the Ju/'hoansi kinship system, he found that interpretations of the naming system varied, and disagreements about the kin connection between people were always resolved by the interpretation of the older person in the relationship.

Once a suitable match is made, one more obstacle to the marriage remains. Perhaps because they have little to gain or much to lose, young women often object strenuously to the marriage or to their parents' choice of a husband. If they protest long and hard enough, the marriage will be called off; if the protest is not sufficient to call off the arrangements, a marriage ceremony takes place. A hut set apart from the bride's family village is built for the couple by members of both families. Friends bring the couple to the hut, and the girl, head covered, is placed in the hut. Coals from the fires of both families are brought to start the fire in the couple's hut. Friends stay, joking, singing, and dancing, while bride and groom stay apart. Often, especially if the girl is young, a relative stays with them in the hut until she begins to adjust to her new status. These "honeymoons" are often the source of continuing conflict.

Working among the Ju/'hoansi, Marjorie Shostak (1983) forged a close relationship with a Ju/'hoansi woman, Nisa, who described her wedding night. Nisa said she cried so much and objected so strongly to spending the night with her new husband, Bo, that her parents asked a female relative, Nukha, to sleep between Nisa and Bo. She soon discovered that Nukha was having sex with Bo, and after a few nights, she told her parents. They took her and moved to another water hole, leaving Nukha and Bo behind.

Typically, half of all first marriages fail among the Ju/'hoansi, who may enter several marriages over the course of their lives. Nisa's second marriage, to Tashay, followed the same lines as her first; on her wedding night she cried and cried and eventually ran away into the bush. Relatives tried to explain the benefits of marriage and to convince her to accept Tashay. When she finally agreed, Tashay took Nisa to his parents' home to live, and Nisa's parents followed. But not until Nisa and Tashay had been living together for a long time did they have sex. Nisa remembers the aftermath of their first love-making as being painful, and it was a long time before she allowed it again and began to enjoy it.

The Family Cycle of Trobriand Islanders

Courtship and sexual play begin early in the Trobriand Islands. Children play erotic games at the ages of seven and eight and begin seeking sex partners at ages 11 to 13. Trobriand adolescents are permitted to openly display their affection for each other; girls scratch, beat, thrash, or even wound their lovers, and boys accept this treatment as a sign of love and display their wounds as proof of manliness and success in courtship. They sing about love, both successful and unrequited, and take great pains with their physical appearance. Here is what Malinowski says about adolescent courtship: "An adolescent gets definitely attached to a given person, wishes to possess her, works purposefully toward his goal, plans to reach fulfillment of his desires by magical and other means, and finally rejoices in achievement. I have seen young people of this age grow positively miserable through ill-success in love" (Malinowski 1929, 63).

Because sexual activity before marriage is common and expected among Trobrianders, the couple often have already been living together, and the marriage simply formalizes an existing relationship. Although the couple may take the initiative in arranging a marriage, parents approve or disapprove of the choice of a spouse and sometimes arrange matches. There are people of certain categories that a Trobriander may not marry. All Trobrianders belong to one of four **clans**, groups whose members consider themselves descended from a common ancestor. They must observe **exogamy**, which requires one to marry outside one's own group—in this case, out of their own clan and into another (other societies practice **endogamy**, which requires marriage inside one's own group). In addition, the incest taboo applies to all close relatives, particularly brothers and sisters, who include all members of a matrilineage of the same generation. Trobriand myths tell of disastrous consequences of brother–sister incest that resulted in both parties committing suicide. Sexual relations between a father and daughter are prohibited, although Trobrianders tell stories about it and joke about the idea of a father being overwhelmed by the beauty of his daughter. From a Trobriand point of view, fathers are not related by kinship to their daughters. The best marriage for a man is to a woman from his father's clan, for then his children, who will trace their descent from their mother, will be members of his father's clan. Consequently, the close relationship a man has with members of his father's clan will continue into the next generation.

There is no formal marriage ceremony; the girl simply stays overnight in her boyfriend's house. The next morning the bride's mother brings the couple cooked yams to indicate the bride's family's approval of the marriage. If the girl's parents don't approve, they demand that their daughter return home with them. Sharing food is considered by Trobrianders to be more intimate than having sex. Later, the wife's mother and maternal uncle bring raw yams for the couple, while the groom's father and maternal uncle begin collecting **bridewealth**—valuables, such as stone axe blades, shells, and money—to give to the wife's kin and her father. The requirement of bridewealth makes young men dependent on members of their matrilineage. This relationship is unlike that of the brideservice required of a Ju/'hoansi man in that brideservice does not obligate a man to members of his family (see Question 5.1).

During the first year of marriage, the couple lives in the hut that served as the groom's adolescent retreat, and during that year the groom's mother brings meals for them to share. At the end of the year, the groom's mother builds a stone hearth for the couple. At that point the wife becomes responsible for the cooking.

clans
Unilineal descent groups whose members claim descent from a common ancestor.

exogamy
A rule that requires a person to marry someone outside his or her own group.

endogamy
A rule that requires a person to marry someone inside his or her own group (e.g., a lineage, an ethnic group, a religious group).

bridewealth
The valuables that a groom or his family are expected or obligated to present to the bride's family.

The end of the first year of marriage marks a dramatic change in the husband–wife relationship. They no longer eat together, and the sexuality that bound them together as adolescents must be publicly submerged. After the first year of marriage it is shameful for anyone to refer to the couple's sex life together. In public, a husband and wife never hold hands or display affection. Their lives become segmented into a private domain in which affection and emotion can be displayed, and a public domain in which the meaning of their relationship is dictated by their obligation to help ensure the continuity and honour of their respective matrilineages.

The matrilineal principle in the life of a Trobriand husband and wife requires each to have a continued involvement with others outside the nuclear family. In addition to his ties to and concerns for his wife and children, the husband is also involved in the family life of his matrilineage: his sisters and their children. The wife is continually involved with her and her children's matrilineage—particularly her brothers. This involvement is economic and revolves around wealth, particularly yams, banana leaf bundles, and skirts, all of which are controlled ultimately by women.

One reason men marry is to obtain yams. Yams are more than food in the Trobriand Islands; they are valuable symbols or objects of wealth and are used as gifts to create and sustain relationships among people. They are particularly important in marriage transactions and in the continued tie of a woman to her matrilineage. Trobriand family yam gardens belong to the wife, but they are tended first by her father and later by a "brother." Each year at harvest time the yams grown in her garden by her father or brother are ceremoniously taken to her. The amount and quality of the yams grown by a woman's brother are usually proportional to the bridewealth given to the wife's family by the groom's family when the couple was married. Early in the marriage these yams are stored in the rafters of the couple's hut, and the husband uses them as valuables to be redistributed to those of his kin who contributed the bridewealth. Later—often 10 to 15 years later—if a man is recognized as important by his wife's kin, they construct a yam house for him to store the yams they bring each year. The amount and quality of the yams stored and displayed by a man are indications of the regard in which he is held by his wife's kin and of his status in the community. The yam house is, according to Weiner (1988), like a public bank account.

As a man seeks a wife to obtain the yams grown for him by his wife's brother, brothers seek husbands for their sisters, not only for the children nurtured by the husbands for their wives' matrilineage but also for the help of the brothers-in-law in obtaining banana leaf bundles. Sisters are obligated, with the help of their husbands, to prepare bundles of banana leaves to be used to finance the funerals of members of their matrilineage. Some are made by the woman, but her husband may have to purchase additional bundles. They are given away at funerals by members of the deceased's matrilineage to people who were important in the life of the deceased. The more important the person was to the deceased, the greater the number of banana leaf bundles he or she receives. In this way, members of a matrilineage uphold their honour and status; to fail to fulfill these obligations would bring dishonour to the matrilineage.

The development of Trobriand family life, then, must be understood in the context of the movement of such goods as yams and banana leaf bundles between husband and wife and members of the wife's matrilineage. It is the successful completion of the cycle of exchanges of yams and banana leaf bundles that ensures the stability of a marriage and a matrilineage.

The Trobriand nuclear family promotes stable bonds between husband and wife, although divorce is both frequent and easy to obtain. The initiative is usually taken by the wife. Most divorces occur in the first year of marriage; they are rare after the couple has been together for a few years.

Although fathers are not technically members of their children's family, they are important in the lives of the children. Once children are weaned

ERIC LAFFORGUE/Alamy Stock Photo

Among the Trobriand Islanders, lineage is traced through the mother, and individuals must marry outside their own clan.

they sleep with their fathers, and later the father is responsible for enhancing their beauty with presents of shells, necklaces, and tiny tortoise-shell earrings. These objects are evidence of a father's presence in the life of his child; in fact, Weiner (1988) says the term for a child with unpierced ears is translated as "fatherless." So important is the tie that develops between a man and his son that when the son marries, the father may try to convince him to remain in his village rather than moving to the village of his maternal kin, as is expected.

The Family Cycle of Rural Chinese

The key relationship in Ju/'hoansi families is between husband and wife, and among Trobriand Islanders it is between brother and sister. In China, the family centres on the relationship between father and son. Marriage in traditional China is less a matter of a man getting a wife than of bringing a child bearer into the household. As Hsu (1967, 57) describes it, "a marriage is made in the name of the parents taking a daughter-in-law, not in the name of the son taking a wife."

Since marriage has far less to do with relations between husband and wife than with those between the husband's family and a daughter-in-law, marriages in rural China are almost always arranged, often far in advance, and there is little, if any courtship. When a boy is six or seven years old, his parents might hire a matchmaker to find a girl who will eventually be an appropriate bride for their son. Since they believe that the time of a person's birth influences his or her personality and fate, the parents may also enlist the services of a diviner to make the appropriate match. The matchmaker takes a red paper with the time and date of a girl's birth to a prospective groom's family. The boy's mother brings this paper (or papers, if there is a choice of brides) to a fortuneteller, who predicts the compatibility of the boy and girl. If a girl is deemed appropriate by the fortuneteller, the matchmaker tries to convince the girl's parents to accept the match. If she is successful, the bridewealth—that is, the marriage gifts of the husband's family to the wife's parents—is then negotiated.

Another way parents can obtain a wife for their son in rural China is to adopt an infant girl who will be reared in the household and later will marry the son. Although this kind of arrangement is not as prestigious as bridewealth marriage, it has two advantages: since the prospective bride was raised in the household of her future mother-in-law, she is more likely to be obedient, and paying a bridewealth for an adopted daughter-in-law is unnecessary. The major disadvantage is that the prospective bride and groom are raised as brother and sister and often find it difficult to make the transition to husband and wife.

The adoption of a boy to serve as a husband for a daughter is a third way that marriages are arranged in rural China. A family does this only when it has no sons. The adopted boy then assumes the family name, so that his sons continue the line of his adopted father. Such marriages are not as respected as others, and a man who is adopted into his wife's family bears the stigma of having abandoned his parents and ancestors. For poor or orphaned boys, however, the prospect of heading a thriving household may outweigh such a stigma.

Compared to Ju/'hoansi or Trobriand marriage ceremonies, the rural Chinese wedding is very formal and, for the groom's family, very expensive.

The date and hour of the wedding are determined by a diviner, who even decides the exact time the bride will arrive in her sedan chair. The day before the wedding, the girl's **dowry**—goods and valuables that the bride's family supplies to the groom's family or the couple—is sent to the groom's home in a procession accompanied by a band, drummers, and ushers. The dowry consists of such goods as leather chests, tables, stools, cosmetics, housewares, clothing and cloth, but never land or a house. On the day of the wedding, the groom is carried in a sedan chair to the house of the bride; when he arrives, she shows token resistance, and she and her mother weep. She is then carried to the groom's house in a red sedan chair decorated to suggest the early birth of sons. Offerings are made at the ancestors' altar to ensure the success of the marriage. Then the couple is taken to pay respect to the boy's parents—the formal introduction of the bride to the groom's household. Feasting and dancing accompany the wedding and sometimes last for three or four days.

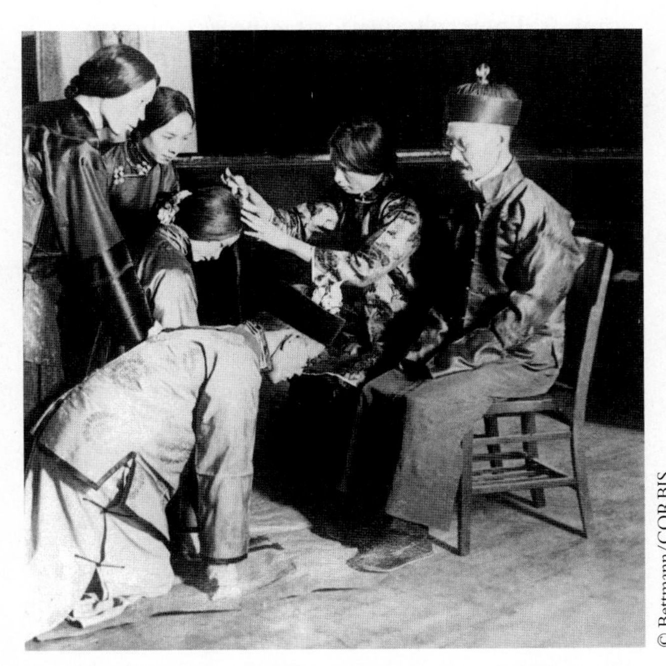

© Bettmann/CORBIS

In a rural Chinese wedding, the bride's mother places a rose in the bride's hair and then transfers it to the groom. The couple then proceed to the household of the groom's parents, where they will make their home.

After the wedding, there is little time or place for romantic relations between husband and wife. Hsu (1967) reports that after the marriage, husband and wife sleep in the same bed for only seven days, and there is no public expression of affection between them. Once the wife enters into her husband's family, she finds herself among strangers, virtually cut off from her parents and siblings. She must treat her mother-in-law with respect and acquiesce to the demands of sisters-in-law or other members of her husband's family. She occupies the lowest place at the table, and she does not acquire full status in her husband's family until she produces a male child. Until then, the husband must show indifference to his wife, addressing her through a third party; after the birth of a son, he can refer to her as the mother of his child. For the groom, marriage is a continued expression of his duty to his father and his ancestors. Whereas divorce is fairly common among Trobrianders and among Ju/'hoansi, it is virtually unheard of in rural China. A husband can take mistresses with impunity, and in theory, he can murder an adulterous wife. Wives have no rights of divorce. A wife may flee her husband's household, commit suicide, or become a prostitute; she has few other alternatives.

Question 5.3: What Are the Roles of Sexuality, Love, and Wealth?

Sex, Love, and Wealth among Ju/'hoansi

Wealth plays no part in the lives of the Ju/'hoansi, but especially for women, according to Nisa, sex, love, and beauty are very important. A Ju/'hoansi woman's sexuality is her major means of negotiating the

dowry
The goods and valuables a bride's family supplies to the groom's family or to the couple.

conditions of her relationships with others. Sexuality is important first for her own well-being. Nisa told Marjorie Shostak (1983) that if a girl grows up not learning to enjoy sex, her mind doesn't develop normally; if a grown woman doesn't have sex, her thoughts are ruined and she is always angry. Moreover, a woman's sexuality maximizes her independence. Sex attracts lovers, and a love relationship, being voluntary, recognizes the equality of the participants. By taking lovers, a Ju/'hoansi woman proclaims her control over her social life, because she can offer her sexuality to men as a means of vitalizing them. Nisa talked candidly about sex, male impotence, and the contributions women make to men:

> *A woman can bring a man life, even if he is almost dead. She can give him sex and make him alive again. If she were to refuse, he would die! If there were no women around, their semen would kill men. Did you know that? Women make it possible for them to live. Women have something so good that if a man takes it and moves about inside it, he climaxes and is sustained.* (in Shostak 1983, 288)*

There is one trade-off for Ju/'hoansi women who use their sexuality. Men see them as sources of male conflict and consequently as potentially dangerous.

Motherhood, unlike sexuality, is not easily bartered by Ju/'hoansi women. In other societies, parents may stress how much they have sacrificed or suffered for their children, thus using motherhood or fatherhood as a way of creating obligations and ties. It makes little sense for a Ju/'hoansi woman (or man, for that matter) to make such a claim. Children owe their parents little; there is no need for bridewealth or dowries for marriage, and food and kin to care for them are plentiful. The dynamics of Ju/'hoansi families are built on the need of individuals to avoid permanent ties and obligations and to maintain their independence.

Sex, Love, and Wealth among Trobriand Islanders

The maintenance of sexuality is important throughout life among Ju/'hoansi; among Trobriand Islanders, it is important for women only prior to their marriage. Armed with the magic and bodily adornments contributed by her father, but without the wealth (yams, banana leaf bundles, other valuables) she will later acquire, an unmarried woman uses her sexuality to negotiate her relationships with others. Once married, she ceases to emphasize her beauty and sexual attraction and, instead, emphasizes her fertility and motherhood. A woman's worth, once measured by her father's concern for her and by her own sexuality and beauty, is determined after marriage by her ability to collect yams for her husband, produce children, and provide banana leaf bundles for her matrilineage.

Men's sexuality is viewed very differently. Since Trobrianders claim that men play no role in reproduction, their sexuality is never very important anyway. Their physical attractiveness, however, is important, for this is what attracts lovers and later a wife to collect the yams by which a man measures his status. Beauty is especially important for chiefs. They must maintain an aura of sexual attractiveness in order to attract more wives, whose fathers and brothers will supply the wealth they need to maintain their influence.

Wealth also forms different kinds of links for Trobrianders. Because Ju/'hoansi have little wealth to contend for and what there is (e.g., meat) is widely shared, the links that men create with their wives' families are based not on wealth but on their labour. Among Trobrianders, however, men who want to marry must use the wealth of members of their matrilineage as bridewealth payments to their wives' families. They are required to return this wealth to members of their family by redistributing the yams they later receive from their wives' brothers. Moreover, the yams they receive from their brothers-in-law are in some ways payment for the children their wives produce—these children are members of the matrilineage of the wife and brothers-in-law.

**NISA: The Life and Words of a !Kung Woman* by Marjorie Shostak, Cambridge, Mass: Harvard University Press, Copyright © 1981 by Marjorie Shostak.

Sex, Love, and Wealth among Rural Chinese

The themes of sexuality, love, and wealth are played out very differently in Chinese rural families. Whereas Ju/'hoansi and Trobriand adolescents have considerable freedom to utilize their sexuality to attract and influence others, quite the opposite is true in China. If a girl comes from a family that is wealthy and influential enough to make an attractive match for her, she will have little to do with boys. Virginity is both valued and necessary for a Chinese bride; for a Ju/'hoansi or Trobriander woman, it is almost no consideration. In China, if a girl is known to have been mixed up in an affair, her only chance of marriage is to someone in a distant village.

According to Margery Wolf (1968), romantic love and sexuality are irrelevant also in the relations between traditional Chinese husbands and wives. A wife's function is to produce children. A man who can afford it takes concubines. A man who can't afford it, but does so anyway, is criticized not for his infidelity to his wife but for squandering the wealth of his ancestors and descendants.

Sexuality figures little in the life of a rural Chinese woman either before or after her marriage. Her sexuality is simply not negotiable; instead, it is as a mother that most Chinese women establish significant relations. A woman's value consists in her potential to become the mother of a boy. Becoming a mother cements her relations with her husband, her father-in-law, and her mother-in-law, and it is her motherhood that secures her later life. While a son is obligated to care for his aged mother, the obligation is not so great as it is to care for a father. To compensate, Wolf argues, a woman must establish bonds of emotion and affection with her sons. She may do this with the assistance of her husband. After a boy is six or seven, fathers become aloof and withdrawn in order to assert and reinforce their authority and control over a son. A mother can use her husband's aloofness from his son to strengthen the son's ties to her. Even if she enjoys good relations with her husband, she will try to reserve the son's affection for herself, while preserving the son's respect for his father.

BEYOND THE BOOK 5.3

In North America, we tend to take romantic love and sexual attraction for granted as central to the development and maintenance of relationships. The cases explored demonstrate that romantic love and sexuality are clearly not universal. Yet there seem to be features of love and sexuality in all three that are similar to life in North American families. List those features of conjugal relationships among Ju/'hoansi, Trobriand Islanders, and rural Chinese that resemble those of North American families. Put another way, what features of North American conjugal relationships would be familiar to a Ju/'hoansi, a Trobriand Islander, or someone from rural China?

Question 5.4: What Threatens to Disrupt the Family Unit?

In the introduction, we briefly discussed contemporary debates about same-sex marriage and teenage and single motherhood in North America. Much of the debate focuses on whether or not these social phenomena pose a "threat" to the typical North American family. There are also threats to the stability and maintenance of traditional Chinese, Trobriand, and Ju/'hoansi families, but these differ from the ones that are perceived to threaten the North American family.

Threats to a Ju/'hoansi Family

The major threat to family stability among the Ju/'hoansi is conflict between husband and wife over infidelity or the efforts of a husband to secure a second wife. Like many societies around the world, the Ju/'hoansi allow **polygamy**, a form of marriage in which a person is permitted to have more than one spouse. Men are allowed to have more than one wife (**polygyny**), and apparently women are permitted to

polygamy
A form of marriage in which a person is permitted to have more than one spouse.

polygyny
A form of marriage in which a man is permitted to have more than one wife.

have more than one husband (**polyandry**), though this is rare. In fact, polygamy is the exception rather than the rule. A survey conducted by Lee in 1968 of 131 married Ju/'hoansi men found that 93 percent were living monogamously, 5 percent were living in polygynous unions, and 2 percent were living in polyandrous relationships.

One reason that polygamy is rare, even though having more than one wife is a sign of prestige, is the family difficulties it creates. According to Marjorie Shostak (1983, 172), a popular saying is "There is never any peace in a household with two women in it." Stories of the complications resulting from polygamous unions are an endless source of humour for those who are single or monogamous. Here is how Nisa described polygyny in her society to Shostak:

> *When a man married one woman, then marries another and sets her down beside the first so there are three of them together at night, the husband changes from one wife to another. First he has sex with the older wife, then with the younger. But when he goes to the younger wife, the older one is jealous and grabs and bites him. The two women start to fight and bite each other. The older woman goes to the fire and throws burning wood at them yelling "What told you that when I, your first wife, am lying here that you should go and sleep with another woman? Don't I have a vagina? So why do you just leave it and go without having sex with me? Instead you go and have sex with that young girl!" Sometimes they fight like that all night, until dawn breaks. A co-wife is truly a terrible thing.** (Shostak 1983, 172)

While polygamy is rare, marital infidelity is not. At one water hole with 50 married couples, Lee (1984) recorded 16 couples in which one or another of the partners was having an affair. The Ju/'hoansi recognize certain benefits in taking lovers. For a woman, extramarital affairs add variety as well as economic insurance. Here is Nisa again:

> *When you are a woman, you just don't sit still and do nothing—you have lovers. You don't just sit with the man of your hut, with just one man. One man can give you very little. One man gives you only one kind of food to eat. But when you have lovers, one brings you something and another brings you something else. One comes at night with meat, another with money, another with beads.** (Shostak 1983, 271)

Men say that the emotion and passion of extramarital affairs are wonderful—"hearts are on fire and passions great," as Ju/'hoansi say. When Shostak asked a young married man about his lover, he said they fantasized about running away. She asked what it would be like, and he smiled and replied, "The first few months would be wonderful!" Extramarital affairs are likely to be threatening to a husband, however, and they are the most common cause of conflict and violence among the Ju/'hoansi. Wives are important to Ju/'hoansi men because as long as they have wives they are dependent on no one. Male adulthood requires acquiring and demonstrating a willingness to fight for a secure marital status.

Threats to a Trobriand Island Family

Among Trobriand Islanders it is not threats to the husband–wife relationship that are critical but threats to the matrilineage. Because the matrilineage is the principal social unit, the honour of that family group relative to other groups is a central concern to all members. Lineages among Trobriand Islanders are ranked according to the closeness of their genealogical connection to the founders of the lineage. Each lineage must be able to maintain its position vis-à-vis others through the ceremonial

polyandry
A form of marriage in which a woman is permitted to have more than one husband.

**NISA: The Life and Words of a !Kung Woman* by Marjorie Shostak, Cambridge, Mass: Harvard University Press, Copyright © 1981 by Marjorie Shostak.

presentation of valuables, particularly yams and banana leaf bundles. So important are yams in the relative ranking of matrilineages that groups try to demonstrate their wealth by giving more yams to others than they receive. Since giving may be taken as a claim of superiority, however, it can be dangerous; as Trobrianders put it, "When you give too much, people worry."

Although it may seem implausible, yams could serve as the focus of a Trobriand soap opera or reality television show. For example, a man's political power, measured in yams, is a direct result of the support he receives from his wife's kin—her yams, grown for her by her father and brother, create status for him as her husband. However, the annual yam gifts received by a husband can also be a source of conflict. If the amount or size of yams harvested does not live up to a husband's expectations, he may be insulted. On the other hand, if a woman's brother is unhappy over the bridewealth he received from the husband's family or the support given by the husband to his sister in collecting banana leaf bundles, he may purposely communicate his unhappiness by not working hard in his sister's yam gardens. Other plots could be devised about unrequited love, about attempts by fathers to convince their sons to remain in their father's village, and even about incest. But a theme that would be sure to attract a Trobriand audience would be about sorcery.

Trobrianders claim to know of spells and magic forms that are capable of killing. Generally, only chiefs have this power, but others can seek out a chief and, for a price, convince him to use his power against their enemies. Someone who is believed to have this power is both feared and respected; Trobrianders tell of instances when they were challenged and retaliated with sorcery. Vanoi, an important Trobriand chief, told Weiner (1988) about being challenged by a Christian convert who openly mocked Vanoi's knowledge of sorcery. Vanoi offered the man a cigarette, saying that he should smoke it if he doubted the chief's knowledge of sorcery. The man did; he became ill later that night and died a week later.

A person who uses sorcery against another is dominating that person, and since each person's fate is tied to that of the matrilineage, a threat to one is considered a threat to all. That is why any death among Trobrianders is a serious matter. Since all deaths are attributed to sorcery, every death is a sign that the power of a matrilineage is being challenged by someone from another lineage. Each funeral marks an attempt by the members of a matrilineage to reassert its power; at the same time, the mourners assert their innocence of sorcery. The matrilineal kin of the deceased do this by distributing banana leaf bundles and other valuables to those who have come to publicly mourn the passing of the deceased and to assist with the funeral arrangements by decorating and carrying the corpse. In recognition of their contribution to the life of the deceased, they receive gifts. The deceased's matrilineage empties its treasury to announce its strength in the face of the threat to its integrity that is signalled by a death.

Maintaining one's identity and that of the matrilineage is a never-ending process among Trobrianders because death threatens the network by removing someone from it. Here is how Weiner sums up the meaning of death for them:

> *Because of the expanding possibilities in a person's life, each Trobriander represents her or his matrilineal identity—originally conceived through a woman and an ancestral baloma spirit—as well as the accumulation of all the other relationships that parenthood and marriage made possible. Therefore, a death demands attention to this full totality, as the members of a matrilineage seek both to repay all "others" for their past care and to hold on to them now that this death has occurred.* (Weiner 1988, 161)

Threats to a Rural Chinese Family

The biggest threat to the traditional rural Chinese family is, of course, the absence of a son. The lack of a male heir endangers not only the continuance of a household but also the entire patrilineage through time. A man without sons, a spirit without descendants, has no one to offer incense for him and no altar on which his spirit can find refuge and honour.

The existence of a son is no guarantee of smooth family relations, however. Fathers have enormous authority and power over sons, and sons are obligated to worship, respect, obey, and care for their fathers. But often fathers become overbearing or use force to assert their authority. Margery Wolf (1968) says that Lim Han-ci in the village of Peihotien (see Question 5.3) was unusual in the frequency with which he administered physical punishment to his sons; once he beat them with a hoe handle and left bruises that lasted for weeks.

Regardless of how harshly a person may be treated, however, breaking away from one's father is considered a violent act. Wolf reports a conflict between Lim Han-ci and his eldest son, Lim Hue-lieng, which illustrates both the dilemma of a father–son split and the difficulties that can arise in adopted marriages. When Lim Hue-lieng was a child, Lim Han-ci adopted Lim A-pou, then nine months old, to be reared as the eventual wife of his son. Growing up in the Lim household, Lim A-pou was a model daughter-in-law. She accepted reprimands and punishment without becoming sullen, she did not complain, and she worked hard. However, her relationship with her prospective husband was not a happy one. When Lim Hue-lieng was 19, he committed what in rural China is an act of moral violence: he left home and severed his relations with his father. If a son dies before his father and so is unable to care for the father in his old age, the father ritually beats the son's coffin to punish him. Lim Hue-lieng was able to leave home only because he had become a leader in the lo mue, a secret society that is involved in crime and extortion but that also protects the downtrodden and contributes heavily to religious festivals.

Dramatic splits between fathers and sons are rare in traditional China. More frequent is conflict between brothers over the division and sharing of the family wealth at the death of a male head of the household. In most other rural, peasant societies around the world, the male head of the household designates his heirs before his death. He may in some fashion divide his property among his offspring—**partible inheritance**—or he may leave all his property to one or another descendant—**impartible inheritance**. In rural China the ideal is for brothers to continue to live together and share the inheritance, usually under the direction of the eldest son, thus avoiding the division of property. In fact, however, brothers rarely continue to share, and ultimately conflict between them leads to a division of household property.

Wolf (1968) documents the ultimate disintegration of the Lim household after the death of Lim Han-ci and the resulting arguments over property among the sons and their wives. When Wolf went to live in the Lim household, Lim Han-ci and his oldest son, Lim Hue-lieng, had already died. The two remaining family units consisted of the family of the second oldest son, Lim Chieng-cua, and the family of Lim Hue-lieng's widow, Lim A-Pou. While Lim Han-ci was alive, his power and influence and his control over the family's wealth were enough to maintain the extended family. Once he died, conflict between Lim A-pou and her son on the one hand and Lim Chieng-cua on the other led to the division of family property. The wealth that had held the extended family together served, finally, to drive it apart. After dividing the property, brothers or their families often continue to live in the same house, but they partition it into separate family units with separate stoves, as did the son and grandson of Lim Han-ci. The once extended household becomes, in effect, a family compound.

partible inheritance
A form of inheritance in which the goods or property of a family is divided among the heirs.

impartible inheritance
A form of inheritance in which family property is passed undivided to one heir.

BEYOND THE BOOK 5.4

Family units, as we have discussed, are fluid and constantly changing in response to various socio-historical and political circumstances. Discuss three political, social, and/or economic changes that have occurred over the last twenty years in Canada that impact Canadian families. What challenges may family units experience as a result of these changes?

Question 5.5: How Has the Anthropological Study of Families Changed?

As we stated in our introduction, a lot has changed within Ju/'hoansi, Trobriand, and rural Chinese societies since the anthropologists noted in the previous sections of this chapter did their fieldwork. Culture is never static, and even small changes in both local societies and global politics may affect how different people in different places construct their beliefs about family relations and kinship. For instance, between the 1930s and the 1970s, China experienced almost constant turmoil: the war with Japan (1937 to 1945), a civil war (1945 to 1949), the Great Leap Forward (1959 to 1961), and the Cultural Revolution (1966 to 1976). Laurel Bossen suggests that throughout this time, women in Lu Village, in the southern province of Yunnan, have gained some benefits, such as "the end of footbinding, greater recognition of women's economic contributions, improved female health and education, lower infant mortality, a wider variety of employment options and family choices, more labor-saving technology and modes of communication, and a greater public voice" (2002, 19). Although patrilineal descent and patrilocality are still the rule, Bossen (2002, 229) found families in Lu Village that followed uxorilocal marriage, where the husband leaves his village and moves to the village of his wife. Lu villagers use the term "zhao guye" (seek a son-in-law) to refer to uxorilocal marriage.

After the Cultural Revolution in China, women gained more control over their lives than they had in the 1960s when Wolf did her fieldwork. Ellen Judd (1994) has suggested that legal changes, such as the Inheritance Law of 1985, which allows daughters to inherit their parents' property, as well as the increase in women's access to employment in rural North China, have allowed some women to gain some freedom from previous constraints.

Changing Anthropological Perceptions of Kinship

Anthropologists began to adjust how they thought about and studied family relations when they began to question some of their main assumptions. The idea that these assumptions might be rooted in Euro-American culture and then used to describe and analyze other cultures gained momentum in the 1970s and 1980s. In Canada, Martin Silverman (1979) questioned the relationship between political economy and anthropology as it applied to the ways that European and anglophone North American anthropologists viewed their own family relationships and those of other peoples in other cultures. Silverman argued that the view of marriage as an exchange of women, for instance, with men directing the exchanges, resembles the model of commodity exchange "in which something is bought and sold ... a thing which has no rights of its own, and in which the direct producer has no rights" (1979, 71).

Linda Stone (2001) has reviewed two important factors questioned by David Schneider in the early 1980s—factors that led anthropologists to re-evaluate some of their assumptions about how different societies establish connections among family members. The first was Schneider's critique of his own work among Yap families in the West Caroline Islands. The more Schneider thought about what he had written, the more he began to wonder how much of what he had described as Yap notions of relatedness were projections of his own Eurocentric beliefs about the role of biology in kinship. When he re-evaluated his account of Yap kinship, he found that two of the fundamental kinship terms in Western biological explanations of conception and birth—mother and father—did not apply to Yap notions of producing children. The biological term "father" as anthropologists were using it was only roughly equivalent to the mother's husband at the time she became pregnant in Yap society. Likewise, the term "mother" applied to the woman who gave birth to a child, but this child had been placed in her womb by ghosts—it was not because the father's sperm had fertilized her egg.

The second factor was Schneider's critique of the ethnocentric evolutionism in studies that assume kinship is important in small-scale societies only where it provides the basis for social organization. In this argument, kinship loses importance as societies become more complex and disappears as a major institution in modern industrial states. Families likewise change from the large extended size in small-scale societies to the efficient nuclear size found in North America. This, according to Schneider, might actually be an anthropological myth, and if the myth itself is investigated, "kinship might … become a special custom distinctive of European culture" (Schneider 1984, 201).

When Schneider asked, "Is blood really thicker than water?," several anthropologists began to take a closer look at whether groups that used kinship terms for their association were related on the basis of biology or on the basis of other factors. In many cultural contexts, biology is still perceived as an important factor in constituting kinship. In the United States, for instance, the rise of Donald Trump and the alt-right has sanctioned the use of exclusionary, anti-immigrant discourses and policies, where metaphors of biology and blood are evoked to denote one's "place" and sense of belonging within American culture. Phrases such as "red-blooded American" are often used by the white alt-right to denote individuals and families that perceive themselves as "more American" than immigrant families.

The perception that family can be reduced to biology is also fuelled by the growing interest in online genealogical research, popularized by websites like Ancestry.com, which encourages subscribers to find their family "origins." In these cases, one's identity is explicitly and exclusively defined by biological relationships—relationships "discovered" by reconstructing family trees and/or through genetic testing. While anthropologists liken these DNA tests to a form of "genetic astrology," and are quick to point out their shortcomings, including their oversimplification of the relationship between biology and ancestry (e.g., Raff 2019), of relevance here is that such methods fail to consider how social factors like one's family history, memories, upbringing, or enculturation into a specific ethnic, religious, or other group shape identity. Ultimately, identity becomes reduced to biological relationships.

In other contexts, the notion of whether "blood" or some other substance is the basis of how family members are related has been debated. For example, whereas in Western science, model children are related to their parents through "blood," people in a neighbourhood of Gaborne, Botswana, told Frederick Klaits (2005) that husbands and wives become "of one blood" when they have sexual intercourse and produce children.

Food is another substance that may be more important than blood in creating kinship. David and Dorothy Counts (1998) tell a very instructive story about their own experience of being defined in kinship terms by the Kaliai people, whom they visited in New Guinea to do their research. They believed that their adoption into a Kandokan family had been basically only fiction and then learned to their surprise that it was very real: "We learned that when members of our Kandokan family brought us bananas, pineapples, and watermelons, and we gave them rice, fresh bread, and tinned beef, we were not just exchanging groceries. We and they were becoming family … When they fed us and our children and received food from us in return, we were exchanging the stuff of which substance is made: we were becoming Kaliai" (1998, 152).

In Canada, the granting of legal rights to families that practise **polyamory** has challenged the presumed salience of both biology and monogamy in dictating parental rights and responsibilities. In 2017, two men involved in a relationship with the biological mother of a child were disturbed to learn that only two parents could be listed on the baby's birth certificate. They took their case to court to have all three members of the polyamorous family declared a parent to the child. In 2018, a Newfoundland judge granted all three parents in this polyamorous relationship the legal status of parent, setting a national precedent.

Another major influence on how anthropologists study family relations is the feminist insight that we must question the ways in which the structure of families and their connections to biology reinforce gender inequalities. For instance, the fact that women give birth is consistently translated into a closer attachment of women to nature and to home, whereas men are more able to take part in the wider social sphere of politics and economics. But to what extent is this association between femininity and nature culturally constructed?

Several anthropologists have conducted studies of the ways in which the increased use of biomedical imaging technologies during pregnancy fosters an emotional attachment between mother and child. Rayna Rapp (2007) and Lisa Mitchell (2001), for instance, have examined the use of ultrasound in the United States and Canada, respectively. We tend to think of ultrasounds as apolitical and "routine" elements of most pregnancies. Ultrasounds can be used to monitor the health and size of a developing fetus, to check its position within the uterus, and to determine sex, among other things. However, they were not routinely used in North America until the 1980s, when women's bodies became subject to increasing surveillance and monitoring in tandem with changes and improvements in biomedical imaging.

These days, for women who intend to keep their babies after birth, ultrasound appointments are ritualized events. The woman typically brings her partner, a friend, or a family member to the appointment. Assuming that the pregnancy looks "healthy," the language employed by the sonographer functions to personify the fetus and to foster a bond between the mother and her otherwise invisible fetus. Rapp (2007, 615), for instance, writes that when sonographers are speaking with pregnant women, they "attribute motives to fetal activity and presence: a fetus that is hard to visualize is 'hiding' or 'shy'; an active fetus is described as 'swimming,' 'playing,' or even 'partying.' " "Showing the baby" drives its personification, and the mother-to-be is given a picture of the fetus to take home.

This process of visualization, according to Rapp (2007), becomes a key means through which mothers form a social bond with their fetus. Ultrasound pictures are often circulated on social media—on Facebook, Instagram, or Twitter; they are placed in albums, framed to hang on walls, posted on refrigerator doors, and emailed to family and friends. There is even a growing (yet controversial) commodification of nonmedical "recreational" ultrasounds, where pregnant women or their family members pay for specialized sonographs for the explicit purpose of obtaining detailed digital images of the developing fetus. Often these images are circulated to family and friends on social media, and/or they wind up as framed pictures in family homes, or in albums that document the first few years of a baby's life. Through these various social practices and processes of visualization, the fetus is perceived as a viable "baby" (even if, at this point, the fetus could not live on its own outside the womb), and the mother-to-be becomes engaged

polyamory
The practice of engaging in consensual intimate relationships with multiple people.

in social conversations about motherhood and pregnancy. Ultimately, ultrasound pictures, or what Mitchell (2001) calls "baby's first picture," are one of a multitude of ways in which the problematic association between femininity and "nature" can be shown to be informed by cultural processes.

These sorts of critiques of our dominant perceptions of family relations have encouraged studies in which a variety of other factors, such as history and power, are taken into account when anthropologists ask how family relationships have formed. A prime example of the influence of the heteronormative concept can be found in the history of colonization and the ways in which European colonizers viewed local family relationships as "primitive" when they differed from the European patriarchal model. In the Caribbean, for instance, family relations were defined as "abnormal" because many households appeared to lack a male figure who acted as the head of the family. Lisa Anderson-Levy, a Jamaican anthropologist, argues that colour, class, and gender work together to structure Caribbean families. Lower-class women tend to be the unmarried heads of their households or to live in extended households headed by their unmarried mothers. Upper- and middle-class women, whose skin colour is lighter, tend to be married and to live in nuclear families. Thus, "marriage was, and to a certain extent still is, something that rich people do" (2000, 195). Even female sexuality is race and class specific in Jamaica. Lower-class, dark-skinned women are thought to be unable to control their sexuality, whereas light-skinned, middle-class women are supposed to be fully in control. While overall marriage rates in Jamaica have declined from approximately 22,500 per year in 2000 to 16,719 in 2018 (STATIN 2020), marriage continues to be perceived as a marker of middle or upper class status and/or upward mobility for many women, and particularly for women who are lower-class and with dark skin (Hamilton and Goldsmith 2009).

Internal colonization, referring to the treatment of Indigenous peoples by the state, often follows the same pattern. Anthropologist Max Hedley (1998) has written about how families in the Walpole Island First Nation changed after the Department of Indian Affairs insisted that they reorganize their agriculture. No longer was growing food a community project, as in the past; instead, it was a matter of individual household production, with men as heads of the families. Around the same time, band government was imposed on the community, with women excluded from formal participation, unable to either hold office or vote. With the introduction of wage labour and formal education, the status of women within the family decreased as they left to work outside the home. Professional educators then took over important aspects of socializing children. All of this changed the meaning of motherhood.

The study of family relations has expanded to include gay and lesbian families and families produced by in vitro fertilization and by surrogate mothers. Gay and lesbian marriages became legal in Canada in July 2005, making Canada the fourth country in the world to recognize same-sex

Gay men celebrate the legalization of same-sex marriage in Canada.

APPLYING ANTHROPOLOGY

Anthropology and the Rainbow Project

As we have seen, knowledge of family relations helps us understand a whole range of things, from parent–child relations, to marriage and courtship patterns, to ideas about love, sexuality, and wealth. Understanding these relations can help societies address a multitude of issues involving families—for example, spousal abuse, divorce, and parent–child conflicts. The same knowledge can be valuable for those who work in a variety of fields that require an understanding of intimate human relations. Anthropologists, for example, can apply their understanding of family relations to help prevent sexually transmitted diseases, especially HIV/AIDS.

The major problem in AIDS prevention (and in the prevention of sexually transmitted infections, or STIs, more generally) is how to persuade people who are sexually active to protect themselves and their sex partners. Condom use is one of the simplest and most common measures. Yet even when people are aware of the risk of contracting an STI, they often fail to take this easy precaution. What do medical practitioners and those working in AIDS prevention need to know in order to design effective prevention programs? And what can anthropologists do to help?

Robert Lorway conducted fieldwork in Windhoek, Namibia's capital, with a gay and lesbian community group, the Rainbow Project. He found that the greatest barrier to successful HIV prevention initiatives in this community was the perception, perpetuated through public health initiatives, that "AIDS in Africa" is exclusively a Pattern II, or heterosexual, epidemic (Lorway 2007, 276). There are virtually no public health campaigns in Namibia that address homosexual behaviour in their prevention education, and as a result, men who have sex with men are more vulnerable to HIV infection (Lorway 2006, 435). For example, there was a common (mis)understanding among men who had wives or girlfriends, and who also enjoyed sex with men, that they were practising safer sex when sleeping with men. One of Lorway's informants explained: "Most of the men I know who have girlfriends are saying that they prefer to have sex with us moffies [effeminate males] because they don't want to catch STDs cheating on them, or HIV, or get someone pregnant. Most of them think they can even have sex with men without a condom because they think it is less risky than sex with a woman" (Jason, 21-year-old male from Katutura) (2007, 276).

Lorway's work shows that, although heterosexual intercourse is the main source of transmission of HIV in Namibia, the exclusion of any information about same-sex transmission was limiting possibilities for education and prevention. These transmission myths were compounded by intense anti-homosexual sentiment (and laws prohibiting homosexuality) in Namibia, which resulted in equally intense stigma, shame, and secrecy. Lorway's fieldwork demonstrated the urgent need for short-term interventions that would work even in a climate of intolerance and fear. During his fieldwork, he was actively involved in precisely this kind of prevention: through the Rainbow Project, he helped coordinate community-level education strategies that could "move safer sex information through secretive social networks without risking public exposure" (2007, 292). Maintaining secrecy may run counter to mainstream HIV-prevention goals, such as raising public awareness about homosexual transmission and encouraging acceptance of homosexuality in the public sphere, but Lorway's ethnographic evidence suggests that doing so is the most culturally appropriate and immediately effective way of promoting prevention. His work demonstrates just how important it is that "intensive ethnography is centrally incorporated within the methodologies of health science projects" (2006, 448).

marriage (the other three were the Netherlands, Belgium, and Spain; since then, many other countries have joined the list). As Meg Luxton (1997) points out, when families are formed by gay and lesbian couples, the definition of marriage is changed: both sexuality and child bearing are separated from legal marriage. This separation of marriage and child bearing has been one point of contention in the debate about gay marriage in Canada. Those who oppose gay marriage cite the family as the institution in which children are produced and argue that the purpose of sexual intercourse—that is, between a male and a female—is to accomplish this.

Yet this does not mean that gay and lesbian couples cannot include children in their families. Children may be brought into the marriage from a former heterosexual relationship; other options for producing children are adoption, in vitro fertilization, and surrogate motherhoods. Indeed, all three methods are being used by heterosexual couples as well as by gay and lesbian couples.

BEYOND THE BOOK 5.5

Developing a Program for Prevention of STIs among Canadian Youth

In the discussion about the work of anthropologists in reducing AIDS and the sexually transmitted infection (STI) rates in Namibia, we explored how anthropologists use their knowledge of changing family patterns and attitudes toward sexuality within applied frameworks like health care education. In Canada, children and teens are formally taught about STIs and sexuality in provincially mandated sex education curriculum at public schools. Many public health specialists feel that such curriculum is necessary because STIs like chlamydia, syphilis, and gonorrhea are on the rise among Canadian youth, and some researchers speculate that a decline in condom use might be the primary reason. With that said, parents in many provinces are permitted to exempt their children from sex education programs. For this exercise, you play the role of an STI prevention specialist whose goal is to help people understand how and why some parents feel threatened by sex education curriculum in your province or territory. Ultimately, your aim to create an inclusive, non-threatening educational environment that will be accepted by the majority of Canadian families. To accomplish this, you need to answer the following questions:

1. What are some of the cultural barriers/factors that might contribute to a family's decision to exempt their child from sex education?
2. What are some measures that you would suggest to help teens who are sexually active to overcome barriers imposed by familial opposition to sex education in schools?

Conclusions

In this chapter we have examined the structure and dynamics of family life among three peoples—the Ju/'hoansi, the Trobriand Islanders, and rural Chinese. Throughout the chapter, you have been asked to think about those aspects of the North American family that we tend to take for granted as natural but that are culturally situated and often unique. As we have seen, each society has different rules about whom a person regards as a family member, and family membership can vary based on variations in descent systems. In each case, we have also thought about how the family is formed and how the ideal family type is maintained in these societies. But it is important to keep in mind that these ideal types are not static and timeless; sometimes, the idea of an ideal family type can be contentious. Sexuality, love, and wealth each play a key role in family life, although as we have seen, the significance of each varies from culture to culture. Often, the forces that threaten the family unit are those that threaten sexuality, love, or wealth as these are understood in each cultural context.

Although kinship questions have always been central to anthropology, the ways that anthropologists think about and study family relations have changed a great deal in recent decades. Critiques such as those by David Schneider and various feminist anthropologists have inspired some researchers to be more aware of the effects of colonialism and of their own underlying Eurocentric assumptions about what families should look like. Nonetheless, knowledge of family and intimate relations in a society remains an important focus of anthropological research, and, it is important to note, can be applied to the development of culturally appropriate and effective programs to promote sexual health.

QUESTIONS: REVIEW

5.1 What is the composition of the typical family group?

This section challenges the assumption that notions of family are universal. Societies differ in terms of their perceptions of family, and some societies perceive friends or even companion animals as family members. Students are introduced to four different case studies of families: Canadian families, Trobriand islanders, rural Chinese, and Ju/'hoansi. These examples highlight cross-cultural differences in terms of how families are organized and conceptualized, and provide a tangible context for understanding key kinship terms such as bilateral kinship, matrilineality, and patrilineality.

Review Questions

1. What are the differences between bilateral, matrilineal, and patrilineal kinship systems? Provide one example for each.
2. How would the constitution of a Ju'hoansi camp change when a female gets married?
3. Why do the rural Chinese express a preference for male children?
4. What are three ways in which marriages may be arranged among the rural Chinese?

5.2 How are families formed, and how is the ideal family type maintained?

Most societies have an ideal family type, which refers to a mainstream cultural assumption or expectation of what constitutes a typical family. While many families do not conform to this ideal (or even wish to), every society has cultural expectations for family prototypes. This section adopts a comparative perspective, analyzing processes of courtship, marriage, and sex among Canadians, Trobrianders, Ju/'hoansi, and rural Chinese families. In the process, concepts such as bridewealth, dowry, clans, exogamy, endogamy are introduced.

Review Questions

1. How does the Ju/'hoansi naming system affect Ju/'hoansi perceptions of family composition and marriage?
2. If you are a Trobriander, who are you forbidden to marry?
3. What is the difference between bridewealth, brideservice, and a dowry?
4. How does the principle of matrilneality affect Trobriand family structure and relationships?
5. Compare and contrast Ju/'hoansi, Trobriand, and rural Chinese wedding ceremonies.

5.3 What are the roles of sexuality, love, and wealth?

This section compares Ju'hoansi, Trobriand, and rural Chinese societies' perspectives on male and female sexuality, love between husband and wife, and wealth. Ultimately, it highlights how factors such as gender roles/expectations, social organization, and matrilineality or patrilineality can affect issues such as sexuality. Among the Ju/'hoansi, for instance, female sexuality is important in establishing a sense of independence and self-worth, yet it is of little significance among the rural Chinese. This section stresses that such factors can only be understood within their culture-specific contexts.

Review Questions

1. How is the concept of motherhood perceived among the rural Chinese?
2. How does wealth play different roles in rural Chinese, Trobriand, and Ju/'hoansi families?
3. Why is a Ju/'hoansi woman's sexuality considered to be important?
4. Why are romantic love and sexuality irrelevant in the relations between traditional Chinese husbands and wives?

5.4 What threatens to disrupt the family unit?

Section 5.4 looks at the different internal and external circumstances that threaten family structures and family relationships among the Trobrianders, the rural Chinese, and the Ju/'hoansi. By comparing and contrasting these three societies, we learn that the factors that are labelled as threatening vary considerably cross-culturally and may include the lack of a male heir, infidelity, power imbalances, polygamy, or other factors.

Review Questions

1. In Trobriand society, how are yams often a source of family conflict?
2. How do the Ju/'hoansi view marital infidelity?
3. Among the Ju/'hoansi, why is polygamy rare?
4. What is the biggest threat to the family among the rural Chinese? Explain your answer.
5. For Trobrianders, what are the consequences of a death in the family?

5.5 How has the anthropological study of families changed?

David Schneider's research on kinship, highlighted in this section, has undergone critique and elaboration since the 1960s. For instance, many scholars (including Schneider himself, in his later writings) question whether biology can be used as a universal organizing principle for kinship. For instance, among the Yap, biology plays no role in establishing father/child relations as ghosts are believed to place children in the wombs of women. Similarly, David and Dorothy Counts's work among the Kaliai people draws attention to the ways in which food, and the sharing of food, are means of constituting kin. Many scholars have also cautioned anthropologists to think critically about how they may, even unconsciously, be imposing Eurocentric ideas of kinship onto various societies. More recently, anthropologists have focused their investigations on new reproductive technologies and technologies of bodily surveillance, such as ultrasounds, and their role in reimagining and/or constructing family. In addition, there is a heightened interest, particularly with the legalization of same-sex marriage in Canada and the United States, with understanding how idealized notions of family are reinforced or challenged by such partnerships.

Review Questions

1. Discuss two critiques that have emerged from Schneider's study of kinship.
2. What is internal colonization and how does it affect indigenous families?
3. In what ways do ultrasounds foster a social bond between parent and child?
4. Among the Kaliai, how does food create kinship?

CRITICAL THINKING QUESTIONS

1. What are some common ways in which we use the idea of family as a metaphor for other kinds of social relationships (e.g., in the workplace or in teams)? What do we accomplish when we make these kinds of metaphorical comparisons?
2. Debates about same-sex marriage in North America often pit "traditional family values" against "universal human rights." What have you learned in this chapter (and the rest of the text) that might undermine this straightforward dualism?

KEY TERMS

bilateral kinship (p. 130)
brideservice (p. 133)
bridewealth (p. 140)
clans (p. 140)
dowry (p. 143)
endogamy (p. 140)
ethnographic present (p. 129)
exogamy (p. 140)
extended family (p. 135)
impartible inheritance (p. 148)
incest taboo (p. 138)
kin term (p. 131)
kin type (p. 131)
kinship (p. 128)
matrilineage (p. 133)
matrilineal kinship (p. 131)
nuclear family (p. 130)
partible inheritance (p. 148)
patrilineage (p. 136)
patrilineal kinship (p. 131)
polyamory (p. 151)
polyandry (p. 146)
polygamy (p. 145)
polygyny (p. 145)

CHAPTER 6

Constructing Identities

sanjeri/E+/Getty Images

Our interactions with others are shaped by their perceptions of us. According to Goffman, quoted below, we use our bodies in unconscious and conscious ways to communicate information. Through our speech, clothing, gestures, and postures, people make assumptions about our character and our place in the world. Similarly, we often consciously manipulate our bodies to show others who we think we are. These aspects of what we call "identity"—both individual and collective—form the subject of this chapter.

> *When an individual enters the presence of others, they commonly seek to acquire information about him or to bring into play information about him already possessed. They will be interested in his general socioeconomic status, his conception of self, his attitude toward them, his competence, his trustworthiness, etc. ... Informed in these ways, the others will know how best to act in order to call forth a desired response from him.*
>
> —Erving Goffman

PROBLEM 6

How do people determine who they are, and how do they communicate who they think they are to others?

Introduction

We are not born knowing who we are or what our place is in the social landscape; we must learn our **social identity**: who we are and how we stand in relation to others. To appreciate the importance of the self as a social identity, try to imagine a society in which every person is physically indistinguishable from every other person. How would people in such a society know how to behave toward one another? Whenever we interact with another person, the interaction must be based on some idea of who the other is: Friend? Stranger? Family member? Teacher? At the same time, the other must have some idea of who *we* are, a conception of the relationship that exists between us. The need to know the social identity of others is apparent whenever two strangers meet and, directly or indirectly, seek to elicit information about each other. Each tries to place the other in some identity at some spot on the social landscape.

Imagine next a society in which every person is utterly unique. In this case, every interaction would be different, and there would be no way to learn from one situation how to behave in another similar situation. Each person would need to have an infinite variety of behaviours with which to interact with people of an infinite number of types. We avoid this situation by categorizing people, placing them in groups so that not everyone in our social universe is unique. We group them into categories based on criteria such as gender (female, male, or some other gender), ethnicity (Irish, Italian, Chinese), and personal characteristics (short, tall, husky, thin).

Try to imagine, also, a social landscape in which no person acknowledges any other person or communicates in any way who she or he thinks the other is. This scenario, too, would represent an impossible situation. People would have no way of acquiring from others confirmation that they occupy the social identities they think they occupy. In reality, our social identities are constructed in large part by others, who, by their behaviour toward us, confirm that we occupy the spot on the social landscape we claim to occupy. Put another way, nobody is anybody except in relation to somebody.

social identity
The view that people have of their own and others' positions in society. These learned personal and social affiliations may include gender, sexuality, race, class, nationalism, and ethnicity. Individuals seek confirmation from others that they occupy the positions on the social landscape that they claim to occupy.

QUESTIONS

6.1 How is identity, and one's sense of self, learned?
6.2 How does the concept of personhood vary from society to society?
6.3 How do societies distinguish individuals from one another?
6.4 How do societies mark changes in identity?
6.5 How do individuals communicate their identities to one another?
6.6 How do people form identities through collective struggles?

To examine how people in a society determine who they are and communicate who they think they are to others, in this chapter we explore the ways different societies define the person, the ways individuals are differentiated from others, the ways they find out who they are and convey to others who they are, the ways they mark transitions from one social identity to another, and the ways they form collective identities.

Question 6.1: How Is Identity, and One's Sense of Self, Learned?

Learning Identities

Hugh Brody begins his book *The Other Side of Eden: Hunters, Farmers, and the Shaping of the World* (2000) with a description of a baby Inuit girl:

> *Imagine the darkness of the far north. Not as something in which the adventurous traveller moves in awe. But as a beginning, for those for whom the Arctic is home. Imagine the inside of a skin tent, or a snowhouse, or a government-regulation low-rental prefab. In this home, an Inuit baby girl wakes in the night. She is held, fed, cuddled—and talked to …*
>
> *In these words, the child is given the sounds of love, and can know that she is safe. Not safe just to feed, to sleep, but safe to do these things as and when she wants. For she is a baby who carries atiq, the spirit and name of her late grandmother. She is the adored baby; she is also her mother's mother, her grandfather's wife. Her grandmother is alive again in the baby. This means the baby is doubly and trebly loved. And she must be treated with respect.* (2000, 11–12)

Is this Inuit baby born with an identity? Or is her identity something she must learn? It is certainly clear to others in her Inuit community that she is the reincarnation of her grandmother, but how long will it take the baby to understand what that means?

Brody suggests that the Inuit baby begins to know that she is an important member of her family almost the moment she is born and that this knowledge expands daily as she interacts with others. As people tell her stories about her land and its creation, she builds up an image of her world and of her place in it. She learns that she is connected to her land and to all the other creatures that share the land with her.

Stories present people of all ages with ways of knowing about who they are and where they came from. Storytelling is also a way of communicating information from one generation to another (Ridington 1990, 14). No one censors Inuit stories, and children's understanding grows as they grow. Brody describes the Inuit child's experiences with stories told by her grandfather and other adults: "The small child listens for as long as she wishes—she is, after all, also her own grandmother. And she discovers that stories are always a mystery, for they have much that cannot be understood, and much that comes from knowledge and experience beyond understanding" (2000, 13).

As this child grows, she recognizes stories that are told over and over, with the same main characters and events. She also learns that no one understands everything in the stories, and she keeps her sense of wonderment about the world.

Brody's example highlights a key point about identity: we are not born knowing who we are or what our places are on the social landscape; we *learn* to be Canadian or Japanese, husbands or wives, Andrea, Gavin, Homa, Natasha, or Sebastian. We learn how we relate to others as sons, daughters, students, friends, or lovers. Both consciously and unconsciously, individuals form various identities so that they can relate to others and cultivate a space for themselves within their social landscape. At the same time, identities are political and collective, formed around struggles against such threats as colonialism or the state. As we become who we are, we learn how we stand in relation to others.

Identities such as gender, sexuality, race, ethnicity, and national identity, to name a few, are not natural or biological. We are not born knowing instinctively what it means to "be Canadian," for instance. Our sense of Canadianness, like any other identity, is cultivated and learned through various agents of **enculturation**. These are sociocultural forces and institutions that teach us, consciously or unconsciously, about what it means to be a Canadian citizen. Agents of enculturation may include the mass media, parents, peers, school, and the government.

Think about the ways in which children are enculturated into the norms of "Canadian identity," for example, in many public school systems across Canada. In elementary school, most children learn how to sing the national anthem, and because provincial governments control the content of the school curriculum, students learn a government-sanctioned version of Canadian history. Students must demonstrate their successful acquisition and knowledge of this history on tests and papers in order to advance to the next grade. Even as they graduate and get older, Canadians continue to learn about Canada through participation in Canada Day parades and other public spectacles, or by watching the national news on Canadian television stations such as the CBC. In Canada, the mass media play an important role in shaping ideals of Canadianness through their depictions of sport, for instance. Hockey, in particular, has long been promoted as a component of a distinctive Canadian identity; however, hockey's participants and spectators are mostly white, middle-class, and male (Gruneau and Whitson 1993; Hartman 2009). As such, it is a sport that (perhaps unintentionally) promotes a dominant, or normative, ideal of Canadian identity as white, middle-class, and male. Given that Canada is officially a diverse, multicultural nation in which no particular gender, sexuality, or ethnic or racial identity should be privileged as "more Canadian" than any other, this image is a problem. In this context, hockey's iconic status as a national symbol is ironic, for it excludes a large portion of the nation's multicultural population and promotes hierarchies of Canadianness. To be "truly" Canadian, we learn, is to consume and participate in hockey. In recent years, the sport has been trying to connect with the nation's increasingly multicultural and multilingual population base. Beginning in 2007, for instance, the CBC began broadcasting hockey games in Punjabi; even after hockey moved from the national public broadcaster to Rogers Media in 2014, Punjabi broadcasts were maintained on the private broadcaster's multicultural OMNI television stations.

Photo by Rick Eglinton/Toronto Star via Getty Images

Hockey Night in Canada *Punjabi Edition* hosts, Harnarayan Singh (left) and Parminder Singh (right).

enculturation
The process through which individuals learn an identity. It can encompass parental socialization, the influence of peers, the mass media, government, and other forces.

Despite the problematical nature of hockey as a "Canadian" identity marker, it is important to note that shared experiences, such as sports and other mediated events, are often used to cultivate a sense of **imagined community**. This term, coined by political scientist Benedict Anderson in 1983, suggests that identities, including national ones, are culturally constructed through shared experiences, even in the absence of face-to-face contacts. So, even though a Canadian living in Halifax may never have visited Toronto, Regina, or Whitehorse, a shared sense of "Canadianness" is created through mediated experiences: watching and listening to stories about Canadian successes at the Olympics; attending Canada Day spectacles and ceremonies; following the national news on television, radio, and the Internet or in newspapers; and so on. Because this process of enculturation often begins when we are young, we often fail to see how various cultural forces shape our identities. Thus, we often view our identities as natural, primordial, or biologically based. Think of the many people who are willing to "sacrifice" themselves or die for their country, for instance. Often, individuals are willing to go to such lengths only if they feel that their identification with their nation is somehow instinctual and, by extension, natural.

Over the past century, anthropologists have engaged actively with precisely these sorts of debates. We live in a pop culture that privileges natural explanations for human behaviours. This has been the case since the late 1800s, with the rise of the **nature versus nurture** debate in academia. In 1874, British naturalist Sir Francis Galton, inspired by the principles of Darwinian evolution, coined the term "nature versus nurture." Galton (whose work on race we discuss in Chapter 7) was a eugenicist who felt that some people, by virtue of their class, race, or other factors, were better suited to reproduce as they were more "fit" to survive in society. Galton believed that many human differences, including intelligence, were rooted in biology, or "nature." His ideas spawned wildly inaccurate assumptions and research on the part of academics throughout the late nineteenth and twentieth centuries. At the time, many scholars felt that many of our identities, such as race and class, were genetic and thus "natural"—that we are born the way we are.

One of the first anthropologists to engage ethnographically with the nature versus nurture debate was Margaret Mead. In 1926, Mead set out for American Samoa to conduct research that would challenge widespread ideas among scientists that acts of teenage rebellion and experimentation were the result of hormonal or other physical changes brought on by puberty (or "nature"). Such behaviour was commonplace among American teenagers; Mead wondered whether similar behavioural patterns existed in other cultures. Under the direction of her doctoral supervisor, Franz Boas, she travelled to the island of Ta'u to study the behaviour of teenage girls. She observed that their experiences of adolescence were completely different from the experiences of American girls. In Samoa, girls were given freedom to experiment with their sexuality and did not go through periods of torment with parents. Samoan culture, she argued, did not possess the same Judeo-Christian ideals of sexual morality, and this contributed to different behaviours and attitudes regarding sexuality. Mead thus argued that the experiences of adolescents varied depending on the culture in which they were raised. Thus she emphasized the role of culture or "nurture" in human behaviour.

Mead's methods and research findings would later be disputed, but her ongoing ethnographic work on the "nature/nurture" debate in 1935 should

imagined community
A term coined by Benedict Anderson in 1983. It refers to the fact that even in the absence of face-to-face interactions, a sense of community (e.g., nationalism) is culturally constructed by forces such as the mass media.

nature versus nurture
A phrase, coined by Sir Francis Galton in 1874, that references a long-standing scholarly debate concerning whether human behaviours and identities are the result of nature (biological and genetic factors) or nurture (learned and cultural factors).

American anthropologist Margaret Mead in the Admiralty Islands.

be noted. Mead visited three tribes along the Sepik River in Papua New Guinea to explore differences in gender roles. She found that in each tribe, men and women took on different responsibilities based on their gender. She was thus able to suggest, once again, that human behavioural differences (in this case, gendered divisions of labour) were the result of culture, not biology.

Research that seeks to link biology with human behaviours and identities is potentially dangerous, for it can provide powerful justifications for social inequalities in society. Back in 1968, for instance, Washburn and Lancaster sought to argue that women, for biological and evolutionary reasons, were better "nurturers" of children—an argument that has since been disputed by feminist scholars. But think of the consequences of this type of research. If women were to be "proven" to be naturally better "nurturers," then it would become easy to argue that a woman's place is in the domestic sphere. This information could then inform government policies relating to daycare funding, affirmative action, and other social issues.

Most anthropologists, though, would be quick to point out the significance of nurture when it comes to explaining gender identity, which, in all cultures, is a key aspect of personhood and identity. All societies use gender to divide their members into meaningful categories, yet the way in which this is accomplished varies widely from culture to culture, as it has throughout history. In North America, gender assignment begins at birth with the announcement "It's a girl" or "It's a boy," conveniently ignoring the 4 percent of births in which the infant has various combinations of male and female characteristics (e.g., an infant with one testis and one ovary, an infant with one testis and aspects of the female genitalia, or an infant with ovaries and some aspect of male genitalia). Once the announcement of gender is made (or after a surgical procedure in which the infant is "corrected" to fit into either the male or the female category), the infant is given a gender-appropriate name, dressed in properly designed or coloured clothing, and spoken to in gender-appropriate language. Parents and other caregivers then teach male children that it is manly to endure pain, to be strong and tough. Male children are discouraged from expressing discomfort and encouraged when they can withstand it. Female children, on the other hand, are comforted when they hurt themselves. Although gender stereotypes are changing, many North American boys are still encouraged to be aggressive and competitive; they learn to compete in games and play with toys that require aggressive behaviour. Girls are still taught to be caring and helpful; they are given toys such as dolls that encourage "feminine" behaviour. As we discuss in greater detail in Chapter 7, gender differences, regardless of whether they are understood as biological or cultural, often promote social inequality.

Anthropological fieldwork in various societies has shed light on the problems associated with viewing all human identities in terms of "nature." Yet the development of genetic behavioural research and the ways in which such research is often discussed by laypeople and sometimes even by scientists continue to link identity with nature. Think of those scientists who are searching for specific genes that they believe are the cause of particular behaviours. We live in a society that valorizes the "gene" and that is fascinated by ongoing research on the "gay gene" or the "selfish gene." Often, this fascination is more a reflection of popular cultural concerns than it is an accurate reflection of the science. As anthropologist Roger Lancaster (2003) has shown, science journalists misinterpret complex scientific findings in ways that imply that the diversity of human behaviours can be reduced to biology, that ignore the role of culture in shaping identities such as race, gender, and sexuality, and that obscure the fact that many individual behaviours, such as selfishness, may be the result of complex interplays of culture and biology.

Recent developments in genetics suggest, however, that today, there is much more middle ground in the nature versus nurture debate. The consensus that is building among geneticists is that genes are not immutable, nor are genetics destiny. Rather, one's environment (including culture) has a profound effect on one's genes. Any effort to understand the relationship between genes and behaviour must take the cultural environment into account; similarly, geneticists argue that some, if not all, cultural behaviours (propensity to smoke cigarettes or drink alcohol, for example) may very well have important genetic underpinnings. As such, many anthropologists advocate a **biocultural approach**, one which recognizes that both biology and culture are mutually constitutive of some forms of human behaviour, such as human sexuality. With that said, most sociocultural anthropologists tend to focus their ethnographic research on analyses of the learned, cultural factors that shape human behaviour. In the next section we examine in greater detail how a sense of self or personhood is shaped by various cultural forces.

BEYOND THE BOOK 6.1

Find a recent news article that deals with the "nature/nurture" debate. For example, the mass media are always reporting on the latest "scientific" discoveries, which often seek to confirm a biological basis for certain identities—the "gay gene," for example. Outline some of the problems associated with this article from an anthropological perspective. How and why do scientists often overlook the "nurture," or cultural and learned, aspects of our identities?

Question 6.2: How Does the Concept of Personhood Vary from Society to Society?

The Importance of Self

Of all the products of our culture, the one we most take for granted is our self.

In all societies a personal name is an intimate marker of a person, differentiating one individual from another. Names also can reveal how people conceive of themselves and their relations to others. For many North Americans, names are perhaps the most enduring aspect of the self. Our names are assigned at birth and remain with us throughout our lives and represent the self. How much of the self is revealed by a name varies by culture and situation. University students meeting for the first time exchange personal names, rarely bothering with family names. Their sense of self is independent of any group or past. When North American businesspeople meet, they exchange first names, last names, and business titles. Businesspeople are linked to their organizations more than to a geographical location. In contrast, when Moroccans from different towns meet, they exchange not only family names but also the names of their towns. The Moroccan self is embedded in family and place of origin. Among the Tsimshian of British Columbia, names depend on social position; on entering adulthood, getting married, or assuming a higher rank in Tsimshian society, they change their names. Among the Tsimshian, one's self is inseparable from one's position in society.

Jorge Chimbinda (2006) has explored the process of "naming" children among the Umbundu of Angola, who have two ways of naming a child. The most common way is to name a child after a

biocultural approach
The idea that some human behaviours are shaped by a combination of cultural factors and biological ones, such as genetics.

© Wolfgang Kaehler/CORBIS

Some contemporary Tsimshian children continue to follow tradition by wearing traditional shawls and will change their names upon entering adulthood.

relative who is either alive or dead (an ancestor). The second way is to give a child a new name that refers to some unusual circumstance that was present during the child's birth. For example, a child born during a severe drought will be given a name that refers to the drought, thus keeping the memory of the suffering alive. The child of a mother who dies in childbirth will be given a name that keeps the memory of the mother's suffering and death. The result of this way of naming is that each child has a last name of his or her own. At the same time, the Umbundu naming system is a historical version of cultural values, such as identity, kinship, geography, folktales, stories, and proverbs. From the Umbundu perspective, names are tools with which people reward the life they have received from their relatives and their world. Names serve to perpetuate the wide kinship web and stress the concept of extended family. Each child represents one of his or her living relatives or ancestors. All relatives and ancestors on both the father's side and that of the mother have equal value because each of them has contributed to the existence of the child. These names also imprint lived experiences on children, so that children named after unusual circumstances embody the meaning of those experiences.

Jorge Chimbinda also explores the effects of colonialism on his people. When Angola became a Portuguese colony, the colonial administrators found it too difficult to keep track of Umbundu people because the naming system did not group people in ways that the administrators understood. For the Portuguese, as for most Europeans, last names were shared among members of families and made family identification orderly. Thus, one of the first ways that the Portuguese colonizers tried to destroy Umbundu identity was by forcing people to discard their Umbundu names and replace them with Portuguese names.

The differences in naming practices among societies reveal the different ways societies conceptualize what a person is and how that person relates to the group. Many North Americans believe that individuals are stable, autonomous entities who exist more or less independently of whatever situations or statuses they occupy. Even as they move from status to status or place to place—from student to husband or wife, to employee, to father or mother—they believe themselves to be the same persons. Otherwise, each time they changed situations or statuses they would in effect become different people and would have to change their names. In this regard, North Americans are highly individualistic. In other societies, however, individuals are not seen as entities distinct from their social position or group. In societies such as the Umbundu, the relationship between the person and the group, or the person and his or her social position, is holistic; the person cannot be conceived as existing separately from society or apart from his or her cultural beliefs and values.

BEYOND THE BOOK 6.2

If you were an Umbundu and lived in Angola, which of your ancestors would you choose for the name of your first child? Why would you make this particular choice? In other words, what are the qualities in your ancestors that you would want to transfer to your child? What about your second child and your third?

The Egocentric Self and the Sociocentric Self

Differences between the individualistic and holistic conceptions of the self led Shweder and Bourne (1984) to delineate two distinct ways in which the person is conceived in different societies: the **egocentric** and the **sociocentric** views of self. Note that these terms are ideal types, or generalizations about the nature of the self in different societies. There will, of course, be exceptions to these patterns, especially given the increasing influence of globalization in constructing our identities. So it is important to recognize that there exist multiple, often overlapping interpretations of the self, even within the generalized contexts of the societies described below.

In the *egocentric* view, typified in many ways by the Western view adopted by North American societies, each person is perceived to be capable of acting independently from others, and the locus of motivations and drives is thus internal. For Westerners, the individual is the centre of awareness, a distinct whole set against other wholes. Social relations are regarded as contracts between autonomous, free-acting beings. Individuals are free to negotiate their places in society, and the dominant idea is that each individual is responsible for *what* and *who* he or she is. Moreover, individuals possess intrinsic qualities such as generosity, integrity, and beauty. The egocentric view of the person places a high value on individualism, self-reliance, and freedom of choice, such as the ability to select one's own marriage partner.

While factors such as poverty and ethnicity may make individualism and self-reliance difficult to achieve, it is worthwhile to explore the beliefs associated with this view of the individual. Robert Bellah and his co-authors of *Habits of the Heart* (1984) examined ideas of the individual in the United States that seem to apply equally to Canada. The self in the United States, they say, seeks to work out its own life plot by individually pursuing happiness and satisfying its wants. Young men and women need to demonstrate that they can stand on their own two feet and support themselves, separate from their parents. This emphasis on self-reliance and independence underpins the belief Americans hold that success is the outcome of free and fair competition among individuals in an open market. Most successful Americans, say Bellah and his associates, claim that they achieved success through their own hard work, seldom acknowledging the contributions made by their families, their schooling, or their positions as members of the upwardly mobile middle class.

Because of this dominant perspective of self, many people who were raised within Western, industrialized societies are inclined to view those afflicted with, for instance, eating disorders such as anorexia nervosa or bulimia, as suffering from an *individual* pathology. Helen Gremillion (2003) conducted 14 months of ethnographic research at a small in-patient eating disorder clinic in the United States. She discovered there that the various cultural forces that have contributed to increases in diagnoses of eating disorders are being ignored in favour of "individualistic" explanations. For example, Gremillion and others often point out that mass media advertising plays a role in constructing normative expectations of an impossibly ideal femininity. Increasingly, the feminine ideal is being defined by physical appearance—in particular, by representations of predominantly white, youthful, slender, "beautiful" women. In this way, advertising on television and the Internet, in magazines, and on billboards is playing a powerful role in shaping Westerners' sense of self. Yet its images of ideal femininity have themselves been constructed and

egocentric
A view of the self that defines each person as a replica of all humanity, as the location of motivations and drives, and as capable of acting independently from others.

sociocentric
A context-dependent view of self. The self exists as an entity only within the concrete situations or roles occupied by the person.

manipulated by computer technologies, which remove wrinkles or fine lines, minimize fat, and reshape facial features. Gremillion argues that many eating disorder treatment plans fail to recognize the role of culture in shaping the self. Such treatment plans replicate Western notions of individualism by including careful daily monitoring of weight and patient "progress." These principles of egocentrism, of the individual monitoring of the body—and, by extension, the self—have led to a proliferation of eating disorders.

In contrast to the egocentric view, the *sociocentric* view of the self is context dependent. The self exists as an entity only within the concrete situations or roles occupied by the person. From a sociocentric perspective, there is no intrinsic self that can possess enduring qualities such as generosity, integrity, and beauty. These qualities can apply only to concrete social situations. Instead of saying that a man is generous, a sociocentric perspective would be that "he gives money to his friends." Instead of saying that a woman is principled, the perspective would be that "she does not give away secrets."

It may be the case, as some anthropologists have argued, that, in fact, most societies understand selfhood as both egocentric *and* sociocentric, and that the differences between the societal views of selfhood might lie less in which view they subscribe to than in how they see and practise the relationship between the two. For example, Anne E. Becker (1995) characterizes the relationship between body, self, and society in Fiji as one in which the relation of one's body to one's self is mediated through the relation of one's self to one's community. The cultivation of one's body (its shape and health, for instance) is understood mainly as a community rather than a personal enterprise; this view of the self and body may be more sociocentric than we are familiar with in North America, but it does not mean that Fijians do not also possess an egocentric view. Indeed, during subsequent fieldwork in Fiji, Becker (2004) discovered that the introduction of broadcast television, and specifically Western programming (along with other socioeconomic changes related to globalization), seemed to have caused a dramatic shift away from the centrality of the sociocentric self and toward seeing the body as a personal project. As a consequence, the incidence of eating disorders among school-aged girls, previously almost unheard of, had skyrocketed. However, as Gremillion's work above demonstrates, even in North America, the underlying logic of eating disorders must also be understood as sociocentric, even if our commonsense reaction to, and treatment of, these disorders privileges egocentric selfhood.

Personhood in Japan

Some anthropologists attribute a sociocentric view of the self to people in Japan. Anthropologist Christie Kiefer (1976) explained that the Japanese are more likely to include within the boundaries of the self the social groups of which the person is a member. Japanese children are not trained to rely solely on the self, as many North American children are. They are taught that interdependence between the person and the family or group is more important than independence.

Robert Smith (1983) noted that the Japanese view of the self is expressed in their language. For example, the Japanese language does not include anything resembling English personal pronouns. In English, children quickly learn to use the two personal referents, *I* and *you*; Japanese boys, on the other hand, must learn six, and girls must learn five. The personal referent used in Japan depends on the speaker's relationship to the listener. It expresses how the self is defined relative to a specific social interaction.

In addition, wrote Smith, the Japanese language contains vocabulary that is very conscious of status. It is characterized by what the Japanese call *keigo*, or "polite speech." *Keigo* has the effect of establishing at the outset of a conversation the relative social standing and degree of intimacy of speaker and listener. Japanese speakers use different forms of address depending on their social position relative to the person to whom they are speaking. Since the Japanese language is status based, people must be careful of the linguistic

FIGURE 6.1 Japan

forms they use in conversations. When conversing with someone in a superior social position, a speaker must linguistically acknowledge the social difference between speaker and listener. Japanese advertisers have a problem with *keigo* because actors should not give imperative commands (e.g., "Drink Coke") for fear of offending people. They solve the problem by using low-status people who are nonthreatening (e.g., clowns, coquettish women, or children) to issue the commands.

The sociocentric Japanese differ also in their approach to social interactions. Most North Americans believe it is desirable to assert themselves to stand out, and to take charge. The Japanese believe that social interactions should be characterized by restraint or reserve, traits they identify as *enryo*. With *enryo*, the giving of opinions is avoided; this attitude is summarized by the Japanese proverb "the nail that sticks up shall be hammered down."

BEYOND THE BOOK 6.3

1. The popularity of social media and attendant forms of virtual selfhood pose some interesting challenges to a strictly dichotomous view of egocentric versus sociocentric selfhood. Many users of sites such as Facebook and Instagram use social media to present idealized versions of their "egocentric" selves. However, these sites also rely upon a more sociocentric sense of self, created through one's social network. Is a person really "on" Facebook if he or she has no friend connections? Think about the way you construct yourself on social media (or in other virtual forms). Would you describe your social media self as egocentric or sociocentric? Why?
2. In your opinion, how accurately does your virtual self reflect your physical self? Is one more real or true than the other?
3. Does your online self ever affect your "real" self? If so, in what ways?
4. How might social media use differ between North America and societies that are considered to have a more sociocentric view of the self?

Yet the Japanese *do* conceive of themselves as separate entities. They are as attached to their personal names as North Americans are, and they believe in self-development. But for them, the autonomy of the individual is established, not in social situations where they actively distinguish themselves from others, but away from society, where self-reflection and introspection are legitimate. Through introspection the Japanese find their true heart (kokoro) and are put in touch with their true nature—their hara ("belly") and jibub ("self").

In Crafting Selves, an ethnography of Japanese factory workers, Dorinne Kondo (1990) approaches the sociocentric versus egocentric question from a slightly different perspective. She questions whether it is accurate to refer to selfhood, in Japan or elsewhere, as singular. Perhaps, she suggests, it would be better to think about how people craft selves through the practices of everyday life. From this perspective, personhood is not static or fixed, but processual and ongoing. According to Kondo, the way that Japanese factory workers craft selves is the result of how they envision and practise their belonging (or lack thereof) to entities such as company and family; selves, that is, are crafted in relation to power and hierarchies. Rather than possessing a singular, decisively sociocentric "Japanese self," Kondo suggests that her informants adopt "multiple, infinitely graded, layers of selfhood," often described as oscillating between two ends of a continuum: omote, the front, formal side; and ura, the back, intimate side. This is not a straightforward dualism: what counts as omote or ura is always shifting, and the tension between the two is never fully resolved (Kondo 1990, 31).

In the remainder of this chapter, we will look at the self less from an egocentric perspective and more from a sociocentric perspective, as something contingent and relative to the situation. Our focus will be on that part of the self that is defined by social relations and social processes and that is subject to change and redefinition.

Question 6.3: How Do Societies Distinguish Individuals from One Another?

Differences and similarities among persons are the materials from which we construct our social landscapes. Those materials allow us to distinguish individuals from one another or assign them to one group or another. From these similarities and differences we construct our social identities. However, all societies do not use the same similarities and differences to construct a social code, nor do they use these similarities and differences in the same way. Some characteristics of persons—some tools in the "identity toolbox," so to speak—are used almost universally to differentiate people or to group them together. For example, most societies use family membership, gender, and age as categories within a social code. But other characteristics figure prominently only in some societies—ethnic group membership, skin colour, and wealth, for example.

In many societies, the most important characteristics for defining the self are related to kinship and family membership. In these societies, kinship is the central organizing principle—the main determinant of a person's social identity. Anthropologists working with these societies are often "adopted" by a family. This act is a signal of acceptance, but it also serves the practical purpose of assigning an outsider a social identity through which she or he can be approached by others. To have no kinship label or designation in such a society is to have no meaningful place on the social landscape.

Language is another important identity marker, one sometimes viewed as essential for the maintenance of group identity. Language is often tied strongly to a national identity, and many countries have established institutions to oversee the "purity" of the national language. The Académie française has, for centuries, been tasked with keeping the French language free of foreign borrowings, such as "le hot dog" or "le weekend." Sometimes, language becomes a flashpoint in political conflicts over collective identity. In Quebec, for example, efforts by one group to preserve French as the official language of the province, and thus protect what it sees as essential to group **ethnic identity**, have led to a movement for independence from the English-speaking remainder of Canada. According to Richard Handler (1988), many Québécois separatists have historically viewed themselves as a distinct ethnic group on the basis of shared language, history, and religion.

While language is a defining feature of their identity, the Québécois argue that Quebec identity is not based solely on language. As they see it, their history in Canada is one of "slights, assaults, yet survival" (Eller 1999, 297). The conflict between British and French settlers in Canada has been

ethnic identity
When a group of people perceive themselves as a cohesive, unified, and distinctive group of people due to the fact that they have a real or imagined common history and that they may share a common language, religion, racial background, or other factors.

ongoing since both arrived on North American shores. In 1759, the English drove the French Acadians out of eastern Canada; and after the Battle of the Plains of Abraham, outside the walls of Quebec City, the Treaty of Paris gave Canada to the English. In 1791, two separate societies were formed: Lower Canada was French and Upper Canada was English, and each had its own culture, religion, stories, political views, and language. Then, in 1841, the Act of Union joined the two societies together, but this union was uneasy: Canada East was still French and Canada West still English. Canadian Confederation, set out in the *British North America Act* of 1867, created two provinces out of the former Province of Canada: Quebec for the French and Ontario for the English. Even so, the two were part of a single entity, Canada, and that entity was ruled by the English.

In the 1960s, during what is often referred to as the "Quiet Revolution," Quebec began building its own sense of nationalism, which saw Quebec as a "homeland" in which the French were "masters in their own house" (Eller 1999, 327). That "house" was no longer inhabited by French Canadians, or francophones; rather, it was the house of the Québécois—people who were ready to take control of their own lives and separate from the rest of Canada, if necessary.

In an environment where the inhabitants of Quebec are increasingly diverse and multicultural due to the combined effects of immigration and globalization, notions of what constitutes a distinctive identity are contested. In many ways, Québécois notions of identity, discussed above, could be considered exclusionary for newcomers to the province or for those who do not fit neatly within these identity parameters.

© Alain Nogues/Sygma/Corbis

Continuing his support of Quebec's Quiet Revolution, French president Charles de Gaulle declared, *"Vive le Québec libre!"* in his historic 1967 speech at Montreal's town hall.

Many Quebec residents, for example, have critiqued the passage of Bill 21, known as the "secularism law." In June 2019, Bill 21 was passed in Quebec. It banned public employees in positions of authority (e.g., police officers or teachers) from wearing religious symbols such as a hijab, a turban, or a crucifix. The stated intent of the legislation was to protect the province as a secular society and to separate religion from government. Critics of the legislation, however, argue that it undermines and silences minority populations, including new immigrants, many of whom are adherents of non-Christian religions. As columnist and clergy member Michael Coren (2019) attests,

> *Christians are hardly affected by this, partly because most Christians have no outwardly visible religious symbolism beyond perhaps a crucifix around the neck, which is not required, usually hidden, and frequently aesthetic or cultural rather than theological. The law will impinge upon some orthodox Jews, and Sikhs of course, but at heart and soul it is about Muslims.*

Ultimately, such instances highlight how notions about collective identity are not fixed or stable and how any attempt to construct a unified sense of social identity can be exclusionary and discriminatory.

Question 6.4: How Do Societies Mark Changes in Identity?

Identities are not static, and people are constantly changing their identities as they move through the life cycle. These changes in identity are announced in myriad ways. Many societies have particular ceremonies or rituals that mark a change in a person's status or role in society. Most societies hold religious events, such as baptisms, confirmations, bat/bar mitzvahs, and secular events, including birthdays and graduations, to mark significant changes in an individual's status in society. In this section we explore cross-cultural examples of these phenomena.

The Transition to Adulthood

In a 1908 book now considered a classic of anthropology, Arnold van Gennep introduced the concept of **rites of passage**. The term refers to a category of rituals that mark a person's passage from one identity to another, in the same way that a person's progress through a house might be marked by entering one room after another. Van Gennep identified three phases in a rite of passage: separation, liminality, and reincorporation. First, the ritual separates the person from an existing identity; next, the person enters a transition phase; finally, the changes are incorporated into a new identity. These phases of rites of passage are not equally elaborated in all ceremonies. The separation phase, for example, is a major part of funeral ceremonies designed to help the living let go of the deceased; transition is a major part of initiation ceremonies marking the passage of a person from, say, childhood to adulthood; and incorporation is emphasized in marriage ceremonies, which, in most societies, mark the transfer of a person from one social group to another.

Rites of passage are visible in Canadian society. For instance, a young man or woman who joins the military is required to undergo "boot camp." Geographically and spatially sequestered from mainstream society, the new recruit lives with other recruits in a dormitory. He or she marks this sense of separation by undergoing physical changes, such as cutting one's hair and wearing a uniform. These acts standardize physical appearances and visually mark an individual as a newcomer or initiate. Recruits then undergo a period of transition, or liminality, where they are expected to perform physically and emotionally draining tasks, such as running long distances when sleep deprived, or enduring verbal insults. Finally, a recruit who is able to endure the stresses of boot camp re-enters mainstream society with a new status: soldier. This period of reincorporation is marked by a new uniform and by a ceremony during which the initiate is reintroduced to family and friends with the new status.

Prominent in most societies around the world are ceremonies that mark the transition of a male from boyhood to manhood. Most such ceremonies involve a test of courage. According to anthropologist David Gilmore (1990), one reason why so many societies incorporate tests of masculinity and tortuous initiation rituals for males is that the male identity is more problematical than the female identity. For every individual, there is at the beginning of life a subliminal identification with the mother, and men must make greater efforts to differentiate themselves from their mothers. Consequently, societies incorporate rituals that symbolically separate the boy from his mother, while at the same time incorporating him into manhood.

Victor Turner (1967) used van Gennep's model of rites of passage to describe the move from boyhood to manhood among the Ndembu of Zambia. When Ndembu boys reach puberty, they are taken, as a group of age mates, away from their mothers and out of the village (separation), to live in the forest (transition). There, the boys shave their heads and remove anything from their bodies that might identify them as individuals. While in the forest, the young Ndembu are circumcised and taught all of the special knowledge that Ndembu men know. But in the forest, they have no identity: they are no longer boys, but they are not yet men. In Turner's words, they are "betwixt and between." Once their circumcisions heal and the lessons are completed,

rites of passage
The term coined in 1908 by Arnold van Gennep to refer to the category of rituals that accompany changes in status, such as the transition from boyhood to manhood, living to dead, or student to graduate.

the young men return to the village (reintegration) as new persons with new identities. These men, who made the transition to manhood together, will remain in close association throughout their lives as age mates, a category that cuts across kinship groups and that has special tasks in many societies, such as herding animals among pastoralists.

Question 6.5: How Do Individuals Communicate Their Identities to One Another?

Both consciously and unconsciously, we make statements about our identity—who we think we are, or who we want to be—with objects and material things. The clothes we wear and the things we possess are used to display an identity that we desire or that we think we have. In North America, think about how designer clothing, shoes, and bags are coveted as markers of class and status.

Clothing can also express gender, sexuality, ethnicity, or religious affiliation. In some cases, clothing marks some individuals as "Other" even within their own society. Women who wear the Muslim veil in North America, for instance, have often been identified as "the enemy within," especially since 9/11. Some Muslims in Canada have dealt with this by removing visible signs of their Muslimness, particularly with regard to their dress. Still others have tried to show Canadians that the stereotype that all Muslims are terrorists is not only wrong but completely illogical.

In a study conducted by Homa Hoodfar (2003), young Muslim women in Canada reported that wearing the veil was not something their parents forced them to do. This finding contradicts the claims made by some North American feminists that banning the veil will free women from Islamic patriarchal oppression (2003, 15). In fact, most of the women Hoodfar talked to said they had had to fight with their parents in order to wear it. When Hoodfar and her research assistants asked young women why they wear the veil, one woman said that doing so "allowed her to be a 'person' rather than an object of male scrutiny" (2003, 17–18). Other women explained that they took up the veil when they began university because wearing it communicated certain values. In Hoodfar's words, "By taking up the veil, they symbolically but clearly announce to their parents and their community that, despite their unconventional activities and involvement with non-Muslims, they retain their Islamic mores and values. They are modern Muslim women who want to be educated and publicly active, but not at the cost of their moral principles" (2003, 21). In the same sense that "a picture is worth a thousand words," they believed that wearing the veil communicated identity in a way that saved them from having to explain why they behaved in certain ways. It is also worth noting that there are different interpretations as to what constitutes proper "Islamic dress." For example, some women wear a head scarf and a long dress over their clothes to cover the body completely and sometimes conceal part of the face; others believe that a head scarf suffices to fulfill the requirements of their faith. Still others do not believe that they need to wear a veil in order to maintain their Muslim identity.

While some Muslim women in Canada choose to wear veils or other garments to emphasize their modesty and to divert attention from the contours of their bodies and their sexual appeal, people in some societies may want to *highlight* their sexuality so that it is immediately visible to others. Men in some groups in New Guinea, for example, wear penis gourds. And in seventeenth-century Europe, men wore codpieces to emphasize their male anatomy.

Sexual identification is an important identity marker, but there are other signals that people use to display their identity. In some parts of Africa, people from different villages have different hairstyles; in North America, teenagers encode their schools or teams by the jackets they wear. People signal their connectedness to others by holding hands, by wearing rings, or by feasting and drinking together.

Rituals of Gift Giving and Hospitality

One of the most influential works in the history of anthropology is *The Gift* (1925), by Marcel Mauss. In it, Mauss identifies what he calls the **principle of reciprocity**: the giving and receiving of gifts. His main point is that gifts, which in theory are voluntary, disinterested, and spontaneous, are, in fact, obligatory. The giving of the gift creates a tie with the person who receives it and who, on some future occasion, is obliged to reciprocate. To Mauss, what matters is not what is given but the relationship that is maintained or established by the gift. The types of things given and received signal the identities of the participants in the exchange and the kind of relationship that exists between them. If the gifts are roughly of equal value, the relationship is one of equality. But if the gifts are unequal in value, the person who gives the more valuable gift is generally of higher status than the receiver.

National Geographic Image Collection/Alamy Stock Photo

Trobriand Islanders define and maintain their social identities by participating in the *kula* ring, a ritualized pattern of gift giving involving the exchange of necklaces and white shell armbands.

BEYOND THE BOOK 6.4

Suppose you were to travel to an island where no one knows anything about you or the society you came from. Suppose, too, that you could communicate with people on the island using only objects you carried with you and that you could take only five things to tell people about yourself. What would you choose, and why?

A well-known example of gift giving in the anthropological literature is the ***kula* ring** of the Trobriand Islanders. The seagoing Trobrianders leave their homes on islands off the eastern coast of New Guinea and travel from island to island, visiting and trading. Noteworthy in their travels is their pattern of gift giving. Each man has trading partners on the islands he visits, and these partnerships are signalled with gifts of red shell necklaces or white shell armbands. As a man travels and trades objects, he gives and receives necklaces and armbands. A man who receives either an armband or a necklace does not keep it but passes it along to another trading partner. There is a set pattern to the exchange: necklaces travel from island to island in a clockwise direction, while armbands move counterclockwise. The time between exchanges and the distances between the islands are so great that it may take two to ten years before the necklaces and armbands make a complete circle.

The *kula* ring serves as a concrete representation of ties among individuals. Any change in the pattern of gift giving reflects a change in the nature of the social ties. Special gifts that are individually owned are also circulated, and the owner's status and renown grow as the goods he owns circulate along

principle of reciprocity
According to Marcel Mauss, gift-giving involves reciprocity. The idea is that the exchange of gifts creates a feeling of obligation, in that the gift must be repaid.

***kula* ring**
A system of inter-island gift exchange documented by anthropologist Bronislaw Malinowski in the Trobriand Islands. It involves the exchange of shell necklaces and armbands. According to Malinowski, the *kula* ring serves, among other things, to create alliances and social ties among individuals living on different islands.

predetermined paths. A successful *kula* operator participates in many such exchanges and can profit from them by keeping items for as long as he can before passing them along. Of course, if he keeps them too long, others will be reluctant to exchange, so a good deal of social skill is required to take successful part in a kula ring.

Anthropologist Margaret Anderson has devoted many years to studying another famous example of gift giving: the potlatch ceremony of the Indigenous peoples of the northwest coast of British Columbia. Among the Tsimshian, the **potlatch** is typically a feast that legitimates a change in social relations, such as a funeral. Someone who dies is vacating a spot on the social landscape—or, more specifically, leaving a name empty. The Tsimshian are organized into matrilineal clans or houses. Each house has associated with it a fixed number of personal names, and each name has associated with it specific spiritual powers, honours, and objects of wealth. The man with the highest-ranking name is recognized as the owner of the house. The name a Tsimshian holds when he dies is vacated until it is claimed by or given to someone else. If the name vacated belongs to a chief, the feasting will begin with his death and end with the acceptance of a new chief, who is usually the eldest son of the deceased chief's eldest sister. A person who disgraces his name by doing something wrong (such as having an automobile accident or being put in jail) must give a feast to "clean the name."

The potlatch feast, however, does more than allow a Tsimshian to obtain a new name and identity. It also serves to symbolically reorder and validate the names and, hence, the social positions of everyone at the feast through the distribution of gifts. Members of the house of the deceased generally serve as hosts to members of the deceased's father's house. The guests are feasted for the services they have performed (preparing the corpse, carving a pole) and as repayment for the gifts they formerly gave the deceased to help him acquire his name. When the guests are seated, the hosts announce the gifts they are giving to the guests, along with the name of the person from the host group who has contributed the gift. Higher-ranking guests receive more gifts at a potlatch than lower-ranking guests. Consequently, the seating arrangements and the value of the gifts given to guests at the feast serve to announce or publicly notarize the social position or identity of each guest.

Anderson (2004) argues that, although the potlatch has changed since Christianity was introduced in 1857 (when William Duncan of the Church Missionary Society came to Fort Simpson), its meaning and symbolic value have remained, in part because as long as the feasts began with a prayer, Duncan considered them respectable.

Exchanges that convey recognition of identities need not be limited to material goods. The exchanges also may consist of emotion and sentiment. Hawai'ians, for example, define a desired identity in part through expressions of gregariousness and hospitality. The emotional qualities of a person's relationships are one criterion by which others judge, interact with, and respond to that person. For example, if you accept an offer of hospitality in Hawai'i, it is a signal that you recognize the generous nature of the offer and that you wish to maintain the social link. If you reject the offer of hospitality, it is seen as a hurtful sign that you do not recognize the generous nature of the person making the offer and do not wish to maintain the relationship. Hawai'ians try to keep social pathways open through altruistic exchanges of love (*aloha*), sincerity, feeling (with heart, *na'au*), and warmth (*pumehana*).

Gifts and Commodities

An important characteristic of traditional *kula* and potlatch goods is that they have histories. A Trobriander who receives a necklace or armband

potlatch
A celebration, usually involving elaborate feasting and the redistribution of gifts, found among many Indigenous Northwest Coast groups, such as the Tsimshian. The potlatch is a means of creating a new identity or of reinforcing social status within a group.

can probably recite the history of the object, sometimes from its creation through all the persons who possessed it at one time or another. These goods are similar to heirlooms in our own society, whether it is the family wedding ring that has been worn by brides for three generations, the watch that was owned by a great-grandfather, or the quilt that was made by a great-aunt. The histories of these objects, especially when the objects are given as gifts, are vital to the identity of the person who gives them. They say something special about the relationship between the giver and the receiver of the gift. The same is true to a lesser extent of gifts that are *produced* by the giver: these carry a special meaning apart from the object itself. A lamp made and given as a gift is often far more meaningful than a lamp purchased at a department store. However, we often must choose the gifts that we give from among thousands of mass-produced, largely impersonal goods available in department and chain stores. Herein lies a dilemma.

James Carrier, in his book *Gifts and Commodities: Exchange and Western Capitalism Since 1700* (1995), argues that since the sixteenth and seventeenth centuries, the production and distribution of goods has become impersonal, and that the spread of industrial and commercial capitalism has meant the spread of alienated objects and relations. In earlier times, commodities were personalized in various ways. The relationship between the producer and the purchaser of goods was a personal one between relatives or friends; the buyer knew who made and sold the object purchased. Even when stores replaced home trade and markets, the buyer knew the store owner, who further personalized the goods by buying them in bulk and individually packaging and displaying them. The buyer–seller relationship was further personalized by the extension of credit from seller to buyer and by the customer loyalty expressed by the buyer to the seller. Today the buyer knows neither the producer nor the seller, and if the item is bought on credit, it is through a credit card issued by some distant bank based on the filing of an impersonal application, with the transaction accomplished completely by mail or electronically. Eyes never meet.

Carrier labels goods that carry no special meaning as **commodities**, to distinguish them from what he calls "possessions." Gifts, says Carrier, must be possessions before they can carry meaning in an exchange. Commodities involve a transfer of value and a counter-transfer: *A* sells something to *B*, and the transaction is finished. But in a gift exchange, a more or less permanent link is established between giver and receiver. Gifts are inalienable, that is, they are bound to people after the presentation; commodities are independent of their sellers (or producers). It is easy to return, destroy, or give away a commodity; it is a dilemma to do any of those things with a gift.

As noted, for North Americans the contrast between commodities and gifts poses a special problem. Most of the items we give as gifts are store-bought commodities, often mass produced. Their history is brief and undistinguished: an item of clothing was probably assembled in some factory in Mexico or Indonesia by a young woman earning perhaps a dollar an hour; a sports item was probably assembled in some factory in South America, shipped to a warehouse in Toronto or Chicago, and sold through a mass-produced catalogue; a radio, iPhone, or laptop, assembled in Korea and distributed by a Japanese company, was probably sold in a North American chain store. These are commodities, not gifts.

For Carrier, the problem is how, in a world filled with impersonal, alienated commodities—goods without history, so to speak—we can turn

commodities
Traditionally, commodities are items that involve a transfer of value and a counter-transfer: A sells something to B, and the transaction is finished. As is typical with capitalist market-exchange systems, a long-standing personal relationship between buyer and seller is not established.

these things into personal items with meaning and history, into possessions that carry something of the buyer's identity. We convert commodities into possessions and gifts, says Carrier, through a process of appropriation. For example, when a person takes an impersonal space—a dorm room, say, or a rented apartment—and decorates and modifies it, he or she has appropriated it and given it meaning. When a person buys an automobile, one virtually identical to thousands of others of the same make, model, year, and colour, and comes to think of it as unique, as an expression of his or her identity, that person has appropriated an object and made it a possession. Shopping itself, says Carrier, is a way of appropriating commodities; "wise shoppers" choose what is "right" for them or what is "right" for the recipient of the gift.

Gift Giving and the Christian Celebration of Christmas in North America

The dilemma of converting commodities into gifts is especially acute during the Christian Christmas holiday season. Most social scientists who have written about the Christian celebration of Christmas agree that it is largely a celebration of the family, serving especially to distinguish the world of the family from the outside world of work. Christmas serves to affirm the identity of Christians all over the world as members of specific family groups, and the circle of kin with whom gifts are exchanged defines the boundaries of the family. In one study conducted in a midwestern American city, 90 percent of all gifts exchanged at Christmas were exchanged with family members. Christmas heightens a person's sense of family identity, expressing how warm the family is and how cold the world outside may be.

Thus, it is within the family that the Christmas gift is most important. The question is how to resolve the problem of using commodities as family gifts, how to transform commodities to make them suitable as statements of the special role that family and family relations play in defining our identity. This problem, apparently, is not new. The dilemma of giving gifts that are manufactured and sold in stores existed as early as the mid-nineteenth century, when department stores tried to convince buyers to purchase their gifts in stores by advertising them as "special Christmas stock." Even today, through Christmas decorations, music, and special attractions, such as the ever-present Santa Claus, retailers try to inject the spirit of Christmas into their stock of goods.

But there are other ways that consumers try to appropriate commodities and turn them into Christmas gifts. First, we may simply say that the nature of the gift is immaterial, that "it's the thought that counts." A second way is to purchase things that aren't very useful, giving frivolous or luxurious gifts, or items that are Christmas specific, such as Christmas tree decorations or clothing with Christmas decorations on it. Third, and very important, there is the wrapping rule: Christmas gifts must be wrapped. The wrapping itself converts the commodity into a gift. Difficult-to-wrap presents (e.g., a piano, a horse, a bicycle) must be decorated with a bow. The only categories of things

©franz12/Shutterstock.com

In North American societies, the yearly ritual of Christmas shopping provides a means of converting impersonal commodities into personalized gifts that show one's love for family members and close friends.

that needn't be wrapped are items made by the giver, such as breads or jams. These items need only a bow and a card.

Finally, says Carrier, there is the shopping itself, the time we spend getting the "right" gift for the "right" person. Why, he asks, do we go through all of this? It is onerous, it is stressful, and it is expensive. Yet one third of all retail sales are made in November and December, most of them accounted for by Christmas shopping. One sixth of all retail sales are related to Christmas. People complain about the materialism of Christmas and Christmas shopping. Yet people shop intensely for Christmas.

In the face of this complaint, why do North Americans, even devout Christians, put so much effort into Christmas shopping? Carrier suggests that shopping in itself is a method of appropriation, of converting a commodity into a gift: we exercise a choice from among the mass of commodities presented to us. As Carrier (1993, 63) puts it: "Christmas shopping is an annual ritual through which we convert commodities into gifts. Performing this ritual indicates that we can celebrate and recreate personal relations with the anonymous objects available to us, just as it strengthens and reassures us as we undertake the more mundane appropriations of everyday life during the rest of the year."

Christmas shopping also demonstrates to people, says Carrier, that they can create a world of family, a world of love, out of the impersonal commodities that flood the world "out there." The Christian celebration of Christmas is a time when North Americans turn a world of money into a world of family, a time of contrast between the impersonal world of commodities and the personal world of possessions and gifts.

BEYOND THE BOOK 6.5

These days, gift cards for stores, restaurants, spas, or other goods and services are popular holiday gift items. After reading about Carrier's work, discuss how gift cards might fit into his discussion of commodities and gifts. How can gift cards, as commodities, be turned into gifts? Is this even possible?

Question 6.6: How Do People Form Identities through Collective Struggles?

As this chapter's epigraph suggests, the formation of identity is a cultural process that involves the lived experiences and everyday practices of people. This cultural construction of identity creates both the individual and the collectivity, which we think of as society. In this section, we focus on the collectivity and ask how identity is produced through collective struggles.

The Meaning of "Indigenous"

After examining **Indigenous peoples** of Asia, Africa, Meso- and South America, North America, Eurasia, and Europe, Bruce Miller strives to arrive at a definition of what "Indigenous" means. He concludes his book *Invisible Indigenes* (2003) by looking at the common elements in the various ways the term has been used in different parts of the world. One common factor in all the societies Miller encountered is the association of Indigenousness with both the presence and the absence of certain traits. The most critical element in the various definitions is that indigenes are recognized because they live in some clearly identifiable way that maintains their own distinct culture, and that they have been living exactly the same way since they were encountered by the colonizers. Furthermore, people are defined as Indigenous because "broadly, definitions have come to focus on difference—the idea that indigenes are distinct—and the related idea that distinctions show up in many ways. These include self-identification and the recognition of distinction by others" (2003, 213).

Indigenous peoples
Groups of people whose ancestors predate the arrival of European or other forms of colonialism, who share a culture and/or way of life that they often identify as distinct from "mainstream" society, and who often feel that they have a right to self-government. In Canada, this includes individuals who identify as First Nations, Métis, or Inuit.

Furthermore, people are defined as Indigenous because "ancestors of members did not practice one of the world religions and therefore needed to be converted. Or members of a group are indigenous because they or their ancestors were not organized around Western values and practices, in particular Enlightenment values of universalism, secularism, rationalism, and subsequent modernist traits of bureaucratization and the centralization of authority" (2003, 213–14). Finally, indigenes are defined by their relationship to the state, in which they are recognized as having different rights than other citizens.

When Indigenous peoples try to gain rights to land or to resources that may lie beneath the surface of the land they occupy, the state or some other entity interested in blocking Indigenous claims may use the definition of essential difference as a weapon against Indigenous claims. For instance, issues such as wearing the same kinds of clothing as other Canadians have been cited by those who are opposed to Indigenous rights as evidence that Indigenous peoples no longer have a separate culture.

Social Movements

Kim Clark (2005) has explored the ways in which class struggles and state legislation created the space in which Indigenous social movements could form in Ecuador (Figure 6.2). The actors in Clark's historical account of the growth of CONAIE (Confederation of Indigenous Nations of Ecuador), and of the eventual amalgamation of small, grassroots social movements, include the state, Ecuador's elites, and Indians. In the early 1900s, the aim of the state, backed by the elite class, was to turn the Indian population into proper "civilized" consumers; however, the Indigenous peoples took advantage of this undertaking to promote their own goals. For instance, they started a literacy program in order to be able to check the account books of the haciendas, and they began to form small local groups.

As more grassroots Indigenous organizations formed, the state used part of its revenues generated from an oil boom to modernize the Ecuadorian countryside, expecting the Indigenous groups to passively accept the state's authoritarian paternalism. But local Indigenous leaders were learning to interact with the administrators of the state's development projects and with NGOs from both inside and outside the country, and they were gaining confidence in their ability to express the common identity that was growing among the various groups that belonged to CONAIE.

FIGURE 6.2 Ecuador

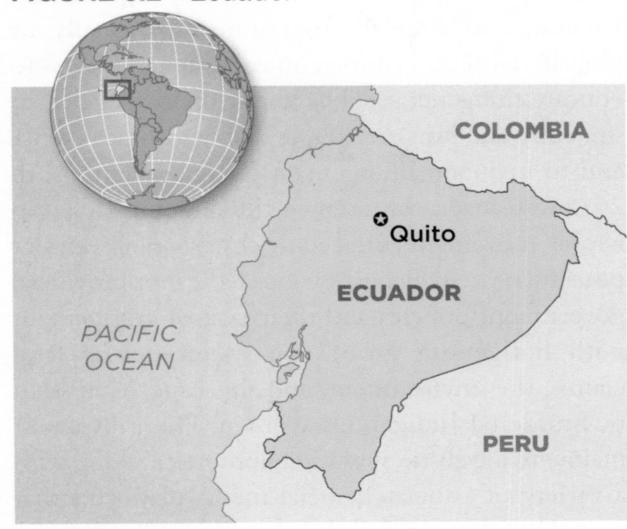

The debt crisis of the 1980s compelled Ecuador to reduce its spending on social programs. When that happened, the state's influence in the countryside diminished rapidly, and Indigenous organizations became more autonomous. The result has been that Indigenous identity has strengthened rapidly, especially in the countryside. Clark argues that the "rural population of the Ecuadorian highlands is becoming more rather than less Indigenous" (2005, 60).

The Indigenous leaders of this new social movement now participate directly in negotiations with the state and rural elites over such matters as agrarian reform and the privatization of water. In 2004, representatives of the Indigenous movement were appointed to positions in the Ecuadorian government.

Many collective Indigenous struggles have gained momentum with the rise of social media. Indigenous peoples are turning increasingly to online platforms such as Twitter, Instagram, and Facebook as a means to connect nationally or globally with other Indigenous groups, as well as to educate the general public about their struggles, to strategize and plan meetings, protests, or other events, and to maintain intergenerational connections. In 2012 in Canada, for instance, the ongoing "Idle No More" movement surfaced. It consists of a series of peaceful protests against various federal or provincial government policies and their lack of engagement with Indigenous groups on issues such as land claims, the environment, and the issue of missing or murdered Indigenous women. The movement maintains a website, www.idlenomore.ca, along with a variety of associated social media platforms that provide a sense of collective agency and solidarity among different groups of geographically dispersed Indigenous peoples, both nationally and globally.

More recently, in the winter of 2020, nationwide sit-ins, mass demonstrations, and blockades of railways and roads were launched in support of northern British Columbia's Wet'suwet'en people, whose hereditary chiefs were opposed to the construction of a 670-kilometre Coastal GasLink pipeline project that would traverse their territory. Decrying that the pipeline would cause irreparable damage to their land and way of life, the Wet'suwet'en with their protests gained significant momentum as well as national and international exposure through the use of social media, including Instagram, Snapchat, Facebook, and Twitter. Social media enabled them to attract both Indigenous and non-Indigenous allies; communities of solidarity formed rapidly, which put pressure on the federal government to negotiate an agreement with the Wet'suwet'en in March of 2020.

Palestinian Refugees

The lot of Palestinian refugees has not been happy. Randa Farah, a Palestinian Canadian anthropologist living in exile, states: "Palestinians constitute the largest refugee population in the world, and their exile is one of the longest in contemporary history, spanning over half a century" (2003, 1550). In a refugee camp in Jordan, where 120,000 Palestinians live in an area of 1.4 square kilometres, Farah listened to the stories of three generations of Palestinian refugees. Her study revealed that the refugees reinforced their collective memory by invoking memories of the land, of original villages, and of shared experiences of exile. This reconstruction of the past cannot be separated from the present political struggles, which counter the plans of the host societies to integrate the refugees. At the same time, the refugees reaffirm their hopes for repatriation. The Palestinian refugees also express their collective identity by reproducing symbols of home while they are away from home or, as Farah puts it, "a sense of place while out of place" (2005, 210).

When camps were not overcrowded, as they are today, Palestinian women planted gardens in front of their shelters as they did in their original villages, and they passed on to their children and grandchildren stories and images of what it was like to live in their villages before they had to flee. Public streets and walls in the camp are inscribed with political graffiti featuring Palestinian political history. Within refugee homes and shelters, Palestinian culture is displayed in Palestinian embroidery—especially embroidered peasant dresses—and in pictures of the Dome of the Rock in Jerusalem, children's diplomas, decorative Koranic verses, and maps of Palestine and its flag.

The notion of prolonged temporary residence, and that exile is not their permanent condition, is vital to Palestinian identity. This is evident in the structures of refugee shelters. In the words of a refugee in Jordan interviewed by Farah,

> *No one at the time used concrete for their shelters ... They used to say this is not our Homeland, we should not build here ... My father used to say we want to return to our Homeland, if not this year, next year ... My father, until he passed away in the eighties, believed we shall return. He didn't even want to build a roof using cement, he kept saying we shall return, but we didn't! (2004, 177)*

Land and return are at the centre of Palestinian identity, and keeping the memory alive is a form of resistance. As Farah explains, without the "Dream of Return," the older generation would have to concede that the younger generation—those born in the refugee camps—"are stateless refugees, without a past or a future" (2004, 181) and without an identity.

Conflict within Collective Identity: Telefolmin and Land in Papua New Guinea

A collective identity does not mean that everyone who assumes that identity experiences it in the same way. In Papua New Guinea (PNG), rights to land characteristically overlap and, as anthropologist Dan Jorgensen documents, are causing all kinds of problems in light of a proposed mining project, the Nena, at the site of Nena Mountain. Mineral exploration has been going on in PNG for quite some time, and the 1980s and 1990s witnessed a mining boom that saw four new mines open. Although mining brings some benefits to local people, such as employment and royalties, it also causes environmental damage, so compensation is paid to landowners. The Telefolmin people live in an area that has experienced mining since the 1960s, and many men have been employed in the industry.

The Telefolmin identify themselves as "Min," along with many of their neighbours. This identity is based on common descent from an ancestress known as Afek, who travelled through the area in the mythological past. When she came to the present site of Telefolip, she built a spirit house, which became the centre of important rituals for Min people. All Telefolmin men must be initiated at Telefolip, and they return at death in order to reach the "Land of the Dead." After Afek built Telefolip, she killed her younger brother, Umoim, and sent him along an underground passage to Mount Fubilan to establish Bagelam, "The Land of the Dead," located west of Telefolip. This place associated with the dead is also a source of wealth, for it is here that Umoim produced stone adzes used to clear gardens, and it is here that *bonang* shells, an important item of exchange in marriage and mortuary rituals, originated. In 1980, copper was discovered at Mount Fubilan and a mine called Ok Tedi (Figure 6.3) was built there. The Telefolmin were hired during the initial construction phase and as wage labourers once the actual mining began. But

FIGURE 6.3 The Ok Tedi Mine in Papua New Guinea

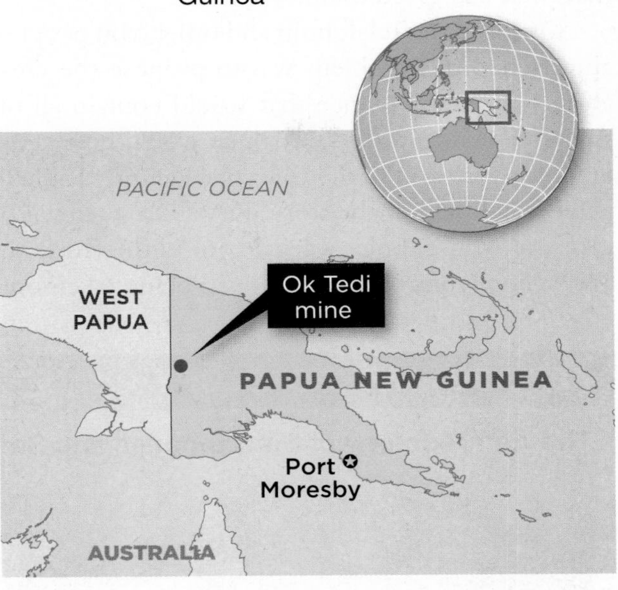

The Ok Tedi mine.

they had no control over the land and the resources that Afek had given them.

One way the Telefolmin and other Min peoples approached this problem was to propose the creation of a new province that would contain all of Afek's descendants. This province would give geographic expression to the collective identity that had been established in the story of Afek; it would also give the Min peoples a legal tool with which to assert more control over what was being taken out of their land and how they were compensated for environmental damage. But this would not solve all the problems, for the Min peoples relate to the land in different ways.

The Telefolmin hold a few basic principles that determine who has first rights to which pieces of land. The principle of first clearance means that whoever clears a plot of land has rights to that land as long as it is in use, and the principle of bilateral inheritance means that land can be passed on through both

APPLYING ANTHROPOLOGY

The Anthropology of Smartphones and Smart Ageing

leungchopan/Shutterstock.com

In Shanghai, elderly people use their smartphones to connect with others at social events in a type of "speed dating" for purposes of developing friendships or romantic relationships.

Anthropologists have come to understand that identities are shaped by various forms of digital media, yet there has been little ethnographic attention devoted to exploring the impact of digital media in non-Western, global contexts. In February 2018, lead anthropologist Daniel Miller and a team of nine anthropologists began ethnographic research on a five-year collaborative project called "The Anthropology of Smartphones and Smart Ageing." The goal of the project is to understand how different age demographics use smartphones and their associated applications (i.e., social media apps like Instagram or Twitter, health-related apps, and features like text messaging and email) differently. They hope to address how smartphones affect people's sense of well-being and health as they age. To undertake this project, anthropologists have begun simultaneous fieldwork in Cameroon, Uganda, Brazil, Chile, Al-Quds, Ireland, Italy, China, and Japan. By adopting a cross-cultural, comparative perspective, Miller and his colleagues hope to avoid imposing their own biases about social media use on different populations, and to understand the unique possibilities and challenges or barriers to social media use that different groups may experience. Ultimately, they hope to address how aging, as a form of individual and social identity, is informed by, and overlaps with, other identities such as gender. How, for example, do the Italian women in their study perceive and use smartphones differently than men in Italy and in other nations? What do these differences tell us about how people use digital technologies like smartphones differently?

Early reports on research blogposts about the project have facilitated the sharing of a number of preliminary results with other researchers as well as the general public. In Uganda, for instance, team member Shireen Walton reports in a blogpost on the work of anthropologist Charlotte Hawkins (2019). Hawkins has found that in this context, elderly people are increasingly reliant upon applications on their smartphones to receive remittances from family members who have migrated elsewhere for work. Through their smart phones, the receipt of remittances is made more reliable, and money is frequently put toward health care–related expenses. The ease and reliability of money transfers that smartphones afford contribute to a feeling of safety; this helps reduce anxiety surrounding household expenses.

This type of applied research helps anthropologists comprehend cross-cultural differences in smartphone use; it also helps phone providers and manufacturers understand the different needs of different demographics of people throughout the world. This can assist with the design and marketing of future products. The Anthropology of Smartphones and Smart Ageing website, which includes periodic updates and a blog, can be found here: https://www.ucl.ac.uk/anthropology/assa/

maternal and paternal connections. A third way that Telefolmin can gain access to land is through being granted permission to use some part of the land of another.

While all of this seems fairly simple in theory, when the principles are combined, the actual practice becomes much more complex. For instance, rights in land and rights based on residence may not be the same. The principle of bilateral inheritance may mean that a Telefolmin has rights in lands located in different places and that he or she, or the entire family, may move away temporarily in order to use land in another hamlet, giving permission to a friend to use land in the place they left. When the mining company agrees to pay occupation fees, royalties, or compensation to a landowner for environmental damage, the question becomes "Who and what is a landowner?"

Adding to the complexity is a history of conflict and warfare that has left some villages empty in the area of the mines but that has not destroyed old rights in land. Furthermore, when one group defeated another, women and children were often adopted into the victorious group, and their rights in land were passed on to their children. Over the years, this overlapping in land rights has created a vast puzzle that defies solution.

The Min conflict over rights to land highlights the connection between place and identity for Telefolmin; it also shows how "a self-conscious Min identity has multiple roots" (Jorgensen 1996, 202). Added to the variety of ways that Min people relate to one another through their common descent are colonial and missionary definitions that reinforce the notions of fixed categories and boundaries.

All three examples of how people form identities through collective action (Indigenous groups in Ecuador, Palestinian refugees in Jordan, and Telefolmin in PNG) challenge the notion of fixed categories and boundaries. Common ancestry, the sense that people as much as plants and trees are grown from the land, and a sense of self and other all come into play as different facets of identity are reworked in relation to current experiences and events.

Conclusions

The concept of the self, or personhood, varies from society to society. In the egocentric view, the person is viewed as an autonomous, discrete individual; in the sociocentric view, the self is viewed as contingent on a situation or social setting. The sociocentric view is often taken by social scientists who are interested in the social processes by which social identities are formed and maintained.

Societies distinguish individuals from one another by using criteria such as age, gender, kinship, ethnicity, and language. Differences and similarities in characteristics among individuals are used to construct social landscapes on which each person's place or identity is indicated. The characteristics that determine identity, such as gender, are treated differently in various societies.

People must also be able to communicate their identities to one another. One way to do this is through gift exchange and the principle of reciprocity. The kula ring of the Trobriand Islanders is an example. North Americans and other people in modern industrial societies have a special problem with gift giving: somehow they need to convert an impersonal, store-bought commodity into a personal and meaningful gift. We examined how during the Christian celebration of Christmas, this is a special problem, and we explored some of the ways in which North Americans solve it.

Another way people form their identity is through collective struggle. Examples of how this is done include the Indigenous social movements in Ecuador, the experiences of Palestinian refugees, and efforts to resolve land disputes in Papua New Guinea.

6.1 How is identity, and one's sense of self, learned?

This section explores the concept of social identity, which refers to our learned personal and social affiliations. These may include gender, sexuality, race, ethnicity, class, and nationality, among others. Anthropologists, following the research of Margaret Mead and her work on the "nature versus nurture" debate, are interested in exploring how many of our identities are not only dynamic and fluid, but also learned via processes of enculturation. We learn our identities in a variety of conscious and unconscious ways—through schooling, the influences of mass media and/or social media, or through our family and friends. Anthropologists also point out the dangers of reducing identities to biology or "nature," which oftentimes occurs in both the mass media and among some scientists in their research.

Review Questions

1. What were Margaret Mead's contributions to the "nature versus nurture" debate?
2. What are the dangers of ignoring the role of culture in constituting identities?
3. What is enculturation, and what are some of the processes by which it occurs?

6.2 How does the concept of personhood vary from society to society?

Societies differ significantly in terms of how they conceptualize personhood. For example, in this section we compared and contrasted differences in naming practices between North American societies and among the Umbunda to reveal the different ways societies conceptualize what a person is and how that person relates to the larger group. While recognizing that societies are dynamic and in flux, this section argues that most societies can be classified as sociocentric and/or egocentric. Egocentric societies, like most Westernized societies under the influence of capitalism, tend to stress notions of individualism in constructing personal identities. In contrast, sociocentric societies, like the Japanese, position kinship and other social relationships as key to constructing a sense of self.

Review Questions

1. What are the main features of the Umbundu naming system?
2. What do differences in Moroccan and Tshimsham naming practices tell us about notions of personhood within these societies?
3. What are some differences between egocentric and sociocentric views of self?

6.3 How do societies distinguish individuals from one another?

This section explores how different societies use different markers of identity in various ways to construct a sense of collective identity. For example, in some societies, kinship is a primary means of organizing people into different groups. In others, religion, ethnicity, or other factors may be considered more important than kinship. The extended example in this chapter discusses the role of factors like language and shared history in constructing a distinctly Québécois identity.

Review Questions

1. What historical factors have helped shape Québécois identity?
2. How and why is language important in maintaining a sense of Québécois identity?

6.4 How do societies mark changes in identity?

The concept of identity is not static or fixed; our identities can change over the course of our lifetime. All societies have rites of passage that mark changes in social status. These may include funerals to grieve the death of a loved one, weddings to celebrate marriage, or ceremonies of initiation into a particular religion (e.g., bar or bat mitzvahs). Drawing upon the work of Arnold van Gennep, anthropologist Victor Turner argues that all rites of passage have three stages: separation, liminality, and reintegration.

Review Questions

1. Outline the features of the three stages of a rite of passage using an example.
2. Discuss the three stages of Ndembu male initiation rites of passage.

6.5 How do individuals communicate their identities to one another?

This section focuses on reciprocity as a means of communicating identities. Social relationships between groups of people can also be affirmed or, at times, contested, through various forms of reciprocity: gift exchanges at Christmas or birthdays, potlatches among Northwest Coast Indigenous peoples, or the *kula* ring in the Trobriand islands.

Review Questions

1. Through what processes are commodities (such as Christmas or birthday presents) turned into gifts, and what is the purpose of gifting?
2. How does the kula ring act as a form of reciprocity?

6.6 How do people form identities through collective struggles?

Section 6.6 examines how a sense of identity is formed through experiences of oppression or victimization, which can lead to the formation of collective struggles. For example, many Indigenous peoples have experienced the oppressive and continuing effects of colonialism. This section explores how Indigenous groups in Ecuador, Palestinian refugees in Jordan, and the Telefolmin in PNG have fostered a sense of collective identity to fight, among other things, for land rights.

Review Questions

1. How do Palestinian refugees reinforce a sense of collective memory, and why is this important?
2. What factors fuelled the growth of CONAIE (Confederation of Indigenous Nations of Ecuador)?

CRITICAL THINKING QUESTIONS

1. Even though anthropologists and other scholars view our identities as learned phenomena, we live in a society that privileges biological or "natural" explanations for our behaviour. What are some of the consequences of thinking about our identities as natural?
2. Hoodfar discusses what veiling means for many Muslim women and how they seek to express and communicate aspects of their identity through veiling. But many people use not just clothing but other forms of body modification to communicate their identity. How are tattoos and piercings markers of identity for many people?

KEY TERMS

biocultural approach (p. 163)
commodities (p. 174)
egocentric (p. 165)
enculturation (p. 160)
ethnic identity (p. 168)
imagined community (p. 161)
Indigenous peoples (p. 176)
***kula* ring** (p. 172)
nature versus nurture (p. 161)
potlatch (p. 173)
principle of reciprocity (p. 172)
rites of passage (p. 170)
social identity (p. 158)
sociocentric (p. 165)

CHAPTER 7

Social Hierarchies

TIMOTHY A. CLARY/AFP via Getty Images

A woman walks past a mural by American artist Angela China (also known as Gumshoe). China's work is a satirical take on Pablo Picasso's famous 1907 painting, *Les Demoiselles d'Avignon*. Here, four male celebrities who have been accused of and/or charged with and sentenced for various forms of sexual assault in the wake of the #MeToo movement replace the five semi-nude women who feature in Picasso's original work. From left to right: Bill Cosby, Harvey Weinstein, Donald Trump, and Kevin Spacey. This mural draws attention to our society's pervasive social hierarchies—such as gender—and highlights the potential for resistance, agency or change (in this case) via social or visual media.

> *Although it may never be possible to quantify the degree of racism that exists in a given society, the evidence unmistakably reveals that racism widely distorts the attitudes of white Canadians toward Aboriginal peoples. Whether blatantly or covertly, many Canadians still believe that Aboriginal people are inferior; as a result, these people believe that there is a sound, rational basis for discriminating against Aboriginal persons at both the individual and institutional level.*
>
> —James S. Frideres and René R. Gadacz

PROBLEM 7

Why are modern societies characterized by social, political, and economic inequalities? How are certain gender, class, racial, and other identities privileged or marginalized in various social contexts?

Introduction

The Rationale for Social Inequality

The maldistribution of wealth, status, power, and privilege is a significant problem throughout the modern world. To North Americans it is visible in the starving faces that stare out from our television screens in documentaries and on the evening news, interspersed with advertisements for luxuries such as automobiles, cosmetics, and household appliances. Some people can purchase the finest amenities, while others lack the necessities of life, such as food, shelter, and health care. There are few, if any, modern nations in which one part of the population does not in some way enjoy privileges that other parts do not share.

Anthropologists use the term **social hierarchy**, or *social stratification*, to refer to the ordering and ranking of individuals within a society. This ranking is usually based on pervasive systems of inequality that privilege particular classes, castes, races, sexualities, or genders over others.

Social hierarchy is not an inevitable feature of human societies. For example, although groups such as the Ju/'hoansi and the Inuit are not completely egalitarian, people go out of their way not to appear better than others. Moreover, there does not seem to be a universal inclination to rank people by one criterion or another; in some societies, skin colour makes a difference, while in others, it does not. In some societies, men are accorded far greater status than women; in others, little if any difference is ascribed to gender. Even the use of age as a criterion of rank varies from society to society. The only general rule seems be that as societies become more complex and more populous, their propensity for social stratification increases.

Some people contend that the hierarchical ordering of people and groups is unavoidable. In their view, scarce resources, occupational specialization, and the power of an elite group to control the behaviour of others inevitably result in some form of social stratification. Others maintain that stratification is avoidable—indeed, that it is counter to human nature. According to anthropologist Thomas Belmonte, "since the emergence of stratification, man's[1]

social hierarchy
The ordering and ranking of individuals within society, also known as *social stratification*. Those at the top of the hierarchy are generally afforded more power, wealth, prestige, or privileges in a society. Hierarchies can be based on race, gender, class, caste, ethnicity, national affiliation, or other factors.

[1] Note that Belmonte's use of "man," "men," and "his" in reference to humankind, including both men and women, is no longer accepted practice, especially in scholarly writing, as this usage is considered to be an example of gendered bias in language (see Section 7.3 for a longer discussion of the relationship between gender, language, and social hierarchy).

history (his changing ways of relating to nature and other men) has stood opposed to his humanity. The emergence of power-wielding elites ... laid the basis for a new kind of anti-collective society whose vastly accelerated growth was founded, not on the reconciliation of antagonisms between men, but on their origination and amplification in slavery, caste, and class" (1989, 137).

Those who support Belmonte's view note that in societies such as those of the Ju/'hoansi and the Inuit, there are no "poor," "rich," "inferior," or "superior" people; nonetheless, these societies are not totally egalitarian, or equal—even in small-scale societies, valued statuses are not available to some members. The question at hand, though, is why modern societies are characterized by extremes of poverty and wealth.

Note that poverty is not random. Indigenous populations, minorities, and women are the social categories most at risk for poverty. For instance, according to data collected by Statistics Canada, in general, poverty rates (measured by low income) decreased by 2.9 percent between 1981 and 2018. However, recent immigrants, Indigenous peoples, racialized communities, and people with disabilities have been the least likely to benefit from this decrease; they are also more likely than other groups to remain poor for the long term. The poverty rate for all Canadians in 2018 was 8.7 percent, but it was 20.8 percent for racialized individuals, 23.6 percent for Indigenous families, and 23 percent for people with disabilities (Citizens for Public Justice 2018). How, then, do we explain the distribution of poverty, power, prestige, status, and wealth based on race, Indigenous status, and gender, among other factors?

In this chapter, we examine how societies construct social hierarchies and why some groups erect social edifices based on social dominance and submission, high and low status, and oppressors and oppressed. We examine why most people in stratified societies—both those at the top and those at the bottom—consider social ranks to be "the nature of things." We go on to discuss how social hierarchies such as race, gender, and class are intertwined in Canada, particularly in the experiences of immigrants who are also members of visible minorities. We also explore whether a relatively nonstratified community can exist within a large-scale society. Finally, we explore how an anthropological perspective can be applied to alleviate the effects of inequality.

QUESTIONS

7.1 How do societies use class and caste to rank people in social hierarchies?
7.2 How do people come to accept social hierarchies as natural?
7.3 How is gender a form of social hierarchy?
7.4 How are different forms of social hierarchy interwoven with one another?
7.5 How can anthropology be applied to alleviate the effects of inequality?

Question 7.1: How Do Societies Use Class and Caste to Rank People in Social Hierarchies?

Social hierarchies in different societies vary along several dimensions: the criteria used to differentiate people into one level of society or another; the number of levels that exist; the kinds of privileges and rights that attach to people at different levels; and the strength of the social boundaries that separate the different levels. In Canada and the United States, for example, people are stratified by income and personal possessions into social **classes** (e.g., lower class, middle class, and upper class). They are also classified by cultural or family background into ethnic groups (e.g., Italian, Jewish, Hispanic,

class
A form of identity informed by perceptions of an individual's economic worth or status. It is also a form of social hierarchy.

or white Anglo-Saxon Protestant), or by physical appearance or skin colour into racial categories or visible minorities (e.g., black or white). They are also classified by gender and age, as well as by standards such as education. People in Canada and the United States may move from class to class, and they may choose to emphasize or de-emphasize their ethnic group membership, but generally, their racial category and gender are perceived as fixed.

Class as a Form of Social Hierarchy

Social class refers to perceptions of an individual's standing or status in society, normally based on economic criteria, status, or other factors, which may vary from society to society. Max Weber argued that social class can be based on economic wealth or "status class": prestige, honour, educational or occupational achievements, or religious or spiritual affiliation. In North American societies, for instance, we tend to place particular value on some occupations that require years of post-secondary schooling over more "hands-on" professions such as construction work and trades. Although many tradespeople earn sizable incomes, their professions lack the "status" associated with medicine or law. Beyond that, we live in a commodified, consumer-driven society in which material possessions, such as cars, houses, and certain brands of clothes, are often perceived as markers of an individual's class background and, by extension, their access to wealth, power, and prestige.

Unlike social identities, such as race (which is normally perceived as an ascribed status, that is, as fixed or unchanging), class in North American society has long been viewed as a more fluid social identity. In other words, it can be either an **ascribed status** or an **achieved status**. An individual may be born into a life of wealth, power, and high status as a Rockefeller or a Massey; or alternatively, they may, through hard work and determination, overcome the odds and achieve a higher class status. The growing wealth gap between the rich and the poor in North America, and the decreased likelihood of upward class mobility, suggests that the former occurs much more frequently than the latter, so that class comes to look much more like an ascribed status. The popular myth that class is an achieved category is enshrined in American fiction (F. Scott Fitzgerald's *The Great Gatsby*) and in real life (former US president Barack Obama). By suggesting that class identity is the result of a **meritocracy**, however, these stories overshadow the ways in which class intersects with other identities, such as gender and race.

In many ways, stories about the opportunities available for all privilege a white male, middle- or upper-class perspective. As discussed earlier, ethnic minorities and women, for instance, are often positioned at the bottom of many social hierarchies, making it difficult for them to access the tools they need—such as post-secondary education, training, and other resources—to "achieve" a higher class status. The idea of North America as a meritocracy discounts the fact that there is no "level playing field" when it comes to class, race, and gender. Unfortunately, when we think of class solely as an achieved status, too often we tend to blame the poor for their own fate.

Caste as a Form of Social Stratification

In a **caste system**, individuals are assigned at birth to the ranked social and occupational groups of their parents. A person's place in the social order is fixed;

ascribed status
An identity that is perceived as fixed and unchanging because a person is believed to be born with it. In Canadian society, race is often assumed to be ascribed at birth.

achieved status
An identity that is believed to be in flux and that is dependent upon the actions and achievements of an individual.

meritocracy
A social system in which individuals are rewarded and resources are distributed according to achievement, effort, and ability.

caste system
A form of social stratification and identity where individuals are assigned at birth to the ranked social and occupational groups of their parents.

there is no mobility from one caste to another. This lack of mobility is one feature that distinguishes the notion of caste from class. Castes are also separated by strict rules that forbid intermarriage and other forms of interaction, such as eating together, speaking to one another, or working together. In other words, caste systems are endogamous, or closed.

Caste systems exist in societies all over the world (for instance, the Balinese, discussed in depth in Chapter 1, have a caste system). However, India presents the best-known and most paradigmatic example of a caste system of social stratification.

In any stratified society, people's access to jobs, wealth, and privilege is determined largely by their position in the hierarchy. In India, where the population is stratified into hundreds of different castes, these groups are based on traditional occupational roles and Hindu ritual categories of purity and pollution. According to this traditional classification system, the Brahmins, the priestly caste whose lives were devoted to worship and teaching, occupied the top of the hierarchy. Directly under them was the Kshatriya caste, whose members comprised the soldiers, politicians, and administrators. Next was the Vaisya caste, made up of farmers and merchants. At the bottom of the hierarchy was the Sudra caste, whose members were devoted to the service of other castes. Although, traditionally, castes were occupational, they did not determine one's occupation so much as they excluded one from certain jobs. Not all Brahmins were priests, nor were all members of the Vaisya caste farmers and merchants, but *only* Brahmins could be priests and *only* Vaisya could be farmers.

Beneath the religious hierarchy were the Harijans, "untouchable" or "unclean" persons, whose occupations were believed to be ritually polluting to others. Members of the Harijan caste have recently changed their name to *dalit*, which means "oppressed" or "ground down." *Dalit* include washermen, tanners, shoemakers, and sweepers—people whose occupations require them to come into contact with animal or human wastes.

For many years, debates about the practice of caste in India centred on which was the more important aspect of the caste system: concrete concerns with occupational roles or more abstract, symbolic issues of purity and pollution. However, rapid social and economic changes in contemporary India have required anthropologists to rethink how and why caste continues to be a salient social category there, and to what extent it continues to work as a justification for and method of social stratification. For instance, no traditional caste rankings apply to modern professions such as pilot, call-centre operator, factory worker, or medical doctor. Furthermore, as Isabelle Clark-Decès (2011, 8) notes, "nowadays ideas of relative purity do not matter as much as they did in the past, [and] equality and democratic values have undermined the practice of caste ranking."

Caste still plays an important role in the social hierarchy, though it now overlaps with a newer hierarchy of class. What has changed is the *way* in which caste links occupation to hierarchy. Many traditional occupations continue to be filled by members of certain castes to the exclusion of all others, but, as Robert Deliège (2011, 47) has pointed out, "today everyone aspires to a better life and as a result, the struggle for attractive occupations has become a major issue in contemporary caste struggles." Today, many Indians think of members of other castes as rivals and as different, but not necessarily as inherently inferior or superior to themselves. The contemporary case of the *dalit* and their caste "rivals" provides an interesting example.

Since 1989, the Indian government has in its constitution outlawed discrimination against the *dalit*, or anyone else, based on caste membership. Although these legal measures did not bring a sudden end to untouchability, they did have important consequences. Untouchables could now go to temple, attend school, apply for jobs, take the same buses and trains as anyone else, and so on. Deliège's *dalit* informants told him they did not find concerns about pollution to be particularly relevant to their lives, and although most people refused to do scavenging work within the village, they would be happy to take jobs as *municipal* scavengers provided that these jobs were salaried with benefits (2011, 54).

The *dalit* have turned their designation as a "scheduled caste" to their collective socioeconomic advantage. As members of a scheduled caste, the *dalit* now enjoy constitutional protection against discrimination, affirmative action in job allotments and higher education, and resources and benefits to bridge the socioeconomic gap with other groups. According to Deliège, the consolidation of the category "scheduled caste" has solidified the formerly ill-defined and somewhat fluid line between untouchable and not-untouchable. If you are within the *dalit* category, you are entitled to protection from the state; if you are outside, you are not. This solidification of categories has had drastic consequences, especially at the lower end of the caste hierarchy.

What, for instance, is the difference between an agricultural worker from a scheduled caste and another from a nonscheduled caste? The two earn similar wages and live in similar conditions. It may well be that members of a scheduled caste are insulted from time to time, but members of the nonscheduled caste may also be despised, even if no derogatory caste names are thrown at them. Moreover, the government usually gives nonscheduled communities fewer opportunities to improve their lot. All things being equal, then, it is often (but not always) better to be a member of a scheduled caste (Deliège 2011, 56). Clearly, caste continues to play a significant role in contemporary India; however, as Deliège's work shows, castes, especially those in similar socioeconomic circumstances, often see one another as rivals in a country where socioeconomic class hierarchies are becoming increasingly prevalent.

Question 7.2: How Do People Come to Accept Social Hierarchies as Natural?

Sociocultural anthropology is about seeing behind the façade of everyday appearances to what lies behind those appearances. Understanding how societies construct rationales to justify and legitimize social discrimination is one of the most important tasks in anthropology as well as, to some extent, one of the most difficult. Race is often viewed as a social category that is biological and fixed. In other words, it is perceived as something that we are born with and thus cannot change. Throughout this section, we challenge this widespread perception of race as a natural, biological category, to argue that race is both a culturally constructed form of identity and a form of social stratification. As a by-product of culture and not biology, race has historically functioned as a means to justify existing inequalities, to maintain the status quo, and to advantage some members of society while disadvantaging others (in terms of access to power, education, jobs, and so on).

Race as a Form of Social Stratification

Franz Boas, a founder of anthropology, was among the first social scientists to discredit racist and sexist theories and ideologies that sought to legitimize the marginalization of people based on race, religion,

Franz Boas (1858–1942) was one of the founders of anthropology and one of the first anthropologists to challenge racism and sexism in popular culture.

gender, and ethnicity: see Boas (1940). Part of the problem is that racist and sexist theories exist not only in popular culture but also in science. It will be useful, then, to examine how such theories are constructed and often taken for granted, and how they are used to justify the ranking of people within the social hierarchy.

Constructing the Ideology of Racism

As discussed earlier, in Canada and the United States the ideology of class is based on the assumption that a person's position in the class hierarchy is determined largely by achievement or individual effort; that is, individuals who work hard and with determination will succeed. Yet there are also attempts to justify social position in terms of a person's innate, biological makeup—largely by race, innate mental ability (intelligence), and other factors. Accordingly, the hierarchical ordering of society is seen as an expression of a natural law that some people are born better able to lead and succeed than others.

The term **race** as used here refers to the presumed genetic, natural, heritable characteristics of a group of people, normally based on physical attributes such as skin colour, eye colour, or hair type. We live in a society that views race as a natural, ascribed category; it is something we believe we are born with. Unlike class, then, race in many industrialized societies (such as Canada) is seen as a fixed, unchanging form of identity.

Anthropologists and other scholars, however, maintain that there is no scientific basis for positioning different groups of people into discrete "races" on the basis of physical features—no population of individuals anywhere in the world is morphologically distinct. In other words, for a "race" to scientifically exist, it would have to be demonstrated that a certain physical feature (e.g., skin colour) occurs consistently and uniformly within a particular population. But no group of people, anywhere in the world, fits this criterion. Simply put, there is too much physical diversity within specific populations. The Executive Board of the American Anthropological Association (1998), the largest professional association of anthropologists in the world, sums up this argument:

> *Both scholars and the general public have been conditioned to viewing human races as natural and separate divisions within the human species based on visible physical differences. With the vast expansion of scientific knowledge in this century, however, it has become clear that human populations are not unambiguous, clearly demarcated, biologically distinct groups. Evidence from the analysis of genetics (e.g., DNA) indicates that most physical variation, about 94%, lies within so-called racial groups. Conventional geographic "racial" groupings differ from one another only in about 6% of their genes. This means that there is greater variation within "racial" groups than between them. In neighbouring populations there is much overlapping of genes and their phenotypic (physical) expressions. Throughout history whenever different groups have come into contact, they have interbred. The continued sharing of genetic materials has maintained all of humankind as a single species.*

These days, most academics view race as a culturally constructed form of identity. In other words, they view race as a by-product of cultural beliefs, not biology. Race may not exist from a strictly scientific perspective, but it remains an important topic for anthropologists to explore. In Canada, we live in a society in which the myth prevails that race is natural or biological, as opposed to a cultural category. Because of this, race has had a variety of social consequences. Over the years, for

race
A culturally constructed form of identity and social hierarchy, *race* refers to the presumed hereditary, physical characteristics of a group of people. These physical, or phenotypic, differences are often erroneously correlated with behavioural attributes.

instance, race has been conflated with behavioural characteristics, resulting in **racism**, or systems of prejudice based on the stratification of physical differences, which are erroneously thought to correlate with behavioural, physical, or intellectual differences in certain populations. We tend to think of racism today as a practice found only among ill-educated or ill-meaning individuals, and as aimed at individuals; but looked at from an anthropological perspective, it can be seen, rather, as a societal or systemic problem.

For centuries, European and North American societies have been characterized by racial stratification. In these societies, membership in certain racial or ethnic groups has been enough to place people in particular positions in a hierarchy that defines their social, political, and economic worth. In the United States, for example, one's position in the racial hierarchy has often determined whether a person can vote, hold political office, pursue a particular occupation, live in a certain area, use certain public facilities, attend certain schools, or marry a particular person.

Although most Canadians consider themselves to be far less racist than their southern neighbours, racism has a long history in Canada, and white supremacist groups have been formed in both countries. The Ku Klux Klan, for instance, was founded in Tennessee in 1865 to terrorize newly freed slaves who questioned white supremacy. By the 1920s, the Klan was well established in Canada. When it arrived from the United States, it added French Canadians and Catholics to its list of inferior peoples. In the 1960s, the Canadian Nazi Party and the Edmund Burke Society, the forerunner of the Western Guard, openly supported racism. Ten years later, the Nationalist Party and the Aryan Nations took their place among the radical right. More recent years have seen the rise of many far-right (or "alt-right") nationalist populist movements (see Chapter 8) in Canada and other industrialized nations. These too are examples of exclusionary and often racist subcultures. The common belief shared by these groups is that the "white race" is superior and that it is on the verge of being "wiped out" by the "dark-skinned races." As Stanley Barrett (2002, 92) put it, "according to white supremacists, interracial mixing, or as they preferred, mongrelization, was more dangerous to humankind than the atomic bomb, because without the genetic purity of 'the master race' the world could not survive."

African Canadians are not the only ones to experience racism in Canada. Racist beliefs about Indigenous peoples are deeply rooted in Canadian history. James Frideres and René Gadacz call this "structural racism" (as opposed to prejudice and discrimination by individuals) because it is embedded in Canadian social institutions. Frideres and Gadacz argue that the Indian reserve is "an internal colony" in which "Canadians are seen as the colonizing people, while Aboriginal persons are considered the colonized people" (2001, 4).

Stratification by race has existed for a number of reasons. It was economically profitable to people who could buy black slaves or obtain workers from among groups legally or socially barred from anything but low-paying jobs. It was advantageous, also, to those who did not have to compete for jobs with people who were socially or legally barred from them. Stratified societies often claim that the ranking of people by race and ethnicity is natural and that social hierarchies are not socially constructed. In the case of racial stratification, some proponents have claimed that it is the Christian God's will that some persons are inferior to others; others, that God created different races as he created different species of animals, and furthermore, that the Bible says the species are to be kept apart; others, that members of one race or another are intellectually or morally superior to members of other races. Generally, of course, it has been the race of the person making reference to the Christian God or the Bible that has been somehow superior.

racism
Refers to the discrimination and mistreatment of particular "racial" groups.

Most people had little trouble constructing an ideology to justify racial stratification, especially since it was reinforced by state and religious authorities. Even supposedly objective scientists assisted in building a racist ideology. In the nineteenth century, reputable scientists devoted much time and energy to proving that the racial stratification of society was "in the nature of things." Indeed, many contemporary forms of racism emerged out of nineteenth-century scientific studies of race. Both misguided and ethnocentric by today's standards, they functioned to maintain what Peggy McIntosh refers to as **white privilege**—the positioning of "white" individuals at the top of racial hierarchies. Science thus became a tool for naturalizing the power, authority, and privileges afforded to individuals with white skin. Their research findings supposedly proved that members of one race (usually whites or Europeans) were intellectually superior to members of another race (usually blacks or Asians).

Samuel George Morton was a respected scientist and physician who began in the 1820s to collect and measure skulls from all over the world. When he died in 1851, he left a collection of some 6,000 skulls. Like many in the nineteenth century, Morton believed that a person's intelligence was related to the size of his or her brain; the larger the brain, the more intelligent the person. He thus believed that a ranking of the races could be objectively achieved by a ranking of skull size.

Morton first measured the size—more specifically, the cranial capacity—of skulls by filling them with mustard seed and then pouring the seed into a container to measure the skull's volume in cubic inches. Dissatisfied with the inconsistency of measurements obtained with mustard seed, he later used 1/8-inch-diameter lead shot. He concluded from his measurements that "white" skulls had a mean value of 92 cubic inches, "American Indian" skulls 79 cubic inches, and "black" skulls from America, Africa, and Australia 83 cubic inches. Among "white" skulls, the largest were those of Germans and English people; in the middle were those of Jews; and at the bottom were those of Hindus. Thus, the social hierarchy of whites at the top, with the English and Germans at the top of the top, and blacks on the bottom, was said to be supported by the evidence of brain size and intelligence.

Morton concluded from all this that "whites" (specifically, northern European "whites") were not only socially superior but also biologically superior. He believed he had provided objective evidence that the distribution of status and power in nineteenth-century North America accurately reflected not merely social, but biological merit.

When Stephen Jay Gould, a Harvard paleontologist, re-examined Morton's published data, he concluded that Morton's summaries were a "patchwork of fudging and finagling" (1981, 54) to reach conclusions that supported the socially constructed hierarchy. Gould found no evidence of conscious fraud. He concluded that Morton had simply selected or rejected certain data to ensure that the results confirmed what he and most other Americans believed: that whites were naturally more intelligent than the people they called "Indian" or "black."

Working with the same skulls Morton had used more than 150 years earlier, Gould discovered that the sample of 144 Native American skulls included proportionally more small-brained Inca skulls from Peru and fewer large-brained Iroquois skulls. This choice naturally produced a lower mean cranial capacity for Indigenous Americans than would have occurred had Morton correctly adjusted for this discrepancy. Moreover, Gould discovered that Morton's failure to include the small-brained Hindu skulls with his "white" skulls had produced a higher average cranial capacity for white skulls. When Gould corrected for Morton's sample biases, he discovered that there was no difference between Euro-American and Indigenous American cranial

white privilege
Refers to the fact that, in many societies, "white" people have access to greater power, authority, and privileges than non-white people.

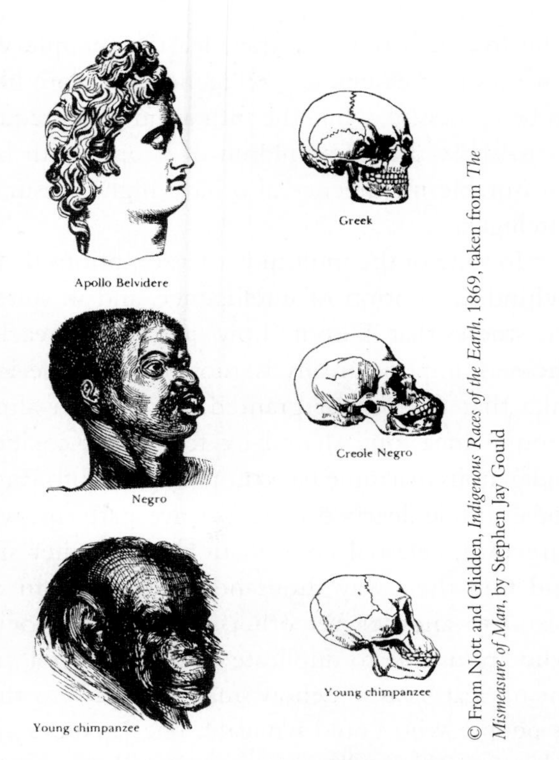

Nineteenth-century scientists attempted to "prove" that whites were naturally superior to other races. In this illustration from an 1868 racist tract, the proportions of the skulls were distorted, giving the impression that blacks might even rank lower than the apes.

capacity. As for comparisons between "white" and "black" skulls, Gould discovered that Morton had ignored the facts that brain size is related to body size and that male skulls are larger than female skulls. Examination of Morton's black skulls indicated that the group included proportionally more female skulls and fewer male skulls.

Gould did not believe that Morton consciously manipulated his skull measurements to prove that whites were intellectually superior to Native Americans or blacks. Rather, he thought that Morton had simply assumed what his measurements would prove and set about achieving the results he expected. For example, Gould observed that when Morton used mustard seed to measure cranial capacity, he obtained even greater differences between his "white" and "black" skulls than he had obtained using lead shot. Gould concluded that because mustard seeds are smaller and lighter than lead shot, Morton, probably unconsciously, packed more mustard seed into "white" skulls to obtain a greater difference in cranial capacity between "blacks" and "whites." Unfortunately, while Morton's measurements were obviously in error, as was his assumption that cranial capacity reveals intelligence, and though his conclusions were dictated by the socially constructed hierarchy of his day, they were used well into the twentieth century to support the ideology that the racial ranking of persons in society could be justified on natural rather than social grounds.

Class, Race, and the Social Construction of "Intelligence"

Morton's experiments were just one example of the efforts in North America and Europe to show that people somehow deserve their ranking in society: that it is not the result of chance or family privilege but, rather, the result of innate attributes. To believe otherwise would threaten a key assertion of North American ideology: that everyone in Canada and the United States enjoys an equal opportunity for success. Moreover, there are serious political and economic consequences to believing otherwise. If poverty and a low ranking in society are not the fault of the poor, then they must be the result of some failure of society. Such an admission provides a strong reason for governments to enact social and economic policies such as affirmative action, programs of economic redistribution, and laws barring racial and other forms of discrimination. Such changes, however, can lead to a loss of privilege for those who are benefiting from present policies; therefore, there is strong motivation to find some concept that legitimizes inherited privilege while still placing the blame for poverty or lack of success on the poor.

The concept of intelligence neatly solves this problem: if people accept that intelligence can explain how well people do, then the fiction that people's rank in society depends solely on their own innate ability can be maintained. Moreover, if it can be shown that intelligence is inherited, then we can explain why the children of successful people tend to be successful, and why certain groups, notably people of colour and immigrants of certain characteristics, are disproportionately poor.

The failure of the thesis that cranial capacity, and hence brain size, reveals intelligence did not end all attempts to link intelligence to success and to race and ethnic class membership. There has been, instead, a continuing effort on the part of some members of the scientific establishment to marshal evidence that intelligence is inherited and varies among racial groups. These efforts have included the work of Arthur Jensen in the 1960s and 1970s and, more recently, the publication in 1994 of *The Bell Curve* by Richard J. Herrnstein and Charles Murray. Missing from most of these accounts is any acknowledgment that intelligence itself is a social construct, an invented idea. We need, then, to look closely at our concept of intelligence. How did it evolve?

To begin, anthropologist Allan Hanson (1993) notes that the concept of intelligence contains several questionable assumptions. First, intelligence is assumed to be a single entity. Second, it is assumed to be measurable and unequally distributed in the population. Third, the amount people have is assumed to be relatively fixed throughout life. Fourth, the amount people have is assumed to largely explain their degree of success in life. Finally, it is assumed to be largely inherited.

Each of these assumptions is critical to the intelligence construct as most people think of it, and each has been the subject of enormous scientific attention and criticism. The first assumption requires that we accept the idea that if someone is intelligent in one way, they will be intelligent in other ways, rather than believing that some people can be intelligent in some ways but not in others. The second assumption implies that we can somehow measure innate intelligence, as opposed to achievement, and the third presumes we can show that whatever is measured does not vary throughout a person's life. The fourth is built on the idea that people who have more measurable intelligence are more likely to be successful, while the fifth assumption requires us to show that the children of people with high measurable intelligence also have high measurable intelligence.

In spite of the multitude of assumptions that lie behind the notion of intelligence, and in spite of the studies that illustrate how questionable each of these assumptions really is, most North Americans take that notion for granted. Yet it is an almost unique idea, one shared by few other societies. Indigenous maritime navigators of the South Pacific, for example, learned to read wave patterns, wind direction, celestial constellations, and other signs and find their way thousands of miles from one island to another. Yet others in the same society who are unable to duplicate this feat did not view the navigators as somehow smarter—they saw them as people who could navigate. The Japanese view what we call intelligence in much the same way as we view health: except in certain (and generally temporary) circumstances, we all have enough of it.

This book is not the place to summarize all those works that call the concept of intelligence into question. Nevertheless, we might learn something about the social construction of ideologies of class by looking briefly at the early history of the intelligence construct and by reviewing how reputable scientists proceeded to develop it. A number of pioneers, including Francis Galton and Karl Pearson, supplied the basic ideas and experimental proofs for the classic concept of intelligence as a fixed "mental" entity that is differentially distributed in the population, that is measurable, that largely explains a person's educational and occupational success, and that is inherited.

Francis Galton was a leading intellectual figure of the late nineteenth century. He was the founder of modern statistics as well as the founder of eugenics—that is, the attempt to identify the most desirable human traits, specify the individuals who possess them, and, through selective reproduction, enhance the number of people possessing those desired characteristics. In his best-known work,

Hereditary Genius (1869), he sought to demonstrate that the "genius" of selected eminent men was linked to the fact that they had eminent parents and, it followed, that their "genius" was largely inherited. In his sample of 997 eminent British men, he found that 31 percent had eminent fathers, 48 percent had eminent sons, and 41 percent had eminent brothers—far higher percentages than one would expect by chance. For Galton, this illustrated the power of heredity in the distribution of "genius." He was, of course, rightly criticized for ignoring the impact of environment. But he did something else that was more interesting, something that went largely unchallenged: he selected the eminent men from the British upper and upper-middle classes, ignoring the "captains of industry and finance," as well as any women. For Galton, eminence was eminence only within a select range of activities and occupations. A nephew of Charles Darwin and of upper-middle-class background, he was faithfully reproducing the judgments of his own status as to what constituted intelligence.

In 1901, Karl Pearson published a study in Proceedings of the Royal Society of London in which he concluded that "the mental characteristics in man are inherited in precisely the same manner as the physical. Our mental and moral nature is quite as much as our physical nature, the outcome of hereditary factors" (155). It is instructive to look at how Pearson reached this conclusion. He took pairs of brothers and measured specific physical characteristics, such as stature, forearm length, hair colour, eye colour, and cephalic (i.e., cranial) index. He found, not surprisingly, that there were high correlations among brothers for these traits, as well as a mean correlation of .5171. He then asked teachers, using a separate sample, to rank brother-pairs on seven "mental characteristics": intelligence, vivacity, conscientiousness, popularity, temper, self-consciousness, and shyness. Thus, under "conscientiousness" teachers were asked to rate each child as "keen" or "dull" and to choose among six subdivisions of intelligence. When the teachers' evaluations of brother-pairs were tabulated, Pearson found a strong correlation between brother ratings and a mean correlation of .5214, thereby proving the power of inheritance.

Much about this study is questionable, but of particular note is the role of teachers' judgments. Clearly, teachers were evaluating selected behaviour patterns and personal characteristics: patterns and characteristics that they judged to be evidence of various "mental characteristics." In other words, the teachers' judgments were highly subjective and, at best, questionable. But Pearson's work marked an important development in the construction of our concept of intelligence: he claimed to show that whatever intelligence was, it was obviously inherited at least as much as physical characteristics.

Obviously, the methodologies of these classic studies were seriously flawed, relying as they did on subjective judgments as to who was intelligent and who was not—judgments that were bound to be biased by such factors as the social class of teachers and students. In both examples, members of the professional middle class were selecting as intelligent those people whose behaviour patterns and appearance most conformed to their own. Moreover, little effort was made to conceal the fact: subjective judgments of members of the professional class were the principal means for defining intelligence.

Much more was to come, of course, in the social construction of intelligence. Most notable in this regard was the development of the Stanford-Binet IQ test and later the Scholastic Aptitude Test (SAT; recently renamed the Scholastic Assessment Test). Among the additional and more sophisticated experiments performed were some that claimed to support the conclusions of Galton, Pearson, and other early researchers. But the most interesting feature was the continued part played by the social judgments of people—largely teachers, psychologists, and school administrators—in determining what did or did not constitute intelligence. As late as the 1960s, intelligence test results were still being cross-checked with teachers' judgments and students' ranks in class; if the test scores failed to correlate with the teachers' judgments, the tests were changed.

Question 7.3: How Is Gender a Form of Social Hierarchy?

Constructing Male and Female

We often assume that gender, like race, is biological. But academics make a distinction between the terms "**sex**" and "**gender**." *Sex* refers to biological, hormonal, and chromosomal differences between males and females; *gender*, by contrast, is cultural. In other words, gender is the cultural interpretation of sex. Cross-culturally, different standards apply to being male and female. As such, there is no cross-cultural, universal understanding of what is considered to be "appropriate" dress, demeanour, behaviours, occupations, or roles for men or women; rather, these understandings must be learned in their respective cultural contexts.

Societies also vary in the number of gender categories they recognize. For example, many Native American societies recognize an alternative gender, also referred to as **third gender**, such as that of the *two-spirit* among the Cheyenne and Lakota. In these contexts, the *two-spirit* is a biological male who does not fill a standard male role. Such individuals are not seen as men, nor are they defined as women. They occupy a third role, one that is culturally defined, accepted, and in some cases revered. Male children among the Lakota and Cheyenne thus can choose from two gender categories, rather than learning that gender roles are defined by physiology. Among the Lakota, male children learn that, if they desire, they can adopt the dress and work roles of women and have sex with men, although the *two-spirit* role does not necessarily involve sexual behaviour. The *two-spirits* do not play only women's roles, however; some are noted for their hunting skills and for their exploits in war.

Another example of a third gender is the sworn virgins of Albania. Antonia Young (2001) has studied how some women in mountainous, remote regions of Albania voluntarily become "sworn virgins"; they choose to don traditionally "masculine" clothing and hair styles, assume male roles and jobs, drink brandy, and carry guns. Having assumed these markers of masculinity, these women are afforded the same level of recognition and respect as a man. These women, however, are expected to remain celibate for the remainder of their lives. In a male-dominated or patriarchal society where options for women are limited beyond the roles of wife and mother, this third gender gives these women a greater sense of freedom and agency over their lives. In addition, because they live in a patrilineal society, where descent and property are passed down the male line, becoming a sworn virgin allows women to inherit property. This may be an important consideration if a father does not produce a male heir.

In North American societies, by contrast, individuals who do not assume the gender roles associated with their anatomy have historically been defined as deviant, abnormal, or nonconformist. In recent years in many Western industrialized nations, a number of high-profile celebrities, such as Caitlyn Jenner (formerly Bruce Jenner), have sought to increase public awareness of transgenderism. While the concept of third gender is not widely used within societies like Canada, **transgender** is a term used to describe situations where an individual feels that their assigned sex at birth does not conform to the associated gender. So, for example, someone labelled a biological male at birth may not adopt a traditionally masculine gender identity, and may feel feminine in terms of gender. Transgender individuals often

sex
Hormonal, chromosomal, or physical differences between males and females.

gender
Culturally constructed ideals of behaviour, dress, occupations, roles, and comportment for particular sexes.

third gender
A gender role given to someone who does not fit within strictly masculine or feminine gender roles in a society that recognizes the possibility of at least three genders.

transgender
Refers to an individual who feels that their assigned sex at birth does not match their accompanying gender.

argue that their sense of gender is the result of internal feelings, and they often claim that they feel "trapped" in the wrong body. North American attitudes toward transgenderism are gradually changing, as is evident in recent federal and provincial legislation. Since 2017, for example, the *Canadian Human Rights Act* has prohibited discrimination against anyone on the basis of gender identity (among other things). In some provinces like Ontario, "misgendering" or referring to someone with the incorrect gendered pronoun constitutes a form of gender discrimination. These policies have generated much backlash in recent years, most notably and famously from the Jordan Peterson controversy. Peterson, a psychology professor at University of Toronto, declared that he would refuse to use the pronoun "they/them" when requested by transgendered individuals. He justified his stance on the basis of freedom of speech, the fact that "they" is not grammatically correct, and his problematic assertion that gender is biological. His often charismatic personality has attracted a large number of loyal fans and followers. He currently has around 1.5 million Twitter followers, and in 2018 and 2019 he embarked on a world tour. Many argue, however, that his controversial perspectives have resulted in the production of divisive and ethnocentric attitudes toward transgendered peoples, who are already an at-risk group for violence. Discrimination against transgendered peoples is widespread; even so, many Canadians are moving away from thinking about sex and gender as dichotomous and toward thinking about gender along a spectrum.

In other contexts, the reversal of gender roles is framed as play. Indeed, one way to learn about how a society constructs gender differences and relationships is by exploring theatrical and ritual transvestism, as Michael Taft (1997) did on the Canadian Prairies when he studied mock weddings. The principal feature of a mock wedding is role reversal: men dress and act like women and sometimes women dress and behave like men. These mock figures are often as much caricatures as stereotypes, reflecting some feature of the identities of the actual wedding pair.

Courtesy of Saskatchewan Archives Board

In this photograph of a mock wedding ritual on the Canadian prairies, transvestism represents a form of gendered social commentary on notions of power, equality, and the position of women in this community.

Taft's study focused on men who dressed as women in these rituals of reversal, which were filled with ludic, or playful, behaviour. He repeatedly asked men why they did this, and the most frequent answer he received was that they were just being "good sports." As good sports, men do not attempt to become women in their role in the mock wedding. In Taft's words, "they play clownish and distorted women. They exaggerate the female physique with over-large breasts and behinds. They mince and wiggle in mockery of femininity" (135).

Thus, these men are expressing their views of women to one another. Taft suggests that men may do this in part because of the economic conditions of farming on the prairies. Farmers or ranchers may seem to be independent, but in fact they are dangerously dependent on government bureaucrats, subsidies, and the world market. In contrast, women have considerable power on farms and often do the same work as men, besides working part-time off the farm in order to pay the bills. By making fun of women, men may be reasserting their own importance. Whatever the men's motives, Taft (1997, 137) argues that "wherever it is found, theatrical transvestism acts as a sounding board for commentaries on gender relations."

Constructing Stratification by Gender

As discussed earlier, the biases that falsely linked race to biology and intelligence to class also led to a belief in the "natural" (as opposed to socially constructed) superiority of men over women. Many people believed that women's bodies defined both their social position and their function, which was to reproduce, in the same way that men's bodies dictated that they manage, control, and defend.

The view that the biology of females makes them lesser persons than males is embedded in North American cultures, sometimes in subtle ways. An example is the language used by professionals to describe women's bodily processes of menstruation and menopause. Anthropologist Emily Martin (1987) writes that during the nineteenth century, Americans regarded the female body as if it were a factory whose job was to "labour" to produce children. Menopause was viewed negatively because it marked the end of productive usefulness, and menstruation was described as a sign of the failure of the implantation of a fertilized egg. Medical writers of the time, such as Walter Heape, a Cambridge zoologist and militant antisuffragist, described how in menstruation the entire epithelium (cellular tissue) was torn away, "leaving behind a ragged wreck of tissue, torn glands, ruptured vessels, jagged edges of stroma, and masses of blood corpuscles, which it would seem hardly possible to heal satisfactorily without the aid of surgical instruments" (Martin 1987, 35).

According to Martin, the same attitudes toward female reproductive functions that existed in the nineteenth century persist today, encoded in contemporary medical and biology textbooks. Menstruation is likewise described even today as a breakdown in the reproductive process. When an egg is not implanted, the process is described in negative terms as a disintegration or shedding. Here is one example Martin found:

> *The fall in blood progesterone and estrogen "deprives" the "highly developed endometrial lining of its hormonal support," constriction of blood vessels leads to a "diminished" supply of oxygen and nutrients, and finally "disintegration starts, the entire lining begins to slough, and the menstrual flow begins." Blood vessels in the endometrium "hemorrhage" and "the menstrual flow consists of this blood mixed with endometrial debris." The "loss" of hormonal stimulation causes "necrosis" (death of tissue). (Martin 1987, 45)*

Another otherwise objective text states that "when fertilization fails to occur, the endometrium is shed, and a new cycle starts. This is why it used to be taught that 'menstruation is the uterus crying for lack of a baby'" (quoted in Martin 1987, 45).

In yet another textbook, menstruation is depicted as a sign of an idle factory, a failed production system, a system producing "scrap" or "waste." However, Martin notes that very different language is used in the same textbooks to describe male reproductive functions. For example, the textbook from which the above description of menstruation is taken describes the production of sperm as follows: "The mechanisms which guide the remarkable cellular transformation from spermatid to mature sperm remain uncertain. Perhaps the most amazing characteristic of spermatogenesis is its sheer magnitude: the normal human male may manufacture several hundred million sperm per day" (Martin 1987, 48).

This text, which describes menstruation as "failed production," fails to mention that only about one of every 100 billion sperm ever makes it far enough to fertilize an egg. Moreover, other bodily processes that are similar to menstruation are not spoken of in terms of breakdown and deterioration. Seminal fluid picks up shredded cellular material as it passes through the male ducts, and the stomach lining is shed periodically. Why are these processes not described in the same negative terms as menstruation? According to Martin, the reason is that both men and women have stomachs, but only women have uteruses. The stomach falls on the positive side, the uterus on the negative.

Rather than describing menstruation as failed production, Martin suggests that it might be more accurate to describe it as the successful avoidance of an egg implant. If a couple has done anything to avoid the implantation of an egg, is it still appropriate to talk of the reproductive cycle in terms of production?

Emily Martin's analysis reveals that in contemporary North American societies, the ideology of gender stratification remains embedded in our language and in our ideas about the bodily functions of males and females. Describing the bodily processes of women in negative terms makes women seem to be lesser human beings. Moreover, describing menstruation and menopause in negative terms leads women themselves to believe that their bodily functions are less clean and less worthy than those of men.

Gender Stratification and the Privileging of Hegemonic Masculinities

All societies have particular images and stereotypes of masculinity and femininity that are privileged as normative—that is, as societal ideals. These ideals of masculinity, for instance, are referred to as **hegemonic masculinity**. Industrialized societies, for example, often view traits such as athleticism, courage, rationality, and heterosexuality as markers of an ideal "manliness." In many societies with patriarchal tendencies, or where men's work or social position is considered more important than women's, hegemonic masculinities idealize the male as the primary "breadwinner." In her study of men's perceptions of the aftermath of Japan's Fukushima nuclear disaster, for instance, Rika Morioka (2014) writes that compared to mothers, the fathers in the households that she interviewed were less concerned about the potential health risks of radiation than mothers were. Instead, the fathers were more concerned about the economic consequences, because for them, the radiation leaks limited their employability and economic opportunities and thereby threatened their masculine identity.

Hegemonic masculinities are often used to construct gendered hierarchies in societies. For instance, those individuals who fall outside hegemonic gendered ideals are often labelled "less masculine" than others, which can lead to the proliferation of homophobia and the objectification of women. Canadian anthropologist David Murray (2002), for instance, has studied how performances of a hegemonic masculinity on the Caribbean island of Martinique are dependent on "proving" one's heterosexuality through the aggressive pursuit of women, cat calling, and flirting with the opposite sex. Men who fail to pursue women aggressively are often labelled *macumé,* a derogatory word in Martinique that is equivalent to "sissy." In a society marked by intense homophobia, all men, whatever their sexual orientation, go to great lengths to uphold the norms of hegemonic masculinity in public settings. To be labelled macumé is a social liability, and a man risks physical and verbal abuse if he does not conform to societal ideals of gender.

Hegemonic masculinities are also constructed, performed, and maintained within societies through sports, competitions, and rituals. Fraternities, for instance, are a means of constructing hegemonic masculinities; they are also a way to promote often dangerous gendered hierarchies in university settings, which lead to the objectification, marginalization, and abuse of women.

Peggy Reeves Sanday ([1990]2007), in her study of college fraternity gang rape, provides a vivid portrait of how male identity is defined and reinforced in American society. Gang rape, or "pulling train," as it is called in fraternities, begins with the coercion of a vulnerable young woman who is seeking acceptance. The ritual incorporates the man into a group whose activities reinforce a male identity, defined largely by the degradation of female identity through sexual conquest and physical abuse. "Pulling train" is both an expression of male sexuality and a display of the brotherhood's power to control

hegemonic masculinity
Refers to ideals and norms of masculinity in a society, which are often privileged over others.

and dominate women. In other words, gang rape is but one instance of the abuse and domination that begin during the initiation and that are continued later in relations with women and new pledges.

When a woman is too weak or intoxicated to protest, a "train" of men have sex with her. Sanday and her associates interviewed fraternity members, women who were associated with them, and victims of rape, seeking to explain what it was about male identity that encouraged these actions. Three things seemed to stand out in her account.

First, there is a heavy emphasis in fraternities on male bonding and male-bonding behaviour, to the extent that a college man's self-esteem and social identity depend on gaining entry to a fraternity and being accepted by the brothers. Fraternities confer status; on most college campuses they are recognized as places "where the action is." They also provide reassurance, security, and a ready-made identity. Membership in a fraternity transforms outsiders into insiders.

Second, sex constitutes a major status and identity marker. Masculinity is defined and demonstrated by sexual conquest. In the fraternity in which the gang rape occurred, a major activity was persuading a woman to have sex. Men who had more success gained status, while those who often failed were in danger of being labelled "nerds" or, worse, "fags." Sex in this case is a public thing. Men in the fraternities that Sanday interviewed bragged publicly about their sexual conquests and arranged for brothers to witness them. Some fraternities posted weekly newsletters listing brothers' sexual conquests.

A third element in the identity of fraternity men concerns their attitudes toward women. Many of the fraternity members in Sanday's study implied that women were sex objects to be abused or debased. A woman's identity among fraternity men was determined largely by her sexual interactions with them. Women who were sexually unresponsive were "frigid," women who allowed advances only up to a point were "cockteasers," and women who had sex with many men were "sluts." Such labels indicate that the role of "girlfriend" is virtually the only role without negative connotations that a woman can play for fraternity men.

Part of the reason men bond in college, says Sanday, is to achieve the domination and power they think is owed to males. Sanday uses the term "phallocentrism," "the deployment of the penis as a concrete symbol of masculine social power and dominance" ([1990]2007, 40), to describe the use of sex and the debasement of women to demonstrate masculinity. Sanday is quick to emphasize that not all college men subscribe to the ideology of phallocentrism and that not all fraternity men measure their masculinity by sexual conquest. In the case that initiated her study, all the women who knew them described the six men charged with gang rape as "among the nicest guys in the fraternity." Individually, probably none of them would have committed the act they were charged with. In the context of the fraternity, however, gang rape was the credible outcome of a process of identity formation manifested in fraternity life in general and in the fraternity initiation ritual in particular.

Gender Stratification and the Feminization of Poverty

Gender and age are significantly related to whether a person lives in poverty. In *Women and Children Last* (1986), Ruth Sidel draws an analogy between the doomed ship *Titanic* and society in the United States at the end of the 1980s. Both, she says, were gleaming symbols of wealth that placed women and children at a disadvantage. When the *Titanic* went down, women and children were indeed saved first, but only those who were travelling in first- or second-class accommodations. Women and children in third class and steerage were not saved. Although only 8 percent of the women and 3 percent of the children in first and second class drowned on the night the *Titanic* sank, 45 percent of the women and 70 percent of the children in steerage died. As with the *Titanic*, Sidel says, certain women and children in the United States are not the first to be saved; instead, they are the first to fall into poverty.

Most of the world's poor are women and children. As Michael Todaro, an economist, explains: "[Women] are more likely to be poor and malnourished and less likely to receive medical services, clean water, sanitation, and other benefits" (2000, 172). Female-headed households make up the poorest segments of developing world populations. For instance, as of 2019, 32.4 percent of all households in Kenya and 20 percent in India had no male wage earners (Bonnet, Vanek, and Chen 2019). Women's potential earnings are far below those of males. Women have less access to education and government employment programs and are more likely to be employed in the informal sector, where neither wages nor working conditions are regulated. Even in households where there is a male wage earner, women may not have access to the household income. In countries where there is a strong male bias, such as India and China, household resources may be distributed unevenly. In India, it is estimated that "girls are four times more likely to suffer from acute malnutrition and boys are 40 times more likely to be taken to a hospital when ill" (Todaro 2000, 173–74). This imbalance results in more female infant deaths and also contributes to an extremely high female child mortality rate.

When gender is combined with other factors, such as Indigenous status, women may then face a combination of risks. Linda Gerber suggests that in Canada, Métis, Inuit, and "Indian" women face "multiple jeopardy"—first as women, then as members of a "visible minority," and finally "as residents of uniquely dependent communities" (1990, 72). In 2011, in the area of education, more than half (51 percent) of Indigenous women between the ages of 25 and 64 had a post-secondary education, compared to 65 percent of non-Indigenous women. Among Indigenous women, this percentage was 57 percent for Métis women, 36 percent for Inuit, and 47 percent for First Nations women (Statistics Canada 2016).

Body Image and Gender Hierarchies

One of the most important identity features for many North Americans is body shape. Although desired body shapes vary cross-culturally and across historical periods, historically in the West a thin person has been judged to be superior to a heavier person. For instance, people who are overweight face hostile work environments and job discrimination. Workers judged unattractive by their peers—especially women—are consistently described in more negative terms.

The relationship between self-image and body shape is particularly relevant for female adolescents, as anthropologist Mimi Nichter (2000) discovered during a three-year study among high school girls in Arizona. Adolescent girls are particularly vulnerable to body image issues because during adolescence girls will gain up to 11.5 kilograms of body fat and thus are likely to be more critical of their own bodies. Young girls, says Nichter, are embedded in a morality play in which thinness is good, fatness is bad, and dieting is the way to get in shape. Nichter found that most of the girls in her study were thinking about their bodies either "all of the time" (24 percent) or "a lot of the time" (31 percent) and that 90 percent of white girls in the study were dissatisfied with their weight.

The adolescent girls in Nichter's study formed their idea of the "perfect" body largely from television, films, magazines, and, of course, Barbie. The ideal woman was tall (170 centimetres) and had long hair (preferably blond), long legs, a flat stomach, a clear complexion, and "good" clothes. Weight, however, was the key factor: being "thin"

Anthropologist Mimi Nichter argues that in North America, women and girls are often subjected to, and subject themselves to, moral judgment based on their weight.

was believed to be the ticket to happiness and popularity. As with many adult women that Nichter knew, the girls seemed to see the world in terms of fat and thin.

The girls rarely talked about weight with classmates whom they judged to be "fat"; nevertheless, they made moral judgments about them, believing that if someone who was overweight really wanted to lose weight, she could. Not losing weight implied that the girl was unconcerned about her personal appearance or was lazy. The lack of respect for overweight girls, writes Nichter, was a theme that emerged repeatedly in discussions with the students. One girl explained,

> *I have a friend that's overweight and I feel that she should—I mean, I don't have anything against her 'cause she's overweight—but I guess it makes me mad that she doesn't do anything about it. She could do something about it and she doesn't. It's like her responsibility … like last night I went over there and right when I walked in she had a bag of Doritos—she was just, I mean, it's just like she's constantly eating. She's addicted to food. She just can't stop.* (Nichter 2000, 42)

More recently, campaigns against body shaming (especially of women's bodies) have achieved prominence thanks to events like the #MeToo movement, which stress, among other things, the importance of body positivity, acceptance, and diversity. This has helped foster a widespread trend toward challenging the centrality of body image and aesthetics as a primary marker of femininity and female self-worth.

BEYOND THE BOOK 7.1

Men rarely talk about dieting, or at least not as much as women do, but concerns about body image are not restricted to women. How, then, do men address the gap between their body image and the cultural ideal represented in advertisements and the media? Do men talk about this issue, and, if so, how is it articulated?

Language, Gender, and Racial Hierarchies

Societies provide a social landscape along with the symbols or codes through which a person's place on the landscape is conveyed to others. For individuals these symbols or codes serve as toolboxes from which to fashion an identity. Societies may vary in the extent to which people are allowed to negotiate their place on the landscape, but all allow people some leeway.

Language, as we mentioned, is one tool that people have to signal how they want to be placed in society. Voice pitch, for example, does tend to differ because men's vocal tracts are longer, thus giving men a deeper voice. But children, whose voice tracts do not yet differ in size, will unconsciously lower or raise their pitch to conform to gender expectations; that is why you can usually tell from the voice the gender of a child. As Penelope Eckert and Sally McConnell-Ginet point out in *Language and Gender (2003)*, people use language to present themselves as a certain kind of person, to project an attitude or a style, along with gender. All parts of language can be used in this way. The phonology, that is, the sounds, of a language can convey gender. For example, the /s/ sound can be made by pressing the tip of the tongue against the teeth. When pressed against the teeth it is still recognized as /s/, but this creates a slight lisp associated among English speakers in the United States and Canada with femininity in women and gayness in men.

Grammar can signal gender. Thus, in French, there are male and female forms of nouns; in English, the third-person singular *he* and *she* force us to differentiate gender. In Japanese, there are sentence-final particles that add to or soften the force of an utterance, with so-called women's language characterized as more mild. Thus, "I am going" can be said as a mild assertion (*iku wa*), as a neutral assertion (*iku*), or as an emphatic assertion (*iku ze/iku zo*), with the latter being characterized as more masculine.

Whether or not to speak can convey gender. Children, for example, are encouraged to speak or to remain silent. Among the Araucanians of Chile, men are encouraged to talk since it is a sign of masculine intelligence and leadership, while the ideal woman is submissive and silent in her husband's presence.

Conversational styles may also convey gender. Linguist Robin Lakoff (1975) was one of the first to draw attention to the way a woman's identity in society influences how she speaks. Women, said Lakoff, are constrained to minimize their expression of opinion with various linguistic devices such as tag questions ("This election mess is terrible, isn't it?"), rising intonations on declaratives ("When will dinner be ready? Six o'clock?"), the use of hedges ("That's kinda sad" or "It's probably dinnertime"), boosters or amplifications ("I'm so glad you're here"), indirection (e.g., saying "I've got a dentist's appointment then," to convey an inability or reluctance to meet at that time and asking the other to propose another time).

The general thrust of Lakoff's argument has to do with the relative powerlessness of women stemming from their relatively weak social position. Speaking "as a woman," suggests Lakoff, requires avoiding firm commitment or expressing strong opinions and, in general, being restricted to using a "powerless" language.

Language can also be used to construct others, or groups from which people want to separate themselves. Ward Churchill (1994) discusses the consequences of naming sports teams the "Braves," "Chiefs," "Redskins," "Seminoles," and "Savages," names that he suggests are deeply demeaning to Native Americans. Since apologists claim that this is just "fun," with no harm intended, Churchill suggests that we spread the fun around and use nicknames from other groups to name sports teams, such as the Kansas City "Kikes," the Hanover "Honkies," the Dayton "Dagos," the Wisconsin "Wetbacks," and so on. Churchill draws attention to the ways we use language, often unknowingly, that stigmatizes the identities of others.

BEYOND THE BOOK 7.2

In the fall of 2017, the hashtag #MeToo began trending on social media in response to widespread allegations that many celebrities, such as film producer Harvey Weinstein, had sexually abused a number of actresses over the course of their careers. Since 2017, #MeToo has gained momentum and functioned as a form of resistance against patriarchy, hegemonic masculinity, and gender inequality. Find three media articles about the #MeToo movement. Based on what you have read, do you think this movement has changed cultural perceptions about gender and the position of women within societies like Canada?

Question 7.4: How Are Different Forms of Social Hierarchy Interwoven with One Another?

It is important to note that different forms of inequality, discussed as separate entities earlier on in this chapter, are often woven together, a concept called intersectionality. As we see in the examples below, race and class, or race and immigrant status, or race and gender, often overlap and sustain each other conceptually.

Race, Class, and Social Hierarchies in Brazil

Anthropologist Alexander Edmonds (2010) has explored the ways in which race and class converge in Brazil to form social hierarchies. While conducting his doctoral dissertation fieldwork in Rio de Janeiro, Edmonds noticed that plastic surgery clinics proliferated in urban areas of Brazil. Furthermore, while access to plastic surgery had once been a marker of middle- or upper-class status (due to the high cost of such surgeries), the attainment of physical "beauty" was regarded as a necessary means of achieving social mobility. In Brazil, plastic surgery rates are among the highest in the world, and the government subsidizes plastic surgeries for the working classes. There are even plastic surgeons who practise "charity" surgeries on behalf of the urban poor. "Beauty" is thus a marker of class status and is increasingly viewed as a "right" that should be available for everyone.

Plastic surgery, however, is also a means by which non-white Brazilians can seek to "whiten" their appearance by correcting what some of Edmonds's informants viewed as undesirable—a "Negroid" nose, for instance. In Brazilian society, race exists along a continuum, and white skin and stereotypically "white" facial features are associated with power, privilege, and prestige. Indeed, many of Edmonds's informants, especially young women, did improve their employment prospects, and ultimately their class status, by undergoing plastic surgery. In this context, plastic surgery represents a means by which some Brazilians can "whiten" their bodies and, by extension, improve their social standing in Brazilian society. Interestingly, Brazil has been mythologized as a multicultural nation, and while its citizens are encouraged to celebrate diversity, there exists enormous social pressure to emulate the powerful—that is, the white upper class—in Brazilian society. Racial identity is also understood to be malleable and linked to one's social class: according to a popular Brazilian adage, "money whitens." Ultimately, this ethnographic example highlights the fluid and interconnected nature of social hierarchies such as class and race, as well as the ways in which the conscious manipulation of features like "attractiveness" are viewed as a means of achieving a sense of individual fulfillment, well-being, and status.

FIGURE 7.1 Brazil

Constructing a New Racism

In 2006, a soup kitchen in Paris discovered by chance that poor Muslims and Jews would not eat soup made with pork. Their response? They began making soup *only* with pork. The soup kitchen leader, Odile Bonnivard, declared that "European civilization and Christian culture is our choice," proclaiming the right to racial preference and launching a campaign across France labelled "Ours Before the Others" (Goldberg 2009, 179–80).

The "identity soup" campaign, as it came to be called, is an example of **new racism**—based not on biological characteristics but on cultural differences that are assumed to be insurmountable. And counter to the claims by some that we have achieved a "raceless" society, it is just one bit of evidence that racism persists in one form or another. Quite simply, being "white," however "whiteness" is defined, still matters. As such, anthropologist Leith Mullings (2005, 684) says that racism is not a singular phenomenon but rather a "relational concept":

> *a set of practices, structures, beliefs, and representations that transform certain forms of perceived differences, generally regarded as indelible and unchangeable, into inequality. It works through modes of dispossession, which have included subordination, stigmatization, exploitation, exclusion, various forms of physical violence, and sometimes genocide. Racism is maintained and perpetrated through coercion and*

new racism
A form of "soft" racism that posits racial differences as cultural, rather than biological, but that still views such differences as immutable or insurmountable.

> *consent and is rationalized through paradigms of both biology and culture. It is, to varying degrees at specific temporal and special points, interwoven with other forms of inequality, particularly class, gender, sexuality, and nationality.*

The perpetuation of inequality and racism within various social institutions has received widespread media attention in recent years. For example, the concept of white privilege was largely restricted to academic circles until 2013, when the Black Lives Matter movement was formed in the United States. The movement does not refer to a centralized, organized protest group, but rather to a widespread and increasingly globalized series of protests and resistance against white privilege and racial discrimination, particularly against black peoples. The movement gained traction with the May 2020 death of an African-American man, George Floyd, at the hands of white Minneapolis police officers. Floyd's death sparked protests not only throughout the United States but globally, and drew attention to the ways in which embedded forms of racism and white privilege continue to operate within the context of the police force and other institutions which have been historically dominated and controlled by white Euro-Americans.

The fieldwork of Alexander Edmonds, described above, also demonstrates how racism, gender, and class are interwoven in Brazil. But this issue is equally salient in Canada, if in different ways. Despite our policy of multiculturalism, recent immigrants are one group whose collective experiences often exemplify the ways in which new racism is interwoven with other forms of equality. However, one's country of origin and ethnic background may result in very different experiences of these forms of inequality, as we discuss below in reference to the experiences of Pakistani immigrants to Canada.

Pakistani Immigrant Women and the Construction of the "Sanitized Body"

Anthropologist Lalaie Ameeriar (2012) has conducted fieldwork in Karachi, Pakistan, and in Toronto with women who immigrated to Canada for work. In Toronto, her work focused particularly on the kinds of spaces where multiculturalism is negotiated: government offices, settlement agencies, mosques, cultural festivals, immigration consulting offices, and women's homes; she conducted interviews not only with recent Pakistani immigrants but also with government workers, translators, mullahs (Islamic clerics or leaders), and not-for-profit workers. Her work was, at least in part, an effort to understand and contextualize the marginalization and poverty experienced among Toronto's Pakistani community. Many Pakistani immigrants come to Canada as highly skilled professionals, yet they experience their move as a decline: Pakistani women have an unemployment rate of over 20 percent; Statistics Canada puts the poverty rate for the Pakistani community at 40 percent; and many in that community "become deskilled, working in what are known as 'survival jobs,' such as cashiering, and living in pockets of poverty in marginal parts of the city" (Ameeriar 2012, 511).

Based on her fieldwork, Ameeriar found that there are two contradictory strains of multicultural practice in Canada, both of which she frames in terms of embodiment: there exists simultaneously a denial of the "difference" of immigrant bodies, and a recognition of that very difference. For Pakistani immigrants, this phenomenon was experienced as a celebration of "multiness" in South Asian cultural festivals and public celebrations; but also as "imposition of the dominant culture through government-funded settlement services that institute new ideals of bodily comportment ... by teaching them how to dress and act" (509–10).

Ameeriar proposes the concept of "the sanitized sensorium" as a means to understand the forms of embodiment required for inclusion in the multicultural public sphere, including smell and appearance. Her research suggests that when it comes to the integration of foreign labour in the workplace, multiculturalism is less about getting employers not to discriminate and much more about making oneself, as an immigrant, into someone who will not be discriminated against. For instance, women in a government-funded workshop about finding employment were told, "Don't show up smelling like foods that are foreign to us," "make sure your clothes are clean," "don't wear the shalwar cameeze," and "don't wear headscarves" (509). The painful irony is that while foreign food smells, clothes, and practices are deemed repugnant or inappropriate when too closely associated with immigrant bodies, when disembodied—at cultural festivals, restaurants, and stores—the same smells are fragrant, the clothes deemed beautifully exotic, and the practices considered entertaining. Pakistani women, many of whom do most of the cooking for their families at home, and who are routinely exhorted by government agencies to "dress plainly," find themselves particularly vulnerable to these contradictions when seeking employment. Their often impressive education and qualifications are not enough to overcome this. In this way, the body of the Other is sanitized, and the "Canadian" body is rendered neutral (that is, nonimmigrant and nonracialized). At the same time, the smell of food becomes both a private "problem" for Pakistani immigrant women (one with real, negative socioeconomic consequences) and a "public, commodified, accessible form of pleasure for white Canadian consumption" (510).

BEYOND THE BOOK 7.3

In Canada, we tend to pride ourselves on being an accepting, multicultural nation. However, there are many examples of embedded or institutionalized racism in our society. Select a recent Canadian newspaper or magazine article that offers an example of embedded racism. By "recent," we mean published within the past two years. Provide a brief overview of the article, outlining how institutionalized racism is at work.

Question 7.5: How Can Anthropology Be Applied to Alleviate the Effects of Inequality?

It is all too easy, and perhaps even understandable, to resign oneself to hopelessness or helplessness when it comes to permanently alleviating poverty and oppression caused by social stratification. Inequality, as we discussed earlier, is striking and is growing worse both within wealthy countries and between the rich and the poor countries of the world. Worse yet, inequality produces differential access to life's necessities—food, water, shelter, health care, and protection from torture and cruel punishment and polluted environments. The question is, of course, what can be done to alleviate these problems, and what role might anthropology play in addressing them?

There are various ways that a background in anthropology is relevant for dealing with problems stemming from inequality. Anthropology prepares people for careers in, for example, delivering health services, administering treatment programs, counselling dysfunctional families, and finding the connections between old age and depression. But perhaps some of the most significant contributions that can be made by people with a background in anthropology are in the design and implementation of measures to protect people from human rights abuses.

Anthropology and Human Rights

The idea of individual rights comes to us from the seventeenth- and eighteenth-century Enlightenment, as codified most notably by Thomas Jefferson in the US *Declaration of Independence*. That idea, however, is clearly biased by the notion of the egocentric view of society (discussed in Chapter 6). However, some of the rights outlined in the *Universal Declaration of Human Rights*,[2] adopted on 10 December 1948 by the General Assembly of the United Nations, could be extended across cultures. These might include the right to be free of the threat of torture or cruel, inhuman, or degrading treatment or punishment, and freedom of opinion and expression. Besides these legal rights, the UN declaration includes the right to a standard of living adequate for health and well-being, which encompasses the rights to food, clothing, housing, medical care, and necessary social

[2] You can access the Universal Declaration of Human Rights at http://www.un.org/Overview/rights.html.

services, along with the right to security in the event of unemployment, sickness, disability, widowhood, old age, or other lack of livelihood in circumstances beyond the person's control.

Amnesty International and Human Rights Watch, two of the major nongovernmental organizations (NGOs) addressing issues of human rights, have documented violations of individual rights in at least 150 countries. In those countries, nonviolent dissidents have been held without trial, imprisoned, tortured, killed, or raped, or have been "disappeared" by police, military, or paramilitary forces. When the UN instituted the post of High Commissioner for Human Rights, the position was allocated only $700,000, small even by NGO standards. In his first year on the job, the High Commissioner did not criticize a single government anywhere in the world.

Furthermore, as we have seen earlier in this chapter, the economic and social inequality that creates the conditions for human rights violations continues to grow. Billions of people are living in poverty and experiencing oppression while the top 358 global billionaires had a combined income equal to that of the 2.3 billion poorest people in the world.

Anthropologists Carol Nagengast and Carlos G. Vélez-Ibáñez (2004) suggest that, of all social scientists, anthropologists are the best prepared for human rights work. That is because they are the best prepared to deal with cultural variation and to understand complex community struggles. They are trained to understand the workings of official bureaucracies and global processes, and they have "a strong penchant for supporting the underdog." The issue, say Nagengast and Vélez-Ibáñez, is that while anthropologists often discover and reveal human rights abuses, they must also find ways to predict such abuses and do something about them, be it indirectly through participation in the design of public policy or directly in the delivery of services. As Canadian General Roméo Dallaire explained regarding conflict resolution in Rwanda: "What you need now are people who can not only fight—because they may need to protect and defend—but people who have a whole new set of skills ... You need them to have more intellectually based skills like anthropology, sociology and philosophy" (Toronto Star, 13 February 2005, A14).

In *Human Rights: The Scholar as Activist* (2004), Nagengast and Vélez-Ibáñez suggest also that the human rights agenda, besides addressing individual and political abuses such as land grabs, torture, murder, rape, and disappearances, must include collective rights, including economic, social, and cultural ones. There are, they point out, no binding or enforceable laws or guidelines to constrain the power of corporations and their support agencies (such as the World Bank and International Monetary Fund), to set working conditions or wages, or to impose development projects that displace persons or leave them worse off than before. Basically, all internationally written and customary law has left it to nation-states to enforce the recognition of rights. But nation-states, which claim the right to self-determination, are also the major violators of human rights either directly, through the operations of the military or the police, or indirectly, by allowing extra-state or paramilitary groups to violate human rights.

Nagengast and Vélez-Ibáñez then ask, "What can scholars do?" First, they say, anthropologists, who among all social scientists most often work with the poor, can publicize human rights abuses. Anthropologists can work with groups whose rights have been violated to help them develop the means to defend themselves.

Terence Turner (2005), for example, has been working with the Kayapo of central Brazil since 1962, to prevent development projects that threaten their land. Turner, a founding member of the American Anthropological Association's Committee on Human Rights, has also been directing the Kayapo Video Project, during which the Kayapo have been shooting and editing their own videos about their lives and culture and their relations with Brazilians.

Anthropologist Robert Hitchcock has worked with the San peoples of Botswana and Namibia. He has done much to map their homelands, institute land claims, and stave off settler takeovers of their land. Hitchcock has ensured that the San participate actively in these efforts. As a result, San communities have created their own human rights and development agencies.

People with anthropological training work on behalf of refugees, too, by helping service providers alleviate their plight, which is an enormous task. In 2013, the UN High Commission on Refugees (www.unhcr.org) estimated that there were more than 25.9 million refugees, with "refugee" defined as a person who "owing to a well-founded fear of being persecuted for reasons of race, religion, nationality, membership of a particular social group, or political opinion, is outside the country of his nationality, and is unable to or, owing to such fear, is unwilling to avail himself of the protection of that country." That same year, in addition to these 25.9 million, 41.3 million people had been displaced internally—that is, within their own countries.

These are just a few examples of how anthropological skills and perspectives can help protect and restore human rights. A description of such efforts would be incomplete without the story of Paul Farmer (discussed in *Applying Anthropology*) and his efforts, according to one author, to "cure the world" (Kidder 2003).

The Kayapo Video Project.

APPLYING ANTHROPOLOGY

Anthropology and Medical Rights: The Work of Paul Farmer

In his Pulitzer Prize–winning book, *Mountains Beyond Mountains* (2003), about the work of anthropologist and physician Paul Farmer, Tracy Kidder described how Farmer's background in anthropology and his experiences in Haiti moulded his view of the links among anthropology, medicine, and human rights.

With a PhD in anthropology, and a medical degree, Farmer is interested in exposing how pervasive inequalities in Haiti (among other places) have resulted in inequitable access to medical care. Haiti, a country of some 7.5 million people, is the poorest country in the Western Hemisphere; 80 percent of Haitians live in poverty.

Farmer argued that to understand inequality, it is critical to examine the social context in which poverty and oppression occurs. He understood that, as he put, "a minor error in one setting of power and privilege could have an enormous impact on the poor in another" (Kidder 2003, 78). For example, in the 1950s, with money from the US Export–Import Bank, the US Army Corps of Engineers built the Péligre dam, which displaced thousands of Haitian farmers. The farmers were forced either to rebuild on the sides of mountains unsuited for growing crops or to move to cities such as Port-au-Prince to look for jobs as housekeepers or as low-paid labourers in American-built assembly plants. The most valuable asset for the remaining farmers was their Creole pigs, but an outbreak of swine fever in the Dominican Republic led the United States to destroy all the Haitian pigs in order to protect the American pork industry. The pigs were replaced with pigs purchased from Iowa farmers, but these were delicate and most of them died, leaving the peasants with little. These are examples of what Farmer refers to as **structural violence**, the systematic ways in which social structures or social institutions harm or otherwise disadvantage local individuals. Structural violence is often invisible, and often lacking one specific person who can (or will) be held responsible. In the examples discussed

Desiree Navarro/Getty Images Entertainment

Anthropologist Paul Farmer has worked intensively with a variety of local and international agencies in Haiti, to help plan, implement, and deliver health and social services to local communities.

by Farmer, *structural violence* refers to the actions of remote governments or international agencies that result in denial to the poor of basic rights of food, shelter, and livelihood.

Since the 1980s, Farmer has worked with local and international agencies that deliver health and social services to local Haitian populations. For example, after he watched a young pregnant woman with malaria die because even after he had helped to raise the $15 needed to purchase blood, he couldn't raise enough for the inexpensive equipment needed for the transfusion, he worked to build a public health program in the village of Cange. That effort included vaccination programs, protected water supplies, and sanitation. He also trained people to administer medicines, treat minor ailments, and recognize symptoms of serious illnesses such as tuberculosis, malaria, and typhoid.

On one of his trips back to Boston from Haiti, he tried to raise money to build a bread oven in Cange. He approached a local charity that gave him the money and that also put him in contact with one of its regular donors, Tom White, a local contractor. White became so interested in what Farmer was doing in Haiti that he founded a public charity called Partners in Health, as well as a corresponding organization in Haiti called Zamni Lasante on which Farmer could draw for his work in Cange. White began by donating $1 million. Soon, Farmer expanded the membership of Partners in Health, adding a fellow anthropology and medical student, Jim Yong Kim, along with Ophelia Dahl, then Farmer's fiancée. Partners in Health has since provided funds to develop various public health projects in Haiti, such as the HIV Equity Initiative to complement prevention efforts with antiretroviral drugs for those for whom treatment has failed. Health workers visit patients each day and administer the drugs. Funds from standard health organizations such as the World Health Organization are limited for expensive drug treatments, but Partners in Health can provide them from private donations.

After the 2010 earthquake, Partners in Health and Zamni Lasante designed and implemented the Stand with Haiti Fund, and a 2.5-year, $125 million plan to help to rebuild the country. In 2013, Partners in Health, in collaboration with the Haitian government, opened the new Mirebalais hospital, funded by donations that poured in from the international community after the earthquake. In addition to designing the hospital as a training hospital (as both the nursing and medical schools had been destroyed), they focused on strengthening the country's health infrastructure, particularly in specialties such as mental health and rehabilitative medicine, which had been weak even before the earthquake.

Conclusions

The problem underlying this chapter is that extremes of poverty and wealth exist in modern societies. The criteria customarily used to rank people in social hierarchies include wealth or income, occupation, ethnic group membership, personal appearance, race, gender, and age. The consequences of such rankings, especially in the creation of poverty and the gap between rich and poor, have raised some of the most challenging questions in modern societies.

People come to accept social hierarchies as natural because they believe that hierarchy is a biological principle. Some people are thought to be naturally more or less intelligent than others or otherwise more or less worthy. Female biological functions, for example, have been described in terms that make women seem less worthy than men. Even when social categories such as race and ethnic identity are understood as being defined by cultural rather than biological differences, the idea that such categories, and subsequent social hierarchies, are immutable often remains.

Finally, we have examined various areas in which persons with a background in anthropology can help

structural violence
Refers to the systematic ways in which social structures or social institutions harm or otherwise disadvantage local individuals. Structural violence is often invisible and lacking one specific person who can (or will) be held responsible.

address the poverty and oppression that often arise from inequality. We focused largely on human rights abuses, since most of these arise from differential access to wealth. The work of anthropologists such as Carole Nagengast and Paul Farmer shows that anthropologists can apply their unique skills and knowledge to mitigate forms of structural violence and alleviate the pernicious effects of growing social inequality.

QUESTIONS: REVIEW

7.1 How do societies use class and caste to rank people in social hierarchies?

This section compares and contrasts two different forms of social hierarchies: class and caste. *Class* refers to a form of identity based upon perceptions of a person's economic worth or status; it is generally viewed as an achieved status or as a form of meritocracy. While someone may be born into a wealthy or influential family, class is often viewed as a fluid category. Upward mobility may be attained through the pursuit of higher education, or other factors. In contrast, caste is a social category that is fixed (ascribed at birth) and static. Indian society is perhaps best known for its caste system, which in recent years has overlapped with class and other forms of social hierarchies.

Review Questions

1. What is the difference between an ascribed and an achieved status?
2. What is a meritocracy?
3. What are the main differences between class and caste as forms of social hierarchy?

7.2 How do people come to accept social hierarchies as natural?

Race is often perceived to be a biological or innate concept in the context of our popular culture. As such, it is deemed to be an ascribed and fixed status at birth. This section, however, explores how identities like race are actually culturally constructed. People are lumped into different racial categories to justify and legitimize various forms of social discrimination, such as slavery. Different forms of racism, like white privilege or structural racism, are ubiquitous, even in the context of multicultural societies like Canada. Racist ideologies have been naturalized by various proponents practitioners of scientific racism, including Francis Galton, Karl Pearson, and Samuel George Morton, as well as Hernstein and Murray in their book *The Bell Curve*.

Review Questions

1. Why is race the by-product of culture and not biology?
2. Why is the concept of intelligence problematic?
3. What is white privilege?
4. Why is the work of Samuel George Morton faulty?
5. What are the social consequences of viewing race as biological?

7.3 How is gender a form of social hierarchy?

This section examines how, in most societies, gender is a form of social stratification. Anthropologists identify sex as a categorization based upon biological criteria, whereas gender is culturally constructed. Many industrialized nation-states like Canada have historically recognized two sexes and two corresponding genders. This is beginning to change, however, with the increasing recognition that gender, for many people, is a fluid category, and that many people, such as transgendered individuals, do not readily fall into Western dichotomies of sex and gender. In other contexts, many societies recognize a category of third-gendered people, such as sworn virgins or two-spirits.

Hegemonic forms of masculinity and femininity exist in many societies, and this section examined how institutions like fraternities oftentimes reinforce a problematic form of hegemonic masculinity that perpetuates gendered inequality. As Emily Martin discusses, even the supposedly objective narratives of scientists reinforce gendered forms of stratification, as does language and vocabulary used by men and women. Many women internalize these forms of hierarchies via their body image. Finally, this section addresses how social inequalities predicated upon gender are intensified by a woman's economic standing or experiences of poverty.

Review Questions

1. What is the difference between sex and gender?
2. What is a hegemonic masculinity, and how does Sanday's example of fraternities reinforce notions of gendered inequality?
3. How does poverty affect gendered stratification?
4. According to Emily Martin, how do scientists' understandings of human conception and reproduction reinforce gendered hierarchies?

7.4 How are different forms of social hierarchy interwoven with each other?

In this section, we explore how various forms of social inequality, such as racism and classism, are often interwoven with one another. For example, Edmonds's study of cosmetic surgery in Brazil highlights how many women seek to whiten their bodies by altering facial features because "whiteness" is associated with a higher class status in Brazil. This, in turn, can provide people with access to a wider range of jobs and other economic opportunities. Discussing what is often termed "new racism" in Canada, Ameeriar studied Pakistani immigrants, who are expected to "sanitize" their bodies to fit within particular expectations of body aesthetics in Canada.

Review Questions

1. How, according to Edmonds, are class, gender, and race intertwined in his example of cosmetic surgery in Brazil?
2. What is "new racism?"
3. What is a "sanitized body," and how is it an example of new racism?

7.5 How can anthropology be applied to alleviate the effects of inequality?

Section 7.5 examines some of the work that has been undertaken by anthropologists to help alleviate and eliminate human rights abuses that result from various forms of poverty and social inequality. As we have seen, the economic and social inequality that creates the conditions for human rights violations continues to grow. Anthropologists like Paul Farmer, for instance, illustrate how, in the case of Haiti, structural violence is at the root of many forms of inequality. With the understanding that government and corporate decision making is at the heart of many health crises, he has launched a number of development projects centred on health care, as part of an effort to implement policy change.

Review Questions

1. How are human rights linked with notions of inequality?
2. What is structural violence?
3. How have Terence Turner and Robert Hitchcock sought to empower Indigenous groups?
4. How do notions of inequality and social hierarchy play a role in the Black Lives Matter movement?

CRITICAL THINKING QUESTIONS

1. In this chapter, we have discussed how most people tend to perceive their identities as natural, or biological. What might be some strategies for getting people to think differently about their identities, and for recognizing the culturally constructed nature of identity? Furthermore, why is it important to understand the role that culture plays in shaping social hierarchies?

2. Describe some examples of how "white privilege" operates in our own society.
3. In Section 7.5, we discuss how anthropologists can help alleviate the effects of inequality. On reading the examples of Terence Turner and Paul Farmer, both of whom work in non-Western contexts, how could you apply these ideas to our own Canadian society? As anthropologists and anthropology students, what can we do in Canada to make a difference in people's lives and confront the issue of social inequality?
4. Section 7.4 discusses the concept of "new racism." Discuss two examples of "new racism" that you may have witnessed and/or experienced in our society. How do they differ from other forms of racism?

KEY TERMS

achieved status (p. 187)
ascribed status (p. 187)
caste system (p. 187)
class (p. 186)
gender (p. 196)
hegemonic masculinity (p. 199)
meritocracy (p. 187)
new racism (p. 204)
race (p. 190)
racism (p. 191)
sex (p. 196)
social hierarchy (p. 185)
structural violence (p. 208)
third gender (p. 196)
transgender (p. 196)
white privilege (p. 192)

CHAPTER 8

The Nation-State, Globalization, and Neoliberalism

© Qilai Shen/Corbis/Getty Images

An employee wearing a Mickey Mouse T-shirt works at a factory in China that supplies shirts and pants to major brands.

The incredible concentration of wealth and power that now exists in the upper echelons of capitalism has not been seen since the 1920s. The flows of tribute into the world's major financial centres have been astonishing. What, however, is even more astonishing is the habit of treating all of this as a mere and in some instances even unfortunate byproduct of neoliberalization. The very idea that this might be—just might be—the fundamental core of what neoliberalism has been about all along appears unthinkable.

—David Harvey, *The History of Neoliberalism* (2005)

PROBLEM 8

How are the nation-state, globalization, and neoliberalism linked together, and what are the economic and cultural effects of globalization?

Introduction

In 1964, Canadian media theorist Marshall McLuhan coined the term "global village" to illustrate his prediction that the proliferation of mass media and other forces would give rise to increasing global interconnectivity. Today, in an era dominated by digital communications and social media, this interconnectivity is obvious. But what are the consequences of globalization for the groups of people that anthropologists work with? Over the years, many anthropologists have explored the various economic and cultural effects of globalization in both face-to-face and virtual communities. As we will see throughout this chapter, globalization can do harm to many communities, even while opening for others a space for creativity, resistance, and change.

The term "globalization" has been bandied about by academics and the mass media and within our popular culture over the past four decades. Anthony Giddens (1990, 64) defines **globalization** as "the intensification of worldwide social relations which link distant localities in such a way that local happenings are shaped by events occurring many miles away and vice versa." Arjun Appadurai (2006) discusses these effects in terms of global cultural flows, where there exists an increasing exchange and flow of information across five different interconnected dimensions, or what Appadurai calls "scapes"—mediascapes, ethnoscapes, financescapes, technoscapes, and ideoscapes. As an example, he uses the term "ethnoscape" to refer to how globalization has led to the increasing physical movement of people throughout the world—as migrant labourers, tourists, immigrants—which "appear[s] to affect the politics of and between nations to a hitherto unprecedented degree" (Appadurai 1990: 297). The impact of this unprecedented movement of people was evident in 2019 through 2020, when the novel zoonotic coronavirus disease (COVID-19) "went global" as a result of the ease of movement of people via commercial air travel. As the virus spread and then was declared a pandemic, many countries enacted divisive policies, ranging from the quarantining of citizens and/or guests, to the closure of national borders. In Canada, for instance, the borders were closed to non-Canadians, with the exception of commercial transit for the movement of essential products, like food. In an effort to slow and eventually stop the effects of the virus, nonessential services and businesses were closed as well. These included dine-in restaurants, elementary

globalization
Defined by Anthony Giddens as the intensification of world-wide social relations that link distant localities in such a way that local happenings are shaped by events occurring many miles away, and vice versa.

and high schools, postsecondary institutions, and most places of business, unless they could operate virtually. The long-term ramifications of these closures remain to be seen, but the short-term effects have been economically devastating in terms of employment and global trade. By April 2020, for instance, Canada's unemployment rate had reached a 70-year high (Macdonald 2020).

Yet at the same time, sociocultural crises often stimulate new ways to foster a community as well as feelings of catharsis or relief from stress in the absence of face-to-face contact and communication. With the introduction of physical and social distancing as a means of reducing the spread of COVID-19, videoconferencing technologies, such as Zoom, became a popular medium for maintaining ties in mostly professional contexts, while social networking apps like Houseparty gained momentum for personal use. Many people also used these (or related) technologies in creative new ways. For instance, many people, bored at home, produced novel videos, which they then shared on social media. As author Robin Wright (2020) discussed in an article in the New Yorker,

> *In China, the epicenter of the COVID-19 outbreak and a nation where almost eight hundred million people have experienced some form of lockdown, night clubs that were forced to shut their doors have turned to virtual "cloud clubbing." Viewers can watch d.j. sets on streaming platforms and send in messages to be read live, to create the illusion that they are connected. (Wright 2020)*

Globalization, then, can have both negative and positive economic and cultural effects on various populations. For example, the worldwide spread of large multinational companies such as Walmart and Starbucks has been documented as having deleterious economic consequences on local communities. Walmart, for instance, may seem like an attractive option for shopping because of its low price points, but because of its buying power, it can sell products more cheaply than most small, local businesses, effectively forcing them to close. Similarly, online shops like Amazon are threatening traditional brick-and-mortar stores and, by extension, the livelihoods of business owners and their employees.

In many ways, globalization is nothing new. As we saw in Chapter 3, Europe's colonization of the world was a global phenomenon. But as Roxana Ng (2002, 74) points out, "what is new in this era of globalization is the ability of capital to move sites of production across national borders with relative ease." The production, circulation, and consumption of a common commodity, the T-shirt, offers an instructive example of the mechanisms and consequences of economic globalization and contemporary capitalism. For instance, many protesters at the annual G20 meetings of world political leaders sport T-shirts emblazoned with antiglobalization slogans or with the logos of the protest groups with which they are affiliated. For many people, these annual meetings represent an opportunity to voice the often underrepresented perspectives of marginalized communities—including Indigenous groups, environmentalists, and LGBTQ+ communities—at a place where the national and international media have gathered. At these events, the images and logos on clothing (such as T-shirts) serve to communicate messages or resist government policies. By examining what Igor Kopytoff (1986) calls the biography of a commodity (in this case, the T-shirt), we can understand much about the global processes the protesters are criticizing.

Economist Pietra Rivoli (2005) wanted to understand the impact, on workers and on the environment, of multilateral institutions such as the World Trade Organization (WTO), the International Monetary Fund (IMF), and the World Bank (see Chapter 3). Her starting assumption was that globalization was a good thing—that the production and sale of commodities such as T-shirts was creating jobs in poor countries as well as supplying consumers with inexpensive goods. To convince herself of the benefits of trade, she wanted to trace the chain of production and distribution of a T-shirt, from the growing of the cotton to the delivery of the final product to a chain store in Fort Lauderdale, Florida. She began by locating the company that printed and distributed the T-shirt, Sherry Manufacturing of Fort Lauderdale. Sherry Manufacturing had purchased the shirt from China, one of about 25 million cotton T-shirts shipped from China that year. Rivoli then travelled to China to visit the factory that had assembled the T-shirt, the place where the fabric had been knit, and, finally, the factory where the yarn had been spun out of raw cotton. The cotton, she was surprised to discover, had been grown in Lubbock County, Texas. The unexpected (yet increasingly typical) biography and global itinerary of her T-shirt—purchased in Fort Lauderdale, printed and distributed by a Florida textile manufacturer, assembled, sewn, and spun in Chinese factories out of cotton grown in Texas—can tell us much about globalization and our role in it as T-shirt consumers in North America. The aspects of capitalism, neoliberalism, and economic globalization that underpin the biography of the T-shirt are the focus of the first half of this chapter.

In the second half of this chapter, we examine the often ambiguous cultural effects of globalization. For some societies, the process has been empowering: a means to strengthen cultural identity as a society's arts, material culture, and values and beliefs circulate around the world. To understand these effects, it is first necessary to understand the relationship between the nation-state and globalization, and between nation-states and national identity. Think, again, about T-shirts and how often they communicate not just political slogans or brand names, but sentiments of national pride and affiliations of national identity (think about how events like the Olympics foster a sense of national pride). When we wear T-shirts purchased in popular tourist destinations, we demonstrate our own global itineraries while simultaneously conveying carefully crafted messages about the locales in which we purchased the T-shirts. To understand both the forces of economic globalization that make it possible for us to buy cheap T-shirts produced elsewhere, and the forces of cultural globalization that compel us to wear our identity and our global itineraries, literally, on our sleeves, we need to explore the four questions that comprise this chapter.

QUESTIONS

- **8.1** What role do nation-states play in market economies?
- **8.2** What is neoliberalism, and what role does it play in capitalist economic globalization?
- **8.3** What is the relationship between the nation-state and identity under globalization?
- **8.4** How do engagements with global capitalism affect local cultural identities and livelihoods?

Question 8.1: What Role Do Nation-States Play in Market Economies?

Although neoliberal philosophy is the driving force behind what we call "globalization," there is a basic contradiction in how it is applied. The core idea of neoliberalism is that governments must not interfere with the functioning of the market, yet nation-states still play a vital role in how the economy functions.

What do we mean by "nation-state"? The concept of the **nation-state** is relatively recent, dating back in its present form to the nineteenth century. Furthermore, the terms **nation** and "state" do not mean the same thing. Most states have more than one nation, as in Canada, where there are many First Nations; moreover, one nation can be scattered across many states, either by choice or by force, as in the case of diasporic communities or refugees.

nation-state
A political community that has clearly defined territorial borders and centralized authority.

nation
A collection of people who share a common language, worldview, and ancestry.

Nation-states typically keep public order, maintain armies, collect tribute or taxes, and so on. The main difference between earlier states and the modern nation-state concerns the extent to which the modern state influences and controls trade. In historical terms, the increasing importance of trade gave governing elites a greater interest in creating conditions for accumulating profits from trade. Of course, ruling elites have always been interested in the economic lives of their subjects. Early states protected the privileges of the elites by regulating the production of goods from resources, offering protection from other elites, and extracting surplus wealth in the form of tribute and taxes from a largely peasant population. The state also issued coins and paper money, established standards for weights and measures, protected the movement of merchants and goods, purchased goods, and created and maintained marketplaces where merchants could sell their products.

In thirteenth- and fourteenth-century China and, later, in sixteenth- and seventeenth-century Europe and Japan, states began to actively promote and regulate trade. By the eighteenth century, rulers were beginning to view trade as the ultimate source of well-being. Consequently, states regulated money. They also passed laws to protect their manufacturers and merchants by imposing taxes and tariffs on goods coming from other states. They used military force to open markets in other places and granted trading monopolies to their own groups. They granted charters to trading companies, such as the East India Company and the Hudson's Bay Company, giving them exclusive rights to trade in specific areas. These were the forerunners of today's transnational corporations.

States also created and maintained the infrastructure that made trade possible. They developed and maintained ports, built roads and canals, and, later, subsidized railway construction. In Canada, for instance, the Canadian Pacific Railway (CPR) was completed in 1885. Connecting the nation's vast expanse from east to west, the CPR facilitated trade and economic links between provinces that would otherwise have been impossible. States also became important customers.

Put simply, nation-states began to develop into partnerships between ruling elites and the merchant classes. As Eric Wolf (1982, 109) put it,

> *The state bought arms and ships. Goods won by force of arms paid for the hiring of mercenaries, for the manufacture of guns and cannon, and for the construction of more ships. The armed merchants foraging overseas needed the state to shield them against competitors and to provide the officialdom capable of holding and consolidating the newly won areas. At the same time the state needed the merchants to lend money to the Crown or to the captains of expeditions; to collect, ship, and sell the goods obtained abroad; and—increasingly—to acquire and export the goods needed in the far-flung outposts of the realm.*

In these ways, states became the building blocks of an emerging global economic network. Each state was now the guardian of its own "national economy," functioning largely to advance the economic lives of its own citizens. The modern nation-state sought to create the conditions that made business profitable, while at the same time ensuring that its citizens could afford the things they wanted to buy. As we will see, though, this ideal is possible only if manufacturers do not have to pay the full production costs of what they make and sell, and only if consumers don't have to pay the real costs of things. One need only examine the real costs of even the most basic commodities to appreciate the role that nation-states played in making possible their production and purchase. Take, for example, the cost of a Snickers bar.

The Nation-State and the Cost of a Snickers Bar

Snickers bars are described by their producer, Mars, Incorporated (listed by *Forbes* in 2014 as the sixth-largest privately held company in the United States) as chocolate treats "packed with roasted peanuts, nougat, caramel and milk chocolate." More precisely, Snickers bars have more than 20 ingredients, the main one being sugar or sugar derivatives. Snickers is the most popular chocolate bar in Canada and the United States, and one package of Snickers sells for about $1.50. But that is only the store price. To arrive at the *real* price, we need to examine the hidden costs, owing to **market externalities**, of each ingredient; in other words, we need to calculate the additional monetary and nonmonetary expenses that go to produce and distribute each ingredient in a Snickers bar: expenses that are not reflected in the store price. In fact, without the intervention of the nation-state, the real cost of a Snickers bar would probably be $10 or higher. It is only about $1.50 because of the various ways the nation-state functions to keep costs accessible and sales profitable.

To illustrate, let us examine just one ingredient that goes into a Snickers bar: cane sugar. Sugar cultivation requires a tropical climate, so sugar cane is not grown in Canada. However, it is a popular and lucrative crop in parts of the United States (southern Florida and Hawaii) and throughout the Caribbean and South America, among other regions. In terms of the environment, sugar is not a benign crop. Its production is responsible for dying coral reefs in Hawai'i, water pollution in Buenos Aires, and damage to river estuaries in Brazil and waterways in the Philippines. Florida's sugar cane industry, centred just south of one of North America's largest freshwater lakes, Lake Okeechobee, dumps phosphorus-laden agricultural runoff into the lake, which destroys native species and results in the growth of non-native species. In 2000, the *Comprehensive Everglades Restoration Plan* was enacted, which saw almost $8 billion spent to "fix" the Everglades. Although sugar producers paid some of that cost, most of it was passed on to American taxpayers.

Sugar cane is not grown in Canada, but there are sugar *refineries* in Canada. While the Canadian government does not subsidize Canada's sugar industry, sugar production is heavily subsidized by some nation-states, including the United States, which, through import quotas, limits the amount

Ullstein Bild/Getty Images

One function of the nation-state is to ensure that businesses and corporations profit and that commodities are affordable to consumers. Thus, laws and regulations are written (or not written) to permit corporations to externalize costs. Rarely, if ever, do consumers pay the real prices for things. Even a Snickers chocolate bar, which might sell for $1.50, would likely cost far more if externalized costs were included in the purchase price.

of sugar that can be imported from other countries. This arrangement raises the cost of sugar for consumers, but it also makes sugar production more profitable and so has resulted in the conversion of more than 200,000 hectares of Everglades wetlands to sugar cane production.

The nation-state also manipulates the prices of things by regulating the price of labour. For example, paying sugar workers less than a living wage keeps the price of sugar down. Countries like the United States and Canada have a "minimum wage," but it does not apply to agricultural workers, many of whom come from Mexico or the English-speaking Caribbean and are permitted to enter North America temporarily only for the purpose of work.

Indirect subsidies for sugar include government funding of the infrastructure for sugar production and processing. This infrastructure includes roads,

market externalities
Costs that are not included in the prices people pay, for example, health risks and environmental degradation.

power systems, water and sanitation systems, and waste disposal. For example, the entire water management infrastructure that supports the Florida sugar cane industry was built with US federal tax dollars. Finally, the tax policies of the nation-state are constantly being adjusted to ensure low prices and ongoing corporate profits. Thus, in the 1950s, the tax bill of corporations in the United States accounted for 39 percent of all federal tax income; by 2018, that figure was 21 percent. By 2014, around one third of the most financially lucrative US corporations were paying less than 10 percent of their net annual revenues in corporate taxes (Pyke 2014).

These are only some of the hidden costs of one ingredient in a Snickers bar. To arrive at a real economic cost, we would need to examine each of the other ingredients and then add the hidden costs of processing, packaging, delivery, and waste disposal. The energy and pollution costs of distribution alone would be considerable. In Europe and North America, a typical food item travels 1,600 kilometres before it reaches consumers' meal plates. A head of lettuce in the local supermarket has travelled an average of 1,900 kilometres from where it was grown. The shipment of foods, while sometimes necessary, is further encouraged by energy subsidies that allow North Americans to enjoy some of the lowest fuel prices in the world. Economists estimate that if tax subsidies, government program subsidies, and environmental damage were calculated and if other externalities of vehicle use were discontinued, the price of gasoline would be as high as $16.40 a gallon in the United States and about $4.00 a litre in Canada.

It is also important to note that our insatiable desire for sugary treats such as Snickers is closely intertwined with a long history of exploitative labour that began during the colonial period. In his analysis of the link between sugar and colonialism, Sidney Mintz (1985) argues that sugar would never have become such a significant and seemingly "necessary" commodity in European and other Western countries without the use of slave labour. In Chapter 3, we discussed the significance of cotton—its production and trade—to colonialism and the slave trade in the Americas. Sugar, too, was an integral part of that history. With the European colonization of the Caribbean, for instance, the Caribbean region became the world's largest producer of sugar. In the 1700s and 1800s, to cultivate and distill sugar cane at high yields and profitable rates, European plantation owners shipped more than one million individuals from West Africa to work as slaves.

Even after slavery was abolished, exploitative forms of labour continued. For instance, about 20,000 poor and dispossessed Haitian workers are lured annually to the Dominican Republic with the promise of jobs, only to find themselves working in horrific conditions on sugar cane plantations. With little or no rights, and no passports, workers are underpaid and overworked. Many of them cross the border illegally and without official passports and so lack legal or official representation in the Dominican Republic. So when we think about the different products we "can't live without"—sugar often being one—we should also consider how colonial relationships among nation-states have persisted into the postcolonial present. Some of these issues pertaining to labour and the production of commodities in an increasingly neoliberal environment are elaborated upon below.

In brief, then, the nation-state develops such instruments as tax laws, financial policies, environmental regulations, and labour laws that help corporations and consumers avoid paying the real costs of production and consumption. The costs of these measures are then passed on to future generations or to people in other countries in the form of low wages, a polluted environment, health risks, and the like. Yet this, it seems, is what citizens want. Corporations look to nation-states to further their interests; to ensure this, they spend billions of dollars each year to help elect officeholders who are sympathetic to their interests. Consumers look to the nation-state to keep the prices of things (e.g., chocolate bars and gasoline) within their reach. And workers expect the nation-state to enact policies to enhance job and wage growth. None of this would be possible without nation-states to enact and enforce rules and regulations that allow their citizens to pass on the real costs of things, such as environmental damage, health risks, and poverty, to people in other countries, to marginalized people in their own countries, or to future generations.

BEYOND THE BOOK 8.1

Each morning, most students begin the day by brushing their teeth, washing their face, and using the toilet facilities. Then, perhaps, they drink a glass of orange juice and maybe sip a cup of coffee. But what are the hidden costs of these activities? What sorts of indirect environmental, health, and economic costs are involved in these activities? Make a list of your weekday morning activities and the typical products that you consume. Then, research what the hidden costs are of your morning routine.

Activity or Product	Hidden Cost
Brushing teeth:	
Flushing the toilet:	
Drinking orange juice:	
Sipping coffee:	

Question 8.2: What Is Neoliberalism, and What Role Does It Play in Capitalist Economic Globalization?

"The Great Transformation"

To understand the various economic effects of globalization, we must explore what we mean by an "economic system." **Economic systems** are about the distribution of goods and services—that is, the rules, mechanisms, institutions, and systems of relations through which people get what they want. This process can be as simple as the borrowing of a cup of sugar or a pair of shoes, or as complex as the production, distribution, consumption, and disposal of automobiles, houses, or military weapons.

Markets go back thousands of years. Communities would set up areas where merchants, farmers, and artisans could bring their goods or services for sale or barter. But as new modes of transportation and manufacturing developed, markets were no longer only places to trade, but entire networks whereby silk manufactured in China, for example, could be sold in Paris. At some point 200 to 300 years ago, technological changes led to what economist Karl Polanyi termed "the great transformation," or the Industrial Revolution. As discussed in Chapter 3, the Industrial Revolution had enormous worldwide economic and social consequences, and it was intimately linked with colonialism. Indeed, the Industrial Revolution contributed to the development and perpetuation of many of our existing forms of social inequality—classism and racism, for example—as well as solidifying the rise of capitalism as the dominant, worldwide economic system.

Capitalism has, of course, expanded, such that we engage in the sale or barter of goods and services on large, international scales that involve complex exchanges between different countries. As we have seen, states have always played a major role in the economy. Some eighteenth-century economists, however, argued that the state should play as small a role as possible. Ideally, they argued, people will supply only those goods and services for which there is demand; and generally, a balance will be established between what is demanded and what is supplied. In his classic treatise *The Wealth of Nations* (1776), Adam Smith saw the workings of the market as an "invisible hand" by which a benevolent God administered a universe in which human happiness was maximized; the market was an ideal system in which each person, seeking his or her own ends, contributed to the betterment of society as a whole. Thus, by seeking money and wealth, each person would work toward supplying what others needed or demanded. For Smith, the market represented a utopian vision in which wealth was perpetually created for the benefit of all.

economic systems
The rules, mechanisms, institutions, and systems of relations through which goods and services are distributed and people get what they want.

The problem was that an unregulated market, in which the generation of wealth was the only goal, resulted in abysmal working conditions, environmental degradation, and wild economic fluctuations that saw people plunged into poverty. In *The Great Transformation* (1944), Polanyi addressed the tension between the need to allow the market—that is, the mechanisms for buying and selling—to operate freely without government interference and the need to somehow minimize the social and natural damages inflicted by the market. Polanyi suggested that the market, if allowed to operate unhindered, would soon destroy the very foundations of society. It would disrupt social relations though the operations of the labour market; it would destroy the environment; it would reduce freedom. Yet regulating the market by enacting laws on pollution, land use, and working conditions could destroy the market. Polanyi saw the working out of this dilemma as one of the driving forces of history since the early nineteenth century.

When it comes to the market's workings, governments have tried to maintain a balance between regulation and noninterference. At one extreme are the almost completely state-run economies of Cuba and North Korea; at the other are capitalist economies such as those of Canada and the United States. Economic systems are generally categorized as market-driven or state-run; in practice, though, almost all represent some mix of the two. North Korea is one of the last of the state-run economies, with the government controlling virtually every economic activity; yet the North Korean government also sponsors the Kaesong Industrial Region, a development zone that welcomes foreign investment and that encourages market principles. The United States, by contrast, is usually represented as a hallmark example of a market economy. Nevertheless, during the 2008 to 2009 global recession, there was significant government intervention in the form of corporate bailouts and promises of stricter financial controls. More recently, stock markets crashed and many businesses have faced financial ruin in the wake of the 2020 recession due to the effects of COVID-19. In this context, the level of government intervention, including corporate bailouts for airlines and other affected industries, remains to be seen. Rarely are even the most capitalist economies free of significant state involvement, and the tension between the state and the market that Polanyi wrote about results in ebbs and flows of regulation.

During the Great Depression, the British economist John Maynard Keynes called on governments to regulate their economies through spending, tax policies, interest rates, and so on. Government involvement in the economy, support of labour unions, and a progressive tax system in which marginal tax rates ranged as high as 90 percent resulted in rapid economic growth in the United States and Canada through the 1960s.

This rapid growth was followed, in the 1970s, by a period of slow economic growth, which generated pressure to change economic policies. Economists began to abandon Keynesian economics, arguing that the state should withdraw from any involvement in regulating the economy. This economic philosophy, known as **neoliberalism**, is often synonymous with contemporary capitalism under globalization. Since the application of neoliberal principles may determine your career path as well as what goods and services you can acquire for what price, not to mention the natural, political, and social environment in which you live, it is useful to understand where neoliberalism came from and what it is trying to accomplish.

The Emergence of Neoliberalism

Neoliberalism emerged from a group of economists, historians, and philosophers who gathered around political philosopher Friedrich von Hayek to

neoliberalism
An economic philosophy that argues for minimal government involvement in the economy and greatly accelerated economic growth. Well-being, neoliberals argue, is best served by liberating individual entrepreneurs to operate in a framework of strong property rights, free markets, and free trade.

establish the Mont Pelerin Society in 1947. Their ideas were prompted by concerns about the spread of totalitarian societies and religious and racial intolerance in the aftermath of World War II. They argued that totalitarian philosophies were both endangering freedom and threatening private property and the free market, without which, they believed, freedom could not be preserved. They called themselves "liberals" because they adhered to ideals of freedom, and "neo" because they adhered to neoclassical economic theory, which was opposed to Keynesian ideas about state involvement in the economy.

Well-being, neoliberals argued, would best be served by liberating individual entrepreneurs to operate within a framework of strong property rights, free markets, and **free trade**. The state's role should be limited to safeguarding the integrity of money and maintaining military, police, and legal structures to secure property rights and protect markets. The state should also open markets in areas such as education, water, land, health care, and social security. Other than that, state intervention should be kept to a minimum, because states can never have enough information to second-guess markets on matters such as prices, and because their involvement allows special interest groups such as unions, environmentalists, and trade groups to distort market operations.

One of the first applications of neoliberalism was in New York City in the 1970s. By the start of the decade, industry was fleeing New York and people who could afford new housing were moving to the suburbs. The city was left with a diminished tax base and an impoverished and socially restive inner city—what became known as the "urban crisis." The initial solution was typical Keynesian economics: expand public employment and public assistance. When President Richard Nixon declared the urban crisis over in the early 1970s, however, he also reduced federal aid to the city. The economic slowdown of the 1970s that hit New York, combined with a reduced tax base and reduced federal aid, drove New York City to the brink of bankruptcy. Financial institutions were unwilling to negotiate the city's debts unless it met strict conditions that included severe budget cuts. They also required unions to put their pension funds in city bonds, which meant that if the city went bankrupt, workers would lose their pensions. The overall result was a diminished standard of living for New Yorkers, particularly the poor. But ultimately, the city became financially solvent and represented to neoliberals what could be done through free market principles.

This pattern soon became the one applied to countries in trouble. The economic stagnation of the 1970s adversely affected developing countries, which, encouraged by banks, had borrowed heavily but could no longer repay their debts. As a condition for restructuring their loans, multilateral institutions such as the World Bank and the IMF (discussed in Chapter 3) imposed neoliberal economic policies on these countries: these included privatizing state-run enterprises; reducing the value of their currency, thus making goods produced in the country cheaper for foreign buyers (and thereby encouraging exports); and making foreign goods more expensive for citizens (thereby discouraging imports). Other conditions included reducing state funding for education, welfare, and health and imposing user fees for school attendance.

These neoliberal policies had few positive results. Only a few countries were able to escape debt, and more than $4.6 trillion flowed from poorer to wealthier countries. According to economist Joseph E. Stiglitz (2002), the poor countries ended up subsidizing the richest. As David Harvey (2005) suggests in the epigraph to the chapter, this result may not be an unfortunate by-product of neoliberalism, but rather, its fundamental purpose.

free trade
The removal of barriers to the free flow of goods and capital between nations by eliminating import and export taxes as well as subsidies paid to farmers and business people. It may also mean reducing environmental or social laws when they restrict the flow of goods and capital.

Removing government involvement in the economy is central to neoliberal economic philosophy. When such involvement ends, so the theory goes, business can be more profitable, create more jobs, and so on. One way that less government involvement can help economic growth is by allowing costs that are involved in the production, distribution, consumption, and disposal of goods and services to be externalized. But as we have seen, all along the commodity chain, from the production of goods to their transport to their sale and disposal, there are market externalities, costs that are not included in the prices that people pay, such as environmental degradation, health risks, and waste disposal.

What Is the Role of the Nation-State in an Increasingly Neoliberalized Global Economy?

Nation-states are currently the political building blocks of the modern world. All individuals derive whatever political rights and privileges they enjoy from their nation-state. Each person is educated, is given or denied permission to travel, and is bound by the laws of his or her state. Yet some people, such as David Korten (1995), claim that the nation-state is a thing of the past, that in an increasingly globalized world, national boundaries are no longer relevant. Millions of people migrate from their home countries in search of jobs, further blurring national boundaries. More than 230 million people currently live and work in countries of which they are not citizens, and this number will continue to grow (ILO 2015). Some say that new **transnational** institutions, such as transnational corporations and transnational treaty organizations (e.g., the WTO), are rapidly replacing nation-states. Is the nation-state a thing of the past?

For many people, the nation-state continues to be a primary actor in the construction of identities and economies. Tensions between nation-states and neoliberalism have emerged in a variety of contexts, one example being Brexit. In June 2016, the British government held a national referendum to determine whether its citizens wished to withdraw from participation in the European Union (EU). In a close vote with surprising results, 51.9 percent of UK voters voted to leave the EU. British legislators have thus been tasked with the daunting process of negotiating the logistics of the UK's withdrawal. EU member countries benefit from enhanced ease of travel for their citizens for purposes of work or tourism, as well as trade liberalization among member countries, and greater security through intelligence and data sharing, among other things. Polling on the day of the referendum asked "Leave" voters why they wanted to leave the EU. Forty-nine percent felt that "decisions about the UK should be taken in the UK." In other words, they perceived that in joining the EU in the first place, the UK had given up agency and control when it came to domestic politics and economics. In many ways, Brexit is a symptom of wider **nationalist populist movements**, or emerging forms of nationalism that "should be understood as a reaction to a neoliberal political and economic order that has been taking shape since the early 1970s and has accelerated with the end of the Cold War and the development of digital communication technologies" (Gusterson 2017, 210). Despite the diverse variants of nationalist populist movements, there exist a number of commonalities:

> *a hostility toward (at least some) immigrants and ethnic others, especially Muslims ...; a claim to speak for working people ...; an insistence that established government institutions have become corrupt or unresponsive to ordinary people ... ; an attack on transnational*

transnational
Involving more than one nation-state; reaching beyond or transcending national boundaries.

nationalist populist movements
Forms of nationalism that represent a reaction against various forces of neoliberalism.

organizations such as the European Union, NATO, the United Nations, and the World Trade Organization ...; a disparagement of cosmopolitan elites; and a call for a return to (an invented) "tradition." (Gusterson 2017, 210)

In the face of rapid change, then, such movements desperately seek to carve out a sense of distinctive identity through recourse to an imagined, exclusionary shared history that is often predicated on various forms of Othering.

The major candidate to replace the nation-state is the transnational corporation. Currently, half the richest institutional entities in the world are not nation-states, but transnational corporations. Apple, Microsoft, and Amazon are the three richest corporations in the world (Hanson 2019), whose net worth is well ahead of the economies of countries like Egypt, Iran, and Finland (Credit Suisse 2019). One reason why nation-states emerged was to integrate national economies. The expansion of the modern global economy, however, requires global, not just state, integration, and transnational corporations have both a vested interest in expanding across national boundaries and the power and financial resources to accomplish that end. One consequence of this development has been that corporate interests, as opposed to human interests, now dominate the policy agendas of nation-states and the international agencies they create, support, and control.

A good example of how international agencies have begun to "escape" nation-states' strictures involves the role of the WTO. The WTO was established in 1995 by international treaty. Its stated goal was to reduce trade barriers among its 140 member nations. Its proponents argued that when these barriers were reduced so that goods and services could flow freely across national boundaries, citizens of all countries would benefit.

But despite its apparently high-minded goals, the WTO has been the focus of mass public protests. In Seattle in 1999 and in Quebec City in 2001, thousands of protesters representing hundreds of labour, environmental, and human rights groups organized to demonstrate against the inequalities resulting from world trade. What were these protests against the WTO all about? Why does it matter that you know? And what does this have to do with anthropology?

Basically, anti-WTO protesters are demanding to know how an unelected body that makes decisions behind closed doors with no provisions for appeal can force sovereign countries to dismantle environmental, health, labour, and social laws that it deems to be "unfair restrictions on trade."

In brief, when a member country, generally acting for a domestic corporation, feels that the laws or regulations of another country constitute an unfair restriction on trade, it can ask the WTO to investigate. If a WTO panel, appointed by the member countries, agrees with the claim, the complaining country can then impose trade taxes and tariffs on goods imported from the offending country. Table 8.1 outlines the WTO's assessment of its value.

An example follows. Most European countries impose a tariff on bananas imported from Central America but not on those from some Caribbean countries, such as Jamaica, Dominica, St. Lucia, and St. Vincent. This policy favours Caribbean countries, since it makes Central American bananas more

TABLE 8.1 Proposed Benefits of the World Trade Organization

Cut living costs and raise living standards
Settle disputes and reduce trade tensions
Stimulate economic growth and employment
Cut the costs of doing business internationally
Encourage good governance
Help countries develop
Give the weak a stronger voice
Support the environment and health
Contribute to peace and stability
Be effective without hitting the headlines

Source: "10 Things the WTO Can Do." World Trade Organization, https://www.wto.org/english/thewto_e/whatis_e/10thi_e/10thi00_e.htm. With permission from the World Trade Organization.

expensive for European consumers. The rationale for these tariffs dates back to when Caribbean countries were colonial outposts of Britain and France.

The United States appealed the European tariff on Central American bananas to the WTO, claiming that it constituted an unfair trade barrier. The Americans acted largely because most Central American banana plantations are owned by US corporations, some of which had contributed considerable amounts of money to the election campaigns of both Republican and Democratic politicians. The WTO ruled that the tariffs imposed by European countries on Central American bananas did, in fact, constitute an unfair restriction on trade.

The WTO does not have the power to force countries to change their trade rules, but it can permit offended countries (the United States, in this case) to impose tariffs on selected goods of offending countries. The WTO permitted the United States to impose import tariffs on such things as British cashmere and French cheeses, thus increasing their costs to American consumers and likely reducing the profits of British wool producers and French cheese makers.

Some of the WTO's rulings have deeply disturbed health, labour, and environmental advocates because the WTO can pressure countries to change their health, labour, and environmental laws if its dispute panel rules that these laws constitute an unfair restriction on trade. For example, when a country has banned a product from another country because of health risks, the country in which the product was manufactured or produced can accuse the banning country of creating an unfair barrier to trade. The country passing the law then has to prove to the WTO panel that the ban was "scientifically based." If it cannot, then trade sanctions and penalties can be applied to the banning country.

A prominent case here involves the European ban on hormone-treated beef produced in the United States and Canada. Injecting hormones into beef cattle is legal in the United States and Canada, but some research suggests that treated beef may be harmful. Europeans are especially sensitive to health threats in meat because of the emergence of mad cow disease (Creutzfeldt-Jakob disease) in Great Britain, which is spread by eating meat from animals that have eaten infected feed, the subsequent ban on British beef by European countries, and fears about cancer-causing dioxins in meat and egg products in Belgium.

The United States, at the request of its ranchers and beef processors, brought the case to the WTO, claiming that the ban on beef was an "unfair restraint of trade" and that there was no clear scientific evidence of health risks. The WTO ruled in favour of the US corporations, thus forcing European consumers to accept American hormone-treated beef or accept restrictive tariffs on selected European products sold in the United States. So far, Europe has refused to overturn the ban, and the United States has been permitted to impose tariffs on selected European imports, including truffles from Italy.

Disputes such as these threaten the "precautionary principle" of risk management, which states that if a product or process poses risks to health or the environment, scientific certainty is not necessary in order for other countries to prohibit or control that product or process. The Europeans reason that, while there is no absolute scientific proof that hormone-treated beef is harmful to health, enough research has been done to raise real health concerns. Yet the WTO has rejected the precautionary principle in the case of North American beef, ruling that the Europeans must either let it in or allow Canada and the United States to impose penalties on European products.

As a result of such developments, some critics claim that "free trade" has less to do with trade and helping citizens of WTO countries than it does with allowing global corporations to force nation-states to change or erase environmental, health, and social regulations that interfere with their business. Critics claim that international agencies are being controlled and manipulated by corporate powers that determine not only what we buy but also the conditions under which our goods are produced and how they are distributed.

Globalization, Free Trade, and the Canadian Garment Industry

An ethnographic approach to studying the Canadian garment industry can yield insights into the local, everyday effects of economic globalization and international trade. First, recall the example at the beginning of this chapter, of Pietra Rivoli's (2005) T-shirt—purchased in Florida, made from cotton grown in Texas, but spun into cloth and assembled in China. One important chapter in the biography of this particular commodity concerns the garment workers. The young women working in the Chinese factories visited by Rivoli were happy to have the work. However terrible the conditions in the factories, they told her, "it sure beats work on the farm" (110).

Roxana Ng (2002) has done similar research on the Canadian garment industry. Her findings with respect to the effects of free trade have led her to ask, "Freedom for whom?" From the perspective of Canadian garment workers, longer hours, lower wages, and job loss have been the concrete, everyday results of the neoliberalization and restructuring of the garment industry under free trade. The industry has always relied on low wages to be competitive and has always used immigrants as a pool of inexpensive labour; 50 percent of workers in the garment industry are immigrants, and 76 percent are women (Ng 2002, 75). Since the mid-1990s, control within the garment industry has shifted away from manufacturers, first toward large retail chains such as The Bay, but increasingly toward transnational retail chains such as Walmart. At the same time that control over the industry has been centralized, production has become fragmented. This fragmentation takes the form of subcontracting. According to Ng (2002, 77), manufacturers have responded to their loss of control by reducing plant sizes and sending work to subcontractors, or "jobbers," who increasingly are using home workers or sweatshop operations to maximize their profit margins and reduce their operating costs.

The implementation in 1993 of the North American Free Trade Agreement (NAFTA), which enabled the freer movement of production and goods between the United States, Canada, and Mexico, also played a major role in the restructuring of the garment industry. Canadian companies such as Gildan, the largest T-shirt manufacturer in Quebec, have since opened plants in Mexico (and throughout the Caribbean). Wages are much lower than Canadian wages, and when labour costs go down, these companies' profits go up. Unfortunately, the direct results in Canada have been job losses, the depressing of wages, and deteriorating working conditions. One garment worker that Ng interviewed demonstrated the unpredictability of wages in this sector:

> *The lowest salary I earned was about $3 per hour, with the same employers I'm now working. [I asked why she didn't complain about the low rate.] I didn't say anything at the beginning. I dared not. But now I start to talk to them about this. This kind of pocket-cover sewing I'm doing now also requires me to cut certain fabric before I can start sewing. But the employers don't count the cutting time. I told the employers about this. But they said that almost every homeworker asks them for a raise. But they get no raise from their contractor who gives them the fabric. I don't know other homeworkers who also work for them. It would be better if I know. Their factory is very small. They only have two workers in their factory, plus some part-timers, and the two owners.*
>
> *The highest salary I earned was around $8 per hour. That was at the beginning when I first worked for these employers, when they let me know the piece rate before I sewed. But now they don't tell me the piece rate before I sew. (Ng 2007, 197)*

One effect of economic globalization has been the movement of capital, production, and goods around the globe. There has been a corresponding movement of people around the world, as well. People migrate in search of a better livelihood or because they have been displaced by the lack of economic and social opportunities in their home country. As mentioned earlier, the Canadian garment industry has always relied heavily on immigrant labour; to this, Ng adds that illegal migrants and undocumented workers now represent a larger and larger portion of Canada's garment sector workforce (necessarily, the official data are scarce). Undocumented garment workers—indeed, all undocumented workers—are among the most vulnerable participants in the global economy.

BEYOND THE BOOK 8.2

Take a look at the label on your shirt, T-shirt, sweatshirt, or whatever article of clothing you are wearing. What company made it? Where was it made? By whom? Look for information online about clothing manufacturing practices (location of factories and labour policies) for your particular label.

The anti-sweatshop movement has increased awareness of the poor working conditions for garment workers in parts of the developing world. In 1999, students at the University of Toronto successfully lobbied for a Code of Conduct for Trademark Licensees. The code now ensures that suppliers of school-trademarked merchandise (including T-shirts) have met minimum employment standards. Gildan, one of the university's suppliers, was forced to directly address allegations of unethical treatment of its workers in the developing world (Ng 2002, 79). So, it is important to note that free trade regulations, in particular, and neoliberalism, in general, have not only sent manufacturing jobs to the developing world, but also led to sweatshop conditions for Canadian workers. "In other words, globalization has created Third World working conditions within the geographical boundaries of the so-called First, or developed, world" (Ng 2007, 204).

Question 8.3: What Is the Relationship between the Nation-State and Identity under Globalization?

The integration and maintenance of the national economy is, then, one of the most important tasks facing the modern nation-state. But there are others. The state must be recognized by its citizens as the legitimate source of authority. And it must establish and uphold its own citizenship rules.

To achieve these ends, the state must create a nation out of groups who share (or who believe they share) a common culture, language, and heritage and who willingly identify themselves as members of the nation (review the discussion of the "imagined community" in Chapter 6). Given that almost all of the world's nation-states are comprised of peoples with different cultures, languages, and heritages, creating a nation is no easy task. Somehow, these diverse entities must come to see themselves as sharing a common culture, tradition, and heritage; only when they do can state leaders claim to represent "the people," whoever they might be. Furthermore, when people can be persuaded to identify themselves as members of a common political entity, they more easily accept integration into the national economy—the same wages, the same currency, and the same goods.

But how does one go about constructing a national identity? Besides the creation of a sense of "imagined community," this challenge often involves creating Others—that is, excluding groups from the nation-state or pushing them to its margins. The Others may be citizens of rival countries who are thought to embody characteristics that are mocked or feared by members of the nation-state. Thus, for centuries the British could pride themselves on not being Irish or French, and Canadians could take pride in not being "American," that is, citizens of the United States. Colonial empires established by the Germans, French, Dutch, and British substantiated each of those countries' claims that God or

Providence had chosen them to rule over "inferior" peoples. In Canada, as in many other nation-states, we maintain our sense of "nationhood" in part by drawing boundaries and by making Others out of those who enter the country, legally or illegally, to work.

These Others may be constructed out of largely arbitrary criteria, including physical characteristics, religion, or language. In Canada, for example, the Meech Lake Accord, a constitutional amendment that was debated in 1990, attempted to make English and French the only "official languages" of the nation-state, thereby implying that anyone who did not speak one of those languages did not quite belong. The Accord was vigorously challenged and defeated by Indigenous leaders, including Elijah Harper, a member of the provincial legislature in Manitoba, who argued that the denial of Indigenous languages was a denial of Indigenous peoples' existence. People who are immigrants, refugees, non-Christians, or members of visible minorities often experience negative reactions from those who claim to be "authentic Canadians."

In the fall of 2019, for example, Don Cherry, a renowned commentator for Canada's iconic *Hockey Night in Canada*, was fired for implying on the air that Canadian immigration policies and resulting multiculturalism had led to a lack of interest in Remembrance Day among minority or racialized Canadians. Lamenting that (in his opinion) fewer people in Toronto were wearing poppies, he fumed: "You people that come here, you love our way of life, you love our milk and honey, at least you can pay a couple of bucks for poppies or something like that." With this one sentence, Cherry launched a divisive and often racist public discussion surrounding race, ethnicity, and notions of Canadianness and belonging. At the heart of the debate is the issue of what and who counts as Canadian.

Indeed, immigration is a prime location for policies of racism in many nation-states. Canada has a long history of immigration policies based on race and ethnicity. Examples include the special head taxes imposed on Chinese immigrants between 1885 and 1923, the setting of quotas for different "racial" groups, and the refusal to allow Jewish refugees into Canada during World War II. During the decades when Canada was trying to populate its territory, British and American immigrants were actively recruited, northern Europeans were welcome, and other Europeans were accepted if they were the only ones available. "Peoples of colour," such as Chinese, East Indians, and blacks, were the least welcome. However, the Canadian state found ways to admit Chinese workers when labour was needed to build the CPR, and in the 1970s, a program was written into the Immigration Act to allow non-Canadians into Canada on a temporary basis as agricultural workers and domestics. For example, the Foreign Agricultural Resource Management Services (FARMS) program was created to allow Ontario growers to import workers from Mexico and various Caribbean countries to work on Ontario farms during planting and harvest. In 1967, Canada introduced the "point system," based on a match between the country's labour needs and applicants' education and skills, to accommodate a growing need for skilled workers from outside its borders.

Nation-states carefully define the places occupied by the various groups within their borders. Through these definitions, they clearly privilege some groups over others and some individuals over others. One way in which this is done is by creating official accounts of history. As Eva Mackey (1999, 23) argues,

> *nationalism often depends upon mythological narratives of a unified nation moving progressively through time—a continuum beginning with a glorious past leading to the present and then onward to an even better future. These mythical stories ensure that specific versions of history are highlighted, versions that reaffirm the particular characteristics ascribed to the nation.*

In Canada, that "glorious past" was filled with "nature," and Indigenous peoples were part of the natural landscape. In settler narratives about the creation of the Canadian nation, Indigenous peoples play the role of helpful "children" who join with the "adult" Euro-Canadians in bringing prosperity to the land. The history that children read in Canadian public schools describes Canada as much kinder to Indigenous peoples than the United States was to the Native American population, but even in this gentle version of history, "real Canadians are, by definition, not 'Native' or not from those 'other cultures' " (Mackey 1999, 89).

Canadians pride themselves on being tolerant of ethnic differences, but these differences are carefully managed through the policy of **multiculturalism**, defined by Fleras and Elliot as an official policy that "involves a process of engaging diversity as different yet equal" (2002, 16). Prime Minister Pierre Elliott Trudeau announced Canada's multicultural policy on 8 October 1971. However, multiculturalism has not been accepted by all Canadians. Himani Bannerji (2000, 44) argues that its ultimate purpose was to sidestep the real issues that were becoming more and more obvious among many new Canadians: poverty, unemployment, and racism. According to Eva Mackey, Canadian multicultural policy has not lived up to its promises. It has produced a core of "Canadian Canadians," with tiny segments of ethnic cultures that contribute to the value of the core. "Ordinary Canadians" are the *unmarked* category of the population, the ones who set the standards from which ethnic groups differ.

Furthermore, the meaning of "culture" changes within the policy of multiculturalism. Culture becomes merely a collection of fragments, such as "folklore, food, dancing, music, and customs," when it is used to refer to ethnic groups, whereas Canadian national culture is "conceived of as a whole, entire, way of life" (Mackey 1999, 90). The *Multiculturalism Act* was, in part, an effort to defuse Quebec's threat to separate from Canada, yet Quebec has rejected the implication that it is just another "ethnic" group. Although Canada claims to have two founding nations, French and British, many of the French in Quebec believe that they will never attain equality with the rest of Canada until they separate and form their own nation-state.

Education and the Nation-State

The creation and cultivation of inferior Others through such means as religion, racial classifications, empire building, and the marginalization of peoples based on their geographic origins is not in itself enough to build identity, loyalty, and devotion to the nation-state. A nation-state also requires institutions that integrate all of its members. For example, it needs to impose some sort of common language on its citizens; facilitate travel from one part of the state to another; establish national media to disseminate information from the state; and create a bureaucracy for collecting taxes and revenues, as well as a judicial system through which to maintain authority. It must establish a military and, perhaps most important, oversee an education system to train and socialize children to be "good citizens."

Ernest Gellner (1983) has suggested that today the control of education is even more important than the control of armed force. In order to regulate the national economy, a nation-state must build education systems that enable people to communicate with others in a common standardized language. People must be taught to deal with meanings rather than with things such as shovels or ploughs, and they must learn the complex processes through which buttons and other controls activate machines. In a complex industrial society, people cannot be taught in the family; they must be instructed by specialists operating within a national education system. Most important, students must be trained to identify themselves as members of a nation-state as well as to learn the identity of Others. They must be taught loyalty to their nation-state and be instructed in patriotism.

multiculturalism
A term that Eva Mackey defines as a Canadian policy in which all hyphenated cultures, such as African-Canadian and French-Canadian, are described and celebrated as part of a "cultural mosaic." Contrast with the "cultural melting pot" image that is used in the United States.

In Canada, the state sponsored residential schools in order to teach Indigenous children how to become Canadians. In *Victims of Benevolence: Discipline and Death at the Williams Lake Indian Residential School, 1891–1920* (1992), Elizabeth Furniss tells the stories of two young boys who died as a result of their experiences in a residential school in British Columbia. One ran away and was found dead at the side of a road; the other committed suicide. Residential schools, which were operated by churches, lasted in Canada for about a century. Indigenous children were removed from their homes and sent to these schools, where they were taught Christian beliefs and morality and were trained in agriculture, trades, and domestic skills. They were also taught that the beliefs of their elders and their parents were wrong and immoral. The residential schools assumed that Indigenous peoples were inferior to Euro-Canadians and that they needed the guidance of Euro-Canadians in order to survive. Through the residential school system, Indigenous children became wards of the Canadian state, and corporal punishment was used on children who made the mistake of reverting to their own languages or religious beliefs. When students actively resisted, the resistance was typically interpreted as confirmation that Indigenous people did not know what was best for them.

BEYOND THE BOOK 8.3

As discussed in this section, educational systems represent important means of cultivating model citizens. In the context of schools, we learn a socially sanctioned version of Canadian history, and we learn to be "proud Canadians." Think about your own experiences in the Canadian education system (elementary, high school, or post-secondary). If you did not go to school in Canada, then reflect on the education you received elsewhere. What are some of the activities, events, curriculum, or other factors that you feel have contributed to your notions of citizenship. What helped contribute to your identification with your nation-state?

Indigenous Peoples' Challenge to the Canadian State

Thus far, we have discussed the nation-state only from the perspective of its power over the people who live within its territory. Tania Li, whose work we also discussed in Chapter 3, argues that development projects carried out by the state are not simply neutral acts of concern by the state for the less fortunate; they are also a way for the state to manage its population. The state typically defines the people it wants to bring under its control as "primitive," "backward," and in need of "proper" housing and education. The critical focus of Li's study was "the ways in which meanings and outcomes are negotiated, albeit within an uneven field of power" (1999b, 297). Li wanted to learn more about "categories that manifestly do not fit, plans that fail, and compliance withheld or withdrawn [that] expose the fragile nature not only of government agencies promoting this or that development program but of the very idea of 'the state' as knower, arbiter, and provider for 'the people'" (1999b, 297).

Li's focus challenges those who would see the state as a source of unquestioned power and its citizens as mindless victims. People who become victims of the state's efforts to create a nation rarely accept their fate quietly. A good example of how marginalized peoples challenge the power of the state is happening right now in Canada.

Canada's history is laced with demonstrations of the power of the colonizers over the colonized. The first step in that was to define Indigenous peoples as Other in a way that allowed Europeans to take possession of the land, which they declared "empty" in the sense that no Europeans were living on it. Dara Culhane (1998) points out that from the first moment of contact, the position of the British colonizers was based on an assumed hierarchy wherein the British Crown asserted its will by declaring its sovereignty over Indigenous peoples and land, and then supported that assertion through armed force whenever necessary.

At first, the French and the British needed the Indigenous peoples; it was they who trapped fur-bearing animals and transported their skins to the trading posts, which brought great wealth to the European traders. Both the British and the French recruited the Indigenous peoples to fight their battles for them as they struggled to determine which European power would control what is now Canada. Because they depended on Indigenous peoples in these matters (and in others), the Europeans had to show them some respect, at least initially. The first treaties were signed in order to ensure peace and friendship between Indigenous peoples and Europeans. These early friendship treaties were between the French and the Mi'kmaq, Maliseets, Montagnaix-Naskapi, Huron, and Abenake; those same treaties were then transferred to the British under the Treaty of Utrecht in 1713. When Canada became a British colony, the Colonial Office issued the Royal Proclamation of 1763, which declared that Indigenous lands could be surrendered only through a legal treaty signed by a representative of the Crown and a representative of the appropriate Indigenous group.

After Confederation, "numbered treaties"—which focused on land far more than on friendship—were signed by the British and various First Nations. The meaning of these treaties is still being debated, and this has led to confrontations between First Nations and the Canadian state. Because the treaties were modelled more on agreements that First Nations had negotiated among themselves than on European models of legal contracts, the First Nations leaders who signed them did not believe they were surrendering their land or their rights; they also expected the agreements to be renewed periodically through the exchange of gifts. From the perspective of the Colonial Office, the treaties were intended to protect the "primitive" Indigenous peoples while they were being "civilized." From the viewpoint of the European settlers, the point was to get rid of "obstacles" to progress. As the population of European settlers grew and land became more important than people, the Canadian state began to deny the few promises it had made in the treaties.

© Jenna Young/Nishnawbe Aski Nation

Former Nishnawbe Aski Nation Grand Chief Stan Beardy (left) and former Missanabie Cree First Nation Chief Glenn Nolan with Treaty No. 9 Scroll.

Increasingly, Indigenous peoples have been refusing to surrender any more of their rights. When Clifford White and David Bob, members of the Saalequn First Nation in Nanaimo, British Columbia, went deer hunting in the spring of 1963, they were arrested and charged under the Game Act (passed by British Columbia in 1960) for hunting out of season. White and Bob argued that they were exercising their right to hunt and fish on unoccupied Crown lands throughout the entire year, a right guaranteed in an 1853 treaty and protected by the Indian Act. The matter went to court and became the first modern Indigenous rights case in British Columbia. A BC court found White and Bob guilty; however, the Supreme Court of Canada overturned that verdict and supported the Indigenous right to hunt and fish on unoccupied Crown lands. Legal tests for Indigenous rights continue to come before the courts. Some of the most important have involved the James Bay Cree.

The James Bay Cree have fought for years against the Quebec government and developers that want to build dams on Cree land (Figure 8.1). By the time Harvey Feit began his work among the Cree in the 1960s, railway and road networks

FIGURE 8.1 Map Showing Appropriation of Cree Land for Quebec Government Hydroelectric Projects

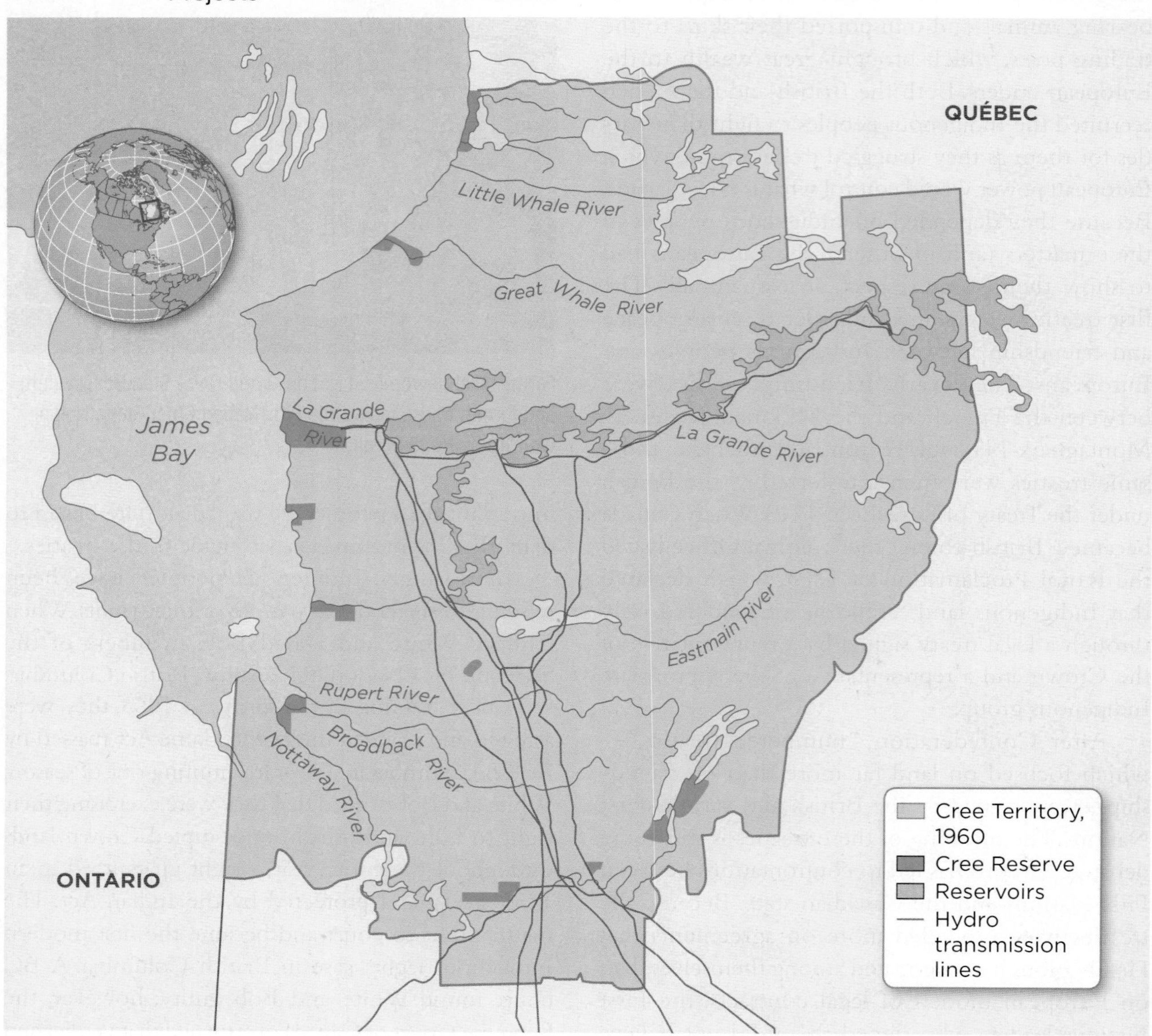

had already expanded into Cree territory, and logging and mining had already been established. The position of the Quebec government was that the Cree didn't need all their land because hunting was no longer a viable way of making a living and any "rational" person would much rather have a steady job. When the Quebec government set out to build a series of hydroelectric dams in the region, it did not involve the Cree in the planning, nor did it make any effort to assess the effects the project might have on the Cree. As soon as the government announced its plans, several young Cree leaders met and came to a consensus that the project would cause severe damage to their land and to the animals they hunted. Joined by the Inuit of northern Quebec, who would also be affected by the project, the Cree initiated a legal injunction in 1972 to stop construction.

The burden was now on the Cree to prove that they had a claim to the land and that the project would cause irreversible damage. They argued, among other things, that flooding the wetlands would destroy the habitat of many of the animals they hunted. The government argued that the Cree no longer lived primarily off the land; they had houses, clothing, and food that they bought from stores, and many had jobs. In November 1973, Judge Malouf ruled that the Cree and Inuit people did have Indigenous title to the land, that hunting was still very important to them, and that the province was "trespassing." Although the ruling was appealed, the Cree had demonstrated that they would hold firm in their demand to be consulted before development projects took place on land they deemed theirs. The James Bay and Northern Quebec Agreement (JBNQA) gave the Cree some power to back up their resolve.

In 1989, Hydro-Québec began the second phase of its project, on the Great Whale River. Again, the Cree went into action, only this time their strategy went beyond negotiations with the Quebec government. Cree representatives approached the potential buyers of Quebec hydro power in the United States and convinced them that Hydro-Québec would not make good economic or environmental sense. Cree spokespeople showed videos of their land to environmental groups and explained the damage that the hydroelectric project would do. The Cree even conducted their own polls to show politicians that voters in the United States favoured reducing their consumption of electric power over importing power from Quebec. When the New York State power company cancelled one of its contracts with Quebec, the province's premier conceded that the Great Whale River project would be cancelled. The conflict between the James Bay Cree and the Quebec government has not ended, but the Cree have greatly strengthened their position.

Ronald Niezen (2003) examines the concept of "**Indigenism**," a term he uses to "document the international movement that aspires to promote and protect the rights of the world's first peoples." The Cree are part of a much larger phenomenon that includes Indigenous peoples everywhere who are pursuing the right of self-determination through human rights standards. For most Indigenous peoples, this effort includes a rejection of state legal systems but not necessarily a rejection of the law, as the Cree example shows.

Question 8.4: How Do Engagements with Global Capitalism Affect Local Cultural Identities and Livelihoods?

Globalization is having a variety of cultural impacts, both positive and negative. The transnational flow of ideas, commodities, and images can help groups cultivate a sense of collective identity. Some commentators worry that globalization will challenge and perhaps even destroy the autonomy of nation-states and that it will homogenize the world's cultures. There is a pervasive worry, for example, that companies such as McDonald's and Starbucks will destroy local food cultures. These fears are not completely unfounded; however, many globalization theorists point out that such fears are essentialist and that they fail to take into account the unique ways in which cultures adapt to and transform new ideas.

Nuxalk Identity in an Age of Globalization

The Nuxalk are a First Nation in the Bella Coola Valley in central British Columbia (Figure 8.2). Nuxalk artists are renowned within their communities—and, indeed, internationally—for their intricately carved and painted spirit masks, and for other

Indigenism
Refers to an international, collaborative movement that aims to protect the rights and livelihoods of Indigenous peoples.

FIGURE 8.2 Nuxalk Territory in British Columbia

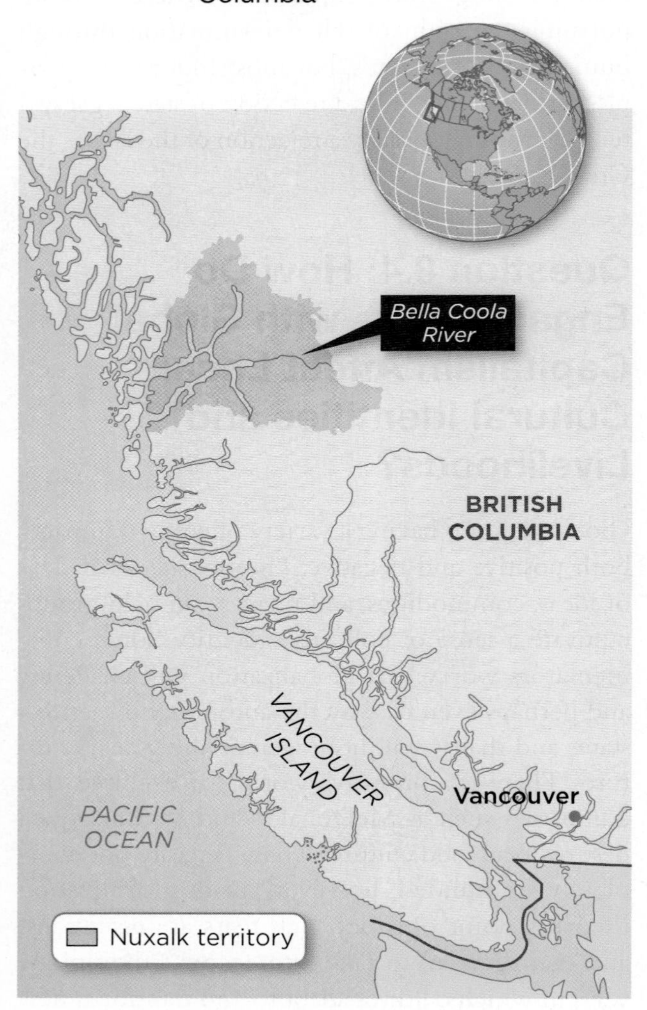

forms of art, such as totem poles, paintings, jewellery, and murals.

Canadian anthropologist Jennifer Kramer (2007) conducted participant observation and interviews with Nuxalk artists, elders, and art school representatives. She spent time in museums and galleries in Vancouver, talking to art dealers and curators about the display and sale of Nuxalk art to national and international audiences. She also talked to Nuxalk individuals with the goal of understanding how they felt about seeing their art displayed in national and international museums and art galleries, and how they interpreted the increasing commodification of their art.

More and more Nuxalk artists, in an effort to earn money for themselves and for their community, are putting images of spiritual figures on mugs, T-shirts, jewellery, and other tourist commodities. Others are selling their art to art dealers. Kramer set out to understand how the Nuxalk engage with the forces of globalization, including tourism, and with the increasing exposure for their art on the Internet and in the international art market.

When she entered the remote Bella Coola Valley by car for the first time to conduct fieldwork, Kramer was struck by the number of dangerous mountain switchbacks that face motorists. Often inaccessible in winter except by ferry or boat, the Nuxalk have historically been proud of their isolation from mainstream Canadian society. Throughout her research, Kramer adopted the metaphor of "switchbacks" to explain how her Nuxalk informants felt about the commodification and global flow of Nuxalk art. She argues that most Nuxalk oscillate between feelings of theft and feelings of pride. Many people felt that they were "selling out": that the commodification of their culture and heritage was devaluing the local meanings and interpretations of their art. Many were opposed to seeing important Nuxalk spiritual figures on mugs or T-shirts and were upset that most Westerners interpreted the images differently. Tourists, for instance, often buy T-shirts as souvenirs and as proof to friends and family that "I was there," or for their aesthetic value. Because tourists and art dealers map new meanings onto Nuxalk art and have different interpretations of its "value," many Nuxalk feel that the global flow of their art has resulted in a loss of cultural heritage.

Yet many of the same Nuxalk individuals that Kramer spoke with who were upset about the potential loss of Nuxalk traditions were also proud that their art was being displayed in national and international museums and that tourists showed so much interest in their work. Many felt that the global flow of their art outside their small community was a form of external validation for their culture as

© Seattle Art Museum, 91.1.35, Mask with Humanoid Face, Nuxalk, ca. 1880, alder, red cedar bark, cotton cloth, paint, 14 1/2 x 8 3/4 x 6 in; gift of John H. Hauberg; photographer: Paul Macapia.

Nuxalk mask.

Yonhap/Newcom/Alamy Live News

Canadian Olympic gold medallists Tessa Virtue and Scott Moir.

a whole. A sense of Nuxalk national identity was being cultivated through the flow and positive international consumption of their art.

Figure Skating, Globalization, and Canadian Identity

The ambiguous cultural effects of globalization can also be explored in the context of elite, high-performance sport. Karen McGarry (2015) conducts fieldwork among national and Olympic-level Canadian figure skaters, coaches, choreographers, journalists, corporate sponsors, and others involved in the production of Canadian figure skating. In Canada, figure skating is the second-ranked sport behind hockey in terms of television sponsorship and spectatorship. One reason for its popularity is that Canada has a long history of producing top world- and Olympic-level figure skaters. Olympic pair gold medallists, such as Jamie Salé and David Pelletier, or Tessa Virtue and Scott Moir, the 2010 and 2018 medallists in ice dancing, have become celebrity figures who derive much of their power as "national symbols" not simply by winning medals, but by circulating their bodies in international arenas of influence.

Canada has historically had an ambivalent relationship with the United States. On the one hand, Canadians live in a world saturated with American popular culture, from television shows to American-based retail outlets, food chains, and other cultural phenomena. Canada's geographical and social proximity to America has resulted in a pervasive fear of American economic and cultural influences, or what Kieran Keohane (1997) refers to as a "theft of national enjoyment." In other words, Canadians often construct themselves as victims in relation to the United States. Economically, we see this in contemporary debates and concerns relating to American appropriation of natural resources such as oil, water, and lumber, and in concerns over the impact of NAFTA. Yet at the same time, Canadians yearn for the approval of Americans on the international stage. So, for instance, Virtue and Moir, like other Canadian celebrities, become a symbol of "Canadianness" not simply because they won an Olympic gold medal, but also because their image has been heavily circulated in the United States: they appear on their own reality show, on talk shows and other television shows, in magazines, and in ice shows and other pop culture venues. The positive international (especially American) reception and consumption of their image has boosted Canadians' national pride. The global flow of commodities (such as Nuxalk art) and bodies (as in athletes) provides countries like Canada with a means of constructing and promoting a sense of national identity.

Intersections of Nationalism and Economic and Cultural Globalization in Vanuatu

As the Nuxalk example suggests, tourism is an aspect of contemporary life in which the simultaneous impacts of economic and cultural globalization are highly obvious. The recent growth of tourism has been staggering. By 2010, around 8 percent of the world's entire workforce was employed in the tourism sector, and this number continues to grow.

Tourism is a relatively new phenomenon. Lofgren (2002, 5) describes it as a mode of consumption "based on the idea of leaving home and work in search of new experiences, pleasures, and leisure." To some extent, our society is obsessed with the need for "experiences." We constantly ask one another, "How was it? How did it feel?" We are also entranced by the thought of being "on holiday," especially as its opposite, being "at work," becomes more burdensome. We often display our experiences as tourists and convey our ability to consume other cultures by buying a souvenir T-shirt. Given what we have discussed earlier in this chapter about T-shirts as global commodities, the centrality of the T-shirt (and other inexpensive souvenirs) to the tourist experience begins to hint at the fact that tourism is more than simply a leisure practice: it is an important indicator that globalization is linking us all together economically and culturally. By examining the local impacts of the global tourist economy on Vanuatu, we can begin to understand some of the ambiguous, or simultaneously positive and detrimental, effects that global forces are having on local cultures.

Vanuatu, formerly known as the New Hebrides, is an archipelago nation in the southwest Pacific that was jointly ruled by France and Britain from 1906 to 1980. In terms of climate, geography, and culture, Vanuatu has all of the "assets" required of the ideal tropical tourist destination: dense rainforests, swaying palm trees, warm turquoise seas, accessible coral reefs, and so-called "primitive" cultures. The tourism industry in Vanuatu has its roots in the 1960s, which the United Nations declared the "Decade of Development." During that decade, Vanuatu's first international resort, the French-owned Hotel Le Lagon, was built on a former plantation. Between 1970 and 1990, tourism arrivals by air grew from 5,000 to 25,000 per year (Douglas 1996, 216); today, around 7,000 tourists arrive by air each month, and every month another 15,000 tourists arrive by cruise ship for day visits. Tourism is the key economic sector in Vanuatu, accounting for 40 percent of the gross domestic product (GDP).

In its efforts to entice foreigners to visit, the Vanuatu Tourism Office has employed various slogans that draw from its imagined status as a land of idyllic, simple pleasures and the easy life: "The

FIGURE 8.3 Vanuatu

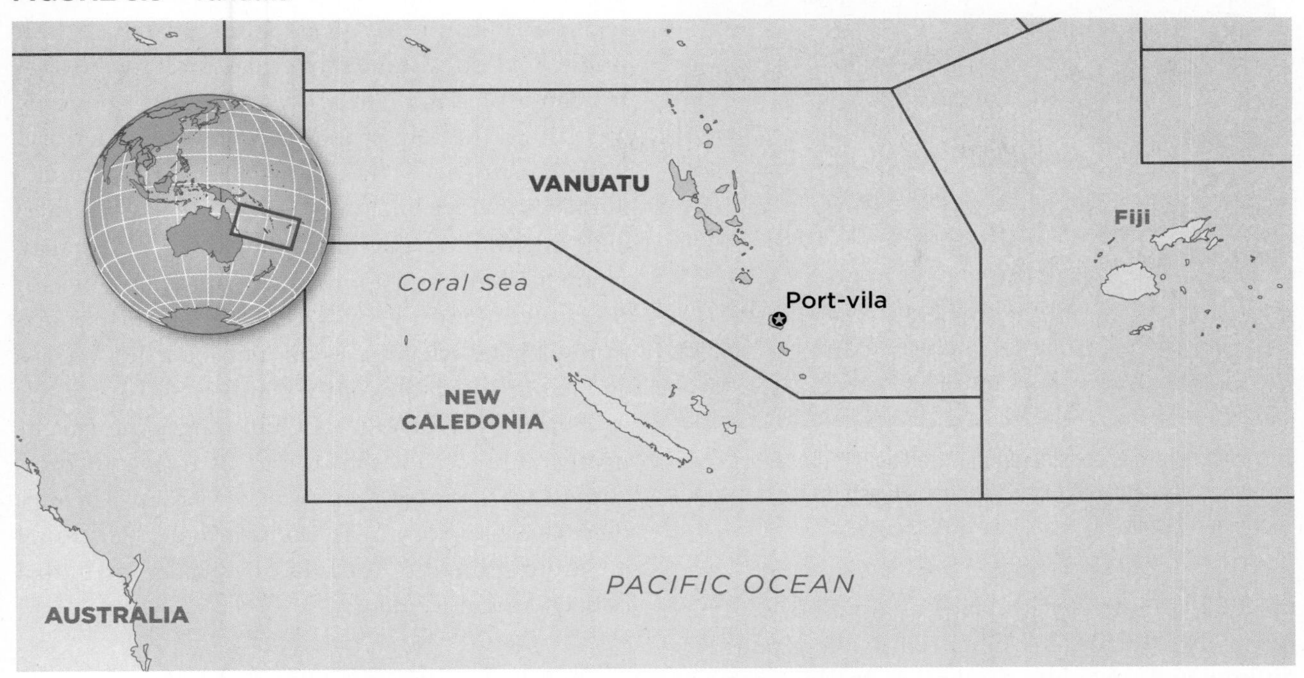

Untouched Paradise," "The Friendly Face of the Pacific," "Vanuatu: Discover What Matters." At the same time, many of the attractions and activities geared toward tourists highlight the "darker" aspects of traditional culture, such as cannibalism, tribal warfare, and sorcery. Tourists flow into Vanuatu with particular expectations about the local people and their culture. At the same time, ni-Vanuatu (the local name for Indigenous citizens) have their own expectations about what tourists are like, as well as their own sense of national identity, which has been forged at least in part by encounters with foreigners.

If, as a tourist in Vanuatu, you want to purchase an "Untouched Paradise" T-shirt as a souvenir, you will likely do so at one of the market stalls on the seafront in Port Vila, the national capital. You will find a vast array of cheap T-shirts (made in and imported from China), but few if any of the women working in the stalls will be wearing T-shirts. Rather, they will being wearing what they refer to as the "island dress," a long, loose, floral-patterned dress—similar to the Hawai'ian mumu—which they consider to be both their "national dress" and the most culturally appropriate and modest clothing for women. Maggie Cummings conducted fieldwork in Vanuatu on gender, dress, and national identity and found that women, especially single, childless young women living in the capital, embody a range of ambivalent and contradictory sentiments about national pride, the commodification of culture for tourist consumption, and the global flow of goods and fashions. The island dress was introduced in Vanuatu during the colonial period by British missionaries, who were scandalized by the scantily clad natives they were trying to convert. Wearing an island dress became a visible sign of one's conversion to Christianity—and to British gender norms, according to which women wore dresses while men wore the pants, both literally and figuratively. Most ni-Vanuatu today are devout Christians, and on achieving independence in 1980, ni-Vanuatu women took

The island dress is considered the "traditional" dress for women in Vanuatu, but many younger women prefer to wear shorts and T-shirts.

up the island dress with pride as a symbol of their uniquely Melanesian Christianity and of their difference from white foreigners. In this context, it makes sense that the island dress, as a symbol of cultural authenticity, would be the appropriate choice for women selling souvenirs to tourists, for whom consuming cultural authenticity is one of the most significant parts of the trip.

The young women Cummings worked with acknowledged the symbolic significance of the island dress (and the importance of wearing it in tourist encounters), but they were also drawn to the kinds of clothing they saw tourist women wearing—T-shirts and shorts rather than skirts. Young women who chose to wear shorts, however, were often chastised and even fined by their elders, pastors, and chiefs for trying to look "like foreigners." Furthermore, chiefs often accused young women of turning their backs on tradition and destroying *kastom* (traditional culture) when they chose to wear even long, modest surf shorts. They were too young to remember the struggle for independence.

Cummings (2008) highlights the ironies of ni-Vanuatu national identity in the context of increasing globalization. As Vanuatu attempts to increase visits (and revenues) from tourism, more and more ni-Vanuatu are moving to the capital, leaving behind—at least temporarily—their traditional subsistence horticultural livelihoods in search of wage labour in the tourist economy. Yet within the tourist industry, they must perform "ni-Vanuatu-ness" that is perceived as culturally authentic, which includes wearing the island dress and sometimes grass skirts. However, as ni-Vanuatu women admire and appropriate tourist fashions for themselves (and the availability of cheap imports from China is what makes this possible), they are less and less inclined to wear the "authentic" island dress in their daily lives. One of Cummings's informants neatly summarized the ironies of trying to dress authentically in contemporary Vanuatu: ironies that have their origin in the uneven intercultural encounters in the context of decades of global contact and movement:

> *When the missionaries came, they told us we were practically naked when we were wearing grass skirts, and that we had no shame. So we put on the island dress to show that we were good Christians, and now we wear it to show our respect for God and for our kastom. Now all these tourists, whose grandparents told our grandparents to cover up, they come and they flaunt themselves, half-naked on the beach in their bikinis and shorts. Meanwhile, we young women are told, now by our own elders, we have to cover up in the island dress to show our national pride!*

Cultural policy in Vanuatu (created, in part, by a former head of the Vanuatu Cultural Centre, Ralph Reganvanu, a ni-Vanuatu with a degree in anthropology) demands that all foreign anthropologists create a product or provide a service that will benefit the nation. Cummings therefore worked with local fieldworkers (who were trained in ethnographic research skills by the Vanuatu Cultural Centre) to produce a video for local audiences about the dress conundrum. One intention of the video was to bridge the gap between chiefs and young women—a gap that seemed to be widening in the face of increased tourism and globalization.

The Vanuatu Cultural Centre has created many important and innovative programs and policies based on ethnographic insights and collaborations with anthropologists (and historians and archaeologists). For instance, the Vanuatu National History Curriculum Project led to the publication of the three-volume Histri Blong Yumi Long Vanuatu (Lightner and Naupa, Our History, 2005), which aimed to provide a core high school history curriculum. One effect of the curriculum project, and related projects and policies, has been to ensure that young ni-Vanuatu are able to participate meaningfully in and contribute to the ongoing vibrancy and viability of *kastom* in a global world.

BEYOND THE BOOK 8.4

Although the context and consequences of tourism and globalization are obviously very different in Vanuatu and Canada, we might find some similarities as well. For example, what similarities do you see between the case of the Nuxalk and that of the Indigenous peoples of Vanuatu? Think, as well, about the various ways that different Canadian communities market themselves as tourist destinations. What similarities (and differences) do you see with the situation in Vanuatu?

APPLYING ANTHROPOLOGY

Global Challenges to the State

Canada's Indigenous peoples are not the only marginalized peoples who have challenged the power of the state. Anthropologist Laura Rival (2016) has worked with the Huaorani of Ecuador for decades, and she has documented, among other things, how they have responded to, and, at times, resisted, the exploration projects of oil companies and the destruction of the Amazon rainforest. She has also studied how the Huaorani understand notions of sustainability, and how they relate to, engage with, or initiate various development interventions on their land.

In March 1990, the Huaorani of Ecuador formed an organization called the *Organizacion de las Nacionalidades Huaorani de la Amazonia Ecuatoriana*, or ONHAE, to challenge *Texaco, Petroecuador, Unocal, Petro-Canada*, and other oil companies that were conducting large-scale exploration projects in the *Amazon*. When the oil companies built roads into the forest, settlers followed and began clearing the land in preparation for agriculture. Tourists then followed the settlers. One of the first steps taken by ONHAE was to secure title to Huaorani lands. The main problem in this was that the government retained all rights to subsurface minerals. The government immediately divided the Huaorani territory into numbered "blocks" and auctioned them off to the oil companies. Although ONHAE has signed contracts permitting oil exploration, it did secure a Huaorani voice in negotiations.

Then, in January 2000, the Huaorani joined with the powerful *Confederation of Indigenous Nations of Ecuador* (CONAIE) to block government cutbacks that had resulted in thousands of people losing their jobs and in an increase of 400 percent in the price of water. When the government tried to repress the resistance, CONAIE and other protesters blocked the roads to the capital city, Quito, and seized the Congress, proclaiming a new government. Without support from the urban labour movement, however, the protest came to an end. However, in early July of the same year, joined by labour unions and community organizations, the protesters closed the international airport, the banks, and government offices for two days. It is clear that when Indigenous peoples and urban workers join together, the state must pay attention.

In 1999, the government of Bolivia sold its water system in its second-largest city, Cochabamba, to *Bechtel Enterprises*, based in San Francisco. The price of water immediately rose by 100 percent, and the "water war" began. Indigenous groups joined with Bolivia's Federation of Workers and began to block the streets and hold public meetings to plan strategy. The protesters set 4 April as the date by which the government had to cancel the sale. The government held out until 10 April, but finally had to admit defeat.

Conclusions

How might we use an anthropological perspective on neoliberalism, economic globalization, and the nation-state outside the academy? What might we gain by taking an anthropological perspective on neoliberalism, globalization, and the nation-state? How can this perspective be put to use in the development of public policy? As we saw in section 8.4, one important contribution that anthropologists have made to globalization studies has been to extend the ethnographic focus not just to the economic impacts of globalization but also to the cultural ones, both negative and positive. As a cultural force, globalization is far from uniformly negative and homogenizing; in fact, transnational flows of ideas, images, and commodities often *activate* and *animate* new local cultural meanings and practices, even as they often devastate traditional modes of livelihood. Indeed, people often actively engage with the forces of globalization in an effort to revitalize and reconstruct a sense of collective identity. As anthropologists, we learn and experience first-hand how culture is both dynamic and shifting in the process.

As we saw in Section 8.1, nation-states exist, in part, to regulate and promote the growth of national economies. In fact, economic growth is clearly the primary directive of market-based industrial societies such as the United States, Canada, and Japan. We measure our economic progress by the growth of GDP, or the sum total of all goods and services transactions in a country in a given year. Failure to maintain GDP can have dire economic, social, and political consequences, including job losses, bank failures, and general political chaos.

So, governments devise economic policies to achieve economic growth. Often forgotten, however, is that market activities have effects that economic policy-makers do not consider. We noted some of these effects in Section 8.1, when we examined the real cost of a Snickers bar and the externalities relating to the cost of sugar, which include underpaid labour and environmental pollution. Yet policy planners rarely consider such externalities. As we saw with the effects of NAFTA on the Canadian garment industry, the local and everyday effects of international trade agreements are unlikely to be taken into account during the drafting of the agreements.

A major contribution of anthropology in the area of public policy and planning is that it makes people aware of market externalities and of the need to craft policies to eliminate or at least minimize those externalities. As we saw in section 8.3 and in the Applied example, challenges to the state, both from within and outside, are always possible, and an anthropological perspective can strengthen those challenges.

QUESTIONS: REVIEW

8.1 What role do nation-states play in market economies?

In this section, we define the concept of nation-state and provide an overview of its origins and different functions and powers (e.g., collecting taxes or tribute, or forming armies for the protection of citizens). Through contrasting examples from China, Japan, and early eighteenth-century European states, we outline some of the differences between ancient and modern states. The main goal of this section, however, is to outline how modern nation-states play a role in international economies. In the case study of the Snickers bar, for instance, we explored how the American government subsidizes national sugar production and how this affects the actual cost of a chocolate bar for consumers. Cost is also affected by market externalities.

Review Questions

1. What are the differences between a nation and a nation-state?

2. In what ways are modern states different from ancient ones?
3. List four examples of market externalities.

8.2 What is neoliberalism, and what role does it play in capitalist economic globalization?

This section examines the relationship between neoliberalism and the state and how most modern nation-states try to maintain a balance between regulation and non-interference. It introduces the concept of neoliberalism, and how it operates via mechanisms such as free trade agreements or through multilateral institutions and corporations such as the World Trade Organization. Ultimately, this section outlines the human cost of neoliberal agendas. Roxana Ng's work on the Canadian garment industry, for instance, explores how free trade agreements have resulted in longer working hours, lower wages, and job loss for many Canadians.

Review Questions

1. Adam Smith described the workings of the market as an "invisible hand." What does this mean?
2. According to Roxana Ng, what are some of the effects of neoliberalism in the context of the Canadian garment industry?
3. What is neoliberalism and when did it develop?

8.3 What is the relationship between the nation-state and identity under globalization?

Section 8.3 shifts away from an analysis of the intersections of nation-states and economics to explore the relationship between the nation-state and identity in the context of globalization. Nation-states have different means of identifying and defining citizenship (e.g., the census), but oftentimes, identifying who you are results in exclusionary tactics such as Othering and various forms of racism toward immigrants or minority groups. Because nationalism is a learned phenomenon, educational systems are also an important means by which people learn about notions of citizenship. Residential schools for Indigenous peoples, for instance, sought to deny Indigenous peoples access to their heritage and to cultivate Euro-Canadian ideologies and aesthetics as more authentically and appropriately "Canadian." People also resist and challenge the authority of the state to define rights and citizenship, as we saw with the example of the James Bay Cree and their fight to maintain their land. International movements like indigenism have developed to protect the rights of Indigenous groups throughout the world.

Review Questions

1. What is indigenism and what factors have contributed to its development and proliferation?
2. Discuss two examples of the ways in which Indigenous peoples have resisted state control.
3. What is Canadian multiculturalism and how has it led to conflict?

8.4 How do engagements with global capitalism affect local cultural identities and livelihoods?

Section 8.4 focuses on three ethnographic examples of the effects of globalization on cultural identities: the Nuxalk and the global interest in and commodification of their art; Canadian figure skating, and the ways in which a sense of identity is predicated upon the global (and especially American) acceptance and circulation of images of Canadian skaters; and, finally Vanuatu, where the "island dress" worn by ni-Vanuatu women acquires ambiguous meanings predicated upon complicated relationships to colonialism, Christianity, and other factors.

Review Questions

1. What does the concept of "switchback" mean in relation to the Nuxalk and their engagement with the global art world?
2. How is a sense of Canadian identity produced in Canadian figure skating?
3. What are the varied meanings of "island dress" in Vanuatu?

CRITICAL THINKING QUESTIONS

1. In Section 8.2, we noted how neoliberalism manifests itself in the context of various nation-states. Describe three ways in which neoliberalism affects Canadian politics, economics, or social life differently than in the United States.
2. From a student's perspective, what are some examples of how principles of neoliberalism affect your education? How does neoliberalism operate on your university or college campus?
3. Sections 8.3 and 8.4 include examples of the ways in which Indigenous peoples have resisted state control. Describe two other cultural or ethnic groups in Canada that have resisted the state's homogenizing tendencies. How do they seek to define their sense of identity against that of "mainstream" Canadian society?
4. Discuss two examples of the cultural impact of globalization within our popular culture. Examples could relate to music, art, and clothing, among other phenomena.

KEY TERMS

economic systems (p. 220)
free trade (p. 222)
globalization (p. 214)
Indigenism (p. 233)
market externalities (p. 218)
multiculturalism (p. 229)
nation (p. 216)
nation-state (p. 216)
nationalist populist movements (p. 223)
neoliberalism (p. 221)
transnational (p. 223)

CHAPTER 9

Resolving Conflict

© Bilderbuch/Design Pics/Thinkstock

Canadian memorials to fallen soldiers, such as the Canadian National War Memorial, often evoke the sentiment "Lest We Forget." In the second half of the twentieth century, Canada saw itself as a peacekeeper nation, striving to prevent or diminish violent conflict. However, as Richler notes in the chapter-opening epigraph, Canada more recently became a "warrior nation," especially after assuming a combat role in Afghanistan. How do Canadians make sense of our ambivalent relationship with war?

Often it is illuminating to see how history puts on different disguises even as the underlying habits of a place are fundamentally unaltered. This is to say either that Canada today is a "warrior nation"—that the peacekeeping version of Canada was a fifty-year aberration and a public that believes otherwise genuinely has ignored Canada's long military history—or that the Canada with an innate disposition toward "soft power," "making a difference" and the sort of peacekeeping work that is now so disparaged is the underlying constant and the "warrior nation" is the fiction.

—Noah Richler, *What We Talk about When We Talk about War* (2012)

PROBLEM 9

How do societies give meaning to and justify various forms of conflict resolution, both peaceful and violent?

Introduction

Justifying Violence and Imagining Peace

We tend to think of violence and peace as conditions that are universally understood, transparent, and commonsense: that violence is an innate human tendency and that peace is simply the absence of violence. Anthropologists, however, may well find it more useful to focus on peacemaking and violence as two sides of the coin of conflict resolution. As with all human behaviours and experience, violence and peace are processes to which we collectively assign meaning in particular contexts. For instance, as Noah Richler points out in the epigraph to this chapter, when Canada sends its soldiers into conflict zones, their role can be understood—and *has* been understood—as peacekeeping or as war-making, depending on the dominant narratives of national identity at the time.

Many of the problems we have explored in this text may give rise to conflicts—be it over resources, over identity, or over inequality or injustice—and these conflicts demand some sort of resolution. Sometimes conflict results in collective violence: think, for instance, of the Trail of Tears discussed in Chapter 3 or Sanday's analysis of fraternity gang rape in Chapter 7. Sometimes more peaceful forms of conflict resolution are favoured, as among the Ju/'hoansi, or in Wovoka's Ghost Dance revitalization movement, discussed in Chapter 4. To understand why humans choose one form of conflict resolution or another, we must think about how humans make sense of and justify violence and peace.

Violence, "a category in between peaceful disputing, and major planned warfare and fighting" (Strathern and Stewart 2002, 1), may seem to be intrinsic to human societies. It is, in fact, difficult to find societies that do not sanction violence for one reason or another. But why is collective violence nearly universally sanctioned? Some suggest that human beings have an innate instinct toward aggression and that the roots of war and collective violence lie somewhere in the biological mechanisms that animals and humans have in common. According to this view, violent conflict is part of human nature. Others reject this explanation as simplistic: collective violence, they say, is above all a cultural construction whose roots lie in the human mind, not in the genes. Bettina Schmidt and Ingo Schroder (2003), for instance, write that anthropologists for decades have been pushing back against early twentieth-century thinkers who analyzed conflict as reflective of a genetic tendency toward competition or aggression. That older trend is perpetuated to this day by media accounts of geneticists who continue to search for "warrior genes" or other biological causes of violent behaviour (Tiihonen et al. 2015). However, as Schroder and Schmidt (2003, 2) maintain, evidence from both biological anthropology and ethnographic research indicates that "there are numerous non-violent avenues to conflict resolution (relocation, exchange, territoriality)." Indeed, most intra- and inter-cultural conflict is settled in peaceful ways that emphasize prevention, negotiation, and various other compensatory strategies.

There is compelling ethnographic and historical evidence that "humans have a solid capacity for getting along with each other peacefully, preventing physical aggression, limiting the scope and spread of violence, and restoring peace following aggression" (Fry 2007, 21). We tend to overlook and underappreciate this capacity precisely because violence is exceptional and aberrant. Because it is those things, it commands our scrutiny, attention, and concern. Put another way, "the view that [violence and] warfare is inevitable because it is an immutable part of human nature is also a cultural convention masquerading as fact" (Sahlins 2008, quoted in Lohmann 2014, 255). The ethnographic realities of conflict resolution suggest that "neither fully peaceful nor fully violent outcomes are actually the norm" (Strathern and Stewart 2011, ix). As anthropologists, we must endeavour to understand the factors that lead to or favour one form of conflict resolution over the other in different circumstances.

The fact that human beings construct systems of meaning to justify violent conflict and to distance themselves from its consequences suggests that this has little to do with a natural aggressive impulse. Acts of collective violence are rationalized as purposeful, noble, or inevitable, not as evidence of wanton cruelty. The task is to discover how societies construct meanings for violent conflict that mask its consequences and that convince people it is right and proper.

It is equally important to understand what peace is and how it is established and maintained. As anthropologist Brian Ferguson (2008, 46–47) has argued, "peace is more than the absence of war." Rather, peace is an active social process, one that must be first imagined and then acted upon. Lohmann (2014) defines *peace*, therefore, as

> *A group activity, carried on by members of one community toward members of another community, in which the primary purpose is to maintain mutual benefit by successfully deploying means for enhancing political relations and preventing violence, by either directing contacts with goodwill or avoiding one another with an attitude of peace. (259)*

Just as violence must be justified, peace must be imagined and maintained; both are deeply social and political processes.

To make sense of these issues, the first question to ask is how societies develop a bias in favour of collective violence. In other words, what kinds of meanings are constructed to encourage people to commit violence against others? Then, if there are societies without collective violence, how do they create a bias against it? How do they create peace? If violent conflict is not natural and inevitable but culturally constructed, it may be possible to learn from societies in which there is little if any violence. This focus raises the following question: Are there significant social, economic, or political differences between violent and peaceful societies? Beyond that, what is the relationship between violence and the nation-state? Since collective violence is sanctioned in North American societies, it is instructive to ask how we have created a bias toward violent conflict and constructed meanings that allow us to contemplate, plan for, and pursue the destruction of millions of people in other nations. We will go on to explore the potential pitfalls and possible insights to be gained by conducting participant observation of, and during, violent conflicts. Finally, as a conclusion to the chapter and to the text as a whole, we will think about the roles that anthropologists can play in promoting peaceful forms of conflict resolution to the kinds of problems we have discussed throughout this book.

QUESTIONS

9.1 How do societies create a bias in favour of collective violence?
9.2 How do societies create a bias in favour of peaceful conflict resolution?
9.3 What are the economic, political, and social differences between peaceful and violent societies?
9.4 What is the relationship between violence and the nation-state?
9.5 How is it possible to justify the creation of weapons of mass destruction?
9.6 How do anthropologists do fieldwork in the midst of violent conflict?

Question 9.1: How Do Societies Create a Bias in Favour of Collective Violence?

Horses, Rank, and Warfare among the Kiowa

One way societies create a bias toward collective violence is by rewarding it. For example, among the Native Americans of the western plains, a man gained status by raiding other groups for horses. Horses symbolized wealth, and in many groups a man's importance and sense of masculinity was measured by the number of horses he owned and gave to others as gifts.

Horses are not indigenous to North America; they were brought to the continent by the Spaniards in the 1500s. Native American groups such as the Kiowa captured some horses and acquired others in trade with the Spaniards. The Kiowa also obtained horses by attacking other Native American groups with horse-raiding parties of as many as 30 men. The objective of these raids was to secure as many of the enemy's horses as possible and, as well, to demonstrate bravery. Among the Kiowa, rank was determined in two ways: by the number of horses a man possessed and by the honours accruing to him in warfare.

Kiowa society was divided into four ranks, or grades. In the top rank were *ongop*, men who were generous, who held considerable wealth, and, most important, who had distinguished themselves in war. In the second rank were *ondeigupa*, men who had property (especially horses), who were generous, but who had not yet distinguished themselves in war. The lower ranks of Kiowa society were occupied by *keen* or *dupom*, people who were poor, propertyless, or helpless.

To rise in status, a young Kiowa male needed to acquire a horse. Often, he began his climb through the ranks of Kiowa society by borrowing a horse from a kinsperson to go on a raid, hoping to repay the loan with another horse he had captured. With a horse of his own, he could participate in more raids, gradually obtaining enough horses to rise to the rank of *ondeigupa*, or, as the Kiowa put it, "rise out of the bush of *keen*." Several years of raiding might bring him 20 or 30 horses, at which point people would begin speaking of him with respect.

To rise to the top rank of *ongop*, however, also required the accumulation of honours won in war. The Kiowa had a very elaborate system of battle honours divided into three groups of brave deeds, with group I being the most honoured. Counting first coup, for example, involved charging the enemy alone and striking one of them with a stick. The number of feathers a man wore in his headdress was a measure of his heroic exploits.

Anthropologist Bernard Mishkin (1940) estimates that about 10 percent of the men would rise to the top rank of Kiowa society by obtaining a significant number of horses and accumulating sufficient battle honours. In this way, the Kiowa rewarded aggressive behaviour and bravery in battle.

In the late nineteenth century, Kiowa society underwent tremendous upheaval in the wake of incursions, often violent, by Euro-American settlers and the US government. The influx of settlers decimated the buffalo herds, and ethnologist James Mooney reported that by the summer of 1879, many Kiowa had been forced to eat their horses to survive (Mooney 1898. cited in Lassiter 1998, 91). The significance of the Kiowa warrior ranks in daily life dwindled throughout the early twentieth century as the Kiowa were forced by the US government to settle on reservation lands and to further assimilate (although there was a brief renaissance during the 1940s, when many Kiowa fought for the US armed forces in the World War II). Today, many Kiowa live on Kiowa tribal lands in what is now Oklahoma. A visit to the Kiowa Tribe's website shows that the symbolic significance of the warrior to Kiowa identity remains strong: the official Kiowa Tribe logo features an armed Kiowa warrior on a horse, as well as various symbols of many of the more peaceful aspects of Kiowa society, including the Sun Dance Ritual (https://kiowatribe.org).

Good Hosts among the Yanomamö

Another way societies create a bias in favour of collective violence is by making it a necessary means for protecting valuable resources. As we discussed in Chapter 2, a classic (but contentious) example is the Yanomamö of Venezuela (Figure 9.1). The Yanomamö live in villages of 40 to 250 people and practise slash-and-burn (swidden) agriculture, living primarily on the crops they grow in their gardens.

BEYOND THE BOOK 9.1

THE CANADIAN PRESS/Andrew Vaughan

Mi'kmaq Warrior Society at shale gas protests in New Brunswick.

Like the Kiowa, many other Indigenous peoples of North America had warrior societies: groups of (usually) men tasked with the protection of their people. In Canada (as in the United States), such warriors were at the forefront of struggles against early settler colonialism and the incursions of the Canadian state (warriors would, however, also be involved in peacemaking efforts and treaty negotiations). In response to these struggles over sovereignty, the Canadian government made concerted (often violent) efforts to pacify and discredit such warrior societies, miscasting them as savage or wild. Today, the Indigenous warrior (as both a symbol and a legitimate identity based in Indigenous worldviews) has become a powerful political force in relations between Indigenous peoples and the state, especially in efforts to resolve conflicts over land rights and the environment. For instance, in 2013, the Mi'kmaq Warrior Society played a key role in shale gas protests near Rexton in Kent County, New Brunswick. However, as Rob LeBlanc (2015) points out in his analysis, the role of Indigenous warriors in such protests is often characterized simply as "the muscle"—they are viewed as stereotypically violent, hyper-masculine, and aggressive. How might an ethnographically informed understanding of the historical and cultural significance of warrior societies lead to a reframing of such protests?

1. Watch the following interview about the Rexton protests between non-Indigenous news anchor Harry Forestell and Indigenous governance scholar Taiaiake Alfred: https://www.cbc.ca/news/canada/new-brunswick/nb-newsmaker-oct22-1.2159466. How do stereotypes of "the warrior" shape the way the protests are viewed by many non-Indigenous observers? How does Alfred challenge these stereotypes?
2. Do a search on warriors and protests. In what contexts do these two terms tend to come together? How is the warrior "used" both symbolically and practically, in the examples you find? How might anthropologists contribute to more informed conversations about this topic, especially with the goal of resolving conflict?
3. TimeTraveller is an animated Web series about a young Mohawk bounty hunter in the year 2121 who uses a virtual reality game to "time travel" through history. In the first episode, he searches the term "Mohawk Warrior." Watch the episode, then list and discuss the various contested meanings of "Indigenous warrior" that appear throughout: http://www.timetravellertm.com/episodes/episode01.html.

FIGURE 9.1 Yanomamö Territory

Warfare between villages is endemic among the Yanomamö. Anthropologist Napoleon Chagnon, who conducted fieldwork with them from the mid-1960s until the latter half of the 1990s, reports that one village of 200 people was attacked 25 times during a 15-month period and that 10 people were killed, representing a loss of 5 percent of the village population. He estimates that 20 to 25 percent of all male deaths are the result of warfare.

For the Yanomamö, women and children are valuable resources. The men believe that to protect themselves and their resources, they must be fierce, and raiding another village is one way for them to demonstrate their ferocity. Raids may be conducted to avenge the death of a village member, be it at the hands of an enemy village or as the result of an act of sorcery by an enemy. Raids may also be undertaken to capture women or children. Violence can take the form of inviting members of another village to a feast and—usually with the aid of allies from another village—killing the guests and abducting their women. Raiding by other villages forces them to move fairly frequently, and sometimes they take refuge from their enemies in the villages of their allies. This practice is risky, however, because host villages generally expect sexual access to the wives of their guests or expect unmarried female guests to marry men of their village. These expectations often lead to open hostilities between hosts and guests.

Expressions of ferocity may arise among village members as well. For example, men often vent anger and demonstrate their ferocity by beating their wives. A man who accuses another of cowardice or of making excessive demands for goods or women may challenge his opponent to a chest-pounding duel in which they take turns hitting each other in the chest as hard as they can. The duel generally ends when one of the contestants is too injured to continue. Fights with clubs are another form of settling disputes between men, although these generally result in free-for-alls, which can be deadly.

In this environment, where each man strives to acquire women from others, it is necessary to adopt an antagonistic stance toward others. This stance, in turn, encourages the development of what the Yanomamö call *waiteri* (ferocity). The *waiteri* complex, as Chagnon calls it, is evidenced in ways other than direct conflict. The Yanomamö express it in their origin myth, which tells how the original people were created from the blood of the moon, which had been shot with an arrow by beings who believed that their children's souls were being devoured by the moon. The first Yanomamö born of the blood of the moon were exceptionally fierce and waged constant war on one another.

The Yanomamö also socialize male children to be aggressive and hostile. Boys are teased to strike tormentors and to bully girls. At one gathering of two villages attended by Chagnon, the men were expected to satisfy their grievances against each other with a chest-pounding duel. Prior to the duel the men gathered all the boys between the ages of 8 and 15 and forced them to fight each other. At first, says Chagnon, the boys were reluctant and tried to run away, but their parents dragged them back and insisted that they hit each other. At the first blows the boys cried, but as the fight progressed, fear became rage, and they ended up pounding each other while screaming and rolling in the dirt, to the cheers and admiration of their fathers.

Constructing Religious and Political Justifications for Violence

Another way to justify violence is by framing it as a cosmic struggle between good and evil. Most modern religions have sacred texts describing violent confrontations between the forces of good and the forces of evil. *The Book of Revelation*, with its description of the forces of Satan and the ultimate battle between good and evil, provides one of the most powerful (and most violent) metaphors of war and redemption in Western literature. As Elaine Pagels (1995) notes, the characterization of one's enemies as "Satanic" and of one's own as God's people has long been a formula for justifying hatred and mass slaughter.

So it should not be surprising that people use religious rhetoric to justify violent acts, but more than that is often at work. When devout adherents to Christianity, Judaism, Sikhism, Buddhism, or Islam commit violent acts in the name of God or some spiritual mission, they are often responding to social, political, or economic grievances as well. Osama bin Laden sought to establish an Islamic caliphate (a form of government), but he was also protesting the Israeli occupation of Palestinian territories, the stationing of US troops in Saudi Arabia, and the Americans' support for oppressive governments in the Middle East.

After he was elected US president in 2016, Donald Trump's anti-immigration rhetoric and his insular, nationalist "America first" policy appealed to many alt-right movements and conservative Christian voters who wanted to preserve, among other things, a white, Judeo-Christian version of America. Many argue that Trump's presidency has provided many fringe groups with a quasi-legitimate platform that has escalated violent behaviour. In

Ryan M. Kelly/The Daily Progress via AP, File

A vehicle crashes into protesters demonstrating against white nationalists in Charlottesville, Virginia, on 12 August 2017.

2017, white supremacists Richard Spencer and Jason Kessler organized a "Unite the Right" rally in Charlottesville, Virginia. The attendees were an ad hoc group of white supremacist organizations, fundamentalist Christians, and other alt-right groups. The goal of the rally was to protest the removal of Confederate monuments in public spaces in the American South. Public addresses at the event were replete with inflammatory anti-immigrant, anti-Muslim, and anti-Semitic rhetoric, which led to violence aimed at protesters that left one person dead and 19 injured.

Of course, violence is not the only response to cosmic conflict and social grievances, yet all religions have their violent militants. On 20 March 1995, five members of the Aum Shinrikyo movement, all of whom had scientific training, walked into the Tokyo subway and, with sharpened umbrellas, punctured plastic bags filled with deadly sarin gas, killing 12 people and poisoning more than 5,500. The group's members explained to Mark Juergensmeyer (2003) that Aum Shinrikyo represented for them a critique of Japanese religion and the "hierarchical" Japanese social system. The movement was founded by Shoko Asahara based on the idea that there would occur a world catastrophe—World War III or "Armageddon"—in which the forces of good and evil would confront each other and members of Aum Shinrikyo would survive.

Asahara justified his acts by reference to Tibetan Buddhism and the concept of phoa. Instead of focusing on the effect that killing has on the killer's moral purity, this doctrine focuses on the one who is killed and on the merit that comes after death. According to Asahara, if a person is a scoundrel or is part of an evil social system, he or she is accumulating negative karmic debt. Killing such people represents a mercy killing that allows their souls to move to a higher plane than if they continued to exist in sin.

Juergensmeyer (2003) asks under what conditions people are likely to embrace religious justifications for violence. He suggests that agresssors who locate their struggle in the cosmic realm are elevating its importance above local concerns and invoking legendary battles between good and evil. Osama bin Laden justified violence by projecting the struggle as one between the forces of Islam and those trying to destroy it. The rhetoric of wars of good versus evil is even part of the US political mainstream, where both presidents and the mass media readily deploy terms such as "axis of evil."

There is real power, suggests Juergensmeyer, in elevating a political conflict to a cosmic war. To live in a state of war, he writes,

> *is to live in a world in which individuals know who they are, why they have suffered, by whose hand they have been humiliated, and at what expense they have persevered. The concept of war provides cosmology, history, and eschatology and offers the reins of political control. Perhaps most important, it holds out the hope of victory and the means to achieve it. In the images of cosmic war this victorious triumph is a grand moment of social and personal transformation, transcending all worldly limitations. One does not easily abandon such expectations. To be without such images of war is almost to be without hope itself. (2003, 158)*

Question 9.2: How Do Societies Create a Bias in Favour of Peaceful Conflict Resolution?

Anthropologist Thomas Gregor (1990) suggests that since war is so widespread in human societies, the task of the social scientist is not so much to explain war as to explain peace. Peaceful societies, he says, are difficult to find. By peaceful, he means a society that is not involved in internal collective violence and in which there is little interpersonal violence. A peaceful society has no special roles for warriors and places a positive value on nonaggressive behaviour and the peaceful resolution of conflict. Societies that have been characterized as relatively peaceful include the Ju/'hoansi, the Semai of Malaysia, and the Xinguano of the Amazon.

Characteristics of Peaceful Societies

Peaceful societies avoid conflicts over material resources through a strong emphasis on sharing and cooperation. It is understood that everyone in the group has a legitimate claim to what the group possesses. Among the Ju/'hoansi, the person whose arrow kills an animal is considered to be the owner of the game, but he is obligated to distribute it. The Ju/'hoansi will share arrows with the understanding that if they kill an animal with an arrow given to them by someone else, they will give the owner the game to distribute. This practice also works to spread out the responsibility for meat sharing and the glory (and perhaps the hostility) that accompanies meat distribution.

The Semai of Malaysia are known for their nonaggressiveness and avoidance of physical conflict. The approximately 15,000 Semai live in hamlets of fewer than 100 people each. Understanding Semai nonviolence, says anthropologist Clayton Robarchek (1990), requires understanding the Semai notion of *pehunan*, a state of being in which a person is unsatisfied in regard to some need or want, such as food or sex. The Semai believe that to refuse a request and deny a person a need intensifies the danger to both the individual and the group; for that reason, the group is obligated to help. The idea of *pehunan* encompasses a depiction of the community as nurturant caregivers. Instead of understanding that each person is obligated to meet his or her own needs, the Semai believe that all members of the community are obliged to help and give nurturance to others. Thus, Semai values stress affiliation, mutual aid, and the belief that violence is not a viable option for settling disputes.

Another way that people in peaceful societies create a bias against violence is by condemning those who boast or who make claims that can be interpreted as a challenge to others. Among the Ju/'hoansi, for example, no one is praised for gathering food or making a kill, and people go out of their way to minimize their accomplishments. Those who make boastful claims are ridiculed. Anthropologist Richard Lee (1969) painfully learned this lesson himself when, to show his appreciation to the Ju/'hoansi for the help they had given him, he brought a fine ox to be slaughtered and distributed at a Christmas feast. The Ju/'hoansi, much to Lee's chagrin, ridiculed the ox, claiming it was thin and unappetizing. Lee later realized that they were acting toward him as they would have to one of their own. They were letting him know that he wasn't as important as the gift and the killing of the ox made him think he was.

Thomas Gregor (1990) says that villagers in the Xingu basin of the Amazon maintain harmony by purposely sanctioning village monopolies in the production of certain goods such as shell belts, stone axes, salt, cotton, fish spears, and ceramic pots. In this way, each village has something that other villages need. The villages therefore maintain good relations, since to alienate another village might deprive one's own village members of a desired good. Moreover, trade is positively valued in itself. When villagers are asked why they don't make the goods they need themselves, they reply that doing so might anger those who do make them. Or they may claim that they do not have the knowledge to produce the items. (When temporarily cut off from a supply, though, they seem to learn how to make or acquire them very quickly.) Gregor says it is unlikely that any village could not produce the goods desired: marriage between groups is common, so each village contains people with the skills of other villages.

The Xinguanos place a strong negative value on aggression and on things that symbolize aggression. Killing is wrong because it produces blood; even animal blood is considered defiling. Most game animals are considered inedible, and even fish must be well cooked so that there is no blood. The Xinguanos also hold strong negative stereotypes of aggressive groups. They consider non-Xingu Indians to be "wild Indians" who are violent, beating their children, raping their women, and shooting arrows at white men's planes. The wild Indian has almost the status of an animal and represents everything a Xinguano does not want to be. When Xingu villages have been the object of aggression by others, they have defended themselves, but successful warriors take no trophies and are given no special honour. In fact, they have to take special medicine to cleanse themselves of the defilement of the blood of those killed.

Peaceful societies also minimize violence and conflict through ceremony. The Ju/'hoansi believe that everyone has "medicine" or power. In the same way that nearby Bantu tribes have witchcraft and sorcery, and Europeans have pills and syringes, the Ju/'hoansi have *n/um*, a substance they say lies in the pit of the stomach. *N/um* has the capacity to keep people healthy and to help cure people who are sick. Most important, *n/um* can be transferred from someone who is acting as a healer to others through the medium of the trance dance, their most common ceremony. The idea of the dance is for a person to "heat up" his or her *n/um* by dancing; as the person dances, the *n/um* in the stomach is vaporized and travels up the spinal cord into the brain, which causes the dancer to go into a trance. The dancer then goes from person to person laying on hands and transferring power to those who are touched, thereby enabling them to ward off sickness and death. Anyone can be a healer among the Ju/'hoansi; in a lifetime, each person is likely to serve as a healer at least once.

The trance dance has meanings that go beyond the power to heal, however. Some Ju/'hoansi are thought to have special powers that allow them to see the ghosts of dead ancestors who hover around the fires, to see distant scenes, to see through things, and, in special cases, to change themselves into lions and stalk the veldt in search of human prey. Trance dances are most frequent when large numbers of people come together (from about once a month in small groups, up to four times a week in large camps) and during certain occasions such as when visitors arrive in a camp, when meat is present, or when someone is sick. The gathering of large numbers of people, the presence of meat, and the arrival of new people are all occasions that, one way or another, create the potential for interpersonal conflict. The fact that trance dances are more frequent during such times seems to indicate that they may serve to heal social conflict as well as individual maladies. By bringing people together in the ceremony, by sharing *n/um*, and through the ritual recognition of common threats, the trance dance unites people and symbolizes the relationship between group harmony and individual well-being.

In sum, peaceful societies create a bias against violence by sharing, by valuing nonaggressive behaviour, by building relations of dependence between individuals and groups, and by engaging in collective behaviours that promote harmony. These efforts are not, of course, always successful, and even among some societies characterized as peaceful, there is violence. Lee (1984, 148) collected accounts of 22 homicides among Ju/'hoansi groups during a 35-year period from 1920 to 1955, but he found little if any sanctioned group violence.

Question 9.3: What Are the Economic, Political, and Social Differences between Peaceful and Violent Societies?

Thomas Hobbes, a seventeenth-century philosopher, proposed that human beings in their natural state, without government or laws, are driven by greed and the quest for gain. Without some common power to keep them in awe, Hobbes said, they live in a state of war, with every person against every other person. In his book *Leviathan*, Hobbes famously describes his vision of life before civilization as "solitary, poore, nasty, brutish, and short" (Hobbes[1651]1881, 94–96).

Hobbes saw human beings as having a natural inclination to be violent, an inclination that can be controlled only by some form of centralized authority. However, as anthropologists have discovered, societies with little formal government, such as the Ju/'hoansi and the Semai, are among the most peaceful in the world. Furthermore, these peaceful societies are small in scale and their members make their living primarily by hunting and gathering or by swidden agriculture. Most are relatively isolated and lack formal mechanisms for resolving conflict once it begins. There are no courts, no police, no jails, and no formally sanctioned threats of violence, even against wrongdoers. Since there is little that people in these societies can do once violence begins, they go to great lengths to avoid it.

Had Hobbes (1881) known the Yanomamö, however, he might have found verification for his vision of a stateless society, "where every man is enemy to every man." Yanomamö social and economic life closely resembles that of the Semai, and they live in virtually the same environment and are neighbours of the peaceful Xinguano. But Yanomamö society creates attitudes that favour collective violence as a means to protect its women and children. In this case, the lack of any centralized control or formal mechanisms for putting an end to conflict results in unrestrained violence rather than the avoidance of conflict.

The Need to Protect Resources

In societies without any form of centralized control and a bias toward collective violence, such as that of the Yanomamö, individuals must protect their own resources through force. Because the Yanomamö do not effectively control intravillage conflict, men of their own as well as other villages are constantly seeking to seduce one another's wives. Consequently, the men, individually or in groups, must build a reputation for fierceness in order to protect themselves and their families. Failure to control conflict and the need for men to build a reputation for aggressiveness in order to protect their resources combine to produce a society that places a positive value on violent behaviour.

The conditions that give rise to violent conflict among the Yanomamö are not unlike those that promote violence in street gangs in the United States. When he worked in the 1960s with the Vice Lords, a Chicago street gang (or "club," as they preferred to call themselves), Lincoln Keiser (1968) concluded that boys joined gangs because alone they could not protect themselves from shakedowns or safeguard their interests in girls. Where the Yanomamö encouraged *waiteri*—fierceness—the Vice Lords valued heart—a willingness to follow any suggestion regardless of personal risk. Where a Yanomamö demonstrated fierceness through chest-pounding duels, axe fights, and raids against enemy villages, members of street gangs in Chicago confirmed their heart in gang fights. Street gangs even formed alliances against other gangs, as do Yanomamö villages with one another. The similarities in the dynamics and values of violent conflict among Yanomamö and among street gangs in Canada and the United States illustrate how under certain conditions, individuals form groups to protect themselves against other groups. To discourage attacks from others in the absence of protection from other agencies, these groups cultivate a reputation for violence.

The gang violence that Keiser observed in Chicago during the late 1960s has escalated since, and weapons more typical of those carried by armed soldiers in the military are now being used. Alex Kotlowitz, in *There Are No Children Here* (1991), reported how the Vice Lords, one of three gang factions in Chicago in the early 1990s, made use of an arsenal that included Uzis and grenades. The purpose was the same, although the stakes were higher. Drugs have become the major source of contention among Chicago gangs (the head of one Vice Lord faction grossed $50,000 to $100,000 a week). When drug wars erupt over territory, the violence reflects the increased stakes and more massive firepower. Some years ago, four members of the Vice Lords came upon a rival gang member in the lobby of a housing project and shot him five times with an Uzi, two sawed-off shotguns, and a .25-calibre automatic handgun to establish their dominance in the neighbourhood.

The social and political conditions that characterize the societies of the Vice Lords and the Yanomamö are such that in each of them, individuals must mobilize and use force to protect or acquire desired resources. In neither case is there any effective centralized authority to guarantee the safety of resources or to stop violence once it begins. Although there is a centralized force in

THE CANADIAN PRESS/Cole Burston

Police officers remove a gun from the scene of a daylight shooting in Toronto.

Chicago—the police—they rarely intervene in gang violence because they are unwilling or lack the resources to do so, or because local residents are afraid or reluctant to report violence.

BEYOND THE BOOK 9.2

When anthropologist Laurence Ralph researched the ethnography *Renegade Dreams: Living through Injury in Gangland Chicago* (2014), his intention was to follow up on the works of Keiser and Kotlowitz by studying violent conflict among gangs such as the Vice Lords. However, he found that his informants spent much of their time and energy not just dealing with violence and death, but also trying to make sense of, and live with, the injury and disability that so often followed in the wake of violence. His findings pointed to the significance of focusing on and understanding not just violence and death, but also injury and its aftermath.

In an interview with *Cosmologics* magazine, Ralph answers questions about "The Politics of Injury" (full interview available at http://cosmologicsmagazine.com/laurence-ralph-the-politics-of-injury). Ralph discusses how the aftermath of an event such as a murder affects many people in a community. By looking at how they are affected, how they respond, and how they manage their grief, we can gain insight into what this sort of violence means to a community.

Ralph's insights and approach suggest a major shift in the way that anthropologists study violence, conflict, and its resolution. With Ralph's response above in mind, think about/discuss the following questions:

1. How might a focus on injury, trauma, and healing change the kinds of research that anthropologists interested in conflict pursue? What new methods, communities, or field sites might be particularly relevant?
2. How might popular media depictions of gangs and gang life change if the focus switched from violence to injury and the aftermath of injury?
3. How might an applied anthropologist interested in addressing the social and political contexts in which violence occurs make use of Ralph's findings?

Creating the Conditions for Violence

Napoleon Chagnon characterized Yanomamö warfare as a "truly primitive cultural adaptation … before it was altered or destroyed by our culture." It was, he said, the normal state of affairs before it was suppressed by colonial governments. There is, however, considerable evidence that Yanomamö warfare and aggression were less a product of their existence or nature than they were consequences of Western contact.

Brian Ferguson (1995) maintains that the period of Chagnon's fieldwork (1964 to 1972), on which he based his best-selling ethnography, *The Fierce People* (1968), was one of the most turbulent in Yanomamö history. Violence and aggression, writes Ferguson, were a product of three major changes: (1) the presence of new outpost settlements of government agents, missionaries, and researchers; (2) competition for Western manufactured goods, particularly steel cutting tools, and (3) a breakdown of social relations brought about by epidemics and the depletion of game and other food resources.

The Yanomamö, Ferguson points out, had been in contact with outsiders for centuries. Europeans began raiding Yanomamö villages for slaves as early as the mid-seventeenth century and continued to do so until around 1850. In the late nineteenth century, the rubber boom in the Amazon—a horrendous period for Indigenous groups, who were forced to collect rubber under the threat of torture and death—brought the Yanomamö into increased contact and conflict with other Indigenous groups. After the Amazon rubber boom collapsed in the 1920s as a result of competition with Asian rubber plantations, the area in which the Yanomamö lived was relatively peaceful until the 1950s and 1960s; then, influenza and measles epidemics swept the area, leaving only one-quarter of the children with both parents. More disruptive yet was the presence of new Western outposts.

The new outposts made available to the Yanomamö desired manufactured items, such as steel knives, machetes, aluminum pots, and shotguns. Steel cutting tools, for example, were ten times more efficient than the stone cutting tools they had long been using. Shotguns were effective both for hunting and for raiding.

The Yanomamö could obtain these items in various ways. They could relocate their villages near the outposts, they could send trading parties on long voyages to get them, or they could raid other groups for them. But the greatest advantage went to what Ferguson called "anchor villages," those that relocated near outposts. The result was a hierarchy of settlements ranging from anchor villages whose members were able to monopolize the new desired goods to more isolated settlements whose members had fewer and lower-quality goods.

Yanomamö in anchor settlements traded Western items to distant groups for local handicrafts and products such as cotton hammocks, spear points, or manioc flour. But trading parties were also targets of raids by groups desiring Western goods. To protect themselves and their monopoly on Western trade goods and to discourage raiding, Yanomamö groups found it advantageous to cultivate a reputation for violence and aggression. A reputation for fierceness was also an advantage in negotiating for desired goods. Thus, one man told of the number of people he had killed on raids just before demanding a machete.

Proximity to Western outposts incited violence in other ways. For example, once people relocated their village near an outpost settlement, they were reluctant to move. One way that small-scale, mobile societies such as the Yanomamö avoid conflict is by moving villages away from enemies when conflict is threatened. But since moving would mean giving up access to and a monopoly on Western goods, members of anchor villages were reluctant to move and, hence, needed to protect themselves and the goods they obtained from Westerners. In addition, more permanent settlements quickly depleted game resources: resources that had been used in reciprocal exchanges with other people and groups. Thus, sharing patterns, which as we noted earlier are crucial for maintaining peaceful relations, began to break down, leading to more conflict.

Deaths from disease and war disrupted traditional social relations; the depletion of game weakened traditional patterns of sharing and cooperation; and access to Western technology provided new sources of conflict. Furthermore, new technologies introduced new ways of ordering society and enhanced the ability of people in anchor villages to make war.

In sum, many of the patterns of Yanomamö warfare, violence, and aggression cannot be understood without knowledge of their history of contact with Western society and the contact conditions that increased the likelihood of violence and war. Even the power of chiefs, whose feast giving played such an important role in Chagnon's descriptions of alliance formation and aggression, was largely a function of Western contact. Outsiders, following traditional customs, brought gifts to local leaders. But the gifts that outsiders brought were far more valuable. Thus, Chagnon gave one chief a gift of 25 machetes, providing him with items that he could use to enhance his power. And thus, as Ferguson (1992, 225) says, "if villages were not anchored to outposts but were able to move freely, if long-established marital alliances were not disturbed by massive mortality, if communal sharing of meat were still the norm, and, above all, if necessary technology were widely and equally available, my theoretical expectation is that there would be little collective violence among the Yanomami."

Sexism and Violent Conflict

Another difference between peaceful and violent societies that has been suggested has to do with gender roles. Among the Ju/'hoansi, the Xinguano, and the Semai, men and women are relatively equal and there is little institutionalized violence against women. In contrast, the Yanomamö and the Vice Lords are characterized by male dominance, and both sanction violence against women.

Several reasons have been advanced to support the link between sexist values and violent conflict. First, it is men that make war, though women may fill certain positions in the armed forces. While there have been societies in which women engage in armed combat, these instances are the exception rather than the rule. During the Sandinista rebellion in Nicaragua in the 1980s, women took an active role in combat, but they were banned from active combat once the Sandinistas gained power. Second, there is a strong cross-cultural link between patriarchy and violent conflict. After examining information on more than one thousand societies, William Tulio Divale and Marvin Harris (1976) concluded that the intensity of collective violence is significantly higher in societies characterized by a strong male bias—by such things as patrilocal residence, patrilineal descent, polygyny, postmarital sex restrictions on females, male secret societies, and men's houses. Finally, there is evidence that societies characterized by sexual violence against women tend to be more warlike and prone to collective violence. Peggy Sanday's 1981 study of 95 societies in which there was evidence of frequency of rape supports this conclusion. The question is, does a sexist ideology promote violent conflict, or does the incidence of violent conflict promote sexism?

Those who claim that sexism promotes violent conflict make that connection in various ways. Betty Reardon (1985) and Leslie Cagan (1983) suggest that societies that relegate women to an inferior position explicitly or implicitly sanction violence against women. Moreover, violence toward women serves as what they call a "primal" paradigm for violent warfare against other peoples; once violence is allowed as a means of domination of one group such as women, it can serve as a model for dominance and violence against other groups.

For Peggy Sanday, and for many others, sexism and violent conflict both have their roots in competition over scarce resources. During periods in which resources are not scarce, males and females are valued equally. When there is an imbalance between food supply or distribution and needs, or when groups are competing for resources, males become of greater value, females become objects to be controlled, and sexual violence becomes one way that men demonstrate dominance. Among cattle-herding people in East Africa, for example, raiding for cattle was common and sometimes led to violent conflict between groups. Violence was defined as a manly activity, and this led East African societies to place great emphasis on masculinity and manliness. Manliness, however, was tested not only in battle but in male–female relations as well, for sex was a way of demonstrating strength.

In sum, factors such as a lack of centralized control, competition over scarce resources, private property, and sexism may lead societies to construct an ideological bias toward violence. Examining the effects of violent conflict to see if they produce changes in societies may provide insights into the factors that promote violent conflict.

BEYOND THE BOOK 9.3

Scholars have suggested a link between militarism and competitive sports; that is, societies that are prone to collective violence are more likely to value games in which men aggressively compete against other men. To explore this link, select and watch a sporting event (this could be a segment of game, an advertisement, or a piece of sports commentary), to watch on your own or with members of a group in class. Discuss the following questions:

1. Does it (the event you have chosen) draw upon or reproduce military values? If so, how? Give as many examples as possible.
2. Do gender roles and expectations play a role in linking violence and sport in your example? Again, explain your answer and give examples.

Question 9.4: What Is the Relationship between Violence and the Nation-State?

Violence and the Nation-State

As we discussed in Chapter 8, the symbolic barriers of excluded Others, infrastructure, and education are essential for nation-building. The use of violence or the threat of armed force is another key instrument in creating and maintaining the nation-state. Killing is the ultimate tool of nation-states. In fact, some anthropologists, among them Pierre van den Berghe, Leo Kuper, and Carol Nagengast, view the nation-state as a genocidal institution, one that conspires to kill or remove those citizens who fail to (or refuse to) conform to the dictates of the imposed national culture. For example, the United States, through policies of either aggressive extermination or benign neglect, attempted to kill all Native American Indigenous peoples and assimilate those who remained. In Canada, the final report of the Truth and Reconciliation Commission (2015) labelled the residential schools for Indigenous children a form of cultural genocide, one that led directly to the deaths of 6,000 students, or 1 in 25 who attended the schools. In 1994, the Rwandan state slaughtered 800,000 of its citizens, including 70 percent of the ethnic Tutsi population. In January 2020, the International Court of Justice in The Hague ruled that Myanmar must take action to protect its Rohingya Muslim minority. The UN estimates that since 2017, when the country's military began a crackdown on the Rohingya, at least 10,000 have been killed, and at least one million have been forced to flee to neighbouring Bangladesh.

Pierre van den Berghe (1992) contends that what is euphemistically called "nation building" is nothing but a blueprint for at best **ethnocide** (an attempt to destroy the culture of a people) and at worst **genocide** (an attempt to exterminate a people). Social scientists, he writes, tend to ignore the genocidal character of the nation-state because of the widespread assumption that nation-states are necessary for maintaining peace and economic stability. In fact, he says, nation-states function as mafias or gangs that, through the use or threat of violence, extract booty for themselves or their elites from rival "gangs" and extract "protection money" from their own citizens.

Other anthropologists share van den Berghe's view of the nation-state as an instrument of force and violence. Nagengast (1994) examined not only state killings but also the use of torture, rape, and homosexual assault to draw the boundaries of the nation-state. State-sponsored violence, she says, not only inflicts pain but also creates "punishable categories of people"—that is, people whose existence creates and maintains an Other. These punishable individuals represent an ambiguous underclass believed capable of undermining the accepted order of society. Arrest and torture, she says, stigmatize people and mark them as people no one would want to be. Arrest and torture provide a way to symbolically mark, discipline, and stigmatize categories of people whose existence or demands threaten the idea, power, and legitimacy of the nation-state. Because torture and violence are committed against only "terrorists," "communists," or "separatists," these methods become legitimate. "We only beat bad people," said a Turkish prison official in 1984. "They are no good, they are worthless bums, they are subversives who think that communism will relieve them of the necessity of working." The official described with apparent pride the order that he had given that "all prisoners should be struck with a truncheon below the waist on the rude parts, and warned not to come to prison again." "My aim," he said, "is to ensure discipline. That's not torture, for it is only the lazy, the idle, the vagabonds, the communists, the murderers who come to prison" (Nagengast 1994, 121).

Nation-states, and national identity, can also be an integral, if complicated, part of the process of creating and maintaining peace. For instance, since the 1994 genocide in Rwanda, the Rwandan government has embarked on a "deethnicization campaign." Ethnic labels on national identity cards are outlawed, and to identify as Hutu or Tutsi is to "risk accusations of 'divisionism' or genocide ideology" (Eramian 2014, 96).

Violence, the Nation-State, and Peace in East Timor

One instance of state violence against its own citizens occurred on the island of Timor on the southern edge of Indonesia. East Timor (Figure 9.2) had been colonized by the Dutch and the Portuguese and was granted its independence by the Portuguese in 1975.

ethnocide
The attempt to destroy the culture of a people.

genocide
The attempt to exterminate a people.

FIGURE 9.2 East Timor

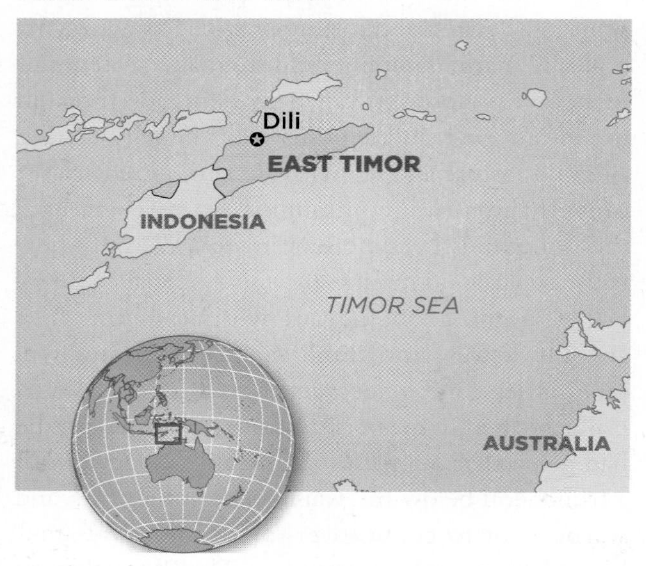

Five days after a state visit by then US Vice-President Gerald Ford and Secretary of State Henry Kissinger, Indonesia invaded East Timor. Over the following two decades, Indonesians, especially members and friends of the ruling family, invested millions of dollars in various enterprises there. And, as many other countries have done, Indonesia embarked on a campaign of violence and terror in its effort to integrate the East Timorese into the Indonesian nation-state.

Indonesian anthropologist George Aditjondro (2000), who faced an indefinite jail term for criticizing Indonesian leaders, described the campaign of terror, violence, and torture embarked on by the Indonesian state against its most recent citizens. It included, among other things, a "pacification war," which lasted from 1975 to 1979, and repression that continued even after a 1999 UN-sponsored referendum in which 80 percent of the population voted for independence from Indonesia.

Torture, says Aditjondro, was a standard method of subjugation. Techniques included physical beatings, the use of cigarette butts to burn holes in the skin, electric shock, the crushing of hands and feet with chair or table legs, the poking of the mouth with bamboo sticks, the infliction of pain on the genitals, the rape of women, and immersion in a metal tank filled with water charged with electricity.

Torture was used for five reasons, according to Aditjondro. First, to obtain information from victims. Second, to crush the fighting spirit of freedom fighters. Third, to weaken the political power of the Catholic Church by obtaining "confessions" of church complicity in pro-independence politics or in sacrilegious or criminal acts. Fourth, to protect the business interests of Indonesians in East Timor. And finally, to minimize critical press reports from East Timorese newspapers.

But torture was not the only technique of state terror used by Indonesia. There was, for example, physical terror, including mass killings of guerrillas along with women and children that took place during the first decade of the Indonesian occupation. Some 200,000 people—around one-third of the population—were killed or died of deprivations brought about by the terror. Prisoners were thrown to their death from helicopters; people were killed by napalm bombings that also destroyed crops, and thousands died from resulting famines. Many people died in overcrowded prison barracks, some of which were covered with black canvas to turn them into human ovens.

There was also a campaign to "depurify," as Aditjondro calls it, the bodies of East Timorese women through rape and forced fertility control. Rape was often committed against the wives or daughters of men suspected of being involved with the resistance. In other cases, rape was committed against women who failed to produce identity cards or who refused to accompany or submit to the sexual demands of soldiers. Other women were forced to spy on resistance forces while serving as sex slaves of Indonesian troops. In still other cases, East Timorese women were forced into brothels for use by Indonesian troops. Rape, says Aditjondro, was also a way to destroy the East Timorese resistance by biologically depurifying their ethnic constituency.

Another way to biologically depurify the population was through forced contraception. Family planning programs were used as means to discipline the population; they symbolically represented state control over human bodies. Thus, high school girls were injected with Depo-Provera, a birth control drug, without being told of its function.

Other forms of symbolic violence included erecting pro-Indonesian monuments and forcing citizens to participate in Indonesian political rituals (flag raisings, parades, and parties), subjecting them to arrest, interrogation, and physical torture if they resisted. Language itself was modified, with new linguistic expressions for torture and execution becoming common. *Jalan-jalan ke Jakarta* ("taking a trip to Jakarta") and *Berangkat studi lanjut ke Jawa* ("going for further study in Java") were euphemisms for executions. *Mani laut* ("taking a sea bath") referred to the practice of weighting the bodies of people with rocks and dumping them from a helicopter into the sea. *De-Santa Cruz-kan* ("Santa Cruz-ified") was an expression used by mothers to threaten their children with the sinister connotations of a notorious 1991 massacre of East Timorese high school students who were protesting Indonesian occupation. Finally, 200,000 people were taken from East Timor and relocated to other parts of Indonesia.

© Supri Supri/Reuters

The brutalization of East Timor by the Indonesian military and by Indonesian-supported militias from 1975 to 1999 is but one example of how nation-states use force to control their citizens. Here, East Timorese youth are staging a drama portraying the killings of some 271 unarmed protesters by Indonesian troops at the Santa Cruz cemetery on 12 November 1991.

Many East Timorese became **refugees**—forced to flee their home country to seek protection in another. Refugees that comprise a **diaspora**, or dispersed population living outside their homeland, escape direct violence and harm; however, the effects of living through sustained, everyday violence are long-lasting. Amanda Wise (2006) conducted fieldwork with the refugee diaspora in Sydney, Australia. She found that the experience of shared violence and trauma was a key element in the collective identity of the refugees, who came together to create what she called a "community of suffering." The embodied memories of pain and suffering drew the community together. The Indonesian military inflicted violence on the East Timorese, and "such practices symbolically and affectively bind the pain of the individual to the fate of the ethnic collectivity." The shared memory and common suffering became the foundation of solidarity among her informants (2006, 15).

East Timor finally regained its independence from Indonesia in 1999, but the break did not come easily. Eighty percent of the population voted for independence in a UN-sponsored referendum; however, before they withdrew from East Timor in September 1999, the Indonesian military and military-trained and-supported militias laid waste to virtually the entire country, killing thousands of people and driving 200,000 people out of East Timor and into Indonesia.

Canada's part in the tragedy of the East Timorese is documented in the video Bitter Paradise: The Sellout of East Timor, by Elaine Brière. Probably the last tourist to visit East Timor while it was still a peaceful, welcoming society in 1974, Brière dedicated her life to making the genocide public.

refugees
Groups of people who have left their homeland due to warfare, forced expulsion, acts of terrorism, or other factors.

diaspora
A population whose members are dispersed and living outside of their homeland.

The video followed Brière's journey into the business world, where she was told that Canadians who were commercially involved in Indonesia did not know about the genocide or believed that it was an exaggeration; to the world of the media, where she was told by the host of a talk show that Canadians didn't "connect" with the killing of East Timorese; and to Ottawa, where her questions were ignored by the external affairs minister. Canada continued to give enormous amounts of economic aid to the Suharto regime in spite of the killings and in spite of cutbacks in social programs at home; and Canadian businesses, such as Inco and Bre-X, continued to see Indonesia as a haven for international investment.

The tactics used by Indonesia to subdue people who resisted integration into the Indonesian nation-state are not unique. In fact, virtually all of these tactics have been used by most, if not all, nation-states at one time or another. You can get some idea of how nation-states today sponsor violence against their citizens by going to the Internet, where information is readily available from organizations such as *Amnesty International* and *Human Rights Watch*.

Question 9.5: How Is It Possible to Justify the Creation of Weapons of Mass Destruction?

Anthropologist Hugh Gusterson, who had been an antinuclear activist, wanted to know how nuclear weapons scientists could justify conducting research on and testing of weapons of mass destruction. What could create a worldview that enabled people to justify performing that kind of work? To answer that question, he set out to study the culture of the Lawrence Livermore National Laboratory in Livermore, California.

Gusterson (1995) suggests that those who justify nuclear weapons and who question nuclear disarmament make four assumptions about the world. First, they claim that anarchy characterizes international relations. Second, they assume that states must rely on self-help since no one else is going to offer them protection. Third, they assume that nuclear weapons are the ultimate form of self-help, because they vastly increase the cost of aggression against them. And fourth, they assume that relatively little can be done in the short term to change the anarchistic nature of the international system.

Critics of nuclear weapons make very different assumptions. They argue that international relations are not as anarchistic as they are made out to be and that rules and norms that control aggression exist. Many critics see the nuclear arms race as "objective social madness." People who work in the area, they assume, must be in denial and must demonize the Other to justify their work.

Gusterson wanted to find out not so much who was "right," but rather how people came to hold such divergent opinions about ways of resolving conflict, especially when the stakes are so high. Nuclear weapons scientists did not, says Gusterson, avoid the ethical concerns of their research. Most, however, accepted the central axiom that nuclear research is necessary to make the world safe. To some, working on nuclear weapons was more ethical than working on conventional weapons, since conventional weapons were more likely to be used. Nuclear weapons, the scientists assumed, were simply symbolic chips in a game, the goal of which was to avoid using them. When asked if he could ever foresee a circumstance in which nuclear weapons would be used, one scientist said, "No, even if we were under attack." In other words, deterrence was the only reason to develop nuclear weapons; if you were attacked, the whole enterprise had failed. Others rationalized their work more baldly, saying they were not responsible for how what they designed would be used. "Are automobile designers," they ask, "responsible for deaths caused by drunk drivers?" (Gusterson 1995, 58)

When Gusterson asked people why they chose to work at Livermore, most cited the intellectual freedom they enjoyed working in a weapons laboratory. Almost all compared Livermore favourably to working in universities (which they characterized as "stodgy," "cutthroat," or "high-pressure") or in private organizations. Some also cited the challenges of weapons research and the opportunity to work with state-of-the-art equipment. Beyond those attractions, Livermore paid about twice as much as a university position.

Once a person was hired, secrecy played a major role in forging a person's identity. Livermore employees were investigated before being given security clearance to laboratory facilities. Personnel were divided into different security categories and given coloured badges indicating their level of clearance. "Q" clearance (a green badge) was necessary for classified research; "L" clearance (yellow badge) allowed access to classified areas but not to classified information. The labs themselves were divided into areas of lesser and greater security. As Gusterson (1995, 70) put it, the laboratory was "an enormous grid of tabooed spaces and tabooed topics."

Without a green badge, a weapons scientist was not considered a full adult in the lab. The process of getting "Q" clearance was elaborate and could take six months to two years. Virtually every aspect of a person's life was subject to investigation in search of clues that he or she was unfit to handle classified material. Most people passed, though, and because secrecy was not so well guarded in practice, the security clearance process functioned mostly as a rite of passage that added to the mystique of weapons research and that disciplined the initiate.

Secrecy was one of the principal ways that the lab's diverse population was brought together. Knowing secrets, regardless of how mundane they might be, marked a person as a member of a special group and lent an air of drama and importance to one's work. Secrecy also served to limit discussion that could change people's views of the work they were doing. As Gusterson (1995, 68) put it, "the laboratory's culture of secrecy does tend to produce certain effects in its scientists: it segregates laboratory scientists as a privileged but somewhat isolated elite; it inculcates a sense of group loyalty; and it thrusts on laboratory scientists an amorphous surveillance, which can become internalized."

The process of testing nuclear weapons was, in many ways, the critical step in creating the nuclear scientist. Any Livermore scientist could propose a weapons test, but reviewers (senior scientists at the laboratory) selected only about one out of 20 ideas for testing. Nuclear tests had elements of myth and ritual. Approval of an idea for testing reaffirmed the scientist's membership in the group, not unlike a rite of passage. Testing produced not only weapons but also weapon designers. It was a way of creating the elite. The more tests one participated in, the greater the prestige and power that accrued. A successful test validated status and credentials and brought forth congratulatory support and reinforcement. Tests provided a symbolic simulation of the reliability of the entire system of deterrence: "Each time a nuclear test is successfully carried off, the scientists' faith in human control over nuclear technology is further reinforced. Seen in this light, the 'reliability' the tests demonstrate has an expandable meaning, extending out from the reliability of the particular device being tested to the entire regime of nuclear deterrence" (Gusterson 1995, 161).

The Language of Nuclear Destruction

Carol Cohn (1987, 1991) spent one year studying the culture of a strategic studies institute, or "think tank," for government defence analysts who plan nuclear strategy. She began her study with this question: How are people whose job it is to plan nuclear destruction able to do it? As we discussed in Chapter 4, language is one of the key ways in which members of a particular culture come to understand their shared worldview as true and natural. One of Cohn's conclusions was that the planners used language to distance themselves from the consequences of the actions they were planning. The language they used obfuscated and reassembled reality in such a way that what was really being talked about—the destruction of human lives—was hidden behind metaphors and euphemisms.

During her first weeks at the centre, as she listened to the participants talking matter-of-factly about nuclear destruction, she heard language that she labelled technostrategic. This language included terms such as *clean bombs* (fusion bombs, which release more energy than fission bombs), *penetration aids* (technologies that help missiles get through enemy defences), *collateral damage* (human deaths), and *surgical strikes* (bombing that takes out only military targets). Domestic metaphors were common in the **technostrategic language**: missiles were based in *silos*, piles of nuclear weapons in a submarine were *Christmas tree farms*, bombs and missiles were *re-entry vehicles* or *RVs*, and massive bombing was *carpet bombing*. According to Cohn, the domestic images were more than a way for people to distance themselves from the grisly reality they were discussing. Calling the pattern in which a bomb would fall a "footprint" removed the speakers from any position of accountability for the acts they were contemplating.

Cohn also discovered that the language and metaphors of those working at the institute seemed incapable of expressing certain realities. The aftermath of a nuclear attack was described in technostrategic language as "a situation bound to include EMP blackout, brute force damage to systems, a heavy jamming environment, and so on" (1987, 707). She contrasted this with eyewitness accounts of the bombing of Hiroshima. There was, Cohn wrote, no way of describing this experience in technostrategic language. It removed the speakers from having to think about themselves as victims of nuclear war.

Cohn also discovered that she could not use ordinary language to speak to the defence analysts. When she tried, they acted as if she were ignorant or simpleminded. To communicate, she had to use terms along the lines of *subholocaust engagement* and *pre-emptive strike*. The word *peace* was not a legitimate part of the vocabulary; to use it was to brand oneself as a softheaded activist. The closest she could come to *peace* in technostrategic language was *strategic stability*.

To an anthropologist, the fact that people are limited by their culture, their language, and their worldview is, of course, no surprise. All cultures assign a characteristic meaning to violent conflict, and to peace, whether it is viewed as the act of an animal in possession of a human body, or as the will of God, or as a game. The more serious implication of Cohn's observations is that scientists, academics, and nuclear planners give weight to their claim that their perspective is "objective" and therefore has greater truth value than other perspectives. Moreover, says Cohn, if one can speak to defence analysts only in technostrategic language, and if the language is constructed in such a way as to be incapable of expressing different realities, then there is no way for these analysts to appreciate or understand the other realities involved in the use of nuclear weapons.

Question 9.6: How Do Anthropologists Do Fieldwork in the Midst of Violent Conflict?

As often as possible, anthropologists try to learn about and understand various social and cultural phenomena through fieldwork and participant observation. However, striving to understand violent conflict first-hand can be difficult at best and dangerous at worst. Often, it is contentious as well. Should anthropologists place themselves in danger in the name of fieldwork? What if, through our very presence, we put others at risk or promote the conditions for further violence? Can we use ethnography to understand war from a soldier's perspective? Below, we discuss three

technostrategic language
A term coined by Carol Cohn to describe the way nuclear strategic language and thinking used by defence intellectuals are imbued with modes of thinking associated with technology.

different examples of the possibilities and pitfalls of studying violence and conflict, either directly or indirectly.

The Endangered Anthropologist

The risk of injury, disease, or hostile reactions has always been a feature of anthropological fieldwork. As anthropologists increasingly work in areas where human rights violations are common, these risks are intensified. At least four anthropologists have been murdered because of their fieldwork. In 1982, South African anthropologist and anti-apartheid activist Ruth First was killed by a mail bomb in her office at Maputo University in Mozambique. In 1984, Melanesian anthropologist Arnold Ap was tortured and killed by the Indonesian army, his body dumped by helicopter into the sea. In 1989, South African anthropologist David Webster was shot and killed by members of a pro-apartheid death squad. And in 1990, Guatemalan anthropologist Myrna Mack was stabbed to death by a soldier, ostensibly for her work with Mayan refugees and their experiences during the government's counterinsurgency war of the early 1980s, in the course of which hundreds of thousands of people died. At least two other anthropologists, Ricardo Falla and George Aditjondro, went into exile under threat of assassination because of their work. These real dangers that anthropologists face may provide insights into how the people with whom they are working experience the threat of violence.

In 1989 and 1990, Linda Green was doing fieldwork in the Guatemalan community of Xe'caj. Like many similar communities, Xe'caj was only beginning to recover from some 35 years of violence. Beginning with a military coup orchestrated largely by the Central Intelligence Agency (CIA) against a democratically elected government in 1954, Guatemala experienced regular violence as the military regime suppressed attempts to overthrow it. Hundreds of thousands of Guatemalans were killed, mostly by the government, in an attempt to suppress the revolt. The late 1970s and early 1980s were particularly brutal as the government embarked on a campaign to destroy peasant villages and relocate people to government-controlled towns. In addition, paramilitary groups, largely supplied and supported by the regular military, embarked on campaigns of terror and torture in an effort to control the peasant population.

The people of Xe'caj lived in a state of constant surveillance conducted by the military encampment located above the town. Many of the residents had husbands, fathers, or sons taken away by the military. There were rumours of death lists. People had difficulty sleeping and reported nightmares of recurring death and violence. Soon, said Green, "I, too, started to experience nighttime hysteria, dreams of death, disappearances, and torture."

Green interviewed women who had been widowed by the conflict. Without prompting, the women recounted in vivid detail their stories of horror, and the deaths and disappearances of husbands, fathers, sons, and brothers, as if they had happened last week or month rather than six to eight years earlier.

Then, one day when Green arrived to continue the interviews, the women were anxious and agitated. When she asked what had happened, they told her that the military commissioner was looking for her and that people were saying she was helping the widows and talking against other people in the community. When Green told the women she was going to see the commissioner, they pleaded with her not to do so, telling her that they knew of people who had gone to the military garrison and never returned. Green decided to visit the garrison alone, and that visit would provide a vivid experience of the fears confronted by the villagers. As she approached the garrison, she noted the following:

> *I saw several soldiers sitting in a small guardhouse with a machine gun perched on a three-foot stanchion pointed downward and directly at me. The plight of Joseph K. in Kafka's Trial flashed through my mind, he accused of a crime for which he must defend himself*

> *but about which he could get no information. I didn't do anything wrong, I must not look guilty, I repeated to myself like a mantra. I must calm myself, as my stomach churned, my nerves frayed. I arrived breathless and terrified. Immediately I knew I was guilty because I was against the system of violence and terror that surrounded me. (1995, 116)*

Fortunately, the *commandante* said he knew nothing about why she was being harassed. He assured her that she could continue with her work, and everything went smoothly from there. But Green had gained a fuller understanding of the experiences of people who must live under the constant threat of violence.

Is There a Place for Anthropology–Military Collaborations?

In 2005, Montgomery McFate, a military adviser with a background in anthropology, published an article in *Military Review* arguing that there was a "culture gap" in our understanding of the conflict in Iraq caused by "the almost total absence of anthropology within the national-security establishment." She argued that successful counterinsurgency requires a total understanding of local culture. To achieve victory, the United States needed to understand Iraq's traditional authority structure and the competing interests of different groups such as the Shia, Sunni, and Kurds. In a second article, co-written with Andrea Jackson, McFate outlined a proposal to establish an "Office for Operational Cultural Knowledge," which would train teams to provide battlefield commanders with knowledge of local culture, or as it was being called, the "human terrain."

The need for cultural knowledge was echoed by retired Major General Robert H. Scales, Jr., (2005, 43), who argued that these new conflicts required not technological superiority but "an exceptional ability to understand people, their culture, and their motivation."

One outcome of this interest in cultural knowledge was the development of the Human Terrain System (HTS), which ran from June 2006 to September 2014. The centrepiece of the program was Human Terrain Teams (HTTs), each of which had a staff of five: an army officer serving as team leader, a cultural analyst, a regional studies analyst, a Human Terrain (HT) research manager, and an HT analyst. Each team studied the local culture, interviewed local people, and provided valuable information to the battalion commander.

Anthropologists who joined the HTS project explained their service as an effort to do something meaningful. Marcus Griffin wrote: "I have an obligation to use my skills to learn about people and to share what I learn." Working as a member of an HTT in Iraq, Griffin saw his job as finding out what Iraqis needed and helping them meet those needs.

Not everyone shared this positive assessment of the Human Terrain System. In 2007 the American Anthropological Association issued a formal statement condemning the project, arguing that it would lead anthropologists to violate ethical standards and that it posed a danger to both anthropologists and the people they were studying. Another notable critic, Roberto Gonzales (2009), pointed out a number of dangers of the Human Terrain System. First, was it possible for informants to consent to their participation? Second, what type of information was being gathered by anthropologists, and how would it be used? Third, how well would informants be protected from retaliation by hostile groups or political rivals?

Despite such reservations, in 2008, the Canadian Forces began a program of "white situational awareness teams," or WSATs, which were similar to HTTs. In military terminology, "white" refers to the civilian population (as opposed to the "red" and "blue" of enemy and friendly forces, respectively). Each WSAT included two military intelligence officers and three civilian Department of Foreign Affairs employees and aimed to provide a more nuanced understanding of the cultural terrain for military leaders and advisers (Fenton 2010).

© US Army photo by SSG Michael Castell

A US soldier takes notes as he talks and drinks tea with local Andar District Special Needs School administrators during a cordon and search of Nani, Afghanistan, in June 2007. Can anthropological expertise be put to (good) use in a war zone?

Maximillian Forte, an anthropologist at Concordia University, expressed concerns about the Human Terrain System, WSATs, and the potential militarization of anthropology in general: "Their [WSATs'] job seems to be no different from that of HTS, except that for now the civilians they use are government employees, not academics. They have breached a barrier however: the idea that social and cultural knowledge can be useful for counterinsurgency, at least that door has now been opened in Canada" (in Fenton 2010).

What bothers many critics of the Human Terrain System, in particular, is that regardless of the efforts of the military and others to put a humanitarian face on the contributions of social scientists, the information gathered by HTTs was clearly going to be used for military purposes. HTS advocates wanted to make whatever information was gathered available to other agencies and to the governments of Iraq and Afghanistan, to "enable them to more fully exercise sovereignty over their country" (Gonzalez 2009, 74).

The use of social scientists for HTTs in Iraq and Afghanistan raises a larger issue: the responsibility of anthropologists and other social scientists to be aware of how their data may be used. The Pentagon, for example, is using information collected by social scientists to help identify dangerous neighbourhoods in Baghdad and Kabul. This knowledge allows the military to predict which neighbourhoods are at risk for riots, gun violence, or bombings; it also helps them develop lists of possible participants and their relatives, friends, and associates.

One danger, of course, is that the philosophy of the Human Terrain System, and the development of elaborate surveillance technologies using vast quantities of information now available on citizens, will move from military applications in places such as Iraq and Afghanistan to domestic venues and thereby seriously undermine democratic freedoms. Gonzalez (2009, 123–24) concludes his critique of the Human Terrain System as follows:

> *What comes across from the accounts of many social scientists supporting counterinsurgency initiatives in Iraq and Afghanistan is a fundamental acceptance of modern warfare in general and the U.S.-led occupations in particular. Furthermore, they generally accept the false notion that counterinsurgency—the "graduate level of war" to quote one military enthusiast—is more antiseptic, more humane, less damaging than conventional warfare. As technicians of power, some adhere to Machiavellian principles: do not question the prince or his war, but instead use the most efficient means to help him achieve victory. War's inevitability is taken for granted. Basic assumptions are left unquestioned. Missing from these accounts is the question of whether war is appropriate at all today.*

BEYOND THE BOOK 9.4

On your own, or as part of a larger group in class, debate the "pros and cons" of anthropology–military collaborations such as the Human Terrain System. As you do so, keep in mind: pros and cons for whom? Are the benefits and pitfalls evenly or unevenly distributed among the various stakeholders? Are the ethical requirements of anthropology discussed in Chapter 2 compatible with such collaborations?

Making Sense of Combat: Canadian Soldiers in Kandahar

Throughout this chapter, we have explored the ways in which people in various societies and cultures make sense of violent conflict, or alternatively, create meaningful, peaceful solutions to conflict. As we have seen, language and ritual are both employed, quite successfully, to make nuclear proliferation and the subsequent possibility of mass destruction seem both feasible and meaningful. As noted at the outset of this chapter, until recently, pride in peacekeeping was a key part of Canadian national identity. But between 2001 and 2014, for the first time since the Korean War, Canada had soldiers in active combat (in Afghanistan, Figure 9.3). In her work with Canadian Forces soldiers stationed in Kandahar, Anne Irwin analyzed the ways in which those soldiers use storytelling and ritual to make sense of their experiences in combat.

A former member of the Canadian Forces, Irwin spent many years studying Canadian soldiers, both while they trained for peacekeeping operations (Irwin 2002) and, more recently, with a unit that would undertake "full-spectrum operations," including combat (2012, 61). Irwin spent several months with the unit during its tour in 2006, living with them both at Kandahar's air base and "outside the wire," on patrol and in combat. Irwin found that time and routine on the base were quite structured, whereas time outside the wire was completely disrupted—"there was no day-to-day routine for sleeping and eating, not even predictable shifts" (64). Even when there was no engagement—"troops in contact," in military parlance—the soldiers experienced all time outside the wire as being in combat, not least because of the omnipresent danger of IEDs (improvised explosive devices). Soldiers who spent time outside the wire together seemed to go through a rite of passage and shared a liminal period together during combat (69). However, Irwin is reluctant to cast combat as a rite of passage that turns boys into men. Indeed, she argues that although combat has some of the elements of a rite of passage, soldiers who return to Canada seem to be both permanent adolescents (referring to themselves and their fellow soldiers as "the boys") and, at the same time, old men: prematurely aged, grief-stricken, and often scarred or disabled (76).

FIGURE 9.3 Iraq and Afghanistan

Irwin has collected and analyzed soldiers' narratives about the war in Afghanistan. Often, these link individual morality to social and political debates about Canada's combat role. One soldier, in telling the story of his experiences, said that "a lot of people in Canada think that we should not be here in Afghanistan, but those people don't see the remarkable changes happening here. One interpreter told me, 'Because Canada is here, our people are happy again.' So to all those Canadians who continue to harp about what they don't know—here's your straw, suck it up" (Cpl Sanders, in Pengelly and Irwin 2011, 52).

Here, the soldier has turned his combat experience into a morality tale, one that takes the qualities of a good solider—responsible, tough, and uncomplaining—and transposes them onto the Canadian public. Moreover, he is attempting to show the moral justness of the war by drawing on "the moral character of a helpful and caring Canada" (2011, 53). By examining these kinds of narratives, we can see how their circulation has helped soldiers understand and justify their participation in this violent conflict. Moreover, when such combat narratives draw on a sense of national identity and pride, of Canada as "helpful and caring," we can begin to make sense of the rather rapid (though contested) shift, at the turn of the twenty-first century, of Canada's role from peacekeeper to warrior nation.

APPLYING ANTHROPOLOGY

Eradicating Gender-Based Violence

As discussed in Chapter 5, much gender-based violence against women is an outgrowth of gendered inequality. Many applied, engaged anthropologists have conducted ethnographic fieldwork in various societies with the goal of historicizing violence and positioning such practices within shifting structures of social hierarchy. But applied anthropologists seek to go beyond simply documenting and naming various forms of violence and abuse; they seek to take measures to eliminate violence against women. This could involve culturally sensitive initiatives that aim to empower women in their communities, helping them access resources such as education or medical aid, or informing international organizations about the needs of a local, often marginalized population. Many of these endeavours are predicated on cultural relativism and collaboration with local communities. This is important in order to avoid mistakes made in the past by many international or Western development organizations that harboured paternalistic or ethnocentric attitudes that sought to "save" or "enlighten" populations about the presumed superiority of Western values surrounding gender or other issues.

One example of this approach is an initiative in Belize by anthropologist Melissa Beske. In Belize, domestic gender-based violence against women affects approximately half the population, and over 70 percent of the population in the western district (Beske 2014, 2016). Unfortunately, however, laws against violence are rarely enforced by police. Between 2002 and 2013, Beske conducted interviews, focus groups, surveys, and participant observation with families in the Cayo region of Belize to assess individual and community-based responses to people's perceptions of the causes of violence as well as the measures that can or should be taken to eliminate violence. Through conducting detailed interviews with women of different backgrounds, she was able to explore the varied experiences of domestic violence for women of different racial, ethnic, and class backgrounds. In the process, she came to understand how various social institutions, such as churches, schools, and workplaces, inadvertently help perpetuate cycles of domestic abuse and violence against women. Working collaboratively with her interlocutors, local advocates of women's health, and international nongovernmental organizations such as the *Cornerstone Foundation* and *Mary Open Doors*, as well as the governmental Women's Department in the capital of San Ignacio, she was able to contribute to a number of initiatives to reduce violence. *Mary Open Doors*, for instance, is a shelter for female victims of domestic violence that is also headed by women; it opened in 2008. She has worked alongside community members to find new land and buildings to expand this organization so that it can house more women in need. Based on the information that she gathered from women during her fieldwork, and armed with an understanding of the causes of violence from a female perspective, she has also helped organize fundraising, job skills training sessions for women, and community outreach programs aimed at educating people about gender-based violence in the workplace and at home.

Conclusions

A unique disciplinary strength of sociocultural anthropology is that it enables us to bring ethnographic and cross-cultural insights to bear on various contemporary social problems. Knowing what we know about the twin human capacities for violence and peace-making as forms of conflict resolution, how might anthropologists encourage the latter? Anthropologist Roger Lohmann (2014) makes the following suggestions:

> *Anthropology is in a position to fulfil some of the prerequisites of world peace if we direct research and communication efforts accordingly. If we wish to stop war and establish peace locally or universally, temporarily or indefinitely, we need to answer several questions of the sort that anthropologists … are well positioned to address: What conditions motivate people to resort to organized violence between polities and how can these positions be manipulated to diffuse conflicts before they escalate? Is peace established and maintained only and ironically through the threat of violence, or can a foundation of non-violent ideology be laid and kept up, and if so, how? Under which conditions are people able to make peace an actively maintained and indefinitely sustainable condition, and not just the cessation of warfare? (255)*

In other words, anthropologists interested in promoting peace need to apply their ethnographic and critical thinking skills to the task at hand. Moreover, anthropologists need to communicate the results of these efforts broadly, not just to other anthropologists but also to those in positions to influence relevant policy and conflict resolution efforts. For example, Kevin Avruch, anthropologist and dean of the School of Conflict Analysis and Resolution at George Mason University, makes a case for the importance of including anthropology in the core curricula of conflict resolution programs. Avruch (2009, 12–13) argues that anthropology can be applied to conflict resolution education in at least three ways: in terms of "subject matter expertise" in particular ethnographic topics (about a specific ethnic group or particular kinds of agricultural practices, for instance); in terms of methodology (including methods of ethnographic inquiry such as participant observation); and by encouraging reflexive sensitivity to practitioners' own cultural beliefs and biases. Of course, graduates of conflict management programs are not the only people with the capacity to imagine and create peace; as we have seen, different peoples have their own culturally meaningful ways of doing so. However, this awareness is precisely why an anthropological perspective is so important for those outside "experts" who are called upon to intervene or lend a hand in conflict resolution.

Finally, anthropologists, or students of anthropology, with an interest in promoting peace can remember, and remind others, that violence and peace are both culturally meaningful and situated processes. Neither form of conflict resolution, it seems, is innate in humans. As we have seen throughout the text, most of the problems we have explored have the potential to incite conflict. The first, and most illuminating, task that we as anthropologists face is to understand each problem on its own terms and situate it within a wider, cross-cultural perspective.

QUESTIONS: REVIEW

9.1 How do societies create a bias in favour of collective violence?

This section challenges problematic, racist assumptions (as outlined in the introduction) that violence is innate or endemic to particular populations by exploring the link between cultural behaviours and the promotion of violence. Among Kiowa males, for instance, counting coup is a means of achieving status, whereas among the Yanomamo, raids and demonstrations of aggression are means of protecting valuable resources. Religious justifications for violence are also common, and according to Jurgensmeyer, political struggles are often elevated to "cosmic wars" between good and evil.

Review Questions

1. Among both the Kiowa and the Yanomamo, how are violence and masculinity related?
2. Discuss two examples of how violence is justified by religious rhetoric.

9.2 How do societies create a bias in favour of peaceful conflict resolution?

Peaceful societies avoid conflicts over material resources through an emphasis on sharing and cooperation and by engaging in collective behaviours that promote harmony. Sharing of meat or other resources among the Ju/'hoansi and an emphasis on the principle of *pehunan* among the Semai are two examples of conflict avoidance strategies. The Xinguanos place negative value on aggression by labelling and stereotyping many non-Xingu peoples as "wild" and violent.

Review Questions

1. What are some of the characteristics of peaceful societies?
2. Compare and contrast the strategies used by the Ju/'hoansi, the Xinguanos, and the Semai to avoid conflict.

9.3 What are the economic, political, and social differences between peaceful and violent societies?

This section compares and contrasts the differences between peaceful and violent societies. Peaceful societies are more likely to be small-scale hunting and gathering societies, or they practise swidden agriculture. They typically lack a hierarchical, central government and do not have centralized armies, police, or jails. In addition, there is a link between sexism and violence. Peaceful societies are less likely to be characterized by male dominance. Among societies that create a bias for violence, like the Yanomamö, *waiteri* (fierceness) is encouraged among men to protect their resources and their families. Similar reasons for creating a bias for violence are noted among the Vice Lords. With respect to the Yanomamö, however, it is also critical to understand how their negative experiences of contact with Westerners increased their predilection toward violence.

Review Questions

1. With respect to the Yanomamo, how and why is knowledge of a society's history, and particularly its interactions with Western society, an important factor in exploring issues of violence and aggression? How is this an important factor in understanding Yanomamö waiteri?
2. What are four common traits of peaceful societies?
3. What is the link between male dominance and violence? Provide two examples.

9.4 What is the relationship between violence and the nation-state?

Many anthropologists have argued that nation-states are instruments of force that promote state-sponsored violence as a means of controlling their populations. Indeed, nation-states are often responsible for policies of genocide, forced sterilization, torture, rape and ethnic cleansing as means to "depurify" a population and exert state influence. Torture, for instance, was used in East Timor during the "pacification war" between 1975 and 1979 as a method of subjugation. As a result, many people flee their native countries and become refugees and part of a global diaspora.

Review Questions

1. Discuss how and why rape and forced sterilization are used by nation-states to "depurify" populations.
2. Why, according to Aditjondro, was torture used in East Timor?

9.5 How is it possible to justify the creation of weapons of mass destruction?

In order to satisfy and pacify their populations, the leaders of nation-states must justify uses of force and the creation of weapons of mass destruction. Carol Cohn, for instance, explored the language used by government defence analysts and found that the destruction of human lives was hidden behind metaphors, euphemisms, and the use of what she calls *technostrategic* language.

Review Questions

1. What, according to Gusterson, are four assumptions about the world that are made by those who justify the use of nuclear weapons?
2. What is technostrategic language, and what is its purpose? Provide three examples.

9.6 How do anthropologists do fieldwork in the midst of violent conflict?

Over the years, anthropological expertise has been acknowledged and sought after by various governments in their efforts to prevent counterinsurgencies during times of armed conflict. For instance, the Human Terrain System (HTS) and the White Situational Awareness Team (WSAT) have been implemented in the United States and Canada, respectively. Such programs have been sharply critiqued by anthropologists because they raise important ethical questions about the use and abuse of anthropological research. Of note is the fact that such programs place one's interlocutors as well as anthropologists themselves in considerable danger. Other anthropologists have worked in military contexts, such as Anne Irwin, who studied Canadian troops in Kandahar.

Review Questions

1. Why would so many anthropologists be opposed to military programs like the HTS or WSAT? What ethical issues are raised by such endeavours?
2. How was storytelling and ritual used among Canadian troops in Kandahar to make sense of their combat experiences?

CRITICAL THINKING QUESTIONS

1. Is world peace possible? Given what you have learned in this chapter, what are the barriers to world peace in the contemporary world? Can they be overcome, and if so, how?
2. Depictions of graphic violence have become commonplace in contemporary popular culture. How might an anthropologist explain this phenomenon?
3. If you could design an applied anthropology project to address an issue of violent conflict, what would it be, and what would you do?

KEY TERMS

diaspora (p. 259)
ethnocide (p. 257)
genocide (p. 257)
refugees (p. 259)
technostrategic language (p. 262)

Glossary

achieved status An identity that is believed to be in flux and that is dependent upon the actions and achievements of an individual. (p. 187)

archaeology The branch of anthropology that studies human history and its artifacts. Archaeologists typically look at the material remains of human groups in order to learn how people lived. (p. 6)

armchair anthropology Refers to an approach to the study of various societies that dominated anthropology in the late 1800s. It involved the collection, study, and analysis of the writings of missionaries, explorers, and colonists who had sustained contact with non-Western peoples. Armchair anthropologists used these documents to make comparisons and generalizations about the ways of life of various groups. (p. 40)

ascribed status An identity that is perceived as fixed and unchanging because a person is believed to be born with it. In Canadian society, race is often assumed to be ascribed at birth. (p. 187)

atheism Refers to a lack of belief in supernatural forces or beings. (p. 118)

bands A term used by anthropologists to refer to egalitarian units of social organization, found mostly among foragers; these units usually consist of fewer than 100 people. (p. 62)

biocultural approach The idea that some human behaviours are shaped by a combination of cultural factors and biological ones, such as genetics. (p. 163)

bilateral kinship A system in which individuals trace their descent through both parents. (p. 130)

biological anthropology A subdiscipline of anthropology that focuses on the evolution, function, and health of the human body and those of our closest primate ancestors. (p. 5)

biomedical model Also known as *Western medicine*, *scientific medicine*, or *modern medicine*, the model combines biology with the diagnosis and treatment of illness and views the body as a machine, independent of social context, that must be repaired periodically. (p. 85)

brideservice The requirement that when a couple marries, the groom must work for the bride's parents for some specified time. (p. 133)

bridewealth The valuables that a groom or his family are expected or obligated to present to the bride's family. (p. 140)

caste system A form of social stratification and identity where individuals are assigned at birth to the ranked social and occupational groups of their parents. (p. 187)

clans Unilineal descent groups whose members claim descent from a common ancestor. (pp. 63, 140)

class A form of identity informed by perceptions of an individual's economic worth or status. It is also a form of social hierarchy. (p. 186)

colonialism Refers to the acquisition of new territories throughout the world by European powers from 1492 until approximately 1945. Colonizers often imposed new forms of politics, economics, and religion upon colonized Indigenous or other cultures, and frequently exploited local populations for their labour. (p. 72)

commodities Traditionally, commodities are items that involve a transfer of value and a counter-transfer: *A* sells something to *B*, and the transaction is finished. As is typical with capitalist market-exchange systems, a long-standing personal relationship between buyer and seller is not established. (p. 174)

creole A term used commonly to refer to the formation of slave societies in the Caribbean in which elements of African and European cultures were merged, blended, or combined into something uniquely Caribbean. (p. 117)

critical cultural relativism An alternative perspective on cultural relativism that poses questions about cultural beliefs and practices in terms of who accepts them and why, who they might be disproportionately harming and benefiting, and the cultural power dynamics that enable them. (p. 16)

cultural relativism The effort to understand the beliefs and behaviours of other cultures in terms of the culture in which they are found. (p. 12)

cultural text A way of thinking about culture as a text of significant symbols, such as words, gestures, drawings, and natural objects, all of which carry meaning. (p. 18)

culture The system of meanings about the nature of experience that are shared by a people and passed on from one generation to another, including the meanings that people give to things, events, activities, and people. (p. 8)

culture change The changes in meanings that a people ascribe to experience and changes in their way of life. (p. 62)

culture shock Refers to a feeling of disorientation in the initial stages of fieldwork when an anthropologist is adjusting to a new language, beliefs, food, or even climate. (p. 47)

diaspora A population whose members are dispersed and living outside of their homeland. (p. 259)

domain of experience An area of human experience (e.g., business, war, science, family life) from which people borrow meaning to apply to other areas. (p. 96)

dowry The goods and valuables a bride's family supplies to the groom's family or to the couple. (p. 143)

economic development The term used to identify an increase in level of technology, and by some, standard of living of a population. Others view it as an ideology based on three key assumptions: (1) that economic growth and development is the solution to national as well as global problems; (2) that global economic integration will contribute to solving global ecological and social problems; and (3) that foreign assistance to undeveloped countries will make things better. (p. 79)

economic systems The rules, mechanisms, institutions, and systems of relations through which goods and services are distributed and people get what they want. (p. 220)

egocentric A view of the self that defines each person as a replica of all humanity, as the location of motivations and drives, and as capable of acting independently from others. (p. 165)

emic perspective Traditionally refers to an "insider's perspective." The goal of most fieldwork is to employ cultural relativism to understand an issue or perspective from the point of view of one's informants. (p. 38)

enculturation The process through which individuals learn an identity. It can encompass parental socialization, the influence of peers, the mass media, government, and other forces. (p. 160)

endogamy A rule that requires a person to marry someone inside his or her own group (e.g., a lineage, an ethnic group, a religious group). (p. 140)

essentialism The act of creating generalizations or stereotypes about the behaviour or culture of a group of people. (p. 52)

ethnic identity When a group of people perceive themselves as a cohesive, unified, and distinctive group of people due to the fact that they have a real or imagined common history and that they may share a common language, religion, racial background, or other factors. (p. 168)

ethnocentric fallacy The mistaken notion that the beliefs and behaviours of other cultures can be judged from the perspective of one's own culture. (p. 12)

ethnocentrism The tendency to judge the beliefs and behaviours of other cultures from the perspective of one's own culture. (p. 12)

ethnocide The attempt to destroy the culture of a people. (p. 257)

ethnographic fieldwork A research method in which sociocultural anthropologists have intensive, long-term engagements with a group of people. It may involve the use of both qualitative and quantitative methods, including interviews, participant observation, and survey-based research. (p. 37)

ethnographic present Use of the present tense to describe a culture, although the description may refer to situations that existed in the past. (p. 129)

ethnography A written description and analysis of a particular group of people, usually based upon anthropological fieldwork. (p. 42)

etic perspective Refers to the analysis of an aspect of culture using comparative categories, explanations, and interpretation from the perspective of an outside observer. (p. 38)

exogamy A rule that requires a person to marry someone outside his or her own group. (p. 140)

extended family A family group based on blood relations of three or more generations. (p. 135)

factory system A system of production characterized by the concentration of labour and machines in specific places. It is associated with the Industrial Revolution. (p. 73)

foragers A term used by anthropologists to refer to societies that make their livelihood through gathering plants, hunting, or fishing. (p. 62)

free trade The removal of barriers to the free flow of goods and capital between nations by eliminating import and export taxes as well as subsidies paid to farmers and business people. It may also mean reducing environmental or social laws when they restrict the flow of goods and capital. (p. 222)

gender Culturally constructed ideals of behaviour, dress, occupations, roles, and comportment for particular sexes. (p. 196)

genocide The attempt to exterminate a people. (p. 257)

globalization Defined by Anthony Giddens as the intensification of worldwide social relations that link distant localities in such a way that local happenings are shaped by events occurring many miles away, and vice versa. (p. 214)

hegemonic masculinity Refers to ideals and norms of masculinity in a society, which are often privileged over others. (p. 199)

imagined community A term coined by Benedict Anderson in 1983. It refers to the fact that even in the absence of face-to-face interactions, a sense of community (e.g., nationalism) is culturally constructed by forces such as the mass media. (p. 161)

impartible inheritance A form of inheritance in which family property is passed undivided to one heir. (p. 148)

incest taboo A rule that prohibits sexual relations among kin of certain categories, such as brothers or sisters, parents and children, or, in some cases, cousins. (p. 138)

Indigenism Refers to an international, collaborative movement that aims to protect the rights and livelihoods of Indigenous peoples. (p. 233)

Indigenous peoples Groups of people whose ancestors predate the arrival of European or other forms of colonialism, who share a culture and/or way of life that they often identify as distinct from "mainstream" society, and who often feel that they have a right to self-government. In Canada, this includes individuals who identify as First Nations, Métis, or Inuit. (p. 176)

Industrial Revolution A period of European history, generally identified as occurring in the late eighteenth century, marked by a shift in production from agriculture to industrial goods, urbanization, and the factory system. (p. 65)

informed consent The ongoing process of ensuring that research participants understand the goals, methods, and potential outcomes of the research process and give permission for the researcher to conduct said research. (p. 51)

International Monetary Fund (IMF) Created as an outcome of the 1944 Bretton Woods Conference to regulate currency transactions among countries. The IMF now makes loans and regulates the economies of lending countries. (p. 80)

interpersonal theory of disease A view of disease in which it is assumed that illness is caused by tensions or conflicts in social relations. (p. 87)

irrigation agriculture A form of cultivation in which water is used to deliver nutrients to growing plants. (p. 63)

key metaphors A term to identify metaphors that dominate the meanings that people in a specific culture attribute to their experience. (p. 98)

key scenarios Dominant stories or myths that portray the values and beliefs of a specific society. (p. 103)

kin term Culture-specific vocabulary to denote family relationships. These terms may or may not correspond to an anthropologist's kin type. (p. 131)

kin type Terms used by anthropologists to denote biological relationships among family members. (p. 131)

kinship Refers to the anthropological, cross-cultural study of family composition, marriage, and descent patterns. (p. 128)

***kula* ring** A system of inter-island gift exchange documented by anthropologist Bronislaw Malinowski in the Trobriand Islands. It involves the exchange of shell necklaces and armbands. According to Malinowski, the *kula* ring serves, among other things, to create alliances and social ties among individuals living on different islands. (p. 172)

linguistic anthropology A study of the relationship between language and culture. Linguistic anthropologists explore how people use language, both in a physical sense with regard to how communication is structured, and in a historical sense with regard to how different languages have developed and spread throughout history. (p. 6)

magic Refers to the manipulation of words or substances to influence spiritual beings for good or evil purposes. (p. 99)

market externalities Costs that are not included in the prices people pay, for example, health risks and environmental degradation. (p. 218)

matrilineage A lineage that is formed by tracing descent in the female line. (p. 133)

matrilineal kinship A system of descent in which persons are related to their kin through the mother only. (p. 131)

meritocracy A social system in which individuals are rewarded and resources are distributed according to achievement, effort, and ability. (p. 187)

metaphors Figures of speech in which linguistic expressions are taken from one area of experience and applied to another. (p. 96)

multiculturalism A term that Eva Mackey defines as a Canadian policy in which all hyphenated cultures, such as African-Canadian and French-Canadian, are described and celebrated as part of a "cultural mosaic." Contrast with the "cultural melting pot" image that is used in the United States. (p. 229)

multi-sited fieldwork This term, coined by George Marcus in 1995, refers to the process of connecting localized experiences of fieldwork with broader, global processes. It necessitates understanding various issues from multiple "sites," or perspectives. (p. 45)

myth A story or narrative that portrays the meanings people give to their experience. (p. 99)

nation A collection of people who share a common language, worldview, and ancestry. (p. 216)

nation-state A political community that has clearly defined territorial borders and centralized authority. (p. 216)

nationalist populist movements Forms of nationalism that represent a reaction against various forces of neoliberalism. (p. 223)

natural selection Refers to Darwin's idea that the survival of different species of organisms is partly contingent upon how well adapted they are to their physical environments. Those with favourable physical traits are more likely to survive to reproduce. (p. 64)

nature versus nurture A phrase, coined by Sir Francis Galton in 1874, that references a long-standing scholarly debate concerning whether human behaviours and identities are the result of nature (biological and genetic factors) or nurture (learned and cultural factors). (p. 161)

neoliberalism An economic philosophy that argues for minimal government involvement in the economy and greatly accelerated economic growth. Well-being, neoliberals argue, is best served by liberating individual entrepreneurs to operate in a framework of strong property rights, free markets, and free trade. (p. 221)

new racism A form of "soft" racism that posits racial differences as cultural, rather than biological, but that still views such differences as immutable or insurmountable. (p. 204)

nuclear family The family group consisting of father, mother, and their biological or adopted children. (p. 130)

partible inheritance A form of inheritance in which the goods or property of a family is divided among the heirs. (p. 148)

participant observation An element of fieldwork that can involve participating in daily tasks and observing daily interactions among a particular group. (p. 41)

pathogen An infectious agent such as a bacteria or a virus that can cause disease. (p. 85)

patrilineage A lineage that is formed by tracing descent in the male line. (p. 136)

patrilineal kinship A system of descent in which persons are related to their kin through the father only. (p. 131)

polyamory The practice of engaging in consensual intimate relationships with multiple people. (p. 151)

polyandry A form of marriage in which a woman is permitted to have more than one husband. (p. 146)

polygamy A form of marriage in which a person is permitted to have more than one spouse. (p. 145)

polygyny A form of marriage in which a man is permitted to have more than one wife. (p. 145)

population density The number of people in a given geographic area. (p. 68)

potlatch A celebration, usually involving elaborate feasting and the redistribution of gifts, found among many Indigenous Northwest Coast groups, such as the Tsimshian. The potlatch is a means of creating a new identity or of reinforcing social status within a group. (p. 173)

principle of reciprocity According to Marcel Mauss, gift-giving involves reciprocity. The idea is that the exchange of gifts creates a feeling of obligation, in that the gift must be repaid. (p. 172)

progress The idea that human history is the story of a steady advance from a life dependent on the whims of nature to a life of control and domination over natural forces. (p. 61)

"putting out" system A means of production, common in the sixteenth and seventeenth centuries and surviving today, in which a manufacturer or merchant supplies the materials and sometimes the tools to workers, who produce the goods in their own homes. (p. 73)

qualitative research Research methods that aim to explore, rather than measure, various phenomena, often through forms of observation such as interviews, focus groups, and direct participant observation. (p. 37)

quantitative research Research methods that involve the generation of statistical data. Examples include surveys and censuses. (p. 37)

race A culturally constructed form of identity and social hierarchy, *race* refers to the presumed hereditary, physical characteristics of a group of people. These physical, or phenotypic, differences are often erroneously correlated with behavioural attributes. (p. 190)

racism Refers to the discrimination and mistreatment of particular "racial" groups. (p. 191)

rapport A feeling of affinity, friendship, and responsibility between an anthropologist and an informant. It is often developed through the use of long-term ethnographic fieldwork. (p. 38)

refugees Groups of people who have left their homeland due to warfare, forced expulsion, acts of terrorism, or other factors. (p. 259)

relativistic fallacy The idea that it is impossible to make moral judgments about the beliefs and behaviours of members of other cultures. (p. 13)

representation The way in which a group of people is depicted in writing or through images. Anthropologists are increasingly conscious of the fact that when they write about a group of people, they are constructing particular representations that may have positive or negative long-term effects for a group of people. (p. 39)

revitalization movements The term suggested by Anthony F.C. Wallace for attempts by a people to construct a more satisfying culture. (p. 114)

rites of passage The term coined in 1908 by Arnold van Gennep to refer to the category of rituals that accompany changes in status, such as the transition from boyhood to manhood, living to dead, or student to graduate. (pp. 106, 170)

ritual A dramatic rendering or social portrayal of meanings shared by a specific body of people in a way that makes them seem correct and proper. (*See also* symbolic actions.) (p. 95)

salvage anthropology An approach to anthropology that arose in the late 1800s when anthropologists witnessed the extinction or assimilation of Indigenous peoples throughout the world. In response, some anthropologists, such as Franz Boas, suggested that anthropologists rapidly document the oral stories, songs, histories, and other traditions of Indigenous peoples before they disappeared. (p. 43)

secularism Refers to the separation of political and economic realms of society from religion or spirituality. (p. 118)

sedentary A mode of livelihood characterized by permanent or semi-permanent settlements. (p. 62)

sex Hormonal, chromosomal, or physical differences between men and women. (p. 196)

shamanism Refers to a spiritual belief system whereby spiritual practitioners called "shamans" enter into an altered state of consciousness to seek guidance from spiritual forces. (p. 111)

slash-and-burn, or swidden, agriculture A mode of livelihood in which forests are cleared by burning trees and brush, and crops are planted among the ashes of the cleared ground. (p. 63)

social hierarchy The ordering and ranking of individuals within society, also known as *social stratification*. Those at the top of the hierarchy are generally afforded more power, wealth, prestige, or privileges in a society. Hierarchies can be based on race, gender, class, caste, ethnicity, national affiliation, or other factors. (p. 185)

social identity The view that people have of their own and others' positions in society. These learned personal and social affiliations may include gender, sexuality, race, class, nationalism, and ethnicity. Individuals seek confirmation from others that they occupy the positions on the social landscape that they claim to occupy. (p. 158)

society The social structures and organization of a group comprised of people who share a territory and culture. (p. 8)

sociocentric A context-dependent view of self. The self exists as an entity only within the concrete situations or roles occupied by the person. (p. 165)

sociocultural anthropology A comparative approach to the study of societies and cultures that focuses on differences and similarities in the ways that societies are structured and cultural meanings are created. (p. 2)

states Forms of society characterized by a hierarchical ranking of people and centralized political control. (p. 63)

structural violence Refers to the systematic ways in which social structures or social institutions harm or otherwise disadvantage local individuals. Structural violence is often invisible and lacking one specific person who can (or will) be held responsible. (p. 209)

symbolic actions The activities—including ritual, myth, art, dance, and music—that dramatically depict the meanings shared by a specific body of people. (p. 96)

syncretism The term given to the combination of old beliefs or religions and new ones (often introduced during colonization) to create a new worldview. (p. 116)

technostrategic language A term coined by Carol Cohn to describe the way nuclear strategic language and thinking used by defence intellectuals are imbued with modes of thinking associated with technology. (p. 262)

third gender A gender role given to someone who does not fit within strictly masculine or feminine gender roles in a given society that recognizes the possibility of at least three genders. (p. 196)

totemism The use of a symbol, generally an animal or a plant, as a physical representation for a group, generally a clan. (p. 95)

transgender Refers to an individual who feels that their assigned sex at birth does not match their accompanying gender. (p 196)

transnational Involving more than one nation-state; reaching beyond or transcending national boundaries. (p. 223)

unilineal evolution A late-nineteenth-century theory of social evolution which posited that all societies go through a series of standardized stages of change. It ethnocentrically positioned Western societies at the apex of a "ladder of civilization." (p. 65)

vector An organism, such as a mosquito, tick, flea, or snail, that can transmit disease to another animal. (p. 85)

white privilege Refers to the fact that, in many societies, "white" people have access to greater power, authority, and privileges than non-white people. (p. 192)

witchcraft Refers to the belief that an individual (the witch) has the ability to cause harm to others through the manipulation of powerful substances. (p. 99)

World Bank One of the institutions created at the 1944 Bretton Woods, New Hampshire, meeting of Allied nations. The World Bank (or the Bank for Reconstruction and Development) functions as a lending institution to nations largely for projects related to economic development. (p. 80)

worldview An encompassing picture of reality based on shared cultural assumptions about how the world works. (p. 94)

Bibliography

Abu-Lughod, Lila. 2002. "Do Muslim Women Really Need Saving? Anthropological Reflections on Cultural Relativism and Its Others." *American Anthropologist* 104(3): 783–90.

——. 1995. "A Tale of Two Pregnancies." In *Women Writing Culture,* edited by Ruth Behar and Deborah A. Gordon. Berkeley: University of California Press.

Adelson, Naomi. 2000. *"Being Alive Well": Health and the Politics of Cree Well-Being*. Toronto: University of Toronto Press.

Aditjondro, George. 2000. "Ninjas, Nanggalas, Monuments, and Mossad Manuals." In *Death Squad: The Anthropology of State Terror,* edited by Jeffery A. Sluka. Philadelphia: University of Pennsylvania Press.

Alberta Government. 2000. Environmental Protection and Enhancement Act. Edmonton: Alberta Queen's Printer.

Alford, Richard D. 1988. *Naming and Identity: A Cross-Cultural Study of Personal Naming Practices*. New Haven: HRAF Press.

Ameeriar, Lalaie. 2012. "The Sanitized Sensorium." *American Anthropologist* 114(3): 509–20.

American Anthropological Association. 2005. *Anthropology News* 46:1.

——. 1998. *Statement on Race.* http://www.aaanet.org/stmts/racepp.htm

Anderson, Benedict. 1991. *Imagined Communities: Reflections on the Origin and Spread of Nationalism.* New York: Verso.

Anderson, Margaret (Seguin). 2004. "Understanding Tsimshian Potlatch." In *Native Peoples: The Canadian Experience,* edited by R. Bruce Morrison and C. Roderick Wilson. Toronto: Oxford University Press.

——. 1984. *Interpretive Contexts for Traditional and Current Coast Tsimshian Feasts, 98.* Ottawa: Canadian Ethnology Service Paper. National Museum of Canada.

Anderson, Margaret (Seguin), ed. 1984. *The Tsimshian: Images of the Past, Views for the Present.* Vancouver: UBC Press.

Anderson, Margaret (Seguin), and Marjorie Halpin, eds. 2000. *Potlatch at Getsegukla.* Vancouver: UBC Press.

Anderson-Levy, Lisa. 2000. "Colliding/Colluding Identities: Race, Class, and Gender in Jamaican Family Systems." In *New Directions in Anthropological Kinship,* edited by Linda Stone. Lanham: Rowman and Littlefield.

Angeloni, Elvio. 1990. *Anthropology 90/91.* Guilford: Dushkin.

Appadurai, Arjun. 2006. *Modernity at Large: Cultural Dimensions of Globalization.* Minneapolis: University of Minnesota Press.

——. 1990. "Disjuncture and Difference in the Global Cultural Economy." *Public Culture* 2(10): 1–24.

Arat-Koc, Sedef. 1999a. "'Good Enough to Work but Not Good Enough to Stay': Foreign Domestic Workers and the Law." In *Locating Law: Race/Class/Gender Connections,* edited by Elizabeth Comack. Halifax: Fernwood.

——. 1999b. "Neoliberalism, State Restructuring, and Immigration: Changes in Canadian Policies in the 1990s." *Journal of Canadian Studies* 34(2): 31–57.

Asad, Talal. 2003. *Formations of the Secular: Christianity, Islam, Modernity.* Palo Alto: Stanford University Press.

Asch, Michael, ed. 2002. *Aboriginal and Treaty Rights in Canada: Essays on Law, Equality, and Respect for Difference.* Vancouver: UBC Press.

Austin-Broos, Diane. 1997. *Jamaica Genesis: Religion and the Politics of Moral Orders.* Chicago: University of Chicago Press.

Avruch, Kevin. 2009. "Transforming Conflict Resolution Education: Applying Anthropology Alongside Your Students." *Learning and Teaching* 2(2): 8–22.

Bannerji, Himani. 2000. *The Dark Side of the Nation: Essays on Multiculturalism, Nationalism, and Gender.* Toronto: Canadian Scholars' Press.

Barker, John, ed. 1990. *Christianity in Oceania: Ethnographic Perspectives.* Lanham: University Press of America.

Barrett, Stanley R. 2002. *Culture Meets Power.* Westport: Praeger.

——. 1996. *Anthropology: A Student's Guide to Theory and Method.* Toronto: University of Toronto Press.

——. 1987. *Is God a Racist? The Right Wing in Canada.* Toronto: University of Toronto Press.

Barsh, Russel Lawrence. 2002. "Netukulimk Past and Present: Mikmaw Ethics and the Atlantic Fisheries." *Journal of Canadian Studies* 37(1): 15–44.

Basok, Tanya. 2004. *Tortillas and Tomatoes: Transmigrant Mexican Harvesters in Canada*. Montreal and Kingston: McGill–Queen's University Press.

Beaud, Michel. 1983. *A History of Capitalism, 1500–1980*. New York: Monthly Review Press.

Becker, Anne E. 2004. "Television, Disordered Eating, and Young Women in Fiji: Negotiating Body Image and Identity during Rapid Social Change." *Culture, Medicine, and Psychiatry* 29: 533–59.

——. E. 1995. *Body, Self, and Society: The View from Fiji*. Philadelphia: University of Pennsylvania Press.

Behar, Ruth, and Deborah Gordon, eds. 1995. *Women Writing Culture*. Berkeley: University of California Press.

Bellah, Robert, Richard Madsen, William M. Sullivan, Ann Swidler, and Steven M. Tipton. 1984. *Habits of the Heart*. Berkeley: University of California Press.

Belmonte, Thomas. 1989. *The Broken Fountain*. New York: Columbia University Press.

Benedict, Ruth. 1934. *Patterns of Culture*. New York: Houghton Mifflin.

Beske, Melissa A. 2016. *Intimate Partner Violence and Advocate Response: Redefining Love in Western Belize*. Lanham: Lexington Books.

——. 2014. "An Analysis of the Collaborative Endeavors to Lessen Gender-Based Intimate Partner Violence in Cayo, Belize, and a Case for Anthropological Engagement." In *Anthropological Approaches to Gender-Based Violence and Human Rights*. Working Paper #304. Center for Gender in Global Context. East Lansing: Michigan State University, 16–33. https://gencen.isp.msu.edu/files/8914/5201/1092/WP304.pdf.

Bielawski, Ellen. 2004. *Rogue Diamonds: Northern Riches on Dene Land*. Seattle: University of Washington Press.

Blackwood, Evelyn. 2005. "Wedding Bell Blues: Marriage, Missing Men, and Matrifocal Follies." *American Ethnologist* 32(1): 3–19.

Blaikie, Piers, and Harold Brookfield. 1987. *Land Degradation and Society*. London: Methuen.

Blaser, Mario, Harvey Feit, and Glenn McRae, eds. 2004. *In the Way of Development: Indigenous Peoples' Life Projects and Globalization*. London and New York: Zed.

Blundell, Valda. 1989. "The Tourist and the Native." In *A Different Drummer: Readings in Anthropology with a Canadian Perspective,* edited by Bruce Alden Cox, Jacques Chevallier, and Valda Blundell. Ottawa: Carleton University Press.

Boas, Franz. 1940. *Race, Language and Culture*. New York: Macmillan.

Boas, Franz, and George Hunt. 1905. *Kwakiutl Texts*. Memoir of the American Museum of Natural History, vol. 5.

Bodley, John. 1999. *The Victims of Progress*. Mountain View: Mayfield.

——. 1994. *Cultural Anthropology: Tribes, States, and the Global System*. Mountain View: Mayfield.

——. 1985. *Anthropology and Contemporary Problems*, 2nd ed. Palo Alto: Mayfield.

Boellstorff, Tom. 2008. *Coming of Age in Second Life: An Anthropologist Explores the Virtually Human*. Princeton: Princeton University Press.

Bogart, Nicole. 2019. "Could basketball overtake hockey as Canada's national sport?" *CTV News*, 10 June. https://www.ctvnews.ca/canada/could-basketball-overtake-hockey-as-canada-s-national-sport-1.4460272.

Bohannan, Laura. 1966. "Shakespeare in the Bush." *Natural History Magazine*, August–September.

Bonanno, Alessandro, Lawrence Busch, William Friedland, Lourdes Gouveia, and Enzo Mingione, eds. 1994. *From Columbus to ConAgra: The Globalization of Agriculture and Food*. Lawrence: University Press of Kansas.

Bonilla, Yaramir, and Jonathan Rosa. 2015. "#Ferguson: Digital Protest, Hashtag Ethnography, and the Racial Politics of Social Media in the United States." *American Ethnologist* 42: 4–17.

Bonnet, Florence, Joann Vanek, and Martha Chen. 2019. "Women and Men in the Informal Economy" [statistical brief]. Manchester: WIEGO (Women in Informal Employment: Globalizing and Organizing).

Bossen, Laurel. 2002. *Chinese Women and Rural Development: Sixty Years of Change in Lu Village, Yunnan*. Lanham: Rowman and Littlefield.

Bourgois, Philippe. 2003. *In Search of Respect: Selling Crack in El Barrio*, 2nd ed. Cambridge: Cambridge University Press.

Branford, Sue, and Jan Rocha. 2002. *Cutting the Wire: The Story of the Landless Movement in Brazil*. London: Latin American Bureau.

Braudel, Fernand. 1982. *Civilization and Capitalism, 15th–18th Century*, vol. 2: *The Wheels of Commerce*. New York: Harper and Row.

Brennan, Denise. 2004. *What's Love Got to Do with It?: Transnational Desires and Sex Tourism in the Dominican Republic*. Durham: Duke University Press.

Brettell, Caroline, and Carolyn Sargent, eds. 2005. *Gender in Cross-Cultural Perspective*. Upper Saddle River: Prentice Hall.

Briggs, Jean. 1970. *Never in Anger*. Cambridge, MA: Harvard University Press.

Brody, Hugh. 2000. *The Other Side of Eden: Hunters, Farmers, and the Shaping of the World*. Vancouver: Douglas and McIntyre.

Brown, Karen McCarthy. 1991. *Mama Lola: A Vodou Priestess in Brooklyn*. Berkeley: University of California Press.

Burt, Martha. 1992. *Over the Edge: The Growth of Homelessness in the 1980s*. New York: Russell Sage Foundation.

Cagan, Leslie. 1983. "Feminism and Militarism." In *Beyond Survival: New Directions for the Disarmament Movement*, edited by M. Albert and D. Dellinger. Boston: South End.

Canadian Council on Learning. 2009. *The State of Aboriginal Learning in Canada: A Holistic Approach to Measuring Success*. Ottawa: Canadian Council on Learning.

Carneiro, Robert. 1990. "Chiefdom-Level Warfare as Exemplified in Fiji and Cauca Valley." In *The Anthropology of War*, edited by Jonathan Hass. New York: Cambridge University Press.

——. 1979. "Slash-and-Burn Cultivation among the Kuikuru and Its Implication for Cultural Development in the Amazon Basin." In *The Evolution of Horticultural Systems in Native South America: Causes and Consequences. Anthropologica Supplement 2*, edited by Johannes Wilbert. Caracas.

——. 1978. "Political Expansion as an Expression of the Principle of Competitive Exclusion." In *Origins of the State: The Anthropology of Political Evolution*, edited by Ronald Cohn and Elman Service. Philadelphia: Institute for the Study of Human Issues.

Carrier, James G. 1995. *Gifts and Commodities: Exchange and Western Capitalism Since 1700*. London: Routledge.

——. 1993. "The Rituals of Christmas Giving." In *Unwrapping Christmas*, edited by Daniel Miller. Oxford: Clarendon.

Carter, Sarah. 1999. *Aboriginal People and Colonizers of Western Canada to 1900*. Toronto: University of Toronto Press.

Case, Emalani. 2019. "*I ka Piko*, To the Summit: Resistance from the Mountain to the Sea." *Journal of Pacific History* 54(2): 166–81.

Cesara, Manda. 1982. *Reflections of a Woman Anthropologist: No Hiding Place*. Toronto: Academic Press.

Chagnon, Napoleon. 1990. "Reproductive and Somatic Conflicts of Interest in the Genesis of Violence and Warfare among Tribesmen." In *The Anthropology of War*, edited by Jonathan Hass. New York: Cambridge University Press.

——. 1968. *Yanomamö: The Fierce People*. Toronto: Holt.

Chambers, Erve. 2000. *Native Tours: The Anthropology of Travel and Tourism*. Prospect Heights: Waveland.

Chen, Zhongping. 2004. "Chinese Minority and Everyday Racism in Canadian Towns and Small Cities: An Ethnic Study of the Case of Peterborough, Ontario, 1892–1951." *Canadian Ethnic Studies* 36(1): 71–91.

Chimbinda, Jorge. 2006. "The Umbundu Naming System." MA thesis, Department of Anthropology, University of Western Ontario, London.

Chodkiewicz, Jean-Luc, and Raymond E. Wiest, eds. 2004. *Globalization and Community*. Winnipeg: University of Manitoba Press.

Chomsky, Noam. 1984. *Turning the Tide: U.S. Intervention in Central America and the Struggle for Peace*. Boston: South End.

Churchill, Ward. 1994. *Indians Are Us? Culture and Genocide in Native North America*. Monroe: Common Courage.

Citizens for Public Justice. 2018. *Poverty Trends 2018*. https://cpj.ca/poverty-trends-2018

Clammer, John, Sylvie Poirier, and Eric Schwimmer, eds. 2004. *Figured Worlds: Ontological Obstacles in Intercultural Relations*. Toronto: University of Toronto Press.

Clark, Kim. 2005. "Ecuadorian Indians, the Nation, and Class in Historic Perspective: Rethinking a 'New Social Movement.'" *Anthropologica* 47(1): 53–65.

Clark-Decès, Isabelle. 2011. "Introduction." In *A Companion to the Anthropology of India*, edited by Isabelle Clark-Decès, 1–21. Malden: Blackwell.

Cohen, Mark. 1989. *Health and the Rise of Civilization*. New Haven: Yale University Press.

——. 1977. *The Food Crisis in Prehistory*. New Haven: Yale University Press.

Cohn, Carol. 1991. "Decoding Military Newspeak." *Ms.* 5.

——. 1987. "Sex and Death in the Rational World of Defense Intellectuals." *Signs* 12: 687–718.

Cole, Sally. 2000. "Reflections on Anthropology in Canada: Introduction." *Anthropologica* 42(2): 123–26.

Collier, Jane E., and Michelle Rosaldo. 1981. "Politics and Gender in Simple Societies." In *Sexual Meanings: The Cultural Construction of Gender and Sexuality,* edited by Sherry B. Ortner and Harriet Whitehead. New York: Cambridge University Press.

Collings, Peter, and Richard G. Condon. 1996. "Blood on Ice: Status, Self-Esteem, and Ritual Injury among Inuit Hockey Players." *Human Organization* 55(3): 253–62.

Comaroff, Jean, and John Comoraff. 2009. "Alien-Nation: Zombies, Immigrants, and Millennial Capitalism." In *Enchantments of Modernity: Empire, Nation, Globalization,* edited by Saurabh Dube, 451–81. New Delhi: Routledge India.

Conklin, Beth. 2001. *Consuming Grief: Compassionate Cannibalism in an Amazonian Society.* Austin: University of Texas Press.

Coombe, Rosemary. 2013. *Dynamic Fair Dealing: Creating Canadian Culture Online.* Toronto: University of Toronto Press.

Coren, Michael. 2019. "Quebec's Proposed Secularism Law is Repugnant." *Maclean's*, 29 March 2019. https://www.macleans.ca/opinion/quebecs-proposed-secularism-law-is-repugnant-here-are-six-reasons-why

Corten, Andre, and Ruth Marshall-Fratani. 2001. *Between Babel and Pentecost: Transnational Pentecostalism in Africa and Latin America.* Bloomington: Indiana University Press.

Counts, David, and Dorothy Counts. 1998. "Fictive Families in the Field." In *Fieldwork and Families: Constructing New Models for Ethnographic Research,* edited by Juliana Flinn, Leslie Marshall, and Jocelyn Armstrong. Honolulu: University of Hawai'i Press.

Cowan, Jane K., Marie-Benedicte Dembour, and Richard A. Wilson, eds. 2001. *Culture and Rights: Anthropological Perspectives.* Cambridge: Cambridge University Press.

Cowell, Daniel David. 1985/86. "Funerals, Family, and Forefathers: A View of Italian-American Funeral Practices." *Omega* 16: 69–85.

Cox, Bruce Alden, Jacques Chevalier, and Valda Blundell, eds. 1989. *A Different Drummer: Readings in Anthropology with a Canadian Perspective.* Ottawa: Carleton University Press.

Crick, Malcolm R. 1982. "Anthropology of Knowledge." *Annual Review of Anthropology* 11: 287–313. Palo Alto: Annual Reviews.

Crowley, Aleister. 1985. *The Book of Thoth.* Stamford: US Games Systems.

Cruikshank, Julie. 2005. *Do Glaciers Listen? Local Knowledge, Colonial Encounters, and Social Imagination.* Vancouver: UBC Press.

——. 1998. *The Social Life of Stories: Narrative and Knowledge in the Yukon Territory.* Lincoln: University of Nebraska Press.

——. 1990. *Life Lived Like a Story: Life Stories of Three Yukon Native Elders.* Lincoln: University of Nebraska Press.

Culhane, Dara. 1998. *The Pleasures of the Crown: Anthropology, Law, and First Nations.* Burnaby: Talonbooks.

Culhane Speck, Dara. 1987. *An Error in Judgement: The Politics of Medical Care in an Indian/White Community.* Vancouver: Talonbooks.

Cummings, Maggie. 2008. "The Trouble with Trousers: Gossip, *Kastom*, and Sexual Culture in Vanuatu." In *Making Sense of AIDS: Culture, Sexuality, and Power in Melanesia,* edited by Leslie Butt and Richard Eves, 133–49. Honolulu: University of Hawai'i Press.

Cummins, Bryan D. 2004. *"Only God Can Own the Land": The Attawapiskat Cree.* Toronto: Pearson Education.

Dahl, Bianca. 2014. "'Too Fat to Be an Orphan': The Moral Semiotics of Food Aid in Botswana." *Cultural Anthropology* 29: 626–47.

Daniel, Valentine. 1996. *Charred Lullabies: Chapters in an Anthropology of Violence.* Princeton: Princeton University Press.

Darnell, Regna. 1990. *Edward Sapir: Linguist, Anthropologist, Humanist.* Berkeley: University of California Press.

Darnell, Regna. 2000. "Canadian Anthropologists, the First Nations, and Canada's Self-Image at the Millennium." *Anthropologica* 42(2): 165–74.

——. 1998a. *And Along Came Boas: Continuity and Revolution in Americanist Anthropology.* Amsterdam and Philadelphia: John Benjamins.

——. 1998b. "Toward a History of Canadian Departments of Anthropology: Retrospect, Prospect, and Common Cause." *Anthropologica* 40(2): 153–68.

Darnell, Regna, and Julia Harrison. 2006. "Introduction." In *Historicizing Canadian Anthropology*, edited by Julia Harrison and Regna Darnell, 3–18. Vancouver: UBC Press.

Darville, Jordan. 2019. "Interview: Jeremy Dutcher: 'The Days of Internalised Colonialism Are Done.'". https://www.theguardian.com/music/2019/mar/26/jeremy-dutcher-interview-canada-first-nation-indigenous-arias

Darwin, Charles. 1859. *On the Origin of Species by Means of Natural Selection, or the Preservation of Favoured Races in the Struggle for Life*. London: John Murray.

Davis, D.L., and R.G. Whitten. 1987. "The Cross-Cultural Study of Human Sexuality." *Annual Review of Anthropology* 16: 69–98.

Davis-Floyd, Robbie E. 2004. *Birth as an American Rite of Passage*. Berkeley: University of California Press.

Dawkins, Richard. 2006. *The God Delusion*. Boston: Houghton Mifflin.

D'Andrade, Roy. 1995. "Moral Models in Anthropology." *Current Anthropology* 36: 399–408.

Day, Richard J.F. 2000. *Multiculturalism and the History of Canadian Diversity*. Toronto: University of Toronto Press.

Delaney, Carol. 1991. *The Seed and the Soil: Gender and Cosmology in a Turkish Village Society.* Berkeley: University of California Press.

Deliège, Robert. 2011. "Caste, Class, and Untouchability. In *A Companion to the Anthropology of India*, edited by Isabelle Clark-Decès, 45–61. Malden, MA: Blackwell.

Desai, Ashok V. 1972. "Population and Standards of Living in Akbar's Time." In *Indian Economic and Social History Review* 9: 42–62.

Devita, Philip. 1990. *The Humbled Anthropologist: Tales from the Pacific*. Belmont: Wadsworth.

Devita, Philip, ed. 1991. *The Naked Anthropologist: Tales from Around the World*. Belmont: Wadsworth.

Dickason, Olive Patricia. 2002. *Canada's First Nations: A History of Founding Peoples from Earliest Times*, 3rd ed. Toronto: Oxford University Press.

Divale, William Tulio, and Marvin Harris. 1976. "Population, Warfare, and the Male Supremacist Complex." *American Anthropologist* 78: 521–38.

Douglas, Mary. 1966. *Purity and Danger*. New York: Praeger.

Douglas, Mary, and Aaron Wildavsky. 1982. *Risk and Culture: An Essay on the Selection of Technical and Environmental Changes*. Berkeley: University of California Press.

Douglas, Ngaire. 1996. *They Came for Savages: 100 Years of Tourism in Melanesia*. Lismore: Southern Cross University Press.

Dréze, Jean, and Amartya Sen. 1991. *Hunger and Public Action*. New York: Cambridge University Press.

Dumont, Louis. 1970. *Homo Hierarchicus: An Essay on the Caste System*. Chicago: University of Chicago Press.

Durham, William H. 1990. "Advances in Evolutionary Culture Theory." *Annual Review of Anthropology* 19: 187–210.

Durkheim, Emile. 1961. *The Elementary Forms of the Religious Life*. New York: Collier.

Dutcher, Jeremy. 2012. "Traditional Music in a Contemporary Moment: Musical Pan-Indigeneity as Revitalization in the Wabanaki Region." Honours thesis, Department of Sociology and Social Anthropology, Dalhousie University.

Dyck, Noel. 2006. "Canadian Anthropology and the Ethnography of 'Indian Administration.'" In *Historicizing Canadian Anthropology*, edited by Julia Harrison and Regna Darnell, 78–92. Vancouver: UBC Press.

——. 2000. "Games, Bodies, Celebrations, and Boundaries: Anthropological Perspectives on Sports." In *Sports, Games and Cultures,* edited by Noel Dyke. Oxford: Berg.

Dyck, Noel, and James B. Waldram, eds. 1993. *Anthropology, Public Policy, and Native Peoples in Canada.* Montreal and Kingston: McGill–Queen's University Press.

Eckert, Penelope, and Sally McConnell-Ginet. 2003. *Language and Gender*. Cambridge: Cambridge University Press.

Edmonds, Alexander. 2010. *Pretty Modern: Beauty, Sex, and Plastic Surgery in Brazil.* Durham: Duke University Press.

Eisler, Riane. 1987. *The Chalice and the Blade*. New York: Harper and Row.

Eller, Jack. 1999. "Quebec: Masters in Our Own House." In *From Culture to Ethnicity to Conflict: An Anthropological Perspective on International Ethnic Conflict*. Ann Arbor: University of Michigan Press.

Epp, Marlene, Francis Iacovetta, and Francis Swyripa, eds. 2004. *Sisters or Strangers? Immigrant, Ethnic, and Racialized*

Women in Canadian History. Toronto: University of Toronto Press.

Eramian, Laura. 2014. "Ethnicity without Labels: Ambiguity and Excess in 'Postethnic' Rwanda." *Focaal: Journal of Global and Historical Anthropology* 70: 96–109.

Erasmus, Charles. 1977. *In Search of the Common Good*. Glencoe: The Free Press.

Ervin, Alexander M. 2005. *Applied Anthropology: Tools and Perspectives for Contemporary Practice*. Boston: Allyn and Bacon.

——. 2001. *Canadian Perspectives in Cultural Anthropology*. Toronto: Nelson Education.

Escobar, Arturo. 1995. *Encountering Development: The Making and Unmaking of the Third World*. Princeton: Princeton University Press.

Evans-Pritchard, E.E. 1985. *Theories of Primitive Religion*. San Francisco: Greenwood.

——. 1940. *The Nuer: A Description of the Modes of Livelihood and Political Institutions of a Nilotic People*. Oxford: Clarendon.

——. 1937. *Witchcraft, Oracles and Magic among the Azande*. Oxford: Clarendon.

Farah, Randa. 2005. "Out of the Shadows: Listening to Place-Based Narratives of Palestinian Women." In *Women and the Politics of Place,* edited by Wendy Harcourt and Arturo Escobar. Bloomfield: Kumarian.

——. 2004. "But Where Shall I Return? Where To? 1948 Palestinian Refugees: Land and Return." *Mediterranean Journal of Human Rights* 8(2): 157–84.

——. 2003. "The Marginalization of Palestinian Refugees." In *Problems of Protection: The UNHCR, Refugees, and Human Rights,* edited by Niklaus Steiner, Mark Gibney, and Gil Loescher. New York and London: Routledge.

Farmer, Paul. 2003. *Pathologies of Power: Health, Human Rights, and the New War on the Poor*. Berkeley: University of California Press.

——. 1992. *AIDS and Accusation: Haiti and the Geography of Blame*. Berkeley: University of California Press.

Fausto-Sterling, Anne. 1993. "The Five Sexes: Why Male and Female Are Not Enough." *The Sciences* 33: 20–24.

Fei, Hsiao-Tung. 1939. *Peasant Life in China: A Field Study of Country Life in the Yangtze Valley*. London: Routledge and Kegan Paul.

Feinberg, Richard. 2001. "Introduction: Schneider's Cultural Analysis of Kinship and Its Implications for Anthropological Relativism." In *The Cultural Analysis of Kinship: The Legacy of David M. Schneider*, edited by Richard Feinberg and Martin Ottenheimer. Urbana: University of Illinois Press.

Feit, Harvey A. 1982. "The Income Security Program for Cree Hunters in Quebec: An Experiment in Increasing the Autonomy of Hunters in a Developed Nation State." *Canadian Journal of Anthropology* 3(1): 57–70.

——. 1973. "The Ethno-Ecology of the Waswanipi Cree; or How Hunters Manage Their Resources." In *Cultural Ecology,* edited by B. Cox. Toronto: McClelland and Stewart.

Fenton, Cameron. 2010. "The Ethnography of an Airstrike: Canada's Military Academics in the Afghan War and at Home." http://www.dominionpaper.ca/articles/3295

Ferguson, R. Brian. 2008. "Ten Points on War." *Social Analysis* 52(2): 32–49.

——. 1995. *Yanomami Warfare: A Political History*. Santa Fe: School of the American Research Press.

——. 1992. "A Savage Encounter: Western Contact and the Yanomami War Complex." In *War in the Tribal Zone: Expanding States and Indigenous Warfare,* edited by R. Brian Ferguson and Neil L. Whitehead. Santa Fe: School of American Research Press.

Ferguson, James. 1990. *The Anti-Politics Machine: "Development," Depoliticization, and Bureaucratic Power in Lesotho*. Cambridge: Cambridge University Press.

Fernandez, James W. 1978. "African Religious Movements." *Annual Review of Anthropology* 7: 195–234.

Fernando, Mayanthi. 2015. *The French Myth of Secularism*. http://theconversation.com/the-french-myth-of-secularism-36227

——. 2014. *The Republic Unsettled: Muslim French and the Contradictions of Secularism*. Durham: Duke University Press.

Fienup-Riordan, Ann. 1990. *Eskimo Essays: Yup'ik Lives and How We See Them*. New Brunswick: Rutgers University Press.

Fisher, William. 1997. "Doing Good? The Politics and Antipolitics of NGO Practices." *Annual Review of Anthropology* 26: 439–64.

Fleras, Augie, and Jean Leonard Elliot. 2002. *Engaging Diversity: Multiculturalism in Canada*. Toronto: Nelson Education.

Foucault, Michel. 1979. *Discipline and Punish: The Birth of the Prison*. New York: Vintage.

Francis, Daniel. 1992. *The Imaginary Indian: The Image of the Indian in Canadian Culture*. Vancouver: Arsenal Pulp.

Franklin, Sarah, and Susan McKinnon, eds. 2001. *Relative Values: Reconfiguring Kinship Studies*. Durham: Duke University Press.

French, Hilary. 2000. *Vanishing Borders: Protecting the Planet in the Age of Globalization*. New York: W.W. Norton.

Frideres, James. 2003. *Native Peoples in Canada: Contemporary Conflicts*. Toronto: Prentice Hall.

Frideres, James S., and René Gadacz. 2001. *Aboriginal Peoples in Canada: Contemporary Conflicts*. Toronto: Prentice Hall.

Fried, Morton, Marvin Harris, and Robert Murphy. 1967. *War: The Anthropology of Armed Conflict and Aggression*. Garden City: Natural History Press.

Fry, Douglas. 2007. *Beyond War: The Human Potential for Peace*. Oxford: Oxford University Press.

Furniss, Elizabeth. 1992. *Victims of Benevolence: Discipline and Death at the Williams Lake Indian Residential School, 1891–1920*. Williams Lake: Cariboo Tribal Council.

Gagne, Marie-Anik. 1994. *A Nation within a Nation: Dependency and the Cree*. Montreal: Black Rose.

Galton, Francis. 1879. *Hereditary Genius: An Inquiry into Its Laws and Consequences*. New York: Appleton.

Gardner, Katy, and David Lewis. 1996. *Anthropology, Development, and the Post-Modern Challenge*. London: Pluto.

Geertz, Clifford. 1973. "The Impact of Culture on the Concept of Man." In *The Interpretation of Cultures: Selected Essays by Clifford Geertz*. New York: Basic Books.

——. 1972. "Deep Play: Notes on the Balinese Cockfight." *Daedalus* 101: 1–37.

Gellner, Ernest. 1983. *Nations and Nationalism*. Ithaca: Cornell University Press.

George, Susan, and Fabrizio Sabelli. 1994. *Faith and Credit: The World Bank's Secular Empire*. Boulder: Westview.

Gerber, Linda. 1990. "Multiple Jeopardy: A Socio-Economic Comparison of Men and Women among the Indian, Métis, and Inuit Peoples of Canada." *Canadian Ethnic Studies* 22(3): 69–84.

Geschiere, Peter. 1997. *The Modernity of Witchcraft: Politics and the Occult in Postcolonial Africa*. Charlottesville: University of Virginia Press.

Gibson, Thomas. 1990. "Raiding, Trading, and Tribal Autonomy in Insular Southeast Asia." In *The Anthropology of War*, edited by Jonathan Hass. New York: Cambridge University Press.

Giddens, Anthony. 1990. *The Consequences of Modernity*. Cambridge: Polity.

Gilmore, David D. 1990. *Manhood in the Making: Cultural Concepts of Masculinity*. New Haven: Yale University Press.

Ginsburg, Faye, and Rayna Rapp. 1991. "The Politics of Reproduction." *Annual Review of Anthropology* 20: 311–43.

Gledhill, John. 1994. *Power and Its Disguises: Anthropological Perspectives on Politics*. London: Pluto.

Goffman, Erving. 1999. *The Presentation of Self in Everyday Life*. New York: Peter Smith.

Goldberg, David Theo. 2009. *The Threat of Race: Reflections on Racial Neoliberalism*. Hoboken: Wiley-Blackwell.

Gonzales, Roberto. 2009. *American Counterinsurgency: Human Science and the Human Terrain*. New York: Prickly Paradigm.

Goodyear-Kaʻōpua, Noelani. 2017. "Protectors of the Future, Not Protestors of the Past: Indigenous Pacific Activism and Mauna a Wākea." *South Atlantic Quarterly* 116(1): 184–94.

Gould, Stephen Jay. 1981. *The Mismeasure of Man*. New York: W.W. Norton.

Goulet, Jean-Guy A. 2004. "The Dene Tha of Chateh: Continuities and Transformations." In *Native Peoples: The Canadian Experience*, edited by R. Bruce Morrison and C. Roderick Wilson. Toronto: Oxford University Press.

——. 1998. *Ways of Knowing: Experience, Knowledge, and Power among the Dene Tha*. Vancouver: UBC Press.

Green, Linda. 1995. "Living in a State of Fear." In *Fieldwork under Fire: Contemporary Studies of Violence and Survival*, edited by Carolyn Nordstrom and Antonius C.G. Robben. Berkeley: University of California Press.

Greenhouse, Carol. 1987. "Cultural Perspectives on War." In *The Quest for Peace: Transcending Collective Violence and War among Societies, Cultures, and States*, edited by Raimo Vayrynen. Beverly Hills: Sage.

Gremillion, Helen. 2003. *Feeding Anorexia: Gender and Power at a Treatment Center*. Durham: Duke University Press.

Gregor, Thomas. 1990. "Uneasy Peace: Intertribal Relations in Brazil's Upper Xingu." In *The Anthropology of War*, edited by Jonathan Hass. New York: Cambridge University Press.

Grim, John A., ed. 2001. *Indigenous Traditions and Ecology: The Interbeing of Cosmology and Community*. Cambridge, MA: Harvard University Press.

Gruneau, Richard, and David Whitson, eds. 1993. *Artificial Ice: Hockey, Commerce, and Culture*. Peterborough: Broadview.

Gusterson, Hugh. 2017. "From Brexit to Trump: Anthropology and the Rise of Nationalist Populism." *American Ethnologist* 44(2): 209–214.

——. 1995. *Nuclear Rites: A Weapons Laboratory at the End of the Cold War*. Berkeley: University of California Press.

Gwynne, Margaret A. 2003. *Applied Anthropology: A Career-Oriented Approach*. Boston: Allyn and Bacon.

Hall, Edgar T. 1966. *The Hidden Dimension*. Garden City: Doubleday.

Hamilton, Darrick, and Arthur H. Goldsmith. 2009. "Shedding 'Light' on Marriage: The Influence of Skin Shade on Marriage for Black Females." *Journal of Economic Behavior and Organization* 72(1): 30–50.

Handler, Richard. 1988. *Nationalism and the Politics of Culture in Quebec*. Madison: University of Wisconsin Press.

Hanson, Allan. 1993. *Testing Testing*. Berkeley: University of California Press.

Harris, Marvin. 1998. *Good to Eat: Riddles of Food and Culture* [1985]. Long Grove: Waveland Press.

——. 1977. *Cannibals and Kings: The Origins of Culture*. New York: Vintage.

Hartman, Anne. 2009. "'Here for a Little Pickup?' Notes on Women's Shinny Hockey in Toronto Public Parks." In *Now Is the Winter: Thinking about Hockey*, edited by Jamie Dobb and Richard Harrison. Toronto: Wolsak and Wynn.

Harvey, David. 2005. *The History of Neoliberalism*. New York: Oxford University Press.

Hass, Jonathan, ed. 1990. *The Anthropology of War*. Cambridge: Cambridge University Press.

Hawkins, Charlotte. 2019. "Mobile Money and Elder Care from Kampala." *UCL*, 22 September 2019. https://blogs.ucl.ac.uk/assa/2019/09/22/mobile-money-elder-care-from-kampala-by-charlotte-hawkins

Hedican, Edward J. 2008. *Applied Anthropology in Canada: Understanding Aboriginal Issues* [1995], 2nd ed. Toronto: University of Toronto Press.

——. 2001. *Up in Nipigon Country: Anthropology as a Personal Experience*. Halifax: Fernwood.

——. 1986. *The Ogoki River Guides: Emergent Leadership among the Northern Ojibwa*. Waterloo: Wilfrid Laurier University Press.

Hedley, Max. 1998. "Shadow of Domination: Colonialism, Household, and Community Relations." In *Transgressing Borders: Critical Perspectives on Gender, Household, and Culture*, edited by Suzan Ilcan and Lynne Phillips. Westport: Bergin and Garvey.

Helly, Denise. 2004. "Are Muslims Discriminated Against Since September 2001?" *Canadian Ethnic Studies* 36(1): 24–47.

Helm, June. 1965. "Bilaterality in the Social Organization of the Arctic Drainage Dene." *Ethnology* 4: 361–85.

Henare, Manuka. 2001. "Tapu, Mana, Mauri, Hau, Wairua: A Maori Philosophy of Vitalism and Cosmos." In *Indigenous Traditions and Ecology: The Interbeing of Cosmology and Community*, edited by John A. Grim. Cambridge, MA: Harvard University Press.

Henderson, Paul. 1976. "Class Structure and the Concept of Intelligence." In *Schooling and Capitalism: A Sociological Reader*, edited by Roger Dale, Geoff Esland, and Madeleine MacDonald. London: Routledge and Kegan Paul in association with Open University Press.

Henry, Paget. 1997. "Rastafarianism and the Reality of Dread." In *Existence in Black: An Anthology of Black Existential Philosophy*, edited by L.R. Gordon. New York: Routledge.

Herrnstein, Richard J., and Charles Murray. 1994. *The Bell Curve: Intelligence and Class Structure in American Life*. New York: The Free Press.

Hertz, Robert. 1960. *Death and the Right Hand*. Glencoe: The Free Press.

Herzfeld, Michael. 2001. *Anthropology: Theoretical Practice in Culture and Society*. Malden: Blackwell.

Hobbes, Thomas. 1881. *Leviathan* [1651]. London: Oxford University Press.

Hoben, Allan. 1982. "Anthropologists and Development." *Annual Review of Anthropology* 11: 349–75.

Hobsbaum, Eric. 1959. *Primitive Rebels: Studies in Archaic Forms of Social Movement in the 19th and 20th Centuries.* New York: Praeger.

Hoerder, Dirk. 2002. *Cultures in Contact: World Migrations in the Second Millennium*. Durham: Duke University Press.

Holmes, Teresa. 1997. "Contested Kinship and the Dispute of Customary Law in Colonial Kenya." *Anthropologica* 39: 79–90.

Honigmann, John J. 1976. *The Development of Anthropological Ideas*. Homewood: Dorsey.

——. 1963. *Understanding Culture*. New York: Harper and Row.

Hoodfar, Homa. 2003. "More Than Clothing: Veiling as an Adaptive Strategy." In *The Muslim Veil in North America*, edited by Sajida Sultana Alvi, Homa Hoodfar, and Sheila McDonough. Toronto: Women's Press.

Hoodfar Homa. 2001. "The Veil in Their Minds and on Our Heads: Veiling Practices and Muslim Women." In *Women, Gender, Religion: A Reader*, edited by E.A. Castelli, 420–46. New York: Palgrave Macmillan.

Hopkins, Debra, et al. 2019. "'Learning Together': Braiding Indigenous and Western Knowledge Systems to Understand Freshwater Mussel Health in the Lower Athabasca Region of Alberta, Canada." *Journal of Ethnobiology* 39(2): 315–36.

Hostetler, John. 1974. *Hutterite Society*. Baltimore: Johns Hopkins University Press.

House, James S., Karl R. Landis, and Debra Umberson. 1988. "Social Relationships and Health." *Science* 241: 540–45.

Howell, Signe, and Roy Willis, eds. *Societies at Peace: Anthropological Perspectives*. London and New York: Routledge.

Hsu, Francis L.K. 1967. *Under the Ancestors' Shadow*. New York: Anchor.

Hutchinson, John, and Anthony D. Smith, eds. 1994. *Nationalism*. Oxford: Oxford University Press.

ILO (International Labor Organization). 2015. *Mainstreaming of Migration in Development Policy and Integrating Migration in the Post-2015 UN Development Agenda*. http://www.ilo.org/wcmsp5/groups/public/---ed_protect/---protrav/---migrant/documents/genericdocument/wcms_220084.pdf

Inhorn, Marcia C., and Peter J. Brown. 1990. "The Anthropology of Infectious Disease." *Annual Review of Anthropology* 19: 89–117.

Irwin, Anne. 2012. "'There Will Be a Lot of Old Young Men Coming Home': Combat and Becoming a Man in Afghanistan." In *Young Men in Uncertain Times*, edited by Verid Amit and Noel Dyck. New York: Berghahn.

——. 2002. "The Social Organization of Soldiering: A Canadian Infantry Company in the Field." PhD diss., Manchester University.

Isbister, John. 2003. *Promises Not Kept: Poverty and Betrayal of Third World Development*. Bloomfield: Kumarian.

Jensen, Arthur. 1972. *Genetics and Education*. New York: Harper and Row.

Johnson, Norris Brock. 1985. *Westhaven: Classroom Culture and Society in a Rural Elementary School*. Chapel Hill: University of North Carolina Press.

Joly, Tara L. 2017a. "Making Productive Land: Utility, Encounter, and Oil Sands Reclamation in Northeastern Alberta, Canada." PhD diss., Department of Social Anthropology, University of Aberdeen.

——. 2017b. "Reclaiming Nature? Indigenous Homeland and Oil Sands Territory." *Engagement: A Blog of the Anthropology and Environment Society*, 7 March 7. https://aesengagement.wordpress.com/2017/03/07/reclaiming-nature-indigenous-homeland-and-oil-sands-territory

Jorgensen, Dan. 1997. "Who and What Is a Landowner? Mythology and Marking the Ground in a Papua New Guinea Mining Project." *Anthropological Forum* 7(4): 599–627.

——. 1996. "Regional History and Ethnic Identity in the Hub of New Guinea: The Emergence of the Min." *Oceania* 66(3): 189–210.

——. 1990. "Placing the Past and Moving the Present: Myth and Contemporary History in Telefolmin." *Culture* 10(2): 47–56.

Judd, Ellen R. 1994. *Gender and Power in Rural North China.* Stanford: Stanford University Press.

Juergensmeyer, Mark. 2003. *Terror in the Mind of God: The Global Rise of Religious Violence,* 3rd ed. Berkeley: University of California Press.

Kafka, Peter. 2005. "Top Earning Dead Celebrities." *Forbes.* http://www.forbes.com/2005/10/25/highest-earning-dead-celebrities_deadceleb05_land.html

Karier, Clarence J. 1976. "Testing for Order and Control in the Corporate Liberal State." In *Schooling and Capitalism: A Sociological Reader*, edited by Roger Dale, Geoff Esland, and Madeleine MacDonald. London: Routledge and Kegan Paul in association with the Open University Press.

Kearney, Michael. 1991. "A Very Bad Disease of the Arms." In *The Naked Anthropologist: Tales from Around the World*, edited by Philip Devita. Belmont: Wadsworth.

Keesing, Roger. 1991. "Not a Real Fish: The Ethnographer as Inside Outsider." In *The Naked Anthropologist: Tales from around the World*, edited by Philip Devita. Belmont: Wadsworth.

Kehoe, Alice. 1989. *The Ghost Dance: Ethnohistory and Revitalization*. New York: Holt, Rinehart, and Winston.

Keiser, Lincoln. 1969. *The Vice Lords: Warriors of the Streets*. New York: Holt, Rinehart, and Winston.

Kelly, John D., and Martha Kaplan. 1990. "History, Structure, and Ritual." In *Annual Review of Anthropology* 19: 119–50. Palo Alto: Annual Reviews.

Kennedy, Paul. 1993. *Preparing for the Twenty-First Century*. New York: Random House.

Keohane, Kieran. 1997. *Symptoms of Canada: An Essay on the Canadian Identity*. Toronto: University of Toronto Press.

Kets de Vries, Manfred, and Danny Miller. 1987. "Interpreting Organizational Texts." *Journal of Management Studies* 24: 233–47.

Kidder, Tracy. 2003. *Mountains beyond Mountains*. New York. Random House.

Kiefer, Christie. 1976. "The Danchi Zoku and the Evolution of the Metropolitan Mind." In *Japan: The Paradox of Progress*, edited by Lewis Austin, with the assistance of Adrienne Suddard and Nancy Remington. New Haven: Yale University Press.

Kinkade, Kathleen. 1973. *A Walden Two Experiment: The First Five Years of Twin Oaks Community*. New York: William Morrow.

Klaits, Frederick. 2005. "The Widow in Blue: Blood and the Morality of Remembering in Botswana's Time of AIDS." *Africa* 75(1): 46–62.

Kolata, Gina. 1995. "Researchers Offer Clue to How AIDS Virus Survives Prolonged Attack by Immune System." *New York Times*, 24 November 1995. http://www.nytimes.com/1995/11/24/us/researchers-offer-clue-aids-virus-survives-prolonged-attack-immune-system.html

Kondo, Dorinne K. 1990. *Crafting Selves: Power, Gender, and Discourses of Identity in a Japanese Workplace*. Chicago: University of Chicago Press.

Kopytoff, Igor. 1986. "The Cultural Biography of Things: Commoditization as Process." In *The Social Life of Things: Commodities in Cultural Perspective*, edited by Arjun Appadurai, 64–91. Cambridge: Cambridge University Press.

Korten, David C. 1995. *When Corporations Rule the World*. Hartford: Kumarian.

Kotlowitz, Alex. 1991. *There Are No Children Here*. New York: Anchor.

Kramer, Jennifer. 2007. *Switchbacks: Art, Ownership, and Nuxalk National Identity*. Vancouver: UBC Press.

Kroeber, Alfred L. 1948. *Anthropology*. New York: Harcourt, Brace.

Kuper, Leo. 1981. *Genocide: Its Political Use in the Twentieth Century*. New Haven: Yale University Press.

Labov, William. 1966. *The Social Stratification of English in New York City*. Washington, D.C.: Center for Applied Linguistics.

Ladao, Mark. 2017. "Science and Culture Are Not Mutually Exclusive." *Manoa Now*, 10 October. http://www.manoanow.org/kaleo/news/science-and-culture-are-not-mutually-exclusive/article_c70569d0-ae0c-11e7-942f-f745d6b90175.html

Lakoff, George, and Mark Johnson. 1980. *Metaphors We Live By*. Chicago: University of Chicago Press.

Lakoff, Robin. 1975. *Language and Women's Place*. New York: Harper and Row.

Lambek, Michael. 2002. "General Introduction." In *A Reader in the Anthropology of Religion*, edited by Michael Lambek. Malden: Blackwell.

Lancaster, Roger. 2003. *The Trouble with Nature: Sex in Science and Popular Culture*. Berkeley: University of California Press.

Lang, Sabine. 1998. *Men as Women, Women as Men: Changing Gender in Native American Cultures*. Austin: University of Texas Press.

Langlois, Kellie, and Didier Garriguet. 2011. *Sugar Consumption among Canadians of All Ages*. http://www.statcan.gc.ca.myaccess.library.utoronto.ca/pub/82-003-x/2011003/article/11540-eng.htm

Lappé, Frances Moore, and Joseph Collins. 1977. *Food First: Beyond the Myth of Scarcity*. New York: Random House.

Lasco, Gideon. 2020. "Why Face Masks Are Going Viral." *Sapiens*, 4 February. https://www.sapiens.org/culture/coronavirus-mask

Lassiter, Luke E. 1998. *The Power of Kiowa Song: A Collaborative Ethnography*. Tucson: University of Arizona Press.

LeBlanc, Rob. 2015. "At the Sacred Intersection of Politics and War: A Discussion of Warrior Societies, Masculine Identity Politics, and Indigenous Resistance Trends in Canada." *Canadian Journal of Native Studies* 35(2): 75–92.

Lee, Richard. 1996. "AIDS: The Conspiracy of Silence." *Southern Africa Report* 12(1): 8. https://tspace.library.utoronto.ca/bitstream/1807/18005/1/TSpace0114.PDF

——. 1984. *The Dobe !Kung*. New York: Holt, Rinehart, and Winston.

——. 1969. "Eating Christmas in the Kalihari." *Natural History Magazine*. December.

Lee, Richard, and Irven DeVore, eds. 1968. *Man the Hunter*. Chicago: Aldine.

Lee, Richard, and Ida Susser. 2002. "Facing the Challenge of HIV/AIDS." *Cultural Survival Quarterly* 26(1). http://www.culturalsurvival.org/publications/cultural-survival-quarterly/botswana/facing-challenge-hivaids

Leslie, Heather Young. 1998. "The Anthropologist, the Mother, and the Cross-Cultured Child." In *Fieldwork and Families: Constructing Models for Ethnographic Research,* edited by Juliana Flinn, Leslie Marshall, and Jocelyn Armstrong. Honolulu: University of Hawai'i Press.

Lévi-Strauss, Claude. 1974. *Tristes Tropiques*. New York: Atheneum.

——. 1966. *The Savage Mind*. Chicago: University of Chicago Press.

——. 1964. *Totemism*. Translated by Rodney Needham. London: Merlin Press.

Lewellen, Ted. 2002. *The Anthropology of Globalization: Cultural Anthropology Enters the 21st Century*. Westport: Bergin and Garvey.

Lewin, Ellen, and William L. Leap, eds. 2002. *Out in Theory: The Emergence of Lesbian and Gay Anthropology*. Chicago: University of Chicago Press.

Li, Tania, 2002. "Local Histories, Global Markets: Cocoa and Class in Upland Sulawesi." *Development and Change* 33(3): 415–37.

——. 1999a. *Transforming the Indonesian Uplands: Marginality, Power, and Production*. Amsterdam: Harwood.

——. 1999b. "Compromising Power: Development, Culture, and Rule in Indonesia." *Cultural Anthropology* 14(3): 295–322.

Lightner, Sara, and Anna Naupa. 2005. *Histri Blong Yumi Long Vanuatu*. Port Vila: Vanuatu Cultural Centre.

Lithman, Yngve G. 2004. "Anthropologists on Home Turf: How Green Is the Grass?" *Anthropologica* 46(1): 17–27.

Lofgren, Orvar. 2002. *On Holiday: A History of Vacationing*. Berkeley: University of California Press.

Lohmann, Roger Ivar. 2014. "Investigating the Causes of Peace to End War: An Introduction." *Anthropologica* 56(2): 255–60.

Long, David, and Olive Patricia Dickason, eds. 2000. *Visions of the Heart: Canadian Aboriginal Issues*. Toronto: Harcourt Canada.

Longres, John F. 1990. *Human Behavior in the Social Environment*. Itasca: F.E. Peacock.

Lorber, Judith. 1994. *Paradoxes of Gender*. New Haven: Yale University Press.

Lorway, Robert. 2007. "Breaking a Public Health Silence: HIV Risk and Male–Male Sexual Practices in the Windhoek Urban Area." In *Unravelling Taboos: Gender and Sexuality in Namibia*, edited by Suzanne LaFont and

Dianne Hubbard. Windhoek: Gender Research and Advocacy Project, Legal Assistance Centre.

——. 2006. "Dispelling 'Heterosexual African AIDS' in Namibia: Same-Sex Sexuality in the Township of Katutura." *Culture, Health, and Sexuality* 8(5): 435–49.

Luhrmann, T.M. 1989. *Persuasions of the Witch's Craft: Ritual Magic in Contemporary England*. Cambridge, MA: Harvard University Press.

Lutz, Catherine A., and Jane L. Collins. 1993. *Reading National Geographic*. Chicago: University of Chicago Press.

Luxton, Meg, ed. 1997. *Feminism and Families: Critical Policies and Changing Practices*. Halifax: Fernwood.

Lyons, Andrew P., and Harriet D. Lyons. 2004. *Irregular Connections: A History of Anthropology and Sexuality*. Lincoln: University of Nebraska Press.

Lyons, Charles. 2015. "Suicides spread through a Brazilian tribe." *New York Times*, 2 January 2015. http://www.nytimes.com/2015/01/04/opinion/sunday/suicides-spread-through-a-brazilian-tribe.html?_r=0

Macdonald, David. 2020. "Unemployment may hit 70-year high, but new EI replacement will help." *Behind the Numbers*. http://behindthenumbers.ca/2020/03/26/unemployment-may-hit-70-year-high-but-new-ei-replacement-will-help

Mackey, Eva. 1999. *The House of Difference: Cultural Politics and National Identity in Canada*. London and New York: Routledge.

Macnair, Peter. 2004. "From Kwakiutl to Kwakwaka'wakw." In *Native Peoples: The Canadian Experience*, edited by R. Bruce Morrison and C. Roderick Wilson. Toronto: Oxford University Press.

Madden, Raymond. 2010. *Being Ethnographic: A Guide to the Theory and Practice of Ethnography*. London: Sage.

Malinowski, Bronislaw. 1961. *Argonauts of the Western Pacific* [1922]. New York: Dutton.

——. 1948. *Magic, Science, and Religion, and Other Essays*. Boston: Beacon.

——. 1944. *A Scientific Theory of Culture, and Other Essays*. Chapel Hill: University of North Carolina Press.

——. 1929. *The Sexual Life of Savages in North-Western Melanesia*. New York: Halcyon House.

Marchak, Patricia M. 2003. *Reins of Terror*. Montreal and Kingston: McGill–Queen's University Press.

Marcus, George E. 1995. "Ethnography in/of the World System: The Emergence of Multi-Sited Ethnography." *Annual Review of Anthropology* 24(1): 95–117.

Marshall, Lorna. 1976. *The !Kung of Nyae Nyae*. Cambridge, MA: Harvard University Press.

Marshall, Mac. 1993. "The Wizard of Oz Meets the Wicked Witch of the East: Mead, Freeman, and Ethnographic Authority." *American Ethnologist* 20: 604–17.

Martin, Emily. 1987. *The Woman in the Body: A Cultural Analysis of Reproduction*. Boston: Beacon.

Martin-Hill, Dawn. 2008a. *Sewatokwa'tshera't: The Dish with One Spoon* [film]. http://www.lock3media.com/doc6.html

——. 2008b. *The Lubicon Lake Nation: Indigenous Knowledge and Power*. Toronto: University of Toronto Press.

——. 2004. "Resistance, Determination, and Perseverance of the Lubicon Cree Women." In *In the Way of Development: Indigenous Peoples, Life Projects, and Globalization*, edited by Mario Blaser, Harvey A. Feit, and Glenn McRae. New York: Palgrave Macmillan.

Marwick, Max. 1965. *Sorcery in Its Social Setting*. Manchester: University of Manchester Press.

Matsubara, Hisako. 1985. *Cranes at Dusk*. New York: Dial.

Mattingly, Cheryl, Mary Lawlor, and Lanita Jacobs-Huey. 2002. "Narrating September 11: Race, Gender, and the Play of Cultural Identities." *American Anthropologist* 104(3): 743–53.

Mauss, Marcel. 1967. *The Gift: Forms and Functions of Exchange in Archaic Societies* [1925]. Translated by Ian Cunnison. New York: W.W. Norton.

Maybury-Lewis, David. 1997. *Indigenous Peoples, Ethnic Groups, and the State*. Boston: Allyn and Bacon.

McCauley, Clark. 1990. "Conference Overview." In *The Anthropology of War*, edited by Jonathan Hass. New York: Cambridge University Press.

McCracken, Grant. 2005. *Culture and Consumption II: Markets, Meaning and Brand Management*. Indianapolis: Indiana University Press.

McElroy, Ann, and Patricia Townsend. 1979. *Medical Anthropology*. North Scituate: Duxbury.

McFate, Montgomery. 2005. "Anthropology and Counterinsurgency: The Strange Story of Their Curious Relationship." *Military Review*, March–April.

McFate, Montgomery, and Andrea Jackson. "An Organizational Solution for DOD's Cultural Knowledge Needs." *Military Review*, May–June.

McGarry, Karen. 2015. "Ethnographic Frictions and the Ice Scandal: Affect, Mass Media, and Canadian Nationalism in High Performance Canadian Figure Skating." In *Reclaiming Canadian Bodies*, edited by Lynda Mannik and Karen McGarry, 105–43. Waterloo: Wilfrid Laurier University Press.

——. 2011. "Mass Media and Gender Identity in High Performance Canadian Figure Skating." In *The Gendered Society Reader,* 2nd Canadian ed., edited by Amy Aronson, Amy Kaler, and Michael S. Kimmel. Cambridge: Oxford University Press.

McGee, R. Jon, and Richard Warms. 2000. *Anthropological Theory: An Introductory History*. Mountain View: Mayfield.

McIntosh, Peggy. 1988. "White Privilege and Male Privilege: A Personal Account of Coming to See Correspondences through Work in Women's Studies." Working Paper no. 189. Wellesley: Wellesley College Center for Research on Women.

McLaughlin, Janet. 2009. "Migration and Health: Implications for Development – a Case Study of Mexican and Jamaican Migrants in Canada's Seasonal Agricultural Workers Program" [policy paper]. Ottawa: Canadian Foundation for the Americas (FOCAL), Labour Mobility and Development Project.

McNally, David. 2002. *Another World Is Possible: Globalization and Anti-Capitalism*. Winnipeg: Arbeiter Ring.

Mead, Margaret. 1928. *Coming of Age in Samoa: A Psychological Study of Primitive Youth for Western Civilization*. New York: Morrow.

Miller, Bruce Granville. 2003. *Invisible Indigenes: The Politics of Nonrecognition*. Lincoln: University of Nebraska Press.

Mills, Antonia. 1988. "A Preliminary Investigation of Cases of Reincarnation among the Beaver and Gitksan Indians." *Anthropologica* 30: 23–59.

Mills, Antonia, and Richard Slobodin, eds. 1994. *Amerindian Rebirth: Reincarnation Belief among North American Indians and Inuit*. Toronto: University of Toronto Press.

Mintz, Sidney W. 1985. *Sweetness and Power: The Place of Sugar in World History*. New York: Viking.

Mishkin, Bernard. 1940. *Rank and Warfare among the Plains Indians*. Monograph no. 3, American Ethnological Society. Seattle: University of Washington Press.

Mitchell, Lisa. 2001. *Baby's First Picture: Ultrasound and the Politics of Fetal Subjects*. Toronto: University of Toronto Press.

Moffat, Tina, and Elizabeth Finnis. 2005. "Considering Social and Material Resources: The Political Ecology of a Peri-Urban Squatter Community in Nepal." *Habitat International* 29: 453–68.

Monture-Angus, Patricia A. 2000. "Lessons in Decolonization: Aboriginal Over-Representation in Canadian Criminal Justice." In *Visions of the Heart: Canadian Aboriginal Issues*, edited by David Long and Olive Patricia Dickason. Toronto: Harcourt Canada.

Mooney, James. 2011. *The Ghost Dance Religion and the Sioux Outbreak of 1890* [1897]. Chicago: University of Chicago Press.

Moore, Henrietta. 1988. *Feminism and Anthropology*. Cambridge: Polity.

Moore, Henrietta, and Todd Sanders, eds. 2005. *Anthropology in Theory: Issues in Epistemology*. Malden: Blackwell.

Moore, Patrick, Angela Wheelock, and Dene Wodih Society. 1990. *Wolverine Myths and Visions: Dene Traditions from Northern Alberta*. Lincoln: University of Nebraska Press.

Moore, Robert B. 1976. *Racism in the English Language*. New York: Council on Interracial Books for Children.

Moore, Sally Falk. 2005. *Law and Anthropology: A Reader*. Oxford: Blackwell.

Moos, Robert, and Robert Brownstein. 1977. *Environment and Utopia*. New York: Plenum.

Morgan, Lewis Henry. 1964. *Ancient Society* [1877]. Cambridge, MA: Belknap.

Morin, Eugene. 2008. "Evidence for Declines in Human Population Densities during the Early Upper Paleolithic in Western Europe." *Proceedings of the National Academy of Sciences of the United States of America* 105(1): 48–53.

Morioka, Rika. 2014. "Gender Difference in the Health Risk Perception of Radiation from Fukushima in Japan: The Role of Hegemonic Masculinity." *Social Science and Medicine* 107: 105–12.

Morrison, David. 2000. "Canadian Aid: A Mixed Record and an Uncertain Future." In *Transforming Development,*

Foreign Aid for a Changing World, edited by J. Freedman. Toronto: University of Toronto Press.

Morrison, R. Bruce, and C. Roderick Wilson, eds. 2004. *Native Peoples: The Canadian Experience*. Toronto: Oxford University Press.

Morton, Samuel G. 1844. *An Inquiry into the Distinctive Characteristics of the Aboriginal Race of America*. Philadelphia: Penington.

Mukhopadhyay, Carol C., and Patricia J. Higgins. 1988. "Anthropological Studies of Women's Status Revisited: 1977–1987." *Annual Review of Anthropology* 17: 461–95.

Mullings, Leith. 2005. "Interrogating Racism: Toward an Antiracist Anthropology." *Annual Review of Anthropology* 34: 667–93.

Murray, David A.B. 2002. *Opacity: Gender, Sexuality, Race, and the "Problem" of Identity in Martinique*. New York: Peter Lang.

Myer, Fred R. 1988. "Critical Trends in the Study of Hunters-Gatherers." *Annual Review of Anthropology* 17: 261–82.

Nader, Laura, ed. 1996. *Naked Science: Anthropological Inquiry into Boundaries, Power, and Knowledge*. New York: Routledge.

Nagengast, Carole. 1994. "Violence, Terror, and the Crisis of the State." *Annual Review of Anthropology* 23: 109–36.

Nagengast, Carol, and Carlos G. Vélez-Ibáñez, eds. 2004. *Human Rights: The Scholar as Activist*. Oklahoma City: Society for Applied Anthropology.

Narayan, Kirin. 1993. "How Native Is a 'Native' Anthropologist?" *American Anthropologist* 95(3): 671–86.

Nations, James D. 1994. "The Ecology of the Zapatista Revolt." *Cultural Survival Quarterly* 18: 31–33.

Neider, Charles. 1966. *The Complete Travel Books of Mark Twain*. New York: Doubleday.

Ng, Roxana. 2007. "Garment Production in Canada: Social and Political Implications. *Studies in Political Economy* 79 (Spring): 3–11.

——. 2002. "Freedom for Whom? Globalization and Trade from the Standpoint of Garment Workers." *Canadian Woman Studies* 21–22(4–1): 74–81.

Nichter, Mimi. 2000. *Fat Talk: What Girls and Their Parents Say about Dieting*. Cambridge, MA: Harvard University Press.

Niehaus, Isak. 2001. *Witchcraft, Power, and Politics: Exploring the Occult in the South African Lowveld*. New York: Pluto Press.

Niezen, Ronald. 2004. "Indigenous Peoples in a Global Era." In *Globalization and Community: Canadian Perspectives*, edited by Jean-Luc Chodkiewicz and Raymond E. Wiest. Winnipeg: University of Manitoba Press.

——. 2003. *The Origins of Indigenism: Human Rights and the Politics of Identity*. Berkeley: University of California Press.

——. 1993. "Power and Dignity: The Social Consequences of Hydro-Electric Development for the James Bay Cree." *Canadian Review of Sociology and Anthropology* 30(4): 510.

Nordstrom, Carolyn. 2004. *Shadows of War: Violence, Power, and International Profiteering in the Twenty-First Century*. Berkeley: University of California Press.

Omohundro, John T. 2001. *Careers in Anthropology*. Mountain View: Mayfield.

Ontario Ministry of Aboriginal Affairs. Aboriginal Labour Force. http://www.aboriginalaffairs.gov.on.ca/english/services/datasheets/labour.asp

Ortner, Sherry B., and Harriet Whitehead, eds. 1981. *Sexual Meanings: The Cultural Construction of Gender and Sexuality*. Cambridge: Cambridge University Press.

Otterbein, Keith F. 2004. *How War Began*. College Station: Texas A&M University Press.

Pagels, Elaine H. 1995. *The Origin of Satan*. New York: Random House.

Paine, Robert, ed. 1985. *Advocacy and Anthropology: First Encounters*. St. John's: Institute of Social and Economic Research.

Palgi, Phyllis, and Henry Abramovitch. 1984. "Death: A Cross-Cultural Perspective." *Annual Review of Anthropology* 13: 385–417.

Parkin, Robert, and Linda Stone, eds. 2004. *Kinship and Family: An Anthropological Reader*. Malden: Blackwell.

Patrick, Donna. 2003. *Language, Politics, and Social Interaction in an Inuit Community*. Berlin: Mouton de Gruyter.

Paulson, Susan, Lisa L. Gezon, and Michael Watts. 2003. "Locating the Political in Political Ecology: An Introduction." *Human Organization* 62(3): 205–17.

Pearson, Karl. 1901. "On the Inheritance of Mental Characteristics in Man." In *Proceedings of the Royal Society of London* 69: 153–55.

Pengelly, Ryan. D., and Anne Irwin. 2011. "Twenty-First Century Narratives from Afghanistan: Storytelling, Morality, and War." In *The Routledge Handbook of War and Society: Iraq and Afghanistan*, edited by Steven Carlton-Ford and Morten G. Ender. New York: Routledge.

Philips, Susan U. 1980. "Sex Differences and Language." In *Annual Review of Anthropology* 9: 523–44. Palo Alto: Annual Reviews.

Polanyi, Karl. 1957. *The Great Transformation* [1944]. Boston: Beacon.

Pratt, Cranford. 2000. "Alleviating Global Poverty or Enhancing Security: Competing Rationales for Canadian Development Assistance." In *Transforming Development: Foreign Aid for a Changing World*, edited by J. Freedman. Toronto: University of Toronto Press.

Pryce, Paula. 1999. *"Keeping the Lakes' Way": Reburial and the Re-creation of a Moral World among an Invisible People.* Toronto: University of Toronto Press.

Pyke, Alan. 2014. "A Third of America's Most Successful Corporations Pay Less Than a 10 Percent Income Tax Rate." *ThinkProgress*, 28 February.

Radice, Martha, Brian Noble, and Liesl Gambold. 2018. "Singing the Ancestors: Indigenous Anthropology Graduate Wins Polaris Music Prize." https://cascacultureblog.wordpress.com/2018/12/19/singing-the-ancestors-indigenous-anthropology-graduate-wins-polaris-music-prize/. Accessed September 20, 2019

Raff, Jennifer. 2019. "Genetic Astrology: When Ancient DNA Meets Ancestry Testing." *Forbes*, 19 April. https://www.forbes.com/sites/jenniferraff/2019/04/09/genetic-astrology-when-ancient-dna-meets-ancestry-testing/#65b573006c69

Ralph, Laurence. 2014. *Renegade Dreams: Living through Injury in Gangland Chicago*. Chicago: University of Chicago Press.

Rapp, Rayna. 2007. "Real-Time Fetus: The Role of the Sonogram in the Age of Monitored Reproduction." In *Beyond the Body Proper: Reading the Anthropology of Material Life*, edited by Margaret Lock and Judith Farquhar, 608–23. Durham: Duke University Press.

Read, Kenneth E. 1965. *The High Valley*. New York: Columbia University Press.

Reardon, Betty. 1985. *Sexism and the War System*. New York: Columbia University Teachers College Press.

Reed, Richard. 1997. *Forest Dwellers, Forest Protectors: Indigenous Models for International Development*. Boston: Allyn and Bacon.

Reichenbach, Lisa, and Amy Maish. 2006. "Larger Than Life: Personal and Social Transitions within Type 2 Diabetes." *Ethnographic Praxis in Industry Conference Proceedings*, 4–18. Arlington: American Anthropological Association.

Reyero, Veronica. 2018. "How does anthropology help Google UX? Interview with Fatimah Richmond." *Antropologia 2.0*, 26 February. https://blog.antropologia2-0.com/en/what-does-an-anthropologist-do-at-google-ux-interview-with-fatimah-richmond

Rich, Bruce. 1994. *Mortgaging the Earth: The World Bank, Environmental Impoverishment, and the Crisis of Development*. Boston: Beacon.

Richler, Noah. 2012. *What We Talk about When We Talk about War.* Fredericton: Goose Lane Editions.

Richmond, Fatimah, and Sam Ladner. 2017. "Ethnography for Equity: Using the Ethnographic Lens to Improve Outcomes for Everyone." *EPIC*, 13 November. https://www.epicpeople.org/ethnography-for-equity

Ridington, Robin. 1990. *Little Bit Know Something: Stories in a Language of Anthropology*. Iowa City: University of Iowa Press.

Rindos, David. 1984. *The Origins of Agriculture*. New York: Academic Press.

Rival, Laura. 2016. *Huaorani Transformations in Twenty-First-Century Ecuador: Treks into the Future of Time*. Tucson: University of Arizona Press.

Rivoli, Pietra. 2005. *The Travels of a T-Shirt in the Global Economy: An Economist Examines the Markets, Power, and the Politics of World Trade*. Hoboken: John Wiley.

Robarchek, Clayton. 1990. "Motivations and Material Causes: On the Explanation of Conflict and War." In *The Anthropology of War*, edited by Jonathan Hass. New York: Cambridge University Press.

Robbins, Richard H. 2005. *Global Problems and the Culture of Capitalism*, 3rd ed. Boston: Allyn and Bacon.

Robbins, Richard H., and Rachel Dowtry. 2017. *Cultural Anthropology: A Problem-Based Approach*, 7th ed. Boston: Cengage Learning.

Rosaldo, Renato. 1989. *Culture and Truth: The Remaking of Social Analysis*. Boston: Beacon.

Ross, Rupert. 1992. *Dancing with a Ghost: Exploring Indian Reality*. Markham: Octopus.

Rothstein, Frances Abrahamer, and Michael L. Blim, eds. 1992. *Anthropology and the Global Factory: Studies of the New Industrialism in the Late Twentieth Century*. New York: Bergin and Garvey.

Rowe, Allen. 2004. "'The Mysterious Oriental Mind': Ethnic Surveillance and the Chinese in Canada During the Great War." *Canadian Ethnic Studies* 36(1): 48–70.

Roy, Ramashray. 1985. *Self and Society: A Study in Gandhian Thought*. Beverly Hills: Sage.

Ruoff, Jeffrey. 1996. "'Can a Documentary Be Made of Real Life?': The Reception of *An American Family*." In *The Construction of the Viewer: Media Ethnography and the Anthropology of Audiences*, edited by P.I. Crawford and S.B. Hafsteinnsson. Denmark: Intervention.

Russell, Wendy. 2004. "The People Had Discovered Their Own Approach to Life: Politicizing Development Discourse." In *In the Way of Development: Indigenous Peoples, Life Projects, and Globalization,* edited by Mario Blaser, Harvey A. Feit, and Glenn McRae. London and New York: Zed Books in association with International Development Research Centre, Ottawa.

Rutherford, Blair. 1999. "To Find a Witch: Anthropology, Witch-Finding in North-West Zimbabwe." *Critique of Anthropology* 19: 89–109.

4/ Sahlins, Marshall. 1968. *Tribesmen*. New York: Prentice Hall.

Sanday, Peggy Reeves. 2007. *Gang Rape: Sex, Brotherhood and Privilege on Campus* [1990], 2nd ed. New York: NYU Press.

——. 1981. "The Socio-Cultural Context of Rape: A Cross-Cultural Study." *Journal of Social Issues* 37: 5–27.

Satzewich, Vic. 1991. *Racism and the Incorporation of Foreign Labour: Farm Labour Migration to Canada Since 1945*. London: Routledge.

Satzewich, Vic, ed. 1992. *Deconstructing a Nation: Immigration, Multiculturalism, and Racism in '90s Canada*. Halifax: Fernwood.

Scaglion, Richard. 1990. "Ethnocentrism and the Abelam." In *The Humbled Anthropologist: Tales from the Pacific,* edited by Philip Devita. Belmont: Wadsworth.

Scales, Robert H. 2005. "The Second Learning Revolution." In *Rethinking the Principles of War*, edited by Anthony D. McIvor, 41–57. Annapolis MD: Naval Institute Press.

Schieffelin, Bambi B., and Elinor Ochs. 1986. "Language Socialization." *Annual Review of Anthropology* 15: 163–91.

Scheper-Hughes, Nancy. 1995. "The Primacy of the Ethical: Propositions for a Militant Anthropology." *Current Anthropology* 36: 409–20.

——. 1992. *Death without Weeping: The Violence of Everyday Life in Brazil*. Berkeley: University of California Press.

Scheper-Hughes, Nancy, and Philippe Bourgois, eds. 2004. *Violence in War and Peace*. Malden: Blackwell.

Schmidt, Bettina E., and Ingo W. Schroder, eds. 2001. *Anthropology of Violence and Conflict*. London and New York: Routledge.

Schmidt, Bettina E., and Ingo W. Schroder. 2003. "Introduction." In *Anthropology of Violence and Conflict*, edited by Bettina E. Schmidt and Ingo W. Schroder, 2nd ed. London: Routledge.

Schneider, David M. 1984. *A Critique of the Study of Kinship*. Ann Arbor: University of Michigan Press.

Schrire, Carmel. 1984. "Wild Surmises on Savage Thoughts." In *Past and Present in Hunter Gatherer Studies*, edited by Carmel Schrire. Orlando: Academic Press.

Sharma, Parnesh. 2001. "On Not Being Canadian: The Social Organization of 'Migrant Workers' in Canada." *Canadian Review of Sociology and Anthropology* 38(4): 415–39.

——. 1998. *Aboriginal Fishing Rights: Laws, Courts, Politics*. Halifax: Fernwood.

Shewell, Hugh. 2004. *"Enough to Keep Them Alive": Indian Welfare in Canada, 1873–1965*. Toronto: University of Toronto Press.

Shipton, Parker. 1990. "African Famines and Food Security." *Annual Review of Anthropology* 19: 353–94.

Shore, Chris, and Susan Wright. 1997. *Anthropology of Policy: Critical Perspectives on Governance and Power*. London: Routledge.

Shostak, Marjorie. 1983. *Nisa: The Life and Words of a !Kung Woman*. New York: Vintage.

Shweder, Richard A., and Edmund J. Bourne. 1984. "Does the Concept of the Person Vary Cross-Culturally?" In *Cultural Conceptions of Mental Health and Therapy*, edited by A.J. Marsella and G.M. White. Boston: Reidel.

Sidel, Ruth. 1986. *Women and Children Last: Social Stratification in America*. New York: Penguin.

Silverman, Martin G. 1979. "'Kinship': An Informal, Critical Guide to Some Problems." In *Challenging Anthropology*, edited by David H. Turner and Gavin A. Smith. Toronto: McGraw-Hill Ryerson.

Sipes, Richard G. 1973. "War, Sports, and Aggression: An Empirical Test of Two Rival Theories." *American Anthropologist* 74: 64–86.

Skinner, B.F. 1962. *Walden Two*. New York: Macmillan.

Slobodin, Richard. 1994. "Kutchin Concepts of Reincarnation." In *Amerindian Rebirth: Reincarnation Belief among North American Indians and Inuit*, edited by Antonia Mills and Richard Slobodin. Toronto: University of Toronto Press.

Smith, Adam. 1994. *The Wealth of Nations* [1776], edited by Edwin Cannan. New York: Modern Library.

Smith, Gavin. 1999. *Confronting the Present: Towards a Politically Engaged Anthropology*. Oxford and New York: Berg.

Smith, Raymond T. 1984. "Anthropology and the Concept of Social Class." In *Annual Review of Anthropology* 13: 467–94.

Smith, Robert J. 1983. *Japanese Society: Tradition, Self, and the Social Order*. New York: Cambridge University Press.

Solway, Jacqueline, ed. 2003. "Politics and Practice in Critical Anthropology: The Work of Richard B. Lee." Special Edition of *Anthropologica* 45(1): 1–128.

Solway, Jacqueline S., and Richard B. Lee. 1990. "Foragers, Genuine or Spurious? Situating the Kalahari San in History." *Current Anthropology* 31(2): 109–46.

Spearman, Charles. 1904. "General Intelligence." *American Journal of Psychology* 115: 201–92.

Stafford, James. 1992. "The Impact of the New Immigration Policy on Racism in Canada." In *Deconstructing a Nation: Immigration, Multiculturalism, and Racism in '90s Canada*, edited by Vic Satzewich. Halifax: Fernwood.

STATIN. 2020. Marriages and Divorce Statistics, Government of Jamaica. https://statinja.gov.jm/Demo_SocialStats/Newmarriagedivorce.aspx

Statistics Canada. 2016. *Study: Women in Canada: First Nations, Metis and Inuit Women*. https://www150.statcan.gc.ca/n1/en/daily-quotidien/160223/dq160223a-eng.pdf?st=e3kq6tgg

——. 2013. *Persons in Low Income After Tax (in Percent, 2007–2011)*. http://www.statcan.gc.ca/tables-tableaux/sum-som/l01/cst01/famil19a-eng.htm?sdi=low%20income

——. 2011. *Religions in Canada – Census 2011*. Ottawa: Statistics Canada.

Stephenson, Peter H. 1991. *The Hutterian People: Ritual and Rebirth in the Evolution of Communal Life*. Lanham: University Press of America.

Stern, Jessica. 2003. *Terror in the Name of God: Why Religious Militants Kill*. New York: HarperCollins.

Stevens, Jacqueline. 1999. *Reproducing the State*. Princeton: Princeton University Press.

Stewart, Pamela J., and Andrew Strathern. 2002. *Violence: Theory and Ethnography*. London and New York: Continuum.

Stiglitz, Joseph E. 2002. http://www.nybooks.com/articles/archives/2002/may/23/a-fair-deal-for-the-world

Stone, Linda, ed. 2001. *New Directions in Anthropological Kinship*. Lanham: Rowman and Littlefield.

Strategic Advisory Group of Experts on Immunization. 2019. "The Global Vaccine Action Plan 2011–2020. Review and Lessons Learned." Geneva: WHO. https://www.who.int/immunization/global_vaccine_action_plan/en

Strathern, Andrew, and Pamela J. Stewart. 2011. *Peace-Making and the Imagination*. St. Lucia: University of Queensland Press.

Strong, William. 1929. "Cross-Cousin Marriage and the Culture of the Northeast Algonkian." *American Anthropologist* 31: 277–88.

Sullivan, Joan. 2016. "Anthropologist Jean L. Briggs' books on Inuit became classics." https://www.theglobeandmail.com/news/national/anthropologist-jean-l-briggs-books-on-inuit-became-classics/article31395950

Susser, Ida. 2006. "The Other Side of Development: HIV/AIDS Among Men and Women in Ju/'hoansi Villages."

In *The Politics of Egalitarianism: Theory and Practice*, edited by J. S. Solway. New York: Berghahn.

——. 2009. "Ju/'hoansi Women in the Age of HIV: An Exceptional Case." In *AIDS, Sex, and Culture: Global Politics and Survival in Southern Africa*, edited by Ida Susser. Malden: Blackwell.

Taft, Michael. 1997. "Men in Women's Clothes: Theatrical Transvestites on the Canadian Prairie." In *Undisciplined Women: Tradition and Culture in Canada*, edited by Pauline Greenhill and Diane Tye. Kingston and Montreal: McGill–Queen's University Press.

Tator, Carol, and Francis Henry. 2000. "The Role and Practice of Racialized Discourse in Culture and Cultural Production." *Journal of Canadian Studies* 35(3): 120–41.

Tengan, Ty P. Kāwika. 2018. "*Ka Ulu Koa Ma Kai*: The Koa Grove Rises in the Sea." *Pacific Studies* 41(3): 134–46.

Thomas, Elizabeth. 1959. *The Harmless People*. New York: A.A. Knopf.

Thompson, E.P. 1967. "Time, Work-Discipline, and Industrial Capitalism." *Past and Present* 38: 56–97.

Thrasher, Frederic. 1963. *The Gang* [1927]. Chicago: University of Chicago Press.

Tiihonnen, J., et al. 2015. "Genetic Background of Extreme Violent Behaviour." *Molecular Psychiatry* 20: 786–92.

Todaro, Michael. 2000. *Economic Development*. Reading: Addison Wesley.

Toynbee, Jason. 2007. *Bob Marley: Herald of Postcolonial World?* Cambridge: Polity.

Trigger, Bruce. 1986. "Evolutionism, Relativism, and Putting Native People into Historical Context." *Culture* 6(2): 65–79.

1/ Trouillot, Michel-Rolph. 2003. "Adieu Culture: A New Duty Arises." In *Global Transformations: Anthropology and the Modern World*, 97–116. New York: Palgrave Macmillan.

Truth and Reconciliation Commission. 2015. *Honouring the Truth, Reconciling for the Future: Summary of the Final Report of the Truth and Reconciliation Commission of Canada*. http://www.trc.ca/assets/pdf/Honouring_the_Truth_Reconciling_for_the_Future_July_23_2015.pdf

Turner, Terence. 2005. "Ethical Issues Arising from Patrick Tierney's *Darkness in El Dorado* and the Ensuing Controversy." In *Yanomami: The Fierce Controversy and What We Can Learn from It*, edited by Rob Borofsky. Berkeley: University of California Press.

Turner, Victor. 1967. *The Forest of Symbols: Aspects of Ndembu Ritual*. Ithaca: Cornell University Press.

——. 1995. *The Ritual Process* [1969]. Hawthorne: Aldine de Gruyter.

Tylor, Edward. 1871. *Primitive Culture*. London: Murray.

UNDP (United Nations Development Programme). 2019. "Human Development Report 2019: Beyond Income, beyond Averages, beyond Today: Inequalities in Human Development in the 21st Century." *United Nations Development Programme*, 10 December 2019.

Valentine, Charles A. 1968. *Culture and Poverty: Critique and Counter-Proposals*. Chicago: University of Chicago Press.

van den Berghe, Pierre L. 1992. "The Modern State: Nation-Builder or Nation-Killer?" *International Journal of Group Tensions* 22: 191–208.

——. 1970. *Race and Ethnicity*. New York: Basic.

——. 1965. *South Africa: A Study in Conflict*. Middletown: Wesleyan University Press.

van den Berghe, Pierre L., and George P. Primov. 1977. *Inequality in the Peruvian Andes: Class and Ethnicity in Cuzco*. Columbia: University of Missouri Press.

van Gennep, Arnold. 1960. *The Rites of Passage* [1906]. Translated by Monica B. Vizedom and Gabrielle L. Chaffe. Chicago: University of Chicago Press.

Vergano, Dan. 2014. "Amazon Warriors' Names Revealed Amid 'Gibberish' on Ancient Greek Vases." *National Geographic*. http://news.nationalgeographic.com/news/2014/09/140923-amazon-greek-vase-translations-science

Vincent, Joan, ed. 2002. *The Anthropology of Politics*. Oxford: Blackwell.

Von Gernet, Alexander. 1994. "Saving the Souls: Reincarnation Beliefs of the Seventeenth-Century Huron." In *American Rebirth: Reincarnation Belief among North American Indians and Inuit*, edited by Antonia Mills and Richard Slobodin. Toronto: University of Toronto Press.

Wagner, Roy. 1984. "Ritual as Communication: Order, Meaning, and Secrecy in Melanesian Initiation Rites." *Annual Review of Anthropology* 13: 143–55.

Waldram, James B. 1997. *The Way of the Pipe: Aboriginal Spirituality and Symbolic Healing in Canadian Prisons*. Peterborough: Broadview.

Waldram, James B., and J. O'Neil. 1989. "Native Health Research in Canada." Special Issue of *Native Studies Review* 5(1): 1–213.

Walens, Stanley. 1981. *Feasting with Cannibals: An Essay on Kwakiutl Cosmology*. Princeton: Princeton University Press.

Wall, Denis. 2000. "Aboriginal Self-Government in Canada: The Cases of Nunavut and the Alberta Métis Settlements." In *Visions of the Heart: Canadian Aboriginal Issues*, edited by David Long and Olive Patricia Dickason. Toronto: Harcourt Canada.

Wall, Ellen. 1992. "Personal Labour Relations and Ethnicity in Ontario Agriculture." In *Deconstructing a Nation: Immigration, Multiculturalism, and Racism in '90s Canada*, edited by Vic Satzewich. Halifax: Fernwood.

Wallace, Anthony F.C. 1966. *Religion: An Anthropological View*. New York: Random House.

Wallerstein, Immanuel. 1989. *The Modern World-System*, vol. 3: *The Second Era of Great Expansion of the Capitalist World-Economy, 1730–1840s*. New York: Academic.

Walsh, Andrew. 2010. "The Commodification of Fetishes: Telling the Difference Between Natural and Synthetic Sapphires." *American Ethnologist* 37(1): 98–114.

Washburn, Sherwood L., and C.S. Lancaster. 1968. "The Evolution of Hunting." In *Man the Hunter*, edited by R.B. Lee and Irvene Devore. New York: Aldine.

Watson-Ellam, Linda. 2001. "Living against the Wind: Pathways Chosen by Chinese Immigrants." *Canadian Ethnic Studies* 33(1): 71–101.

Weiner, Annette B. 1988. *The Trobrianders of Papua New Guinea*. New York: Holt, Rinehart, and Winston.

——. 1976. *Women of Value, Men of Renown*. Austin: University of Texas Press.

Weston, Kath. 1991. *Families We Choose: Lesbians, Gays, Kinship*. New York: Columbia University Press.

White, Leslie. 1959. *The Evolution of Culture*. New York: McGraw-Hill.

——. 1949. *The Science of Culture*. New York: Farrar, Straus and Giroux.

Whitehead, Harriet. 1981. "The Bow and the Burden Strap: A New Look at Institutionalized Homosexuality in Native North America." In *Sexual Meanings: The Cultural Construction of Gender and Sexuality*, edited by Sherry B. Ortner and Harriet Whitehead. New York: Cambridge University Press.

Whitehead, Neil Lancelot. 1990. "The Snake Warriors – Sons of the Tiger's Teeth: A Descriptive Analysis of Carib Warfare, ca. 1500–1820." In *The Anthropology of War*, edited by Jonathan Hass. New York: Cambridge University Press.

Williams, Walter L. 1986. *The Spirit and the Flesh: Sexual Diversity in American Indian Culture*. Boston: Beacon.

Wilmsen, Edwin N., and James R. Denbow. 1990. "Paradigmatic History of San-Speaking Peoples and Current Attempts at Revision." *Current Anthropology* 31: 489–512.

Wilson, Richard A. 1997. *Human Rights, Culture, and Context: Anthropological Perspectives*. London: Pluto.

Wise, Amanda. 2006. *Exile and Return among the East Timorese*. Philadelphia: University of Pennsylvania Press.

Wolf, Eric. 1982. *Europe and the People without History*. Berkeley: University of California Press.

——. 1969. *Peasant Wars of the Twentieth Century*. New York: Harper and Row.

——. 1966. *Peasants*. Englewood Cliffs: Prentice Hall.

——. 1964. *Anthropology*. Englewood Cliffs: Prentice-Hall.

Wolf, Margery. 1968. *The House of Lim*. Englewood Cliffs: Prentice Hall.

WHO (World Health Organization). 2017. "10 facts on health inequities and their causes," April 2017. https://www.who.int/features/factfiles/health_inequities/en

Worsley, Peter. 1982. "Non-Western Medical Systems." *Annual Review of Anthropology* 11: 315–48.

Wright, Robin. 2020. "Finding Connection and Resilience during the Coronavirus Pandemic." *The New Yorker*. https://www.newyorker.com/news/our-columnists/coping-camaraderie-and-human-evolution-amid-the-coronavirus-crisis

Yan, Yunxiang. 2002. "Practicing Kinship in Rural North China." In *Practicing Kinship: Lineage and Descent in Late Imperial China*, edited by Michael Szonyi. Stanford: Stanford University Press.

Yanagisako, Sylvia Junko. 1979. "Family and Household: The Analysis of Domestic Groups." *Annual Review of Anthropology* 8: 161–205.

Yanagisako, Sylvia, and Carol Delaney, eds. 1995. *Naturalizing Power: Essays on Feminist Cultural Analysis*. New York: Routledge.

Young, Allan. 1982. "The Anthropologies of Illness and Sickness." *Annual Review of Anthropology* 11: 257–85.

Young, Antonia. 2001. *Women Who Become Men: Albanian Sworn Virgins*. Oxford: Berg.

Young, K. 1988. *Health Care and Culture Change: The Indian Experience in the Central Subarctic*. Toronto: University of Toronto Press.

Zechenter, Elizabeth. 1997. "In the Name of Culture: Cultural Relativism and the Abuse of the Individual." *Journal of Anthropological Research – Universal Human Rights versus Cultural Relativity* 53: 319–48.

Ziegler-Otero, Lawrence. 2004. *Resistance in an Amazonian Community: Huaorani Organizing against the Global Economy*. New York and Oxford: Berghahn.

Ziemba, Christine. 2011. "The Beer Archaeologist: Tasting World History: ... The "Indiana Jones of Alcohol." *Slate* magazine. www.slate.com: John Alderman.

Index

C

D

E

F

G

H

I

J

K

L

M

N

S

T

U

V

W

Z